The Secret of the Ages

Other Library of Spiritual Wisdom Titles

THE SECRET OF THE AGES

And Other Essential Works

ROBERT COLLIER

ST. MARTIN'S
ESSENTIALS
NEW YORK

Published in the United States by St. Martin's Essentials,
an imprint of St. Martin's Publishing Group

Printed in the United States of America. For information,
address St. Martin's Publishing Group, 120 Broadway, New York, NY 10271.

www.stmartins.com

Designed by Steven Seighman

The Library of Congress Cataloging-in-Publication Data is available upon request.

ISBN 978-1-250-88077-2 (trade paperback)
ISBN 978-1-250-84528-3 (ebook)

Our books may be purchased in bulk for promotional, educational, or business use. Please contact your local bookseller or the Macmillan Corporate and Premium Sales Department at 1-800-221-7945, extension 5442, or by email at MacmillanSpecialMarkets@macmillan.com.

The Secret of the Ages was first published in 1926.
Riches Within Your Reach was first published in 1947.
The Secret of Gold was first published in 1927.

First St. Martin's Essentials Edition: 2022

10 9 8 7 6 5 4 3 2 1

This edition seeks to faithfully reproduce the original publications of the author's works and so has maintained the original spelling and grammar throughout, with only minor alterations for clarity or content.

Contents

The Secret
of the Ages

ROBERT COLLIER

Contents

CONTENTS

VOLUME IV

VOLUME V

VOLUME VI

VOLUME VII

VOLUME VIII

VOLUME IX

VOLUME X

VOLUME XI

VOLUME XII

VOLUME XIII

VOLUME XIV

VOLUME XV

VOLUME XVI

VOLUME XVII

VOLUME XVIII

VOLUME XIX

VOLUME XX

"A fire-mist and a planet,
A crystal and a cell,
A jelly-fish and a saurian,
A cave where the cave-men dwell;
Then a sense of law and order,
A face upturned from the clod;
Some call it Evolution,
And others call it God."

—REPRINTED FROM *THE NEW ENGLAND JOURNAL*

Foreword

IF you had more money than time, more millions than you knew how to spend, what would be your pet philanthropy? Libraries? Hospitals? Churches? Homes for the Blind, Crippled or Aged?

Mine would be "Homes"—but not for the aged or infirm. *For young married couples!*

I have often thought that, if ever I got into the "Philanthropic Billionaire" class, I'd like to start an Endowment Fund for helping young married couples over the rough spots in those first and second years of married life—especially the second year, when the real troubles come.

Take a boy and a girl and a cozy little nest—add a cunning, healthy baby—and there's nothing happier on God's green footstool.

But instead of a healthy babe, fill in a fretful, sickly baby—a wan, tired, worn-out little mother—a worried, dejected, heart-sick father—and there's nothing more pitiful.

A nurse for a month, a few weeks at the shore or mountains, a "lift" on that heavy Doctor's bill—any one of these things would spell H-E-A-V-E-N to that tiny family. But do they get it? Not often! And the reason? Because they are not poor enough for charity. They are not rich enough to afford it themselves. They belong to that great "Middle Class" which has to bear the burdens of both the poor and the rich—and take what is left for itself.

It is to them that I should like to dedicate this book. If I cannot endow Libraries or Colleges for them, perhaps I can point the way to get all good gifts for themselves.

For men and women like them do not need "charity"—nor even sympathy.

What they do need is Inspiration—and Opportunity—the kind of Inspiration that makes a man go out and create his own Opportunity.

And that, after all, is the greatest good one can do anyone. Few people appreciate free gifts. They are like the man whom an admiring townsfolk presented with a watch. He looked it over critically for a minute. Then—"Where's the chain?" he asked.

But a way to win *for themselves* the full measure of success they've dreamed of but almost stopped hoping for—*that* is something every young couple would welcome with open arms. And it is something that, if I can do it justice, will make the "Eternal Triangle" as rare as it is today common, for it will enable husband and wife to work *together*—not merely for domestic happiness, but for business success as well.

—ROBERT COLLIER

Volume I

The World's Greatest Discovery

"You can do as much as you think you can,
But you'll never accomplish more;
If you're afraid of yourself, young man,
There's little for you in store.
For failure comes from the inside first,
It's there if we only knew it,
And you can win, though you face the worst,
If you feel that you're going to do it."

—EDGAR A. GUEST[1]

WHAT, in your opinion, is the most significant discovery of this modern age?

The finding of Dinosaur eggs on the plains of Mongolia, laid—so scientists assert—some 10,000,000 years ago?

The unearthing of the Tomb of Tutankh-Amen, with its matchless specimens of a bygone civilization?

The radio-active time clock by which Professor Lane of Tufts College estimates the age of the earth at 1,250,000,000 years?

Wireless? The Aeroplane? Manmade thunderbolts?

No—not any of these. The really significant thing about them is that from

1. From "A Heap o' Livin'." The Reilly & Lee Co.

all this vast research, from the study of all these bygone ages, men are for the first time beginning to get an understanding of that "Life Principle" which—somehow, some way—was brought to this earth thousands or millions of years ago. They are beginning to get an inkling of the infinite power it puts in their hands—to glimpse the untold possibilities it opens up.

This is the greatest discovery of modern times—that every man can call upon this "Life Principle" at will, that it is as much the servant of his mind as was ever Aladdin's fabled "Genie-of-the-lamp" of old; that he has but to understand it and work in harmony with it to get from it anything he may need—health or happiness, riches or success.

To realize the truth of this, you have but to go back for a moment to the beginning of things.

IN THE BEGINNING—

It matters not whether you believe that mankind dates back to the primitive Ape-man of 500,000 years ago, or sprang full-grown from the mind of the Creator. In either event, there had to be a First Cause—a Creator. Some Power had to bring to this earth the first germ of Life, and the creation is no less wonderful if it started with the lowliest form of plant life and worked up through countless ages into the highest product of today's civilization, than if the whole were created in six days.

In the beginning, this earth was just a fire mist—six thousand or a billion years ago—what does it matter which?

The one thing that does matter is that some time, some way, there came to this planet the germ of Life—the Life Principle which animates all Nature—plant, animal, man. If we accept the scientists' version of it, the first form in which Life appeared upon earth was the humble Algae—a jelly-like mass which floated upon the waters. This, according to the scientists, was the beginning, the dawn of life upon the earth.

Next came the first bit of animal life—the lowly Amoeba, a sort of jelly fish, consisting of a single cell, without vertebrae, and with very little else to distinguish it from the water round about. But it had *life*—the first bit of *animal* life—and from that life, according to the scientists, we can trace everything we have and are today.

All the millions of forms and shapes and varieties of plants and animals that have since appeared are but different manifestations of *life*—formed to meet differing conditions. For millions of years this "Life Germ" was threatened by every kind of danger—from floods, from earthquakes, from droughts, from desert heat, from glacial cold, from volcanic eruptions—but to it each new danger was merely an incentive to finding a new resource, to putting forth Life in some new shape.

To meet one set of needs, it formed the Dinosaur—to meet another, the Butterfly. Long before it worked up to man, we see its unlimited resourcefulness shown in a thousand ways. To escape danger in the water, it sought land. Pursued on land, it took to the air. To breathe in the sea, it developed gills. Stranded on land, it perfected lungs. To meet one kind of danger it grew a shell. For another, a sting. To protect itself from glacial cold, it grew fur. In temperate climes, hair. Subject to alternate heat and cold, it produced feathers. But ever, from the beginning, it showed its power to meet every changing condition, to answer every creature need.

Had it been possible to kill this "Life Idea," it would have perished ages ago, when fire and flood, drought and famine followed each other in quick succession. But obstacles, misfortunes, cataclysms, were to it merely new opportunities to assert its power. In fact, it required obstacles to awaken it, to show its energy and resource.

The great reptiles, the monster beasts of antiquity, passed on. But the "Life Principle" stayed, changing as each age changed, always developing, always improving.

Whatever Power it was that brought this "Life Idea" to the earth, it came endowed with unlimited resource, unlimited energy, unlimited LIFE! No other force can defeat it. No obstacle can hold it back. All through the history of life and mankind you can see its directing intelligence—call it Nature, call it Providence, call it what you will—rising to meet every need of life.

THE PURPOSE OF EXISTENCE

No one can follow it down through the ages without realizing that the whole purpose of existence is GROWTH. Life is dynamic—not static. It is ever moving forward—not standing still. The one unpardonable sin of nature is to stand still, to stagnate. The Gigantosaurus, that was over a hundred feet long and as big as a house; the Tyrannosaurus, that had the strength of a locomotive and was the last word in frightfulness; the Pterodactyl or Flying Dragon—all the giant monsters of Prehistoric Ages—are gone. They ceased to serve a useful purpose. They did not know how to meet the changing conditions. They stood still—stagnated—while the life around them passed them by.

Egypt and Persia, Greece and Rome, all the great Empires of antiquity, perished when they ceased to grow. China built a wall about herself and stood still for a thousand years. Today she is the football of the Powers. In all Nature, to cease to grow is to perish.

It is for men and women who are not ready to stand still, who refuse to cease to grow, that this book is written. It will give you a clearer understanding of your own potentialities, show you how to work with and take advantage of the infinite energy all about you.

The terror of the man at the crossways, not knowing which road to take, will be no terror to you. Your future is of your own making. For the only law of Infinite Energy is the law of supply. The "Life Principle" is your principle. To survive, to win through, to triumphantly surmount all obstacles has been its everyday practice since the beginning of time. It is no less resourceful now than ever it was. You have but to supply the urge, to work in harmony with it, to get from it anything you may need.

For if this "Life Principle" is so strong in the lowest forms of animal life that it can develop a shell or a poison to meet a need; if it can teach the bird to circle and dart, to balance and fly; if it can grow a new limb on a spider to replace a lost one, how much more can it do for *you*—a reasoning, rational being, with a mind able to *work with* this "Life Principle," with an energy and an initiative to urge it on!

The evidence of this is all about you. Take up some violent form of exercise— rowing, tennis, swimming, riding. In the beginning your muscles are weak, easily tired. But keep on for a few days. The "Life Principle" promptly strengthens them, toughens them, to meet their new need. Do rough manual labor—and what happens? The skin of your hands becomes tender, blisters, hurts. Keep it up, and does the skin all wear off? On the contrary, the "Life Principle" provides extra thicknesses, extra toughness—callouses, we call them—to meet your need.

All through your daily life you will find this "Life Principle" steadily at work. Embrace it, work with it, take it to yourself, and there is nothing you cannot do. The mere fact that you have obstacles to overcome is in your favor, for when there is nothing to be done, when things run along too smoothly, this "Life Principle" seems to sleep. It is when you need it, when you call upon it urgently, that it is most on the job.

It differs from "Luck" in this, that fortune is a fickle jade who smiles most often on those who need her least. Stake your last penny on the turn of a card—have nothing between you and ruin but the spin of a wheel or the speed of a horse—and it's a thousand to one "Luck" will desert you! But it is just the opposite with the "Life Principle." As long as things run smoothly, as long as life flows along like a song, this "Life Principle" seems to slumber, secure in the knowledge that your affairs can take care of themselves.

But let things start going wrong, let ruin and disgrace stare you in the face—*then* is the time this "Life Principle" will assert itself if you but give it a chance.

THE "OPEN, SESAME!" OF LIFE

There is a Napoleonic feeling of power *that insures success* in the knowledge that this invincible "Life Principle" is behind your every act. Knowing that you have working with you a force which never yet has failed in anything it has undertaken, you can go ahead in the confident knowledge that it will not fail in your case, either. The ingenuity which overcame every obstacle in making you what you are, is not likely to fall short when you have immediate need for it. It is the reserve strength of the athlete, the "second wind" of the runner, the power that, in moments of great stress or excitement, you unconsciously call upon to do the deeds which you ever after look upon as superhuman.

But they are in no wise superhuman. They are merely beyond the capacity of your conscious self. Ally your conscious self with that sleeping giant within you, rouse him daily to the task, and those "superhuman" deeds will become your ordinary, everyday accomplishments.

W. L. Cain, of Oakland, Oregon, writes: "I know that there is such a power, for I once saw two boys, 16 and 18 years of age, lift a great log off their brother, who had been caught under it. The next day, the same two boys, with another man and myself, tried to lift the end of the log, but could not even budge it."

How was it that the two boys could do at need what the four were unable to do later on, when the need had passed? Because they never stopped to question whether or not it *could* be done. They saw only the urgent need. They concentrated all their thought, all their energy on that one thing—never doubting, never fearing—and the Genie which is in all of us waiting only for such a call, answered their summons and gave them the strength—not of two men, but of ten!

It matters not whether you are Banker or Lawyer, Business Man or Clerk. Whether you are the custodian of millions, or have to struggle for your daily bread. This "Life Principle" makes no distinction between rich and poor, high and low. The greater your need, the more readily will it respond to your call. Wherever there is an unusual task, wherever there is poverty or hardship or sickness or despair, *there* is this Servant of your Mind, ready and willing to help, asking only that you call upon him.

And not only is it ready and willing, but it is always ABLE to help. Its ingenuity and resource are without limit. It is Mind. It is Thought. It is the Telepathy that carries messages without the spoken or written word. It is the Sixth Sense that warns you of unseen dangers. No matter how stupendous and complicated, nor how simple your problem may be—the solution of it is somewhere in Mind, in Thought. And since the solution does exist, this Mental Giant can find it for you. It can KNOW, and it can DO, every right thing. Whatever it is necessary for you to know, whatever it is necessary for you to do, you can know and you can do if you will but seek the help of this Genie-of-your-Mind and work with it in the right way.

Volume II

The Genie-of-Your-Mind

FIRST came the Stone Age, when life was for the strong of arm or the fleet of foot. Then there was the Iron Age—and while life was more precious, still the strong lorded it over the weak. Later came the Golden Age, and riches took the place of strength—but the poor found little choice between the slave drivers' whips of olden days and the grim weapons of poverty and starvation.

Now we are entering a new age—the Mental Age—when every man can be his own master, when poverty and circumstance no longer hold power and the lowliest creature in the land can win a place side by side with the highest.

To those who do not know the resources of mind these will sound like rash statements; but science proves beyond question that in the well springs of every man's mind are unplumbed depths—undiscovered deposits of energy, wisdom and ability. Sound these depths—bring these treasures to the surface—and you gain an astounding wealth of new power.

From the rude catamaran of the savages to the giant liners of today, carrying their thousands from continent to continent, is but a step in the development of Mind. From the lowly cave man, cowering in his burrow in fear of lightning or fire or water, to the engineer of today, making servants of all the forces of Nature, is but a measure of difference in mental development.

Man, without reasoning mind, would be as the monkeys are—prey of any creature fast enough and strong enough to pull him to pieces. At the mercy of wind and weather. A poor, timid creature, living for the moment only, fearful of every shadow.

Through his superior mind, he learned to make fire to keep himself warm; weapons with which to defend himself from the savage creatures round about; habitations to protect himself from the elements. Through mind he conquered the forces of Nature. Through mind he has made machinery do the work of millions of horses and billions of hands. What he will do next, no man knows, for man is just beginning to awaken to his own powers. He is just getting an inkling of the unfathomed riches buried deep in his own mind. Like the gold seekers of '49, he has panned the surface gravel for the gold swept down by the streams. Now he is starting to dig deeper to the pure vein beneath.

We bemoan the loss of our forests. We worry over our dwindling resources of coal and oil. We decry the waste in our factories. But the greatest waste of all, we pay no attention to—the waste of our own potential mind power. Professor Wm. James, the world-famous Harvard psychologist, estimated that the average man uses only 10% of his mental power. He has unlimited power—yet he uses but a tithe of it. Unlimited wealth all about him—and he doesn't know how to take hold of it. With God-like powers slumbering within him, he is content to continue in his daily grind—eating, sleeping, working—plodding through an existence little more eventful than the animals', while all of Nature, all of life, calls upon him to awaken, to bestir himself.

The power to be what you want to be, to get what you desire, to accomplish whatever you are striving for, abides within you. It rests with you only to bring it forth and put it to work. Of course you must know *how* to do that, but before you can learn how to use it, you must *realize* that you *possess* this power. So our first objective is to get acquainted with this power.

For Psychologists and Metaphysicians the world over are agreed in this—that Mind is all that counts. You can be whatever you make up your mind to be. You need not be sick. You need not be unhappy. You need not be poor. You need not be unsuccessful. You are not a mere clod. You are not a beast of burden, doomed to spend your days in unremitting labor in return for food and housing. You are one of the Lords of the Earth, with unlimited potentialities. Within you is a power which, properly grasped and directed, can lift you out

of the rut of mediocrity and place you among the Elect of the earth—the lawyers, the writers, the statesmen, the big business men—the DOERS and the
THINKERS. It rests with you only to learn to use this power which is yours—
this Mind which can do all things.

Your body is for all practical purposes merely a machine which the mind
uses. This mind is usually thought of as consciousness; but the *conscious part* of
your mind is in fact the *very smallest part of it*. Ninety per cent of your mental life
is subconscious, so when you make active use of only the conscious part of your
mind you are using but a fraction of your real ability; you are running on low
gear. And the reason why more people do not achieve success in life is because
so many of them are content to run on low gear all their lives—on SURFACE
ENERGY. If these same people would only throw into the fight the resistless
force of their subconscious minds they would be amazed at their undreamed of
capacity for winning success.

Conscious and subconscious are, of course, integral parts of the one mind.
But for convenience sake let us divide your mind into three parts—the con-
scious mind, the subconscious mind, and the Infinite, Subliminal or Universal
Mind.

THE CONSCIOUS MIND

When you say "I see—I hear—I smell—I touch," it is your conscious mind
that is saying this, for it is the force governing the five physical senses. It is the
phase of mind with which you feel and reason—the phase of mind with which
everyone is familiar. It is the mind with which you do business. It controls, to
a great extent, all your voluntary muscles. It discriminates between right and
wrong, wise and foolish. It is the generalissimo, in charge of all your mental
forces. It can plan ahead—and get things done as it plans. Or it can drift along
haphazardly, a creature of impulse, at the mercy of events—a mere bit of flotsam
in the current of life.

For it is only through your conscious mind that you can reach the subconscious and the Universal Mind. Your conscious mind is the porter at the door,
the watchman at the gate. It is to the conscious mind that the subconscious
looks for all its impressions. It is on it that the subconscious mind must depend
for the teamwork necessary to get successful results. You wouldn't expect much
from an army, no matter how fine its soldiers, whose general never planned

ahead, who distrusted his own ability and that of his men, and who spent all his time worrying about the enemy instead of planning how he might conquer them. You wouldn't look for good scores from a ball team whose pitcher was at odds with the catcher. In the same way, you can't expect results from the subconscious when your conscious mind is full of fear or worry, or when it does not know what it wants.

The one most important province of your conscious mind is to center your thoughts on the thing you want, and to shut the door on every suggestion of fear or worry or disease.

If you once gain the ability to do that, nothing else is impossible to you.

For the subconscious mind does not reason inductively. It takes the thoughts you send in to it and works them out to their logical conclusion. Send to it thoughts of health and strength, and it will work out health and strength in your body. Let suggestions of disease, fear of sickness or accident, penetrate to it, either through your own thoughts or the talk of those around you, and you are very likely to see the manifestation of disease working out in yourself.

Your mind is master of your body. It directs and controls every function of your body. Your body is in effect a little universe in itself, and mind is its radiating center—the sun which gives light and life to all your system, and around which the whole revolves. And your *conscious thought* is master of this sun center. As Emile Coué puts it—"The conscious can put the subconscious mind over the hurdles."

THE SUBCONSCIOUS MIND

Can you tell me how much water, how much salt, how much of each different element there should be in your blood to maintain its proper specific gravity if you are leading an ordinary sedentary life? How much and how quickly these proportions must be changed if you play a fast game of tennis, or run for your car, or chop wood, or indulge in any other violent exercise?

Do you know how much water you should drink to neutralize the excess salt in salt fish? How much you lose through perspiration? Do you know how much water, how much salt, how much of each different element in your food should be absorbed into your blood each day to maintain perfect health?

No? Well, it need not worry you. Neither does any one else. Not even the greatest physicists and chemists and mathematicians. But your subconscious mind knows.

And it doesn't have to stop to figure it out. It does it almost automatically. It is one of those "Lightning Calculators." And this is but one of thousands of such jobs it performs every hour of the day. The greatest mathematicians in the land, the most renowned chemists, could never do in a year's time the abstruse problems which your subconscious mind solves every minute.

And it doesn't matter whether you've ever studied mathematics or chemistry or any other of the sciences. From the moment of your birth your subconscious mind solves all these problems for you. While you are struggling along with the three R's, it is doing problems that would leave your teachers aghast. It supervises all the intricate processes of digestion, of assimilation, of elimination, and all the glandular secretions that would tax the knowledge of all the chemists and all the laboratories in the land. It planned and built your body from infancy on up. It repairs it. It operates it. It has almost unlimited power, not merely for putting you and keeping you in perfect health but for acquiring all the good things of life. Ignorance of this power is the sole reason for all the failures in this world. If you would intelligently turn over to this wonderful power all your business and personal affairs in the same way that you turn over to it the mechanism of your body, no goal would be too great for you to strive for.

Dr. Geo. C. Pitzer sums up the power of the subconscious mind very well in the following:

"The subconscious mind is a distinct entity. It occupies the whole human body, and, when not opposed in any way, it has absolute control over all the functions, conditions, and sensations of the body. While the objective (conscious) mind has control over all of our voluntary functions and motions, the subconscious mind controls all of the silent, involuntary, and vegetative functions. Nutrition, waste, all secretions and excretions, the action of the heart in the circulation of the blood, the lungs in respiration or breathing, and all cell life, cell changes and development, are positively under the complete control of the subconscious mind. This was the only mind animals had before the evolution of the brain; and it could not, nor can it yet, reason inductively, but its power of deductive reasoning is perfect. And more, it can see without the use of physical eyes. It perceives by intuition. It has the power to communicate with others without the aid of ordinary physical means. It can read the thoughts of others. It receives intelligence and transmits it to people at a distance. Distance offers no resistance against the successful missions of the subconscious mind. It never dies. We call this the 'soul mind.' It is the living soul."

In "Practical Psychology and Sex Life," by David Bush, Dr. Winbigler is quoted as going even further. To quote him:

"It is this mind that carries on the work of assimilation and upbuilding whilst we sleep. . . .

"It reveals to us things that the conscious mind has no conception of until the consummations have occurred.

"It can communicate with other minds without the ordinary physical means.

"It gets glimpses of things that ordinary sight does not behold.

"It makes God's presence an actual, realizable fact, and keeps the personality in peace and quietness.

"It warns of approaching danger.

"It approves or disapproves of a course of conduct and conversation.

"It carries out all the best things which are given to it, providing the conscious mind does not intercept and change the course of its manifestation.

"It heals the body and keeps it in health, if it is at all encouraged."

It is, in short, the most powerful force in life, and when properly directed, the most beneficent. But, like a live electric wire, its destructive force is equally great. It can be either your servant or your master. It can bring to you evil or good.

The Rev. William T. Walsh, in a new book just published, explains the idea very clearly:

"The subconscious part in us is called the subjective mind, because it does not decide and command. It is a subject rather than a ruler. Its nature is to do what it is told, *or what really in your heart of hearts you desire.*

"The subconscious mind directs all the vital processes of your body. You do not think consciously about breathing. Every time you take a breath you do not have to reason, decide, command. The subconscious mind sees to that. You have not been at all conscious that you have been breathing while you have been reading this page. So it is with the mind and the circulation of blood. The heart is a muscle like the muscle of your arm. It has no power to move itself or to direct its action. Only mind, only something that can think, can direct our muscles, including the heart. You are not conscious that you are commanding your heart to beat. The subconscious mind attends to that. And so it is with the assimilation of food, the building and repairing of the body. In fact, all the vital processes are looked after by the subconscious mind."

"Man lives and moves and has his being" in this great subconscious mind. It supplies the "intuition" that so often carries a woman straight to a point that may require hours of cumbersome reasoning for a man to reach. Even in ordinary, every-day affairs, you often draw upon its wonderful wisdom.

But you do it in an accidental sort of way without realizing what you are doing.

Consider the case of "Blind Tom." Probably you've heard or read of him. You know that he could listen to a piece of music for the first time and go immediately to a piano and reproduce it. People call that abnormal. But as a matter of fact he was in this respect more normal than any of us. We are abnormal because we cannot do it.

Or consider the case of these "lightning calculators" of whom one reads now and then. It may be a boy seven or eight years old; but you can ask him to divide 7,649.437 by 326.2568 and he'll give you the result in less time than it would take you to put the numbers down on a piece of paper. You call him phenomenal. Yet you ought to be able to do the same yourself. Your subconscious mind can.

Dr. Hudson, in his book "The Law of Psychic Phenomena," tells of numerous such prodigies. Here are just a few instances:

"Of mathematical prodigies there have been upwards of a score whose calculations have surpassed, in rapidity and accuracy, those of the greatest educated mathematicians. These prodigies have done their greatest feats while but children from three to ten years old. In no case had these boys any idea how they performed their calculations, and some of them would converse upon other subjects while doing the sum. Two of these boys became men of eminence, while some of them showed but a low degree of objective intelligence.

"Whateley spoke of his own gift in the following terms:

"'There was certainly something peculiar in my calculating faculty. It began to show itself at between five and six, and lasted about three years. I soon got to do the most difficult sums, always in my head, for I knew nothing of figures beyond numeration. I did these sums much quicker than anyone could upon paper, and I never remember committing the smallest error. When I went to school, at which time the passion wore off, I was a perfect dunce at cyphering, and have continued so ever since.'

"Professor Safford became an astronomer. At the age of ten he worked correctly a multiplication sum whose answer consisted of thirty-six figures. Later in life he could perform no such feats.

"Benjamin Hall Blyth, at the age of six, asked his father at what hour he was born. He was told that he was born at four o'clock. Looking at the clock to see the present time, he informed his father of the number of seconds he had lived. His father made the calculation and said to Benjamin, 'You are wrong 172,000 seconds.' The boy answered, 'Oh, papa, you have left out two days for the leap years 1820 and 1824,' which was the case.

"Then there is the celebrated case of Zerah Colburn, of whom Dr. Schofield writes:

"'Zerah Colburn could instantaneously tell the square root of 106,929 as 327, and the cube root of 268,336,125 as 645. Before the question of the number of minutes in forty-eight years could be written he said 25,228,810. He immediately gave the factors of 247,483 as 941 and 263, which are the only two; and being asked then for those of 36,083, answered none; it is a prime number. He could not tell how the answer came into his mind. He could not, on paper, do simple multiplication or division.'"

The time will come when, as H. G. Wells visioned in his "Men Like Gods," schools and teachers will no longer be necessary except to show us how to get in touch with the infinite knowledge our subconscious minds possess from infancy.

"The smartest man in the world," says Dr. Frank Crane in a recent article in *Liberty*, "is the Man Inside. By the Man Inside I mean that Other Man within each one of us that does most of the things we give ourselves credit for doing. You may refer to him as Nature or the Subconscious Self or think of him merely as a Force or a Natural Law, or, if you are religiously inclined, you may use the term God.

"I say he is the smartest man in the world. I know he is infinitely more clever and resourceful than I am or than any other man is that I ever heard of. When I cut my finger it is he that calls up the little phagocytes to come and kill the septic germs that might get into the wound and cause blood poisoning. It is he that coagulates the blood, stops the gash, and weaves the new skin.

"I could not do that. I do not even know how he does it. He even does it for babies that know nothing at all; in fact, does it better for them than for me.

"No living man knows enough to make toenails grow, but the Man Inside thinks nothing of growing nails and teeth and thousands of hairs all over my body; long hairs on my head and little fuzzy ones over the rest of the surface of the skin.

"When I practice on the piano I am simply getting the business of piano playing over from my conscious mind to my subconscious mind: in other words, I am handing the business over to the Man Inside.

"Most of our happiness, as well as our struggles and misery, comes from this Man Inside. If we train him in ways of contentment, adjustment, and decision he will go ahead of us like a well trained servant and do for us easily most of the difficult tasks we have to perform."

Dr. Jung, celebrated Viennese specialist, claims that the subconscious mind contains not only all the knowledge that it has gathered during the life of the individual, but that in addition it contains all the wisdom of past ages. That by drawing upon its wisdom and power the individual may possess any good thing of life, from health and happiness to riches and success.

You see, the subconscious mind is the connecting link between the Creator and ourselves, between Universal Mind and our conscious mind. It is the means by which we can appropriate to ourselves all the good gifts, all the riches and abundance which Universal Mind has created in such profusion.

Berthelot, the great French founder of modern synthetic chemistry, once stated in a letter to a close friend that the final experiments which led to his most wonderful discoveries had never been the result of carefully followed and reasoned trains of thought, but that, on the contrary, "they came of themselves, so to speak, from the clear sky."

Charles M. Barrows, in "Suggestion Instead of Medicine," tells us that:

"If man requires another than his ordinary consciousness to take care of him while asleep, not less useful is this same psychical provision when he is awake. Many persons are able to obtain knowledge which does not come to them through their senses, in the usual way, but arrives in the mind by direct communication from another conscious intelligence, which apparently knows more of what concerns their welfare than their ordinary reason does. I have known a number of persons who, like myself, could tell the contents of letters in their mail before opening them. Several years ago a friend of mine came to Boston for the first time, arriving at what was then the Providence railroad station in Park Square. He wished to walk to the Lowell station on the opposite side of the city. Being utterly ignorant of the streets as well as the general direction to take he confidently set forth without asking the way, and reached his destination by the most direct path. In doing this he trusted solely to 'instinctive guidance,' as he called it, and not to any hints or clews obtained through the senses."

The geniuses of literature, of art, commerce, government, politics and invention, are, according to the scientists, but ordinary men like you and me who have learned somehow, some way, to draw upon their subconscious minds.

Sir Isaac Newton is reported to have acquired his marvelous knowledge of mathematics and physics with no conscious effort. Mozart said of his beautiful symphonies that "they just came to him." Descartes had no ordinary regular education. To quote Dr. Hudson:

"This is a power which transcends reason, and is independent of induction. Instances of its development might be multiplied indefinitely. Enough is known to warrant the conclusion that when the soul is released from its objective environment it will be enabled to perceive all the laws of its being, to 'see God as He is,' by the perception of the laws which He has instituted. It is the knowledge of this power which demonstrates our true relationship to God, which confers the warranty of our right to the title of 'sons of God,' and confirms our inheritance of our rightful share of his attributes and powers—our heirship of God, our joint heirship with Jesus Christ."

Our subconscious minds are vast magnets, with the power to draw from Universal Mind unlimited knowledge, unlimited power, unlimited riches.

"Considered from the standpoint of its activities," says Warren Hilton in "Applied Psychology," "the subconscious is that department of mind, which on the one hand directs the vital operations of the body, and on the other conserves, subject to the call of interest and attention, all ideas and complexes not at the moment active in consciousness.

"Observe, then, the possibility that lies before you. On the one hand, if you can control your mind in its subconscious activities, you can regulate the operation of your bodily functions, and can thus assure yourself of bodily efficiency and free yourself of functional disease. On the other hand, if you can determine just what ideas shall be brought forth from subconsciousness into consciousness, you can thus select the materials out of which will be woven your conscious judgments, your decisions and your emotional attitudes.

"To achieve control of your mind is, then, to attain (a) health, (b) success, and (c) happiness."

Few understand or appreciate, however, that the vast storehouse of knowledge and power of the subconscious mind can be drawn upon at will. Now and then through intense concentration or very active desire we do accidentally penetrate to the realm of the subconscious and register our thought upon it. Such thoughts are almost invariably realized. The trouble is that as often as not it is our negative thoughts—our fears—that penetrate. And these are realized just as surely as the positive thoughts. What you must manage to do is learn to communicate only such thoughts as you wish to see realized to your subconscious mind, for it is exceedingly amenable to suggestion. You have heard of the man who was always bragging of his fine health and upon whom some of his friends decided to play a trick. The first one he met one morning commented upon how badly he looked and asked if he weren't feeling well. Then all the others as they saw him made similar remarks. By noon time the man had come to believe them, and before the end of the day he was really ill.

That was a rather glaring example. But similar things are going on every day with all of us. We eat something that someone else tells us isn't good for us and in a little while we think we feel a pain. Before we know it we have indigestion, when the chances are that if we knew nothing about the supposed indigestible properties of the food we could eat it the rest of our days and never feel any ill effects.

Let some new disease be discovered and the symptoms described in the daily paper. Hundreds will come down with it at once. They are like the man who read a medical encyclopedia and ended up by concluding he had everything but "housemaid's knee." Patent medicine advertisers realize this power of suggestion and cash in upon it. Read one of their ads. If you don't think you have everything the matter with you that their nostrums are supposed to cure, you are the exception and not the rule.

That is the negative side of it. Emile Coué based his system on the positive side—that you suggest to your subconscious mind that whatever ills it thinks you have are getting better. And it is good psychology at that. Properly carried out it will work wonders. But there are better methods. And I hope to be able to show them to you before we reach the end of this book.

Suffice it now to say that your subconscious mind is exceedingly wise and powerful. That it knows many things that are not in books. That when properly used it has infallible judgment, unfailing power. That it never sleeps, never tires.

Your conscious mind may slumber. It may be rendered impotent by anæsthetics or a sudden blow. But your subconscious mind works on, keeping your heart and lungs, your arteries and glands ever on the job.

Under ordinary conditions, it attends faithfully to its duties, and leaves your conscious mind to direct the outer life of the body. But let the conscious mind meet some situation with which it is unable to cope, and, if it will only call upon the subconscious, that powerful Genie will respond immediately to its need.

You have heard of people who had been through great danger tell how, when death stared them in the face and there seemed nothing they could do, things went black before them and, when they came to, the danger was past. In the moment of need, their subconscious mind pushed the conscious out of the way, the while it met and overcame the danger. Impelled by the subconscious mind, their bodies could do things absolutely impossible to their ordinary conscious selves.

For the power of the subconscious mind is unlimited. Whatever it is necessary for you to do in any right cause, it can give you the strength and the ability to do.

Whatever of good you may desire, it can bring to you. "The Kingdom of Heaven is within you."

THE UNIVERSAL MIND

Have you ever dug up a potato vine and seen the potatoes clustering underneath? How much of intelligence do you suppose one of these potatoes has? Do you think it knows anything about chemistry or geology? Can it figure out how to gather carbon gas from the atmosphere, water and all the necessary kinds of nutriment from the earth round about to manufacture into sugar and starch and alcohol? No chemist can do it. How do you suppose the potato knows? Of course it doesn't. It has no sense. Yet it does all these things. It builds the starch into cells, the cells into roots and vines and leaves—and into more potatoes.

"Just old Mother Nature," you'll say. But old Mother Nature must have a remarkable intelligence if she can figure out all these things that no human scientist has ever been able to figure. There must be an all-pervading Intelligence behind Mother Nature—the Intelligence that first brought life to this planet— the Intelligence that evolved every form of plant and animal—that holds the winds in its grasp—that is all-wise, all-powerful. The potato is but one small manifestation of this Intelligence. The various forms of plant life, of animals, of man—all are mere cogs in the great scheme of things.

But with this *difference*—that man is an active part of this Universal Mind.

That he partakes of its creative wisdom and power and that by working in harmony with Universal Mind he can *do* anything, *have* anything, *be* anything.

There is within you—within everyone—this mighty resistless force with which you can perform undertakings that will dazzle your reason, stagger your imagination. There constantly resides within you a Mind that is all-wise, all-powerful, a Mind that is entirely apart from the mind which you consciously use in your everyday affairs yet which is one with it.

Your subconscious mind partakes of this wisdom and power, and it is through your subconscious mind that you can draw upon it in the attainment of anything you may desire. When you can intelligently reach your subconscious mind, you can be in communication with the Universal Mind.

Remember this: the Universal Mind is omnipotent. And since the subconscious mind is part of the Universal Mind, there is no limit to the things which it can do when it is given the power to act. Given any desire that is in harmony with the Universal Mind and you have but to hold that desire in your thought to attract from the invisible domain the things you need to satisfy it.

For mind does its building solely by the power of thought. Its creations take form according to its thought. Its first requisite is a mental image, and your desire held with unswerving purpose will form that mental image.

An understanding of this principle explains the power of prayer. The results of prayer are not brought about by some special dispensation of Providence. God is not a finite being to be cajoled or flattered into doing as you desire. But when you pray earnestly you form a mental image of the thing that you desire and you hold it strongly in your thought. Then the Universal Intelligence which is your intelligence—Omnipotent Mind—begins to work with and for you, and this is what brings about the manifestation that you desire.

The Universal Mind is all around you. It is as all-pervading as the air you breathe. It encompasses you with as little trouble as the water in the sea encompasses the fish. Yet it is just as thoroughly conscious of you as the water would be, were it intelligent, of every creature within it. "Are not two sparrows sold for a farthing? And one of them shall not fall on the ground without your Father. But the very hairs of your head are all numbered. Fear ye not, therefore, ye are of more value than many sparrows."

It seems hard to believe that a Mind busied with the immensities of the universe can consider such trivial affairs as our own when we are but one of the billions of forms of life which come into existence. Yet consider again the fish in the sea. It is no trouble for the sea to encompass them. It is no more trouble for the Universal Mind to encompass us. Its power, Its thought, are as much at our disposal as the sunshine and the wind and the rain. Few of us take advantage to the full of these great forces. Fewer still take advantage of the power of the Universal Mind. If you have any lack, if you are prey to poverty or disease, it is because you do not believe or do not understand the power that is yours. It is not a question of the Universal giving to you. It offers everything to everyone—there is no partiality. "Ho, everyone that thirsteth, come ye to the waters." You have only to take. "Whosoever will, let him take of the water of life freely."

"With all thy getting, get understanding," said Solomon. And if you will but get understanding, everything else will be added unto you.

To bring you to a realization of your indwelling and unused power, to teach you simple, direct methods of drawing upon it, is the beginning and the end of this course.

> *"And the earth was*
> *Without form and void;*
> *And darkness was upon*
> *The face of the deep.*
> *And the Spirit of God moved*
> *Upon the face of the waters."*
> —GENESIS 1:2

Volume III

The Primal Cause

This city, with all its houses, palaces, steam engines, cathedrals and huge, immeasurable traffic and tumult, what is it but a Thought, but millions of Thoughts made into one—a huge immeasurable Spirit of a Thought, embodied in brick, in iron, smoke, dust, Palaces, Parliaments, coaches, docks and the rest of it! Not a brick was made but some man had to think of the making of that brick.

—CARLYLE

FOR thousands of years the riddle of the universe has been the question of causation. Did the egg come first, or the chicken? "The globe," says an Eastern proverb, "rests upon the howdah of an elephant. The elephant stands upon a tortoise, swimming in a sea of milk." But then what? And what is life? As the Persian poet puts it—

"What without asking, hither hurried whence,
And without asking whither hurried hence?"

It has been said that every man, consciously or unconsciously, is either a materialist or an idealist. Certainly throughout the ages the schools of philosophy as well as individuals have argued and quarrelled, but always human thought through one or the other of these channels "has rolled down the hill of speculation into the ocean of doubt."

The materialist, roughly speaking, declares that nothing exists but matter and the forces inherent therein.

The idealist declares that all is mind or energy, and that matter is necessarily unreal.

The time has come when people have become dissatisfied with these unceasing theories which get them nowhere. And today, as the appreciation of a Primal Cause becomes more clearly defined, the spiritual instinct asserts itself determinedly.

"Give me a base of support," said Archimedes, "and with a lever I will move the world."

And the base of support is that all started with *mind*. In the beginning was nothing—a fire mist. Before anything could come of it there had to be an idea, a model on which to build. *Universal Mind* supplied that idea, that model. Therefore the primal cause is mind. Everything must start with an idea. Every event, every condition, every thing is first an idea in the mind of someone.

Before you start to build a house, you draw up a plan of it. You make an exact blue-print of that plan, and your house takes shape in accordance with your blue-print. Every material object takes form in the same way. Mind draws the plan. Thought forms the blueprint, well drawn or badly done as your thoughts are clear or vague. It all goes back to the one cause. The creative principle of the universe is mind, and thought is the eternal energy.

But just as the effect you get from electricity depends upon the mechanism to which the power is attached, so the effects you get from mind depend upon the way you use it. We are all of us dynamos. The power is there—unlimited power. But we've got to connect it up to something—set it some task—give it work to do—else are we no better off than the animals.

The "Seven Wonders of the World" were built by men with few of the opportunities or facilities that are available to you. They conceived these gigantic projects first in their own minds, pictured them so vividly that their subconscious minds came to their aid and enabled them to overcome obstacles that most of us would regard as insurmountable. Imagine building the Pyramids of Gizeh, enormous stone upon enormous stone, with nothing but bare hands. Imagine the labor, the sweat, the heartbreaking toil of erecting the Colossus of Rhodes, between whose legs a ship could pass! Yet men built these wonders, in a day when tools were of the crudest and machinery was undreamed of, by using the unlimited power of Mind.

Mind is creative, but it must have a model on which to work. It must have thoughts to supply the power.

There are in Universal Mind ideas for millions of wonders greater far than the "Seven Wonders of the World." And those ideas are just as available to you as they were to the artisans of old, as they were to Michelangelo when he built St. Peter's in Rome, as they were to the architect who conceived the Woolworth Building, or the engineer who planned the Hell Gate bridge.

Every condition, every experience of life is the result of our mental attitude. We can *do* only what we think we can do. We can *be* only what we think we can be. We can *have* only what we think we can have. What we do, what we are, what we have, all depend upon what we think. We can never express anything that we do not first have in mind. The secret of all power, all success, all riches, is in first thinking powerful thoughts, successful thoughts, thoughts of wealth, of supply. We must build them in our own mind first.

William James, the famous psychologist, said that the greatest discovery in a hundred years was the discovery of the power of the subconscious mind. It is the greatest discovery of all time. It is the discovery that man has within himself the power to control his surroundings, that he is not at the mercy of chance or luck, that he is the arbiter of his own fortunes, that he can carve out his own destiny. He is the master of all the forces round about him. As James Allen puts it:

"Dream lofty dreams, and as you dream, so shall you become. Your vision is the promise of what you shall one day be; your Ideal is the prophecy of what you shall at last unveil."

For matter is in the ultimate but a product of thought. Even the most material scientists admit that matter is not what it appears to be. According to physics, matter (be it the human body or a log of wood—it makes no difference which) is made up of an aggregation of distinct minute particles called atoms. Considered individually, these atoms are so small that they can be seen only with the aid of a powerful microscope, if at all.

MATTER—*DREAM OR REALITY?*

Until recently these atoms were supposed to be the ultimate theory regarding matter. We ourselves—and all the material world around us—were supposed to consist of these infinitesimal particles of matter, so small that they could not be seen or weighed or smelled or touched individually—but still particles of matter *and indestructible*.

Now, however, these atoms have been further analyzed, and physics tells us that they are not indestructible at all—that they are mere positive and negative buttons of force or energy called protons and electrons, without hardness, without density, without solidity, without even positive actuality. In short, they are vortices in the ether—whirling bits of energy—dynamic, never static, pulsating with life, but the life is *spiritual!* As one eminent British scientist put it—"Science now explains matter by *explaining it away!*"

And that, mind you, is what the solid table in front of you is made of, is what your house, your body, the whole world is made of—*whirling bits of energy!*

To quote the New York *Herald-Tribune* of March 11, 1926: "We used to believe that the universe was composed of an unknown number of different kinds of matter, one kind for each chemical element. The discovery of a new element had all the interest of the unexpected. It might turn out to be anything, to have any imaginable set of properties.

"That romantic prospect no longer exists. We know now that instead of many ultimate kinds of matter there are only two kinds. Both of these are really kinds of electricity. One is negative electricity, being, in fact, the tiny particle called the electron, familiar to radio fans as one of the particles vast swarms of which operate radio vacuum tubes. The other kind of electricity is positive electricity. Its ultimate particles are called protons. From these protons and electrons all of the chemical elements are built up. Iron and lead and oxygen and gold and all the others differ from one another merely in the number and arrangement of the electrons and protons which they contain. That is the modern idea of the nature of matter. *Matter is really nothing but electricity.*"

Can you wonder then that scientists believe the time will come when mankind *through mind* can control all this energy, can be absolute master of the winds and the waves, can literally follow the Master's precept—"If ye have faith as a grain of mustard seed, ye shall say unto this mountain, Remove hence to yonder place; and it shall remove; and nothing shall be impossible unto you."

For Modern Science is coming more and more to the belief that what we call *matter is a force subject wholly to the control of mind.*

How tenuous matter really is, is perhaps best illustrated by the fact that a single violin string, tuned to the proper pitch, could start a vibration that would shake down the Brooklyn Bridge! Oceans and mountains, rocks and iron, all can be reduced to a point little short of the purely spiritual. Your body is 85 per cent water, 15 per cent ash and phosphorus! And they in turn can be dissipated into gas and vapor. Where do we go from there?

Is not the answer that, to a great degree at least, and perhaps altogether, this world round about us is one of our mind's own creating? And that we can put into it, and get from it, pretty much what we wish? You see this illustrated every day. A panorama is spread before you. To you it is a beautiful picture; to another it appears a mere collection of rocks and trees. A girl comes out to meet you. To you she is the embodiment of loveliness; to another all that grace and beauty may look drab and homely. A moonlit garden, with its fragrant odors and dew-drenched grass, may mean all that is charming to you, while to another it brings only thoughts of asthma or fever or rheumatism. A color may be green to you that to another is red. A prospect may be inviting for you that to another is rugged and hard.

To quote "Applied Psychology," by Warren Hilton:

"The same stimulus acting on different organs of sense will produce different sensations. A blow upon the eye will cause you to 'see stars'; a similar blow upon the ear will cause you to hear an explosive sound. In other words, the vibratory effect of a touch on eye or ear is the same as that of light or sound vibrations.

"The notion you may form of any object in the outer world depends solely upon what part of your brain happens to be connected with that particular nerve-end that receives an impression from the object.

"You see the sun without being able to hear it because the only nerve-ends tuned to vibrate in harmony with the ether-waves set in action by the sun are nerve-ends that are connected with the brain center devoted to sight. 'If,' says Professor James, 'we could splice the outer extremities of our optic nerves to our ears, and those of our auditory nerves to our eyes, we should hear the lightning and see the thunder, see the symphony and hear the conductor's movements.'

"In other words, the kind of impressions we receive from the world about us, the sort of mental pictures we form concerning it, in fact, the character of the outer world, the nature of the environment in which our lives are cast—all these things depend for each one of us simply upon how he happens to be put together, upon his individual mental make-up."

In short, it all comes back to the old fable of the three blind men and the elephant. To the one who caught hold of his leg, the elephant was like a tree. To the one who felt of his side, the elephant was like a wall. To the one who seized his tail, the elephant was like a rope. The world is to each one of us the world of *his individual perceptions*.

You are like a radio receiving station. Every moment thousands of impressions are reaching you. You can tune in on whatever ones you like—on joy or sorrow, on success or failure, on optimism or fear. You can select the particular impressions that will best serve you, you can hear only what you want to hear, you can shut out all disagreeable thoughts and sounds and experiences, or you can tune in on discouragement and failure and despair.

Yours is the choice. You have within you a force against which the whole world is powerless. By using it, you can make what you will of life and of your surroundings.

"But," you will say, "objects themselves do not change. It is merely the difference in the way you look at them." Perhaps. But to a great extent, at least, we find what we look for, just as, when we turn the dial on the radio, we tune in on whatever kind of entertainment or instruction we may wish to hear. And who can say that it is not our thoughts that put it there? Who, for the matter of that, can prove that our surroundings in waking hours are not as much the creature of our minds as are our dreams? You've had dreams many a time where every object seemed just as real as when you were awake. You've felt of the objects, you've pinched yourself, yet still you were convinced that you were actually *living* those dreams. May not your waking existence be largely the creation of your own mind, just as your dream pictures are?

Many scientists believe that it is, and that in proportion as you try to put into your surroundings the good things you desire, rather than the evil ones you fear, *you will find those good things*. Certain it is that you can do this with your own body. Just as certain that many people are doing it with the good things of life. They have risen above the conception of life in which matter is the master.

Just as the most powerful forces in nature are the invisible ones—heat, light, air, electricity—so the most powerful forces of man are his invisible forces, his thought forces. And just as electricity can fuse stone and iron, so can your thought forces control your body, so can they make or mar your destiny.

THE PHILOSOPHER'S CHARM

There was once a shrewd necromancer who told a king that he had discovered a way to make gold out of sand. Naturally the king was interested and offered him great rewards for his secret. The necromancer explained his process. It seemed quite easy, except for one thing. Not once during the operation must the king think of the word Abracadabra. If he did, the charm was broken and the gold would not come. The king tried and tried to follow the directions, but he could not keep that word Abracadabra out of his mind. And he never made the gold.

Dr. Winbigler puts the same idea in another way: "Inspiration, genius, power, are often interfered with by the conscious mind's interposing, by man's failing to recognize his power, afraid to assist himself, lacking the faith in himself necessary to stimulate the subconscious so as to arouse the genius asleep in each."

From childhood on we are assured on every hand—by scientists, by philosophers, by our religious teachers, that "ours is the earth and the fullness thereof." Beginning with the first chapter of Genesis, we are told that "God said, Let us make man in our image, after our likeness; and let them have dominion over the fish of the sea, and over the fowl of the air, and over the cattle, and over all the earth—and over every living thing that moveth upon the earth." All through the Old and the New Testament, we are repeatedly adjured to use these God-given powers. "He that believeth on me," said Jesus, "the works that I do shall he do also; and greater works than these shall he do." "If ye abide in me, and my words abide in you, ye shall ask what ye will, and it shall be done unto you." "For verily I say unto you, that whosoever shall say unto this mountain, Be thou removed, and be thou cast into the sea; and shall not doubt in his heart, but shall believe that those things which he saith shall come to pass; he shall have whatsoever he saith." "The kingdom of God is within you."

We hear all this, perhaps we even think we believe, but always, when the time comes to use these God-given talents, there is the "doubt in our heart."

Baudouin expressed it clearly: "To be ambitious for wealth and yet always expecting to be poor; to be always doubting your ability to get what you long for, is like trying to reach east by travelling west. There is no philosophy which will help a man to succeed when he is always doubting his ability to do so, and thus attracting failure.

"You will go in the direction in which you face. . . .

"There is a saying that every time the sheep bleats, it loses a mouthful of hay. Every time you allow yourself to complain of your lot, to say, 'I am poor; I can never do what others do; I shall never be rich; I have not the ability that others have; I am a failure; luck is against me;' you are laying up so much trouble for yourself.

"No matter how hard you may work for success, if your thought is saturated with the fear of failure, it will kill your efforts, neutralize your endeavors, and make success impossible."

And that is responsible for all our failures. We are like the old lady who decided she wanted the hill behind her house removed. So she got down on her knees and prayed the good Lord to remove it. The next morning she got up and hurried to the window. The hill was still in its same old place. "I knew it!" she snapped. "I gave Him his chance. But I knew all the time there was nothing to this prayer business."

Neither is there, as it is ordinarily done. Prayer is not a mere asking of favors. Prayer is not a pæan of praise. Rather prayer is a realization of the God-power within you—of your right of dominion over your own body, your environment, your business, your health, your prosperity. It is an understanding that you are "heir of God and co-heir with Christ." And that as such, no evil has power over you, whereas you have all power for good. And "good" means not merely holiness. Good means happiness—the happiness of everyday people. Good means everything that is good in this world of ours—comforts and pleasures and prosperity for ourselves, health and happiness for those dependent upon us. There are no limits to "Good" except those we put upon it ourselves.

What was it made Napoleon the greatest conqueror of his day? Primarily his magnificent faith in Napoleon. He had a sublime belief in his destiny, an absolute confidence that the obstacle was not made which Napoleon could not find a way through, or over, or around. It was only when he lost that confidence, when he hesitated and vacillated for weeks between retreat and advance, that winter caught him in Moscow and ended his dreams of world empire. Fate gave him every chance first. The winter snows were a full month late in coming. But Napoleon hesitated—and was lost. It was not the snows that defeated him. It was not the Russians. It was his loss of faith in himself.

THE KINGDOM OF HEAVEN

"The Kingdom of Heaven is within you." Heaven is not some far-away state—the reward of years of tribulation here. Heaven is right here—here and now! When Christ said that Heaven was within us, He meant just what He said—that the power for happiness, for good, for everything we need of life, is within each one of us.

That most of us fail to realize this Heaven—that many are sickly and suffering, that more are ground down by poverty and worry—is no fault of His. He gave us the power to overcome these evils; He stands ready and waiting to help us use it. If we fail to find the way, the fault is ours. To enjoy the Heaven that is within us, to begin here and now to live the life eternal, takes only a fuller understanding of the Power-that-is-within-us.

Even now, with the limited knowledge at our command, we can control circumstances to the point of making the world without an expression of our own world within, where the real thoughts, the real power, resides. Through this world within you can find the solution of every problem, the cause for every effect. Discover it—and all power, all possession is within your control.

For the world without is but a reflection of that world within. Your thought *creates* the conditions your mind images. Keep before your mind's eye the image of all you want to be and you will see it reflected in the world without. Think abundance, feel abundance, BELIEVE abundance, and you will find that as you think and feel and believe, abundance will manifest itself in your daily life. But let fear and worry be your mental companions, thoughts of poverty and limitation dwell in your mind, and worry and fear, limitation and poverty will be your constant companions day and night.

Your mental concept is all that matters. Its relation to matter is that of idea and form. There has got to be an idea before it can take form. As Dr. Terry Walter says:

"The impressions that enter the subconscious form indelible pictures, which are never forgotten, and whose power can change the body, mind, manner, and morals; can, in fact, revolutionize a personality.

"All during our waking hours the conscious mind, through the five senses, acts as constant feeder to the subconscious; the senses are the temporal source of supply for the content of the soul mind; therefore it is most important that we know and realize definitely and explicitly that every time we think a thought or feel an emotion, we are adding to the content of this powerful mind, good or bad, as the case may be. Life will be richer or poorer for the thoughts and deeds of today."

Your thoughts supply you with limitless energy which will take whatever form your mind demands. The thoughts are the mold which crystalizes this energy into good or ill according to the form you impress upon it. You are free to choose which. But whichever you choose, the result is sure. Thoughts of wealth, of power, of success, can bring only results commensurate with your idea of them. Thoughts of poverty and lack can bring only limitation and trouble.

"A radical doctrine," you'll say, and think me wildly optimistic. Because the world has been taught for so long to think that some must be rich and some poor, that trials and tribulations are our lot. That this is at best a vale of tears.

The history of the race shows that what is considered to be the learning of one age is ignorance to the next age.

Dr. Edwin E. Slosson, Editor of *Science Service,* speaking of the popular tendency to fight against new ideas merely because they were *new,* said: "All through the history of science, we find that new ideas have to force their way into the common mind in disguise, as though they were burglars instead of benefactors of the race."

And Emerson wrote: "The virtue in most request is conformity. Self-reliance is its aversion. It loves not realities and creators, but names and customs."

In the ages to come man will look back upon the poverty and wretchedness of so many millions today, and think how foolish we were not to take advantage of the abundance all about us. Look at Nature; how profuse she is in everything. Do you suppose the Mind that imaged that profuseness ever intended you to be limited, to have to scrimp and save in order to eke out a bare existence?

There are hundreds of millions of stars in the heavens. Do you suppose the Mind which could bring into being worlds without number in such prodigality intended to stint you of the few things necessary to your happiness?

What is money but a mere idea of mind, a token of exchange? The paper money you have in your pockets is supposed to represent so much gold or silver currency. There are billions upon billions of this paper money in circulation, yet all the gold in the world amounts to only about $8,000,000,000. Wealth is in ideas, not in money or property. You can control those ideas through mind.

Reduced to the ultimate—to the atom or to the electron—everything in this world is an idea of mind. All of it has been brought together through mind. If we can change the things we want back into mental images, we can multiply them as often as we like, possess all that we like.

"TO HIM THAT HATH"—

Take as an example the science of numbers. Suppose all numbers were of metal—that it was against the law to write figures for ourselves. Every time you wanted to do a sum in arithmetic you'd have to provide yourself with a supply of numbers, arrange them in their proper order, work out your problems with them. If your problems were too abstruse you might run out of numbers, have to borrow some from your neighbor or from the bank.

"How ridiculous," you say. "Figures are not things; they are mere ideas, and we can add them or divide them or multiply them or subtract them as often as we like. Anybody can have all the figures he wants."

To be sure he can. And when you get to look upon money in the same way, you will have all the money you want.

"To him that hath shall be given, and from him that hath not shall be taken away even that which he hath." To him that hath the right idea everything shall be given, and from him who hath not that right idea shall be taken away everything he hath.

Thought externalizes itself. What we are depends entirely upon the images we hold before our mind's eye. Every time we think, we start a chain of causes which will create conditions similar to the thoughts which originated it. Every thought we hold in our consciousness for any length of time becomes impressed upon our subconscious mind and creates a pattern which the mind weaves into our life or environment.

All power is from within and is therefore under our own control. When you can direct your thought processes, you can consciously apply them to any condition, for all that comes to us from the world without is what we've already imaged in the world within.

Do you want more money? Sit you down now quietly and realize that money is merely an idea. That your mind is possessed of unlimited ideas. That being part of Universal Mind, there is no such thing as limitation or lack. That somewhere, somehow, the ideas that shall bring you all the money you need for any right purpose are available for you. That you have but to put it up to your subconscious mind to find these ideas.

Realize that—*believe* it—and your need will be met. "What things soever ye desire, when ye pray, believe that ye receive it and ye shall have it." Don't forget that *"believe that ye receive it."* This it is that images the thing you want on your subconscious mind. And this it is that brings it to you. Once you can image the belief clearly on your subconscious mind, "whatsoever it is that ye ask for . . . ye shall have it."

For the source of all good, of everything you wish for, is the Universal Mind, and you can reach it only through the subconscious.

And Universal Mind will be to you whatever you believe it to be—the kind and loving Father whom Jesus pictured, always looking out for the well-being of his children—or the dread Judge that so many dogmatists would have us think.

When a man realizes that his mind is part of Universal Mind, when he realizes that he has only to take any right aspiration to this Universal Mind to see it realized, he loses all sense of worry and fear. He learns to dominate instead of to cringe. He rises to meet every situation, secure in the knowledge that everything necessary to the solution of any problem is in Mind, and that he has but to take his problem to Universal Mind to have it correctly answered.

For if you take a drop of water from the ocean, you know that it has the same properties as all the rest of the water in the ocean, the same percentage of sodium chloride. The only difference between it and the ocean is in volume. If you take a spark of electricity, you know that it has the same properties as the thunderbolt, the same power that moves trains or runs giant machines in factories. Again the only difference is in volume. It is the same with your mind and Universal Mind. The only difference between them is in volume. Your mind has the same properties as the Universal Mind, the same creative genius, the same power over all the earth, the same access to all knowledge. Know this, believe it, use it, and "yours is the earth and the fulness thereof." In the exact proportion that you believe yourself to be part of Universal Mind, sharing in Its all-power, in that proportion can you demonstrate the mastery over your own body and over the world about you.

All growth, all supply is from the world-within. If you would have power, if you would have wealth, you have but to image it on this world within, on your subconscious mind, through belief and understanding.

If you would remove discord, you have but to remove the wrong images— images of ill health, of worry and trouble from within. The trouble with most of us is that we live entirely in the world without. We have no knowledge of that inner world which is responsible for all the conditions we meet and all the experiences we have. We have no conception of "the Father that is within us."

The inner world promises us life and health, prosperity and happiness— dominion over all the earth. It promises peace and perfection for all its offspring. It gives you the right way and the adequate way to accomplish any normal purpose. Business, labor, professions, exist primarily in thought. And the outcome of your labors in them is regulated by thought. Consider the difference, then, in this outcome if you have at your command only the limited capacity of your conscious mind, compared with the boundless energy of the subconscious and the Universal Mind. "Thought, not money, is the real business capital," says

Harvey S. Firestone, "and if you know absolutely that what you are doing is right, then you are bound to accomplish it in due season."

Thought is a dynamic energy with the power to bring its object out from the invisible substance all about us. Matter is inert, unintelligent. Thought can shape and control. Every form in which matter is today is but the expression of some thought, some desire, some idea.

You have a mind. You can originate thought. And thoughts are creative. Therefore you can create for yourself that which you desire. Once you realize this you are taking a long step toward success in whatever undertaking you have in mind.

More than half the prophecies in the Scriptures refer to the time when man shall possess the earth, when tears and sorrow shall be unknown, and peace and plenty shall be everywhere. That time will come. It is nearer than most people think possible. You are helping it along. Every man who is honestly trying to use the power of mind in the right way is doing his part in the great cause. For it is only through Mind that peace and plenty can be gained. The earth is laden with treasures as yet undiscovered. But they are every one of them known to Universal Mind, for it was Universal Mind that first imaged them there. And as part of Universal Mind, they can be known to you.

How else did the Prophets of old foretell, thousands of years ago, the aeroplane, the cannon, the radio? What was the genius that enabled Ezekiel to argue from his potter's wheel, his water wheel and the stroke of the lightning to an airplane, with its wheels within wheels, driven by electricity and guided by man? How are we to explain the descriptions of artillery in the Apocalypse and the astonishing declaration in the Gospels that the utterances of the chamber would be broadcast from the housetops?

"TO THE MANNER BORN"

Few of us have any idea of our mental powers. The old idea was that man must take this world as he found it. He'd been born into a certain position in life, and to try to rise above his fellows was not only the height of bad taste, but sacrilegious as well. An All wise Providence had decreed by birth the position a child should occupy in the web of organized society. For him to be discontented with his lot, for him to attempt to raise himself to a higher level, was tantamount to tempting Providence. The gates of Hell yawned wide for such scatterbrains, who were lucky if in this life they incurred nothing worse than the ribald scorn of their associates.

That is the system that produced aristocracy and feudalism. That is the system that feudalism and aristocracy strove to perpetuate.

The new idea—the basis of all democracies—is that man is not bound by any system, that he need not accept the world as he finds it. He can remake the world to his own ideas. It is merely the raw material. He can make what he wills of it.

It is this new idea that is responsible for all our inventions, all our progress. Man is satisfied with nothing. He is constantly remaking his world. And now more than ever will this be true, for psychology teaches us that each one has within himself the power to become what he wills.

Learn to control your thought. Learn to image upon your mind only the things you want to see reflected there.

You will never improve yourself by dwelling upon the drawbacks of your neighbors. You will never attain perfect health and strength by thinking of weakness or disease. No man ever made a perfect score by watching his rival's target. You have got to think strength, think health, think riches. To paraphrase Pascal—"Our achievements today are but the sum of our thoughts of yesterday."

For thought is energy. Mental images are concentrated energy. And energy concentrated on any definite purpose becomes power. To those who perceive the nature and transcendency of this force, all physical power sinks into insignificance.

What is imagination but a form of thought? Yet it is the instrument by which all the inventors and discoverers have opened the way to new worlds. Those who grasp this force, be their state ever so humble, their natural gifts ever so insignificant, become our leading men. They are our governors and supreme law-givers, the guides of the drifting host which follows them as by an irrevocable decree. To quote Glenn Clark in the *Atlantic Monthly*, "Whatever we have of civilization is their work, theirs alone. If progress was made they made it. If spiritual facts were discerned, they discerned them. If justice and order were put in place of insolence and chaos, they wrought the change. Never is progress achieved by the masses. Creation ever remains the task of the individual."

Our railroads, our telephones, our automobiles, our libraries, our newspapers, our thousands of other conveniences, comforts and necessities are due to the creative genius of but two per cent of our population.

And the same two per cent own a great percentage of the wealth of the country.

The question arises, Who are they? What are they? The sons of the rich? College men? No—few of them had any early advantages. Many of them have never seen the inside of a college. It was grim necessity that drove them, and somehow, some way, they found a method of drawing upon their Genie-of-the-Mind, and through that inner force they have reached success.

You don't need to stumble and grope. You can call upon your inner forces at will. There are three steps necessary:

First, to realize that you have the power;

Second, to know what you want.

Third, to center your thought upon it with singleness of purpose.

To accomplish these steps takes only a fuller understanding of the Power-that-is-within-you.

But what is this power? Where should you go to locate it? Is it a thing, a place, an object? Has it bounds, form or material shape? No! Then how shall you go about finding it?

If you have begun to *realize* that there is a power within you, if you have begun to arouse in your conscious mind the ambition and desire to use this power—you have started in the pathway of Wisdom. If you are willing to go forward, to endure the mental discipline of mastering this method, nothing in the world can hinder you or keep you from overcoming every obstacle.

Begin at once, today, to use what you have learned. All growth comes from practice. All the forces of life are active—peace—joy—power. The unused talent decays. Open the door—

"Behold I stand at the door and knock; if ANY MAN hear my voice and open the door, I will come in to him, and will sup with him and he with me."

So let us make use of this dynamo, which is *you*. What is going to start it working? Your *Faith,* the faith that is begotten of understanding. Faith is the impulsion, the propulsion of this power within. Faith is the confidence, the assurance, the enforcing truth, the knowing that the right idea of life will bring you into the reality of existence and the manifestation of the All power.

All cause is in Mind—and Mind is everywhere. All the knowledge there is, all the wisdom there is, all the power there is, is all about you—no matter where you may be. Your Mind is part of it. You have access to it. If you fail to avail yourself of it, you have no one to blame but yourself. For, as the drop of water in the ocean shares in all the properties of the rest of the ocean water so you share in that all-power, all-wisdom of Mind. If you have been sick and ailing, if poverty and hardship have been your lot, don't blame it on "fate." Blame yourself. "Yours is the earth and everything that's in it." But you've got to *take* it. The power is there—but *you* must *use* it. It is round about you like the air you breathe. You don't expect others to do your breathing for you. Neither can you expect them to use your Mind for you. Universal Intelligence is not only the mind of the Creator of the universe, but it is also the mind of MAN, *your* intelligence, *your* mind. "Let this mind be in you, which was also in Christ Jesus!"

So start today by KNOWING that you can do anything you wish to do, have anything you wish to have, be anything you wish to be. The rest will follow.

"Ye shall ask what ye will and it shall be done unto you."

Volume IV

Desire—the First Law of Gain

"Ah, Love! Could Thou and I with Fate conspire
To grasp this sorry Scheme of Things entire,
Would we not shatter it to bits—and then
Re-mold it nearer to the Heart's Desire!"

—THE RUBAIYAT OF OMAR KHAYYAM

IF YOU had a fairy wishing ring, what one thing would you wish for? Wealth? Honor? Fame? Love? What one thing do you desire above everything else in life?

Whatever it is, you can have it. Whatever you desire wholeheartedly, with singleness of purpose—you can have. But the first and all-important essential is to know what this one thing is. Before you can win your heart's desire, you've got to get clearly fixed in your mind's eye what it is that you want.

It may sound paradoxical, but few people do know what they want. Most of them struggle along in a vague sort of way, hoping—like Micawber—for something to turn up. They are so taken up with the struggle that they have forgotten—if they ever knew—what it is they are struggling for. They are like a drowning man—they use up many times the energy it would take to get them somewhere, but they fritter it away in aimless struggles—without thought, without direction, exhausting themselves, while getting nowhere.

You've got to know what you want before you stand much chance of getting it. You have an unfailing "Messenger to Garcia" in that Genie-of-your-Mind—but YOU have got to formulate the message. Aladdin would have stood a poor chance of getting anything from his Genie if he had not had clearly in mind the things he wanted the Genie to get.

In the realm of mind, the realm in which is all practical power, you can possess what you want at once. You have but to claim it, to visualize it, to bring it into actuality—and it is yours for the taking. For the Genie-of-your-Mind can give you power over circumstances. Health, happiness and prosperity. And all you need to put it to work is an earnest, intense desire.

Sounds too good to be true? Well, let us go back for a moment to the start. You are infected with that "divine dissatisfaction with things as they are" which has been responsible for all the great accomplishments of this world—else you would not have gotten thus far in this book. Your heart is hungering for something better. "Blessed are they which do hunger and thirst after righteousness (right-wiseness) for they shall be filled." You are tired of the worry and grind, tired of the deadly dull routine and daily tasks that lead nowhere. Tired of all the petty little ills and ailments that have come to seem the lot of man here on earth.

Always there is something within you urging you on to bigger things, giving you no peace, no rest, no chance to be lazy. It is the same "something" that drove Columbus across the ocean; that drove Hannibal across the Alps; that drove Edison onward and upward from a train boy to the inventive wizard of the century; that drove Henry Ford from a poor mechanic at forty to probably the richest man in the world at sixty.

This "something" within you keeps telling you that you can do anything you want to do, be anything you want to be, have anything you want to have—and you have a sneaking suspicion that it may be right.

That "something" within you is your subconscious self, your part of Universal Mind, your Genie-of-the-brain. Men call it ambition, and "Lucky is the man," says Arthur Brisbane, "whom the Demon of Ambition harnesses and drives through life. This wonderful little coachman is the champion driver of all the world and of all history.

"Lucky you, if he is *your* driver.

"He will keep you going until you do something worth while—working, running and moving ahead.

"And that is how a real man ought to be driven.

"This is the little Demon that works in men's brains, that makes the blood tingle at the thought of achievement and that makes the face flush and grow white at the thought of failure.

"Every one of us has this Demon for a driver, IN YOUTH AT LEAST.

"Unfortunately the majority of us he gives up as very poor, hopeless things, not worth driving, by the time we reach twenty-five or thirty.

"How many men look back to their teens, when they were harnessed to the wagon of life with Ambition for a driver? When they could not wait for the years to pass and for opportunity to come?

"It is the duty of ambition to drive, and it is your duty to *keep Ambition alive and driving.*

"If you are doing nothing, if there is no driving, no hurrying, no working, *you may count upon it that there will be no results. Nothing much worth while in the years to come.*

"Those that are destined to be the big men twenty years from now, when the majority of us will be nobodies, *are those whom this demon is driving relentlessly, remorselessly, through the hot weather and the cold weather, through early hours and late hours.*

"Lucky YOU if you are in harness and driven by the Demon of Ambition."

Suppose you *have* had disappointments, disillusionments along the way. Suppose the fine point of your ambition has become blunted. Remember, there is no obstacle that there is not some way around, or over, or through—and if you will depend less upon the 10 per cent of your abilities that reside in your conscious mind, and leave more to the 90 per cent that constitute your subconscious, you can overcome all obstacles. Remember this—there is no condition so hopeless, no life so far gone, that mind cannot redeem it.

Every untoward condition is merely *a lack* of something. Darkness, you know, is not real. It is merely a lack of light. Turn on the light and the darkness will be seen to be nothing. It vanishes instantly. In the same way poverty is simply a lack of necessary supply. Find the avenue of supply and your poverty vanishes. Sickness is merely the absence of health. If you are in perfect health, sickness cannot hurt you. Doctors and nurses go about at will among the sick without fear—and suffer as a rule far less from sickness than does the average man or woman.

So there is nothing you have to *overcome*. You merely have to *acquire* something. And always Mind can show you the way. You can obtain from Mind anything you want, if you will learn how to do it. "I think we can rest assured that one can do and be practically what he desires to be," says Farnsworth in

"Practical Psychology." And psychologists all over the world have put the same thought in a thousand different ways.

"It is not will, but desire," says Charles W. Mears, "that rules the world." "But," you will say, "I have had plenty of desires all my life. I've always wanted to be rich. How do you account for the difference between my wealth and position and power and that of the rich men all around me?"

THE MAGIC SECRET

The answer is simply that you have never focused your desires into one great dominating desire. You have a host of mild desires. You mildly wish you were rich, you wish you had a position of responsibility and influence, you wish you could travel at will. The wishes are so many and varied that they conflict with each other and you get nowhere in particular. You lack one *intense* desire, to the accomplishment of which you are willing to subordinate everything else.

Do you know how Napoleon so frequently won battles in the face of a numerically superior foe? By concentrating his men at the actual *point of contact!* His artillery was often greatly outnumbered, but it accomplished far more than the enemy's because instead of scattering his fire, he *concentrated it all on the point of attack!*

The time you put in aimlessly dreaming and wishing would accomplish marvels if it were concentrated on one definite object. If you have ever taken a magnifying glass and let the sun's rays play through it on some object, you know that as long as the rays were scattered they accomplished nothing. But focus them on one tiny spot and see how quickly they start something.

It is the same way with your mind. You've got to concentrate *on one idea at a time.*

"But how can I learn to concentrate?" many people write me. Concentration is not a thing to be learned. It is merely a thing to do. You concentrate whenever you become sufficiently interested in anything. Get so interested in a ball game that you jump up and down on your hat, slap a man you have never seen before on the back, embrace your nearest neighbor—*that* is concentration. Become so absorbed in a thrilling play or movie that you no longer realize the orchestra is playing or there are people around you—*that* is concentration.

And that is all concentration ever is—getting so interested in some one thing that you pay no attention to anything else that is going on around you.

If you want a thing badly enough, you need have no worry about your ability to concentrate on it. Your thoughts will just naturally center on it like bees on honey.

Hold in your mind the thing you most desire. Affirm it. Believe it to be an existing fact. Let me quote again the words of the Master, because there's nothing more important to remember in this whole book. "Therefore I say unto you, what things soever ye desire, when ye pray, *believe that ye receive them* and ye shall have them."

And again I say, the most important part is the *"believe that ye receive them."* Your subconscious mind is exceedingly amenable to suggestion. If you can truly believe that you have received something, can impress that belief upon your subconscious mind, depend upon it, it will see that you have it. For being a part of Universal Mind, it shares that Universal Mind's all-power. "The Father that is within me, He doeth the works." Your mind will respond to your desire in the exact proportion in which you believe. "As thy faith is, so be it unto thee."

The people who live in beautiful homes, who have plenty to spend, who travel about in yachts and fine cars, are for the most part people who started out to accomplish *some one definite thing.* They had one clear goal in mind, and everything they did centered on that goal.

Most men just jog along in a rut, going through the same old routine day after day, ekeing out a bare livelihood, with no definite desire other than the vague hope that fortune will some day drop in their lap. Fortune doesn't often play such pranks. And a rut, you know, differs from a grave only in depth. A life such as that is no better than the animals live. Work all day for money to buy bread, to give you strength to work all the next day to buy more bread. There is nothing to it but the daily search for food and sustenance. No time for aught but worry and struggle. No hope of anything but the surcease of sorrow in death.

You can have anything you want—if you want it badly enough. You can be anything you want to be, have anything you desire, accomplish anything you set out to accomplish—if you will hold to that desire with singleness of purpose; if you will understand and BELIEVE in your own powers to accomplish.

What is it that you wish in life? Is it health? In the chapter on health I will show you that you can be radiantly well—without drugs, without tedious exercises. It matters not if you are crippled or bedridden or infirm. Your body rebuilds itself entirely every eleven months. You can start now rebuilding along perfect lines.

Is it wealth you wish? In the chapter on success I will show you how you can increase your income, how you can forge rapidly ahead in your chosen business or profession.

Is it happiness you ask for? Follow the rules herein laid down and you will change your whole outlook on life. Doubts and uncertainty will vanish, to be followed by calm assurance and abiding peace. You will possess the things your heart desires. You will have love and companionship. You will win to contentment and happiness.

But desire must be impressed upon the subconscious before it can be accomplished. Merely conscious desire seldom gets you anything. It is like the day-dreams that pass through your mind. Your desire must be visualized, must be persisted in, must be concentrated upon, must be impressed upon your subconscious mind. Don't bother about the means for accomplishing your desire—you can safely leave that to your subconscious mind. It knows how to do a great many things besides building and repairing your body. If you can visualize the thing you want, if you can impress upon your subconscious mind the *belief that you have it,* you can safely leave to it the finding of the means of getting it. Trust the Universal Mind to show the way. The mind that provided everything in such profusion must joy in seeing us take advantage of that profusion. "For herein is the Father glorified—that ye bear much fruit."

You do not have to wait until tomorrow, or next year, or the next world, for happiness. You do not have to die to be saved. "The Kingdom of Heaven is within you." That does not mean that it is up in the heavens or on some star or in the next world. It means *here* and *now!* All the possibilities of happiness are always here and always available. At the open door of every man's life there lies this pearl of great price—the understanding of man's dominion over the earth. With that understanding and conviction you can do everything which lies before you to do and you can do it to the satisfaction of everyone and the well-being of yourself. God and good are synonymous. And God—good—is absent only to those who believe He is absent.

Find your desire, impress it upon your thought, and you have opened the door for opportunity. And remember, in this new heaven and new earth which I am trying to show you, *the door of opportunity is never closed.* As a matter of fact, you constantly have *all that you will take.* So keep yourself in a state of receptivity. It is your business to receive abundantly and perpetually. The law of opportunity enforces its continuance and availability. "Every good gift and every perfect gift is from above and cometh down from the Father of light, with whom is *no variableness, neither shadow of turning.*"

Infinite Mind saith to every man, "Come ye to the open fountain." The understanding of the law of life will remedy every discord, giving "Beauty for ashes, the oil of joy for mourning, the garment of praise for the spirit of heaviness."

Believe that you share in that goodness and bounty. Act the part you wish to play in this life. Act healthy, act prosperous, act happy. Make such a showing with what you have that you will carry the conviction to your subconscious mind that all good and perfect gifts ARE yours. Register health, prosperity and happiness on your inner mind and some fine morning soon you will wake to find that *you are* healthy, prosperous and happy, that you *have* your dearest wish in life.

"THE SOUL'S SINCERE DESIRE"

Do you know what prayer is? Just an earnest desire that we take to God—to Universal Mind—for fulfillment. As Montgomery puts it—"Prayer is the soul's *sincere desire,* uttered or unexpressed." It is our Heart's Desire. At least, the only prayer that is worth anything is the prayer that asks for our real desires. That kind of prayer is heard. That kind of prayer is answered.

Mere lip prayers get you nowhere. It doesn't matter what your lips may say. The thing that counts is what your heart desires, what your mind images on your subconscious thought, and through it on Universal Mind. "Thou, when thou prayest, be not as the hypocrites are; for they love to pray standing in the synagogue and at the corners of the streets, that they may be seen of men. Verily I say unto you, they have their reward."

What was it these hypocrites that Jesus speaks of really wanted? "To be seen of men." And their prayers were answered. Their sincere desire was granted. They were seen of men. "They have their reward." But as for what their lips were saying, neither God nor they paid any attention to it.

"Thou, when thou prayest enter into thy closet, and when thou hast shut the door, pray to thy Father which is in secret, and thy Father which seeth in secret, shall reward thee openly." Go where you can be alone, where you can concentrate your thoughts on your one innermost sincere desire, where you can impress that desire upon your subconscious mind without distraction, and so reach the Universal Mind (the Father of all things).

But even sincere desire is not enough by itself. There must be BELIEF, too. "What things soever ye desire, when ye pray, believe that ye receive them and ye shall have them." You must realize God's ability to give you every good thing.

You must believe in his readiness to do it. Model your thoughts after the Psalmists of old. They first asked for that which they wanted, then killed all doubts and fears by affirming God's power and His willingness to grant their prayers. Read any of the Psalms and you will see what I mean. So when you pray, ask for the things that you want. Then affirm God's readiness and His Power to grant your prayer.

Glenn Clark, in "The Soul's Sincere Desire," gives some wonderfully helpful suggestions along these lines. To quote him:

"For money troubles, realize: There is no want in Heaven, and affirm:

"Our Heavenly Father, we know that thy Love is as infinite as the sky is infinite, and Thy Ways of manifesting that love are as unaccountable as the stars of the heavens.

"Thy Power is greater than man's horizon, and Thy Ways of manifesting that Power are more numerous than the sands of the sea.

"As Thou keepest the stars in their courses, so shalt Thou guide our steps in perfect harmony, without clash or discord of any kind, if we keep our trust in Thee. For we know Thou wilt keep him in perfect peace whose mind is stayed on Thee, because he trusteth in Thee. We know that, if we acknowledge Thee in all our ways, Thou wilt direct our paths. For Thou art the God of Love, Giver of every good and perfect gift, and there is none beside Thee. Thou art omnipotent, omniscient, and omnipresent, in all, through all, and over all, the only God. And Thine is the Kingdom, and the Power, and the Glory, forever, Amen.

"For aid in thinking or writing, realize: There is no lack of ideas, and affirm:

"Thy wisdom is greater than all hidden treasures, and yet as instantly available for our needs as the very ground beneath our feet."

"For happiness: There is no unhappiness in Heaven, so affirm:

"Thy joy is brighter than the sun at noonday and Thy Ways of expressing that Joy as countless as the sunbeams that shine upon our path."

This is the kind of prayer the Psalmists of old had recourse to in their hours of trouble—this is the kind of prayer that will bring you every good and perfect gift.

Make no mistake about this—*prayer is effective.* It *can* do anything. It doesn't matter how trivial your desires may be—if it is RIGHT for you to have them, it is RIGHT for you to pray for them.

According to a United Press dispatch of May 3, 1926:

"Prayer belongs to the football field as much as to the pulpit, and a praying team stands a good chance of 'getting there,' Tim Lowry, Northwestern University football star, told a large church audience here.

"'Just before the Indiana-Northwestern game last year,' Tim said, 'we worried a great deal about the outcome. Then we saw that bunch of big husky Indiana players coming toward us and we knew something had to be done quick.

"'Fellows,' I said, 'I believe in prayer and we better pray.' We did and won a great victory.

"When the next game came, every fellow prayed again.

"You don't need to think that churches have a copyright on prayer."

In "Prayer as a Force," A. Maude Royden compares the man who trusts his desires to prayer with the swimmer who trusts himself to the water:

"Let me give you a very simple figure which I think may perhaps convey my meaning. If you are trying to swim you must believe that the sea is going to keep you afloat. You must give yourself to the sea. There is the ocean and there are you in it, and I say to you, 'According to your faith you will be able to swim!' I know perfectly well that it is literally according to your faith. A person who has just enough confidence in the sea and in himself to give one little hop from the ground will certainly find that the water will lift him but not very much; he will come down again. Persons who have enough confidence really to start swimming but no more, will not swim very far, because their confidence is so very small and they swim with such rapid strokes, and they hold their breath to such an extent, that by and by they collapse; they swim five or six, or twelve or fourteen strokes, but they do not get very far, through lack of confidence.

"Persons who know with assurance that the sea will carry them if they do certain things, will swim quite calmly, serenely, happily, and will not mind if the water goes right over them. 'Oh,' you say, 'that person is doing the whole thing!' *He can't do it without the sea!* You might hypnotize people into faith; you might say, 'You are now in the ocean; swim off the edge of this precipice' (which is really a cliff). You might make them do it, they might have implicit faith in you, you might hypnotize them into thinking they were swimming; but if they swam off the edge of the cliff they would fall. You can't swim without the sea! I might say to you, 'It lies with you whether you swim or not, according to your faith be it unto you'; but if the sea is not there you can't swim. That is exactly what I feel about God. 'According to your faith be it unto you.' Yes, certainly, if you try to swim in that ocean which is the love of God your faith will be rewarded, and according to your faith it will be to you. In exact proportion to your faith you will find the answer, like a scientific law. There is not one atom of faith you put in God that will not receive its answer."

But remember: you would not plant a valuable seed in your garden, and then, a day or a week later, go out and dig it up to see if it were sprouting. On the contrary, you would nourish it each morning with water. It is the same with your prayers. Don't plant the seed of your desire in your subconscious mind and then go out the next morning and tear it up with doubts and fears. Nourish it by holding in thought the thing you desire, by believing in it, visualizing it, SEEING it as an accomplished fact.

If you ask for my own formula for successful prayer, I would say—

1st. Center your thoughts on the thing that you want. Visualize it. Make a mental image of it. You are planting the seed of Desire. But don't be content with that. Planting alone will not make a seed of corn grow. It has to be warmed by sunshine, nurtured by rain. So with the seed of your Desire. It must be warmed by Faith, nurtured by constant Belief. So—

2nd. Read the 91st and the 23rd Psalms, just as a reminder of God's power and His readiness to help you in all your needs.

3rd. Don't forget to be thankful, not merely for past favors, *but for the granting of this favor you are now asking!* To be able to thank God for it sincerely, in advance of its actual material manifestation, is the finest evidence of belief.

4th. BELIEVE! Picture the thing that you want so clearly, see it in your imagination so vividly, that for the moment, at least, you will actually BELIEVE THAT YOU HAVE IT!

It is this sincere conviction, registered upon your subconscious mind, and through it upon Universal Mind, that brings the answer to your prayers. Once convince your subconscious mind that you HAVE the thing you want, and you can forget it and go on to your next problem. Mind will attend to the bringing of it into being.

Volume V

Aladdin & Company

"But the feeble hands and helpless,
Groping blindly in the darkness,
Touch God's right hand in that darkness,
And are lifted up and strengthened."

—LONGFELLOW

IT is not always the man who struggles hardest who gets on in the world. It is the direction as well as the energy of struggle that counts in making progress. To get ahead—you must swim with the tide. Men prosper and succeed who work in accord with natural forces. A given amount of effort with these forces carries a man faster and farther than much more effort used against the current. Those who work blindly, regardless of these forces, make life difficult for themselves and rarely prosper.

It has been estimated by wise observers that on the average something like 90 per cent of the factors producing success or failure lie outside a man's conscious efforts—separate from his daily round of details. To the extent that he cooperates with the wisdom and power of Universal Mind he is successful, well and happy. To the extent that he fails to cooperate, he is unsuccessful, sick and miserable.

All down the ages some have been enabled to "taste and see that the Lord is good." Prophets and Seers being blessed with the loving kindness of God, have proclaimed a God of universal goodness, saying: "The earth is full of the goodness of the Lord"; "Thou wilt show me the path of life; in Thy presence is fullness of joy."

Now we know that this Infinite Good is not more available to one than it is to all. We know that the only limit to it is in our capacity to receive. If you had a problem in mathematics to work out, you would hardly gather together the necessary figures and leave them to arrange themselves in their proper sequence. You would know that while the method for solving every problem has been figured out, *you* have got to *work* it. The principles are there, but *you* have got to *apply* them.

The first essential is to understand the principle—to learn how it works—how to use it. The second—and even more important part—is to APPLY that understanding to the problem in hand.

In the same way, the Principle of Infinite Energy, Infinite Supply, is ever available. But that Energy, that Supply, is static. You've got to make it dynamic. You've got to understand the law. You've got to *apply* your understanding in order to solve your problems of poverty, discord, disease.

Science shows that it is possible to accomplish any good thing. But distrust of your ability to reach the goal desired often holds you back and failure is the inevitable result.

Only by understanding that there is but one power—and that this power is Mind, not circumstances or environment—is it possible to bring your real abilities to the surface and put them to work.

Few deny that intelligence governs the universe. It matters not whether you call this intelligence Universal Mind or Providence or God or merely Nature. All admit Its directing power. All admit that It is a force for good, for progress. But few realize that our own minds are a part of this Universal Mind in just the same way that the rays of the sun are part of the sun.

If we will work in harmony with It, we can draw upon Universal Mind for all power, all intelligence, in the same way that the sun's rays draw upon their source for the heat and light they bring the earth.

It is not enough to *know* that you have this power. You must put it into *practice*—not once, or twice, but *every hour and every day*. Don't be discouraged if at first it doesn't always work. When you first studied arithmetic, your problems did not always work out correctly, did they? Yet you did not on that account doubt the principle of mathematics. You knew that the fault was with your methods, not with the principle. It is the same in this. The power is there. Correctly used, it can do anything.

All will agree that the Mind which first brought the Life Principle to this earth—which imaged the earth itself and the trees and the plants and the animals—is all-powerful. All will agree that to solve any problem, to meet any need, Mind has but to *realize* the need and it will be met. What most of us do not understand or realize is that we ourselves, being part of Universal Mind, have this same power. Just as the drop of water from the ocean has all the properties of the great bulk of the water in the ocean. Just as the spark of electricity has all the properties of the thunderbolt. And having that power, we have only to realize it and use it to get from life any good we may desire.

In the beginning all was void—space—nothingness. How did Universal Mind construct the planets, the firmaments, the earth and all things on and in it from this formless void? *By first making a mental image on which to build.*

That is what you, too, must do. You control your destiny, your fortune, your happiness to the exact extent to which you can think them out, VIZUALIZE them, SEE them, and allow no vagrant thought of fear or worry to mar their completion and beauty. The quality of your thought is the measure of your power. Clear, forceful thought has the power of attracting to itself everything it may need for the fruition of those thoughts. As W. D. Wattles puts it in his "Science of Getting Rich":

"There is a thinking stuff from which all things are made and which, in its original state, permeates, penetrates, and fills the interspaces of the universe. A thought in this substance produces the thing that is imagined by the thought. Man can form things in his thought, and, by impressing his thought upon formless substance, can cause the thing he thinks about to be created."

The connecting link between your conscious mind and the Universal is thought, and every thought that is in harmony with progress and good, every thought that is freighted with the right idea, can penetrate to Universal Mind. And penetrating to it, it comes back with the power of Universal Mind to accomplish it. You don't need to originate the ways and means. The Universal Mind knows how to bring about any necessary results. There is but one right way to solve any given problem. When your human judgment is unable to decide what that one right way is, turn to Universal Mind for guidance. You need never fear the outcome, for if you heed its advice you cannot go wrong.

Always remember—your mind is but a conductor—good or poor as you make it—for the power of Universal Mind. And thought is the connecting energy. Use that conductor, and you will improve its conductivity. Demand much, and you will receive the more. The Universal is not ungenerous in any of its gifts. "Ask and ye shall receive, seek and ye shall find, knock and it shall be opened unto you."

That is the law of life. And the destiny of man lies not in poverty and hardship, but in living up to his high estate in unity with Universal Mind, with the power that governs the universe.

To look upon poverty and sickness as sent by God and therefore inevitable, is the way of the weakling. God never sent us anything but good. What is more, He has never yet failed to give to those who would use them the means to overcome any condition not of His making. Sickness and poverty are not of His making. They are not evidences of virtue, *but of weakness.* God gave us everything in abundance, and he expects us to manifest that abundance. If you had a son you loved very much, and you surrounded him with good things which he had only to exert himself in order to reach, you wouldn't like it if he showed himself to the world half-starved, ill-kempt and clothed in rags, merely because he was unwilling to exert himself enough to reach for the good things you had provided. No more, in my humble opinion, does God.

Man's principal business in life, as I see it, is to establish a contact with Universal Mind. It is to acquire an understanding of this power that is in him. "With all thy getting, get understanding," said Solomon.

"Happy is the man that findeth wisdom,
And the man that getteth understanding.
For the gaining of it is better than the gaining of silver.
And the profit thereof than fine gold.
She is more precious than rubies:
And none of the things thou canst desire are to be compared unto her.
Length of days is in her right hand:
In her left hand are riches and honor.
Her ways are ways of pleasantness,
And all her paths are peace.
She is a tree of life to them that lay hold upon her.
And happy is every one that retaineth her."

—*Proverbs*

When you become conscious, even to a limited degree, of your one-ness with Universal Mind, your ability to call upon It at will for anything you may need, it makes a different man of you. Gone are the fears, gone are the worries. You know that your success, your health, your happiness will be measured only by the degree to which you can impress the fruition of your desires upon mind.

The toil and worry, the wearisome grind and the back-breaking work, will go in the future as in the past to those who will not use their minds. The less they use them, the more they will sweat. And the more they work only from the neck down, the less they will be paid and the more hopeless their lot will become. *It is Mind that rules the world.*

But to use your mind to the best advantage doesn't mean to toil along with the mere conscious part of it. It means hitching up your conscious mind with the Man Inside You, with the little "Mental Brownies," as Robert Louis Stevenson called them, and then working together for a definite end.

"My Brownies! God bless them!" said Stevenson, "Who do one-half of my work for me when I am fast asleep, and in all human likelihood do the rest for me as well when I am wide awake and foolishly suppose that I do it myself. I had long been wanting to write a book on man's double being. For two days I went about racking my brains for a plot of any sort, and on the second night I dreamt the scene in Dr. Jekyll and Mr. Hyde at the window; and a scene, afterward split in two, in which Hyde, pursued, took the powder and underwent the change in the presence of his pursuer."

Many another famous writer has spoken in similar strain, and every man who has problems to solve has had like experiences. You know how, after you have studied a problem from all angles, it sometimes seems worse jumbled than when you started on it. Leave it then for a while—forget it—and when you go back to it, you find your thoughts clarified, the line of reasoning worked out, your problem solved for you. It is your little "Mental Brownies" who have done the work for you!

The flash of genius does not originate in your own brain. Through intense concentration you've established a circuit through your subconscious mind with the Universal, and it is from It that the inspiration comes. All genius, all progress, is from the same source. It lies with you merely to learn how to establish this circuit at will so that you can call upon It at need. It can be done.

"In the Inner Consciousness of each of us," quotes Dumont in "The Master Mind," "there are forces which act much the same as would countless tiny mental brownies or helpers who are anxious and willing to assist us in our mental work, if we will but have confidence and trust in them. This is a psychological truth expressed in the terms of the old fairy tales. The process of calling into service these Inner Consciousness helpers is similar to that which we constantly employ to recall some forgotten fact or name. We find that we cannot recollect some desired fact, date, or name, and instead of racking our brains with an increased effort, we (if we have learned the secret) pass on the matter to the Inner Consciousness with a silent command, 'Recollect this name for me,' and then go on with our ordinary work. After a few minutes—or it may be hours—all of a sudden, pop! will come the missing name or fact before us—flashed from the planes of the Inner Consciousness, by the help of the kindly workers or 'brownies' of those planes. The experience is so common that we have ceased to wonder at it, and yet it is a wonderful manifestation of the Inner Consciousness' workings of the mind. Stop and think a moment, and you will see that the missing word does not present itself accidentally, or 'just because.' There are mental processes at work for your benefit, and when they have worked out the problem for you they gleefully push it up from their plane on to the plane of the outer consciousness where you may use it.

"We know of no better way of illustrating the matter than by this fanciful figure of the 'mental brownies,' in connection with the illustration of the 'subconscious storehouse.' If you would learn to take advantage of the work of these Subconscious Brownies, we advise you to form a mental picture of the Subconscious Storehouse in which is stored all sorts of knowledge that you have placed there during your lifetime, as well as the impressions that you have acquired by race inheritance—racial memory, in fact. The information stored away has often been placed in the storage rooms without any regard for systematic storing, or arrangement, and when you wish to find something that has been stored away there a long time ago, the exact place being forgotten, you are compelled to call to your assistance the little brownies of the mind, which perform faithfully your mental command, 'Recollect this for me!' These brownies are the same little chaps that you charge with the task of waking you at four o'clock tomorrow morning when you wish to catch an early train—and they obey you well in this work of the mental alarm-clock. These same little chaps will also flash into your consciousness the report, 'I have an engagement at two o'clock with Jones'—when looking at your watch you will see that it is just a quarter before the hour of two, the time of your engagement.

"Well then, if you will examine carefully into a subject which you wish to master, and will pass along the results of your observations to these Subconscious Brownies, you will find that they will work the raw materials of thought into shape for you in a comparatively short time. They will analyze, systematize, collate, and arrange in consecutive order the various details of information which you have passed on to them, and will add thereto the articles of similar information that they will find stored away in the recesses of your memory. In this way they will group together various scattered bits of knowledge that you have forgotten. And, right here, let us say to you that you never absolutely forget anything that you have placed in your mind. You may be unable to recollect certain things, but they are not lost—sometime later some associative connection will be made with some other fact, and lo! the missing idea will be found fitted nicely into its place in the larger idea—the work of our little brownies. Remember Thompson's statement: 'In view of having to wait for the results of these unconscious processes, I have proved the habit of getting together material in advance, and then leaving the mass to digest itself until I am ready to write about it.' This subconscious 'digestion' is really the work of our little mental brownies.

"There are many ways of setting the brownies to work. Nearly everyone has had some experience, more or less, in the matter, although often it is produced almost unconsciously, and without purpose and intent. Perhaps the best way for the average person—or rather the majority of persons—to get the desired results is for one to get as clear an idea of what one really wants to know—as clear an idea or mental image of the question you wish answered. Then after rolling it around in your mind—mentally chewing it, as it were—giving it a high degree of voluntary attention, you can pass it on to your Subconscious Mentality with the mental command: 'Attend to this for me—work out the answer!' or some similar order. This command may be given silently, or else spoken aloud—either will do. Speak to the Subconscious Mentality—or its little workers—just as you would speak to persons in your employ, kindly but firmly. Talk to the little workers, and firmly command them to do your work. And then forget all about the matter—throw it off your conscious mind, and attend to your other tasks. Then in due time will come your answer—flashed into your consciousness— perhaps not until the very minute that you must decide upon the matter, or need the information. You may give your brownies orders to report at such and such a time—just as you do when you tell them to awaken you at a certain time in the morning so as to catch the early train, or just as they remind you of the hour of your appointment, if you have them all well trained."

Have you ever read the story by Richard Harding Davis of "The Man Who

Could Not Lose?" In it the hero is intensely interested in racing. He has studied records and "dope" sheets until he knows the history of every horse backward and forward.

The day before the big race he is reclining in an easy chair, thinking of the morrow's race, and he drops off to sleep with that thought on his mind. Naturally, his subconscious mind takes it up, with the result that he dreams the exact outcome of the race.

That was mere fiction, of course, but if races were run solely on the speed and stamina of the horses, it would be entirely possible to work out the results in just that way. Unfortunately, other factors frequently enter into every betting game.

But the idea behind Davis' story is entirely right. The way to contact with your subconscious mind, the way to get the help of the "Man Inside You" in working out any problem is:

First, fill your mind with every bit of information regarding that problem that you can lay your hands on.

Second, pick out a chair or lounge or bed where you can recline in perfect comfort, where you can forget your body entirely.

Third, let your mind dwell upon the problem for a moment, not worrying, not fretting, but placidly, and then turn it over to the "Man Inside You." Say to him—"This is your problem. You can do anything. You know the answer to everything. Work this out for me!" And utterly relax. Drop off to sleep, if you can. At least, drop into one of those half-sleepy, half-wakeful reveries that keep other thoughts from obtruding upon your consciousness. Do as Aladdin did— summon your Genii, give him your orders, then forget the matter, secure in the knowledge that he will attend to it for you. When you waken, *you will have the answer!*

For whatever thought, whatever problem you can get across to your subconscious mind at the moment of dropping off to sleep, that "Man Inside You," that Genie-of-your-Mind will work out for you.

Of course, not everyone can succeed in getting the right thought across to the subconscious at the first or the second attempt. It requires understanding and faith, just as the working out of problems in mathematics requires an understanding of and faith in the principles of mathematics. But keep on trying, and you WILL do it. And when you do, *the results are sure.*

If it is something that you want, VISUALIZE it first in your mind's eye, see it in every possible detail, see yourself going through every move it will be necessary for you to go through when your wish comes into being. Build up a complete story, step by step, just as though you were acting it all out. Get from it every ounce of pleasure and satisfaction that you can. Be *thankful* for this gift that has come to you. Then relax; go on to sleep if you can; give the "Man Inside You" a chance to work out the consummation of your wish without interference.

When you waken, hold it all pleasurably in thought again for a few moments. Don't let doubts and fears creep in, but go ahead, confidently, knowing that your wish is working itself out. Know this, believe it—and if there is nothing harmful in it, IT WILL WORK OUT!

For somewhere in Universal Mind there exists the correct solution of every problem. It matters not how stupendous and complicated, nor how simple a problem may appear to be. There always exists the right solution in Universal Mind. And because this solution does exist, there also exists the ability to ascertain and to prove what that solution is. You can know, and you can do, every right thing. Whatever it is necessary for you to know, whatever it is necessary for you to do, you can know and you can do, if you will but seek the help of Universal Mind and be governed by its suggestions.

Try this method every night for a little while, and the problem does not exist that you cannot solve.

Volume VI

SEE YOURSELF DOING IT

"You say big corporations scheme
To keep a fellow down;
They drive him, shame him, starve him, too,
If he so much as frown.
God knows I hold no brief for them;
Still, come with me to-day
And watch those fat directors meet,
For this is what they say:
"In all our force not one to take
The new work that we plan!
In all the thousand men we've hired
Where shall we find a man?"

—St. Clair Adams[2]

You've often heard it said that a man is worth $2 a day from the neck down. How much he's worth from the neck up depends upon how much he is able to SEE.

"Without vision the people perish" did not refer to good eyesight. It was the eyes of the mind that counted in days of old just as they do today. Without

---

2. From "It Can Be Done." Copyright 1921, George Sully & Company.

them you are just so much power "on the hoof," to be driven as a horse or an ox is driven. And you are worth only a little more than they.

But given vision—imagination—the ability to visualize conditions and things a month or a year ahead; given the eyes of the mind—there's no limit to your value or to your capabilities.

The locomotive, the steamboat, the automobile, the aeroplane—all existed complete in the imagination of some man before ever they became facts. The wealthy men, the big men, the successful men, visioned their successes in their minds' eyes before ever they won them from the world.

From the beginning of time, nothing has ever taken on material shape without first being visualized in mind. The only difference between the sculptor and the mason is in the mental image behind their work. Rodin employed masons to hew his blocks of marble into the general shape of the figure he was about to form. *That was mere mechanical labor.* Then Rodin took it in hand and from that rough hewn piece of stone there sprang the wondrous figure of "The Thinker." *That was art!*

The difference was all in the imagination behind the hands that wielded mallet and chisel. After Rodin had formed his masterpiece, ordinary workmen copied it by the thousands. Rodin's work brought fabulous sums. The copies brought day wages. Conceiving ideas—*creating something*—is what pays, in sculpture as in all else. Mere hand-work is worth only hand wages.

"The imagination," says Glenn Clark in "The Soul's Sincere Desire," "is of all qualities in man the most God-like—that which associates him most closely with God. The first mention we read of man in the Bible is where he is spoken of as an 'image.' 'Let us make man in our image, after our likeness.' The only place where an image can be conceived is in the imagination. Thus man, the highest creation of God, was a creation of God's imagination.

"The source and center of all man's creative power—the power that above all others lifts him above the level of brute creation, and that gives him dominion, is his power of making images, or the power of the imagination. There are some who have always thought that the imagination was something which makes-believe that which is not. This is fancy—not imagination. Fancy would convert that which is real into pretense and sham; imagination enables one to see through the appearance of a thing to what it really *is*."

There is a very real law of cause and effect which makes the dream of the dreamer come true. It is the law of visualization—the law that calls into being in this outer material world everything that is real in the inner world. Imagination pictures the thing you desire. VISION idealizes it. It reaches beyond the thing that is, into the conception of what can be. Imagination gives you the picture. Vision gives you the impulse to make the picture your own.

Make your mental image clear enough, picture it vividly in every detail, and the Genie-of-your-Mind will speedily bring it into being as an everyday reality.

That law holds true of everything in life. There is nothing you can rightfully desire that cannot be brought into being through visualization.

Suppose there's a position you want—the general managership of your company. See yourself—just as you are now—sitting in the general manager's chair. See your name on his door. See yourself handling his affairs as you would handle them. Get that picture impressed upon your subconscious mind. See it! *Believe it!* The Genie-of-your-Mind will find the way to make it come true.

The keynote of successful visualization is this: See things as you would have them be instead of as they are. Close your eyes and make clear mental pictures. Make them look and act just as they would in real life. In short, day dream—but day dream with a purpose. Concentrate on the one idea to the exclusion of all others, and continue to concentrate on that one idea until it has been accomplished.

Do you want an automobile? A home? A factory? They can all be won in the same way. They are in their essence all of them ideas of mind, and if you will but build them up in your own mind first, stone by stone, complete in every detail, you will find that the Genie-of-your-Mind can build them up similarly in the material world.

"The building of a trans-continental railroad from a mental picture," says C. W. Chamberlain in "The Uncommon Sense of Applied Psychology," "gives the average individual an idea that it is a big job. The fact of the matter is, the achievement, as well as the perfect mental picture, is made up of millions of little jobs, each fitting in its proper place and helping to make up the whole.

"A skyscraper is built from individual bricks, the laying of each brick being a single job which must be completed before the next brick can be laid."

It is the same with any work, any study. To quote Professor James:

"As we become permanent drunkards by so many separate drinks, so we become saints in the moral, and authorities and experts in the practical and scientific spheres, by so many separate acts and hours of working. Let no youth have any anxiety about the upshot of his education whatever the line of it may be. If he keep faithfully busy each hour of the working day he may safely leave the final result to itself. He can with perfect certainty count on waking some fine morning, to find himself one of the competent ones, of his generation, in whatever pursuit he may have singled out. . . . Young people should know this truth in advance. The ignorance of it has probably engendered more discouragement and faintheartedness in youths embarking on arduous careers than all other causes taken together."

Remember that the only limit to your capabilities is the one you place upon them. There is no law of limitation. The only law is of supply. Through your subconscious mind you can draw upon universal supply for anything you wish. The ideas of Universal Mind are as countless as the sands on the seashore. Use them. And use them lavishly, just as they are given. There is a little poem by Jessie B. Rittenhouse[3] that so well describes the limitations that most of us put upon ourselves that I quote it here:

"I bargained with Life for a penny,
And Life would pay no more,
However I begged at evening
When I counted my scanty store.

"For Life is a just employer;
He gives you what you ask,
But once you have set the wages,
Why, you must bear the task.

"I worked for a menial's hire,
Only to learn, dismayed,
That any wage I had asked of Life,
Life would have paid."

Aim high! If you miss the moon, you may hit a star. Everyone admits that this world and all the vast firmament must have been thought into shape from the formless void by some Universal Mind. That same Universal Mind rules today, and it has given to each form of life power to attract to itself whatever it needs for its perfect growth. The tree, the plant, the animal—each one finds its need.

You are an intelligent, reasoning creature. Your mind is part of Universal Mind. And you have power to *say* what you require for perfect growth. Don't

---

3. From "The Door of Dreams," Houghton, Mifflin & Co., Boston.

be miserly with yourself. Don't sell yourself for a penny. Whatever price you set upon yourself, life will give. So aim high. Demand much! Make a clear, distinct mental image of what it is you want. Hold it in your thought. Visualize it, see it, *believe it!* The ways and means of satisfying that desire will follow. For supply always comes on the heels of demand.

It is by doing this that you take your fate out of the hands of chance. It is in this way that you control the experiences you are to have in life. But be sure to visualize *only what you want.* The law works both ways. If you visualize your worries and your fears, you will make them real. Control your thought and you will control circumstances. Conditions will be what you make them.

Most of us are like factories where two-thirds of the machines are idle, where the workmen move around in a listless, dispirited sort of way, doing only the tenth part of what they could do if the head of the plant were watching and directing them. Instead of that, he is off idly dreaming or waiting for something to turn up. What he needs is someone to point out to him his listless workmen and idle machines, and show him how to put each one to working full time and overtime.

And that is what YOU need, too. You are working at only a tenth of *your* capacity. You are doing only a tenth of what *you* are capable of. The time you spend idly wishing or worrying can be used in so directing your subconscious mind that it will bring you anything of good you may desire.

Philip of Macedon, Alexander's father, perfected the "phalanx"—a triangular formation which enabled him to center the whole weight of his attack on one point in the opposing line. It drove through everything opposed to it. In that day and age it was invincible. And the idea is just as invincible today.

Keep the one thought in mind, SEE it being carried out step by step, and you can knit any group of workers into one homogeneous whole, all centered on the one idea. You can accomplish any one thing. You can put across any definite idea. Keep that mental picture ever in mind and you will make it as invincible as was Alexander's phalanx of old.

"It is not the guns or armament
Or the money they can pay,
It's the close cooperation
That makes them win the day.
It is not the individual

Or the army as a whole
But the everlasting team work of every bloomin' soul."

—J. Mason Knox

The error of the ages is the tendency mankind has always shown to limit the power of Mind, or its willingness to help in time of need.

"Know ye not," said Paul, "that ye are the temples of the Living God?"

No—most of us do not know it. Or at least, if we do, we are like the Indian family out on the Cherokee reservation. Oil had been found on their land and money poured in upon them. More money than they had ever known was in the world. Someone persuaded them to build a great house, to have it beautifully furnished, richly decorated. The house when finished was one of the show places of that locality. But the Indians, while very proud of their showy house, continued to *live in their old sod shack!*

So it is with many of us. We may know that we are "temples of the Living God." We may even be proud of that fact. But we never take advantage of it to dwell in that temple, to proclaim our dominion over things and conditions. We never avail ourselves of the power that is ours.

The great Prophets of old had the forward look. Theirs was the era of hope and expectation. They looked for the time when the revelation should come that was to make men "sons of God." "They shall obtain joy and gladness, and sorrow and sighing shall flee away."

Jesus came to fulfill that revelation. "Ask and ye shall receive, that your joy may be full."

The world has turned in vain to matter and materialistic philosophy for deliverance from its woes. In the future the only march of actual progress will be in the mental realm, and this progress will not be in the way of human speculation and theorizing, but in the *actual demonstration* of the Universal, Infinite Mind.

The world stands today within the vestibule of the vast realm of divine intelligence, wherein is found the transcendent, practical power of Mind over all things.

"What eye never saw, nor ear ever heard,
What never entered the mind of man—
Even all that God has prepared for those who love Him."

Volume VII

"As a Man Thinketh"

"Our remedies in ourselves do lie
Which we ascribe to heaven."

—SHAKESPEARE

IN our great-grandfather's day, when witches flew around by night and cast their spell upon all unlucky enough to cross them, men thought that the power of sickness or health, of good fortune or ill, resided outside themselves.

We laugh today at such benighted superstition. But even in this day and age there are few who realize that the things they *see* are but *effects*. Fewer still who have any idea of the *causes* by which those effects are brought about.

Every human experience is an effect. You laugh, you weep, you joy, you sorrow, you suffer or you are happy. Each of these is an effect, the cause of which can be easily traced.

But all the experiences of life are not so easily traceable to their primary causes. We save money for our old age. We put it into a bank or into safe bonds—and the bank breaks or the railroad or corporation goes into a receivership. We stay at home on a holiday to avoid risk of accident, and fall off a stepladder or down the stairs and break a limb. We drive slowly for fear of danger, and a speeding car comes from behind and knocks us into a ditch. A man goes over Niagara Falls in a barrel without harm, and then slips on a banana peel, breaks his leg, and dies of it.

What is the cause back of it all? If we can find it and control it, we can control the effect. We shall no longer then be the football of fate. We shall be able to rise above the conception of life in which matter is our master.

There is but one answer. The world without is a reflection of the world within. We image thoughts of disaster upon our subconscious minds and the Genie-of-our-Mind finds ways of bringing them into effect—even though we stay at home, even though we take every possible precaution. The mental image is what counts, be it for good or ill. It is a devastating or a beneficent force, just as we choose to make it. To paraphrase Thackeray—"The world is a looking-glass, and gives back to every man the reflection of his own thought."

For matter is not *real* substance. Material science today shows that matter has no natural eternal existence. Dr. Willis R. Whitney, in an address before the American Chemical Society on August 8th, 1925, discussing "Matter—Is There Anything In It?" stated that "the most we know about matter is that it is almost entirely *space*. It is as empty as the sky. It is almost as empty as a perfect vacuum, although it usually contains a lot of energy." Thought is the only force. Just as polarity controls the electron, gravitation the planets, tropism the plants and lower animals—just so thought controls the action and the environment of man. And thought is subject wholly to the control of mind. Its direction rests with us.

Walt Whitman had the right of it when he said—"Nothing external to me has any power over me."

The happenings that occur in the material world are in themselves neither cheerful nor sorrowful, just as outside of the eye that observes them colors are neither green nor red. It is our thoughts that make them so. And we can color those thoughts according to our own fancy. We can make the world without but a reflection of the world within. We can make matter a force subject entirely to the control of our mind. For matter is merely our wrong view of what Universal Mind sees rightly.

We cannot change the past experience, but we can determine what the new ones shall be like. We can make the coming day just what we want it to be. We can *be* tomorrow what *we think* today. For the thoughts are causes and the conditions are the effects.

What is the reason for most failures in life? The fact that they first thought failure. They allowed competition, hard times, fear and worry to undermine their confidence. Instead of working aggressively ahead, spending money to make more money, they stopped every possible outlay, tried to "play safe," but expected others to continue spending with them. War is not the only place where "The best defensive is a strong offensive."

The law of compensation is always at work. Man is not at the caprice of fate. He is his own fate. "As a man thinketh in his heart, so is he." We are our own past thoughts, with the things that these thoughts have attracted to us added on.

The successful man has no time to think of failure. He is too busy thinking up new ways to succeed. You can't pour water into a vessel already full.

All about you is energy—electronic energy, exactly like that which makes up the solid objects you possess. The only difference is that the loose energy round about is unappropriated. It is still virgin gold—undiscovered, unclaimed. You can think it into anything you wish—into gold or dross, into health or sickness, into strength or weakness, into success or failure. Which shall it be? "There is nothing either good or bad," said Shakespeare, "but thinking makes it so." The understanding of that law will enable you to control every other law that exists. In it is to be found the panacea for all ills, the satisfaction of all want, all desire. It is Creative Mind's own provision for man's freedom.

Have you ever read Basil King's "Conquest of Fear"? If you haven't, do so by all means. Here is the way he visions the future:

"Taking Him (Jesus) as our standard we shall work out, I venture to think, to the following points of progress:

"*a.* The control of matter in furnishing ourselves with food and drink by means more direct than at present employed, as He turned water into wine and fed the multitudes with the loaves and fishes.

"*b.* The control of matter by putting away from ourselves, by methods more sure and less roundabout than those of today, sickness, blindness, infirmity, and deformity.

"*c.* The control of matter by regulating our atmospheric conditions as He stilled the tempest.

"*d.* The control of matter by restoring to this phase of existence those who have passed out of it before their time, or who can ill be spared from it, as He 'raised' three young people from 'the dead' and Peter and Paul followed His example.

"*e.* The control of matter in putting it off and on at will, as He in His death and resurrection.

"*f.* The control of matter in passing altogether out of it, as He in what we call His Ascension into Heaven."

Mortals are healthy or unhealthy, happy or unhappy, strong or weak, alive or dead, in the proportion that they think thoughts of health or illness, strength or weakness. Your body, like all other material things, manifests only what your mind entertains in belief. In a general way you have often noticed this yourself. A man with an ugly disposition (which is a mental state) will have harsh, unlovely features. One with a gentle disposition will have a smiling and serene countenance. All the other organs of the human body are equally responsive to thought. Who has not seen the face become red with rage or white with fear? Who has not known of people who became desperately ill following an outburst of temper? Physicians declare that just as fear, irritability and hate distort the features, they likewise distort the heart, stomach and liver.

Experiments conducted on a cat shortly after a meal showed that when it was purring contentedly, its digestive organs functioned perfectly. But when a dog was brought into the room and the cat drew back in fear and anger, the X-ray showed that its digestive organs were so contorted as to be almost tied up in a knot!

Each of us makes his own world—and he makes it through mind. It is a commonplace fact that no two people see the same thing alike. "A primrose by a river's brim, a yellow primrose was to him, and it was nothing more."

Thoughts are the causes. Conditions are merely effects. We can mould ourselves and our surroundings by resolutely directing our thoughts towards the goal we have in mind.

Ordinary animal life is very definitely controlled by temperature, by climate, by seasonal conditions. Man alone can adjust himself to any reasonable temperature or condition. Man alone has been able to free himself to a great extent from the control of natural forces through his understanding of the relation of cause and effect. And now man is beginning to get a glimpse of the final freedom that shall be his from all material causes when he shall acquire the complete understanding that mind is the only cause and that effects are what he sees.

"We moderns are unaccustomed," says one talented writer, "to the mastery over our own inner thoughts and feelings. That a man should be a prey to any thought that chances to take possession of his mind, is commonly among us assumed as unavoidable. It may be a matter of regret that he should be kept awake all night from anxiety as to the issue of a lawsuit on the morrow, but that he should have the power of determining whether he be kept awake or not seems an extravagant demand. The image of an impending calamity is no doubt odious, but its very odiousness (we say) makes it haunt the mind all the more pertinaciously, and it is useless to expel it. Yet this is an absurd position for man, the heir of all the ages, to be in: Hag-ridden by the flimsy creatures of his own brain. If a pebble in our boot torments us, we expel it. We take off the boot and shake it out. And once the matter is fairly understood, it is just as easy to expel an intruding and obnoxious thought from the mind. About this there ought to be no mistake, no two opinions. The thing is obvious, clear and unmistakable. It should be as easy to expel an obnoxious thought from the mind as to shake a stone out of your shoe; and until a man can do that, it is just nonsense to talk about his ascendency over nature, and all the rest of it. He is a mere slave, and a prey to the bat-winged phantoms that flit through the corridors of his own brain. Yet the weary and careworn faces that we meet by thousands, even among the affluent classes of civilization, testify only too clearly how seldom this mastery is obtained. How rare indeed to find a *man!* How common rather to discover a *creature* hounded on by tyrant thoughts (or cares, or desires), cowering, wincing under the lash.

"It is one of the prominent doctrines of some of the oriental schools of practical psychology that the power of expelling thoughts, or if need be, killing them dead on the spot, *must be* attained. Naturally the art requires practice, but like other arts, when once acquired there is no mystery or difficulty about it. It is worth practice. It may be fairly said that life only begins when this art has been acquired. For obviously when, instead of being ruled by individual thoughts, the whole flock of them in their immense multitude and variety and capacity is ours to direct and despatch and employ where we list, life becomes a thing so vast and grand, compared to what it was before, that its former condition may well appear almost ante-natal. If you can kill a thought dead, for the time being, you can do anything else with it that you please. And therefore it is that this power is so valuable. And it not only frees a man from mental torment (which is nine-tenths at least of the torment of life), but it gives him a concentrated power of handling mental work absolutely unknown to him before. The two are co-relative to each other."

There is no intelligence in matter—whether that matter be electronic energy made up in the form of stone, or iron, or wood, or flesh. It all consists of Energy, the universal substance from which Mind forms all material things. Mind is the only intelligence. It alone is eternal. It alone is supreme in the universe.

When we reach that understanding, we will no longer have cause for fear, because we will realize that Universal Mind is the creator of *life* only; that death is not an actuality—it is merely the *absence* of life—and life will be ever-present. Remember the old fairy story of how the Sun was listening to a lot of earthly creatures talking of a very dark place they had found? A place of Stygian blackness. Each told how terrifically dark it had seemed. The Sun went and looked for it. He went to the exact spot they had described. He searched everywhere. But he could find not even a tiny dark spot. And he came back and told the earth-creatures he did not believe there *was* any dark place.

When the sun of understanding shines on all the dark spots in our lives, we will realize that there is no cause, no creator, no power, except good; evil is not an entity—it is merely the *absence of good*. And there can be no ill effects without an evil cause. Since there is no evil cause, only good can have reality or power. There is no beginning or end to good. From it there can be nothing but blessing for the whole race. In it is found no trouble. If God (or Good—the two are synonymous) is the only cause, then the only effect must be like the cause. "All things were made by Him; and without Him was not anything made that was made."

Don't be content with passively reading this. Use it! Practice it! Exercise is far more necessary to mental development that it is to physical. Practice the "daily dozen" of right thinking. Stretch your mind to realize how infinitely far it can reach out, what boundless vision it can have. Breathe out all the old thoughts of sickness, discouragement, failure, worry and fear. Breathe in deep, long breaths (thoughts) of unlimited health and strength, unlimited happiness and success. Practice looking forward—always looking forward to something better—better health, finer physique, greater happiness, bigger success. Take these mental breathing exercises every day. See how easily you will control your thoughts. How quickly you will see the good effects. You've got to think all the time. Your mind will do that anyway. And the thoughts are constantly building—for good or ill. So be sure to exhale all the thoughts of fear and worry and disease and lack that have been troubling you, and inhale only those you want to see realized.

Volume VIII

Volume III

The Law of Supply

"They do me wrong who say I come no more
When once I knock and fail to find you in;
For every day I stand outside your door,
And bid you wake, and rise to fight and win.
"Wail not for precious chances passed away,
Weep not for golden ages on the wane!
Each night I burn the records of the day—
At sunrise every soul is born again!"

—WALTER MALONE[4]

HAVE you ever run a race, or worked at utmost capacity for a protracted period, or swum a great distance? Remember how, soon after starting, you began to feel tired? Remember how, before you had gone any great distance, you thought you had reached your limit? But remember, too, how, when you kept on going, you got your second wind, your tiredness vanished, your muscles throbbed with energy, you felt literally charged with speed and endurance?

Stored in every human being are great reserves of energy of which the average individual knows nothing. Most people are like a man who drives a car in

_____

4. Courtesy of Mrs. Ella Malone Watson.

low gear, not knowing that by the simple shift of a lever he can set it in high and not merely speed up the car, but do it with far less expenditure of power.

The law of the universe is the law of supply. You see it on every hand. Nature is lavish in everything she does.

Look at the heavens at night. There are millions of stars there—millions of worlds—millions of suns among them. Surely there is no lack of wealth or profusion in the Mind that could image all of these; no place for limitation there! Look at the vegetation in the country round about you. Nature supplies all that the shrubs or trees may need for their growth and sustenance! Look at the lower forms of animal life—the birds and the wild animals, the reptiles and the insects, the fish in the sea. Nature supplies them bountifully with everything they need. They have but to help themselves to what she holds out to them with such lavish hand. Look at all the natural resources of the world—coal and iron and oil and all metals. There is plenty for everyone. We hear a lot about the exhaustion of our resources of coal and oil, but there is available coal enough to last mankind for thousands of years. There are vast oil fields practically untouched, probably others bigger still yet to be discovered, and when all these are exhausted, the extraction of oil from shales will keep the world supplied for countless more years.

There is abundance for everyone. But just as you must strain and labor to reach the resources of your "second wind," just so you must strive before you can make manifest the law of supply in nature.

THE WORLD BELONGS TO YOU

It is your estate. It owes you not merely a living, but everything of good you may desire. You've got to *demand* these things of it, though. You've got to fear naught, dread naught, stop at naught. You've got to have the faith of a Columbus, crossing an unknown sea, holding a mutinous crew to the task long after they had ceased to believe in themselves or in him—*and giving to the world a new hemisphere.* You've got to have the faith of a Washington—defeated, discredited, almost wholly deserted by his followers, yet holding steadfast in spite of all—*and giving to America a new liberty.* You've got to *dominate*—not to cringe. *You've* got to make the application of the law of supply.

"Consider the lilies how they grow." The flowers, the birds, all of creation, are incessantly active. The trees and flowers in their growth, the birds and wild creatures in building their nests and finding sustenance, are always working—*but never worrying.* "Your Father knoweth that ye have need of these things." "And all these things shall be added unto you."

If all would agree to give up worrying—to be industrious, but never anxious about the outcome—it would mean the beginning of a new era in human progress, an age of liberty, of freedom from bondage. Jesus set forth the universal law of supply when he said—"Therefore I say unto you, be not anxious for the morrow, what ye shall eat, or wherewithal ye shall be clothed—but seek first the kingdom of God, *and all those things shall be added unto you.*"

What is this "Kingdom of God?"

Jesus tells us—"The Kingdom of God is within you." It is the "Father within you" to which He so frequently referred. It is Mind—your part of Universal Mind. "Seek first the Kingdom of God." Seek first an understanding of this Power within you—learn to contact with it—to use it—"and all those things shall be added unto you."

All riches have their origin in Mind. Wealth is in ideas—not money. Money is merely the material medium of exchange for ideas. The paper money in your pockets is in itself worth no more than so many Russian rubles. It is the idea behind it that gives it value. Factory buildings, machinery, materials, are in themselves worthless without a manufacturing or a selling idea behind them. How often you see a factory fall to pieces, the machinery rust away, after the idea behind them gave out. Factories, machines, are simply the tools of trade. It is the idea behind them that makes them go.

So don't go out a-seeking of wealth. Look within you for ideas! "The Kingdom of God is within you." Use it—*purposefully!* Use it to THINK constructively. Don't say you are *thinking* when all you are doing is exercising your faculty of memory. As Dumont says in "The Master Mind"—"They are simply allowing the stream of memory to flow through their field of consciousness, while the Ego stands on the banks and idly watches the passing waters of memory flow by. They call this 'thinking', while in reality there is no process of Thought under way."

They are like the old mountaineer sitting in the shade alongside his cabin. Asked what he did to pass the long hours away, he said—"Waal, sometimes I set and think; and sometimes I just set."

Dumont goes on to say, in quoting another writer: "When I use the word 'thinking,' I mean *thinking with a purpose, with an end in view, thinking to solve a problem.* I mean the kind of thinking that is forced on us when we are deciding on a course to pursue, on a life work to take up perhaps; the kind of thinking that was forced upon us in our younger days when we had to find a solution to a problem in mathematics; or when we tackled psychology in college. I do not mean 'thinking' in snatches, or holding petty opinions on this subject and on that. I mean thought on significant questions which lie outside the bounds of your narrow personal welfare. This is the kind of thinking which is now so rare—so sadly needed!"

The Kingdom of God is the Kingdom of Thought, of Achievement, of Health, of Happiness and Prosperity. "I came that ye might have life and have it more abundantly."

But you have got to *seek* it. You have got to do more than ponder. You have got to *think*—to think constructively—to seek how you may discover new worlds, new methods, new needs. The greatest discoveries, you know, have arisen out of things which everybody had *seen,* but only one man had NOTICED. The biggest fortunes have been made out of the opportunities which many men *had,* but only one man GRASPED.

Why is it that so many millions of men and women go through life in poverty and misery, in sickness and despair? Why? Primarily because they make a reality of poverty through their fear of it. They visualize poverty, misery and disease, and thus bring them into being. And secondly, they cannot demonstrate the law of supply for the same reason that so many millions cannot solve the first problem in algebra. The solution is simple—but they have never been shown the method. They do not understand the law.

The essence of this law is that you must *think* abundance, *see* abundance, *feel* abundance, *believe* abundance. Let no thought of limitation enter your mind. There is no lawful desire of yours for which, as far as mind is concerned, there is not abundant satisfaction. And if you can visualize it in mind, you can realize it in your daily world.

"Blessed is the man whose delight is in the *law* of the Lord: And he shall be like a tree planted by the rivers of water, that bringeth forth his fruit in his season: his leaf also shall not wither; and whatsoever he doeth shall prosper."

Don't worry. Don't doubt. Don't dig up the seeds of prosperity and success to see whether they have sprouted. Have faith! Nourish your seeds with renewed desire. Keep before your mind's eye the picture of the thing you want. BELIEVE IN IT! No matter if you seem to be in the clutch of misfortune, no matter if the future looks black and dreary—FORGET YOUR FEARS! Realize that the future is of your own making. There is no power that can keep you down but yourself. Set your goal. Forget the obstacles between. Forget the difficulties in the way. Keep only the goal before your mind's eye—*and you'll win it!*

Judge Troward, in his Edinburgh Lectures on Mental Science, shows the way:

"The initial step, then, consists in determining to picture the Universal Mind as the ideal of all we could wish it to be, both to ourselves and to others, together with the endeavor to reproduce this ideal, however imperfectly, in our own life; and this step having been taken, we can then cheerfully look upon it as our ever-present Friend, providing all good, guarding from all danger, and guiding us with all counsel. Similarly if we think of it as a great power devoted to supplying all our needs, we shall impress this character also upon it, and by the law of subjective mind, it will proceed to enact the part of that special providence which we have credited it with being; and if, beyond general care of our concerns, we would draw to ourselves some particular benefit, the same rule holds good of impressing our desire upon the universal subjective mind. And thus the deepest problems of philosophy bring us back to the old statement of the law: 'Ask and ye shall receive; seek and ye shall find; knock and it shall be opened unto you.' This is the summing-up of the natural law of the relation between us and the Divine Mind. It is thus no vain boast that mental science can enable us to make our lives what we will. And to this law there is no limit. What it can do for us today it can do tomorrow, and through all that procession of tomorrows that loses itself in the dim vistas of eternity. *Belief in limitation is the one and only thing that causes limitation,* because we thus impress limitation upon the creative principle; and in proportion as we lay that belief aside, our boundaries will expand, and increasing life and more abundant blessing will be ours."

You are not working for some firm merely for the pittance they pay you. You are part of the great scheme of things. And what you do has its bearing on the ultimate result. That being the case, you are working for Universal Mind, and Universal Mind is the most generous paymaster there is. Just remember that you can look to it for all good things. Supply is *where* you are and *what* you need.

Do you want a situation? Close your eyes and realize that somewhere is the position for which you of all people are best fitted, and which is best fitted to your ability. The position where you can do the utmost of good, and where life, in turn, offers the most to you. Realize that Universal Mind knows exactly where this position is, and that through your subconscious mind you, too, can know it. Realize that this is YOUR position, that it NEEDS you, that it belongs to you, that it is right for you to have it, that you are entitled to it. Hold this thought in mind every night for just a moment, then go to sleep knowing that your subconscious mind HAS the necessary information as to where this position is and how to get in touch with it. Mind you—not WILL have, but HAS. The earnest realization of this will bring that position to you, and you to it, as surely as the morrow will bring the sun. Make the law of supply operative and you find that the things you seek are seeking you.

Get firmly fixed in your own mind the definite conviction that you can do anything you greatly want to do. There is no such thing as lack of opportunity. There is no such thing as only one opportunity. You are subject to a law of boundless and perpetual opportunity, and you can enforce that law in your behalf just as widely as you need. Opportunity is infinite and ever present.

Berton Braley has it well expressed in his poem on "Opportunity"[5]:

> "For the best verse hasn't been rhymed yet,
>   The best house hasn't been planned,
> The highest peak hasn't been climbed yet,
>   The mightiest rivers aren't spanned;
> Don't worry and fret, faint hearted,
>   The chances have just begun,
> For the Best jobs haven't been started,
>   The Best work hasn't been done."

Nothing stands in the way of a will which wants—an intelligence which knows. The great thing is to start. "Begin your work," says Ausonius. "To begin is to complete the first half. The second half remains. Begin again and the work is done." It matters not how small or unimportant your task may seem to be. It may loom bigger in Universal Mind than that of your neighbor, whose position is so much greater in the eyes of the world. Do it well—and Universal Mind will work with you.

But don't feel limited to any one job or any one line of work. Man was given dominion over all the earth. "And God said, Let us make man in our image, after our likeness: and let them have dominion over the fish of the sea, and over the fowl of the air, and over the cattle, and over all the earth, and over every creeping thing that creepeth upon the earth."

All of energy, all of power, all that can exercise any influence over your life, is in your hands through the power of thought. God—good—is the only

---

5. From "A Banjo at Armageddon." Copyright 1917, George H. Doran Company.

power there is. Your mind is part of His mind. He is "the Father that is within you that doeth the works."

So don't put any limit upon His power by trying to limit your capabilities. You are not in bondage to anything. All your hopes and dreams can come true. Were you not given dominion over all the earth? And can anyone else take this dominion from you?

All the mysterious psychic powers about which you hear so much today are perfectly natural. I have them. You have them. They only await the time when they shall be allowed to assert their vigor and prove themselves your faithful servitors.

"Be not afraid!" Claim your inheritance. The Universal Mind that supplies all wisdom and power is *your* mind. And to the extent that you are governed by your understanding of its infinite law of supply you will be able to demonstrate plenty. "According to your faith, be it unto you."

"Analyze most of the great American fortunes of the past generation," says *Advertising and Selling Fortnightly,* "and you will find that they were founded on great faiths. One man's faith was in oil, another's in land, another's in minerals.

"The fortunes that are being built today are just as surely being built on great faiths, but there is this difference: the emphasis of the faith has been shifted. Today it takes faith in a product or an opportunity, as it always did, but it takes faith in the public, in addition. Those who have the greatest faith in the public—the kind of faith possessed by Henry Ford and H. J. Heinz—*and make that faith articulate*—build the biggest fortunes."

"WANTED"

There is one question that bothers many a man. Should he stick to the job he has, or cast about at once for a better one. The answer depends entirely upon what you are striving for. The first thing is to set your goal. What is it you want? A profession? A political appointment? An important executive position? A business of your own?

Every position should yield you three things:

1. Reasonable pay for the present.
2. Knowledge, training, or experience that will be worth money to you in the future.

3. Prestige or acquaintances that will be of assistance to you in attaining your goal.

Judge every opening by those three standards. But don't overlook chances for valuable training, merely because the pay is small. Though it is a pretty safe rule that the concern with up-to-the-minute methods that it would profit you to learn, also pays up-to-the-minute salaries.

Hold each job long enough to get from it every speck of information there is in it. Hold it long enough to learn the job ahead. Then if there seems no likelihood of a vacancy soon in that job ahead, find one that corresponds to it somewhere else.

Progress! Keep going ahead! Don't be satisfied merely because your salary is being boosted occasionally. Learn something every day. When you reach the point in your work that you are no longer adding to your store of knowledge or abilities, you are going backward, and it's time for you to move. Move upward in the organization you are with if you can—but MOVE!

Your actual salary is of slight importance compared with the knowledge and ability you add to your mind. Given a full storehouse there, the salary or the riches will speedily follow. But the biggest salary won't do you much good for long unless you've got the knowledge inside you to back it up.

It's like a girl picking her husband. She can pick one with a lot of money and no brains, or she can pick one with no money but a lot of ability. In the former case, she'll have a high time for a little while, ending in a divorce court or in her having a worthless young "rounder" on her hands and no money to pay the bills. In the other, the start will be hard, but she is likely to end up with a happy home she has helped to build, an earnest, hardworking husband who has "arrived"— *and happiness.*

Money ought to be a consideration in marriage—but never *the* consideration. Of course it's an easy matter to pick a man with neither money nor brains. But when it's a choice of money *or* brains—take the brains every time. Possessions are of slight importance compared to mind. Given the inquiring, alert type of mind—you can get any amount of possessions. But the possessions without the mind are nothing. Nine times out of ten the best thing that can happen to any young couple is to have to start out with little or nothing and work out their salvation together.

What is it *you* want most from life? Is it riches?

Picture yourself with all the riches you could use, with all the abundance that Nature holds out with such lavish hand everywhere. What would you do with it?

Day-dream for a while. Believe that you *have* that abundance *now*. Practice being rich in your own mind. See yourself driving that expensive car you have always longed for, living in the sort of house you have often pictured, well-dressed, surrounded by everything to make life worth while. Picture yourself spending this money that is yours, lavishly, without a worry as to where more is coming from, knowing that there is no limit to the riches of Mind. Picture yourself doing all those things you would like to do, living the life you would like to live, providing for your loved ones as you would like to see them provided for. *See* all this in your mind's eye. *Believe* it to be true for the moment. *Know* that it will all be true in the not-very-distant future. Get from it all the pleasure and enjoyment you can.

It is the *first step* in making your dreams come true. You are creating the model in mind. And if you don't allow fear or worry to tear it down, Mind will re-create that model for you in your every-day life.

"All that the Father hath is yours," said Jesus. And a single glance at the heavens and the earth will show you that He has all riches in abundance. Reach out mentally and appropriate to yourself some of these good gifts. You've got to do it mentally before you can enjoy it physically. "'Tis mind that makes the body rich," as Shakespeare tells us.

See the things that you want as *already yours*. Know that they will come to you at need. Then LET them come. Don't fret and worry about them. Don't think about your LACK of them. Think of them as YOURS, as *belonging* to you, as already in your possession.

Look upon money as water that runs the mill of your mind. You are constantly grinding out ideas that the world needs. Your thoughts, your plans, are necessary to the great scheme of things. Money provides the power. But *it* needs YOU, it needs your ideas, before it can be of any use to the world. The Falls of Niagara would be of no use without the power plants that line the banks. The Falls need these plants to turn their power to account. In the same way, money needs your ideas to become of use to the world.

So instead of thinking that you need money, realize that money needs YOU. Money is just so much wasted energy without work to do. Your ideas provide the outlet for it, the means by which money can do things. Develop your ideas, secure in the knowledge that money is always looking for such an outlet. When the ideas are perfected, money will gravitate your way without conscious effort on your part, if only you don't dam up the channels with doubts and fears.

"First have something good—then advertise!" said Horace Greeley. First have something that the world needs, even if it be only faithful, interested service—then open up your channels of desire, and dollars will flow to you.

And remember that the more you have to offer—the more of riches will flow to you. Dollars are of no value except as they are used.

You have seen the rich attacked time and again in newspapers and magazines. You have read numberless articles and editorials against them. You have heard agitators declaim against them by the hour. But have you ever heard one of them say a single word against the richest man of them all—Henry Ford? I haven't. And why? Because Henry Ford's idea of money is that it is something to be *used*—something to provide more jobs, something to bring more comfort, more enjoyment, into an increasingly greater number of lives.

That is why money flows to him so freely. That is why he gets so much out of life. And that is how you, too, can get in touch with Infinite Supply. Realize that it is not money you have to seek, but a way to *use* money for the world's advantage. *Find the need!* Look at everything with the question—How could that be improved? To what new uses could this be put? Then set about supplying that need, in the absolute confidence that when you have found the way, money will flow freely to and through you. Do your part—and you can confidently look to Universal Mind to provide the means.

Get firmly in mind the definite conviction that YOU CAN DO ANYTHING RIGHT THAT YOU MAY WISH TO DO. Then set your goal and let everything you do, all your work, all your study, all your associations, be a step towards that goal. To quote Berton Braley[6] again—

"If you want a thing bad enough
To go out and fight for it,
Work day and night for it,
Give up your time and your peace and your sleep for it,
If only desire of it
Makes you quite mad enough
Never to tire of it,

6. From "Things As They Are." Copyright 1916, George H. Doran Company, New York.

Makes you hold all other things tawdry and cheap for it,
If life seems all empty and useless without it
And all that you scheme and you dream is about it,
If gladly you'll sweat for it,
Fret for it,
Plan for it,
Lose all your terror of God or man for it,
If you'll simply go after that thing that you want,
With all your capacity,
Strength and sagacity,
Faith, hope and confidence, stern pertinacity,
If neither cold poverty, famished and gaunt,
Nor sickness nor pain
Of body or brain
Can turn you away from the thing that you want,
If dogged and grim you besiege and beset it,
   You'll get it!"

Volume IX

Volume IX

The Formula of Success

"One ship drives east, and another drives west,
With the self-same winds that blow.
'Tis the set of the sails, and not the gales
Which tells us the way they go.
"Like the waves of the sea are the ways of fate
As we voyage along thru life.
'Tis the set of the soul which decides its goal
And not the calm or the strife."

—ELLA WHEELER WILCOX

WHAT is the eternal question which stands up and looks you and every sincere man squarely in the eye every morning?

"How can I better my condition?" That is the real life question which confronts you, and will haunt you every day till you solve it.

Read this chapter carefully and I think you will find the answer to this important life question which you and every man must solve if he expects ever to have more each Monday morning, after pay day, than he had the week before.

To begin with, all wealth depends upon a clear understanding of the fact that mind—thought—is the only creator. The great business of life is thinking. Control your thoughts and you control circumstance.

Just as the first law of gain is desire, so the formula of success is BELIEF.

Believe that you have it—see it as an existent fact—and anything you can rightly wish for is yours. Belief is "the substance of things hoped for, the evidence of things not seen."

You have seen men, inwardly no more capable than yourself, accomplish the seemingly impossible. You have seen others, after years of hopeless struggle, suddenly win their most cherished dreams. And you've often wondered, "What is the power that gives new life to their dying ambitions, that supplies new impetus to their jaded desires, that gives them a new start on the road to success?"

That power is belief—faith. Someone, something, gave them a new belief in themselves and a new faith in their power to win—and they leaped ahead and wrested success from seemingly certain defeat.

Do you remember the picture Harold Lloyd was in two or three years ago, showing a country boy who was afraid of his shadow? Every boy in the countryside bedeviled him. Until one day his grandmother gave him a talisman that she assured him his grandfather had carried through the Civil War and which, so she said, had the property of making its owner invincible. Nothing could hurt him, she told him, while he wore this talisman. Nothing could stand up against him. He believed her. And the next time the bully of the town started to cuff him around, he wiped up the earth with him. And that was only the start. Before the year was out he had made a reputation as the most daring soul in the community.

Then, when his grandmother felt that he was thoroughly cured, she told him the truth—that the "talisman" was merely a piece of old junk she'd picked up by the roadside—that she knew all he needed was *faith in himself,* belief that he could do these things.

THE TALISMAN OF NAPOLEON

Stories like that are common. It is such a well-established truth that you can do only what you think you can, that the theme is a favorite one with authors. I remember reading a story years ago of an artist—a mediocre sort of artist—who was visiting the field of Waterloo and happened upon a curious lump of metal half buried in the dirt, which so attracted him that he picked it up and put it in his pocket. Soon thereafter he noticed a sudden increase in confidence, an absolute faith in himself, not only as to his own chosen line of work, but in his ability to handle any situation that might present itself. He painted a great picture—just to show that he *could* do it. Not content with that, he visioned an empire with Mexico as its basis, actually led a revolt that carried all before it—until one day he lost his talisman. *And immediately his bubble burst.*

I instance this just to illustrate the point that it is *your own belief in yourself* that counts. It is the consciousness of dominant power within you that makes all things attainable. *You can do anything you think you can.* This knowledge is literally the gift of the gods, for through it you can solve every human problem. It should make of you an incurable optimist. It is the open door to welfare. *Keep it open*—by expecting to gain everything that is right.

You are entitled to every good thing. Therefore expect nothing but good. Defeat does not *need* to follow victory. You don't have to "knock wood" every time you congratulate yourself that things have been going well with you. Victory should follow victory—and it will if you "let this mind be in you which was also in Christ Jesus." It is the mind that means health and life and boundless opportunity and recompense. No limitation rests upon you. So don't let any enter your life. Remember that Mind will do every good thing for you. It will remove mountains for you.

"Bring ye all the tithes into the storehouse, and prove me now herewith, saith the Lord of hosts, if I will not open you the windows of heaven, and pour you out a blessing, that there shall not be room enough to receive it."

Bring all your thoughts, your desires, your aims, your talents, into the Storehouse—the Consciousness of Good, the Law of Infinite supply—and prove these blessings. There is every reason to know that you are entitled to adequate provision. Everything that is involved in supply is a thing of thought. Now reach out, stretch your mind, try to comprehend *unlimited thought, unlimited supply.*

Do not think that supply must come through one or two channels. It is not for you to dictate to Universal Mind the means through which It shall send Its gifts to you. There are millions of channels through which It can reach you. Your part is to impress upon Mind your need, your earnest desire, your boundless belief in the resources and the willingness of Universal Mind to help you. Plant the seed of desire. Nourish it with a clear visualization of the ripened fruit. Water it with sincere faith. But leave the means to Universal Mind.

Open up your mind. Clear out the channels of thought. Keep yourself in a state of receptivity. Gain a mental attitude in which you are constantly *expecting good.* You have the fundamental right to all good, you know. "According to your faith, be it unto you."

The trouble with most of us is that we are mentally lazy. It is so much easier to go along with the crowd than to break trail for ourselves. But the great discoverers, the great inventors, the great geniuses in all lines have been men who dared to break with tradition, who defied precedent, who believed that there is no limit to what Mind can do—and who stuck to that belief until their goal was won, in spite of all the sneers and ridicule of the wiseacres and the "It-can't-be-done'rs."

Not only that, but they were never satisfied with achieving just one success. They knew that the first success is like the first olive out of the bottle. All the others come out the more easily for it. They realized that they were a part of the Creative Intelligence of the Universe, and that the part shares all the properties of the whole. And that realization gave them the faith to strive for any right thing, the knowledge that the only limit upon their capabilities was the limit of their desires. Knowing that, they couldn't be satisfied with any ordinary success. They had to keep on and on and on.

Edison didn't sit down and fold his hands when he gave us the talking machine. Or the electric light. These great achievements merely opened the way to new fields of accomplishment.

Open up the channels between your mind and Universal Mind, and there is no limit to the riches that will come pouring in. Concentrate your thoughts on the particular thing you are most interested in, and ideas in abundance will come flooding down, opening up a dozen ways of winning the goal you are striving for.

But don't let one success—no matter how great—satisfy you. The Law of Creation, you know, is the Law of Growth. You can't stand still. You must go forward—or be passed by. Complacency—self-satisfaction—is the greatest enemy of achievement. You must keep looking forward. Like Alexander, you must be constantly seeking new worlds to conquer. Depend upon it, the power will come to meet the need. There is no such thing as failing powers, if we look to Mind for our source of supply. The only failure of mind comes from worry and fear—or from disuse.

William James, the famous psychologist, taught that "The more mind does, the more it can do." For ideas release energy. You can *do* more and better work than you have ever done. You can *know* more than you know now. You know from your own experience that under proper mental conditions of joy or enthusiasm, you can do three or four times the work without fatigue that you can ordinarily. Tiredness is more boredom than actual physical fatigue. You can work almost indefinitely when the work is a pleasure.

You've seen sickly persons, frail persons, who couldn't do an hour's light work without exhaustion, suddenly buckle down when heavy responsibilities were thrown upon them, and grow strong and rugged under the load. Crises not only draw upon the reserve power you have, but they help to create new power.

"IT COULDN'T BE DONE"

It may be that you have been deluded by the thought of incompetence. It may be that you have been told so often that you cannot do certain things that you've come to believe you can't. Remember that success or failure is merely a state of mind. Believe you cannot do a thing—and you can't. Know that you *can* do it—and you *will*. You must *see yourself doing it*.

> "If you think you are beaten, you are;
>   If you think you dare not, you don't;
> If you'd like to win, but you think you can't,
>   It's almost a cinch you won't;
> If you think you'll lose, you've lost,
>   For out in the world you'll find
> Success begins with a fellow's will—
>   It's all in the state of mind.

> "Full many a race is lost
>   Ere even a race is run,
> And many a coward fails
>   Ere even his work's begun.
> Think big, and your deeds will grow,
>   Think small and you fall behind,
> Think that you can, and you will;
>   It's all in the state of mind.

> "If you think you are outclassed, you are;
>   You've got to think high to rise;
> You've got to be sure of yourself before
>   You can ever win a prize.
> Life's battle doesn't always go

To the stronger or faster man;
But sooner or later, the man who wins
Is the fellow who thinks he can."

There's a vast difference between a proper understanding of one's own ability and a determination to make the best of it—and offensive egotism. It is absolutely necessary for every man to believe in himself, before he can make the most of himself. All of us have something to sell. It may be our goods, it may be our abilities, it may be our services. You've got to believe in yourself to make your buyer take stock in you at par and accrued interest. You've got to feel the same personal solicitude over a customer lost, as a revivalist over a backslider, and hold special services to bring him back into the fold. You've got to get up every morning with determination, if you're going to go to bed that night with satisfaction.

There's mighty sound sense in the saying that all the world loves a booster. The one and only thing you have to win success with is MIND. For your mind to function at its highest capacity, you've got to be charged with good cheer and optimism. No one ever did a good piece of work while in a negative frame of mind. Your best work is always done when you are feeling happy and optimistic.

And a happy disposition is the *result*—not the *cause*—of happy, cheery thinking. Health and prosperity are the *results* primarily of optimistic thoughts. *You* make the pattern. If the impress you have left on the world about you seems faint and weak, don't blame fate—blame your pattern! You will never cultivate a brave, courageous demeanor by thinking cowardly thoughts. You cannot gather figs from thistles. You will never make your dreams come true by choking them with doubts and fears. You've got to put foundations under your air castles, foundations of UNDERSTANDING and BELIEF. Your chances of success in any undertaking can always be measured by your BELIEF in yourself.

Are your surroundings discouraging? Do you feel that if you were in another's place success would be easier? Just bear in mind that your real environment is within you. All the factors of success or failure are in your inner world. *You* make that own inner world—and through it your outer world. You can choose the material from which to build it. If you've not chosen wisely in the past, you can choose again now the material you want to rebuild it. The richness of life is within you. No one has failed so long as he can begin again.

Start right in and *do* all those things you feel you have it in you to do. Ask permission of no man. Concentrating your thought upon any proper undertaking will make its achievement possible. Your belief that you *can* do the thing gives your thought forces their power. Fortune waits upon you. Seize her boldly, hold her—and she is yours. She belongs rightfully to you. But if you cringe to her, if you go up to her doubtfully, timidly, she will pass you by in scorn. For she is a fickle jade who must be mastered, who loves boldness, who admires confidence.

A Roman boasted that it was sufficient for him to strike the ground with his foot and legions would spring up. And his very boldness cowed his opponents. It is the same with your mind. Take the first step, and your mind will mobilize all its forces to your aid. But the first essential is that you *begin*. Once the battle is started, all that is within and without you will come to your assistance, if you attack in earnest and meet each obstacle with resolution. But *you* have got to start things.

"The Lord helps them that help themselves" is a truth as old as man. It is, in fact, plain common sense. Your subconscious mind has all power, but your conscious mind is the watchman at the gate. *It* has got to open the door. *It* has got to press the spring that releases the infinite energy. No failure is possible in the accomplishment of any right object you may have in life, if you but understand your power and will perseveringly try to use it in the proper way.

The men who have made their mark in this world all had one trait in common—*they believed in themselves!* "But," you may say, "how can I believe in myself when I have never yet done anything worth while, when everything I put my hand to seems to fail?" You can't, of course. That is, you couldn't if you had to depend upon your conscious mind alone. But just remember what one far greater than you said—"I can of mine own self do nothing. The Father that is within me—He doeth the works."

That same "Father" is within you. And it is by knowing that He *is* in you, and that through Him you can do anything that is right, that you can acquire that belief in yourself which is so necessary. Certainly the Mind that imaged the heavens and the earth and all that they contain has all wisdom, all power, all abundance. With this Mind to call upon, you know there is no problem too difficult for you to undertake. The *knowing* of this is the first step. *Faith.* But St. James tells us—"Faith without works is dead." So go on to the next step. Decide on the one thing you want most from life. No matter what it may be. There is no limit, you know, to Mind. Visualize this thing that you want. See it, feel it, BELIEVE in it. Make your mental blue-print, and *begin to build!*

Suppose some people DO laugh at your idea. Suppose Reason does say—"It can't be done!" People laughed at Galileo. They laughed at Henry Ford. Reason contended for countless ages that the earth was flat. Reason said—or so numerous automotive engineers argued—that the Ford motor wouldn't run. But the earth *is* round—and the twelfth or fifteenth million Ford *is* on the road.

Let us start right now putting into practice some of these truths that you have learned. What do you want most of life right now? Take that one desire, concentrate on it, impress it upon your subconscious mind.

Psychologists have discovered that the best time to make suggestions to your subconscious mind is just before going to sleep, when the senses are quiet and the attention is lax. So let us take your desire and suggest it to your subconscious mind tonight. The two prerequisites are the earnest DESIRE, and an intelligent, understanding BELIEF. Someone has said, you know, that education is three-fourths encouragement, and the encouragement is the suggestion that the thing can be done.

You know that you can have what you want, if you want it badly enough and can believe in it earnestly enough. So tonight, just before you drop off to sleep, concentrate your thought on this thing that you most desire from life. BELIEVE that you have it. SEE YOURSELF possessing it. FEEL yourself using it.

Do that every night until you ACTUALLY DO BELIEVE that you have the thing you want. When you reach that point, *YOU WILL HAVE IT!*

Volume X

"This Freedom"

"Ye shall know the truth
And the Truth shall make you free."

I HAVE heard that quotation ever since I was a little child. Most of us have. But to me it was never anything much but a quotation—until a few years ago. It is only in the past several years that I have begun to get an inkling of the real meaning of it—an understanding of the comfort back of it. Perhaps to you, too, it has been no more than a sonorous phrase. If so, you will be interested in what I have since gotten from it.

To begin with, what is the "truth" that is so often referred to in all our religious teaching? The truth about what? And what is it going to free us from?

The truth as I see it now is the underlying reality in everything we meet in life. There is, for instance, one right way to solve any given problem in mathematics. That one right way is the truth as far as that problem is concerned. To know it is to free yourself from all doubt and vain imagining and error. It is to free yourself from any trouble that might arise through solving the problem incorrectly.

In the same way, there is but one BEST way of solving every situation that confronts you. That BEST way is the truth. To know it is to make you free from all worry or trouble in connection with that situation. For if it is met in the RIGHT way, only good can come of it.

Then there is your body. There is only one RIGHT idea of every organism in your body. One CORRECT method of functioning for each of them. And Universal Mind holds that RIGHT idea, that CORRECT method. The functioning of your body, the rebuilding of each cell and tissue, is the work of your subconscious mind. If you will constantly hold before it the thought that its model is perfection, that weakness or sickness or deformity is merely ABSENCE of perfection—not a reality in itself—in short, if you will realize the *Truth* concerning your body, your subconscious mind will speedily make you free and keep you free from every ill.

It matters not what is troubling you today. If you will KNOW that whatever it may seem to be is merely the absence of the true idea, if you will realize that the only thing that counts is the truth that Universal Mind knows about your body, you can make that truth manifest.

Affirm the good, the true—and the evil will vanish. It is like turning on the light—the darkness immediately disappears. For there is no actual substance in darkness—it is merely absence of light. Nor is there any substance in sickness or evil—it is merely the absence of health or good.

That is the truth that was the mentality of Jesus—what Paul describes as "the mind which was also in Christ Jesus."

Jesus declared that "we should know the truth, and the truth would make us free." That truth was the power which He exercised. He had so perfect an understanding of truth that it gave Him absolute dominion over evil, enabled Him to heal diseases of every nature, even to raise the dead. The power that He exercised then was not confined to His time, nor limited to His own immediate followers. "Lo, I am with you always," He said, "even unto the end of the world." And He is just as available to us now as He was to His own disciples 1900 years ago.

"I have given you power to tread serpents and scorpions under foot and to trample on all the power of the enemy; and in no case shall anything do you harm."

That gift was never meant to be confined to His own disciples or to any other one group. God has never dealt in special or temporary gifts. He gives to *all*—to all who will accept—to all who have an understanding heart.

All sickness, all poverty, all sorrow, is the result of the incorrect use of some gift of God, which in itself is inherently good. It is just as though we took the numbers that were given us to work out a problem, and put them in the wrong places. The result would be incorrect, inharmonious. We would not be expressing the truth. The moment we rearrange those numbers properly, we get the correct answer—harmony—the *truth!* There was nothing wrong with the principle of mathematics before—the fault was all with us, with our incorrect arrangement of the figures.

What is true of the principle of mathematics is true of every principle. The principle is changeless, undying. It is only our expression of the principle that changes as our understanding of it becomes more thorough. Lightning held only terror for man until he made of electricity his servant. Steam was only so much waste until man learned to harness it. Fire and water are the most destructive forces known—until properly used, then they are man's greatest helpers. There is nothing wrong with any gift of God—once we find the way to use it. The truth is always there if we can find the principle behind it. The figures in mathematics are never bad. It is merely our incorrect arrangement of them.

The great need is an open mind and the desire for understanding. How far in the science of mathematics would you get if you approached the study of it with the preconceived notion that two plus two makes five, and nothing you heard to the contrary was going to change that belief? "Except ye turn, and become as little children, ye shall not enter into the kingdom of heaven." You must drop all your preconceived ideas, all your prejudices. You must never say—"Oh, that sounds like so-and-so. I don't want any of it." Just remember that any great movement must have at least a grain of truth back of it, else it could never grow to any size. Seek that grain of truth. Be open-minded. Keep your eyes and ears open for the truth. If you can do this, you will find that new wordings, different interpretations, are but the outer shell. You can still see the Truth beneath, the Christ that "before Abraham was, I am."

THE ONLY POWER

He who is looking for wisdom, power, or permanent success, will find it only within. Mind is the only cause. Your body is healthy or sick according to the images of thought you impress upon your subconscious mind. If you will hold thoughts of health instead of sickness, if you will banish all thoughts of disease and decay, you can build up a perfect body. Dr. William S. Patten of New York says, "To know and to understand the organization of mind and to recognize the action of mind is the first and the only requisite of a sound body."

For all disease starts in mind. It may be in your own conscious mind, from reading of an epidemic or from meeting with circumstances which education has taught you will bring about disease. It may be suggested to your subconscious mind, as so frequently happens with young children, by the fears and worries and thoughts of contagion of those around you.

But whichever it is, it is FEAR that starts it. You visualize, consciously or unconsciously, the disease that you fear, and because that is the image held before your thought, your body proceeds to build in accordance with that model. You believe that disease is necessary, that you have got to expect a certain amount of it. You hear of it every day, and subconsciously at least you are constantly in fear of it. And through that very fear you create it, when if you would spend that same amount of time thinking and believing in the necessity of HEALTH, you would never need to know disease.

Disease is not sent by God. It is not a visitation of Providence. If it were, what would be the use of doctoring it? You couldn't fight against the power of God!

God never sent us anything but good. He never gave us disease. When we allow disease to take hold of us, it is because we have lost touch with God—lost the perfect model of us that He holds in mind. And what we have got to strive for is to get back the belief in that perfect model—to forget the diseased image we are holding in our thought.

Remember the story of Alexander and his famous horse, Bucephalus? No one could ride the horse because it was afraid of its shadow. But Alexander faced it towards the sun—and rode it without trouble. Face towards the sun and the shadows will fall behind you, too. Face towards the perfect image of every organ, and the shadows of disease will never touch you.

There is no germ in a draft capable of giving you a cold. There is no bacteria in exposure to the weather that can give you a fever or pneumonia. It is you that gives them to yourself. The draft doesn't reason this out. Neither does your body. They are both of them merely phases of matter. They are not intelligent. It is your conscious mind that has been educated to think that a cold must follow exposure to a draft. This it is that suggests it to your subconscious mind and brings the cold into being.

Before you decide again that you have a cold, ask yourself, Who is it that is taking this cold? It cannot be my nose, for it has no intelligence. It does only what my subconscious mind directs. And anyway, how could my nose know that a draft of air has been playing on the back of my neck? If it wasn't my nose that decided it, what was it? The only thing it can have been is my mind.

Well, if mind can tell me to have a cold, surely it can stop that cold, too. So let's reverse the process, and instead of holding before the subconscious mind images of colds and fevers, think only of health and life and strength. Instead of trying to think back to discover how we "caught" cold, and thus strengthening the conviction that we have one, let us deny its existence and so knock the props out from under the creative faculties that are originating the cold. Let us hold before our subconscious mind only the perfect idea of nose and head and throat that is in Universal Mind. Let us make it use the Truth for its pattern, instead of the illusory ideas of conscious mind.

Every form of disease or sickness is solely the result of wrong thinking. The primary law of being is the law of health and life. When you recognize this, when you hold before your mind's eye only a perfect body, perfect organisms functioning perfectly, you will "realize the truth that makes you free."

Farnsworth in his "Practical Psychology" tells of a physician who has lived on a very restricted diet for years while at home. But about once a year he comes to New York for a week. While here, he eats anything and everything that his fancy dictates, and never suffers the least inconvenience. As soon as he gets home he has to return to his diet. Unless he sticks to his diet, he expects to be ill—*and he is ill.* "As a man thinketh, so is he." What one expects to get he is apt to get, especially where health is concerned. For matter has no sensation of its own. The conscious mind is what produces pain, is what feels, acts or impedes action.

Functional disorders are caused by certain suggestions getting into the subconsciousness and remaining there. They are not due to physical, but to mental causes—due to wrong thinking. The basis of all functional disorders is in the mind, though the manifestation be dyspepsia, melancholia, palpitation of the heart, or any one of a hundred others. There is nothing organically wrong with the body. It is your mental image that is out of adjustment. Change the one and you cure the other.

In this day of the gymnasium and the daily dozen, it may sound impractical to suggest that it is the mind, not the body, which needs the care. But I am far from being the first to suggest it.

There is a very successful physician in London whose teaching is that gymnastic exercise does more harm than good. He contends that the only exercise necessary for the perfect development of the body is yawning and stretching.

I would go farther than that. I would say that no physical exercise is *essential* to the perfect development of the body. That since the only cause is mind, the principal good of exercise is that when we go through the motions we are impressing upon our subconscious mind the picture of the perfect figure that we would have. And that mental visualization is what brings the results.

You can get the same results without the physical exercise by visualizing in your mind's eye the figure of the man you want to be, by intensely desiring it, by BELIEVING that you have it.

You can win to perfect health by knowing that there is but one right idea in Universal Mind for every organism in your body—that this right idea is perfect and undying—that you have only to hold it before you subconscious mind to see it realized in your body. *This is the truth that makes you free.*

Volume XI

The Law of Attraction

"For life is the mirror of king and slave.
'Tis just what you are and do;
Then give to the world the best you have,
And the best will come back to you."

—MADELINE BRIDGES

THE old adage that "He profits most who serves best" is no mere altruism.

Look around you. What businesses are going ahead? What men are making the big successes? Are they the ones who grab the passing dollar, careless of what they offer in return? Or are they those who are striving always to give a little greater value, a little more work than they are paid for?

When scales are balanced evenly, a trifle of extra weight thrown into either side overbalances the other as effectively as a ton.

In the same way, a little better value, a little extra effort, makes the man or the business stand out from the great mass of mediocrity like a tall man among pigmies, and brings results out of all proportion to the additional effort involved.

It pays—not merely altruistically, but in good, hard, round dollars—to give a little more value than seems necessary, to work a bit harder than you are paid for. It's that extra ounce of value that counts.

For the law of attraction is service. We receive in proportion as we give out.

In fact, we usually receive in far greater proportion. "Cast thy bread upon the waters and it will return to you an hundred-fold."

Back of everything is the immutable law of the Universe—that what you are is but the effect. Your thoughts are the causes. The only way you can change the effect is by first changing the cause.

People live in poverty and want because they are so wrapped up in their sufferings that they give out thoughts only of lack and sorrow. They expect want. They open the door of their mind only to hardship and sickness and poverty. True—they hope for something better—but their hopes are so drowned by their fears that they never have a chance.

You cannot receive good while expecting evil. You cannot demonstrate plenty while looking for poverty. "Blessed is he that expecteth much, for verily his soul shall be filled." Solomon outlined the law when he said:

"There is that scattereth, and increaseth yet more;
And there is that withholdeth more than is meet, but it tendeth only to want.
The liberal soul shall be made fat;
And he that watereth shall be watered also himself."

The Universal Mind expresses itself largely through the individual. It is continually seeking an outlet. It is like a vast reservoir of water, constantly replenished by mountain springs. Cut a channel to it and the water will flow in ever-increasing volume. In the same way, if you once open up a channel of service by which the Universal Mind can express itself through you, its gifts will flow in ever-increasing volume and YOU will be enriched in the process.

This is the idea through which great bankers are made. A foreign country needs millions for development. Its people are hard-working, but lack the necessary implements to make their work productive. How are they to find the money?

They go to a banker—put their problem up to him. He has not the money himself, but he knows how and where to raise it. He sells the promise to pay of the foreign country (their bonds, in other words) to people who have money to invest. His is merely a service. But it is such an invaluable service that both sides are glad to pay him liberally for it.

In the same way, by opening up a channel between universal supply and human needs—by doing your neighbors or your friends or your customers service—you are bound to profit yourself. And the wider you open your channel—the greater service you give or the better values you offer—the more things are bound to flow through your channel, the more you are going to profit thereby.

But you've got to *use* your talent if you want to profit from it. It matters not how small your service—using it will make it greater. You don't have to retire to a cell and pray. That is a selfish method—selfish concern for your own soul to the exclusion of all others. Mere self-denial or asceticism as such does no one good. You've got to DO something, to USE the talents God has given you to make the world better for your having been in it.

Remember the parable of the talents. You know what happened to the man who went off and hid his talent, whereas those who made use of theirs were given charge over many things.

That parable, it has always seemed to me, expresses the whole law of life. The only right is to *use* all the forces of good. The only wrong is to *neglect* or to abuse them.

"Thou shalt love the Lord thy God. This is the first and the greatest Commandment." Thou shalt show thy love by using to the best possible advantage the good things (the "talents" of the parable) that He has placed in your hands. "And the second is like unto it. Thou shalt love thy neighbor as thyself." Thou shalt not abuse the good things that have been provided you in such prodigality, by using them against your neighbor. Instead, thou shalt treat him (love him) as you would be treated by him. Thou shalt use the good about you for the advantage of all.

If you are a banker, you've got to use the money you have in order to make more money. If you are a merchant, you've got to sell the goods you have in order to buy more goods. If you are a doctor, you must help the patient you have in order to get more practice. If you are a clerk, you must do your work a little better than those around you if you want to earn more money than they. And if you want more of the universal supply, you must use that which you have in such a way as to make yourself of greater service to those around you.

"Whosoever shall be great among you," said Jesus, "shall be your minister, and whosoever of you will be the chiefest, shall be servant of all." In other words, if you would be great, you must serve. And he who serves most shall be greatest of all.

If you want to make more money, instead of seeking it for yourself, see how you can make more for others. In the process you will inevitably make more for yourself, too. We get as we give—but we must give first.

It matters not where you start—you may be a day laborer. But still you can give—give a bit more of energy, of work, of thought, than you are paid for. "Whosoever shall compel thee to go a mile," said Jesus, "go with him twain." Try to put a little extra skill into your work. Use your mind to find some better way of doing whatever task may be set for you. It won't be long before you are out of the common labor class.

There is no kind of work than cannot be bettered by thought. There is no method that cannot be improved by thought. So give generously of your thought to your work. Think every minute you are at it—"Isn't there some way in which this could be done easier, quicker, better?" Read in your spare time everything that relates to your own work or to the job ahead of you. In these days of magazines and books and libraries, few are the occupations that are not thoroughly covered in some good work.

Remember in Lorimer's "Letters of a Self-Made Merchant to His Son," the young fellow that old Gorgan Graham hired against his better judgment and put in the "barrel gang" just to get rid of him quickly? Before the month was out the young fellow had thought himself out of that job by persuading the boss to get a machine that did the work at half the cost and with a third of the gang. Graham just had to raise his pay and put him higher up. But he wouldn't stay put. No matter what the job, he always found some way it could be done better and with fewer people. Until he reached the top of the ladder.

There are plenty of men like that in actual life. They won't stay down. They are as full of bounce as a cat with a small boy and a dog after it. Thrown to the dog from an upper window, it is using the time of falling to get set for the next jump. By the time the dog leaps for where it hit, the cat is up the tree across the street.

The true spirit of business is the spirit of that plucky old Danish sea captain, Peter Tordenskjold. Attacked by a Swedish frigate, after all his crew but one had been killed and his supply of cannon balls was exhausted, Peter boldly kept up the fight, firing pewter dinner-plates and mugs from his one remaining gun.

One of the pewter mugs hit the Swedish captain and killed him, and Peter sailed off triumphant!

Look around YOU now. How can YOU give greater value for what you get? How can you SERVE better? How can you make more money for your employers or save more for your customers. Keep that thought ever in the forefront of your mind and *you'll never need to worry about making more for yourself!*

A BLANK CHECK

There was an article by Gardner Hunting in a recent issue of "Christian Business," that was so good that I reprint it here entire:

"All my life I have known in a vague way that getting money is the result of earning it; but I have never had a perfect vision of that truth till recently. Summed up now, the result of all my experience, pleasant and unpleasant, is that a man gets back exactly what he gives out, only multiplied.

"If I give to anybody service of a kind that he wants I shall get back the benefit myself. If I give more service I shall get more benefit. If I give a great deal more, I shall get a great deal more. But I shall get back more than I give. Exactly as when I plant a bushel of potatoes, I get back thirty or forty bushels, and more in proportion to the attention I give the growing crop. If I give more to my employer than he expects of me, he will give me a raise—and on no other condition. What is more, his giving me a raise does not depend on his fair-mindedness—he has to give it to me or lose me, because if he does not appreciate me somebody else will.

"But this is only part of it. If I give help to the man whose desk is next to mine, it will come back to me multiplied, even if he apparently is a rival. What I give to him, I give to the firm, and the firm will value it, because it is teamwork in the organization that the firm primarily wants, not brilliant individual performance. If I have an enemy in the organization, the same rule holds; if I give him, with the purpose of helping him, something that will genuinely help him, I am giving service to the organization. Great corporations appreciate the peace-maker, for a prime requisite in their success is harmony among employees. If my boss is unappreciative, the same rule holds; if I give him more, in advance of appreciation, he cannot withhold his appreciation and keep his own job.

"The more you think about this law, the deeper you will see it goes. It literally hands you a blank check, signed by the Maker of Universal Law, and leaves you to fill in the amount—and the kind—of payment you want! Mediocre successes are those that obey this law a little way—that fill in the check with a small amount—but that stop short of big vision in it. If every employee would only get the idea of this law firmly fixed in him as a principle, not subject to wavering with fluctuating moods, the success of the organization would be miraculous. One of my fears is apt to be that, by promoting the other fellow's success, I am side-tracking my own; but the exact opposite is the truth.

"Suppose every employee would look at his own case as an exact parallel to that of his firm. What does his firm give for the money it gets from the public? Service! Service in advance! The better the service that is given out, the more money comes back. What does the firm do to bring public attention to its service? It advertises; that is part of the service. Now, suppose that I, as an employee, begin giving my service to the firm in advance of all hoped for payment. Suppose I advertise my service. How do I do either? I cannot do anything constructive in that firm's office or store or plant or premises that is not service, from filing a letter correctly to mending the fence or pleasing a customer; from looking up a word for the stenographer, to encouraging her to look it up herself; demonstrating a machine to a customer or encouraging him to demonstrate it himself; from helping my immediate apparent rival to get a raise, to selling the whole season's output. As for advertising myself, I begin advertising myself the moment I walk into the office or the store or the shop in the morning; I cannot help it. Everybody who looks at me sees my advertisement. Everybody around me has my advertisement before his eyes all day long. So has the boss—my immediate chief and the head of the firm, no matter where they are. And if I live up to my advertising, nobody can stop me from selling my goods—my services! The more a man knocks me, the more he advertises me; because he calls attention to me; and if I am delivering something better than he says I am, the interested parties—my employers—will see it, and will not be otherwise influenced by what he says.

"More than that, I must give to every human being I come in contact with, from my wife to the bootblack who shines my shoes; from my brother to my sworn foe. Sometimes people will tell you to smile; but the smile I give has got to be a real smile that lives up to its advertising. If I go around grinning like a Cheshire cat, the Cheshire-cat grin will be what I get back—multiplied! If I give the real thing, I'll get back the real thing—multiplied! If anybody objects that this is a selfish view to take, I answer him that any law of salvation from anything by anybody that has ever been offered for any purpose, is a selfish view to take. The only unselfishness that has ever been truly taught is that of giving a lesser thing in hope of receiving a greater.

"Now, why am I so sure of this law? How can you be sure? I have watched it work; it works everywhere. You have only to try it, and keep on trying it and it will prove true for you. It is not true because I say so, nor because anybody else says so; it is just true. Theosophists call it the law of Karma; humanitarians call it the law of Service; business men call it the law of common sense; Jesus Christ called it the law of Love. It rules whether I know it or not, whether I believe it or not, whether I defy it or not. I *can't* break it! Jesus of Nazareth, without reference to any religious idea you may have about Him, without consideration as to whether He was or was not divine, was the greatest business Man that ever lived, and he said: 'Give and ye shall receive—good measure, pressed down, shaken together, running over!' And this happens to be so—not because He said it—but because it is the Truth, which we all, whether we admit it or not, worship *as* God. No man can honestly say that he does not put the truth supreme.

"It is the truth—the principle of giving and receiving—only there are few men who go the limit on it. But going the limit is the way to unlimited returns!

"What shall I give? What I have, of course. Suppose you believe in this idea—and suppose you should start giving it out, the idea itself, tactfully, wisely, and living it yourself in your organization. How long do you think it will be before you are a power in that organization, recognized as such and getting pay as such? It is more valuable than all the cleverness and special information you can possibly possess without it. What you have, give—to everybody. If you have an idea, do not save it for your own use only; give it. It is the best thing you have to give and therefore the thing best to give—and therefore the thing that will bring the best back to you. I believe that if a man would follow this principle, even to his trade-secrets, he would profit steadily more and more; and more certainly than he will by holding on to anything for himself. He would never have to worry about his own affairs—because he would be working on fundamental law. Law never fails—and it will be easy for you to discover what is or is not law. And if law is worth using part of the time, it is worth using all the time.

"Look around you first, with an eye to seeing the truth, and then put the thing to the test. Through both methods of investigation you will find a blank check waiting for you to fill in with 'whatsoever you desire,' and a new way to pray and to get what you pray for."

Volume XII

Volume XII

The Three Requisites

"Waste no tears
Upon the blotted record of lost years,
But turn the leaf, and smile, oh smile, to see
The fair white pages that remain for thee.
"Prate not of thy repentance. But believe
The spark divine dwells in thee: let it grow.
That which the upreaching spirit can achieve
The grand and all creative forces know;
They will assist and strengthen as the light
Lifts up the acorn to the oak-tree's height.
Thou hast but to resolve, and lo! God's whole
Great universe shall fortify thy soul."

—ELLA WHEELER WILCOX

SOMETIME today or tomorrow or next month, in practically every commercial office and manufacturing plant in the United States, an important executive will sit back in his chair and study a list of names on a sheet of white paper before him.

Your name may be on it.

A position of responsibility is open and he is face to face with the old, old problem—"Where can I find the man?"

The faces, the words, the work, the impressions of various men will pass through his mind in quick review. What is the first question he will ask concerning each?

"Which man is strongest on initiative, which one can best assume responsibility?"

Other things being equal, THAT is the man who will get the job. For the first requisite in business as in social life is confidence in yourself—*knowledge of your power*. Given that, the second is easy—initiative or *the courage to start things*. Lots of men have ideas, but few have the confidence in themselves or the courage to start anything.

With belief and initiative, the third requisite follows almost as a matter of course—*the faith to go ahead* and do things in the face of all obstacles.

"Oh, God," said Leonardo da Vinci, "you sell us everything for the price of an effort."

Certainly no one had a better chance to know than he. An illegitimate son, brought up in the family of his father, the misfortune of his birth made him the source of constant derision. He had to do something to lift himself far above the crowd. And he did. "For the price of an effort" he became the greatest artist in Italy—probably the greatest in the world—in a day when Italy was famous for her artists. Kings and princes felt honored at being associated with this illegitimate boy. He made the name he had no right to famous for his work alone.

"Work out your own salvation," said Paul. And the first requisite in working it out is a knowledge of your power. "Every man of us has all the centuries in him."—Morley. All the ages behind you have bequeathed you stores of abilities which you are allowing to lie latent. Those abilities, are stored up in your subconscious mind. Call upon them. Use them. As Whittier put it—

"All the good the past has had
Remains to make our own time glad."

Are you an artist? The cunning of a da Vinci, the skill of a Rembrandt, the vision of a Reynolds, is behind those fingers of yours. Use the Genie-of-your-mind to call upon them.

Are you a surgeon, a lawyer, a minister, an engineer, a business man? Keep before your mind's eye the biggest men who have ever done the things you now are doing. Use them as your model. And not as your model simply, but as your inspiration. Start in where they left off. Call upon the innermost recesses of your subconscious mind, for their skill, their judgment, their initiative. Realize that you have it in you to be as great as they. Realize that all that they did, all that they learned, all the skill they acquired is stored safely away in Universal Mind and that through your subconscious mind *you have ready access to it.*

The mind in you is the same mind that animated all the great conquerers of the past, all the great inventors, all the great artists, statesmen, leaders, business men. What they have done is but a tithe of what still remains to do—of what men in your day and your children's day will do. You can have a part in it. Stored away within you is every power that any man or woman ever possessed. It awaits only your call.

In "Thoughts on Business," we read: "It is a great day in a man's life when he truly begins to discover himself. The latent capacities of every man are greater than he realizes, and he may find them if he diligently seeks for them. A man may own a tract of land for many years without knowing its value. He may think of it as merely a pasture. But one day he discovers evidences of coal and finds a rich vein beneath his land. While mining and prospecting for coal he discovers deposits of granite. In boring for water he strikes oil. Later he discovers a vein of copper ore, and after that silver and gold. These things were there all the time—even when he thought of his land merely as a pasture. But they have a value only when they are discovered and utilized.

"Not every pasture contains deposits of silver and gold, neither oil nor granite, nor even coal. But beneath the surface of every man there must be, in the nature of things, a latent capacity greater than has yet been discovered. And one discovery must lead to another until the man finds the deep wealth of his own possibilities. History is full of the acts of men who discovered somewhat of their own capacity; but history has yet to record the man who fully discovered all that he might have been."

Everything that has been done, thought, gained, or been is in Universal Mind. And you are a part of Universal Mind. You have access to it. You can call upon it for all you need in the same way you can go to your files or to a library for information. If you can realize this fact, you will find in it the key to the control of every circumstance, the solution of every problem, the satisfaction of every right desire.

But to use that key, you've got to bear in mind the three requisites of faith in your powers, initiative, and courage to start. "Who would stand before a blackboard," says "Science and Health," "and pray the principle of mathematics to solve the problem? The rule is already established, and it is our task to work out the solution." In the same way, all knowledge you can need is in Universal Mind, but it is up to *you* to tap that mind.

And without the three requisites you will never do it.

Never let discouragement hold you back. Discouragement is the most dangerous feeling there is, because it is the most insidious. Generally it is looked upon as harmless, and for that very reason it is the more sinister. For failure and success are oftentimes separated by only the distance of that one word—Discouragement.

There is an old-time fable that the devil once held a sale and offered all the tools of his trade to anyone who would pay their price. They were spread out on the table, each one labeled—hatred, and malice, and envy, and despair, and sickness, and sensuality—all the weapons that everyone knows so well.

But off on one side, apart from the rest, lay a harmless looking, wedge-shaped instrument marked "Discouragement." It was old and worn looking, but it was priced far above all the rest. When asked the reason why, the devil replied:

"Because I can use this one so much more easily than the others. No one knows that it belongs to me, so with it I can open doors that are tight bolted against the others. Once I get inside I can use any tool that suits me best."

No one ever knows how small is the margin between failure and success. Frequently the two are separated only by the width of that one word—*discouragement*. Ask Ford, ask Edison, ask any successful man and he will tell you how narrow is the chasm that separates failure from success, how surely it can be bridged by perseverance and faith.

Cultivate confidence in yourself. Cultivate the feeling that you ARE succeeding. Know that you have unlimited power to do every right thing. Know that with Universal Mind to draw upon, no position is too difficult, and no problem too hard. "He that believeth on me, the works that I do shall he do also; and greater works than these shall he do." When you put limitations upon yourself, when you doubt your ability to meet any situation, you are placing a limit upon Universal Mind, for "The Father that is within me, He doeth the works."

With that knowledge of your power, with that confidence in the unlimited resources of Universal Mind, it is easy enough to show initiative, it is easy enough to find the courage to start things.

You have a right to dominion over all things—over your body, your environment, your business, your health. Develop these three requisites and you will gain that dominion.

Remember that you are a part of Universal Mind, and that the part shares every property of the whole. Remember that, as the spark of electricity is to the thunderbolt, so is your mind to Universal Mind. Whatever of good you may desire of life, whatever qualification, whatever position, you have only to work for it whole heartedly, confidently, with singleness of purpose—*and you can get it.*

Volume XIII

That Old Witch—Bad Luck

"How do you tackle your work each day?
Are you scared of the job you find?
Do you grapple the task that comes your way
With a confident, easy mind?
Do you stand right up to the work ahead
Or fearfully pause to view it?
Do you start to toil with a sense of dread
Or feel that you're going to do it?
"What is the thought that is in your mind?
Is fear ever running through it?
If so, just tackle the next you find
By thinking you're going to do it."

—Edgar A. Guest[7]

HAS that old witch—bad luck—ever camped on your doorstep? Have ill health, misfortune and worry ever seemed to dog your footsteps?

If so, you will be interested in knowing that YOU were the procuring cause of all that trouble. For fear is merely creative thought in negative form.

Remember back in 1920 how fine the business outlook seemed, how everything

---

7. From "A Heap o' Livin'." The Reilly & Lee Co.

looked rosy and life flowed along like a song? We had crops worth ten billions of dollars. We had splendid utilities, great railways, almost unlimited factory capacity. Everyone was busy. The government had a billion dollars in actual money. The banks were sound. The people were well employed. Wages were good. Prosperity was general. *Then something happened.* A wave of fear swept over the country. The prosperity could not last. People wouldn't pay such high prices. There was too much inflation. What was the result?

As Job put it in the long ago, "The thing that I greatly feared has come upon me."

The prosperity vanished almost over night. Failures became general. Hundreds of thousands were thrown out of work. And all because of panic, fear.

'Tis true that readjustments were necessary. 'Tis true that prices were too high, that inventories were too big, that values generally were inflated. But it wasn't necessary to burst the balloon to let out the gas. There are orderly natural processes of readjustment that bring things to their proper level with the least harm to anyone.

But fear—panic—knows no reason. It brings into being overnight the things that it fears. It is the greatest torment of humanity. It is about all there is to Hell. *Fear is, in short, the devil.* It causes most of the sin, disaster, disease and misery of the world. It is the only thing you can put into business which won't draw dividends in either fun or dollars. If you guess right, you don't get any satisfaction out of it.

The real cause of all sickness is fear. You image some disease in your thought, and your body proceeds to build upon this model that you hold before it. You have seen how fear makes the face pallid, how it first stops the beating of the heart, then sets it going at trip-hammer pace. Fear changes the secretions. Fear halts the digestion. Fear puts lines and wrinkles into the face. Fear turns the hair gray.

Mind controls every function of the human body. If the thought you hold before your subconscious mind is the fear of disease, of colds or catarrh, of fever or indigestion, those are the images your subconscious mind will work out in your body. For your body itself is merely so much matter—an aggregation of protons and electrons, just as the table in front of you is an aggregation of these same buttons of force, but with a different density. Take away your mind, and your body is just as inert, just as lifeless, just as senseless, as the table. Every function of your body, from the beating of your heart to the secretions in your glands, is controlled by mind. The digestion of your food is just as much a function of your mind as the moving of your finger. So the all-important thing is not what food you put into your stomach, but what your mind decides shall be done with it. If your mind feels that certain food should make you sick, it *will* make you sick. If, on the other hand, your mind decides that though the food has no nutritive value, there is no reason why unintelligent matter should make you sick, mind will eliminate that food without harm or discomfort to you.

Your body is just like clay in the hands of a potter. Your mind can make of it what it will. The clay has nothing to say about what form it shall take. Neither have your head, your heart, your lungs, your digestive organs anything to say about how conditions shall affect them. They do not decide whether they shall be dizzy or diseased or lame. It is mind that makes this decision. They merely conform to it AFTER mind has decided it. Matter has undergone any and every condition without harm, when properly sustained by mind. And what it has done once, it can do again.

When you understand that your muscles, your nerves, your bones have no feeling or intelligence of their own, when you learn that they react to conditions only as mind directs that they shall react, you will never again think or speak of any organ as imperfect, as weak or ailing. You will never again complain of tired bodies, aching muscles, or frayed nerves. On the contrary, you will hold steadfast to thoughts of exhaustless strength, of super-abundant vitality, knowing that, as Shakespeare said—"There is nothing, either good or bad, but thinking makes it so."

Never fear disaster, for the fear of it is an invitation to disaster to come upon you. Fear being vivid, easily impresses itself upon the subconscious mind. And by so impressing itself, it brings into being the thing that is feared. It is the Frankenstein monster that we all create at times, and which, created, turns to rend its creator. Fear that something you greatly prize will be lost and the fear you feel with create the very means whereby you will lose it.

Fear is the Devil. It is the ravening lion roaming the earth seeking whom it may devour. The only safety from it is to deny it. The only refuge is in the knowledge that it has no power other than the power you give to it.

HE WHOM A DREAM HATH POSSESSED

You fear debt. So your mind concentrates upon it and brings about greater debts. You fear loss. And by visualizing that loss you bring it about.

The only remedy for fear is to know that evil has no power—that it is a nonentity—merely a lack of something. You fear ill health, when if you would concentrate that same amount of thought upon good health you would insure the very condition you fear to lose. Functional disturbances are caused solely by the mind through wrong thinking. The remedy for them is not drugs, but right thinking, for the trouble is not in the organs but in the mind. Farnsworth in his "Practical Psychology" tells of a man who had conceived the idea when a boy that the eating of cherries and milk together had made him sick. He was very fond of both, but always had to be careful not to eat them together, for whenever he did he had been ill. Mr. Farnsworth explained to him that there was no reason for such illness, because all milk sours anyway just as soon as it reaches the stomach. As a matter of fact it cannot be digested until it does sour. He then treated the man mentally for this wrong association of ideas, and after the one treatment the man was never troubled in this way again, though he had been suffering from it for forty-five years.

If you had delirium tremens, and thought you saw pink elephants and green alligators and yellow snakes all about you, it would be a foolish physician that would try to cure you of snakes. Or that would prescribe glasses to improve your eyesight, when he knew that the animals round about you were merely distorted visions of your mind.

The indigestion that you suffer from, the colds that bother you—in short, each and every one of your ailments—is just as much a distorted idea of your mind as would be the snakes of delirium tremens. Banish the idea and you banish the manifestation.

The Bible contains one continuous entreaty to cast out fear. From beginning to end, the admonition "Fear not" is insistent. Fear is the primary cause of all bodily impairment. Jesus understood this and He knew that it could be abolished. Hence His frequent entreaty, "Fear not, be not afraid."

Struggle there is. And struggle there will always be. But struggle is merely wrestling with trial. We need difficulties to overcome. But there is nothing to be afraid of. Everything is an effect of mind. Your thought forces, concentrated upon anything, will bring that thing into manifestation. Therefore concentrate them only upon good things, only upon those conditions you wish to see manifested. *Think* health, power, abundance, happiness. Drive all thoughts of poverty and disease, of fear and worry, as far from your mind as you drive filth from your homes. For fear and worry is the filth of the mind that causes all trouble, that brings about all disease. Banish it! Banish from among your associates any man with a negative outlook on life. Shun him as you would the plague. Can you imagine a knocker winning anything? He is doomed before he starts. Don't let him pull you down with him. "Fret not thyself," says the Psalmist, "else shalt thou be moved to do evil."

That wise old Psalmist might have been writing for us today. For there is no surer way of doing the wrong thing in business or in social life than to fret yourself, to worry, to fume, to want action of some kind, regardless of what it may be. Remember the Lord's admonition to the Israelites, *"Be still*—and know that I am God."

Have you ever stood on the shore of a calm, peaceful lake and watched the reflections in it? The trees, the mountains, the clouds, the sky, all were mirrored there—just as perfectly, as beautifully, as the objects themselves. But try to get such a reflection from the ocean! It cannot be done, because the ocean is always restless, always stirred up by winds or waves or tides.

So it is with your mind. You cannot reflect the richness and plenty of Universal Mind, you cannot mirror peace and health and happiness, if you are constantly worried, continually stirred by waves of fear, winds of anger, tides of toil and striving. You must relax at times. You must give mind a chance. You must realize that, when you have done your best, you can confidently lean back and leave the outcome to Universal Mind.

Just as wrong thinking produces discord in the body, so it also brings on a diseased condition in the realm of commerce. Experience teaches that we need to be protected more from our fears and wrong thoughts, than from so-called evil influences external to ourselves. We need not suffer for another man's wrong, for another's greed, dishonesty, avarice or selfish ambition. But if we hug to ourselves the fear that we do have to so suffer, take it into our thought, allow it to disturb us, then we sentence ourselves. We are free to reject every suggestion of discord, and to be governed harmoniously, in spite of what anything or anybody may try to do to us.

Do you know why old army men would rather have soldiers of 18 or 20 than mature men of 30 or 40? Not because they can march farther. They can't! Not because they can carry more. They can't! But because when they go to sleep at night, they really sleep. *They wipe the slate clean!* When they awaken in the morning, they are ready for a new day and a new world.

But an older man carries the nervous strain of one day over to the next. He worries! With the result that at the end of a couple of months' hard campaigning, the older man is a nervous wreck.

And that is the trouble with most men in business. *They never wipe the slate clean! They worry!* And they carry each day's worries over to the next, with the result that some day the burden becomes more than they can carry.

THE BARS OF FATE

Fear results from a belief that there are really two powers in this world—Good and Evil. Like light and darkness. When the fact is that Evil is no more real than darkness. True, we lose contact with Good at times. We let the clouds of fear and worry come between us and the sunlight of Good and then all seems dark. But the sun is still shining on the other side of those clouds, and when we drive them away, we again see its light.

Realizing this, realizing that Good is ever available if we will but turn to it confidently in our need, what is there to fear? "Fear not, little flock," said Jesus, "for it is the Father's good pleasure to give you the kingdom." And again— "Son, thou art ever with me, and all that I have is thine."

If this means anything, it means that the Father is ever available to all of us, that we have but to call upon Him in the right way and our needs will be met. It doesn't matter what those needs may be.

If Universal Mind is the Creator of all, and if everything in the Universe belongs to It, then your business, your work, isn't really yours—but the "Father's." And He is just as much interested in its success, as long as you are working in accordance with His plan, as you can be.

Everyone will admit that Universal Mind can do anything good. Everyone will admit that It can bring to a successful conclusion any undertaking It may be interested in. If Mind created your business, if It inspired your work, then It is interested in its successful conclusion.

Why not, then, call upon Mind when you have done all you know how to do and yet success seems beyond your efforts. Why not put your problem up to Mind, secure in the belief that It CAN and WILL give you any right thing you may desire? I know that many people hesitate to pray for material things, but if Universal Mind made them, they must have been made for some good purpose, and as long as you intend to use them for good, by all means ask for them.

If you can feel that your business, your work, is a good work, if you can be sure that it is advancing the great Scheme of Things by ever so little, you will never again fear debt or lack or limitation. For "The earth is the Lord's and the fullness thereof." Universal Mind is never going to lack for means to carry on Its work. When Jesus needed fish and bread, fish and bread were provided in such abundance that a whole multitude was fed. When He needed gold, the gold coin appeared in the fish's mouth. Where you are, Mind is, and where Mind is, there is all the power, all the supply of the universe.

You are like the owner of a power house that supplies electricity for light and heat and power to the homes and the factories around you. There is unlimited electricity everywhere about you, but you have got to set your dynamo going to draw the electricity out of the air and into your power lines, before it can be put to practical account.

Just so, there are unlimited riches all about you, but you have got to set the dynamo of your mind to work to bring them into such form as will make them of use to yourself and the world.

So don't worry about any present lack of money or other material things. Don't try to win from others what they have. Go where the money is! The material wealth that is in evidence is so small compared with the possible wealth available through the right use of mind, that it is negligible by comparison. The great rewards are for the pioneers. Look at Carnegie; at Woolworth; at Ford! Every year some new field of development is opened, some new world discovered. Steam, gas, electricity, telegraphy, wireless, the automobile, the aeroplane—each opens up possibilities of new worlds yet to come.

A hundred years ago, people probably felt that everything had been discovered that could be discovered. That everything was already known that was likely ever to be known. Just as you may feel about things now. Yet look at the tremendous strides mankind has taken in the past hundred years. And they are as nothing to what the future holds for us, once man has learned to harness the truly unlimited powers of his subconscious mind.

There are billions of dollars worth of treasure under every square mile of the earth's surface. There are millions of ways in which this old world of ours can be made a better place to live. Set your mind to work locating some of this treasure, finding some of those ways. Don't wait for someone else to blaze the trail.

No one remembers who else was on the *Santa Maria,* but Columbus' name will be known forever! Carnegie is said to have made a hundred millionaires, but he alone became almost a *billionaire!*

Have you ever read Kipling's "Explorer?"

"'There's no sense in going further—it's the edge of cultivation,'
So they said, and I believed it—broke my land and sowed my crop—
Built my barns and strung my fences in the little border station
Tucked away below the foothills where the trails run out and stop.

"Till a voice, as bad as Conscience, rang interminable changes
On one everlasting Whisper day and night repeated—so:
'Something hidden. Go and find it. Go and look behind the Ranges—
Something lost behind the Ranges. Lost and waiting for you. Go!'"

Your mind is part and parcel of Universal Mind. You have the wisdom of all the ages to draw upon. Use it! Use it to do your work in a way it was never done before. Use it to find new outlets for your business, new methods of reaching people, new and better ways of serving them. Use it to uncover new riches, to learn ways to make the world a better place to live in.

Concentrate your thought upon these things, knowing that back of you is the vast reservoir of Universal Mind, that all these things are *already* known to It, and that you have but to make your contact for them to be known to you.

Optimism based on such a realization is never overconfidence. It is the joyous assurance of *absolute faith*. It is the assurance that made Wilson for a time the outstanding leader of the world. It is the assurance that heartened Lincoln during the black days of the Civil War. It is the assurance that carried Hannibal and Napoleon over the Alps, that left Alexander sighing for more worlds to conquer, that enabled Cortez and his little band to conquer a nation.

Grasp this idea of the availability of Universal Mind for your daily needs, and your vision will become enlarged, your capacity increased. You will realize that the only limits upon you are those you put upon yourself. There will be no such thing then as difficulties and opposition barring your way.

EXERCISE

You feed and nourish the body daily. But few people give any thought to nourishing that far more important part—the Mind. So let us try, each day, to set apart a few minutes time to give the Mind a repast.

To begin with, *relax!* Stretch out comfortably on a lounge or in an easy chair and let go of every muscle, loosen every bit of tension, forget every thought of fear or worry. Relax mentally and physically.

Few people know how to relax entirely. Most of us are on a continual strain, and it is this strain that brings on physical disturbances—not any real work we may do. Here is a little exercise that will help you to thoroughly relax:

Recline comfortably on a lounge or bed. Stretch luxuriously first. Then when you are settled at your ease again, lift the right leg a foot or two. Let it drop limply. Repeat slowly twice. Do the same with the left leg. With the right arm. With the left arm. You will find then that all your muscles are relaxed. You can forget them and turn your thoughts to other things.

Try to realize the unlimited power that is yours. Think back to the dawn of time, when Mind first imaged from nothingness the heavens and the earth and all that in them is. Remember that, although your mind is to Universal Mind only as a drop of water to the ocean, this drop has all the properties of the great ocean; one in quality although not in quantity; your mind has all the creative power of Universal Mind.

"And God made man in His image, after His likeness." Certainly God never manifested anything but infinite abundance, infinite supply. If you are made in His image, there is no reason why you should ever lack for anything of good. You can manifest abundance, too.

Round about you is the same electronic energy from which Universal Mind formed the heavens and the earth. What do you wish to form from it? What do you want most from life? Hold it in your thought, visualize it, SEE it! Make your model clear-cut and distinct.

1. Remember, the first thing necessary is a sincere desire, concentrating your thought on one thing with singleness of purpose.

2. The second is visualization—SEEING YOURSELF DOING IT—imaging the object in the same way that Universal Mind imaged all of creation.

3. Next is faith—BELIEVING that you HAVE this thing that you want. Not that you are GOING to have it, mind you—but that you HAVE it.

4. And the last is gratitude—gratitude for this thing that you have received, gratitude for the power that enabled you to create it, gratitude for all the gifts that Mind has laid at your feet.

"Trust in the Lord . . . and verily thou shalt be fed.
"Delight thyself also in the Lord, and He shall give thee the desires of thy heart.
"Commit thy way unto the Lord, and He shall bring it to pass."

Volume XIV

Your Needs Are Met

"Arise, O Soul, and gird thee up anew,
Though the black camel Death kneel at this gate;
No beggar thou that thou for alms shouldst sue;
Be the proud captain still of thine own fate."

—KENYON

You've heard the story of the old man who called his children to his bedside to give them a few parting words of advice. And this was the burden of it.

"My children," he said, "I have had a great deal of trouble in my life—a great deal of trouble—*but most of it never happened.*"

We are all of us like that old man. Our troubles weigh us down—in prospect—but we usually find that when the actual need arrives, Providence has devised some way of meeting it.

Dr. Jacques Loeb, a member of the Rockefeller Institute, conducted a series of tests with parasites found on plants, which show that even the lowest order of creatures have the power to call upon Universal Supply for the resources to meet any unusual need.

"In order to obtain the material," reads the report of the tests, "potted rose bushes are brought into a room and placed in front of a closed window. If the plants are allowed to dry out, the aphides (parasites), previously wingless, change to winged insects. After the metamorphosis, the animals leave the plants, fly to the window and then creep upward on the glass.

"It is evident that these tiny insects found that the plants on which they had been thriving were dead, and that they could therefore secure nothing more to eat and drink from this source. The only method by which they could save themselves from starvation was to grow temporary wings and fly, which they did."

In short, when their source of sustenance was shut off and they had to find the means of migrating or perish, Universal Supply furnished the means for migration.

If Universal Mind can thus provide for the meanest of its creatures, is it not logical to suppose that It will do even more for us—the highest product of creation—if we will but call upon It, if we will but have a little faith? Viewed in the light of Mind's response to the need of those tiny parasites, does it seem so unbelievable that a sea should roll back while a people marched across it dry-shod? That a pillar of fire should lead them through the wilderness by night? That manna should fall from heaven, or water gush forth from a rock?

In moments of great peril, in times of extremity, when the brave soul has staked its all—those are the times when miracles are wrought, if we will but have faith.

That doesn't mean that you should rest supinely at your ease and let the Lord provide. When you have done all that is in you to do—when you have given of your best—don't worry or fret as to the outcome. Know that if more is needed, your need will be met. You can sit back with the confident assurance that having done your part, you can depend upon the Genie-of-your-Mind to do the rest.

When the little state of Palestine was in danger of being overrun by Egypt on the one hand, or gobbled up by Assyria on the other, its people were frantically trying to decide which horn of the dilemma to embrace, with which enemy they should ally themselves to stave off the other. "With neither," the Prophet Isaiah told them, "in calmly resting your safety lieth; in quiet trust shall be your strength."

So it is with most of the great calamities that afflict us. If we would only "calmly rest, quietly trust," how much better off we should be. But no—we must fret and worry, and nine times out of ten do the wrong thing. And the more we worry and fret, the more likely we are to go wrong.

All of Universal Mind that is necessary to solve any given problem, to meet any need, is wherever that need may be. Supply is always *where* you are and *what* you need. It matters not whether it be sickness or trouble, poverty or danger, the remedy is there, waiting for your call. Go at your difficulty boldly, knowing that you have infinite resources behind you, and you will find these forces closing around you and coming to your aid.

It's like an author writing a book. For a long time he works in a kind of mental fog, but let him persevere, and there flashes suddenly a light that clarifies his ideas and shows him the way to shape them logically. At the moment of despair, you feel a source of unknown energy arising in your soul.

That doesn't mean that you will never have difficulties. Difficulties are good for you. They are the exercise of your mind. You are the stronger for having overcome them. But look upon them as mere exercise. As "stunts" that are given you in order that you may the better learn how to use your mind, how to draw upon Universal Supply. Like Jacob wrestling with the Angel, don't let them go until they have blessed you—until, in other words, you have learned something from having encountered them.

Remember this: No matter how great a catastrophe may befall mankind, no matter how general the loss, you and yours can be free from it. There is always a way of safety. There is always an "ark" by which the understanding few can be saved from the flood. The name of that ark is Understanding—understanding of your inner powers.

When the children of Israel were being led into the promised land, and Joshua had given them their directions, they answered him: "All that thou commandest us we will do, and whithersoever thou sendest us, we will go. . . . Only the Lord thy God be with thee, as He was with Moses."

They came to the river Jordan, and it seemed an insurmountable barrier in their path, but Joshua commanded them to take the Ark of the Covenant, representing God's understanding with them, before them into the Jordan. They did it, and "the waters which came down from above stood and rose up upon an heap. . . . And the priests that bare the Ark of the Covenant of the Lord stood firm on dry ground in the midst of Jordan, and all the Israelites passed over on dry ground, until all the people were passed clean over Jordan."

THE ARK OF THE COVENANT

All through the Old Testament, when war and pestilence, fire and flood, were the common lot of mankind, there is constant assurance of safety for those who have this understanding, this "Covenant" with the Lord. "Because thou hast made the Lord which is my refuge—even the Most High—thy habitation, there shall no evil befall thee, neither shall any plague come nigh thy dwelling. For He shall give His angels charge over thee to keep thee in all thy ways."

That is His agreement with us—an agreement which gives us the superiority to circumstances which men have sought from time immemorial. All that is necessary on our side of the agreement is for us to remember the infinite powers that reside within us, to remember that our mind is part of Universal Mind and as such it can foresee, it can guard against and it can protect us from harm of any kind. We need not run away from trials or try to become stoical towards them. All we need is to bring our understanding to bear upon them—to know that no situation has ever yet arisen with which Universal Mind—and through it our own mind—was not fully competent to deal. To know that the right solution of every problem is in Universal Mind. That we have but to seek that solution and our trial is overcome.

"But where shall Wisdom be found? And where is the place of understanding? Acquaint now thyself with God, and be at peace."

If evil threatens us, if failure, sickness or accident seems imminent, we have only to decide that these evils do not come from Universal Mind, therefore they are unreal and have no power over us. They are simply the absence of the right condition which Universal Mind knows. Refuse, therefore, to see them, to acknowledge them—and seek through Mind for the right condition which shall nullify them.

If you will do this, you will find that you can appropriate from Mind whatever you require for your needs, *when* you require it. The greater your need, the more surely it will be met, if you can but realize this truth. "Fear not, little flock," said Jesus, "for it is your Father's good pleasure to give you the Kingdom."

Remember that your thought is all-powerful. That it is creative. That there is no limitation upon it of time or space. And that it is ever-available.

Forget your worries. Forget your fears. In place of them, visualize the conditions you would like to see. Realize their availability. Declare to yourself that you already *have* all these things that you desire, that your needs *have* been met. Say to yourself: "How thankful I am that Mind has made all these good things available to me. I have everything that heart could desire to be grateful for."

Every time you do this, you are impressing the thought upon your subconscious mind. And the moment you can convince your subconscious mind of the truth of it—*that moment* your mind will proceed to *make* it true. This is the way to put into practice the Master's advice—"Believe that ye RECEIVE it, and ye SHALL HAVE it."

There is no condition so hopeless, no cause so far gone, that this truth will not save it. Time and again patients given over by their doctors as doomed have made miraculous recoveries through the faith of some loved one.

"I hope that everyone who reads this Book may gain as much from their first reading as I did," writes a happy subscriber from New York City. "I got such a clear understanding from that one reading that I was able to break the mental chain holding a friend to a hospital bed, and she left the hospital in three days, to the very great astonishment of the doctors handling the case."

In the same way, there are innumerable instances where threatened calamity has been warded off and good come instead. The great trouble with most of us is, we do not *believe*. We insist upon looking for trouble. We feel that the "rainy day" is bound to come, and we do our utmost to make it a surety by keeping it in our thoughts, preparing for it, fearing it. "Cowards die many times before their deaths; the valiant never taste of death but once." We cross our bridges a dozen times before we come to them. We doubt ourselves, we doubt our ability, we doubt everyone and everything around us. And our doubts sap our energy; kill our enthusiasm; rob us of success. We are like the old lady who "enjoys poor health." We always place that little word "but" after our wishes and desires, feeling deep down that there are some things too good to be true. We think there is a power apart from Good which can withhold blessings that should be ours. We doubt, because we cannot see the way by which our desires can be fulfilled. We put a limit upon the good that can come to us.

"Prove me now herewith, saith the Lord of Hosts," cried the Prophet Malachi, "if I will not open you the windows of heaven and pour you out a blessing that there shall not be room enough to receive it . . . And all nations shall call you blessed, for ye shall be a delightsome land."

Your mind is part of Universal Mind. And Universal Mind has all supply. You are entitled to, and you can have, just as much of that supply as you are able to appropriate. To expect less is to get less, for it dwarfs your power of receiving.

It doesn't matter what your longings may be, provided they are right longings. If your little son has his heart set on a train and you feel perfectly able to get him a train, you are not going to hand him a picture book instead. It may be that the picture book would have greater educational value, but the love you have for your son is going to make you try to satisfy his longings as long as those longings are not harmful ones.

In the same way, Universal Mind will satisfy *your* longings, no matter how trivial they may seem, as long as they are not harmful ones. "Delight thyself also in the Lord, and He shall give thee the desires of thine heart."

If we would only try to realize that God is not some far-off Deity, not some stern Judge, but the beneficent force that we recognize as Nature—the life Principle that makes the flowers bud, and the plants grow, that spreads abundance about us with lavish hand. If we could realize that He is the Universal Mind that holds all supply, that will give us the toy of our childhood or the needs of maturity, that all we need to obtain from Him our Heart's Desire is a right understanding of His availability—then we would lose all our fears, all our worries, all our sense of limitation.

For Universal Mind is an infinite, unlimited source of good. Not only the source of general good, but the specific good things you desire of life. To It there is no big or little problem. The removal of mountains is no more difficult than the feeding of a sparrow.

And to one—like the Master—with a perfect understanding, the "miracle" of raising Lazarus from the dead required no more effort than the turning of the water into wine. He knew that Universal Mind is all power—and there cannot be more than ALL. He knew that "To know God aright is life eternal." And Jesus knew God aright, so was able to demonstrate this knowledge of life eternal in overcoming sin, disease and death. For it is one and the same law that heals sin, sickness, poverty, heartaches, or death itself. That law is the right understanding of Divine Principle.

But what does this ability to perform "miracles" consist of? What is the power or force by which we can prove this ability? Perhaps the simplest way is to begin with the realization that Universal Mind is man's working power.

THE SCIENCE OF THOUGHT

Can you stretch your mind a bit and try to comprehend this wonderful fact—that the ALL POWERFUL, ALL-KNOWING, EVERLASTING CREATOR and Governor of the infinite universe, "Who hath measured the waters in the hollow of his hand, and meted out heaven with the span, and comprehended the dust of the earth in a measure, and weighed the mountains in scales, and the hills in a balance," is your working power? In proportion as we understand this fact, and make use of it, in that same proportion are we able to perform our miracles.

Your work is inspired to the extent that you realize the presence of Universal Mind in your work. When you rely entirely on your own conscious mind, your work suffers accordingly. "I can of mine own self do nothing; for the works which the Father hath given me to finish, the same works that I do bear witness of me." The miracles of Jesus bear witness of the complete recognition of God the Father as his working power.

And mind you, this inspiration, this working of Universal Mind with you, is available for all of your undertakings. Mind could not show Itself in one part of your life and withhold Itself from another, since It is all in all. Every rightly directed task, no matter how insignificant or menial it may appear to you, carries with it the inspiration of Universal Mind, since by the very nature of omnipotence, Its love and bestowals must be universal and impartial, "and whatsoever ye do, do it heartily as to the Lord."

Too many of us are like the maiden in the old Eastern legend. A Genii sent her into a field of grain, promising her a rare gift if she would pick for him the largest and ripest ear she could find. His gift to be in proportion to the size and perfection of the ear.

But he made this condition—she must pluck but one ear, and she must walk straight through the field without stopping, going back or wandering hither and thither.

Joyously she started. As she walked through the grain, she saw many large ears, many perfect ones. She passed them by in scorn, thinking to find an extra-large, super-perfect one farther along. Presently, however, the soil became less fertile, the ears small and sparse. She couldn't pick one of these! Would now that she had been content with an ordinary-sized ear farther back. But it was too late for that. Surely they would grow better again farther on!

She walked on—and on—and always they became worse—'till presently she found herself at the end of the field—*empty handed as when she set out!*

So it is with life. Every day has its worth-while rewards for work well done. Every day offers its chance for happiness. But those rewards seem so small, those chances so petty, compared with the big things we see ahead. So we pass them by, never recognizing that the great position we look forward to, the shining prize we see in the distance, is just the sum of all the little tasks, the heaped up result of all the little prizes that we must win as we go along.

You are not commanded to pick out certain occupations as being more enti-tled to the Lord's consideration than others, but "Whatsoever ye do." Whether it be in the exalted and idealistic realms of poetry, music and art, whether in the cause of religion or philanthropy, whether in government, in business, in science, or simply in household cares, "whatsoever ye do" you are entitled to, and *have* all of inspiration at your beck and call. If you seem to have less than all, it is because you do not utilize your gift.

"Now he that planteth and he that watereth are one; and every man shall receive his own reward according to his own labour. For we are labourers together with God." "All things are yours; and ye are Christ's and Christ's is God's."

How shall you take advantage of this Universal Supply? When next any need confronts you, when next you are in difficulties, close your eyes for a moment and realize that Universal Mind knows how that need can best be met, knows the solution of your difficulties. And that your subconscious mind, being part of the Universal Mind, can know this, too. So put your problem up to your sub-conscious mind with the sublime confidence that it will find the solution. Then forget it for a while. When the time comes, the need will be met.

Dr. Winbigler corroborates the working out of this idea in the following:

"Suggestions lodged in the mind can effect a complete change, morally and physically. If mankind would become in spirit 'as a little child,' trusting in God implicitly, the greatest power would be utilized in the establishment of health and equilibrium, and the results would be untold in comfort, sanity, and blessing. For instance, here is one who is suffering from worry, fear, and the vexations of life. How can he get rid of these things and relieve this suffer-ing? Let him go to a quiet room or place, twice a day, lie down and relax every muscle, assume complete indifference to those things which worry him and the functions of the body, and quietly accept what God, through this law of demand and supply, can give. In a few days he will find a great change in his feelings, and the sufferings will pass away and life will look bright and promis-ing. Infinite wisdom has established that law; and its utilization by those who are worried and fearful will secure amazing results in a short time.

"The real reason for the change is found in the possibility of recovery by using the laws that God has placed within our reach, and thus securing the coveted health and power for all that we want and ought to do. The subliminal life is the connecting link between man and God, and by obeying His laws, one's life is put in contact with infinite resources and all that God is able and willing to give. Here is the secret of all the cures of disease, and the foundation for the possibility of a joyful existence, happiness and eternal life. Suggestion is the method of securing what God gives, and the mind is the agent through which these gifts are received. This is not a matter of theory, but a fact. If any one who is sick or who desires to be kept well will have stated periods of relaxation, openmindedness, and faith, he can prove the beneficial and unvarying result of this method."

Volume XV

The Master of Your Fate

"A craven hung along the battle's edge,
And thought, 'Had I a sword of keener steel—
That blue blade that the king's son bears,—but this blunt thing—!'
And lowering crept away and left the field.
Then came the king's son, wounded, sore bestead
And weaponless, and saw the broken sword,
And ran and snatched it, and with battle-shout
Lifted afresh he hewed his enemy down,
And saved a great cause that heroic day."

—EDWARD ROWLAND SILL[8]

WHERE will *you* be at 65?

Five men in six at the age of 65 are living on charity. Just one in twenty is able to live without working at 65.

That is what the American Bankers Association found when it took one hundred healthy men at 25 and traced them to 65.

These hundred were healthy to start with. They all had the same chance for success. The difference lay in the way they used their MINDS. Ninety-five out of one hundred just do the tasks that are set them. They have no faith in

---

8. From "Poems," Houghton, Mifflin Co.

themselves—no initiative—none of the courage that starts things. They are always directed or controlled by someone else.

At 65, where will *you* be? Dependent or independent? Struggling for a living—accepting charity from someone else—or at the top of the heap?

"I am the Master of my fate."

Until you have learned that, you will never attain life's full success. Your fate is in your own hands. *You* have the making of it. What you are going to be six months or a year from now depends upon what you think today.

So make your choice now:

Are you going to bow down to matter as the only power? Are you going to look upon your environment as something that has been wished upon you and for which you are in no way responsible?

Or are you going to try to realize in your daily life that matter is merely an aggregation of protons and electrons subject entirely to the control of Mind, that your environment, your success, your happiness, are all of your own making, and that if you are not satisfied with conditions as they are, you have but to visualize them as you would have them be in order to change them?

The former is the easier way right now—the easy way that leads to the hell of poverty and fear and old age.

But the latter is the way that brings you to your Heart's Desire.

And merely because this Power of Universal Mind is invisible, is that any reason to doubt it? The greatest powers of Nature are invisible. Love is invisible, but what greater power is there in life? Joy is invisible, happiness, peace, contentment. The radio is invisible—yet you hear it. It is a product of the law governing sound waves. Law is invisible, yet you see the manifestation of different laws every day. To run a locomotive, you study the law of applying power, and you apply that law when you make the locomotive go.

These things are not the result of invention. The law has existed from the beginning. It merely waited for man to learn how to apply it. If man had known how to call upon Universal Mind to the right extent, he could have applied the law of sound waves, the law of steam, ages ago. Invention is merely a revelation and an unfoldment of Universal Wisdom.

That same Universal Wisdom knows millions of other laws of which man has not even a glimmering. You can call upon It. You can use that Wisdom as your own. By thinking of things as they might be instead of as they are, you will eventually find some great Need. And to find a need is the first step towards finding the supply to satisfy that need. You've got to know what you are after, before you can send the Genie-of-your-Mind a-seeking of it in Universal Mind.

THE ACRE OF DIAMONDS

You remember the story of the poor Boer farmer who struggled for years to glean a livelihood out of his rocky soil, only to give it up in despair and go off to seek his fortune elsewhere. Years later, coming back to his old farm, he found it swarming with machinery and life—more wealth being dug out of it every day than he had ever dreamed existed. It was the great Kimberley Diamond Mine!

Most of us are like that poor Boer farmer. We struggle along under our surface power, never dreaming of the giant power that could be ours if we would but dig a little deeper—rouse that great Inner Self who can give us more even than any acre of diamonds.

As Orison Swett Marden put it:

"The majority of failures in life are simply the victims of their mental defeats. Their conviction that they cannot succeed as others do robs them of that vigor and determination which self-confidence imparts, and they don't even half try to succeed.

"There is no philosophy by which a man can do a thing when he thinks he can't. The reason why millions of men are plodding along in mediocrity today, many of them barely making a living, when they have the ability to do something infinitely bigger, is because they lack confidence in themselves. They don't believe they can do the bigger thing that would lift them out of their rut of mediocrity and poverty; they are not winners mentally.

"The way always opens for the determined soul, the man of faith and courage.

"It is the victorious mental attitude, the consciousness of power, the sense of mastership, that does the big things in this world. If you haven't this attitude, if you lack self-confidence, begin now to cultivate it.

"A highly magnetized piece of steel will attract and lift a piece of unmagnetized steel ten times its own weight. Demagnetize that same piece of steel and it will be powerless to attract or lift even a feather's weight.

"Now, my friends, there is the same difference between the man who is highly magnetized by a sublime faith in himself, and the man who is de-magnetized by his lack of faith, his doubts, his fears, that there is between the magnetized and the de-magnetized pieces of steel. If two men of equal ability, one *magnetized by a divine self-confidence,* the other demagnetized by fear and doubt, are given similar tasks, one will succeed and the other will fail. The self-confidence of the one *multiplies his powers a hundredfold;* the lack of it subtracts a hundredfold from the power of the other."

Have you ever thought how much of your time is spent in choosing what you shall do, which task you will try, which way you shall go? Every day is a day of decision. We are constantly at crossroads, in our business dealings, our social relations, in our homes, there is always the necessity of a choice. How important then that we have faith in ourselves and in that Infinite intelligence within. "Commit thy works unto the Lord, and thy thoughts shall be established." "In all thy ways acknowledge him, and he shall direct thy paths."

In this ever-changing material age, with seemingly complex forces all about us, we sometimes cry out that we are driven by force of circumstances. Yet the fact remains that we do those things which we choose to do. For even though we may not wish to go a certain way, we allow ourselves to pursue it because it offers the least resistance.

> "To every man there openeth
> A way, and ways, and a way.
> And the high soul climbs the high way,
> And the low soul gropes the low:
> And in between, on the misty flats,
> The rest drift to and fro.
> But to every man there openeth
> A high way and a low,
> And every man decideth
> The way his soul shall go."

—JOHN OXENHAM

Now, how about you? Are you taking active control of your own thought? Are you imaging upon your subconcious mind only such things as you want to see realized? Are you thinking healthy thoughts, happy thoughts, successful thoughts?

The difference between the successful man and the unsuccessful one is not so much a matter of training or equipment. It is not a question of opportunity or luck. It is just in the way they each of them look at things.

The successful man sees an opportunity, seizes upon it, and moves upward another rung on the ladder of success. It never occurs to him that he may fail. He sees only the opportunity, he visions what he can do with it, and all the forces within and without him combine to help him win.

The unsuccessful man sees the same opportunity, he wishes that he could take advantage of it, but he is fearful that his ability or his money or his credit may not be equal to the task. He is like a timid bather, putting in one foot and then drawing it swiftly back again—and while he hesitates some bolder spirit dashes in and beats him to the goal.

Nearly every man can look back—and not so far back either with most of us—and say, "If I had taken that chance, I would be much better off now."

You will never need to say it again, once you realize that the future is entirely within your own control. It is not subject to the whims of fortune or the capriciousness of luck. There is but one Universal Mind and that mind contains naught but good. In it are no images of Evil. From it comes no lack of supply. Its ideas are as numberless as the grains of sand on the seashore. And those ideas comprise all wealth, all power, all happiness.

You have only to image vividly enough on your subconscious mind the thing you wish, to draw from Universal Mind the necessary ideas to bring it into being. You have only to keep in mind the experiences you wish to meet, in order to control your own future.

When Frank A. Vanderlip, former President of the National City Bank, was a struggling youngster, he asked a successful friend what one thing he would urge a young man to do who was anxious to make his way in the world. "Look as though you have already succeeded," his friend told him. Shakespeare expresses the same thought in another way—"Assume a virtue if you have it not." Look the part. Dress the part. Act the part. Be successful in your own thought first. It won't be long before you will be successful before the world as well.

David V. Bush, in his book "Applied Psychology and Scientific Living," says:

"Man is like the wireless operator. Man is subject to miscellaneous wrong thought currents if his mind is not in tune with the Infinite, or if he is not keyed up to higher vibrations than those of negation.

"A man who thinks courageous thoughts sends these courageous thought waves through the universal ether until they lodge in the consciousness of someone who is tuned to the same courageous key. Think a strong thought, a courageous thought, a prosperity thought, and these thoughts will be received by someone who is strong, courageous and prosperous.

"It is just as easy to think in terms of abundance as to think in terms of poverty. If we think poverty thoughts we become the sending and receiving stations for poverty thoughts. We send out a 'poverty' mental wireless and it reaches the consciousness of some poverty-stricken 'receiver.' We get what we think.

"It is just as easy to think in terms of abundance, opulence and prosperity as it is to think in terms of lack, limitation and poverty.

"If a man will raise his rate of vibration by faith currents or hope currents, these vibrations go through the Universal Mind and lodge in the consciousness of people who are keyed to the same tune. Whatever you think is sometime, somewhere, received by a person who is tuned to your thought key.

"If a man is out of work and he thinks thoughts of success, prosperity, harmony, position and growth, just as surely as his, thoughts are things—as Shakespeare says—someone will receive his vibrations of success, prosperity, harmony, position and growth.

"If we are going to be timid, selfish, penurious and picayunish in our thinking, these thought waves which we have started in the universal ether will go forth until they come to a mental receiving station of the same caliber. 'Birds of a feather flock together,' and minds of like thinking are attracted one to the other.

"If you need money, all you have to do is to send up your vibrations to a strong, courageous receiving station, and someone who can meet your needs will be attracted to you or you to him."

When you learn that you are entitled to win—in any right undertaking in which you may be engaged—*you will win.* When you learn that you have a right to a legitimate dominion over your own affairs, *you will have dominion over them.* The promise is that we can do all things through the Mind that was in Christ.

Universal Mind plays no favorites. No one human being has any more power than any other. It is simply that few of us use the power that is in our hands. The great men of the world are in no wise SUPER Beings. They are ordinary creatures like you and me, who have stumbled upon the way of drawing upon their subconscious mind—and through it upon the Universal Mind. Speaking of Henry Ford's phenomenal success, his friend Thomas A. Edison said of him— "He draws upon his subconscious mind."

The secret of being what you have it in you to be is simply this: Decide now what it is you want of life, exactly what you wish your future to be. Plan it out in detail. Vision it from start to finish. See yourself as you are now, doing those things you have always wanted to do. Make them REAL in your mind's eye—feel them, live them, believe them, especially at the moment of going to sleep, when it is easiest to reach your subconscious mind—and you will soon be seeing them in real life.

It matters not whether you are young or old, rich or poor. The time to begin is NOW. It is never too late. Remember those lines of Appleton's:[9]

"I knew his face the moment that he passed
Triumphant in the thoughtless, cruel throng—
I gently touched his arm—he smiled at me—
He was the Man that Once I Meant to Be!

"Where I had failed, he'd won from life, Success;
Where I had stumbled, with sure feet he stood;
Alike—yet unalike—we faced the world,
And through the stress he found that life was good.
And I? The bitter wormwood in the glass,
The shadowed way along which failures pass!
Yet as I saw him thus, joy came to me—
He was the Man that Once I Meant to Be!

"We did not speak. But in his sapient eyes
I saw the spirit that had urged him on,
The courage that had held him through the fight
Had once been mine. I thought, 'Can it be gone?'
He felt that unasked question—felt it so
His pale lips formed the one-word answer, 'No!'

"Too late to win? No! Not too late for me—
He is the Man that Still I Mean to Be!"

---

9. From "The Quiet Courage." D. Appleton & Co., New York.

Volume XVI

Unappropriated Millions

"Somebody said that it couldn't be done,
But he with a chuckle replied
That 'maybe it couldn't,' but he would be one
Who wouldn't say so till he'd tried.
So he buckled right in with the trace of a grin
On his face. If he worried he hid it.
He started to sing as he tackled the thing
That couldn't be done, and he did it."

—EDGAR A. GUEST[10]

THE main difference between the mind of today and that of our great-great-grandfathers was that in their day conditions were comparatively static, whereas today they are dynamic. Civilization ran along for centuries with comparatively little change. Most people lived and died in the places where they were born. They followed their fathers' avocations. Seldom, indeed, did one of them break out of the class into which he had been born. Almost as seldom did they even *think* of trying to. No wonder, then, that civilization made little progress.

Today we are in the presence of continual change. Men are imbued with that divine unrest which is never satisfied with conditions as they are, which is

---

10. From "The Path to Home." The Reilly & Lee Co.

always striving for improvement. And *thought* is the vital force behind all this change.

Your ability to think is your connecting link with Universal Mind, that enables you to draw upon It for inspiration, for energy, for power. Mind is the energy in *static* form. Thought is the energy in *dynamic* form.

And because life is dynamic—not static; because it is ever moving forward—not standing still; your success or failure depends entirely upon the *quality* of your thought.

For thought is creative energy. It brings into being the things that you think. Think the things you would see manifested, see them, *believe* them, and you can leave it to your subconscious mind to bring them into being.

Your mind is a marvelous storage battery of power on which you can draw for whatever things you need to make your life what you would have it be. It has within it all power, all resource, all energy—but YOU are the one that must use it. All that power is static unless you make it dynamic. In the moment of creative thinking your conscious mind becomes a Creator—it partakes of the power of Universal Mind. And there is nothing static about one who shares that All-power. The resistless Life Energy within him pushes him on to new growth, new aspirations. Just as the sap flowing through the branches of the trees pushes off the old dead leaves to make way for the new life, just so you must push away the old dead thoughts of poverty and lack and disease, before you can bring on the new life of health and happiness and unlimited supply.

This life is in all of us, constantly struggling for an outlet. Repress it—and you die. Doctors will tell you that the only reason people grow old is because their systems get clogged. The tiny pores in your arteries get stopped up. You don't throw off the old. You don't struggle hard enough, and the result is you fall an easy victim to failure and sickness and death.

Remember the story of Sinbad the Sailor, and the Old Man of the Sea? The Old Man's weight was as nothing when Sinbad first took him on his shoulders, but he clung there and clung there, slowly but surely sapping Sinbad's strength, and he would finally have killed him as he had killed so many others if Sinbad, by calling to his aid all his mental as well as his physical resources, had not succeeded in shaking him off.

Most of us have some Old Man of the Sea riding us, and because he clings tightly and refuses to be easily shaken off, we let him stay there, sapping our energies, using up our vitality, when to rid us of him it is only necessary to call to our aid ALL our resources, mental as well as physical, for one supreme effort.

When a storm arises, the hardy mariner doesn't turn off steam and drift help-lessly before the wind. That might be the easy way, but that way danger lies. He turns on more steam and fights against the gale. And so should you. There is a something within you that thrives on difficulties. You prize that more which costs an effort to win. You need to blaze new trails, to encounter unusual hard-ships, in order to reach your hidden mental resources, just as the athlete needs to exert himself to the utmost to reach his "second wind."

Have you ever seen a turtle thrown on its back? For a while it threshes around wildly, reaching for something outside to take hold of that shall put it on its feet. Just as we humans always look for help outside ourselves first. But presently he draws all his forces within his shell, rests a bit to regain his strength, and then throws his whole force to one side—legs, head, tail, and all—*and over he goes!*

So it is with us. When we realize that the power to meet any emergency is within ourselves, when we stop looking outside for help and intelligently call upon Mind in our need, we shall find that we are tapping Infinite Resource. We shall find that we have but to center all those resources on the one thing we want most—to get anything from life that it has.

As Emerson put it, when we once find the way to get in touch with Univer-sal Mind we are—

"... *owner of the sphere,*
Of the seven stars and the solar year,
Of Cæsar's hand and Plato's brain,
Of the Lord Christ's heart and Shakespeare's strain."

Volume XVII

The Secret of Power

"The great were once as you.
They whom men magnify today
Once groped and blundered on life's way
Were fearful of themselves, and thought
By magic was men's greatness wrought.
They feared to try what they could do;
Yet Fame hath crowned with her success
The selfsame gifts that you possess."

—EDGAR A. GUEST[11]

THERE is a woman in one of the big Eastern cities whose husband died a year or two ago and left her nearly $100,000,000. She has unlimited power in her hands—yet she uses none of it. She has unlimited wealth—yet she gets no more from it than if it were in the thousands instead of millions. She knows nothing of her power, of her wealth. She is insane.

You have just as great power in your hands—without this poor woman's excuse for not using it.

---

11. Published by permission of The International Magazine Co. (Cosmopolitan Magazine). Copyright, 1921.

You have access to unlimited ideas, unlimited energy, unlimited wealth. The "Open, Sesame!" is through your subconscious mind.

So long as you limit yourself to superficial conditions, so long as you are a mere "hewer of wood or carrier of water" for those around you who *do* use their minds, you are in no better position than the beasts of burden.

The secret of power is in understanding the infinite resources of your own mind. When you begin to realize that the power to do anything, to be anything, to have anything, is within yourself, then *and then only* will you take your proper place in the world.

As Bruce Barton has it in "The Man Whom Nobody Knows"—

"Somewhere, at some unforgetable hour, the daring filled His (Jesus) heart. He knew that He was bigger than Nazareth."

Again in speaking of Abraham Lincoln, Barton says—"Inside himself he felt his power, but where and when would opportunity come?" And later in the book—

"But to every man of vision the clear voice speaks. Nothing splendid has ever been achieved except by those who dared believe that *something inside them was superior to circumstance.*"

No doubt Jesus' friends and neighbors all ridiculed the idea of any such power within Him. Just as most people today laugh at the thought of a power such as that within themselves.

So they go on with their daily grind, with the gaunt spectres of sickness and need ever by their side, until death comes as a welcome relief. Are you going to be one of those? Or will you listen to that inner consciousness of power and find the "Kingdom of Heaven that is within you." For whatever you become conscious of, will be quickly brought forth into tangible form.

Don't judge your ability by what you have done in the past. Your work heretofore has been done with the help of your conscious mind alone. Add to that the infinite knowledge at the disposal of your subconscious mind, and what you have done is as nothing to what you will do in the future.

For knowledge does not apply itself. It is merely so much static energy. You must convert it into dynamic energy by the power of your thought. The difference between the $25-a-week clerk and the $25,000-a-year executive is solely one of thought. The clerk may have more brains than the executive—frequently *has* in actual weight of gray matter. He may even have a far better education. But he doesn't know how to apply his thought to get the greatest good from it.

If you have brains, *use* them. If you have skill, *apply* it. The world must profit by it, and therefore you.

We all have inspired moments when we see clearly how we may do great things, how we may accomplish wonderful undertakings. But we do not believe in them enough to make them come true. An imagination which begins and ends in day-dreaming is weakening to character.

Make the day-dreams come true. Make them so clear and distinct that they impress themselves upon your subconscious mind. There's nothing wrong with day-dreaming, except that most of us stop there. We don't try to make the dreams come true. The great inventor, Tesla, "dreams" every new machine complete and perfect in every particular before ever he begins his model for it. Mozart "dreamed" each of his wonderful symphonies complete before ever he put a note on paper. But they didn't stop with the dreaming. They visualized those dreams, *and then brought them into actuality.*

We lose our capacity to have visions if we do not take steps to realize them.

Power implies service, so concentrate all your thought on making your visions of great deeds come true. Thinking is the current that runs the dynamo of power. To connect up this current so that you can draw upon universal supply through your subconscious mind, is to become a Super-man. Do this, and you will have found the key to the solution of every problem of life.

Volume XVIII

This One Thing I Do

"How do you tackle your work each day?
Do you grapple the task that comes your way
With a confident, easy mind?
Do you start to toil with a sense of dread
Or feel that you're going to do it?
"You can do as much as you think you can,
But you'll never accomplish more;
If you're afraid of yourself, young man,
There's little for you in store.
For failure comes from the inside first,
It's there, if we only knew it,
And you can win, though you face the worst,
If you feel that you're going to do it."

—Edgar A. Guest[12]

How did the Salvation Army get so much favorable publicity out of the War? They were a comparatively small part of the "Services" that catered to the boys "over there," yet they carried off the lion's share of the glory. Do you know how they did it?

---

12. From "A Heap o' Livin'." The Reilly & Lee Co.

By concentrating on just one thing—DOUGHNUTS!

They served doughnuts to the boys—and they did it *well*. And that is the basis of all success in business—to focus on one thing and do that thing well. Better far to do one thing pre-eminently well than to dabble in forty.

Two thousand years ago, Porcius Marcus Cato became convinced, from a visit to the rich and flourishing city of Carthage, that Rome had in her a rival who must be destroyed. His countrymen laughed at him. He was practically alone in his belief. But he persisted. He concentrated all his thought, all his faculties, to that one end. At the end of every speech, at the end of every talk, he centered his hearers' thought on what he was trying to put over by epitomizing his whole idea in a single sentence—"Carthage must be destroyed!" And *Carthage was destroyed*.

If one man's concentration on a single idea could destroy a great nation, what can you not do when you apply that same principle to the *building* of a business?

I remember when I was first learning horsemanship, my instructor impressed this fact upon me: "Remember that a horse is an animal of one idea. You can teach him only one thing at a time."

Looking back, I'd say the only thing wrong with his instruction was that he took in too little territory. He need not have confined himself to the horse. Most humans are the same way.

In fact, you can put ALL humans into that class if you want a thing done well. For you cannot divide your thought and do justice to any one of the different subjects you are thinking of. You've got to do one thing at a time. The greatest success rule I know in business—the one that should be printed over every man's desk, is—"This One Thing I Do." Take one piece of work at a time. Concentrate on it to the exclusion of all else. *Then finish it!* Don't half-do it, and leave it around to clutter up your desk and interfere with the next job. Dispose of it completely. Pass it along wherever it is to go. Be through with it *and forget it!* Then your mind will be clear to consider the next matter.

"The man who is perpetually hesitating which of two things he will do first," says William Wirt, "will do neither. The man who resolves, but suffers his resolution to be changed by the first counter-suggestion of a friend—who fluctuates from plan to plan and veers like a weather-cock to every point of the compass with every breath of caprice that blows—can never accomplish anything real or useful. It is only the man who first consults wisely, then resolves firmly, and then executes his purpose with inflexible perseverance, undismayed ilituffffiity

by those petty difficulties that daunt a weaker spirit, that can advance to eminence in any line."

Everything in the world, even a great business, can be resolved into atoms. And the basic principles behind the biggest business will be found to be the same as those behind the successful running of the corner newsstand. The whole practice of commerce is founded upon them. Any man can learn them, but only the alert and energetic can apply them. The trouble with most men is that they think they have done all that is required of them when they have earned their salary.

Why, that's only the beginning. Up to that point, you are working for someone else. From then on, you begin to work for yourself. Remember, you must *give* to *get*. And it is when you give that *extra* bit of time and attention and thought to your work that you begin to stand out above the crowd around you.

Norval Hawkins, for many years General Manager of Sales for the Ford Motor Company, wrote that "the greatest hunt in the Ford business right now is the MAN hunt." And big men in every industrial line echo his words. When it comes to a job that needs real ability, they are not looking for relatives or friends or men with "pull." They want a MAN—and they will pay any price for the right man.

Not only that, but they always have a weather eye open for promising material. And the thing they value most of all is INITIATIVE.

But don't try to improve the whole works at once. Concentrate on one thing at a time. Pick some one department or some one process or some one thing and focus all your thought upon it. Bring to bear upon it the limitless resources of your subconscious mind. Then prepare a definite plan for the development of that department or the improvement of that process. Verify your facts carefully to make sure they are workable. *Then*—and not till then—present your plan.

In "Thoughts on Business," you read: "Men often think of a position as being just about so big and no bigger, when, as a matter of fact, a position is often what one makes it. A man was making about $1,500 a year out of a certain position and thought he was doing all that could be done to advance the business. The employer thought otherwise, and gave the place to another man who soon made the position worth $8,000 a year—at exactly the same commission.

"The difference was in the man—in other words, in what the two men thought about the work. One had a little conception of what the work should be, and the other had a big conception of it. One thought little thoughts, and the other thought big thoughts.

"The standards of two men may differ, not especially because one is naturally more capable than the other, but because one is familiar with big things and the other is not. The time was when the former worked in a smaller scope himself, but when he saw a wider view of what his work might be he rose to the occasion and became a bigger man. It is just as easy to think of a mountain as to think of a hill—when you turn your mind to contemplate it. The mind is like a rubber band—you can stretch it to fit almost anything, but it draws in to a smaller scope when you let go.

"Make it your business to know what is the best that might be in your line of work, and stretch your mind to conceive it, and then devise some way to attain it.

"Big things are only little things put together. I was greatly impressed with this fact one morning as I stood watching the workmen erecting the steel framework for a tall office building. A shrill whistle rang out as a signal, a man over at the engine pulled a lever, a chain from the derrick was lowered, and the whistle rang out again. A man stooped down and fastened the chain around the center of a steel beam, stepped back and blew the whistle once more. Again the lever was moved at the engine, and the steel beam soared into the air up to the sixteenth story, where it was made fast by little bolts.

"The entire structure, great as it was, towering far above all the neighboring buildings, was made up of pieces of steel and stone and wood, put together according to a plan. The plan was first imagined, then penciled, then carefully drawn, and then followed by the workmen. It was all a combination of little things.

"It is encouraging to think of this when you are confronted by a big task. *Remember that it is only a group of little tasks, any of which you can easily do.* It is ignorance of this fact that makes men afraid to try."

One of the most essential requisites in the accomplishment of any important work is patience. Not the patience that sits and folds its hands and waits—Micawber like—for something to turn up. But the patience that never jeopardizes or upsets a plan by forcing it too soon. The man who possesses that kind of patience can always find plenty to do in the meantime.

Make your plan—then wait for the opportune moment to submit it. You'd be surprised to know how carefully big men go over suggestions from subordinates which show the least promise. One of the signs of a really big man, you know, is his eagerness to learn from everyone and anything. There is none of that "know it all" about him that characterized the German general who was given a book containing the strategy by which Napoleon had for fifteen years kept all the armies of Europe at bay. "I've no time to read about bygone battles," he growled, thrusting the book away, "I have my own campaign to plan."

There is priceless wisdom to be found in books. As Carlyle put it—"All that mankind has done, thought, gained or been—it is lying in matchless preservation in the pages of books."

The truths which mankind has been laboriously learning through countless ages, at who knows what price of sweat and toil and starvation and blood—all are yours for the effort of reading them.

And in business, knowledge was never so priceless or so easily acquired. Books and magazines are filled with the hows and whys, the rights and wrongs of buying and selling, of manufacturing and shipping, of finance and management. They are within the reach of anyone with the desire to KNOW.

Nothing pays better interest than judicious reading. The man who invests in more knowledge of his business than he needs to hold his job, is acquiring capital with which to get a better job.

As old Gorgon Graham puts it in "The Letters of a Self-Made Merchant To His Son"—

"I ain't one of those who believe that a half knowledge of a subject is useless, but it has been my experience that when a fellow has that half knowledge, he finds it's the other half which would really come in handy.

"What you know is a club for yourself, and what you don't know is a meat-ax for the other fellow. That is why you want to be on the lookout all the time for information about the business and to nail a fact just as a sensible man nails a mosquito—the first time it settles near him."

The demands made upon men in business today are far greater than in any previous generation. To meet them, you've got to use your talents to the utmost. You've got to find in every situation that confronts you, the best, the easiest and the quickest way of working it out. And the first essential in doing this is to plan your work ahead.

You'd be surprised at how much more work you can get through by carefully planning it, and then taking each bit in order and disposing of it before starting on the next.

Another thing—once started at work, don't let down. Keep on going until it is time to quit. You know how much power it takes to start an auto that is standing motionless. But when you get it going, you can run along in high at a fraction of the expenditure of gas. It is the same way with your mind. We are all mentally lazy. We hate to start using our minds. Once started, though, it is easy to keep along on high, if only we won't let down. For the moment we let down, we have that starting to do all over again. You can accomplish ten times as much, with far less effort or fatigue, if you will keep right on steadily instead of starting and stopping, and starting and stopping again.

Volumes have been written about personal efficiency, and general efficiency, and every other kind of efficiency in business. But boiled down, it all comes to this:

1. Know what you want.
2. Analyze the thing you've got to do to get it.
3. Plan your work ahead.
4. Do one thing at a time.
5. Finish that one thing and send it on its way before starting the next.
6. Once started, KEEP GOING!

And when you come to some problem that "stumps" you, give your subconscious mind a chance.

Frederick Pierce, in "Our Unconscious Mind," gives an excellent method for solving business problems through the aid of the subconscious:

"Several years ago, I heard a successful executive tell a group of young men how he did his work, and included in the talk was the advice to prepare at the close of each day's business, a list of the ten most important things for the next day. To this I would add: Run them over in the mind just before going to sleep, not thoughtfully, or with elaboration of detail, but with the sure knowledge that the deeper centers of the mind are capable of viewing them constructively even though conscious attention is surrendered in sleep.

"Then, if there is a particular problem which seems difficult of solution, review its features lightly as a last game for the imaginative unconscious to play at during the night. Do not be discouraged if no immediate results are apparent. Remember that fiction, poetry, musical composition, inventions, innumerable ideas, spring from the unconscious, often in forms that give evidence of the highest constructive elaboration.

"Give your unconscious a chance. Give it the material, and stimulate it with keenly dwelt-on wishes along frank Ego Maximation lines. It is a habit which, if persisted in, will sooner or later present you with some very valuable ideas when you least expect them."

I remember reading of another man—a genius at certain kinds of work— who, whenever an especially difficult problem confronted him, "slept on it." He had learned the trick as a child. Unable to learn his lessons one evening, he had kept repeating the words to himself until he dozed in his chair, the book still in his hands. What was his surprise, on being awakened by his father a few minutes later to find that he knew them perfectly! He tried it again and again on succeeding evenings, and almost invariably it worked. Now, whenever a problem comes up that he cannot solve, he simply stretches out on a lounge in his office, thoroughly relaxes, *and lets his subconscious mind solve the problem!*

Volume XIX

Volume XIX

The Master Mind

"One who never turned his back but marched breast forward,
Never doubted clouds would break,
Never dreamed though right were worsted
Wrong would triumph,
Held we fall to rise, are baffled to fight better,
Sleep to wake."

—BROWNING

AMONG your friends there is one of those men who doesn't have much use for the word "can't."

You marvel at his capacity for work.

You'll admire him the more the longer you know him.

You'll always respect him.

For he not only has made good, but he always will make good. He has found and appropriated to himself the "Talisman of Napoleon"—*absolute confidence in himself.*

The world loves a leader. All over the world, in every walk of life, people are eagerly seeking for some one to follow. They want some one else to do their thinking for them; they need some one to hearten them to action; they like to have some one else on whom to lay the blame when things go wrong; they want some one big enough to share the glory with them when success crowns his efforts.

But to instill confidence in them, that leader must have utter confidence in himself. A Roosevelt or a Mussolini who did not believe in himself would be inconceivable. It is that which makes men invincible—the Consciousness of their own Power. They put no limit upon their own capacities—therefore they have no limit. For Universal Mind sees all, knows all, and can do all, and we share in this absolute power to the exact extent to which we permit ourselves. Our mental attitude is the magnet that attracts from Universal Mind everything we may need to bring our desires into being. We make that magnet strong or weak as we have confidence in or doubt of our abilities. We draw to ourselves unlimited power or limit ourselves to humble positions according to our own beliefs.

A long time ago Emerson wrote: "There is one mind common to all individual men. Every man is an inlet to the same *and to all* of the same. He that is once admitted to the right of reason is made a freeman of the whole estate. What Plato has thought, he may think; what a saint has felt, he may feel; what at any time has befallen any man, he can understand. Who hath access to this Universal Mind, *is a party to all that is or can be done,* for this is the only and sovereign agent."

The great German physicist, Nernst, found that the longer an electric current was made to flow through a filament of oxide of magnesium, the greater became the conductivity of the filament.

In the same way, the more you call upon and use your subconscious mind, the greater becomes its conductivity in passing along to you the infinite resources of Universal Mind. The wisdom of a Solomon, the skill of a Michelangelo, the genius of an Edison, the daring of a Napoleon, *all* may be yours. It rests with you only to form the contact with Universal Mind in order to draw from it what you will.

Think of this power as something that you can connect with any time. It has the answer to all of your problems. It offers you freedom from fear, from worry, from sickness, from accident. No man and no thing can interfere with your use of this power or diminish your share of it. No one, that is, but yourself.

Don Carlos Musser expresses it well in "You Are":

"Because of the law of gravitation the apple falls to the ground. Because of the law of growth the acorn becomes a mighty oak. Because of the law of causation, a man is 'as he thinketh in his heart.' Nothing can happen without its adequate cause."

Success does not come to you by accident. It comes as the logical result of the operation of law. Mind, working through your brain and your body, makes your world. That it is not a better world and a bigger one, is due to your limited thoughts and beliefs. They dam back the flood of ideas that Mind is constantly striving to manifest through you. God never made a failure or a nobody. He offers to the highest and the lowest alike, all that is necessary to happiness and success. The difference is entirely in the extent to which each of us AVAILS himself of that generosity.

There is no reason why you should hesitate to aspire to any position, any honor, any goal, for the Mind within you is fully able to meet any need. It is no more difficult for it to handle a great problem than a small one. Mind is just as much present in your little everyday affairs as in those of a big business or a great nation. Don't set it doing trifling sums in arithmetic when it might just as well be solving problems of moment to yourself and the world.

Start something! Use your initiative. Give your mind something to work upon. The greatest of all success secrets is initiative. It is the one quality which more than any other has put men in high places.

Conceive something. Conceive it first in your own mind. Make the pattern there and your subconscious mind will draw upon the plastic substance or energy all about you to make that model real.

Drive yourself. Force yourself. It is the dreamer, the man with imagination, who has made the world move. Without him, we would still be in the Stone Age.

Galileo looked at the moon and dreamed of how he might reach it. The telescope was the fruition of that dream. Watt dreamed of what might be done with steam—and our great locomotives and engines of today are the result. Franklin dreamed of harnessing the lightning—and today we have manmade thunderbolts.

Initiative, plus imagination, will take you anywhere. Imagination opens the eyes of the mind, and there is nothing good you can image there that is not possible of fulfillment in your daily life.

Imagination is the connecting link between the human and the Divine, between the formed universe and formless energy. It is, of all things human, the most God-like. It is our part of Divinity. Through it we share in the creative power of Universal Mind. Through it we can turn the most drab existence into a thing of life and beauty. It is the means by which we avail ourselves of all the good which Universal Mind is constantly offering to us in such profusion. It is the means by which we can reach any goal, win any prize.

What was it gave us the submarine, the aeroplane, wireless, electricity? Imagination. What was it that enabled man to build the Simplon Tunnel, the Panama Canal, the Hell Gate span? Imagination. What is it that makes us successful and happy, or poor and friendless? Imagination—or the lack of it.

It was imagination that sent Spanish and English and French adventurers to this new world. It was imagination that urged the early settlers westward—ever westward. It was imagination that built out railroads, our towns, our great cities.

Parents foolishly try to discourage imagination in their children, when all it needs is proper guidance. For imagination forms the world from which their future will take its shape. Restrain the one and you constrict the other. Develop the one in the right way, and there is no limit to the other. Uncontrolled, the imagination is like a rudderless ship. Or even, at times, like the lightning. But properly controlled, it is like the ship that carries riches from port to port. Or like the electric current, carrying unlimited power for industry and progress.

Do you want happiness? Do you want success? Do you want position, power, riches? *Image them!* How did God first make man? "In his image created He him." He "imaged" man in His Mind.

And that is the way everything has been made since time began. It was first imaged in Mind. That is the way everything you want must start—with a mental image.

So use your imagination! Picture in it your Heart's Desire. Imagine it—daydream it so vividly, so clearly, that you will actually BELIEVE you HAVE it. In the moment that you carry this conviction to your subconscious mind—in that moment your dream will become a reality. It may be a while before you realize it, but the important part is done. You have created the model. You can safely leave it to your subconscious mind to do the rest.

When Jesus adjured His disciples—"Whatsoever ye desire, when ye pray, believe that ye RECEIVE it," He was not only telling them a great truth, but he was teaching what we moderns would call excellent psychology as well. For this "belief" is what acts upon the subconscious mind. It is through this "belief" that formless energy, is compressed into material form.

Every man wants to get out of the rut, to grow, to develop into something better. Here is the open road—open to you whether you have schooling, training, position, wealth, or not. Remember this: Your subconscious mind knew more from the time you were a baby than is in all the books in all the colleges and libraries of the world.

So don't let lack of training, lack of education, hold you back. Your mind can meet every need—and will do so if you give it the chance. The Apostles were almost all poor men, uneducated men, yet they did a work that is unequalled in historical annals. Joan of Arc was a poor peasant girl, unable to read or write—*yet she saved France!* The pages of history are dotted with poor men, uneducated men, who thought great thoughts, who used their imaginations to master circumstances and became rulers of men. Most great dynasties started with some poor, obscure man. Napoleon came of a poor, humble family. He got his appointment to the Military Academy only through very hard work and the pulling of many political strings. Even as a Captain of Artillery he was so poverty-stricken that he was unable to buy his equipment when offered an appointment to India. Business today is full of successful men who have scarcely the rudiments of ordinary education. It was only after he had made his millions that Andrew Carnegie hired a tutor to give him the essentials of an education.

So it isn't training and it isn't education that make you successful. These help, but the thing that really counts is that gift of the Gods—*Creative Imagination!*

You have that gift. *Use it!* Make every thought, every fact, that comes into your mind *pay you a profit.* Make it work and produce for you. Think of things—not as they are but as they MIGHT be. Make them real, live and interesting. Don't merely dream—but *CREATE!* Then use your imagination to make that CREATION of advantage to mankind—and, incidentally, yourself.

Volume XX

What Do You Lack?

"I read the papers every day, and oft encounter tales which show there's hope for every jay who in life's battle fails. I've just been reading of a gent who joined the has-been ranks, at fifty years without a cent, or credit at the banks. But undismayed he buckled down, refusing to be beat, and captured fortune and renown; he's now on Easy Street. Men say that fellows down and out ne'er leave the rockly track, but facts will show, beyond a doubt, that has-beens do come back. I know, for I who write this rhyme, when forty-odd years old, was down and out, without a dime, my whiskers full of mold. By black disaster I was trounced until it jarred my spine; I was a failure so pronounced I didn't need a sign. And after I had soaked my coat, I said (at forty-three), 'I'll see if I can catch the goat that has escaped from me.' I labored hard; I strained my dome, to do my daily grind, until in triumph I came home, my billy-goat behind. And any man who still has health may with the winners stack, and have a chance at fame and wealth—for has-beens do come back."

—WALT MASON[13]

Do you know why it is that the Bolsheviki are so opposed to religion?

Because religion, as it is commonly accepted, teaches man resignation to conditions as they are—teaches, in effect, that God created some men poor and

---

13. From "Walt Mason—His Book." Barse & Hopkins, Newark, NJ.

some rich. That this unequal distribution is a perfectly natural thing. And that we must not rail against it because it will all be made right in the next world.

Napoleon, in his early Jacobin days, denounced religion for that very reason. But when he had won to power, when he planned to make himself Emperor, then he found he had need for that religion, and re-established the Church in France.

For, he reasoned, how can people be satisfied without religion? If one man is starving, near another who is making himself sick by eating too much, how can you expect to keep the starving one resigned to his fate unless you teach him it will all be made right in some indefinite future state?

Organized society could not exist, as he planned it, without some being rich and some poor, and to keep the poor satisfied, there must be an authority to declare—"God wills it thus. But just be patient. In the hereafter all this will be different. YOU will be the ones then to occupy the places of honor."

Religion, in other words—as it is ordinarily taught—*is a fine thing to keep the common people satisfied!*

But Christianity was never meant for a weapon to keep the rich wealthy and secure, the poor satisfied and in their proper place. On the contrary, Christianity as taught by Jesus opened the way to all Good. And Christianity as it was practiced in its early years was an idealized form of Socialism that benefited each and all. No one was wealthier than his neighbors, it is true—but neither was any poverty-stricken. Theirs was the creed of the Three Musketeers—"All for one, and one for all!"

"Ask and ye shall receive," said Jesus. "Seek and ye shall find." That was not directed to the rich alone. That was to ALL men.

Providence has never made a practice of picking out certain families or certain individuals and favoring them to the detriment of other people—much as some of our "leading families" would have us believe it. It is only man that has arrogated to himself that privilege. We laugh now at the "divine right of Kings." It is just as ridiculous to think that a few have the right to all the good things of life, while the many have to toil and sweat to do them service.

To quote Rumbold's last words from the scaffold—"I never could believe that Providence had sent a few men into the world ready booted and spurred to ride, and millions ready saddled and bridled to be ridden."

There is nothing right in poverty. Not only that, but there is nothing meritorious in poverty. The mere fact that you are poor and ground down by fear and worry is not going to get you any forwarder in the hereafter. On the contrary, your soul is likely to be too pinched by want, too starved and shrivelled to be able to expand.

"The Kingdom of Heaven is within you." To me that means that Heaven is here and now. That if we want any happiness from it we've got to get it as we go along. I've never been much of a believer in accepting these promissory notes for happiness. Every time one of them falls due, you find you just have to renew it for another six months or a year, until one of these days you wake up and find that the bank has busted and all your notes are not worth the paper they are written on.

The Cumæan Sibyl is said to have offered Tarquin the Proud nine books for what he thought an exorbitant sum. So he refused. She burned three of the books, and placed the same price on the six as on the original nine. Again he refused. She burned three more books, and offered the remainder for the sum she had first asked. This time Tarquin accepted. The books were found to contain prophecies and invaluable directions regarding Roman policy, but alas, they were no longer complete.

So it is with happiness. If you take it as you go along, you get it in its entirety. But if you keep putting off the day when you shall enjoy it—if you keep taking promissory notes for happiness—every day will mean one day less of it that you will have. Yet the cost is just the same.

The purpose of existence is GROWTH. You can't grow spiritually or mentally without happiness. And by Happiness I don't mean a timid resignation to the "Will of God." That so-called "Will of God" is more often than not either pure laziness on the part of the resigned one or pure cussedness on the part of the one that is "putting something over" on him. It is the most sanctimonious expression yet devised to excuse some condition that no one has the energy or the ability to rectify.

No—by Happiness I mean the everyday enjoyment of everyday people. I mean love and laughter and honest amusement. Every one of us is entitled to it. Every one of us can have it—if he has the WILL and the ENERGY to get out and get it for himself.

Joyless work, small pay, no future, nothing to look forward to—God never planned such an existence. It is manmade—and you can be man enough to unmake it as far as you and yours are concerned.

God never made any man poor any more than He made any man sick. Look around you. All of Nature is bountiful. On every hand you see profusion—in the trees, in the flowers, in everything that He planned. The only Law of Nature is the law of Supply. Poverty is unnatural. It is man-made, through the limits man puts upon himself. God never put them there any more than He showed partiality by giving to some of His children gifts and blessings which He withheld from others. His gifts are just as available to you as to any man on earth. The difference is all in your understanding of how to avail yourself of the infinite supply all about you.

Take the worry clamps off your mentality and you will make the poverty clamps loosen up from your finances. Your affairs are so closely related to your consciousness that they too will relax into peace, order, and plenty. Divine ideas in your spiritual consciousness will become active in your business, and will work out as your abundant prosperity.

As David V. Bush says in "Applied Psychology and Scientific Living"— "Thoughts are things; thoughts are energy; thoughts are magnets which attract to us the very things which we think. Therefore, if a man is in debt, he will, by continually thinking about debt, bring more debts to him. For thoughts are causes, and he fastens more debts on to himself and actually creates more obligations by thinking about debts.

"Concentrate and think upon things that you want; not on things which you ought not to have. Think of abundance, of opulence, of plenty, of position, harmony and growth, and if you do not see them manifested today, they will be realized to-morrow. If you must pass through straits of life where you do not outwardly see abundance, know that you have it within, and that in time it will manifest itself.

"I say, if you concentrate on debt, debt is what you will have; if you think about poverty, poverty is what you will receive. It is just as easy, when once the mind becomes trained, to think prosperity and abundance and plenty, as it is to think lack, limitation and poverty."

Prosperity is not limited to time or to place. It manifests when and where there is consciousness to establish it. It is attracted to the consciousness that is free from worry, strain, and tension.

So never allow yourself to worry about poverty. Be careful, take ordinary business precautions—of course. But don't center your thought on your *troubles*. The more you think of them, the more tightly you fasten them upon yourself. Think of the *results* you are after—not of the difficulties in the way. Mind will find the way. It is merely up to you to choose the goal, then keep your thought steadfast until that goal is won.

The greatest short-cut to prosperity is to *LIVE IT!* Prosperity attracts. Poverty repels. To quote Orison Swett Marden—"To be ambitious for wealth and yet always expecting to be poor, to be always doubting your ability to get what you long for, is like trying to reach East by travelling West. There is no philosophy which will help a man to succeed when he is always doubting his ability to do so, and thus attracting failure."

Again: "No matter how hard you may work for success, if your thought is saturated with the fear of failure it will kill your efforts, neutralize your endeavors, and make success impossible."

The secret of prosperity lies in so vividly imaging it in your own mind that you literally exude prosperity. You feel prosperous, you look prosperous, and the result is that before long you ARE prosperous.

I remember seeing a play a number of years ago that was based on this thought. A young fellow—a chronic failure—was persuaded by a friend to carry a roll of $1000 counterfeit bills in his pocket, and to show them, unostentatiously, when the occasion offered. Of course, everyone thought he had come into some legacy. The natural inference was that anyone who carried fifty or a hundred thousand dollar bills in his pockets must have a lot more in the bank. Opportunities flocked to him. Opportunities to make good. Opportunities to make money. He made good! And that without having to spend any of this spurious money of his. For most business today is done on credit. I know many wealthy men who seldom carry anything but a little change in their pockets for tips. Everything they do, everything they buy, is "Charged." And big deals are put through in the same way. If a man is believed to have plenty of money, if he has a reputation for honesty and fair-dealing, he may put through a transaction running into six or seven figures without paying one cent down. The thing that counts is not the amount of your balance at the Bank, but what others THINK of you, the IMAGE you have created in your own and in others minds.

What do you lack? What thing do you want most? Realize that before it or any other thing can be, it must first be imaged in Mind. Realize, too, that when you can close your eyes and actually SEE that thing, *you have brought it into being*—you have drawn upon that invisible substance all about you—you have *created something.* Hold it in your thought, focus your mind upon it, "BELIEVE THAT YOU HAVE IT"—and you can safely leave its material manifestation to the Genie-of-your-Mind.

God is but another name for the invisible, everywhere-present, Source-of-things. Out of the air the seed gathers the essences which are necessary to its bountiful growth; out of the invisible ether our minds gather the rich ideas that stimulate us to undertake and to carry out enterprises that bring prosperity to us. Let us see with the eye of the mind a bountiful harvest; then our minds will be quickened with ideas of abundance, and plenty will appear, not only in our world, but everywhere.

"As the rain cometh down and the snow from heaven, and returneth not thither, but watereth the earth, and maketh it bring forth and bud, and giveth seed to the sower and bread to the eater; so shall my word be that goeth forth out of my mouth: it shall not return unto me void, but it shall accomplish that which I please, and it shall prosper in the thing whereto I sent it."—Isaiah

Volume XXI

The Sculptor and the Clay

"Eternal mind the Potter is,
And thought the eternal clay.
The hand that fashions is divine;
His works pass not away.
God could not make imperfect man
His model Infinite, Unhallowed thought
He could not plan—Love's work and Love must fit."

—ALICE DAYTON

WHEN you step into your office on Monday morning, no doubt you have dreams of wonderful achievement. Your step is firm, your brain is clear and you have carefully thought out just WHAT you will do and HOW you will accomplish big things in your business. Perhaps the very plans you have in mind will influence your whole business career, and you have visions of the dollars that will be yours rolling into your bank account.

But do these dreams come true?

Are you always able to put through what you had planned to do—does your day's work have the snap and power you imagined it would have? Are you ever forced to admit that your dreams of big accomplishment are often shattered because of "fagged nerves" and lack of energy, because you have not the "pep"?

How easy it is to think back and see how success was in your grasp if only you had felt equal to that extra bit of effort, if only you had had the "pep," the energy to reach out and take it. The great men of the world have been well men, strong men. Sickness and hesitancy go hand in hand. Sickness means weakness, querulousness, lack of faith, lack of confidence in oneself and in others.

But there is no real reason for sickness or weakness, and there is no reason why you should remain weak or sick if you are so afflicted now.

Remember the story of the sculptor Pygmalion? How he made a statue of marble so beautiful that every woman who saw it envied it? So perfect was it that he fell in love with it himself, hung it with flowers and jewels, spent day after day in rapt admiration of it, until finally the gods took pity upon him and breathed into it the breath of life.

There is more than Pagan mythology to that story. There is this much truth in it—that any man can set before his mind's eye the image of the figure he himself would like to be, and then breathe the breath of life into it merely by keeping that image before his subconscious mind as the model on which to do its daily building.

For health and strength are natural. It is ill-health and weakness that are unnatural. Your body was meant to be lithe, supple, muscular, full of red-blooded energy and vitality. A clear brain, a powerful heart, a massive chest, wrists and arms of steel—all these were meant for you—all these you can have if you will but *know*, and *feel*, and *think aright*.

Just take stock of yourself for a moment. Are your muscles tough, springy and full of vim? Do they do all you ask of them—and then beg for more? Can you eat a good meal—and forget it?

If you can't, it's your own fault. You can have a body alive with vitality, a skin smooth and fine of texture, muscles supple and virile. You can be the man you have always dreamed of being, without arduous dieting, without tiresome series of exercises, merely by following the simple rules herein laid down.

For what is it that builds up the muscles, puts energy and vitality into your system, gives you the pep and vigor of youth? *Is it exercise?* Then why is it that so many day laborers are poor, weak, anæmic creatures, forced to lay off from one to three months every year on account of sickness? They get plenty of exercise and fresh air. Why is it that so many athletes die of tuberculosis or of weak hearts? They get the most scientific exercise year in and year out.

Just the other day I read of the sudden death of Martin A. Delaney, the famous trainer, known all over the country as a physical director. He taught thousands how to be strong, but "Athletic Heart" killed him at 55. Passers-by saw him running for a car, then suddenly topple over dead.

"Exercise as a panacea for all human ills is dangerously overrated," Dr. Charles M. Wharton, in charge of health and physical education at the University of Pennsylvania, said today (March 20, 1926), according to an Associated Press despatch.

Dr. Wharton, who has been a trainer of men for thirty years and was an all-American guard on the Pennsylvania football team in 1895 and 1896, declared the search for the fountain of youth by exercise and diet has been commercialized to a point of hysteria.

"Some one should cry a halt against this wild scramble for health by unnatural means," said Dr. Wharton. "This indiscriminate adoption of severe physical training destroys the health of more people than it improves."

Dr. Wharton said he was appalled by the amount of physical defects and weaknesses developed by overindulgence in athletics by students in preparatory schools.

"I know I am presenting an unpopular viewpoint, and it may sound strange coming from a physical director.

"In gymnasium work at the University of Pennsylvania we try to place our young men in sports *which they will enjoy,* and thus get a physical stimulation from *relaxed play.*"

Is it diet? Then why is it that so many people you know, who have been dieting for years, are still such poor, flabby creatures? Doesn't it always work, or is it merely a matter of guess-work—and those were the cases where no one happened to guess right? Why is it that doctors disagree so on what is the correct diet? For years we have been taught to forswear too much meat. For years we have been told that it causes rheumatism and gout and hardening of the arteries—and a dozen or more other ailments.

Now comes Dr. Woods Hutchinson—a noted authority, quoted the world over—and says: "All the silly old prejudice against meat, that it heated the blood (whatever that means) and produced uric acid to excess, hardened the arteries, inflamed the kidneys, caused rheumatism, etc., has now been proved to be pure fairy tales, utterly without foundation in scientific fact.

"Red meats have nothing whatever to do with causing gout and rheumatism, because neither of these diseases is due to foods or drinks of any sort, but solely to what we call local infections. Little pockets of pus (matter) full of robber germs—mostly streptococci—around the roots of our teeth, in the pouches of our tonsils, in the nasal passages and sinuses of our foreheads and faces opening into them; . . . Our belief now is: 'No pockets of pus, no rheumatism or gout.' Food of any kind has absolutely nothing to do with the case.

"On the other hand, the very worst cases on record in all medical history of hardening and turning to lime (calcification) of the arteries all over the body, and in the kidneys and intestines particularly, have been found in Trappist and certain orders of Oriental monks who live almost exclusively upon starch and pulse—that is, peas, beans, and lentils, and abstain from meat entirely."

Then what is right? *Is it the combination of diet and exercise?* But surely the patients in sanitariums and similar institutions would have every chance to get just the right combination, yet how often you see them come out little, if any, better off than when they went in.

No. None of these is the answer. As a matter of fact, the principal good of either diet or exercise is that it keeps before the patient's mind the RESULT he is working for, and in that way tends to impress it upon his subconscious mind. That is why physical culturists always urge you to exercise in front of a mirror. If results are achieved, it is MIND that achieves them—not the movements you go through or the particular kind of food you eat.

Understand, I don't ask you to stop exercising. A reasonable amount of light, pleasant exercise is good for you mentally and physically. It develops your will power. It helps to impress upon your subconscious mind the image you want to see realized in your body. And it takes your mind off your troubles and worries, centering your thoughts instead upon your desires. Just where your thoughts should always be.

Outdoor exercise, tennis, horseback, swimming—any sort of active *game*—is the best rest there is for a tired mind. For mental tiredness comes from a too steady contemplation of ones problems. And anything that will take ones mind completely off them, and give the subconscious time to work out the solution, is good. That is why it so often happens that you go back to your work after a day of play—not merely refreshed, but with so clear a mind that the problems which before seemed insurmountable are but as child's play to you.

You who envy the rosy cheek and sparkling eye of youth, who awake in the morning weary and unrefreshed, who go to your daily tasks with fagged brain and heavy tread—just remember that Perfect Youth or Perfect Health is merely a state of mind.

There is only one thing that puts muscles on your bones. There is only one thing that keeps your organs functioning with precision and regularity. There is only one thing that builds for you a perfect body. That one thing is your subconscious mind.

Every cell and tissue, every bone and sinew, every organ and muscle in your entire body is subject to the control of your subconscious mind. As it directs, so they build or function.

True, that subconscious mind accepts suggestions from your conscious mind. Hold before it the thought that the exercise you are taking is building muscle upon your arms or shoulders, and your subconscious mind will fall in readily with the suggestion and strengthen those muscles. Hold before it the thought that some particular food gives you unusual energy and "pep," and the subconscious mind will be entirely agreeable to producing the added vigor.

But have you ever noticed how some sudden joy (which is entirely a mental state) energizes and revitalizes you—*more than all the exercise or all the tonics you can take?* Have you ever noticed how martial music will relieve the fatigue of marching men? Have you ever noticed how sorrow (which is entirely a mental state) will depress and devitalize you, *regardless of any amount of exercise or health foods you may take?*

Each of us has within him all the essentials that go to the making of a Super-Man. But so has every acorn the essentials for making a great oak tree, yet the Japanese show us that even an oak may be stunted by continual pruning of its shoots. Negative and weak thoughts, thoughts of self-doubt, of mistrust, continually prune back the vigorous life ever seeking so valiantly to show forth the splendor and strength of the radiant inner self.

Choose what you will be! Your responsibility is to think, speak, act the true inner self. Your privilege is to show forth in this self, the fullness of peace and plenty. Keep steadfastly in mind the idea of yourself that you want to see realized. Your daily, hourly, and continual idea of yourself, your life, your affairs, your world, and your associates, determines the harvest, the showing forth. Look steadfastly to your highest ideal of self, and your steadfast and lofty ideal will draw forth blessing and prosperity not only upon you, but upon all who know you.

For mind is the only creator, and thought is the only energy. All that counts is the image of your body that you are holding in your thought. If heretofore that image has been one of weakness, of ill-health, change it *now*—TODAY. Repeat to yourself, the first thing upon awakening in the morning and the last thing before going to sleep at night—"My body was made in the image and likeness of God. God first imagined it in its entirety, therefore every cell and bone and tissue is perfect, every organ and muscle performing its proper function. That is the only model of me in Universal Mind. That is the only model of me that my Subconscious Mind knows. Therefore, since Mind—God—is the only creator, *that is the only model of me that I can have!*"

Volume XXII

Why Grow Old?

"And Moses was an hundred and twenty years old when he died:
his eye was not dim, nor his natural force abated."

REMEMBER how you used to plough through great masses of work day after day and month after month, cheerily, enthusiastically, with never a sign of tiring or nervous strain? Remember how you used to enjoy those evenings, starting out as fresh from your office or shop as if you hadn't just put a hard day's work behind you?

No doubt you've often wondered why you can't work and enjoy yourself like that now, but solaced yourself with the moth-eaten fallacy that "As a man grows older he shouldn't expect to get the same fun out of life that he did in his earlier years."

Poor old exploded idea!

Youth is not a matter of time. It is a mental state. You can be just as brisk, just as active, just as light-hearted now as you were ten or twenty years ago. Genuine youth is just a perfect state of health. You can have that health, and the boundless energy and capacity for work or enjoyment that go with it. You can cheat time of ten, twenty or fifty years—not by taking thought of what you shall eat or what you shall drink, not by diet or exercise, but solely through a right understanding of what you should expect of your body.

"If only I had my life to live over again!" How often you have heard it said. How often you have thought it.

But the fact is that you CAN have it. You can start right now and live again as many years as you have already experienced. Health, physical freedom and full vigor need not end for you at 35 or 40—nor at 60 or 70. Age is not a matter of years. It is a state of mind.

In an address before the American Sociological Society a few months ago Dr. Hornell Hart of Bryn Mawr predicted that—"Babies born in the year 2000 will have something like 200 years of life ahead of them, and men and women of 100 years will be quite the normal thing. But instead of being wrinkled and crippled, these centenarians will be in their vigorous prime."

Thomas Parr, an Englishman, lived to be 152 years old, and was sufficiently hale and hearty at the age of 120 to take unto himself a second wife. Even at 152, his death was not due to old age, but to a sudden and drastic change in his manner of life. All his days he had lived upon simple fare, but his fame reaching the King, he was invited to London and there feasted so lavishly that he died of it.

In a despatch to the New York *Times* on February 14th last, I read of an Arab now in Palestine, one Salah Mustapha Salah Abu Musa, who at the age of 105 *is growing his third set of teeth!*

There is an ancient city in Italy which can be approached by sea only through a long stretch of shallow water full of rocks and cross currents. There is one safe channel, and it is marked by posts. In the days of the Sea Rovers the city used to protect itself by pulling up the posts whenever a rover hove in sight.

Mankind has taken to planting posts along its way to mark the flight of time. Every year we put in a new one, heedless of the fact that we are thus marking a clear channel for our Arch-Enemy, Age, to enter in from the sea of human belief.

But the fact is that there is no natural reason for man to grow old as soon as he does, *no biological reason for him to grow old at all!*

Why is it that the animals live eight to ten times their maturity, when man lives only about twice his? Why? Because man hastens decrepitude and decay by holding the thought of old age always before him.

Dr. Alexis Carrel, Nobel Prize winner and member of the Rockefeller Institute, has demonstrated that living cells taken from a body, properly protected and fed, can be kept alive indefinitely. Not only that, but they *grow!* In 1912 he took some tissue from the heart of an embryo chick and placed it in a culture medium. It is living and growing yet.

Recently Dr. Carrel showed a moving picture of these living cells before the American Institute of Electrical Engineers. They grow so fast that they double in size every twenty-four hours, and have to be trimmed daily!

The cells of your being can be made to live indefinitely when placed outside your body. Single-celled animals never die a natural death. They live on and on until something kills them. Now scientists are beginning to wonder if multicellular animals like man really need to die.

Under the title, "Immortality and Rejuvenation in Modern Biology," M. Metalnikov, of the Pasteur Institute, has just published a volume that should be read by all those who have decided that it is necessary to grow old and die.

Here is the first sentence of the concluding chapter of the book: "What we have just written forces us to maintain our conviction that immortality is the fundamental property of living organisms."

And further on:

"Old age and death are not a stage of earthly existence. . . ."

And that, mind you, is set forth under the aegis of a scientific establishment that has no equal in the world, and of a scholar universally respected.

As the *Journal of Paris* says in reviewing the article:

"Most religious and philosophic systems assert the immortality of the soul. But the positive sciences have shown themselves more skeptical on this point. This idea seems to them quite contradictory to all that we know, or think we know, of animal life. Animal life originates as a tiny germ, which becomes an embryo, developing into an adult organism, which grows old and finally dies. This means the disappearance of all the faculties of life that so clearly distinguish it from an inanimate object. There is no scientific evidence to show that at this moment the 'soul' does not disappear with the body, and that it continues its existence separately. Biologists cannot even conceive the possibility of separation of soul and body, so strong and indissoluble are the bonds that unite all our psychic manifestations with our bodily life. For them an immortal soul only can exist in an immortal body. What if it were so? What if our organism is really indestructible? It is this that M. Metalnikov attempts scientifically to prove.

"Death is a permanent and tangible phenomenon only in the case of man and the higher animals. It is not so for plants and for the simpler forms of animal life, the protozoans. These last, composed often of a single cell, just observable under the microscope, are however without the chief faculties that characterize the higher animals. They move about by means of vibratory hair-like processes, sustain themselves, seek their food, hunt animals still smaller than themselves, react to irritations of different kinds, and multiply. But this multiplication is not effected by means of special organs, as among the higher animals, but by the division of the whole organism into two equal parts. The common infusoria which abound in fresh water thus divide once or twice every twenty-four hours. Each daughter cell continues to live like the mother cell, of which it is the issue; it feeds, grows, and divides in its turn. And never, in this constantly renewed cycle in their lives, do we find the phenomenon of natural death, so characteristic and so universal in the higher animals. The infusorium is subject only to accidental death, such as we can cause by the addition of some poisonous element to the water in which it lives, or by heat.

"Experiments along this line were made long ago. The first were by de Saussure, in 1679. Having put an infusorium in a drop of water, he saw it divide under his eye. Four days later it was impossible to count the number of creatures. However, some authors thought that this reproductive facility was not unlimited. Maupas himself, who made a minute study of it forty years ago and succeeded in observing 700 successive generations of a single species, thought that it was finally subject to old age and to death.

"But the more recent works of Joukovsky at Heidelberg, of Koulaghine at Petrograd, of Calkins in England, of Weissmann, and still others, lead to an opposite opinion. The degeneration observed by these workers was due to auto-intoxication, caused by not renewing the culture-medium.

"Decisive experiments were made in Russia, dating from 1907, by Woodruff and by M. Metalnikov himself. Begun at Tsarskoe Selo, they continued until the tragic hours of the 1917 revolution, and were renewed at the University of Crimea. These investigators took an infusorium found in an aquarium, the Paramoecium caudatum, whose characteristics are well determined, and in thirteen years, in 1920, they had obtained 5,000 successive generations. . . .

"Thus we are bound to say that a unicellular body possesses within itself the power of immortality.

"And we ourselves are made up only by the juxtaposition of simple cells."

THE FOUNTAIN OF YOUTH

Four hundred years ago Ponce de Leon set sail into the mysteries of an unknown world in search of the Fountain of Youth, when all the time the secret of that fountain was right within himself.

For the fact is, that no matter how many years have passed since you were born, *you are only eleven months old today!* Your body is constantly renewing itself. The one thing about it you can be surest of is CHANGE. Every one of the millions of cells of which it is composed is constantly being renewed. Even your bones are daily renewing themselves in this way.

These cells are building—building—building. Every day they tear down old tissue and rebuild it with new. There is not a cell in your body, not a muscle or tissue, not a bone, that is more than eleven months old! Why then should you feel age? Why should you be any less spry, any less cheerful, than these young-sters around you that you have been envying?

The answer is that you *need not*—if you will but realize your YOUTHFUL-NESS. Every organ, every muscle, tissue and cell of your body is subject to your subconscious mind. They rebuild exactly as that mind directs them. What is the model *you* are holding before your mind's eye? Is it one of age, of decrepitude? That is the model that most men use, because they know no better. That is the result that you see imaged upon their bodies.

But you need not follow their outworn models. You can hold before your mind's eye only the vision of youth, of manly vigor, of energy and strength and beauty—*and that is the model that your cells will use to build upon.*

Do you know what is responsible for the whole difference between Youth and Age? Just one thing. Youth looks *forward* always to something better. Age looks backward and sighs over its "lost" youth.

In youth we are constantly growing. We KNOW we have not yet reached our prime. We know we can expect to continually IMPROVE. We look forward to ever-increasing physical powers. We look forward to a finer, more perfect physique. We look forward to greater mental alertness. We have been educated to expect these things. Therefore we BELIEVE we shall get them—and we GET them!

But what happens after we get to be thirty or forty years of age? We think we have reached our prime. We have been taught that we can no longer look for-ward to greater growth—that all we can hope for is to "hold our own" for a little while, and then start swiftly downward to old age and decay. History shows that no nation, no institution and no individual can continue for any length of time to merely "hold his own." You must go forward—or back. You must move—or life will pass you by. Yours is the choice. If you will realize that there is never any end to GROWTH—that your body is constantly being rebuilt—that per-fection is still so far ahead of you that you can continue GROWING towards it indefinitely—you need never know age. You can keep on growing more perfect, mentally and physically, every day. Every minute you live is a minute of concep-tion and rebirth.

You may be weak and anæmic. You may be crippled or bent. No matter! You can start today to rebuild along new lines. In eleven months at the most, every one of those weak and devitalized cells, every one of those bent and crippled bones, will be replaced by new, strong, vigorous tissue.

Look at Annette Kellerman—crippled and deformed as a child—yet she grew up into the world's most perfectly formed woman. Look at Roosevelt—weak and anæmic as a young man—yet he made himself the envy of the world for boundless vigor and energy. And they are but two cases out of thousands I could quote. Many of the world's strongest men were weaklings in their childhood. It matters not what your age, what your condition—you can start now renewing your youth, growing daily nearer the model of YOU that is imaged in Universal Mind.

Arthur Brisbane says that at the age of 85 George F. Baker is doing the work of ten men.

That is what every man of 85 ought to be doing, for he should have not only the physical vigor and strength and enthusiasm of 21, but combined with them he should have the skill and experience, the ripened judgment of 85.

There is no more despairing pronouncement than the belief of the average man that he matures only to begin at once to deteriorate and decay. When the actual fact is, as stated in a recent utterance by the eminent Dr. Hammond, *there is no physiological reason* why a man should die. He asserted—and the statement is corroborated by scientists and physiologists—that the human body possesses inherent capacity to renew and continue itself and its functions indefinitely!

Your body wear out? Of course it does—just as all material things do. But with this difference—your body is being renewed just as fast as it wears out! Have you damaged some part of it? Don't worry. Down inside you is a chemical laboratory which can make new parts just as good or better than the old. Up in your subconscious mind is a Master Chemist with all the formulas of Universal Mind to draw upon, who can keep that chemical laboratory of yours making new parts just as fast as you can wear out the old.

But that Master Chemist is like all of us—like you. He is inclined to lazy a bit on the job—if you let him. Try to relieve him of some of his functions—and he won't bother about them further. Take to the regular use of drugs or other methods of eliminating the waste matter from the body, and your Master Chemist will figure that your conscious mind has taken over this duty from him—and he will leave it thereafter to your conscious mind. Lead him to believe that you no longer expect him to rebuild your body along such perfect lines as in youth—and he will slow down in his work of removing the old, worn-out tissues, and of replacing them with new, better material. The result? Arteries clogged with worn-out cells. Tissues dried and shrunken. Joints stiff and creaky. In short—Old Age.

The fault is not with the Master Chemist. It is with you. You didn't hold him to the job. When a business or an enterprise or an expedition fails, it is not the rank and file who are to blame—it is the directing head. He didn't give his men the right plans to work on. He didn't supply the proper leadership. He didn't keep them keyed up to their best work.

What would you think of an engineer who, with the best plans in the world, the best material with which to build, threw away his plans when he was half through with the job and let his men do as they pleased, ruining all his early work and all his fine material by putting the rest of it together any which way?

Yet that is what you do when you stop LOOKING FORWARD at 30 or 40, and decide thereafter to just grow old any which way. You throw away the wonderful model on which you have been building, you take the finest material in the world, and let your workmen put it together any way they like. In fact, you do worse than that. You tell them you don't expect much from them any more. That any sort of a patched-up job they put together after that will be about as good as you can look for.

Man alive! What would you expect from ordinary workmen to whom you talked like that? Your inner workmen are no different. You will get from them just what you look for—no more, no less.

"Your time of life" should be the best time you have yet known. The engineer who has built forty bridges should be far more proficient than the one who has built only a few. The model you are passing on to your Master Chemist now ought to be a vastly more perfect model than the one you gave to him at twenty. Instead of feeling that your heart is giving out and your stomach weak, you ought to be boasting of how much better a heart you are now making than a few years ago, how much more perfectly your stomach is functioning than before you learned that you were its boss.

Of one thing you can be sure. God never decreed a law of decay and death. If there is any such law, it is man-made—and man can unmake it. The Life Principle that came to this planet thousands or millions of years ago brought no Death Principle with it. For death is like darkness—it is nothing in itself. Death is merely the absence of life, just as darkness is merely the absence of light. Keep that life surging—strongly.

In the Book of Wisdom, of the Apocryphal writings, you read:

"For God made not death; neither hath He pleasure in the destruction of the living.

"For He created all things that they might have being; and the generative powers of the world are healthsome, and there is no poison of destruction in them, nor hath death dominion upon the earth.

"For righteousness is immortal:

"But ungodly men with their works and words called death unto them.

"For God created man to be immortal, and made Him to be an image of His own proper being.

"But by the envy of the devil came death into the world."

"Whosoever liveth and believeth in me (understandeth me)," said Jesus, "shall never die."

And again—"If a man keep my saying, he shall never see death."

Universal Mind knows no imperfection—no decay—no death. It does not produce sickness and death. It is your *conscious* mind that has decreed these evils. Banish the thought—and you can banish the effect. Life was never meant to be measured by years.

I remember reading a story of a traveler who had journeyed to a land of perpetual sun. Since there was no sunrise and no sunset, no moons or changing seasons, there was no means of measuring time. Therefore to the inhabitants of that land, time did not exist. And having no time, they never thought to measure ages and consequently never grew old. Like organisms with a single cell, they did not die except by violence.

There is more truth than fiction to that idea. The measurement of life by the calendar robs youth of its vigor and hastens old age. It reminds me of the days of our grandparents, when a woman was supposed to doff her hat and don a bonnet at 40. And donning a bonnet was like taking the veil. She was supposed to retire to her chimney corner and make way for the younger generation.

Men and women ought to *grow* with years into greater health, broader judgment, maturer wisdom. Instead of becoming atrophied, and dead to all new ideas, their minds should through practice hold ever stronger images before them of youthful vigor and freshness. The Psalmist says—"But thou art the same, and thy years shall have no end."

No one need retire to the chimney corner, no matter how many years have passed over his head. Years should bring wisdom and greater health—not decrepitude. Many of the world's famous men did their greatest work long after the age when most men are in their graves. Tennyson composed the immortal lines of "Crossing the Bar" at the age of 80. Plato still had pen in hand at 81. Cato learned Greek at the same age. Humboldt completed his "Cosmos" in his ninetieth year, while John Wesley at 82 said—"It is twelve years now since I have felt any such sensation as fatigue."

You are only as old as your mind. Every function, every activity of your body, is controlled by your mind. Your vital organs, your blood that sends the material for rebuilding to every cell and tissue, the processes of elimination that remove all the broken down and waste material, all are dependent for their functioning upon the energy derived from your mind.

The human body can be compared to an electric transportation system. When the dynamo runs at full power every car speeds along, and everything is handled with precision. But let the dynamo slow down and the whole system lags.

That dynamo is your mind, and your thoughts provide the energy that runs it. Feed it thoughts of health and vigor and your whole system will reflect energy and vitality. Feed it thoughts of decrepitude and age, and you will find it slowing down to the halting pace you set for it.

You can grow old at 30. You can be young at 90. It is up to you. Which do you choose?

If you choose youth, then start this minute renewing your youth. Find a picture—or, better still, a statuette—of the man you would like to be, the form you would like to have. Keep it in your room. When you go to bed at night, *visualize* it in your mind's eye—hold it in your thought as *YOU*—as the man *YOU ARE GOING TO BE!*

The Journal of Education had the idea in their story of "The Prince and the Statue" in a recent issue:

"There was once a prince who had a crooked back. He could never stand straight up like even the lowest of his subjects. Because he was a very proud prince his crooked back caused him a great deal of mental suffering.

"One day he called before him the most skilful sculptor in his kingdom and said to him: 'Make me a noble statue of myself, true to my likeness in every detail with this exception—make this statue with a straight back. I wish to see myself as I might have been.

"For long months the sculptor worked hewing the marble carefully into the likeness of the prince, and at last the work was done, and the sculptor went before the prince and said: 'The statue is finished; where shall I set it up?' One of the courtiers called out: 'Set it before the castle gate where all can see it,' but the prince smiled sadly, and shook his head. 'Rather,' said he, 'place it in a secret nook in the palace garden where only I shall see it.' The statue was placed as the prince ordered, and promptly forgotten by the world, but every morning, and every noon, and every evening the prince stole quietly away to where it stood and looked long upon it, noting the straight back and the unlifted head, and the noble brow. And each time he gazed, something seemed to go out of the statue and into him, tingling in his blood and throbbing in his heart.

"The days passed into months and the months into years; then strange rumors began to spread throughout the land. Said one: 'The prince's back is no longer crooked or my eyes deceive me.' Said another: 'The prince is more noble-looking or my eyes deceive me.' Said another: 'Our prince has the high look of a mighty man,' and these rumors came to the prince, and he listened with a queer smile. Then went he out into the garden to where the statue stood and, behold, it was just as the people said, his back had become as straight as the statue's, his head had the same noble bearing; he was, in fact, the noble man his statue proclaimed him to be."

A novel idea? Not at all! 2,500 years ago, in the Golden Age of Athens, when its culture led the world, Grecian mothers surrounded themselves with beautiful statues that they might bring forth perfect children and that the children in turn might develop into perfect men and women.

Eleven months from now *you* will have an entirely new body, inside and out. Not a single cell, not a single bit of tissue that is now in you will be there then. What changes do you want made in that new body? What improvements?

Get your new model clearly in your mind's eye. Picture it. VISUALIZE it! Look FORWARD daily to a better physique, to greater mental power.

Give that model to your Subconscious Mind to build upon—and before eleven months are out, that model *WILL BE YOU!*

Volume XXIII

The Medicine Delusion

"I find the medicine worse than the malady."

—SHAKESPEARE

WE are getting rid of the drug illusion," declared Dr. Woods Hutchinson, the noted medical writer of America, at a luncheon given on June 6, 1925, by the English-Speaking Union to 700 American and Canadian doctors assembled in London, England.

"We are willing even to subscribe to the dictum of Oliver Wendell Holmes," the doctor added, "that if 99 per cent of all drugs we possess were thrown into the sea it would be a good thing for the human race, but rather hard on the fishes."

Sir Arbuthnot Lane, Surgeon to King George, seconded Dr. Hutchinson's remarks. "They might say," he went on, "that he was trying to establish a 'suicide club' for doctors. It practically came to that, because as the public became educated in matters of health the medical profession might disappear. It was in fact an anomaly that a medical profession should exist. If people were healthy, there was no reason to have doctors at all."

Twenty-five years ago, the charms of the Patent Medicine fakir and the incantations of the Indian Medicine Man were in the heyday of their popularity. So long as you talked about their aches and pains, their diseases and ailments, people would buy any kind of a nostrum that an unscrupulous fakir chose to palm off upon them. Patent medicine manufacturers made fabulous fortunes selling cheap whisky adulterated with burnt sugar and water, under a hundred different names for $1.00 the bottle. You could hardly pick up a magazine or newspaper without seeing a dozen of their lurid ads.

The day of the Indian Medicine Man and street-corner fakir has passed. And for a time, thanks to the crusade against them led by *Collier's,* and backed by a number of other reputable magazines, patent medicine manufacturers suffered an eclipse.

But they are back again today in a more respectable guise.

Pick up almost any small town paper and you will find a dozen "sovereign remedies" for tired women or fretful children or run-down men. Concoctions, most of them, containing just enough alcohol to give you a pleasant sense of stimulation, enough burnt sugar to color them—and a whole lot of water.

But if that were all, no great harm would be done. If the peddling of drugs depended entirely—or even mostly—on Patent Medicine advertisers, the end of it would soon be in sight. But it doesn't. The worst offenders of all are the ones who, of all people, should know better—some of the doctors.

Understand, I don't mean all of them. And I don't mean the best of them. There are thousands of them like Dr. Woods Hutchinson who have the courage to get up and say that medicine itself cannot cure disease. That it never has cured disease. That Nature is the only Healer. Drugs can give you temporary relief from pain—yes. They can cleanse—yes. But as for *curing* anything, the drug is not made that can do it.

The principal good that the administering of a drug has is in its effect upon the mind of the patient. Men have been taught for so many years that drugging is the only way to cure disease, that when you give them something, they BELIEVE they are going to be cured, and to the extent that they believe, they ARE CURED.

The best proof of that is to let two patients suffering from the same complaint go to two different physicians—the one a doctor of the regular school, the other a homeopath. The regular doctor will administer a dose containing ten thousand times as much of the mother drug as the homeopath. In fact, there is so slight a trace of any drug in the homeopath's prescription that it might be called none at all. Yet it frequently happens that his patient will respond just as readily to his denatured dose as the other will to his drug.

Dr. Gour, in a recent issue of *Pearson's Magazine,* said: "A few years ago there appeared an article in the *Atlantic Monthly* written by a young woman physician who was with the Red Cross in Russia. Immediately following the

Kerensky revolution, the Russian peasants who, for the first time in their lives, found that they could keep what they earned, began to think of going to doctors for ailments which had afflicted them for years, but which they could never before afford to have treated. Within two weeks' time this young physician exhausted her supply of medicine. But the rush of peasant patients continued and she was reduced to the placebo idea of administering colored waters with a slight amount of a single drug—quinine, if I recall correctly. For several weeks she obtained such wonderful results in every conceivable form of affliction that she said her faith in specific medication was completely lost."

In a despatch from Rome to the New York *Herald-Tribune,* under date of June 15, 1926, I read:

"Under the skeptical eyes of local doctors Don Luigi Garofalo, a priest in the Quarto sector of Naples, alleges that he is curing all the ills that flesh is heir to, from pneumonia to broken bones, by a practical application of the theory derived from the text, 'Man is of dust and to dust he shall return.' Don Luigi argues that from a homeopathic viewpoint dust should be a curative element. So from dust taken from the reddish earth near Pozznoli, which contains traces of sulphur and copper, he makes pills for the afflicted, but he contends that any other earth will do.

"The cures, most of which have been effected by means of the red earth, include the healing of broken limbs, tubercular cases, toothache, internal lesions, heart diseases, mumps, paralysis and fevers."

Of course, it is not to be inferred from this that reliance can be placed upon red earth—or any other kind of earth—to cure you of any ill. But it shows that even so common, ordinary a thing as a bit of dirt can be used to arouse people from the lethargic condition in which sickness so frequently leaves them, and give them the power to help themselves.

Take another case. Your doctor prescribes regular doses of some drug. You take it once. It has the desired effect. You take it again. The effect is not quite so pronounced. You keep it up—and in a short time *the drug seems to have lost its efficacy.*

Why? The same chemical elements are there. And if you mix the same chemical elements in a retort, you will get the same results whether you do it once or a thousand times. Why doesn't it work the same way with drugs and your body?

Because the strongest factor in bringing about the desired effect in the beginning was your BELIEF—yours and that of your doctor. But as you kept on and on, your belief began to falter, until presently it died away altogether. You may have *hoped,* but the active belief suggestions to your subconscious mind had stopped carrying conviction.

Dr. Richard C. Cabot, Professor of Medicine at Harvard University, in a recent address, declared that "three-quarters of all illnesses are cured without the victims even knowing they have had them.

"Proof of this contention is to be found in post-mortem examinations, which time after time reveal indelible and unmistakable traces of disease which the subject has conquered all unknowingly. Ninety per cent of all typhoid cures itself, as does 75 per cent of all pneumonia. In fact, out of a total of 215 diseases known to medical science, there are only about eight or nine which doctors conquer—the rest conquer themselves."

He went on to say that—"If nature, assisted by the proper mental and emotional moods, is capable of curing an ulcer in three or four weeks, why isn't it possible for the same force to heal a similar ulcer in a few minutes, when the curative processes have been speeded up abnormally?"

Great physicians have, on numerous occasions, maintained that there is no science in *medicating* people. In Preventive Medicine—yes. In Surgery. In Obstetrics. In a score of different lines that fall under the heading of the medical profession.

But the art of drugging is little ahead of where it was in the Middle Ages, when Egyptian mummies were in great demand among druggists and "powdered Pharaoh" was considered the greatest remedy for any ill that flesh was heir to.

Every day brings the discovery of some new drug, and the consequent dictum that the remedy previously prescribed was all a mistake—that it had little or no real value whatever.

One doctor says: "A medicine that will not kill you if you take an overdose is no good." Another: "The most prominent doctors now claim that there is not a single drug will do what it has been prescribed for in the past."

Dr. Douglas White, writing in *The Churchman,* sums it up thus:

"All cure of every disease is spiritual. Healing can never be imposed from without by either the surgeon or physician; it is the living organism which, helped by the skill of the one or the other, is enabled to work its way back to health. The whole principle of healing in all cases is the *vis medicatrix naturae.* And when we speak of nature, we are only personifying the principle of life which Christians call God."

In the *Medical Record* of September 25, 1920, Dr. Joseph Byrne, Professor of Neurology at Fordham University Medical School, said:

"At a conservative estimate it may be admitted that of all the ailments for which relief is sought, 90% or over are self limited and tend to get well. It may also be admitted that in over 90% of all human ailments, the *psychic* is the dominating factor."

In other words, Mind is the Healer. Drugs can sometimes make its work easier by removing obstructions, by killing off parasites. But the regular use of drugs is far more likely to harm than to heal. We might well quote to the druggists the old proverb:

"God gives the mango;
  The farmer plants the seed.
God cures the patient;
  The doctor takes the fees."

In the Great War, the one drug that most proved its worth was Iodine. And what is Iodine? A *cleanser*. It killed germs. It cleansed wounds. But it has no healing power. And no healing was expected of it. It did all that was asked. It cauterized—cleansed—so that Nature (Mind) could do its own healing, unobstructed.

That would seem to be the most that should be expected of any drug—kill the germs of sickness or disease, cleanse so that Nature can the more easily do its rebuilding. And that is where the use of drugs should stop. Mind works best when it is interfered with least—when we throw ourselves entirely upon it for support, rather than share the responsibility with some outside agency.

Dr. Burnett Rae, a well-known English specialist, addressing a large audience on the subject of "Spiritual Healing and Medical Science," said the term "spiritual healing" was sometimes used in a manner which seemed to imply that there was a form of healing which was of a non-spiritual character, and that spiritual healing was incompatible with, or opposed to, medical practice. Healing could never be regarded as a purely physical process. He would go so far as to say that healing was always effected through the control of the mind, and medicinal remedies only set the machinery of the mind in motion. We are too apt to think of medical science as concerned with drugs or appliances and operations. *These might completely pass away during the next twenty or fifty years.*

It is not through drugs that the medical profession has done so much of good for the world. It is not through drugs that they have improved the general health, cleaned up plague spots, cut down infant mortality, lengthened the average life expectancy of mankind by fifteen years.

It is by scotching disease at its very source. It is by getting rid of artificially created *unwholesome* conditions, getting back to *natural wholesome* conditions.

What is it causes typhus? Filth—an entirely unwholesome condition, man-made. And how do doctors prevent the spread of typhus? By cleaning up—by getting back to *natural* wholesome conditions.

What is it causes typhoid? Impure water. And its prevention is simply the purifying of the water—getting back to Nature's perfect, wholesome supply.

Yellow fever has been practically stamped out of existence. Typhus is almost a forgotten plague, except in such backward places as parts of Russia and Asia.

Malaria has been conquered. And doctors predict that in another generation tuberculosis will be an almost forgotten malady.

How were these wonderful results brought about? Not through drugs— *but by cleaning up!* Cleaning out swamps and filth. Purifying water. Building drainage systems. Making everything round about as clean and wholesome as Nature herself.

Cleanliness—Purity—Sunshine!

God gave us in abundance all that is necessary for perfect health—clean air, pure water, clear sunshine. All we need to do is to keep these pure and clean, and to use all we possibly can of them. The greatest good the medical profession has done mankind is in discovering the value of these gifts of God and showing us how to use them.

The Chinese have long had the right idea—they pay their physicians to keep them well, not to cure them of sickness. And the thing that made the reputation of such men as Gorgas, Reed, Flexner, Carrel, was not their *cure* of disease—but their *prevention* of it.

That way lies the future of medicine—bringing our surroundings back to the *natural* wholesome conditions for which we were created. That way lies health and happiness for all—cleanliness inside and out, clean air, pure water, plenty of sunshine—*and right thinking!*

In the next Chapter, I shall try to show you how you can apply the illimitable power of Mind hopefully towards the successful treatment of disease.

Volume XXIV

Volume XXIV

The Gift of the Magi

"Sweep up the debris of decaying faiths;
Sweep down the cobwebs of worn-out beliefs,
And throw your soul wide open to the light
Of Reason and of Knowledge. Be not afraid
To thrust aside half-truths and grasp the whole."

—ELLA WHEELER WILCOX

ALL over the world, sick, weak and devitalized men and women are searching for health and strength. By the hundreds of thousands, they drag their weary and aching bones around, or languish on sick beds, waiting for someone to bring health to them corked up in a bottle.

But real, lasting health was never found in pill boxes or medicine bottles. There is one method—and only one—by which it can be gained and kept. That method is by using the power of the Subconscious Mind.

For a long time the doctors pooh-poohed any such idea. Then as the evidence piled up, they grudgingly admitted that nervous troubles and even functional disorders might be cured by mind.

Even now there are some who, as Bernard Shaw put it, "Had rather bury a whole hillside ethically than see a single patient cured unethically. They will give credit to no method of healing outside the tenets of their own school."

Yet, as Warren Hilton has it in "Applied Psychology":

"All the literature of medicine, whether of ancient or modern times, abounds in illustrations of the power of the mind over the body in health and in disease. And medical science has always based much of its practice on this principle. No reputable school of medicine ever failed to instruct its students in practical applications of the principle of mental influence at the bedside of their patients. A brisk and cheery manner, a hopeful countenance, a supremely assured and confident demeanor—these things have always been regarded by the medical profession as but second in importance to sanitation and material remedies; *while the value of the sugar-coated bread pill when the diagnosis was uncertain, has long been recognized.*

"The properly trained nurse has always been expected to supplement the efforts of the attending physician by summoning the mental forces of the patient to his aid. She, therefore, surrounds the patient with an atmosphere of comfortable assurance. And by constantly advising him of his satisfactory progress toward speedy recovery she seeks to instil hope, confidence and mental effort.

"To quote Dr. Didama: 'The ideal physician irradiates the sick chamber with the light of his cheerful presence. He may not be hilarious—he is not indifferent—but he has an irrepressible good-nature which lifts the patient out of the slough of despond and places his feet on the firm land of health. In desperate cases, even a little harmless levity may be beneficial. A well-timed jest may break up a congestion; a pun may add pungency to the sharpest stimulant.' Dr. Oliver Wendell Holmes reduced this principle to its cash equivalent when he said that a cheerful smile might be worth five thousand dollars a year to a physician.

"Today, psychotherapy, or the healing of bodily disease by mental influence, has the unqualified endorsement of the American Therapeutic Society, the only national organization in America devoted exclusively to therapeutics. It has the enthusiastic support of men of such recognized international leadership in the scientific world and in the medical profession as Freud, Jung, Bleuler, Breuer, Prince, Janet, Babinski, Putnam, Gerrish, Sidis, Dubois, Munsterberg, Jones, Brill, Donley, Waterman and Taylor.

"The present attitude of reputable science toward the principle that the mind controls all bodily operations is, then, one of positive conviction. The world's foremost thinkers accept its truth. The interest of enlightened men and women everywhere is directed toward the mind as a powerful curative force and as a regenerative influence of hitherto undreamed-of resource."

The more progressive physicians everywhere now admit that there is practically no limit to how far mind can go in the cure of disease. As Dr. Walsh of Fordham University puts it: "Analysis of the statistics of diseases cured by mental influence shows that its results have been more strikingly manifest in organic than in the so-called nervous or functional diseases."

Everyone admits that the mind influences the body somewhat, for everyone has seen others grow pale with fear, or red with anger. Everyone has felt the stopping of the heartbeats at some sudden fright, the quickened breathing and the thumping of the heart caused by excitement. These and a hundred other evidences of the influence of mind over matter are common to all of us, and everyone will admit them.

But everyone does not know that our whole bodies seem to be nothing more or less than the outward expression of our thought. We sit in a draught, and education teaches us we should have a cold or fever. So we *have* a cold or fever. We eat something which we have been told is indigestible, and immediately we are assailed with pains. We see another yawn, and our impulse is to follow suit. In the same way, when we hear of sickness round about us, the fear of it visualizes it in our own minds and we, too, have it. The *fear* of these things seems to bring them about, the mental suggestion sent through to our subconscious minds. We have been educated in a medical age to think that most diseases are infectious or contagious. So the mere sight of a diseased person makes most of us withdraw into ourselves like a turtle within his shell. We fear we shall catch it—when one of the great dangers of disease is that very fear of it.

For years it has been accepted as an acknowledged fact that anyone trapped in a mine or other air-tight compartment would presently die of carbon dioxide poisoning—lack of oxygen. Now comes Houdini to prove that death for lack of oxygen is not necessary at all!

"Fear, and not poisoning by carbon dioxide, causes the death of miners and others trapped in air-tight compartments," in the opinion of Houdini, according to an Associated Press despatch of August 6, 1926.

Houdini had himself sunk in a sealed coffin in a swimming pool, without chance for a breath of outside air to reach him, and stayed there for an hour and a half, although, according to all previous scientific belief, he should have been dead at the end of four minutes. Yet Dr. W. J. McConnell of the United States Department of Mines, who examined Houdini before and after the experiment, reported no marked physical reactions from the test, and Houdini himself said he felt only a slight dizziness when he was released from the coffin!

"Anyone can do it," said Houdini. "The important thing is to *believe that you are safe.*"

The Chinese have a saying that when the plague comes, 5,000 people may die of the plague, but 50,000 will die of the fear of it.

Did you ever hurt a limb, or a finger, so that you thought you couldn't move it? And then, under the stress of some sudden emotion, forget all about the hurt and presently wake to find yourself using the finger or the limb just as readily and as painlessly as though there had never been anything wrong with it?

I have before me a clipping from the New York *Times* of March 29, 1925, telling of a cripple who had been paralyzed for six years, but under the spur of sudden fear, he ran up a stairway unaided, without crutch or cane. He had been treated in a number of hospitals, but because of an injury to his spine received in an auto accident, had been unable to walk without crutches or canes for six years. The patient in the bed next his own suddenly went crazy and attacked him, and in his fear this paralytic leaped from his bed and ran up a flight of stairs. According to the report, *the sudden fright cured him!*

Take the miracles of Lourdes, or of St. Anne of Beaupre, or of any of the dozens of shrines that dot the world. What is it that effects the cures? Two things—*Desire* and *Faith*. "What wouldst thou that I should do unto thee?" the Saviour asked the blind man who kept following and crying out to him. "Lord that I should receive my sight." And again of the cripple at the Pool of Bethesda Jesus asked—"Wouldst thou be made whole?"

Sounds like foolish questioning, doesn't it? But you remember the story of the famous Saint of Italy, who traveled from town to town healing the lame, the halt, and the blind. A pilgrim hastening to a town where the Saint was expected, met two lame beggars hurrying away. He asked them the reason for their haste, to be told, to his astonishment, it was because the Saint was coming to town. As they put it—"He will surely heal us, and where will our livelihood be then?"

So it is with many people today—not beggars, mind you—but people in every walk of life. They have become so wedded to their ailments, they "enjoy poor health" so thoroughly, that they are secretly a bit proud of it. Take away their complaints and they would be lost without them.

You must have the *sincere desire first.* That is prayer. Then the *faith*—the kind of faith that Jesus meant when he said—"Whatsoever ye ask for when ye pray, believe that ye *receive* it, and ye shall *have it.*" Mind you, not "believe ye are *going* to receive it." "Believe that ye *receive* it"—*now*—this very minute. Know that the REAL you, the image of you held in Universal Mind—in short, the *Truth* concerning every organ in your body—is perfect. *"Know the Truth."* Believe that you HAVE this perfect image. On the day that you can truly believe this—carry this sincere conviction to your subconscious mind—on that day you WILL BE perfect.

This is the faith that Jesus meant when he said—"Thy faith hath made thee whole." This is the faith that is responsible for the miracles of Lourdes, for miraculous healings everywhere. It matters not whether you be Catholic or Protestant, Jew or Gentile. Desire and faith such as these will heal you.

A month or two ago I read in the newspapers of a farmer, blind for two years, who went out in the field and prayed "that he should receive his sight." At the end of the second day, his sight was completely restored. He was a Protestant. He went to no shrine—just out under the sky and prayed to God.

Today I have before me a clipping from the New York *Sun* of February 23, 1926, telling of Patrolman Dennis O'Brien of the Jersey City police force, who at the end of a Novena to Our Lady of Help at the Monastery of St. Michael's in Union City, recovered the use of his legs, which had been paralyzed since the time, two years before, when a bullet had entered the base of his spine, severing the cord of motor and sensory nerves. He was a Catholic.

Then here is one from the New York *Sun* of June 26, 1926, telling how Miss Elsie Meyer of the Bronx, New York, was healed *overnight* of a tumorous growth that had troubled her for months:

"I realized last fall that there was an unusual growth on my body," she said. "It might have resulted from the strain of lifting a trunk. I wanted to know what it was, and I first went to a doctor, who informed me it was a tumorous growth and likely to become serious.

"But I would not be frightened and refused to receive any medical remedies in the way of cure. I have been a believer in faith healing and member of the Unity Society, a branch of the New Thought organization, for a number of years, so I went to a New Thought practioner. While this seemed to help me, the tumorous growth remained. I guess my faith wasn't strong enough at the time. That was last fall.

"I came to the congress with the same growth, apparently unaffected by any attempts to cure it. But after attending the healing meeting at the congress yesterday I left with firm faith that I would get the healing I had asked for. When I retired I noticed the tumor was still on my body, but when I awoke this morning it had disappeared."

The chronicles of every religion are full of just such miracles. And the reason for them is the same in every case—*prayer* and *faith*. Given these, no healing is impossible.

Suppose we go back for a moment to the lowly Amoeba, the first bit of animal life upon the earth. I know not whether you are Fundamentalist or Evolutionist. The facts are a bit harder to prove from the Evolution side of it, so let us argue from that angle.

The Amoeba, as you will recall from Chapter I, is the lowest form of animal life known to scientists, a sort of jellyfish with but a single cell—without brains, without intelligence, possessing only LIFE. No one would ever contend that this jellyfish could improve itself. No one would argue that it developed the next form of life out of its own mind or ideas.

Yet, according to science, the next form of life did develop from this jelly-like mass. The Amoeba certainly was not responsible for doing it. And it couldn't develop itself. So the conclusion is forced upon us that some outside Intelligence must have done it.

But there were no other living creatures. The Amoeba was alone of all animal life upon the planet. The condition of the water and atmosphere was such that few if any other forms of animals could have sustained life at that time. So the Intelligence which developed the next form of animal life must have been the same that created the Amoeba—that first brought LIFE to this Planet. That Intelligence is variously called God, Providence, Nature, the Life Principle, Mind, etc. For our purposes here let us call it Universal Mind.

Having formed life here on earth, Universal Mind proceeded to develop it. Starting with a single cell, It built cell upon cell, changing each form of life to meet the different conditions of atmosphere and environment that the cooling of the earth crust brought about. When the multi-cellular structure became complicated, It gave a brain to it to direct the different functions, just as you put a "governor" on a steam engine. When land appeared and the receding tides left certain animals high and dry for periods of hours, It gave these both lungs and gills—the one for the air, the other for the water.

When the creatures began to prey upon one another, It gave one speed, another a shell, a third an ink-like fluid, that each in its own way might escape and survive.

But always It progressed. Each new stage of life was an improvement over the previous one. And always It showed Its resourcefulness, Its ability to meet ANY need.

Finally, as the culmination of all Its efforts, It made MAN—a creature endowed not only with a brain like that of the lower animals, but with the power of reason—"made in His image and likeness," sharing Infinite Intelligence—himself a Creator and a part of Universal Mind.

All through the creation—from the time of the one-celled Amoeba right up to Man—every scientist will admit that the directing intelligence of Universal Mind was on the job every minute, that It formed the models on which each new and different kind of animal was made, that each of these models was perfect—the one model best fitted to cope with the conditions it had to confront.

Certainly when It came to Man, It is not likely to have been any less successful in forming a perfect model than it was in making the tiger or the elephant. So we can take it, I assume, that all will admit that Man as formed by Universal Mind is perfect—that the idea of Man as it exists in Universal Mind is perfect in every particular.

And Universal Mind, from the very beginning, has never taken a step backward, has never stood still. Always it has PROGRESSED. So it would seem safe to assume that man is not going backward now—that he is a more perfect creature than he was 5,000, 10,000 or 100,000 years ago—that he is constantly drawing nearer and nearer the likeness of his Creator.

The next step seems just as logical. If there was inherent in even the earliest and lowest forms of life the power to develop whatever means was requisite to meet each new emergency, such as a shell or lungs or legs or wings—if this power is still inherent in the lower forms of life such as the Plant Parasites referred to in a previous chapter, does it not seem a certainty that *we* have the same power within ourselves, if only we knew how to call it forth?

Jesus proved that we have, and his disciples and followers added still further proof. After the third century of the Christian era, that power was allowed to lapse through disuse, but of late years thousands have been taking advantage of it for themselves and for others through psychology or religion. A new Church has been founded upon the words of James: "Faith without WORKS is dead." It differs from most Churches in that it teaches that Jesus meant ALL that he said when he commanded his disciples to—"Go, preach, saying, The kingdom of heaven is at hand. *Heal the sick,* cleanse the lepers, raise the dead, cast out devils; freely ye have received, freely give." The sick, the lame, the halt and the blind have flocked to it literally by the hundred thousands. That thousands have been cured is beyond dispute. That many were cases which had been given up by the medical fraternity, the doctors quite frankly admit.

And the basis of all these cures is that there is nothing miraculous about the cure of disease at all. That it is "Divinely Natural." That it requires merely understanding. That Mind is the only Creator. And that the only image Universal Mind holds of your body is a perfect image, neither young nor old, but full of health, of vigor, of beauty and vitality. That all you have to do when assailed by disease is to go back to Universal Mind for a new conception of its perfect image—for the Truth concerning your body. Just as you would go back to the principle of mathematics for the Truth concerning any problem that worked out incorrectly. When you can make your subconscious mind copy after this Universal image—the *Truth*—instead of the diseased image you are holding in your thoughts, your sickness will vanish like the mere dream it is.

Does that sound too deep? Then look at it this way:

When you think an organ is diseased, it is your conscious mind that thinks this. Inevitably it sends this thought through to your subconscious mind, and the latter proceeds to build the cells of that organ along this imperfect, diseased model. Change the model—in other words, change your belief—and your subconscious mind will go back again to building along right lines.

Your body, you know, is simply an aggregation of millions upon millions of protons and electrons, held together by mind. They are the universal substance all about us, the plastic clay from which the sculptor Mind shapes the forms you see.

To quote the New York *Sun:* "Man's body is made up of trillions of miniature solar systems, each with whirling planets and a central sun. These tiny systems are the atoms of modern science. The atoms of all elements are made up of protons and electrons in varying quantities and arranged in various ways.

"But what are protons and electrons?

"The masters of physics have succeeded in weighing and measuring them. We know that they carry the smallest possible charges of electricity, and we are learning much about the way they behave; but students are beginning to doubt that they have real substance, that they are anything one could hit with a lilliputian hammer. Dr. H. G. Gale of the University of Chicago, addressing the Ohio Academy of Science the other day, said there was good reason to believe that electrons were composed entirely of electricity and that their mass or weight was only a manifestation of electrical force. According to this view, *nothing exists in the universe except electricity*—and perhaps ether."

Your subconscious mind partakes of the creative power of Mind and because of that, it is daily, hourly, changing the particles of electrical energy which constitute your body to conform to the image you hold before it.

The clay cannot reply to the sculptor. No more can these tiny particles of electricity. Your body has nothing to say as to whether it shall be diseased or crippled. It is MIND that decides this. Jesus understood this, and it was on the basis of this understanding that he was able to cure any and all manner of disease. He was not a magician or occult wonder-worker, aiming to set aside the laws of nature. He was a TEACHER, demonstrating those laws. He didn't pick the learned Scribes and Pharisees and let them in on the secret of his wonder working. On the contrary, the men he chose were simple fisher folk, and to them he gave the UNDERSTANDING that enabled them, too, to cure the sick, the halt and the blind.

For what is sickness? An illusion, a mortal dream—merely the *absence* of health. Bring back that health image, and the sickness immediately disappears. Universal Mind never created disease. The only image it knows of man is the *Truth*—the perfect image. The only idea it has of your body is a perfect, healthy idea. "For God is of purer eyes than to behold evil."

Then where does disease come from? Who created it? *No one did.* It is a mere illusion—just as, if you think a pin is sticking you, and you concentrate your thought on the pain, it becomes unbearable. Yet when you investigate, you find that no pin was sticking you at all—merely a hair, or bit of cinder lodged against the skin. How often have you had some fancied pain, only to have it promptly disappear when your physician assured you there was nothing wrong with you at all. It would be the same way with all sickness, all pain, if you would understand that it is merely fear or suggestion working on your conscious mind, and that if you will deny this belief of pain or sickness, your subconscious mind will speedily make that denial good. Don't render that mind impotent by thoughts of fear, doubt and anxiety. If you do, it is going to get like a working crew which is constantly being stopped by strikes or walk-outs or changes of plans. It will presently get discouraged and stop trying.

To quote Dr. Geo. E. Pitzer again—"In proper, healthy or normal conditions of life, the objective mind and the subjective mind act in perfect harmony with each other. When this is the case, healthy and happy conditions always prevail. But these two minds are not always permitted to act in perfect harmony with each other; this brings mental disturbances; excites physical wrongs, functional and organic diseases.

"Our unconscious is a tremendous storage plant full of potential energy which can be expended for beneficial or harmful ends. Like every apparatus for storing up power, it can be man's most precious ally, if man is familiar with it and, hence, not afraid of it. Ignorance and fear, on the other hand, can transform a live electric wire into an engine of destruction and death."

Even as long ago as Napoleon's day, men had begun to get an inkling of this. "Think that you are well," said the astute Tallyrand, "instead of thinking that you are sick." And the formula of the Quakers is that an energetic soul is "master of the body which it loves."

So keep in mind the one basic fact that covers the whole ground—that *Mind is all*. There is no other cause. When you drive the belief in disease from your subconscious mind, you will drive away the pain and all the other symptoms with it.

Few sick people have any idea how much they can do for themselves. There is an old saying that every man is "a fool or his own physician at 40." When the science of Mind is more generally understood, that saying will become literally true. Every man will find within himself the Mind which "healeth all thy diseases." For every function of your body is governed by your mind. When sickness or pain assails you, *deny it!* Cling steadfastly to the one idea that covers all—that Universal Mind made your every organ perfect; that the only image of each organ now in Universal Mind is this perfect image; and that this perfect idea is endowed with resources sufficient to meet any need.

Jesus' command—"Be ye therefore perfect, even as your father in Heaven is perfect,"—was meant to be taken literally. And it can be followed literally if we will model our bodies upon the image He holds of us in Universal Mind. We are all sculptors, you know, but instead of marble or clay, our material is the plastic energy—protons and electrons—of which we and everything in this world about us are made. What are you making of it? What image are you holding in mind? Images of sickness? Of poverty? Of Limitation? Then you are reproducing these in your life.

Banish them! Forget them! Never let them enter your thought, and they will never again manifest themselves in your life.

You admit that mind influences your body to some extent, but you think your physical organs hold the preponderance of power. So you depend upon them, and make yourself their slave.

"Know ye not," says Paul, "that to whom ye yield yourselves servants to obey, his servants ye are to whom ye obey?"

By holding before yourself the thought that your organs are the master, you make them your master, and deprive yourself of the directing intelligence of your subconscious mind. When an organ ceases to function properly, you try to doctor it, when the part that needs attention is your mind. If you are running an electric machine, and the current becomes weak or is switched off, you don't take the machine part, or oil it or tamper with it to make it run better. You go to the source of the power to find what is wrong there.

In the same way, when anything seems wrong with the functioning of your body, the place to investigate is your subconscious mind. Your stomach has no intelligence, nor your heart, nor your liver, nor any other of your organs. Your liver, for instance, could never figure out how much sugar should be turned into your blood every minute to keep your bodily temperature at 98 degrees, when you are sitting in a room that is warmed to only 65 degrees. It doesn't know how much more sugar is required to keep that temperature normal when you go out into a driving gale 10 below zero. Yet it supplies the requisite amount—neither too much nor too little. And it does it instantaneously. Where does it get the information? *You* don't know it. No mortal man could figure it out in a year's time.

It gets it from your subconscious mind. It gets both the information and the directions to use it. And every other of your bodily organs gets its information in the same place. Your muscles are not self-acting. Take away mind and those muscles are just like any other bit of matter—lifeless, inert. They have nothing to say as to what they shall do. They merely obey the behests of mind.

Have you ever seen one of those great presses at work in a newspaper plant? They seem almost human in their intelligence. At one end, great rolls of paper feed in. At the other, out comes the finished newspaper, folded, ready for delivery. Everything is automatic. Everything as perfect as machinery can be made. The "fingers" that fold the papers seem almost lifelike in their deftness.

But shut off the life-giving electric current—and what happens? The machinery is powerless. Take away the directing human intelligence, and how long before that wonderful machine would be a mass of scrap—mere bits of steel and rubber? How long could it function of itself?

So it is with your body. A wonderful mechanism—the most complicated, yet the most perfect in the world. But switch off the current of your mental dynamo, take away the intelligence that directs the working of your every organ, and what is left? A bit of bone and flesh—inert and useless.

In the final analysis, your body is merely a piece of mechanism—dependent entirely upon mind. It has no power, no volition, of its own. It does as mind tells it to, insofar as mind believes itself to be the Master. Your eyes, for instance, are merely lenses which transmit light from the outer world to the brain within. They contract or elongate, they open or close, just as mind directs. And mind, in its turn, keeps them constantly nourished with new, life-giving blood, replacing old tissue, old cells, as fast as they wear out, rebuilding ever, so that your eyes may continue to function perfectly as long as your conscious mind is dependent upon them for its impressions of outer objects. It doesn't matter how old you may be or how much you use them. Your eyes are like any other muscles of your body—they improve in strength with use. Give them but enough rest intervals for mind to repair and rebuild the used tissue, keep before your subconscious mind the perfect image of eyes on which you expect it to rebuild, and you need never fear glasses, you need never worry about "your eyes going back on you."

What is it happens when your muscles refuse to work—fail to perform their functions properly? *You* are what has happened. You have switched off the current from some particular part. You have been holding the belief so long and so firmly that the muscles have the preponderance of power, that your subconscious mind has come to believe it, too. And when the nerve or muscle suffers an injury, the subconscious mind—at the suggestion of your conscious mind—gives up all dominion over it.

All disease, all sickness, all imperfections of the human body are due to this one cause—your belief that your body is the master, that it can act, that it can catch cold, or become diseased, without the consent of mind. This is the procuring cause of all suffering. One disease is no different from another in this. They are all due to that one erroneous belief.

If you will deny the power of your body over your mind, you can destroy all fear of disease. And when the fear goes, the foundation of the disease is gone.

The way to begin is to *refuse to believe* or to heed any complaint from your body. Have no fear of climate or atmosphere, of dampness or drafts. It is only when you believe them unhealthy that they are so to you. When your stomach sends a report of distress, when it tells you that something you have eaten is disagreeing with it, treat it as you would an unruly servant. Remind it that it is not the judge of what is or is not good for it. That it has no intelligence. That it is merely a channel through which the food you give it passes for certain treatment and selection. That if the food is not good it has but to pass it through to the eliminatory organs as speedily as may be.

Your stomach is entirely capable of doing this. Every organ you have is capable of withstanding any condition—given the right state of mind to direct it. The only reason that they succumb to sickness or disease or injury is because you tell them to. Men have fallen from great heights without injury. Men have taken the most deadly poison without harm. Men have gone through fire and flood and pestilence with not a scratch to show. And what men have done once they can do again. The fact that it *has* been done shows that your body does not *need* to suffer injury from these conditions. And if it does not need to, then it would seem that the only reason it ordinarily suffers is because your fear of injury is the thought you are holding before your subconscious mind and therefore that is the thought that it images on your body.

In a despatch from Stockholm to the New York *Herald-Tribune,* dated January 18, 1926, I read that Dr. Henry Markus and Dr. Ernest Sahlgren, Stockholm scientists, have been able, through hypnotic suggestion, to offset the effect of poisons on the human system to a marked degree.

The scientists put three subjects into hypnotic sleep and then administered drugs, carefully recording the effects on blood pressure and pulse, both with and without "suggestion." When a drug which acts to increase blood pressure was administered without "suggestion," the blood pressure readings ranged between 109 to 130 and pulse readings from 54 to 100. But when the drug was administered with the "suggestion" to the mind of the patient that it was merely so much harmless water, the blood pressures were from 107 to 116 and pulse readings all less than 67. From which one would judge that it was the patient's *belief* which affected him, far more than any power in the drug.

Bear this in mind when anyone tells you that certain foods are not good for you. You can eat what you like, if you do it in moderation. Just remember—no matter what you may eat—if you relish it, if you BELIEVE it to be good for you, *it will be good for you!*

But, you may say, is not this like the tenets of a well-known religion? What of that? If certain fundamental truths have been uncovered by another why not use them, regardless of whether or not we agree with the philosophy from which they are taken.

To quote again from Dr. Richard C. Cabot of the Harvard Medical School:

"There need be no conflict. There is opportunity for all sincere, humble-minded effort. Let us have no persecutions and no interference with the spread of truth and light from any source. Indictments against movements as powerful and sincere as Christian Science and Preventive Medicine are anachronistic.

Let us all get busy along our own lines. 'With malice towards none, with charity for all, let us bind up the nation's wounds.'"

It has often seemed to me that if all the churches would take a leaf out of the book of ordinary Business Practice, forget their differences over dogma, and simply profit by the example that Mary Baker Eddy, Discoverer and Founder of Christian Science, has given them of building up an enormous following almost overnight, they would be much the better off thereby.

For what was it brought men and women into the Church in such vast numbers in the early day of Christianity? *Healing!* What was responsible for the phenomenal growth of the Christian Science Church? The *healing* of thousands of people of any and every kind of ill. What is it that people go to any Church for? To pray—*and to find how to get an answer to their prayers.* Show them the way to do this, show them the way to *heal* themselves of all their ills and lacks, and you will need to worry no more about the crowded theaters and the empty churches.

"If this be treason, make the most of it."

The moment any symptom of illness shows in your body, vigorously deny its existence. Say to yourself—"My body has no intelligence. Neither has any germ of disease. Therefore neither my body nor the disease can tell me I am sick. Mind is the only cause. And Mind has not directed them to make me sick. The only image of my body that Mind knows is a perfect, vigorous, healthy image. And that is the only image I am going to build on." Then forget the image of disease. It is only an illusion, and can be dispelled like any other illusion. Keep in your mind's eye the image of perfect health, of vigorous, boundless vitality.

Your body can not say it is sick. Therefore when the belief of sickness assails you, it must come either from your conscious mind or from outside suggestion. In either event, it is your job to see that no belief of sickness reaches your subconscious mind, that no fear of it, no thought of it, is imaged there.

To treat one who has already succumbed to the belief of sickness, explain to him, as I have explained to you here, that his body has no power for sickness or for health, any more than a log of wood has. That his body is merely an aggregation of millions of electrons—particles of electrical energy, really—subject wholly to his mind. That these particles of energy have neither substance nor intelligence; that they are constantly changing; and that the forms they take depend entirely upon the images he holds in his own mind.

His body is, in short, a mental concept. It is an exact reflection of the thought he is holding in mind of it. If he has been sick, it is because he has been holding sickly, weak and unhealthy thoughts in his mind. If he wishes to get well, it is first necessary for him to change his thought. Instead of doctoring the machine, he is to go direct to the power house and change the current. Let him repeat to himself, night and morning, this little formula:

"There is no permanence to matter. The one surest thing about it is *change*. Every cell, every tissue in my body is constantly being renewed. The old, worn-out tissues are being torn down and carried away. New, perfect ones are replacing them. And the model on which those new organisms are being re-built is the perfect model that is held in Divine Mind.

"For God made man in His image. That image was perfect then—*is* perfect now. It is the only image that Divine Mind knows of me. It is the only image on which my subconscious mind is ever again going to pattern its re-building. Every minute of every day I am growing more and more into the image of God—the *True Likeness* He holds of me in His thought."

If he will do that, if he will bear in mind that matter as such has no feeling, no intelligence; that it is the mind that feels, the mind that directs, and therefore he has nothing to fear from any external causes, his fear of the disease will vanish. And the patient does not exist who will not speedily recover when his fear of the disease is gone.

"Verily, verily, I say unto you," said Jesus, "if a man keep my saying, he shall never see death." And again—"This is the life eternal." *"Is,"* you will notice, not "shall be."

"The subconscious mind is God's way of utilizing His energy," says the Rev. William T. Walsh, Rector of St. Luke's Church, New York City, in his book "Scientific Spiritual Healing." "God evolved the subconscious mind. It is His gift to us like all else that we possess, and because it is from Him we should give thanks and learn to use it intelligently.

"God has so fashioned us that we do not have to give conscious attention to the vital processes. He has given us what is called the subconscious mind which looks after all the vital functions. This mind can receive commands from us and has wonderful ability to carry them out, for it is a law that *every thought tends to realize itself* subconsciously in the body.

"If you allow evil thoughts to remain, they are received by the subconscious which tends to realize them in the body just as much as though they were good, wholesome, health-giving spiritual thoughts. For remember, the subconscious does not reason and judge. It only receives and obeys."

When you have an accident, don't immediately think that you must be hurt. On the contrary, deny at once that you can be hurt. The denial will take away the creative power of your thought from any damaging condition. More than that, if you will immediately call to mind the fact that the only image of your body that Universal Mind holds is a perfect image, and that this is the image on which your subconscious mind is building, you will find that this subconscious mind will speedily rebuild any damaged parts in accordance with that image.

As a matter of fact, if we could thoroughly realize that our bodies are made up merely of vortices of energy subject wholly to the control of mind, it should hurt us no more to run a knife through them than it does to run it through water. The water immediately resumes the shape of the vessel that holds it. Just so, our bodies should immediately resume the shape that mind holds them in.

But even with our present imperfect understanding, we can perform what the uninitiated would call miracles with our bodies. And each victory we win gives us a bit more of power over them. To conquer one diseased condition makes it easier to ward off or to conquer other diseased conditions. The body cannot oppose us. It is only the bias of education and the suggestions of those about us that we have to combat.

There is no necessity for disease. There is no necessity even for fatigue. "They that wait upon the Lord shall run and not be weary; and they shall walk and not faint." Those words from Holy Writ were meant literally—and they can be applied literally if you will govern your body by mind, and not let custom and popular belief make your body the master. Whatever it is right for you to do, you can do without fear, no matter if it entails long-continued toil, hardship or danger. Depend upon it, your mind can call to your aid all the forces of Nature if they are necessary to your emergency.

"Therefore I say unto you," quoth the Master, "take no thought for your life, what ye shall eat, or what ye shall drink; nor yet for your body, what ye shall put on. Is not the life more than meat and the body than raiment?"

Diet, exercise and rules of health never kept any one well of themselves. Often they attract the mind to the subject of sickness and thereby foster it.

Dieting is good insofar as it prevents gluttony. Temperance is just as important in eating as in the drinking of alcoholic liquor. But you can eat in moderation anything you like, anything that you relish and BELIEVE to be good for you, without fear of its disagreeing with you.

Reasonable exercise, too, is fine for both the body and the mind. Provided you do not make a fetich of it. It isn't the exercise that keeps you well—it is the mental image you hold in your thought.

The exercise merely helps to impress that mental image on your subconscious mind.

Electrical treatments, skin tonics, alcohol rubs, etc., all are useful only to the extent that they center the attention of the subconscious mind upon the parts affected. Exactly the same results, even to that pleasant little tingling of the skin, can be effected by mind alone. I remember reading an article by Mrs. Vance Cheney, telling how she cured herself of paralysis of the legs in just that way. After lying for months under the care of doctors and masseurs, she tired of them and decided to depend entirely upon mind. So, several times a day, she would utterly relax in every nerve and muscle, then consciously send her thought down along the nerves of her legs to her feet. Presently there would be that little tingling sensation in her feet—evidence of increased circulation—followed after a time by a feeling of drowsiness. A few weeks of these treatments completely restored the use of her legs.

The same effort can be made to throw off any physical trouble. Put your hand upon the part affected. Try to visualize that organ as it should be. See it functioning perfectly. BELIEVE that it IS working normally again! Your thought brings the blood to the affected part, clears up the trouble, provides new cells, new tissue, while your belief that the organ IS functioning properly will bring about that normal condition.

This is a treatment, however, that must be used with discretion, for to consciously interfere in the regular functioning of the body without any real need for such interference results in confusion rather than help. It is like going down a flight of stairs rapidly. Pay no attention to the movement of your feet, and they flit over the steps with never a sign of hesitancy or faltering. But try to watch them step by step, and you will either have to slow up or you will presently miss a step, stumble or fall.

> *"The centipede was happy quite,*
> *Until the toad, for fun,*
> *Said, 'Pray, which leg goes after which?'*
> *This stirred his mind to such a pitch,*
> *He lay distracted in a ditch,*
> *Considering how to run."*

There is one rule that will help anyone keep healthy. That rule is to forget your nerves, throw away your pills and your medicine bottles, and hold before your mind's eye only the perfect image that Universal Mind has of your body. That is the surest way to keep free from sickness.

And if you are already sick, the same rule applies. Know that Universal Mind never created disease—that it is but an illusion of your conscious mind. Know that mind is the only creator, that as Shakespeare puts it, "There is nothing, either good or bad, but thinking makes it so." Know that you have the say as to what that thinking shall be. Know, therefore, that by holding a perfect image of your body in your thoughts you can make your body perfect.

Have you ever cut your finger? Who was it coagulated the blood, stopped the gash, wove new skin? Who was it called upon the little phagocytes to come and kill the septic germs?

Not your conscious mind, certainly. Most people don't even know there are "any such animals." Their conscious minds don't know the first thing about healing. Whence comes the information? Whence the directing genius? Where but from the same intelligence that keeps your heart and lungs on the job while you sleep, that regulates your liver and your kidneys, that attends to all the functions of your body?

That intelligence is your subconscious mind. With the proper co-operation on your part, your subconscious mind will attend to these duties indefinitely, keeping your every organ perfect, your every function regular as clockwork.

But it is exceedingly amenable to suggestion. Worry about sickness or contagion, hold before it the thought that you are getting old, or that some organ is becoming feeble, and it will be perfectly agreeable to bringing about the condition you suggest. Convince it that there is no danger from contagion, hold before it the thought of health and strength, and it will be just as prompt in manifesting them.

So what you must realize is this: Before anything can be made, there must be a model for it in mind. Before a house can be built, there must be a plan, a blueprint from which to build. Before you were created, Universal Mind held in thought the model on which you were made. That model was perfect then—is perfect now. The only idea of you that Universal Mind knows is a perfect model, where every cell and organism is formed along perfect lines.

True, many of us have built up imperfect models in our own thoughts, but we can get rid of them just as rapidly as we get rid of the fear of them.

Your body is changing every moment. Every cell, every organism, is constantly being rebuilt. Why rebuild along the old, imperfect lines? Why not build on the lines held in the thought of Universal Mind? You CAN do it! But the essence of it lies in the words of the Master: "Whatsoever things ye desire when ye pray, believe that ye RECEIVE them, and ye SHALL HAVE them."

It matters not what your ailment may be. It will respond to that treatment. Suppose, as an example, that your stomach has been troubling you, that you cannot eat what you would like, that you cannot assimilate your food, that you are weak and nervous is consequence. Every morning when you awake, and every night just before you drop off to sleep say to yourself—

"My stomach has neither intelligence nor feeling. It functions only as mind directs it. Therefore I need have no worry about its being weak or diseased, for the only image that Mind knows of stomach is Its perfect image. And that perfect image can assimilate or remove anything I may put into it. It is perfect, as everything that Universal Mind makes is perfect. And being perfect, it can do anything right I may ask of it without fear or anxiety."

Concentrate on the one organ at a time, and repeat this formula to yourself night and morning. Say it, *feel* it, BELIEVE it—and you can do what you please with that organ. "As thy faith is, so be it done unto thee."

"SUFFER LITTLE CHILDREN TO COME UNTO ME"

"I can believe all you say about my fears and worries being responsible for my own illnesses," write many people, "but how about infants and little children? They have no fear. Why do they sicken and die?"

What many people do not understand is that the subconscious mind is just as amenable to suggestion from those round about you as it is from your own conscious mind. Otherwise you would be in no danger from anything you did not consciously know of. And the more ignorant you were, the safer you would be.

Suppose, for instance, you took a draught of what you believed to be pure "bootleg" whisky, but which in reality was no more than wood alcohol. Many others have done it. Your conscious mind would expect no harm from it—any more than did theirs. You would have no fear of the result. No more did they. So, you would say, you should experience no harm.

Yet you would probably die—or at least go blind—as have these others. Why? Because your subconscious mind would know the wood alcohol for what it is. Your own conscious belief, and the preponderance of opinion of those about you, have instilled the conviction in your subconscious mind that wood alcohol is dire poison. Therefore when you pour this poison into your system—even though you do not consciously recognize it as such—your subconscious mind proceeds to bring about the effects you would logically expect such a poison to produce.

It is the same with contagion, with the hundreds of diseases which most people scarcely know the names of, but to which they are constantly falling victims. They don't know they have been exposed to contagion. They don't know that their systems are in such condition that certain diseases logically follow. But their subconscious minds do know it. And they have so thoroughly educated those minds to believe in the necessity for ill health, in the inevitability of sickness under certain conditions, that the subconscious proceeds to work out the contagion or the condition to its logical conclusion.

Grown people can change these subconscious convictions by the proper counter-suggestions, consciously given. But young children cannot reason. They accept the beliefs that are held by the generality of mankind, or that are strongly suggested to them by those nearest to them.

That is why babies and young children fall such easy victims to the fears of disease and contagion of their parents and those about them. That is why worry over a seeming epidemic so often results in the children catching it, even when they have apparently been in no way exposed to the contagion.

"Man," says a famous writer, "often has fear stamped upon him before his entrance into the outer world; he is reared in fear; all his life is passed in bondage of fear of disease and death and thus his whole mentality becomes cramped, limited, and depressed, and his body follows its shrunken pattern and specification. IS IT NOT SUPRISING THAT HEALTH EXISTS AT ALL? Nothing but the boundless Divine Love, exuberance, and vitality, constantly poured in, even though unconsciously to us, could in some degrees neutralize such an ocean of morbidity."

But the remedy is just as simple. Know that your children are primarily children of God. That the image He holds of them is perfect. And that His perfect image has within itself every power necessary to ward off disease of any kind.

Put your children actively under His care. Throw the responsibility upon Him. Depend upon it, when you do this in the right way, no harm can come near them. Whenever fear assails you, whenever your children are exposed to danger or contagion, realize that "He shall give His angels (his thoughts) charge over them, to lead them in all their ways."

If your children are sick or ailing, read these thoughts aloud to them just as though you were talking to a grown person. Only address yourself to their subconscious minds. Read over the past few pages. Repeat to them the little formula outlined above, adapting it to their own particular need. Above all, BELIEVE it! Your faith will work just as great wonders for your children as for yourself.

Never doubt. Never fear. Go at your problem just as you would approach a difficult problem in mathematics. In mathematics, you know that the problem does not exist for which you cannot find the solution, provided you follow the rules and work in the right way.

As long as you do your part, the principle of mathematics will do the rest. It is the same in all of life. Don't worry. Don't fret. Go at your problem in the right way, no matter how difficult it may seem; follow the rules herein laid down, and you can confidently look to the Principle of Being to bring you the answer.

L'ENVOI

"The Kingdom of Heaven is like unto a treasure hid in a field; the which when a man hath found, he hideth, and for joy thereof goeth and selleth all that he hath, and buyeth that field." This field is your own consciousness—a treasure you find within yourself—which others cannot see. But *you* know it for the indwelling Spirit—"the Father within you"—and are willing to sell all that you have because this treasure is worth more than all other possessions.

If you have begun to realize this treasure, and use it even in a small way, the most wonderful thing that can happen to anyone on this planet has happened to you. What does it mean? It means that an ordinary human being, afflicted with all the sufferings and fears and worries and superstitions of the average man, has learned the Law of Being. It means that he has acquired a power above all that of his would-be destroyers. It means that he has put his foot upon the Rock of Life, that the Doorway of Heaven is open before him, that all of Good is as free to him as the air he breathes.

"There hath not failed one word of all His good promises." "And we declare unto you glad tidings, how that the promise which was made unto the fathers, God hath fulfilled the same unto us."

Surely we have every reason to be grateful for all the good round about us. Surely we should be thankful for the infinite power that has been given to us.

And being truly grateful, by the way, is the surest evidence of real faith that there is. Faith, you know, is "the substance of things hoped for, the evidence of things not seen." Remember, when Jesus raised Lazarus from the dead, how He first prayed, *then thanked the Father for answering His prayer?* There was not yet any material evidence that the prayer had been answered. But Jesus had perfect faith in the Father. And it was justified. Immediately He had given thanks, Lazarus *came forth from the tomb!*

The world today is so much more wonderful than it was to former generations. Mankind has begun to glimpse its illimitable powers. The whole world is plastic and sensitive to new ideas. The soul of man is finding itself, and learning its relation to the Infinite. The veil between the visible and the invisible is being drawn aside. Through seeing the "Father do the works," we are becoming more assured of our own power, beginning to assert "the Father that is within us." We know that, given the right understanding, the works that Jesus did we can do also. We recognize his "miracles" as divinely natural laws, part of God's continuous plan.

So let us go with Him unto the Mount of Vision, taking as our motto His words—"See that thou make all things according to the pattern shewed thee in the Mount."

Index of Scriptural References and Quotations

These passages are quoted from the King James version of the Bible. Authorized, Revised, and from various modern translations.

Thou art of purer eyes than to behold—Habakkuk 1:13, vol. vii, page 590

Thou shall love the Lord—Matthew 22:37, 38, vol. iv, page 311

Thou wilt show me the path—Psalms 16:11, vol. iii, page 166

Thy faith hath made thee whole—Luke 8:48, vol. vii, page 575

To him that hath—Matthew 25:29, vol. ii, page 107, 108

To know aright is life—John 17:3, vol. v, page 389

Trust in the Lord and—Psalms 37:3, vol. iv, page 365

Twenty-third psalm—vol. ii, page 156

Verily, verily I say unto you—John 8:51, vol. vii, page 611

We shall see Him as he is—I John 3:2, vol. i, page 57

What eye never saw—I Corinthians 2:9, vol. iii, page 206

What things soever ye—Mark 11:24, vol. ii, page 110, 111, 139, 148; vol. v, page 462;
    vol. vi, page 469; vol. vii, page 574, 623

What wouldst thou that I—Mark 10:51, vol. vii, page 573

Where there is no vision—Proverbs 29:18, vol. iii, page 191

Who hath measured the waters—Isaiah 40:12, vol. v, page 390

Who healeth all thy diseases—Psalms 103:3, vol. vii, page 593

Whosoever shall be great—Matthew 20:26, 27, vol. iv, page 312

Whosoever liveth and believeth—John 11:26, vol. vi, page 528

Whosoever shall compel thee—Matthew 5:41, vol. iv, page 313

Whosoever will let him take—Revelation 22:17, vol. i, page 70

With all thy getting—Proverbs 4.7, vol. i, page 70; vol. iii, page 175

Work out your own salvation—Philippians 2:12, vol. iv, page 330

Wouldst thou be made whole—John 5:16, vol. vii, page 573

Ye shall ask what ye will—John 15:7, vol. ii, page 125

Ye shall know the truth—John 8:32, vol. iv, page 287, 290; vol. vii, page 575

Your Father knoweth that ye—Luke 12:30, vol. iii, page 229

The Secret
of Gold

How to Get What You Want

ROBERT COLLIER

Contents

The Riddle of the Sphinx

THAT is it," asked the Sphinx, "that walks on four legs in the morning, on two legs at noon and on three legs in the evening?"

And all who passed her way had to answer that question—*or be devoured!*

That was the Riddle of the Sphinx of olden days. But to modern man has come a far more difficult one—

"How can I earn more money? How can I make enough to get the necessities and the comforts of life to which my family and I are entitled?"

That is the eternal question which confronts you and will haunt you every day until you solve it. That is the present-day Riddle of the Sphinx that devours all who fail to answer it.

For *lack* is the greatest evil that mankind has to contend with.

Yet every man knows that in this old earth of ours are riches and abundance sufficient not merely for every soul now on this planet—but for all who ever will be! And in the very first chapter of the Bible, it is written that "God gave man dominion over all the earth."

Not only that, but more than half the prophecies in the Scriptures refer to the time when man shall possess the earth. When tears and sorrow shall be unknown. When riches and abundance shall be yours for the taking.

That time is here—here and now for those who understand the power and the availability of that mysterious, half recognized Spirit within which so few people know, but which, fully understood, *can do anything*.

But in no book ever written is there any complete explanation of this Spirit within, any complete directions for availing one's-self of its infinite power and understanding.

In no book, that is, but one!

And in the following pages I shall show you what that one Book is and where to find the directions which tell you how to harness this truly illimitable power, how to make it bring to you anything of good you may desire. For—

"There hath not failed one word of all His good promises, which He promised by the hand of Moses, His servant."—I. KINGS, 8:56

—ROBERT COLLIER

"Then opened He their understanding,
that they might understand the Scriptures."
—LUKE 24:25

1

The Genii of the Lamp

"Thou gavest also Thy Good Spirit to instruct them, and withheldest not thy manna from their mouth, and gavest them water for their thirst."

—NEHEMIAH 9:20

IN AN ancient town in far off Cathay, there once lived a poor young man named Aladdin. His father had been a tailor, but died before he could teach his profession to his son, and the boy and his widowed mother were frequently hard put to get enough to eat.

But despite his poverty, Aladdin was one of those cheerful souls who find life good. Many and often were the times that found him wandering joyfully in the mountains, when he should have been seeking the elusive yen in some odd job among his neighbors. And Fortune, looking down upon his cheery hopefulness, smiled—as has been the habit of Fortune since time began—for then, as now, she was a fickle jade, loving most those who worry least about her.

One day, wandering among the hills, Aladdin discovered a cave, its entrance closed by a great stone. Prying the stone away, he entered, and found therein a lamp burning upon a shelf. Thinking to use it at home, Aladdin stuck the lamp in his belt and, departing, took it with him.

Next morning, lacking the wherewithal for breakfast, he bethought him of this lamp, and since it looked old and tarnished, started to polish it in the hope of thus bringing for it a better price. What was his astonishment and terror to

see immediately appear before him a Genii of gigantic proportions, who, however, made humble obeisance: "I am the slave of the lamp," quoth he, "ready to
do the bidding of him who holds the lamp. What would you of me?"

Terrified though he was, Aladdin could understand that. So he took heart
of grace, and decided to see if this great Genii really was as good as his word.
"I am hungry," he therefore told him. "Bring me something to eat." The Genii
disappeared. An instant later he was back again with a sumptuous repast!

Aladdin ate and was satisfied. And when next he hungered, summoned
the Genii and ate again. Thereafter, to one so used to hunger, life was one
grand song—just one endless succession of eating and sleeping, sleeping and
eating again.

Until one day the Sultan's daughter passed that way. Her eyes had the mis-
chievous sparkle in their depths that has drawn hermits from their cells. Her
lips were twin rubies. Her teeth pearls.

So much Aladdin saw—and was enchanted. Life took on a new meaning.
There was more to it than eating and sleeping after all. Here was something to
live for, work for, hope for. Even though at the moment it never occurred to him
that he might ever hope to win such loveliness, such divinity, for himself.

But then he bethought him of his Genii. If the Genii could bring him
food, raiment, riches—why not position and power, too? Why not the Sultan's
daughter? Why not, in fact, the Sultan's place? He decided to try.

First he astonished the Sultan with the magnificence of the gifts with which
his good Genii furnished him. Then he built a palace more beautiful far than
that of the Sultan himself. Finally he presented himself as suitor for the hand
of the beautiful princess.

The Sultan laughed at the idea. But one cannot continue to laugh at a man
whose raiment is more costly, whose retinue more splendid, whose palace more
magnificent than one's own. One can only vie with him in splendour, and failing that—either fight him or take him into one's own camp.

The Sultan tried to vie with him. But princely riches could not compare
with those of the Genii. He tried fighting. But who could hope to cope with
the powers of the invisible world?

At last he decided to share that wealth, to benefit by that power. And so it
came about that Aladdin won the lovely Princess of his dreams.

Fairy tales—you will say. And of course, they are. But back of them is more
than mere childish fable. There is the Wisdom and the Mysticism of the East—so
frequently hidden in parable or fable.

For those Wise Men of the East had grasped, thousands of years ago, the fundamental fact—so hard for our Western minds to realize—that deep down within ourselves, far under our outer layers of consciousness, is a Power that far transcends the power of any conscious mind.

"The Holy Spirit within us," deeply religious people term it. And, truly, its power is little short of Divine.

"Our Subconscious Mind," so the Scientists call it.

Call it what you will, it is there—all unknown to most of us—a sleeping Giant who, aroused, can carry us on to fame and fortune over-night. A Genii-of-the-Brain more powerful, more the servant of our every right wish, than was ever Aladdin's fabled Genii-of-the-Lamp of old.

Health and happiness, power and riches, lie ready to its hand. You have but to wake it, to command it, to get of it what you will. It is part of you—yet its power is limitless. It is Mind—Thought—Idea. It is an all-powerful mental magnet that can draw to you anything you may desire.

Just as electricity turns the inert electric bulb into a thing of light and life— just as the gasoline vapor turns your motor into a creature of speed and action— just as steam awakens the locomotive into an engine of power and usefulness—so this mental magnet can vitalize YOU into a Being capable of accomplishing ANY TASK YOU MAY SET, capable of rising to any height, capable of winning love, honor and riches.

You have seen hypnotists put subjects to sleep. You have seen men and women, while in this hypnotic trance, do marvelous feats of mind reading or of mental arithmetic. You have seen others show wonderful endurance or physical strength.

I remember one hypnotist who, after putting his subject in a trance, would assure him that he (the subject) was a bar of iron. Then the hypnotist would stretch him out between two chairs—his head on one, his feet on another—and pile weights upon him, or have several people stand upon him. A feat of strength that the subject could never have accomplished in his ordinary mind. Yet did it without strain or difficulty under the influence of the hypnotist.

How did he do it? Simply by removing the control of the conscious mind—by putting it to sleep—and leaving the Subconscious in sole charge. The power is in your body to do anything—only your conscious mind doesn't believe that it is. Remove these conscious inhibitions—place the Subconscious in entire charge—and there is nothing beyond your capacity to perform.

The hypnotist does his tricks by putting your conscious mind to sleep and then suggesting to your Subconscious the things he wants it to do. But it is in no wise necessary to deal with the Subconscious through some third party. It is no part of the Divine plan that you must first put yourself under some outside control. On the contrary, those who learn to use their own Subconscious Minds can accomplish far greater wonders with their bodies, with their brains, with their fortunes than could any hypnotist for them.

It is to show you how to properly use this Genii-of-your-Mind, how to summon it, how to control it, that this Course is written.

"But where shall wisdom be found? And where is the place of understanding?"—JOB 28:12

There is a Spirit in man; and the inspiration of the Almighty giveth him understanding."—JOB 32:8

2

The Spirit Within

"Know ye not that ye are the temple of God, and that the Spirit
of God dwelleth in you?"

—I CORINTHIANS 3:16

You often hear a man spoken of as brainy. The idea being that he has more gray matter in his cranium than most of us. And for years the size of a man's head or the shape of his "bumps" was believed to indicate his mentality.

But science now shows that one man has just as good brains as another. Differences in weight or shape or size have nothing to do with it. Each of us has a perfect brain to start with. It is what we put *into* it and the way we *use* it that counts—not the size or weight!

Brains are merely the storehouse of the mind. They are not the mind itself. Each individual brain cell—and there are some nine billions of them—is like a phonograph record on which impressions are registered through the thousands of nerves from all over the body that center in the brain.

Once registered, that impression stays as long as the brain cell remains. When we have no occasion to use an impression for a long time, it is filed away in the nine-billion filing compartment—and apparently forgotten.

But it is never really forgotten. It can always be recalled by the proper suggestion to the subconscious mind. The only thing that can permanently destroy the impression is the removal of the brain cell itself. That is why injuries to the brain so frequently result in complete loss of memory as to many events in the individual's life.

But the registering of impressions is merely the first step. The animals have that. The next—and the step that puts man so far above all other creatures—is the reasoning mind. Mind uses the brain cells to recall any impression it may need. To compare them. To draw conclusions from them. In short, *to reason!*

That is the most important province of mind. But it has another—the regulating, governing and directing of the growth and functions of the body. So complicated an affair that no conscious mind in the universe could ever grope with it.

Yet the subconscious mind does it with ease—does it for the youngest infant as well as for you or me—in fact, frequently does it better.

From the earliest moment of our birth, the subconscious mind takes control. It directs the beating of the heart, the breathing of the lungs, the complicated processes of digestion and assimilation. And the less it is interfered with, the better work it does.

Your body is the most wonderful and complicated chemical factory in the world. Made up of water, coal, iron, lime, sugar, phosphorus, salt, hydrogen and iodine, no man living could figure out the changes made necessary in its composition from minute to minute by heat, by cold, by pressure from without or by food taken within. No chemist in all the world could tell you how much water you should drink to neutralize the excess salt in salt fish. How much you lose through perspiration. How much water, how much salt, how much of each different element in your food should be absorbed into your blood each day to maintain perfect health.

Yet your subconscious mind knows. Knows without effort. Knows even when you are an infant. And furthermore, acts immediately upon that knowledge.

To quote the Rev. Wm. T. Walsh:

The subconscious mind directs all the vital processes of our body. You do not think consciously about breathing. Every time you take a breath you do not have to reason, decide, command. The SUBCONSCIOUS MIND sees to that. You have not been at all conscious that you have been breathing while you have been reading this page. So it is with the mind and the circulation of blood. The heart is a muscle like the muscle of your arm. It has no power to move itself or to direct its action. Only mind, only something that can think, can direct our muscles, including the heart. You are not conscious that you are commanding your heart to beat. The subconscious mind attends to that. And so it is with the assimilation of food, the building and repairing of the body. In fact, all the vital processes are looked after by the subconscious mind.

Whence comes all this wonderful knowledge? Whence comes the intelligence that enables day-old infants to figure out problems in chemistry that would confound the most learned professors? Whence but from the same Mind that regulates the planets in their courses, that puts into the acorn the image of the mighty oak it is to be, and then shows it how to draw from the sunlight, from the air, from the earth, from the water, the nutriment necessary to build that image into reality.

That Mind is God. And the subconscious in us is our part of Divinity. It is the Holy Spirit that Jesus so often referred to.

"But when they shall lead you and deliver you up, take no thought beforehand what ye shall speak, neither do ye premeditate; but whatsoever shall be given you in that hour, that speak ye; for it is not ye that speak, but the Holy Ghost."—Mark 13

Christianity teaches one Universal God, Father of all things, *the life of all things animate.*

"For there are three that bear record in Heaven, the Father, the Word and the Holy Ghost; and these three are one."—I John 5:7

And modern science shows us that *all things are animate*—even the rocks and the dirt beneath our feet. Even the supposedly dead piece of paper on which these words are printed. All are made up of tiny particles called atoms. And the atoms in turn consist of protons and electrons—bits of electrical energy, so minute as to be invisible to the naked eye, but very much alive and constantly moving, constantly changing.

In *The Secret of the Ages*, the consistency of matter is explained in detail. For those who have not read this explanation, suffice it here to quote from the New York Herald-Tribune:

"We used to believe that the universe was composed of an unknown number of different kinds of matter, one kind for each chemical element. The discovery of a new element had all the interest of the unexpected. It might turn out to be anything, to have any imaginable set of properties.

"That romantic prospect no longer exists. We know now that instead of many ultimate kinds of matter there are only two kinds. Both of these are really kinds of electricity. One is negative electricity, being, in fact, the tiny particle called the electron, familiar to radio fans as one of the particles vast swarms of which operate radio vacuum tubes. The other kind of electricity is positive electricity. Its ultimate particles are called protons. From these protons and electrons all of the chemical elements are built up. Iron and lead and oxygen and gold and all the others differ from one another merely in the number and arrangement of the electrons and protons which they contain. That is the modern idea of the nature of matter. *Matter is really nothing but electricity.*"

Everything has life in it. And life is God. Therefore, everything in this world, everything in the heavens above, in the earth beneath, or in the waters under the earth, is a manifestation of God.

God is life. He is the life in us. And the life in all created things. He is the "Father" that was in Jesus—the Father that, "before Abraham was, I am"—the Father that did such wonderful works.

"Believest thou not that I am in the Father, and the Father in me? The words that I speak unto you, I speak not of myself; but the Father that dwelleth in me, He doeth the works. Believe me that I am in the Father, and the Father in me."—John 14:10–11

That same Father is in you. He is the life-force, the God-force, that flows through every atom of your being. Make yourself one with Him, and there is nothing you cannot do. "I and the Father are one," said Jesus. And His prayer was—"That they may all be one; as Thou, Father art in me and I in Thee, that they also may be one in us."

A great religious teacher once said that there are just two things in the Universe—God and His manifestations. Really there is just one—for God is *in* all His manifestations.

"If a man love me . . . my Father will love him and we will come unto him and make our abode with him."—John 14:23

THE MESSAGE OF JESUS

What was the real message of Jesus? What was the one unforgivable thing that He taught which brought down all the wrath of the Jews upon His head?

- What one thing did He add to the teachings of Moses, of Amos and of Hosea that changed the whole current of history?
- What has since become the basis of all Democracy?

NOT the doctrine of the One God. NOT the new idea of loving one's neighbor and forgiving one's enemies. No—that wasn't why the Pharisees and Rulers hated him and resolved to have his blood. BUT BECAUSE HE WENT UP AND DOWN THE LENGTH AND BREADTH OF THE LAND TEACHING THAT ALL MEN ARE EQUALLY THE CHILDREN OF GOD!

"As many as received Him, to them gave He power to become the sons of God, even to them that believe on His name."

Can you imagine what this meant to mankind in that day of slavery and oppression? Just think—if God is the Father of ALL men, then ALL are His children, equally entitled to the good things of life, equally dear to Him!

"No wonder," says Bruce Barton in *The Man Nobody Knows*, "the authorities trembled. They were not fools. They recognized the logical implication of such teaching. Either Jesus' life or their power must go. No wonder that succeeding generations of authorities have embroidered His idea and corrupted it. It was too dangerous a Power to be allowed to wander the world, unleashed and uncontrolled."

That is why the idea most of us have of Jesus is so far from the reality that lived and taught and worked wonders throughout Palestine 1900 years ago.

"This was the message of Jesus," Barton explains, "that God is supremely better than anybody had ever dared to believe. Not a petulant Creator, who had lost control of His creation and, in wrath, was determined to destroy it all. Not a stern Judge dispensing impersonal justice. Not a vain King who must be flattered and bribed into concessions of mercy. Not a rigid Accountant, checking up the sins against the penances and striking a cold hard balance. Not any of these . . . nothing like these . . . but a great Companion, a wonderful Friend, a kindly, indulgent, joy-loving Father.

"Hold your heads high," He had exclaimed, "you are lords of the universe . . . only a little lower than the angels . . . children of God."

It is the same note that rings through the Psalms of old:

"What is man that thou art mindful of him? And the son of man that thou visitest him? For thou hast made him a little lower than the angels." And Jesus echoed the refrain when he quoted from the Old Testament—"Ye are gods!"

"And it shall come to pass," cried Hosea (1:10), "that in the place where it was said unto them, Ye are not my people, there it shall be said unto them, Ye are the sons of the living God."

Jesus did not come to call attention to Himself, to get people to believe in Him as a god or demi-god; He did not come solely to reveal God to man; *he came to reveal man to himself.*"

"Beloved, now are ye the Sons of God," says John.

Not only did Jesus proclaim this in His words, but His whole life was given to teaching and showing the Divine Son-ship of *man*. Thirty-seven times in the Gospel records He refers to Himself as the Son of Man! He never called Himself God. But He claimed *union* with God! And He claimed and demonstrated possession of the Father's power and all that the Father had.

"All power is given unto Me in Heaven and in earth," He said. —Matthew 28:18

But He disclaimed this as a mere personal power. "It is not Me, but the Father in Me; He doeth the works."

Furthermore, He again and again assured His followers that this same power was in them. "If ye believe in Me and My word abideth in you, the works that I do shall ye do also. And greater works than these shall ye do."

Again, speaking not of Himself but of all mankind, He said:

"Verily, verily I say unto you, the son can do nothing of himself, but what He seeth the Father do; for what things soever He doeth, these also doeth the son likewise. For the Father loveth the son and showeth him all things that Himself doeth. . . . For as the Father raiseth the dead, and quickeneth them, even so the son quickeneth whom he will. For the Father judgeth no man, but hath committed all judgment unto the son, that all men should honor the son even as they honor the Father."—John 5:19–23

What, then, was the message of Jesus?

The greatest message ever brought to any planet! That *man is the son of God.*

That he inherits from the Father all of life, all of wisdom, all of riches, all of power.

God is the Parent. And man's every quality is derived from Him. Not only that, *but man inherits every quality of the Father!* He has only to grow up in knowledge, to learn the Father's ways, to lean trustfully upon the Father's help, in order to be supreme "amid the war of elements, the wreck of matter and the crush of worlds."

Apart from God, man is a weakling, the sport of circumstances, the victim of any force strong enough to overpower or brush him aside.

But let him ally himself with the Father, and he becomes, instead of the creature of law, the ruler through law. Instead of the sport of circumstance, he makes circumstances. Instead of the victim of fire or water or sickness or poverty, he masters the forces of nature, demands health and prosperity as his birthright.

The God that most of us were taught to believe in was a huge patriarchal Man-God, seated upon a throne high up in the skies. A King—stern, righteous and just—chastening His children mercilessly whenever He felt it was for their good. Holding an exact scale between the good they had done and the sins they had committed. And dispensing penances or rewards to balance the two.

The King idea has gone out of fashion here on earth this many a year. And the idea of a God-King is fast disappearing from our conception of the Infinite. After 1900 years, we are at last coming around to Jesus' idea of a loving Father-God. A God that is in each one of us, whose "good pleasure it is to give us the Kingdom."

"For the works which the Father hath given me to finish, the same works that I do, bear witness of me, that the Father hath sent me."—John 5:36

In the light of such an understanding of God, we can readily grasp how it was possible for Jesus to heal the sick, to feed the hungry, to bring forth gold from the fish's mouth, to still the tempest—and, what is even more, to promise these same powers to us!

Man is the Son of God.

We start with that. How, then, shall we take advantage of our son-ship? How use the infinite power it puts in our hands?

The purpose of this book is to develop the divinity that is in you. What is the first thing to do? Where shall you start? What shall you do?

REACHING INTO INFINITY

The first essential is to find a point of contact with the Father.

Benjamin Franklin sent a kite up into the clouds and brought down along its string a current of electricity. Through him, man has learned to harness this electricity for his daily servant. Franklin made his contact with the source of power.

Thousands of years before Franklin—centuries even before the birth of Christ—men began to send up kites (figuratively speaking) trying to contact with the source of life itself.

A few succeeded. A few great Prophets like Elisha, Elijah, Moses, contacted with the Source of all Power, and whenever and as long as they kept that contact, nothing could withstand them.

"For the prophesy came not in old time by the will of man; but holy men of God spake as they were moved by the Holy Ghost."—II Peter 1:21

Franklin caught the source of electrical power, and by learning to understand and work with it, turned those terror-inspiring thunderbolts of destruction into man's greatest friend and servant. The electricity did not change. It is exactly the same now as afore time. It is merely man's conception of it that has changed.

Uncontrolled, lightning was a curse to mankind. Through understanding, man has harnessed it to serve his needs. Touch a button—and it lights your home. Touch another—and it brings to you news and instruction, entertainment and music from hundreds or thousands of miles away. The mere throwing of a switch releases the power of millions of horses. Pulling it out bridles them again. Was ever such a master servant?

Yet it is as nothing to the power latent in the Source of Life—the power of the Father of all things.

Even now, ignorant of this Power as most of us are, we occasionally contact with it, but we do it accidentally—*and we fail to maintain the contact.*

Remember "The Lost Chord," by Adelaide Procter?

Seated one day at the organ,
I was weary and ill at ease;
And my fingers wandered idly
Over the noisy keys.

I know not what I was playing,
Or what I was dreaming then,
But I struck one chord of music
Like the sound of a great Amen.

It flooded the crimson twilight,
Like the close of an angel's psalm,
And it lay on my fevered spirit,
With a touch of infinite calm.

It quieted pain and sorrow,
Like love overcoming strife,
It seemed the harmonious echo
From our discordant life.

It linked all perplexed meanings
Into one perfect peace,
And trembled away into silence,
As if it were loath to cease.

I have sought, but I seek it vainly,
That one lost chord divine,
Which came from the soul of the organ,
And entered into mine.

It may be that Death's bright angel
Will speak in that chord again,
It may be that only in Heaven
I shall hear that grand Amen!

You know how often things have come to you like that—snatches of song, or speech, or verse such as man never wrote before. Visions of wonderful achievement. Echoes of great ideas. Glimpses of riches you could almost reach—the riches of the Spirit within.

If only you could tap that boundless Reservoir at will, what success would not be yours, how puny your present accomplishments would seem by comparison!

And you *can* tap it. You can make your contact with Infinity—if not at will—at least with frequency. All that is necessary is understanding and belief.

How to do it? How to go about it? Through the Holy Spirit within you. Through your part of Divinity. Through an understanding of what is commonly known as your Subconscious Mind.

Why did the Apostles, after cowering in hiding so abjectly for ten days after the ascension of Jesus, suddenly issue forth boldly and astonish the world with their preaching and their miracles?

"It is expedient for you that I go away," Jesus had told them (John 16:7), "for if I go not away, the Comforter will not come unto you; but if I depart, I will send Him unto you."

"Howbeit when He, the Spirit of truth, is come," He promised, "He will guide you into all truth; for He shall not speak of Himself; but whatsoever He shall hear, that shall He speak."—John 16:13

And He commanded the Apostles that they should not depart from Jerusalem, but await the consummation of His promise.

"And behold, I send the promise of my Father upon you; but tarry ye in the city of Jerusalem, until ye be endued with power from on high."—Luke 24:49

"And when the day of Pentecost was fully come, they were all with one accord in one place.

"And suddenly there came a sound from heaven as of a rushing mighty wind, and it filled all the house where they were sitting.

"And there appeared unto them cloven tongues like as of fire, and it sat upon each of them.

"And they were all filled with the Holy Ghost, and began to speak with other tongues, as the Spirit gave them utterance.

"And there were dwelling at Jerusalem Jews, devout men, out of every nation under heaven.

"Now when this was noised abroad, the multitude came together, and were confounded, because that every man heard them speak in his own language.

"And they were all amazed and marvelled, saying one to another, Behold, are not all these which speak Galilaeans?

"And how hear we every man in our own tongue, wherein we were born?

"Parthians, and Medes, and Elamites, and the dwellers in Mesopotamia, and in Judaea, and Cappadocia, in Pontus, and Asia,

"Phrygia, and Pamphylia, in Egypt, and in the parts of Libya about Cyrene, and strangers of Rome, Jews and proselytes,

"Cretes and Arabians, we do hear them speak in our tongues the wonderful works of God.

"And they were all amazed, and were in doubt, saying one to another, What meaneth this?

"But this is that which was spoken by the prophet Joel;

"And it shall come to pass in the last days, saith God, I will pour out my spirit upon all flesh."—Acts 2:1, 12, 16, 17

Just as the one great fact of the Gospels is the presence of the Son exalting and revealing the Father, so the one great fact of the Acts of the Apostles is the presence of the Holy Spirit inspiring all their acts.

"The Comforter, which is the Holy Ghost, whom the Father will send you in my name," Jesus had promised them, "he shall teach you all things, and bring all things to your remembrance, whatsoever I have said unto you."— John 14:26

How else do you suppose they could have remembered all that Jesus had taught, all that he had said to them? They took no notes. For the most part, they could not even read or write!

And why has the power of healing so largely disappeared since about the 3rd century of the Christian era? Why did the Apostles at Jerusalem send Peter and John to "lay hands" upon the Christian converts in Samaria?

"Now when the apostles which were at Jerusalem heard that Samaria had received the word of God, they sent unto them Peter and John:

"Who, when they were come down, prayed for them, that they might receive the Holy Ghost:

"(For as yet he was fallen upon none of them: only they were baptized in the name of the Lord Jesus.)

"*Then laid they their hands on them, and they received the Holy Ghost.*"—Acts 8

Why did Paul ask other Christian congregations, which had as yet worked no signs or wonders, whether they had received the Holy Ghost?

"He said unto them, Have ye received the Holy Ghost since ye believed? And they said unto him, We have not so much as heard whether there be any Holy Ghost.

"And when Paul had laid his hands upon them, the Holy Ghost came on them; and they spake with tongues and prophesied."—Acts 19:2, 6

It is as Jesus said—

"When the Comforter is come, whom I will send unto you from the Father, even the Spirit of truth, which proceedeth from the Father, he shall testify of me."—John 15:26

We are most of us like the dwellers in Samaria—"we have not so much as heard whether there be any Holy Spirit," much less tried to cultivate an understanding of Him.

We stumble upon His vast power occasionally—and call our resultant deeds superhuman! We contact now and then with Infinity—and regard the result as a miracle!

There is no such thing as a miracle. The occasional wonder-works that we do—the sudden healing from sickness, the miraculous escape, the answered prayer—are all divinely natural. The miracle is that it happens so seldom. We should be able to establish and keep that contact always! We should be able to contact with and use the power of the Spirit as readily as we now can use the power of electricity.

"And it shall come to pass afterwards, that I will pour out my spirit upon all flesh; and your sons and your daughters shall prophesy, your old men shall dream dreams, your young men shall see visions."—Joel 2:28

But just as Franklin had first to determine what the power was that made the lightning, so have you first to learn what is this Holy Spirit within you.

To say that it is the subconscious mind is not enough. It is far more than that. The subconscious mind can be used either for good or for evil. Uncontrolled, it is as great a destructive force as the lightning. If you have read the *Secret of the Ages*, you know that you can suggest thoughts of health or of disease to your subconscious mind, of success or of failure—and whichever image you get across to the subconscious, it will proceed to work out. But the Holy Spirit can be used only for good.

The Samaritans had subconscious minds, yet they worked no wonders. It was only when Paul conferred the Holy Spirit upon them that signs and wonders followed.

What then is the Holy Spirit?

How do you acquire it? How contact with it?

Have you ever read any of the accounts you occasionally see of people who have been very sick—who have hovered for minutes or for hours right over the Valley of Death—and then come back? Remember their description of how they seemed to be looking down upon themselves, upon the whole scene, as one apart, as one having but a casual interest in what was going on? Remember how some little thing called them back and how frequently they went back with reluctance?

Stewart Edward White had a story in the May *American Magazine* that exactly illustrated the idea. It told of a man who, according to all scientific tests, had died—lay dead, in fact, for two hours. And here, in part, was his description of the experience:

"I was pretty ill before I died, and things about me got somewhat vague and unreal. I suppose I was half dozing, and partly delirious perhaps. I'd slip in and out of focus, as it were. Sometimes I'd see myself and the bed and the room and the people clearly enough; then again I'd sort of drop into an inner reverie inside myself. Not asleep exactly, nor yet awake. You'll get much the same thing sitting in front of a warm fire after a hearty dinner.

"Now, here's a funny one. I don't know if you'll get this: You know these pictures sent by radio? They are all made up of a lot of separate dots, you know. If you enlarged the thing enough, you'd almost lose the picture, wouldn't you? And you'd have a collection of dots with a lot of space between them. Well, that's how I seemed to myself.

"I could contract myself, bring all the dots close together, and there I'd be, solid as a brick church, lying in bed; and I could expand myself until the dots got separated so far that there were mostly spaces between them. And when I did that my body in the bed got very vague to me, because the dots were so far apart they didn't make a picture; and I—the consciousness of me—was some-how the thing in the spaces that held the dots together at all. I found it quite amusing contracting and expanding like that.

"Then I began to think about it. I began to wonder whether I held the dots together, or whether the dots held me together; and I got so interested that I thought I'd try to find out. You see, I wasn't the dots: I—the essence of me, the consciousness of me—was the spaces between the dots, holding them together. I thought to myself, 'I wonder if I can get away from these dots?' So I tried it; and I could. I must say I was a little scared. That body made of dots was a good, solid container. When I left its shelter, it occurred to me that I might evaporate into universal substance, like letting a gas out of a bottle. I didn't; but I certainly was worried for fear I'd burst out somewhere. I felt awfully thin-skinned!"

Remember how you have sometimes had similar experiences in dreams, when you seemed to be a disembodied spirit looking down on yourself from above?

That disembodied self is the soul of you—your subconscious mind. But it is something more, too. Baptize it in the waters of understanding of your oneness with the Father, confirm it with a realization of the God-life flowing so abun-dantly through you—and it becomes, in addition, *the Holy Spirit within you*—one with the Father, one with the Source of Life, of Power, of Abundance. In short, the Holy Spirit within you is your subconscious mind, vitalized through direct contact with the Father.

You have been told time and again how small a part of your real abilities you use when you confine your mental work to your conscious mind. Prof. Wm. James, the world-famous Psychologist, estimated that the average man used only 10 per cent. of his real abilities. While Dr. Mayo compares the mind to an ice-berg—one-fourth above water (the conscious mind), and three-fourths sub-merged (the subconscious). Think, then, if the use of your subconscious mind adds so much to your abilities, how much your value will be increased if you add to that the infinite power of the Holy Spirit!

"Now we have received, not the spirit of the world, but the Spirit which is of God; that we might know the things that are freely given to us of God."
—I Corinthians 2:12

As the ordinary man uses it, the subconscious mind is largely a bundle of habits. You practice on the piano merely to set up a certain train of actions and reactions so that, after a time, your subconscious can take over the work from your conscious mind. The skilled pianist can play from memory the most difficult pieces and at the same time carry on a spirited conversation. Why? Because two entirely different provinces of the mind are carrying on their functions—the one through the fingers, the other through speech and hearing.

The same thing applies to every physical avocation. To become really skilful at anything, you must get it into the charge of your subconscious mind. As long as your conscious mind must take active control, you are tense, doubtful, hesitant—you blunder, become excited, fail. Let the action become automatic, however—in other words, let your subconscious have charge of it—and you relax naturally and do whatever is required of you without effort and will.

A man's responsiveness to subconscious reactions is usually the measure of his luck or ill luck in avoiding accidents. In the New York Herald-Tribune there was an editorial recently along this very line entitled—"Whom Ill Luck Pursues":

"The Industrial Fatigue Research Board has made an interesting report on the reasons for industrial accidents. It is already well known to thoughtful managers of factories that some men are persistently unlucky. If any one is to suffer a broken leg, it will be one of these individuals. When minor accidents are being dealt out by Fate these unfortunates never fail to receive more than their reasonable shares. No definite fault can be found with them. They are not noticeably careless or foolhardy. The poor things seem simply to possess an incurable propensity for being at hand when anything happens. Like the conventional innocent bystander, they are, almost by definition, the persons who get hurt.

"Armed with the modern magician's wand of careful record and exact statistical inquiry, two investigators for the research board have traced these instances of persistent ill luck to their cause. No demon of bad luck is concerned, although the uninstructed may well think so when they read that the cause's name is aesthetakinetic co-ordination. Translated into English, this means a lack of that instinct and exact correspondence between warning and action which some people possess and some do not. If a board in the floor is loose and happens to fly up when stepped on, some people will jump instantly and in the right direction. Others will move the wrong way or not at all. If a chair breaks some sitters will land on their feet, others on the floor. Under the conditions of modern civilization it is usually the latter who are being taken to the hospital."

The functions of your body—your heart, lungs, stomach, liver, the continual breaking down and rebuilding of all the cells—these, too, are the province of your subconscious mind. And as long as they are left to it in the full assurance that it knows its work and is tending faithfully to it, all will be well with them.

But let the conscious mind interfere, and as in playing the piano or doing any other difficult stunt, trouble will ensue.

Have you ever seen a football team whose classmates did nothing but "knock" it, tell it how rotten it was individually and collectively, how little chance it had of ever winning a game? You know how little chance that team would have of getting even a single goal.

But take that same team, put a real class spirit behind it, surround it with boosters and urge it on with a stirring college yell—and then watch it go!

So it is with your subconscious mind and your body. It knows perfectly how to rebuild your body—how to keep it well. But if you tell it, in effect, that you have no confidence in its ability to do this—if you are continually trying to take over the control through your doubts and fears and worries—you will soon have a mutinous or discouraged crew on your hands, that no longer believes in you or itself. And the result will be nervousness, apathy, failure.

As the Rev. W. John Murray put it—

"Whatever order we issue to the subconscious mind, it promptly undertakes to carry out. Whatever state of existence you declare to be in being, the subconscious mind assumes exists and works within you accordingly. If a friend asks you: How do you feel today? and you reply: I am not well; I have a headache; I am all in; I don't feel up to the mark at all, you are unconsciously setting the subconscious mind to work to realize the state you declare yourself to be in. On the other hand if you say: I am well, happy and strong, the subconscious mind undertakes to realize this state for you.

"Hence you can see what a wonderful power is within your control for your happiness or unhappiness, your condition of body and mind, and how necessary it is for you to use this power always in a positive direction. *You are, in a word, what you think you are.* This is not a theory, a fancy or a fad. It is a law. And the reason why the world is filled with sin, disease, misery and misfortune is because it requires effort to think positive thoughts while negative thinking is the result of inertia."

But it is not only in running the body-machine that the subconscious shows the power of the Spirit that is behind it. It has all knowledge of outside things as well. Contact with it, and you can learn what you will.

Some time ago there was an article in the "American" telling of the experiences of a convict, formerly the editor of a large newspaper.

Morphine had brought this man to prison. He had started taking it when, as a newspaper man, his body would be so worn out that he could no longer write. By "doping" the conscious mind into unconsciousness, he would bring the subconscious to the fore, with the result that the most wonderful articles flowed from his pen. In one case, without a clue to guide him, he traced a gang of criminals who were in hiding!

But his was not merely an impossible way to contact with the Holy Spirit—it was the wrong way to contact with the subconscious as well—and he paid a fearful price for it.

Take Theodore Roosevelt, on the other hand. When he entered Harvard in 1876, he was thin of chest, be-spectacled, nervous, weighing only 90 pounds. He was afraid to get on his feet and try to make a speech. Compare that with the man he became—the wonder of the world for efficiency, endurance, working power, and joyousness in life. He was a cowboy, a soldier, a lawyer, a statesman, a writer. And he did each of these things phenomenally well.

That is one example of what the right attitude towards the subconscious will do. Then there are those frequent cases you hear about like the one described in Psychology Magazine. Henry A. Wight never studied art—never knew he had any talent for painting. He went into the matter-of-fact-business of steel and coal, and was successful in it. Then when he was getting along in the thirties, he found himself with the desire to paint. So, to use his own laconic explanation, "he did it—that's all." And his monotypes have won the praise of the best critics.

I know a famous song writer who never studied a note. Her music "just comes to her." I know a man—a successful business man of nearly fifty—who suddenly started writing poems. Wonderful poems—that have been eagerly accepted by the best magazines. And he doesn't know a rule of prosody! I know an eminent geologist who never consciously examines a stone. He just walks over his ground abstractedly and then tells—for a very high fee—what is underneath it.

Contacting with the Subconscious—contacting haphazardly, accidentally—yet getting marvelous results while the contact holds!

Whatever you want to know, whatever you wish to do—the knowledge and the power are there. "When He, the Spirit of Truth is come," promised Jesus, "He will guide you into all the truth."

Ordinary contact with the subconscious is comparatively easy. The first essential is relaxation. To find a really comfortable easy chair or lounge or bed, where one can be quiet, undisturbed, unconscious of oneself and one's surroundings. To stretch luxuriously and then let every muscle relax. To review before your mind's eye every phase of the problem or the subject—not worriedly, not striving for the answer—but merely laying them before the spirit within in the way you would put them before some all-wise Solomon. To *know* that he *has* the answer—and will presently give it to you. To relax thankfully in this knowledge into slumber, with the contented feeling that you have got what you wanted. Do that—and your answer will come.

Dr. W. Hanna Thomson, in "Brain and Personality," gives some instances of how this sometimes works out even when the person doing it has no knowledge of how to put his problem up to his subconscious mind. The first was told him by a fellow student at college. One night his roommate sat up late working at a difficult problem in mathematics. Failing to solve it, he rubbed his slate clean, put out the light and went to bed.

Later on that night the first student was awakened by the light shining in his eyes. Looking up, he saw his friend working away at his slate. The next morning he commented on it, only to have his roommate indignantly deny that he had been up at all during the night.

To prove his assertion, the first student got the slate, and there on it was the problem that had puzzled his friend—*all worked out to the correct conclusion!*

The other case Thomson tells of was that of a British Consul in Syria. He had been studying Arabic diligently in an effort to better fit himself for his position, and one night tried to compose a letter to the Emir at Lebanon. After a couple of hours of fruitless effort, he finally lost all patience with the language and the job, and went to bed.

What was his astonishment to find on his desk in the morning a freshly written letter, in his own handwriting, couched in the purest Arabic, that the Slave-of-the-Lamp himself could not have improved upon!

Then there is the classic case of Herman V. Hilprecht, Professor of Assyrian at the University of Pennsylvania: He had worn himself out trying to decipher certain mysterious inscriptions on some old Assyrian rings. Finally he had given up the problem in despair—no living man could solve it. One night, still thinking and studying over it, he had gone to bed exhausted. He fell asleep and dreamed.

In his dream, a tall thin priest of the old Pre-Christian Nippur temple appeared to him and led him to the treasure chamber of the temple. In a low-ceiled room without windows he saw a great wooden chest with scraps of agate and lapislazuli lying on the floor.

"The fragments over which you have been working," spoke the priest, "are not finger rings. King Kurigalzu once sent to the Temple of Bel an inscribed vo-tive cylinder of agate. Later we priests suddenly received a hasty and imperative summons to make a pair of agate earrings for the great God Ninib.

"We had no new agate at hand, and were in great dismay. At last we decided to cut the votive cylinder into three parts, thus making three rings. The two fragments which have given you so much trouble are portions of them. If you will put them together you will find this to be true. The third ring you will never find."

Professor Hilprecht awoke, roused his wife and told her the dream. Then ran to his study. Before long she heard him cry: "It is so! It is so!" Next winter he went to Cairo to study the objects from the Temple Nippur which were in the Imperial Museum. He found there complete evidence of the truthfulness of his dream in every detail.

The subconscious mind is your Slave of the Lamp. Use him, in the ways outlined above—and there is no problem he cannot work out for you.

But recognize your Sonship with God, your oneness with the Source of all life and Power—in short, contact with the Source of Power—and that subcon-scious mind becomes the Holy Spirit within you, *to whom nothing is impossible!*

"The natural man receiveth not the things of the Spirit of God," says Paul (I Corinthians 2:14), "for they are foolishness unto him; neither can he know them, because they are *spiritually* discerned."

3

The Lode Star

"And I will pray the Father, and He shall give you another Comforter, that He may abide with you forever. Even the Spirit of Truth; whom the world cannot receive, because it seeth Him not. But ye know Him. For He dwelleth with you and shall be in you."

—JOHN 14:16–17

THERE once lived in a town of Persia two brothers, one named Cassim, the other Ali Baba. Cassim had married a very rich wife, and become a wealthy but miserly and greedy money-lender. Ali Baba had married a woman as poor as himself, and lived by cutting wood, and bringing it upon his donkeys into the town to sell. But he had married for love and he worked cheerily, asking only of Allah that He watch over his little family and help him to teach his son to tread in the right path.

One day, when Ali Baba was in the forest cutting wood, he saw a great cloud of dust coming towards him from the distance. Observing it attentively, he soon distinguished a body of horsemen, and as honest people had little business that far from the haunts of men he suspected they might be robbers. Greatly frightened, he determined to leave his donkeys and save himself. Yet he was not so frightened as to lose all curiosity, so he climbed up a tree that grew on a high rock, whose branches, while thick enough to conceal him, yet enabled him to see all that passed beneath.

The troop, which numbered about forty, all well mounted and armed, came to the foot of the rock and dismounted. Each man unbridled his horse, tied him to some shrub, and hung about the animal's neck a bag of corn. Then each took off his saddle-bag, which from its weight seemed to Ali Baba to be full of gold and silver. One, whom he took to be their captain, came under the tree in which Ali Baba was concealed; and, making his way through some shrubs, pronounced these words—"Open, Sesame!" The moment the captain of the robbers had thus spoken, a door opened in the rock; and after he had made all his troop enter before him, he followed them, when the door shut again of itself.

The robbers stayed some time within the rock, during which Ali Baba, fearful of being caught, remained in the tree.

At last the door opened again, and as the captain went in last, so he came out first, and stood to see them all pass by him. Then Ali Baba heard him make the door close by pronouncing these words, "Shut, Sesame!" The robbers forthwith bridled their horses, and mounted, and when the captain saw them all ready, he put himself at their head, and they returned the way they had come.

Ali Baba followed them with his eyes as far as he could see, and afterward stayed a considerable time before he descended. Remembering the words the captain of the robbers had used to cause the door to open he was curious to see if his pronouncing them would have the same effect. Accordingly, he went among the shrubs, stood before it, and said, "Open, Sesame!" Instantly the door flew wide open.

Ali Baba, who expected a dark, dismal cavern, was surprised to see a well-lighted and spacious chamber, receiving its light from an opening at the top of the rock. Scattered around in profusion were all sorts of rich bales of silk stuff, brocade, and valuable carpeting, gold and silver ingots in great heaps, and money in bags. The cave must have been occupied for ages by robbers, one succeeding another.

Ali Baba fell on his knees and thanked Allah, the Most High. "Here," thought he, "is the provision I have prayed for to keep us in our old age and to provide our son with a start in life."

So he went boldly into the cave, and collected as much of the gold coin, which was in bags, as he thought his three donkeys could carry. When he had loaded them with the bags, he laid wood over them in such a manner that they could not be seen. After he had passed in and out as often as he wished, he stood before the door, and pronounced the words, "Shut, Sesame!" and the door closed of itself.

When Ali Baba got home, he drove his asses into a little yard, shut the gates very carefully, threw off the wood that covered the panniers, carried the bags into the house, and ranged them in order before his wife. He emptied the bags before his astonished wife, raising such a great heap of gold as to dazzle her eyes. Then he told her the whole adventure from beginning to end, and, above all, recommended her to keep it secret.

The wife rejoiced greatly at their good-fortune, but woman-like, wanted to count the gold piece by piece. "Wife," replied Ali Baba, "never try to number the gifts of Allah. Take them—and be thankful. To number them is to limit them. As for this treasure, I will dig a hole and bury it. There is no time to be lost." "You are in the right, husband," replied she.

"But," she thought, as he departed into the garden with his spade, it will do no harm to know, as nigh as possible, how much we have. I will borrow a small measure, and measure it."

Away she ran to her brother-in-law Cassim, who lived hard by, and begged his wife for the loan of a measure for a little while. Her sister-in-law asked her whether she would have a great or a small one. The other asked for a small one. She bade her stay a little, and she would readily fetch one.

The sister-in-law did so, but as she knew Ali Baba's poverty, she was curious to know what sort of grain his wife wanted to measure, and, artfully putting some suet at the bottom of the measure, brought it to her, with the excuse that she was sorry that she had made her stay so long, but that she could not find it sooner.

Ali Baba's wife went home, filled the measure with gold and emptied it in the corner. Again and again she repeated that, and when she had done, she was very well satisfied to find the number of measures amounted to so many as they did, and went to tell her husband, who had almost finished digging the hole. While Ali Baba was burying the gold, his wife, to show her exactness and diligence to her sister-in-law, carried the measure back again, but without taking notice that a piece of gold had stuck to the bottom. "Sister," said she, giving it to her again, "you see that I have not kept your measure long. I am obliged to you for it, and return it with thanks."

As soon as Ali Baba's wife was gone, Cassim's wife looked at the bottom of the measure, and was in inexpressible surprise to find a piece of gold sticking to it. Envy immediately possessed her breast. "What!" said she, "has Ali Baba gold so plentiful as to measure it? Whence has he all this wealth?"

Cassim, her husband, was at his counting-house. When he came home his wife said to him, "Cassim, I know you think yourself rich, but Ali Baba is infinitely richer than you. He does not count his money, but measures it." Cassim desired her to explain the riddle, which she did by telling him the stratagem she had used to make the discovery, and showed him the piece of money, which was so old that they could not tell in what prince's reign it was coined.

Cassim, after he had married the rich widow, had never treated Ali Baba as a brother, but scorned and neglected him; and now, instead of being pleased, he conceived a base envy at his brother's prosperity. He could not sleep all that night, and went to him in the morning before sunrise. "Ali Baba," said he, "I am surprised at you! You pretend to be miserably poor, and yet you measure gold. My wife found this at the bottom of the measure you borrowed yesterday."

By this discourse, Ali Baba perceived that Cassim and his wife, through his own wife's folly, knew what they had so much reason to conceal; but what was done could not be undone. Therefore, without showing the least surprise or chagrin, he told all, and offered his brother part of his treasure to keep the secret.

"I expect as much," replied the greedy Cassim haughtily; "but I must know exactly where this treasure is, and how I may visit it myself when I choose; otherwise, I will go and inform against you, and then you will not only get no more, but will lose all you have, and I shall have a share for my information."

Ali Baba told him all he asked, even to the very words he was to use to gain admission into the cave.

Cassim rose the next morning long before the sun, and set out for the forest with ten mules bearing great chests, which he designed to fill, and followed the road which Ali Baba had pointed out to him. It was not long before he reached the rock, and found out the place, by the tree and other marks which his brother had given him. Walking up to the entrance of the cavern, he pronounced the words, "Open, Sesame!" Immediately the door opened, and when he was in, closed upon him.

On examining the cave, his avaricious soul was in transports of delight to find much more riches than he had expected from Ali Baba's relation. Quickly he laid as many bags of gold as he could carry at the door of the cavern; but his thoughts were so full of the great riches he should possess, and how with them he should become the richest money-lender and usurer in the city, that he could not think of the necessary words to make the door open. Instead of "Sesame" he said, "Open, Barley!" and was much amazed to find that the door remained fast shut. He named several sorts of grain, but still the door would not open.

Cassim had never anticipated such a contingency as this, and was so frightened at the danger he was in, that the more he endeavored to remember the word "Sesame," the more his memory was confounded. He threw down the bags he had loaded himself with, and walked distractedly up and down the cave, for the first time in his greedy life appreciating that to put your trust in money alone is to pin your faith to the most elusive thing in the world. Yet he had looked to it alone for so long a time that he knew now no other way to turn.

About noon the robbers visited their cave. At some distance they saw Cassim's mules straggling about the rock, with great chests on their backs. Alarmed at this, they galloped full speed to the cave, drove away the mules, which strayed through the forest so far that they were soon out of sight, and went directly, with their naked sabres in their hands, to the door, which on their captain pronouncing the proper words, immediately opened.

Cassim, who heard the noise of the horses' feet, at once guessed the arrival of the robbers, and resolved to make one effort for his life. He rushed to the door, and no sooner saw it open, than he ran out and threw the leader down, but could not escape the other robbers, who with their scimeters soon deprived him of life.

There is more to this old Eastern legend, but the meat of it lies here—that if you learn the Magic Secret, the "Open Sesame" of life, wealth and honor are yours for the taking.

But if you become like the greedy Cassim, and get so taken up with the riches that you can think of nothing else—you not only lose the Magic Secret, but you bring down speedy retribution on your head as well.

THE "OPEN, SESAME!"

What is this "Open, Sesame" of life? What is the Philosopher's Stone which turns everything it touches into gold?

It is any controlling idea or desire so intense, so alive and real, that it carries utter faith with it and thus involuntarily establishes a contact with the Holy Spirit within, which attracts to itself everything it needs for its fulfillment.

It is, in short, the Lode Star—the Polar Magnet by means of which we may draw from the heavens above, from the earth beneath or from the waters under the earth anything that is necessary to our controlling idea or desire.

Ridiculous? Stop and think for just a moment.

Have you ever concentrated for days or weeks on the writing of an article or story, on the making of some device, on the discovery of some new formula—on anything that required the deepest thought and faith and concentration?

Remember how there seemed to pour in upon you all sorts of facts and information and material pertinent to the idea you had in mind? Remember how things came to you from the most unlikely and unexpected sources—from the chance words of associates or even strangers; from newspaper and magazine articles, picked up in the most casual way imaginable; from books you happened to see in the windows or in the hands of some friend; from *out of the air,* as it were, unsought, unbidden—except as they were sought out and brought to you by that Mental Magnet within.

"If any of you lack wisdom," said James, "let him ask of God, that giveth to all men liberally, and upbraideth not; and it shall be given him. But let him ask in faith, nothing wavering. For he that wavereth is like a wave of the sea driven with the wind and tossed. For let not that man think that he shall receive anything from the Lord."—James 1:5–6

The earnest desire for some definite thing, coupled with the sincere belief in your power to get it through the Spirit within, is the most powerful force in the world. As Marie Corelli says in "Life Everlasting":

"Nothing in the universe can resist the force of a steadfastly fixed resolve. What the spirit truly seeks must, by eternal law, be given to it, and what the body needs for the fulfillment of the spirit's demands will be bestowed. From the sunlight and the air and the hidden things of space strength shall be daily and hourly renewed. Everything in nature shall aid in bringing to the resolved soul that which it demands. There is nothing within the circle of creation that can resist its influence. Success, wealth, triumph upon triumph come to every human being who daily 'sets his house in order'—whom no derision can drive from his determined goal, whom no temptation can drag from his appointed course."

I know that when I first conceived the idea for this book and began to look for different works of reference to bear out the thought I had in mind, I was almost flooded with material—wonderful material that I had never even heard about, much less knew where to look for. Three of the best works on the subject I have ever seen, literally walked into my office—unsought, unbidden and without cost—and have been of more help to me than anything else I have found. And I am far from being alone in this experience.

In a recent issue of *Advertising and Selling,* Floyd W. Parsons tells how a piece of cheese tossed by one workman at another during the lunch hour missed its mark and dropped into the plating bath used in the production of copper disks from which wax phonograph records were stamped. Later the disks from that bath were found to be far superior to the others, and an investigation revealed that the casein in the cheese had done the trick. This disclosed a possible improvement worth several thousand dollars.

The top of a salt cellar fell off, and the outcome was a new flux for welding permalloy, making possible a six-fold increase in the speed with which we can send messages by cable.

By inadvertently opening the wrong valve, a French scientist found the answer to the long search for liquid oxygen. Again an accident created an industry and gave us an explosive safer and mightier than dynamite.

A great corporation ordered its industrial chemists to produce a paint that could be applied quickly, would dry rapidly, and be tough, hard and resistant to the elements. It had to have some of the properties of glass and yet not crack, and it had to be proof against the action of oil, grease, and acid.

Everything went well up to the point of finding a way to keep the solution in a liquid condition so that it could be applied with a brush. All efforts to solve this problem failed until one day the machinery broke down and the material had to stand for days in the tank until the repairs were completed. When work started again, the chemists were amazed to find that the paint now retained its liquid form. The long-sought secret had finally been discovered, and an accident had again shaped the destiny of a business.

In short, when you have put all of your reasoning, all of your information into the cauldron of thought, there frequently flashes out an idea that is not the logical development of anything you have had before—but a direct inspiration from the Holy Spirit within.

"And thine ears shall hear a word behind thee, saying, This is the way, walk ye in it, when ye turn to the right hand, and when ye turn to the left."
—ISAIAH 30–21

"The key to successful methods," says Thos. A. Edison, "comes right out of the air. A real new thing like a general idea, a beautiful melody, is pulled out of space—a fact which is inexplicable."

Inexplicable? Not at all! It is simply that all knowledge already exists in Divine Mind—in the Father who fills all space and animates all things. There is nothing for us to discover—merely to *seek*, to *unfold*. Columbus did not discover America. It was here all the time. As the Englishman said after three days of traveling on a California-bound train—"How could he have missed it?" Columbus—and all of Europe—merely learned something that Divine Mind had known all the time.

Galileo did not discover that the earth was round; Copernicus did not discover the movement of the planets; Newton did not discover the law of gravitation; any more than your young son discovers the law of mathematics by which 2+2=4. He learns it—yes. He makes the information his own. And to him it partakes of discovery. But the law was known to Divine Mind since time began.

We are God's children, grasping a little at a time of the infinite knowledge He is constantly writing on the blackboard before us—and hailing each bit as a grand discovery of our own. Sir Isaac Newton, one of the greatest geniuses of all time, compared himself to a boy, gathering pebbles on the shore of the vast, unknown ocean of truth.

"God looked down from heaven," said David, "upon the children of men to see if there were any that did understand."—Psalms 14:2

The great essential is to realize that the Father HAS all information—that the "vast ocean of truth" IS there—and that if we will do our best in the trustful knowledge that the Father *can* and very gladly *will* supply anything beyond our own powers to grasp, our faith and trust will be justified. "There is nothing hidden," saith the Scripture, "which shall not be revealed; neither hid which shall not be known." "When God is with us," quoth Josephus, "the impossible becomes possible."

When any problem confronts you that seems beyond your ability to solve, just say to yourself—"I am one with the Infinite Intelligence of the Universe. And Infinite Intelligence HAS the correct answer to this problem. Therefore, I too have the answer, and at the right time and in the right way will manifest it."

There are no new gold deposits. No new diamond fields. All of them have been known to the Father for millions of years.

You don't need to discover anything. You don't need to create something new. All you need to do is to seek the riches and the methods that have been known to the Father for all time. And the place to seek them is not far afield—but in Mind. "Seek and ye shall find," said Jesus. "Knock and it shall be opened to you."

A RADIO WITH A THOUSAND AERIALS

Our bodies are, in effect, radio stations powerful or otherwise as our controlling ideas are strong or weak. The nerves that come to the surface all over our body act as thousands of aerials gathering in impressions from every source. And just as any station properly attuned and powerful enough to "get" it, can pick what it wants out of the air any minute of the day or night, so can you "get" anything you may want—be it riches or success, happiness or health—if your thought be properly keyed and powerful enough to receive it.

For our minds are vast magnets that can attract to us anything we may desire. The only requisite is—they have got to be *charged*. A demagnetized magnet won't draw to it or hold even the weight of a pin. Nor will a demagnetized man attract to himself a single idea or a single penny.

There are two ways of charging your mental magnet:

1. By occasional but heartfelt prayer—like the radio fan who lets his batteries run down until, when something special comes along that he particularly wants, he finds them so weak he can scarcely raise a sound, and forthwith hies himself to the battery man to have them recharged.
2. By heeding Jesus' admonition to pray without ceasing—to go back to the simile of the radio fan again, to attach your batteries to the electric light socket and keep them constantly charged to capacity, ready and able at all times to bring you anything you may wish.

Which method is yours? Old Mother Nature adopts the second. The flowers turn their faces to the sun not just once a day or once a week—but always. The waving grain, the shrubs, the trees, drink in the light and life of the sun every day and all day. They recharge themselves with life and fragrance whenever and as long as opportunity offers.

That is what you too must do. You must first charge the magnet of your mind with a compelling desire. Then keep it recharged with faith in the power and the willingness of the Father to give to you anything of good that may be necessary to the fruition of your prayer. Not only that, but you must realize your ability (through the Father) to draw to yourself anything of good. In short, you must realize your Sonship with God, and the consequent fact that all of good is already yours—that God has done his part—that it is up to you merely to manifest, to unfold, to SEE the good things that the Father has provided for you in such profusion.

When Hagar and Ishmael were wandering in the desert, and could find no water and seemed about to perish, then Hagar cried aloud to the Lord.

"And God heard the voice of the lad; and the angel of God called to Hagar out of heaven, and said unto her, What aileth thee, Hagar? Fear not; for God hath heard the voice of the lad where he is.

"And God opened her eyes, and she saw a well of water; and she went, and filled the bottle with water, and gave the lad drink."—Genesis 21:17, 19

Again, when the three kings in the desert sought water for their men and horses, the Prophet Elisha told them:

"Thus saith the Lord—Ye shall not see wind, neither shall ye see rain, yet make this valley full of ditches."—II Kings 3:16–17

And though it looked a hopeless task, the three kings set their men to work as directed, and after they had prepared the ditches, the rains came and filled them.

Wherever you are and whatever you need, supply is always there—for supply is in the Father, and the Father is everywhere. It is like the air we breathe—it is all around us, always available, always plentiful—unless we lock ourselves into the air-tight houses of limitation.

The trouble is that we have for so long been taught that everything of good must be fought for, struggled for, taken away from some one else, that we can't believe when we are told that all we need do is to open up the windows of our souls and let in the Holy Spirit—open up the channels of supply and let riches flow freely to us. To quote Trench's beautiful poem—

"Make channels for the streams of love,
Where they may broadly run,
For Love has overflowing streams
To fill them every one;

"But if at any time we cease
Such channels to provide,
The very founts of Love for us,
Will soon be parched and dried;

"For we must share if we would keep
Such blessings from above,
Ceasing to give, we cease to have,
Such is the law of Love."

We see others breathing deeply of the air about us, and we don't begrudge them it because we know there is plenty for all. We see others enjoying the sunlight; the clear water from the spring; and we rejoice with them in it. But let another make a lot of money, and immediately we become envious, for we think he has made it that much harder for us to get any.

The best things in life, the greatest essentials to life, are free. Air, sunshine, water—all are free, because the supply of them is inexhaustible.

What we fail to realize is that there is just as inexhaustible supply of the things that money will buy as there is of sunlight or water or air. And they can be drawn just as freely from the Father through the magic of faith and a compelling idea.

But you can't do it if you dam up the source of supply with doubts and fears. You must not limit supply as did the widow in the Scriptural story. Left destitute, her creditors were pressing her hard; and her sons, as was the law in that day, were to become bondsmen for the debt she owed. In her distress she came to the prophet Elisha, and he asked—"What have you in your house?" She replied—"I have nothing but a vessel of oil." He said—"Send out to your neighbors and borrow all the vessels you can; take them empty into a room, and pour into them the oil which you have." She did not question him but did as she was told; she poured the oil from the vessel which contained all that she possessed and filled all those which she had borrowed. Then she told her sons to get others, but they said—"We have no more." And as soon as they made that announcement, the oil stopped flowing—not one drop came after all the vessels were full—II Kings 4:2–6. Do you see who determined the quantity that should come to the widow? Was it God? I know your answer—"It was the woman herself." She received just the amount for which she had made preparation.

IT'S NOT THE SUPPLY THAT IS LIMITED— IT IS OURSELVES!

Too many of us are like the little colored boy and the watermelon. An old gentleman, seeing the difficulty the boy was having in storing away so large a melon, stopped and asked, "Too much melon, isn't it, son?" "No, suh!" replied the youngster with conviction, "just not enough niggah."

Why does so large a part of humanity suffer hunger and want?

Certainly not from lack on the part of old Mother Earth. Ask the farmers and they will tell you their trouble is over-production—not scarcity. Ask the scientists, and they will tell you that there is food in plenty in the very air. And not only food—but power and riches. Ask the miners—whether of gold, or silver, or diamonds, or coal, or iron—and they will tell you that the supply exceeds the demand. Go to the manufacturer and ask him—and again your answer will be the same.

Evidently there is plenty to go around. Evidently the Father has not failed us, any more than he fails the birds of the air or the beasts of the field, in providing the supply. The problem is merely one of our ability to receive—to receive and digest and distribute and exchange.

There is plenty for all—of everything of good. The poor are hungry, the needy are in lack, not because there is not enough supply, but because their mental magnets have become so weak through discouragement, their channels so stopped up with fear and worry, that the stream of supply no longer reaches them.

If you cut your finger, what happens? You call upon your heart for an extra supply of blood to rebuild the damaged part. And the heart immediately responds.

If you have urgent need of money or other worldly goods, what should you do? Call upon the Heart of all things to send you an extra supply for your emergency—and He will just as promptly and cheerfully respond.

There's a little comedy on one of the Broadway stages that illustrates this idea clearly. A couple of young darkies are boxing—the first, an active, alert little fellow, on the go every minute—the second a tall, shambling, lazy sort, slow-moving, slow-thinking.

The big one is too lazy to really fight his active opponent. He contents himself with trying to guard himself. But every time he moves a hand, the little one gets in a punch.

Finally the big one catches hold of the little fellow by the shoulders, holds him off at arm's length and studies him for a minute. Then he puts one hand in the other's face and lets the little one jab at him, the while he holds him off at arm's length.

The little one swings and punches, but his arms are too short. He can't quite reach the big fellow. The lazy one throws back his head and laughs as he prepares to swing his good right arm at leisure. *"That's all I wanted to know,"* he says.

And all you need to know when that little devil of fear or worry or lack assails you and you want to hold him off for a while until you can swing your good right arm to put him out for the count is that the answer to any trouble, the remedy for any lack, the antidote for any ill is just around the corner. Charge your mental magnet with earnest desire and faith—and the need does not exist which you cannot satisfy.

"The Lord's hand is not shortened, that it cannot save," promised the Prophet Isaiah 59:1. "Neither His ear heavy, that it cannot hear."

The principal reason there is so much truth in the Scriptural quotation—"To him that hath shall be given," is that the man who has a tidy sum safely put away loses all worry about supply. Like the man in the play, he feels that his money gives him that bit of extra reach with which he can easily fend off the attacks of want and fear and worry, while he is getting in his good licks elsewhere. True, he places his dependence upon money rather than upon the Spirit, but the belief that he has money enough not to have to worry emboldens him to demand more. He loses all sense of fear. He expects and demands only the *good* things of life—and consequently the good things of life come to him. To put it in the words of Solomon—"He that hath a bountiful eye shall be blessed"—Proverbs 22:9

"He who dares assert the I,
May calmly wait, while hurrying fate
Meets his demand with sure supply."

Remember the story of the merchant who saw ruin staring him in the face unless he could raise money immediately? He went to a wise friend, who gave him a great nugget of gold—on condition, however, that he was not to use it except as a last resource.

Knowing that he had the gold to use at need, the merchant went boldly about his business with a mind at ease—faced his creditors so confidently that they gladly trusted him further—with the result that he never needed to use the gold.

But you don't need to go to the pages of fiction for such examples. Most of us have seen similar instances ourselves. There is the classic case of George Muller, of Bristol, England, who maintained orphanages which spent millions, through which hundreds of children were rescued from the slums and fitted for places of trust in the world—*all without any visible means of support!*

Like the oil from the widow's cruse, the money came through his perfect faith in the Giver of all good. Many and many a time utter penury stared him in the face, so that any man of less Job-like faith would have been discouraged. Once hundreds of hungry children sat waiting for their breakfasts—and there was not a mouthful to give them.

But always in time—though sometimes at the very last moment—his faith was justified and some generous donation would supply all their wants. Like Job, he might well have said—

"I know that my Redeemer liveth."—Job 19:25

"Though He slay me, yet will I trust in Him."—Job 13:15

Or with David—

"Yea, though I walk through the valley of the shadow of Death I shall fear no evil, for Thou art with me."—Psalms 23:4

For nothing stands between you and the dearest wish of your heart but doubt and fear. When you can pray without doubting, when you can believe as the Master bade us believe—"Whatsoever ye ask for when ye pray, believe that ye RECEIVE it and ye SHALL HAVE IT"—every desire of your heart will be instantly filled.

What, then, is the "Open, Sesame," of life? What is the Magic Secret that will bring to you everything of good you may wish?

It is simply a "Message to Garcia." There is within you a Holy Spirit who is your part of Divinity—who knows all, sees all and can do all things. Give him a definite task, magnetize Him with your absolute belief in His ability and His readiness to accomplish it—charge Him with such absolute faith that you can actually SEE HIM DOING IT—and "as thy faith is, so it will be unto you." The Spirit within you can draw from the heavens or the earth or the waters under the earth whatever you may need for the consummation of your desires.

How do men talk 3,000 miles across the Atlantic—without wires, without cables? In the Marconi beam system, they do it by focusing the electric waves into one great beam, just as a searchlight focuses all the light waves into one powerful ray. Ordinary broadcasting stations let their waves radiate in all directions like the ripples a pebble makes in a pool of water. The Marconi beam system focuses them all into one powerful beam and then directs it straight across the Atlantic, with the result that they will carry your message wherever you wish it to go.

Focus your desires in the same way. Instead of frittering away your energy in a thousand directions, bring them all to bear in one powerful beam on one single desire at a time. Do that, and you can attract to yourself anything of good you may wish.

"All that the Father hath is yours." And—"there is no lack in Him in whom all fullness lies."

So what do you want?

Is it money? Then know that the Father is the source of all wealth. Go to Him—tell Him your need—ask Him for money in abundance to meet your needs. Bless the money you now have—know that the Father is in it even as he is in all good things—then see it, in your mind's eye, *multiplied* as Jesus multiplied the loaves and fishes.

Send forth the Holy Spirit within you to the source of supply for as much as you need or can use to good advantage. Then SEE HIM DRAWING THAT SUPPLY! See a golden stream flowing to you in the sunlight, in the moonbeams!

Actually speak the word that sends your Spirit forth. Tell Him—"Holy Spirit, you know that the one Law of Supply is abundance—plenty for every right purpose, plenty for every right desire. You know that the Father has all of abundance, that there is unlimited money available for me right now, that as His son I am heir to it. Go you, therefore, bring to me of the infinite abundance that is mine, all that I may need for this purpose. If there is anything you wish *me* to do, give me a definite lead."

Speak the word, then cast your burden upon the Holy Spirit—and forget it! "My word shall not return unto me void, but shall accomplish that where unto it is sent."—Isaiah 55:11. Every doubt, every fear, every worry that you entertain is a shackle holding Him back. If you can release Him from all do-minion of the conscious mind, if you can have the faith in Him that you have when you give a task to a trusted servant and thereafter look upon it as done—depend upon it, He will bring you what you ask for.

But it is so hard for us to let go. We are like a man on a desert isle, daily releasing our one carrier pigeon with a message for help, yet as often bringing him back to earth again by the string on his foot that we are too distrustful to untie.

Yet when at last in desperation we do cut off the shackles, our faithful mes-senger flies straight home with his message of need and brings succour to us immediately.

That is why so often our prayers are not answered until the eleventh hour. We won't turn loose the string. We won't trust entirely in the Spirit. We think He needs our help, too. When all that we need is a little trust.

"If we have faith as a grain of mustard seed, ye shall say unto this mountain— remove hence to yonder place, and it shall remove. And nothing shall be impossible unto you."—Matthew 17:20

It is the same no matter what you may want. Are you seeking a position? Know that in the Mind of the Father there is one right position for you—one position that in the present stage of your development, is best fitted for you even as you are best fitted for it. You have a definite place in the great scheme of things. And there is one right position that marks the next step in your forward progress.

That position IS yours. You have only to *know* this and to realize it. Then send forth the Spirit within you to bring that position to you or you to it. *Speak the word.* Throw the burden upon Him, asking Him only, if there is anything you can do to forward the work, to give you a definite lead. Then rest content in the knowledge that the Spirit *is* doing the work.

"Prove me now herewith, saith the Lord of Hosts, if I will not open you the windows of heaven, and pour you out a blessing that there shall not be room enough to receive it."—Malachi 3:10

What, then, is the answer? Is this a lazy-man's world, where all that one needs to do is to fast and pray?

By no means! It is a worker's world—and the only ones who ever get anything out of it that is worth while are the workers. Mere wishing never magnetized the Spirit within to bring anything of good.

Look at all of Nature—busy every moment, never idle—*but never worrying.* Model after her. Whatever it is you may want, remember that you must get it first in Mind. See yourself with it there—see yourself receiving it. Make it as real as you can. Be thankful for it!

Then set about manifesting that dream in the material world. Do anything you can think of that will help to bring it about. Concentrate your thought upon it in every conceivable way. But never worry as to the outcome. Know that after you have done all that is possible for you to do—if you are still lacking in some essential, you can sit back in the utter confidence that the Holy Spirit within will supply that lack. Give of your best—and you need never fear for the outcome. Your best will come back to you—amplified an hundredfold.

"Ye know in all your hearts and in all your souls, that not one thing hath failed of all the good things which the Lord your God spake concerning you; all are come to pass unto you, and not one thing hath failed thereof."
—Joshua 23:14

4

The Man of Brass

"Behold, *now* is the accepted time.
Behold, *now* is the day of salvation."

—II CORINTHIANS

AWAY back in the 13th century, there lived a scientist so far ahead of his times that he had to record most of his discoveries in cypher—to keep from being burned at the stake.

Even as it was, he was thought by the ignorant to be a sorcerer, a magician, an apostate who had sold his soul to the devil. Only among the initiate was he known as "The Wonderful Doctor."

His name was Roger Bacon.

And wonderful he truly was. Many of the chemical formulas he discovered are in use today. He made gunpowder.

He discovered the possibilities of the magnifying glass. He was a forerunner of Galileo and Copernicus.

Innumerable legends grew up about him, some of which will be touched upon in the later volumes of this Course—notably his "Elixir of Life." But the most persistent of these legends deals with "The Man of Brass."

Bacon, you must know, had mastered seven different languages in his efforts to wrest from every possible source the secrets of science that had been known to previous ages. Among these languages was the Arabic. And one day there was brought to him an old Arabic manuscript which some wandering knight had picked up in far-away Palestine.

Bacon read the work and marvelled. It told first how to fashion a man of brass. Then, by means of clock-work and wires leading to certain jars of chemicals (the first crude storage batteries), how the eyeballs could be made to glow, the tongue to move, smoke to issue from the nostrils, and noise from the mouth. But most important of all—how, by adhering to certain directions, the Man of Brass could be made to speak *and reveal a secret of the utmost importance to every Englishman.*

For seven years, Roger Bacon toiled over his Man of Brass. He is reputed to have spent a fortune in scientific experiments, and no small part of it must have gone into this brazen image. At last it was finished. Everything had been done with the greatest care, strictly in accordance with the directions given in the manuscript.

Then he sat down and waited. For more than a month, there was never a minute when Roger Bacon or his friend and confidante Friar Bungay was not sitting before the brazen image, listening for any sound it might utter. But neither friars nor philosophers can keep on without sleep.

One night, when Friar Bungay had gone home, Bacon was nodding in his chair before the image. "If I can keep awake but a few hours longer," he muttered, "the wonderful voice will speak and the great secret will be known." But he could not keep awake. His eyes would close in spite of himself. Finally he called his servant, admonished him to wake him immediately if the image should speak and went off to snatch a bit of rest.

The servant sat near the door, his eyes fastened in frightened fascination upon those of the image, his fingers gripped about the stout oaken cudel in his hands.

Suddenly the eyes of the image glowed, its lips moved and in a sybilant whisper there issued from its mouth the words—

"TIME IS!"

The servant jumped to his feet and started to run, but as the brazen image seemed to remain rooted to the one spot, he paused on the threshold to see what more it might have to say.

Presently again the eyes lighted up, the lips moved, and a voice like the rattling of a kettle-drum shrilled out—

"TIME WAS!"

This time the servant all but fled. But before he could get the door open, the eyes glowed once more and in a voice of thunder there issued the words—

"TIME IS PAST!"

And with that the image fell and smashed into a thousand pieces.

Bacon is said to have been so bitterly disappointed at what he considered the wasting of all his seven years of labor that he burned his books, closed his study and spent the rest of his life in a monastery.

But had his work been wasted? Is there any secret of greater importance than the knowledge that—*"Time is NOW"?* Most of us are so busy regretting the past or planning what we are going to be and do in some far distant day or state that we overlook the chances for happiness and success that are all around us now.

The past is gone and done with. No amount of regrets will bring it back. So let us forget it—except in so far as we may draw lessons from it. Let our motto be "Yesterday ended last night."

As for the future—it is still ahead of us, and no man may tell what it holds.

But the present is ours to do with as we will. So let us live it to the utmost. *"Time IS"*—not has been or will be. "Time *passes"*—you will never have one bit more of time than you have this minute.

So what do you want to do with it? What have you to ask of the Father of Life—not next year, or ten years from now, or in some indefinite future state—but NOW?

There's an old Eastern legend that the gates of Paradise are opened only once in each thousand years. And judging by most people's attitude toward life, that belief seems to have obtained credence among us, for most of us look forward to happiness and success as something in the far distant future. We pray—but look for the result of our prayers in some vague future state.

"Behold, *now* is the accepted time," declared Paul.

All of supply is already in existence. Why put off drawing upon it six months—or a year—or ten years? Why not charge the magnet of your mind to draw from Infinite Supply what you may want NOW?

"I cause those that love me to inherit substance, and I will fill their treasures."— Proverbs 8:21

If you were to take a vote of the Christian peoples of the world, you would find them practically unanimous in believing that God intended to save their souls in the next world—but that in so far as their present existence is concerned, you've got to leave Him out of the reckoning!

Yet if you took from the Scriptures all those parts that tell of His succoring those in trouble—not in some far-off future state, but in this life; if you left out all His promises of protection and reward here on earth to those that loved Him and kept His commandments—how much of the Bible would there be left?

"And the Lord shall guide thee continually, and satisfy thy soul in drought, and make fat thy bones; and thou shalt be like a watered garden, and like a spring of water whose waters fail not."—Isaiah 58:11

If only all could realize that even in the heart of the humblest laborer, of the poorest scrub-woman, lies the key to riches inexhaustible, what a world of poverty and misery we might avoid.

"God shall supply all your need, according to His riches."—Philippians 4:19

Most of us find it easy enough to believe this when our pockets are full and all is going well with us. But let the wolf start scratching at the door and then watch us. Yet that is the very time when we most need faith! The fact is that we have more confidence in the weekly pay envelope, uncertain as it is, than we have in the Almighty! Well might the Prophet of old say to us, as he sarcastically said to the idolaters of his day—"Ye have gods that ye carry, but *we have a God that carries us.*"

"God is able to make all grace abound toward you, that ye always having all sufficiency in all things, may abound in every good work."—II Corinthians 9:8

Consider the lilies of the field. Consider the birds; the denizens of the field; of the forest; of the air and the water; they don't lack for what they need. The big difference between them and you is that you have been given free will. You don't need to go to the Father unless you wish. You can struggle and toil on your own account. You can look upon this as a vale of tears—and find it so. Or you can do your best—and then rest in the arms of the Father while "He doeth the works."

"Yea, the Almighty shall be thy defence, and thou shalt have plenty of silver."—Job 22:25

All that you need, all of good that you want, is right at your hand. Remember, when the disciples had been fishing all night and caught nothing, how Jesus told them to cast their nets on the *right* side—and they caught so many fish that their nets were full to overflowing?

If He could fill the nets of these discouraged fishermen with fish, don't you suppose He can just as easily fill your nets with whatever it is you may be fishing for?

"The soul answers never by words," says Emerson, "but by the thing itself sought after."

Have you ever seen the Hopi Indians' Snake Dance—their prayer for rain? It is probably the oldest religious ceremony on this continent, and it is said that it never yet has failed to bring the rains.

"Speak to Him thou, for He heareth
When Spirit with Spirit doth meet;
Closer is He than breathing,
And nearer than hands and feet."

Scientists may talk learnedly of atmospheric conditions and natural laws, but the fact remains—the Indians send up their heartfelt prayers to the Holy Spirit in simple faith—and so far as is known, the rains have never failed to promptly come!

"Whither shall I go from thy Spirit?" cried the Psalmist of old, "Or whither shall I flee from Thy presence? If I ascend up into heaven Thou are there; if I make my bed in hell, behold Thou are there. If I take the wings of the morning and dwell in the uttermost parts of the sea; even there shall Thy hand lead me and Thy right hand shall hold me. If I say,

Surely the darkness shall cover me; even the night shall be light about me."—Psalms 139:7–11

There is in this universe a Power that hears the cry of the human heart. There is behind us a Father "whose good pleasure it is to give us the Kingdom." You don't have to beg Him for the good things of life any more than you have to beg the sun for its heat. You have only to draw near and take of the bountiful supply He is constantly holding out to you.

"Before ye call, I shall answer."

So what is it you want of the Father of Life? A house? A toy? A car? Success in this or that undertaking? Health? Love? Happiness?

Whatever it is, you can have it. Whatever of good you ask for with earnest desire and simple faith, the Father will gladly give.

Does this sound too simple, too direct? Do you feel that it is a bit sacreligious to be asking the Father for worldly things? Just listen:

"And I say unto you, Ask, and it shall be given you; seek, and ye shall find; knock, and it shall be opened unto you.

"For every one that asketh receiveth; and he that seeketh findeth; and to him that knocketh it shall be opened.

"If a son shall ask bread of any of you that is a Father, will he give him a stone? Or if he ask a fish, will he for a fish give him a serpent?

"Or if he shall ask an egg, will he offer him a scorpion?

"If ye then, being evil, know how to give good gifts unto your children: how much more shall your heavenly Father give the Holy Spirit to them that ask him?"—Luke 11:9–13

And those words came—not from any Prophet or Disciple, but from the lips of the Master Himself!

So have no hesitancy in going to Him about little things. Don't you suppose He is as glad to see you clothed in a new suit or new dress as He is to see the birds preening their new feathers, the wild things of the forest in their shining new coat, the snake and his like in their new skins? Don't you suppose it gives Him as much pleasure to give you something you have been longing for as it gladdens the heart of an earthly father to give a much-desired toy to his little boy?

"Thou openest thy hand and satisfieth the desire of every living thing."

I have had people write me that prayer has brought to them such simple little things as flowers, as toys for the children, as an automobile. Last Christmas one reader wrote me that he had needed $500. That he had put his problem before the Father confidently, believingly. Then left it with Him. To use his own words, "the $500 came from so unexpected a source that if the President himself had sent it to him, he would not have been more surprised."

"No good things will He withhold from them that walketh uprightly."

The very fact that you have some earnest desire is the best evidence that the answer to that desire is in the great heart of God.

"Time is NOW!"

That earnest desire of yours is in the present. And the supply is just as much so. The Father is just as much present here and now as He will ever be. So why put off the realization of your desires to some vague and distant future? Why not realize them in the now?

What is it that you want?

Whatever it is, it already exists somewhere, in some form. And if your desire be strong enough, your faith great enough you can attract it to you.

There are riches in abundance for you. They already exist. They are labeled YOURS in the mind of the Father. And until you get them, they will remain idle. You don't have to take them from someone else. You don't have to envy anyone else what he has. All you have to KNOW is that somewhere all of riches that you can ever desire are lying waiting for you.

Don't try to get them all at once.

If you had a million dollars on deposit in some bank, you wouldn't rush there and draw it out, to carry around with you or to hide about the house. No—as long as you had confidence in the integrity of the bank, you would leave your money on deposit there, drawing upon it merely as you needed it.

Have you less confidence in the Bank of the Father than in those of man? Must you ask It for all your heritage at once for fear the Bank will fail? Or can you do as Jesus did, as He told us all to do, ask each day for that day's needs—"Give us this day our daily bread"—in the simple faith that our every draft will be met promptly, fully, no matter what the size?

The man who has that simple faith will not try to pinch pennies. He won't "pass by on the other side" when a worthy need approaches him. Neither will he throw away money foolishly—"casting pearls before swine."

He will spend cheerfully—for any right purpose. He will bless the money he sends out—as Jesus blessed the loaves and the fishes—putting it to work in the confident knowledge that when used gainfully, it will come back increased and multiplied.

The same thing applies to your home, to your surroundings. There is a perfect home for you already built in the Father's mind. Know this—realize it—then, like Hagar in the wilderness, pray that your eyes may be opened that you may SEE this perfect home that is yours.

There is a perfect position for you. A perfect mate. A perfect work. A perfect idea of each cell and organism in your body. In later volumes of this set, I shall try to show you how through the promises of the Scriptures these may all be realized. Suffice it now to say that they all exist in the Father's mind. It is up to you merely to *seek* that you may find them.

You have the most powerful magnet on earth right within your own mind. Uncover it! Charge it with desire and faith. Speak the word that sends the Holy Spirit that is within you in quest of what you wish. Then cast the burden upon Him and thereafter look upon your desire as an accomplished fact.

"Whatsoever ye ask for when ye pray, believe that ye *receive* it and ye shall have it."

Prepare for the thing you have asked for, even though there be not the slightest sign of its coming. Act the part! Like the three Kings in the desert, dig your ditches to receive the water, even though there be not a cloud in the sky. And your ditches will be filled—even as were theirs.

"Be still—and know that I am God!" Wait calmly, confidently, in the full assurance that the Father has what you want and will gladly give it to you.

One's ships come in over a calm sea.

THE LAW OF KARMA

You have probably heard of the Law of Karma. It is Sanskrit, you know, for "Comeback." It is one of the oldest laws known to man—yet perhaps the least regarded.

It is the law of the boomerang. Jesus quoted it: "Whatsoever a man soweth, that shall he also reap."

In the parlance of today, it is—"Chickens come home to roost." Even in science we find it, as Newton's Third Law of Motion—"Action and reaction are always equal to each other."

Wherein does this law affect us now? Only in that, if you wish riches, if you long for happiness, health, success, you must *think* abundance, you must charge your mind with happy thoughts, healthy thoughts, optimistic thoughts.

If you are seeking riches, you will never get them by stopping up all the avenues of outgo, and waiting for your vessel to fill up from the top. I remember one man who wrote me from down in West Virginia that when he received *The Secret of the Ages* he was a farmhand, working for $1 a day. Through the confidence and knowledge acquired through the books, he had landed a job at $6.20 a day of eight hours, where before he had labored for twelve hours on the farm. But, he wrote, "I've returned the books. You gave me time to get out of them what I wanted and return at your expense without buying them. I think now I can make a million. So I don't want to spend any money now. I want to make my million." That man was like a funnel—big at the receiving end, but little at the outgoing part. The Law of Karma will get him before he has gone far. You have got to cast your bread upon the waters, in the secure confidence that it will come back to you multiplied an hundredfold.

If you are longing for a beautiful home, you will never get it by thinking thoughts of poverty and lack. Forget the state of your pocketbook. Your supply is not there. All supply is in the Father, "with Whom is no variableness nor shadow of turning." So go to the Father with your desire. Try to picture in your mind's eye the perfect home that already is yours in Divine Mind. Make it complete in every detail. Realize that this perfect home *is yours*—that it already exists—in the mind of the Father. Then send forth the Holy Spirit to bring it to you or you to it.

Don't ask for some particular house. Ask, if you wish, for one like it. Don't try to take that which is another's. Know that the one perfect home for you already exists in Divine Mind, even though you may never have seen it. Then leave it to the Holy Spirit to manifest it.

"All that the Kingdom affords is yours."

Speak the word—then cast the burden upon the Holy Spirit within. The Father sends His gifts in His own way, even as earthly fathers frequently do. Make all preparations for them—dig your ditches—open up the windows of your soul. Be ready to receive.

Remember, in Genesis I:1–2—"In the beginning, God created the heaven and the earth. And the earth was without form and void; and darkness was upon the face of the deep. *And the Spirit of God moved upon the face of the waters.*"

That Spirit of God still moves upon the face of the waters. And upon the face of the land. That Spirit of God is the Holy Spirit within you. And just as He helped to form the earth from the void, so will He bring form to your dreams, your desires. If only you do your part. If only you have the faith. If only you can cast the burden upon Him—confidently, believingly!

"Oh Judah, fear not; but tomorrow go out against them, for the Lord will be with you. You shall not need to fight this battle; set yourselves, stand you still, *and see the salvation of the Lord with you.*"

And the time to do it is NOW.

5

Start Something!

"And I have filled him with the Spirit of God, in wisdom, and in understanding, and in knowledge, and in all manner of workmanship,

"To devise cunning works, to work in gold, and in silver, and in brass,

"And in cutting of stones, to set them, and in carving timber, to work in all manner of workmanship.

"And I, behold, I have given with him Aholiah, the son of Ahisamach, of the tribe of Dan: and in the hearts of all that are wise hearted I have put wisdom, that they may make all that I have commanded thee."

—EXODUS 31:3–6

A Spanish adventurer gets together a following of a couple of thousand out-at-elbows soldiers of fortune like himself—and with them conquers a nation! A disciplined, well-led warlike nation numbering millions! Defeats armies ten times the size of his little force, time after time! Captures a walled city garrisoned by a great army and protected by dykes and canals, and makes its emperor prisoner!

I refer to Hernando Cortez, conqueror of Mexico.

Another Spaniard, with a handful of followers, enslaves the whole of Peru, carries away the vast treasures of the Incas, makes Spain the richest nation on the globe!

That was 400 years ago, but it is easy enough to find their counterparts today. A few years ago Persia had been almost dismembered by Russia and England.

And Reza Khan was but a poor trooper in the Persian army. Today Persia has been restored to an independent state—and Reza Khan is its Ruler.

Before the war Mussolini was an unknown Socialist worker. During the war, a common soldier. Today he is head of a re-nationalized Italy.

Ebert, a saddle-maker before the war—becomes President of the new German Republic. Trotsky, a waiter in a cheap New York restaurant—is made War Minister of Soviet Russia. Mustapha Kemal, a good soldier—but until the war unknown—makes himself Ruler of Turkey. Every day brings its grist of new stars in the world firmament—new and comet-like rises to fame.

How do they do it? What is the secret behind such phenomenal successes?

Not education—many of these men had no education to speak of. Not training—none of them was ever trained for real leadership. Then what is it?

Just one thing these men all had in common—the daring to *start something!*

If Cortez had been content to sit around in Cuba and wait for something to turn up, do you suppose we should ever have heard of him?

If Reza Khan had been content to do his mere duty as a Persian trooper; if Mussolini had sat down and rested on his laurels as a soldier; if Ebert had been satisfied to keep on making saddles; if Mustapha Kemal had merely obeyed whatever orders he received; do you suppose their countrymen would have started out on a still hunt for them, routed them out of their obscurity and put them at the head of their governments?

Not in a thousand years!

You may—and do—possess latent ability equal to any man on earth; you have ready to your call, through the Holy Spirit within you, not merely the wisdom of a Solomon but the Wisdom of God! Yet all of this will not get you anywhere—all of this will never result in the world calling upon you to lead it—unless you *use it to start something!*

"BUBBLES"

You know the air castles a young fellow builds when he is planning his future with his Best Girl. You know what pictures of wonderful achievement he can paint for her. The wealth of the Indies is but a trifle compared with the fortune he is going to lay at her feet.

"Day dreams," we call them—and laugh good-naturedly at the fondness of youth and love for believing in such bubbles, such figments of the imagination. But these dreams are very real and very dear to every boy—and girl. They embody all those things they hope some day soon to see materialize.

The only trouble with them is, that with most of us these bubbles are so soon pricked. We meet with discouragement. The fine point of our enthusiasm and ambition is blunted. Soon we lapse into a regular grind, and the man we hoped to be, the man we painted in such glowing terms to our Sweetheart—the man she really married—quietly passes out, leaving nothing but the husk of what might have been.

Is it any wonder there are so many unhappy marriages, when you compare the realities a man actually gives to the girl who marries him, with the "Bubbles" he promised her before?

The wonder is that so many girls shed only a few tears over their shattered dreams, forget their disillusionment, and knuckle down to the tiresome, dispiriting daily round of cooking and housework—of tending babies and being good wives to their plodding husbands.

The greatest waste in business today is the waste of the enthusiasm of all the fine young fellows that go into it. True—their enthusiasm is frequently misdirected—but that is *your* opportunity. Go look at Niagara Falls!

For uncounted years the Niagara River dashed over its rocky cliff, the power of millions of horses behind it—a beautiful sight for the occasional tourist—but nothing more!

Today that same Niagara turns the wheels of a hundred great industries—gives light and power to all of Western New York—is soon to become the basis of a giant super-power system for the entire Northeast.

What made the difference? The Niagara has not changed—it had exactly the same power afore-time. 'Tis simply that man has learned how to *direct* that power, to *use* that energy for useful purposes.

"Give instruction to a wise man, and he will be yet wiser," says the Proverbs (9); "teach a just man, and he will increase in learning."

Remember the story of the young King of the Black Isles? He started out full of high ambitions. But the wicked enchantress (Lack of Initiative) turned him into black marble from the waist down. So he was condemned to sit in his palace and bemoan his fate until there came a new King to lift the spell, to inspire him for high emprise, to keep him from ever again lapsing into the state of half man and half statue.

"And Moses said unto the Lord, O my Lord, I am not eloquent, neither hereto-fore, nor since thou hast spoken unto thy servant: but I am slow of speech, and of a slow tongue.

"And the Lord said unto him, Who hath made man's mouth? Or who maketh the dumb, or deaf, or the seeing, or the blind? Have not I the Lord?

"Now therefore go, and I will be with thy mouth, and teach thee what thou shalt say."

The world's most tragic figure is the man who never starts anything. He is dead from the waist down. He sits and wishes and dreams; he goes through motions, doing routine things that a machine could do just as well, but he never gets anywhere.

How did Carnegie make his millions? By finding a new way to make steel—and then starting to *do* it! How did Woolworth, how did Penny, make their successes? By trying out new methods of merchandising—by starting something. How did Ford become the richest man in the world? By visioning the new transportation within the reach of every one—and then starting to put it there!

You want to get out of the rut—to grow—to develop into something better. And there are unnumbered new methods in industry, new inventions, new ideas—waiting merely to be uncovered.

To whom will these prizes go? Nine times out of ten to the man who starts something—to the man who dreams great dreams, and then has the courage, the belief in himself, in his Spirit, in his Destiny, to make the start, to take the plunge, *to go!*

"And the Spirit of the Lord shall rest upon him, the spirit of wisdom and understanding, the spirit of counsel and might, the spirit of knowledge and of the fear of the Lord."—Isaiah II

THE THINGS THAT CAN'T BE DONE

When John MacDonald first proposed to build the great New York subways, people laughed at him. He went to one "big" financier after another, and the answer of all was the same. "Dig a tunnel under all these streets and houses, with their maze of pipe lines and electric cables and gas mains and sewers? Impossible!"

But through it all he held to the one main idea. "You have a cellar under your house, haven't you?" he asked them. "And you dug it without much trouble, didn't you? Well, I'm not thinking of building a tunnel the length of this island. I'm planning to dig a string of cellars—*and then connect them together!*"

And he finally found a man big enough to see the idea—and to back it.

"Thou shalt make thy prayer unto Him, and He shall hear thee, and thou shalt pay thy vows.

"Thou shalt also decree a thing, and it shall be established unto thee: and the light shall shine upon thy ways."—Job 22:27–28

In this day of miracles, it would be a hardy spirit that would say that anything is impossible. The time is not far distant when men will harness the tides, get motive power and much of their food from the air and from the tropic seas, talk to anyone anywhere and see them while they talk. These and a thousand other inventions even more wonderful are in the very air. Why shouldn't you be the one to start some of them?

You don't need to be an engineer. You don't need to be an inventor. Pasteur was not a doctor, yet he did more for medical science than any doctor. Whitney was not a cotton planter. Not even a Southerner. He was a Connecticut school teacher. Yet he invented the cotton gin! Bell was a professor of elocution, and he once said that he invented the telephone because he knew nothing of electricity. He didn't know it couldn't be done! Morse, of telegraphic fame, was a portrait painter—not an electrician. Dunlop (maker of tires) was a veterinary surgeon. Gillette was a traveling salesman. Eastman a bank clerk. Ingersoll a mechanic. Harriman a broker. Gary a lawyer.

In fact, most of the great inventors and pioneers have been outsiders. Why? They don't know the things that can't be done—*so they go ahead and do them!*

"Opportunity," says Doc Lane, "is as scarce as oxygen; men fairly breathe it and do not know it."

"But as it is written, Eye hath not seen, nor ear heard, neither have entered into the heart of man, the things which God hath prepared for them that love him.

"But God hath revealed them unto us by His Spirit: for the Spirit searcheth all things, yea, the deep things of God.

"For what man knoweth the things of a man, save the spirit of man which is in him? Even so the things of God knoweth no man, but the Spirit of God."—I Corinthians 2:9–11

It is not necessary to have a "pull" to succeed. In fact, a "pull" is more often than not just that—a pull *backward*. What we need is the "push" of necessity. For most of us are so constituted that, unless we have to put into the fight all our strength and energy, we just jog along in a slothful, ambitionless sort of way, getting nowhere.

The saving event in many a man's life has been the blow that knocked the props out from under him and left him to look out for himself. As Emerson put it: "It is only as a man puts off all foreign support and stands alone that I see him firm and to prevail. He is weaker by every recruit to his banner."

So never envy the man with a "pull." Pity him. He has lost the greatest thing there is in business—the need for individual initiative.

You say you have to start at the bottom, while Bill Smith's father left him enough money to begin at the head of a real business? Never mind. Start something—even if it be only a peanut stand—and ten years from now you will have not only some very valuable experience, but a business that will be paying you dividends and give you an insurance for the future. Whereas the chances are that though Bill Smith may have the experience, that is all he will have. Most of the big businesses of today, you know, started on a shoestring.

"Thus saith the Lord; Refrain thy voice from weeping, and thine eyes from tears: for thy work shall be rewarded, saith the Lord."—Jeremiah 31

Democracy is equality, not of place, but of opportunity. Just because you were born on Fifth Avenue doesn't mean that you are going to stay there. And just because you were born on the East Side doesn't mean that you have got to stay there. Al Smith is but one of thousands who have come up from humble surroundings to the topmost rung of the ladder of success.

"Always the real leaders of men," says Dr. Frank Crane, "the real kings, have come up from the common people. The finest flowers in the human flora grow in the woods pasture and not in the hothouse; no privileged class, no Royal house, no carefully selected stock produced a Leonardo or a Michelangelo in art, a Shakespeare or Burns in letters, a Galli Curci or Paderewski in music, a Socrates or Kant in philosophy, an Edison or Pasteur in science, a Wesley or a Knox in religion."

The Law of Compensation is constantly at work. When men grow to put too much dependence upon the fortune or the institution or the position that has been given them, these props are suddenly removed. When through grim necessity they have learned not to rely upon anything short of the Infinite, the channels of supply are reopened to them.

"Put not your trust in Princes," advised the Psalmist. Not because Princes are so much more unreliable than ordinary men, but because they are mere tributaries—even as you are—to the King of Kings.

Put not your trust in some other man or institution. Go direct to the Fount! Don't tap some other man's channel. Go direct to the main Source of Supply!

"By me kings reign, and princes decree justice.

"By me princes rule, and nobles, even all the judges of the earth.

"I love them that love me; and those that seek me early shall find me.

"Riches and honour are with me; yea, durable riches and righteousness."
—Proverbs 8:15–19

BE KING IN YOUR OWN THOUGHTS

"Every man," says a mediaeval writer, "has within him the making of a great saint."

And every one of us has in him the making of a great success.

"Less than a year ago," reads a letter to me from W. Bruce Haughton, "I started in the automotive business in Jacksonville with $23.00 in my pocket. I bought $14.40 worth of tools and rented a two-car garage in the back yard of the house where I rented a room. I then went to several of the city professional men and told them what I could do for their cars. In thirty days I had a net return of $476.80 with an overhead of about $50.00.

"In June, 1926, I had to find bigger quarters to handle my business, for I then had 591 regular customers coming to my 'Back Yard' for service they could not buy elsewhere. Today I am negotiating with a concern for another corner in the best part of this city to handle my patrons who live in that section."

In the newspaper the other day, I read how Palmer C. Hayden, 33 years old, was quitting his scrub bucket to study art in Europe. He had just won the $400 prize in art awarded by the Harmon Foundation. He had the courage to start something.

I know a young fellow who, while still in College, got the idea through a chance occurrence that there was an entirely virgin field among the undertakers for raincoats—black raincoats. He reasoned that there were so few undertakers in each city that no store could afford to carry a complete range of sizes for them, whereas one central store, selling to the whole country, could do so.

So he borrowed a few dollars and tried out his idea by mail. Today he is a millionaire—and it has all been the logical outcome of that one idea.

He started something.

If you could only realize that you have a definite place in a scheme so big that God has been working millions of years to bring it about; if you would only remember that every forward step you take has His approval and help; if you would look upon Him as a loving Father watching you, His little son, taking a few faltering steps, ready to catch you when you stumble, ready to help you over the difficult places, ready to strengthen and support you—how much of fear and worry you would avoid, how much more surely you would progress.

"If ye walk in my statutes, and keep my commandments, and do them;

"Then I will give you rain in due season, and the land shall yield her increase, and the trees of the field shall yield their fruit.

"And your threshing shall reach unto the vintage, and the vintage shall reach unto the sowing time: and ye shall eat your bread to the full, and dwell in your land safely.

"And I will give peace in the land, and ye shall lie down, and none shall make you afraid."—Leviticus 26:3–6

But to progress, it is necessary that you learn to take a few steps for yourself. You can't remain tied to the Father's apron-strings if you are to become a man or woman worthy of the name.

You know how much these "Mother's darlings" are good for when they get out among other boys. You know how long these pampered children of the rich usually last, when they are thrown upon their own resources.

The Father above has the wisdom and the courage to do what very few earthly fathers can. He gives his children free will. He turns them loose, in a world full of pitfalls and dangers, to learn self-reliance, to become real men and women, worthy Sons of God.

Yet He is always just behind us. His arms ready to support us. His hand to guide us. His wisdom to counsel us—if only we will realize His presence, His solicitude, His Fatherly love and care.

"He giveth power to the faint; and to them that have no might, he increaseth strength."—Isaiah 40:29

He has given us free will, so He will not force Himself upon us. He has untied our apron-strings, so He won't *make* us take the great place He plans for us in the Divine scheme of things. But if we will learn to work with Him, if we will treat Him as a Father, run to Him with our joys as with our sorrows, have Him at the back of all our plans, know that we can rely upon His help in all our undertakings, what a difference it will make!

You need never hesitate then to start anything of good, because you will know that with Him behind you, it can not fail. You will never lack the faith, the enthusiasm, the power to carry through even the most difficult undertaking. Most of all, you will never lack the will to begin, for you will know that even the Father can not help you to accomplish, until you yourself have taken the first step by STARTING SOMETHING!

"Since receiving your first books," writes M. D. C. of Capitola, California, "I have made from insurance premuims in a new company which I was instrumental in forming, more than $100,000.00 in a little over six months' time. My previous income over a period of years has been approximately $7,500.00 per year."

He started something!

"And we know that all things work together for good to them that love God."—Luke 11:28

THE STARTING POINT

Now, how about you—have *you* started anything? Do you want to? Then let's take stock of you for a moment:

1. The first thing to do is to list all of your successes, no matter how unimportant they may seem. Go back to your boyhood days. What was your favorite game. Was it one that required initiative, quick thinking, prompt action? Were you a better "individual-player" or "team-player"? In other words, were you a brilliant "star," or one of those who could sink his own individuality for the good of the team? Did you ever captain any team successfully? Did your teammates

like you, work with you enthusiastically? Could you inspire loyalty, cooperation, weld your team into a single unit with a common purpose?

Qualities such as these can be acquired, of course, but if you had them naturally as a boy, then you have them now, so by all means develop them to their fullest extent. They can be made your most valuable assets in business.

2. What sort of game do you prefer now? One that depends primarily upon yourself—or one that demands mostly team-work? Games are wonderful indicators, you know, of your innate characteristics. I used to know a very shrewd old fellow who never formed a business friendship until after he had played poker with his prospective friend. How do you play bridge—*with* your partner or regardless of him? How do you play tennis—as two individual players, or as a team?

Don't misunderstand me—I am not decrying brilliant individual play. I am just trying to get you to analyze your innate characteristics. If you play best alone, by all means concentrate on the kind of work or the kind of business that is built up around one single figure. On the other hand, if your forte is team-work, cooperation—go in for organized effort where your leadership and fairness and good-fellowship will have the greatest play.

3. List your characteristics frankly. Ability in particular lines, quickness in picking up new ideas, open-mindedness, versatility, honesty, sociability, interest in others, power to convince others, courage, aggressiveness, stick-to-it-iveness.

In short, analyze yourself frankly—then from that analysis, from your past failures and successes, pick the work you have the greatest aptitude for—and go into it!

Don't go into it blindly. First study it. There are good books on every phase of business today. There are correspondence courses as good as any taught in colleges. Get them. Read them. Set your goal. Make your plans carefully. Start them in a small way first. Test each step before you put your weight upon it. But once sure of it, put your *whole* weight into it—your money and your ability and all your thought—*particularly all your thought*.

Don't scatter your energies. You can do it with the work of your hands but you can't do it with your thought. To make a great success, your thought has to be concentrated on your goal in the same way that the Marconi beam system concentrates all the power of its rays in the one direction. "No man can serve two masters"—with justice to either.

Choose your goal; then, like the searchlight, concentrate all your efforts, all your energies, all your thoughts in the one direction. Don't go running off after false gods. Don't fritter away your energies on inconsequential side-issues. Focus them—focus them as you focus the rays of the sun through a magnifying glass. Do that—and you will speedily start something!

There is a definite place for you in the Divine plan. There is a work which you are to do, which no one else can do quite as well. Pray, therefore, to the Father that He may open your eyes to your right work, that He may open your ears to the promptings of His voice, that He may open your understanding of the right way.

"I will instruct thee and teach thee in the way which thou shalt go: I will guide thee with mine eye."—Psalms 32:8

6

Rough Diamonds

"And he hath filled him with the Spirit of God, in wisdom, in understanding, and in knowledge, and in all manner of workmanship.

"And to devise curious works, to work in gold, and in silver, and in brass.

"And in the cutting of stones, to set them, and in carving of wood, to make any manner of cunning work."

—EXODUS 35:31–33

OVER in the northwestern corner of Pennsylvania a few years ago, there lived a farmer who was interested in oil. His brother was in the oil business in Canada and had told him that fortunes were being made in it every day. So he sent for all kinds of books that told how and where to locate oil, took a course in geology, spent two years getting ready—and then sold his farm and went to Canada to work in the oil fields.

The man who bought the farm, walking over the place next morning, came to a little brook that ran through the middle of it. There was a heavy board across the brook to hold back the surface drift, and back of it for some yards the water was coated with a thick scum.

It seems that this scum had troubled the previous owner for a long time. The cattle wouldn't drink the water with it on it. So he had conceived the idea of the board to clear the scum from the surface and let the cattle drink from the water below.

To the new buyer, that "scum" looked and smelled and tasted suspiciously like oil! He sent for experts. They bored. And opened up one of the richest oil fields in Pennsylvania!

It is natural to think that the first step towards success is to go somewhere else or into some new business. The distant pastures always look greenest. But more often than not, our best opportunities lie right under our own nose.

When the original Pennsylvania oil wells seemed to be worked out, most of the oil men set off for fields and pastures new. But a few stayed. And those few found that the surface had merely been scratched! Instead of being worked out, scarcely 15 per cent of the oil had been taken out of the ground. By the pressure system, or by boring deeper and striking new deposits, they found the other 85 per cent!

And that is only one industry out of hundreds where fortunes have been made out of what other men had thrown away as worthless. No one has yet exhausted any line of thought. The inventions that mankind has already made are merely the introduction to bigger and greater things—the open door to opportunity. The most brilliant scientists are the first to tell you that their discoveries are but as a drop of water to the great ocean of achievement that lies beyond.

"For the earth shall be filled with the knowledge of the glory of the Lord, as the waters cover the sea."—Habakuk 2:14

Nearly a century and a half ago, Malthus propounded his famous theory that population, when unchecked, tends to increase in geometrical proportion, whereas subsistence increases only in arithmetical proportion. In other words, that population increases many times as rapidly as the means of subsistence. And he visioned a time in the very near future when artificial checks would have to be put on population, or the world would starve.

Population has increased very near to the point he feared, but what has happened? We are farther away from the saturation point than in his day! The age of machinery came along; the age of scientific experiment; and not only opened up new fields through better transportation, but greatly increased the yields in present fields. Now Prof. Albrecht Penck advances the belief that by the year 2227 there will be 8,000,000,000 people here on earth—and famine will be continuous, because the earth cannot support that many!

What little faith some of these economists have! They get so wrapped up in their own calculations that they can see nothing else. "By that time (2227 A. D.)," says the New York Herald Tribune, "man may be taking foodstuffs from the sunlight, from the air or from the power of the revolving earth! The only safe prediction about the future of man is that no limit dare be set to what he and Nature may cooperate to do."

> "For I know the thoughts that I think towards you, saith the Lord, thoughts of peace and not of evil, to give you an expected end. Then, shall ye call upon me, and ye shall go and pray unto me and I will hearken unto you. And ye shall seek me, and find me, when ye shall search for me with all your heart."—Jeremiah 29:11–13

For 5,000 years men have built houses of brick, and in all of that time there had been no change made, either in the tools used, or in the manner in which the work was done.

Along came Frank Gilbreth, studied the motions involved in laying brick, reduced them from eighteen to five, and increased the hourly output from 120 to 350 bricks!

Simple enough—but it took 5,000 years for someone to think up this simple solution.

For 5,000 years mankind has been taught that some men are born with ability—some without—and that those without must serve those who have it.

No greater mistake was ever made. Every man is born with ability sufficient to carry him upward to the highest rung of success. "Ordinary ability, properly applied," said Theodore N. Vail, "is all that is necessary to reach the highest rung in the ladder of success."

Life's biggest blunder is to underestimate your own power to develop and accomplish. What if you are handicapped by lack of education, by poverty, by self-consciousness, by sickness, by some physical disability?

Thank God for it! A handicap is the greatest urge you can have towards success. Like the eagle which uses adverse winds to rise higher, you can mount to success on your handicap.

In an editorial some time ago, the New York Globe observed: "Nature is not democratic. She gives some women beauty and leaves others, of equal or greater merit, plain. She makes some persons intelligent and some stupid. In brief, we are not born free and equal nor do we become so. To some the Gods bring gifts and others they pass by. There are aristocracies of voices, of beauty and of intelligence. The best that democracy can ever do is to give every Caruso a chance to sing."

That is the general belief. That is the idea that prevails among most casual thinkers. But the man who thinks thus is overlooking the greatest force in life—the reserve force that lies so dormant in most of us—the power of the Spirit within to rise superior to any inequality, to overcome any seeming handicap or difficulty.

The greatest thing that can happen to any man is the discovery of this all-powerful Spirit within him. If it is necessary for him to undergo hunger, if it is necessary for him to suffer sickness or injury in order to make the discovery, let him suffer it cheerfully, gladly! No price is too high to pay to bring into your affairs the power of the Holy Spirit. For everything you have suffered, everything you have paid, will be made good to you an hundredfold. There is no maybe about this. I have seen it work out hundreds of times. I have learned it from very bitter experience. As in the case of Job of olden times:

"The Lord gave Job twice as much as he had before.

"So the Lord blessed the latter end of Job more than his beginning; for he had fourteen thousand sheep, and six thousand camels, and a thousand yoke of oxen and a thousand she asses.

"He had also seven sons and three daughters."—Job 42:10, 12, 13

THE LAW OF COMPENSATION

What was it made Demosthenes the greatest orator of all time. NOT his natural gifts—but his natural *handicaps!* He was self-conscious. And he stuttered. Had he not been thus handicapped, he would probably have become a mediocre orator—and lived and died unknown to the world. But he had to study so hard to overcome his natural handicaps, he had to practice and work so long and so whole-heartedly, that when at last he was ready to appear before the public, his conscious efforts were backed by all the powers of the subconscious. He had so often called upon the Spirit within to help him in his practice that it came to his aid of Itself when the real need arose. It stood at his back to give him confidence, to lend him inspiration, to supply the power that moved his hearers as they had never been moved before.

In "Organ Inferiority and Its Psychic Compensation," Dr. Adler brings out the well-known scientific fact that any physical weakness or inferiority brings with it an extra urge to strive for superiority in some compensating way.

Napoleon, Caesar, Prince Eugene were little men, but the urge within them made them the biggest men of their day.

Whistler, the greater painter, had poor eyes. He was said to be color blind. So he became a master in nuances. Edison was deaf—so he perfected the talking machine.

Beethoven, Mozart, Franz—all had defects in hearing. And worked so hard at their music that they became masters of technique, and musical geniuses.

The same principle applies to nations. Take Alaska and Switzerland as an instance. Alaska has enormous resources of gold and silver and copper and coal, vast virgin forests, 1,000,000 square miles suitable for agriculture, and the greatest fisheries in the world. Yet if Alaska were as densely populated as Switzerland it would be supporting 120,000,000 inhabitants!

The Swiss have few natural resources, so they are constrained to use their ingenuity instead. They take a ton of metal and put it together in such form as to make it worth a million dollars. They take cotton thread at 20 cents a pound, and convert it into lace worth $2,000 a pound. They take a block of wood worth 10 cents and convert it into a carving worth $100. And because as a nation they have learned the art of utilizing their talents, they have prospered abundantly.

Where is the moral? Simply this:

There is no lack, no handicap, *nothing*, that can defeat you. Obstacles are the greatest blessings God can give you. They bring out the soul of you. They bring the Holy Spirit to your help. And anything which acquaints you with the Spirit within you, anything that gives you an understanding of the infinite power within you, anything that brings the Holy Spirit into your daily affairs, is worth while no matter what its cost.

"And Jacob was left alone; and there wrestled a man with him until the breaking of the day.

"And when he saw that he prevailed not against him, he touched the hollow of his thigh; and the hollow of Jacob's thigh was out of joint, as he wrestled with him.

"And he said, Let me go, for the day breaketh. And he said, I will not let thee go, *except thou bless me.*

"And he said unto him, What is thy name? And he said, Jacob.

"And he said, Thy name shall be called no more Jacob, but Israel: for as a prince hast thou power with God and with men, and hast prevailed.

"And Jacob asked him, and said, Tell me, I pray thee, thy name. And he said, Wherefore is it that thou dost ask after my name? *And he blessed him there.*"

That is what you, too, must do. Wrestle with every difficulty until you have learned something from it. Don't let go of any trouble until you have made it bless you.

Remember that back of you always is the power of the Holy Spirit and if the need arises, it can give you the strength—not merely of one man, but of ten! Like David going out to meet Goliath, realize that it is not you who is fighting the battle, but God. "Be not afraid, nor dismayed by reason of this great multitude; for the battle is not yours but God's."—II Chronicles 20:15. Knowing that, no obstacle need deter you, no experience terrify you. With God on your side, you are always in the majority. Struggles and trials are mere growing pains of your soul, to teach you that, though terrifying to you alone, they are as nothing to you when allied to the Father through the Holy Spirit.

"When thou liest down thou shalt not be afraid; yea thou shalt lie down, and thy sleep shall be sweet. Be not afraid of sudden fear, neither of the desolation of the wicked when it cometh. For the Lord shall be thy confidence, and shall keep thy foot from being taken. My confidence is in Him in whom I live and move and have my being."

Before you give up where you are and move to distant fields, before you seek your fortune afar, look around you! See if some of the riches in your own back yard won't bear cultivating.

There is a story told of an old Boer farmer living on a rocky bit of ground on the road between Kimberley and Pretoria. Scattered here and there over the ground, they often found dull looking pieces of crystal. The boys used them to throw at the sheep. Until one day a Cecil Rhodes engineer happened that way—*and discovered them to be diamonds!*

Many of us are just as literally walking on diamonds in the rough as were that farmer's boys. Only most of us never know it until someone comes along and points them out to us.

Let us resolve to do some of this discovering for our own selves. Let us look at every job with the question—how can this be done easier, quicker, better? Let us devote part of our thoughts to finding new outlets, new methods, new needs. Let us get a fixed objective—and then work towards it. Some great thinker once said that we should be a world of successes if the idea of a fixed objective and a set goal possessed us.

A fixed objective—it serves much the same as the controlling idea outlined in Chapter 3, magnetizing your thoughts and your work and yourself with the one intense desire. Add to that a sublime faith that shall bring the Holy Spirit within into cooperation with you—and your objective is assured.

"First have something good," said Horace Greeley, "then advertise!" First have your fixed objective, then call upon the Holy Spirit to help you, and there is no goal you cannot win.

"For the vision is yet for an appointed time, but at the end it shall speak, and not lie; though it tarry, wait for it; because it will surely come; it will not tarry."—Habakkuk 2:3

I know a man who had a $2,500 job. He had just been offered another paying $500 more. And he went to a friend of mine to ask his advice about changing. The first question my friend asked was what he had to offer these new people. He told him, the usual round of routine knowledge.

"That isn't worth much," my friend informed him. "These people are in the same line of business that you have been working at for years. If in all those years you haven't thought out ways in which that work could be vastly improved, if you haven't been perfecting in your own mind short cuts, money-saving ways, practical ideas—then hold on to your $2,500 job until you do. You're not worth a cent more.

"My advice to you is to go home and write down on paper what you have to offer this new firm. What new methods you can show them that any other $2,500 man can't. What new ideas you have that will make money for them.

"When you get them all down, center your attention on the best of them, and work it out. Then go to these people and tell them you will give them your idea and your services—NOT for $3,000, but for $6,000!"

That talk woke this man up. He did some really serious thinking for the first time in his business life. With the result that he refused the $3,000 offer then, but kept the position open for a few weeks until he could get his big idea ready.

Then he not only landed his $6,000, but made good on his idea so completely that within six months that $6,000 was increased to $7,200.

"There is guidance for each one of us," says Emerson, "and by lowly listening we shall hear the right word." Give of your best—not merely in manual labor but in ideas—and you can safely leave the rest to the guidance of the Holy Spirit within.

As pointed out in *The Secret of the Age*s, the basic principles of all business are the same, be they as big as the Steel Trust or as small as the corner news-stand. The whole practice of commerce is founded upon them. Summed up, and boiled down to the fewest possible words, they are two:

1—Give to get.

2—This one thing I do.

1—You can get away with dishonest values, with poor service, for a little while. You can take two dollars worth of value for every one you give. But the Law of Karma will get you soon or late. If you intend to stay in business, it pays to make it a rule to try to give a little more of value or of service than you are paid for.

2—Remember that each task, no matter how great, is but a group of little tasks, any one of which you can easily do. Like the great New York subways, it is but a succession of cellars connected together. Find a place to start. Take the first step. The rest will follow easily.

So many are afraid of giving too much for the amount that is paid them. And so many wives get inflated ideas of their husband's value to or work in a business, and urge them not to give so much unless the business pays them more for it.

Poor things—they mean well. But no man ever has to be urged not to work too hard at his business. He can work too hard at worrying about it—yes. But every bit of honest work he puts into his business will pay him an honest return. He is not working merely for some man or some institution. He is doing God's work. And God is the most generous Paymaster there is. He doesn't label His pay-checks. He doesn't say—"This is in payment of such-and-such invoices." But the pay comes—just as surely as the day follows night.

"I cause those that love me to inherit substance; and I will fill their treasures."—Proverbs 8:21

There is a place for you in the Divine plan—a place that no one but you can fill. There is a work for you in the great scheme of things—a work that no one can do as well as you.

So, if you have been drifting, if your work has been joyless, your business profitless, look around you for the right niche that was made for you to fill. Don't mind how humble it may seem. To do even the most humble thing supremely well is artistry—and will bring its reward. "Who sweeps a room as for God's law, makes that and the action fine."

"Now he that planteth and he that watereth are one; and every man shall receive his own reward according to his own labour. For we are labourers together with God."—I Corinthians 3:8–9

Let your daily prayer to the Spirit within you be that He manifest the Divine design in your life—that He bring you to your proper work, your right place.

Say to Him each day, as F. S. Shinn suggests in *The Game of Life and How to Play It*—"Infinite Spirit, open the way for the Divine design in my life to manifest. Let the genius within me now be released. Let me see clearly the perfect plan."

And then, if you like, ask Him to give you a lead, an indication of the next step for you to take.

"Call upon the Almighty," says the old Eastern Sage. "He will help thee. Thou needst not perplex thyself about anything else. Shut thy eyes and while thou art asleep, God will change thy bad fortune into good."

"Blessed *is* the man that trusteth in the Lord, and whose hope the Lord is.
"For he shall be as a tree planted by the waters, and *that* spreadeth out her roots by the river, and shall not see when heat cometh, but her leaf shall be green; and shall not be careful in the year of drought, neither shall cease from yielding fruit."—Jeremiah 17:7–8

7

Ich Dien—I Serve

"For the kingdom of heaven is as a man traveling into a far country, who called his own servants, and delivered unto them his goods.

"And unto one he gave five talents, to another two, and to another one; to every man according to his several ability; and straightway took his journey.

"Then he that had received the five talents went and traded with the same, and made them other five talents.

"And likewise he that had received two, he also gained other two.

"But he that had received one went and digged in the earth, and hid his lord's money.

"After a long time the lord of those servants cometh, and reckoneth with them.

"And so he that had received five talents came and brought other five talents, saying, Lord, thou deliveredst unto me five talents: behold, I have gained beside them five talents more.

"His lord said unto him, Well done, thou good and faithful servant: thou hast been faithful over a few things, I will make thee ruler over many things: enter thou into the joy of thy lord.

"He also that had received two talents came and said, lord, thou deliveredst unto me two talents: behold, I have gained two other talents beside them.

"His lord said unto him, Well done, good and faithful servant; thou hast been faithful over a few things, I will make thee ruler over many things: enter thou into the joy of thy lord.

"Then he which had received the one talent came and said, Lord, I knew thee that thou art an hard man, reaping where thou hast not sown, and gathering where thou hast not strawed:

"And I was afraid, and went and hid thy talent in the earth; lo, there thou hast that is thine.

"His lord answered and said unto him, Thou wicked and slothful servant, thou knewest that I reap where I sowed not, and gather where I have not strawed:

"Thou oughtest therefore to have put my money to the exchangers, and then at my coming I should have received mine own with usury.

"Take therefore the talent from him, and give it unto him which hath ten talents.

"For unto every one that hath shall be given, and he shall have abundance: but from him that hath not shall be taken away even that which he hath.

"And cast ye the unprofitable servant into outer darkness: there shall be weeping and gnashing of teeth."

—MATTHEW 25:14:30

You want riches. You want five talents, ten talents, a thousand—a million. But what have you to offer in return? Has it never occurred to you that you must make an accounting of them?

If some one were to offer you a million right now, what would you do with it? Buy a yacht—an automobile—have a good time! But what sort of an accounting would that make for the Master? And why should He put Himself out to place riches in hands no better prepared to use them to good purpose than that?

Suppose you went to a banker for money—a banker who knew you well—and asked him to lend you $100,000. What is the first question he would ask of you? "What are you going to do with it?"

If you could give him no better answer than—"Buy a yacht, an automobile, have a good time"—how much do you suppose he would lend you? Not a red cent! No more will the Father which is in Heaven.

You have got to have an idea first before you can borrow money from a bank. And if the banker is wise, he will make you prove your idea in a small way before he will advance you any great sum to spend upon it.

And when you approach the Father for ten talents or a thousand, you must first have an idea that will be of some benefit to mankind.

Henry Ford is worth a billion dollars. He is probably the richest man in the world. How did he get it?

He started out with an idea—an idea that the automobile should be put within reach of everyone. That idea was of definite benefit to mankind. It opened up remote districts. It brought light and life into the lives of millions of farm dwellers. He was entitled to a generous reward.

Woolworth accumulated a fortune of millions. He performed a definite service. So did Penny. So has many another merchant on a smaller scale. And the supply flows to him in proportion. But before reward, must come the idea. You must give to get.

The United States has become the richest of all peoples. Half the world's gold is in our possession. In 75 years the wealth of the country has increased fifty times over. All the world has become richer, but in no other country has the wealth increased to anything like that extent.

Why?

Some will say because of our great natural resources. But Mexico has great natural resources. So has Russia. And China. Yet all these countries are backward.

What then is the answer?

The fact that in America manufacturers have learned to share with the workers the fruits of industry. America began to forge ahead of the rest of the world the moment its manufacturers learned that every worker was entitled to a share of the good things of life.

Automobile manufacturers saw every workman as a potential automobile owner. And then proceeded to make that ideal feasible. Telephone companies, gas companies, electric light and equipment companies, radio manufacturers, saw every home as a user of their products—and proceeded to put them within the reach of all.

Never since life first appeared upon this planet has there been so much of comfort, happiness and contentment among *all* the people as there is in these United States. And the reason? Free education. Equal opportunity. And the realization on the part of manufacturers that their best market and their biggest one is right among the workers—that the more they share with the workers, the more will come back to them.

You must give to get.

Russia has enormous resources of land and minerals and oil. So has China. And Mexico. Why then are they so poor?

Because the ruling classes have tried to keep all these riches for themselves. They wanted to take all—and give nothing. That may work for a little while, but always there is an accounting.

> "For they have sown the wind, and they shall reap the whirlwind: it hath no stalk: the bud shall yield no meal: if so be it yield, the strangers shall swallow it up."—Hosea 8:7

You must give to get.

There is a story by Samuel Butler that describes the idea exactly:

"In Erehwon," he says, "he who makes a colossal fortune in the hosiery trade and by his energy has succeeded in reducing the price of woolen goods by the thousandeth part of a penny in a pound, this man is worth ten professional philanthropists. So strongly are the Erehwonians impressed with this that if a man has made a fortune of over £20,000 a year they exempt him from all taxation, considering him as a work of art and too precious to be meddled with. They say, 'How much he must have done for society before society could be prevailed upon to give him so much money!'"

Unfortunately, we have not yet reached the ideal state visioned by Butler, where every millionaire earned his money through unusual service to the community. Too many are still robber captains or greedy money-lenders like Cassim.

The Law of Karma is steadily at work. Give it time. There is always an accounting. Meantime, thank God for the Fords and the Edisons and the Burbanks and the thousands of others of their kind who are not only making this the richest country on earth, but are helping to spread those riches around and make it also the happiest.

THE BANK OF GOD

The true purpose of every worthy business is to help in the distribution of God's gifts among men.

Judge your work, your ideas, by that standard. If you want money, if you seek riches, ask yourself—"Could I go to God and tell Him as my banker that the purpose for which I want this money is anything but a selfish one? Could I honestly assure Him that my primary idea is service—giving to people a little better value, a little more of service, a little greater comfort or convenience or happiness than they are now getting?"

Don't misunderstand me. You are entitled to money to meet your daily needs. You have a right to ask for all those things necessary to your happiness, as long as they do not infringe upon the happiness of others. You even have a right to demand just as much more than that as you can use to advantage. *But you have got to account for it!*

Given a right idea, given a controlling thought, dollars will seek you, even as iron filings seek the magnet. You can claim all that you can use to good advantage.

So get your thought right first. Make sure that you have something the world needs. Then draw on the Great Banker for all the money you need, never fearing, never doubting that He will honor your draft.

"For the Lord God is a sun and shield. The Lord will give grace and glory. No good thing will he withhold from them that walk uprightly."—Psalms 84:11

After all the proofs of God's power to supply them with food and water. After He had brought them safely through every conceivable danger. When another crucial time came, the children of Israel fearfully called out—"Can God furnish us a table in the wilderness?"—Psalms 78:19

Of course He can!

"Hast thou not known? Hast thou not heard? That the everlasting God, the Lord, the Creator of the ends of the earth, fainteth not, neither is weary?" —Isaiah 40:28

Draw on Him as you need. Don't wait to start until you have all the money in hand. How many businesses—big and successful today—do you suppose would have been started if their founders had waited until they had all the money in hand they were going to need? Use the talent you have. Your credit is good for just as much more as you can use to advantage. More than that is a weight around your neck.

If you had a business proposition, and knew that your banker would extend you credit to the extent of a million dollars to develop it, you wouldn't think of drawing that million all at once. No—you would ask for credit as you needed it. You would draw upon it only as your business required it. You wouldn't burden yourself with one cent more of interest than was necessary.

Do likewise with the Lord. If your banker promised you the money as you needed it, you would go ahead with your plans, secure in the knowledge that his word was just as good as the actual money in the bank. Do you rate the promises of the Father any lower than those of man?

> "Be glad then, ye children of Zion, and rejoice in the Lord your God: for he hath given you the former rain moderately, and he will cause to come down for you the rain, the former rain, and the latter rain in the first month.
>
> "And the floors shall be full of wheat, and the vats shall overflow with wine and oil.
>
> "And ye shall eat in plenty, and be satisfied, and praise the name of the Lord your God, that hath dealt wondrously with you: and my people shall never be ashamed.
>
> "And ye shall know that I am in the midst of Israel, and that I am the Lord your God, and none else: and my people shall never be ashamed."—Joel 2:21, 23, 24, 26, 27

What is it you want money for? Get your idea clearly in mind. Satisfy yourself that it is for a worthy purpose. And when you are thoroughly satisfied of that, then go right ahead with your plans.

How much do you need for this stage of them? How much would you draw on the bank for, this moment, if you had unlimited credit there? $100? $1,000? $10,000? Explain your need to the Father just as you would to a very wise and sympathetic banker. Then tell Him you are drawing upon Him for that amount. Actually write out a draft and mail it—anywhere—to me if you like. Then go about your plans as confidently, as believingly, as though the Father's Bank were just around the corner.

But don't try to fool yourself. Above all, don't try to deceive the Father. Don't camouflage merely selfish desires in some high and mighty guise as benefits to mankind.

Remember the old Spanish Conquistadores? Freebooters they were—neither more nor less—searching for booty, and caring not how they came by it. They robbed the Indians, they massacred thousands, they enslaved whole nations—all for lust of gold.

But that wasn't their tale about it. They put it all upon the high and mighty plane of spreading Christianity, of saving the souls of the heathen.

It worked for the Spaniards for a little while. But they became so puffed up that they thought to use the same ideas upon the heretics of England, of the Netherlands, upon the entire world. Then came the disastrous Armada, followed by swift and certain decline.

It was only 300 years ago that Spain was the richest nation in the world, her power pre-eminent in Europe, her sovereignty extending over most of America. Now look at her—even the Riffians laughed at her until France came to her aid.

We reap what we sow. A grain of corn planted reproduces only corn. A grain of wheat brings forth wheat. And the seed of the deadly night-shade brings forth poisonous flowers.

God cannot be mocked. We reap in kind exactly as we sow. "Be not deceived. God is not mocked; for whatsoever a man soweth, that shall he also reap."—Galatians 6:7

What then shall you do to succeed? What is the modern law of business? The same two commandments that Jesus gave to us 2,000 years ago.

"Thou shalt love the Lord thy God with all thy heart and with all thy soul and with all thy mind. This is the first and great commandment. And the second is like unto it. Thou shalt love thy neighbor as thyself. On these two commandments hang all the law and the prophets."—Matthew 23:37–40

"Thou shalt love the Lord thy God." Thou shalt use the talents He has given thee. Thou shalt use them to benefit thy neighbor, to benefit all of mankind, and in so doing thou shalt benefit thyself. Do that, and thy Lord will say unto thee: "Well done, thou good and faithful servant; thou hast been faithful over a few things, I will make thee ruler over many things: enter thou into the joy of thy Lord."

But to those who fail to use, or who *abuse* their talent, the Lord says even as he did of the unprofitable servant: "Take therefore the talent from him and cast him into outer darkness: there shall be weeping and gnashing of teeth."

8

The Coming of the Spirit

"Now about the midst of the feast Jesus went up into the temple, and taught.

"And the Jews marvelled, saying, How knoweth this man letters, having never learned?

"Jesus answered them, and said, My doctrine is not mine, but His that sent me."

—JOHN 7:14–16

THERE was a certain Sultan of the Indies that had three sons, the eldest called Houssain, the second Ali, the third Ahmed.

He had also a niece, remarkable for her wit and beauty, named Nouronnihar, whom all three Princes loved and desired to wed.

Their father remonstrated with them, pointed out the troubles that would ensue if they persisted in their attachment, and did all he could to persuade them to abide by his choice of which of them should wed her.

Failing that, he sent for them one day and suggested that the three Princes should depart on a three-months' journey, each to a different country. Upon their return, whichever one should bring to him the most extraordinary rarity as a gift, should receive the Princess in marriage.

The three Princes cheerfully consented to this, each flattering himself that fortune would prove favorable to him. The Sultan gave them money, and early next morning they all went out at the same gate of the city, each dressed like a merchant, attended by a trusty officer habited as a slave, and all well mounted and equipped. The first day's journey they proceeded together; and at night, when they were at supper, they agreed to meet again in three months at the khan where they were stopping; and that the first who came should wait for the rest; so that as they had all three taken leave together of the Sultan, they might return in company. The next morning, after they had embraced and wished each other success, they mounted their horses, and took each a different road.

Prince Houssain, the eldest brother, had heard of the riches and splendor of the kingdom of Bisnagar and bent his course toward it.

Arriving there, he betook himself to the quarters of the traders, where a merchant, seeing him go by much fatigued, invited him to sit down in front of his shop. He had not been seated long before a crier appeared, with a small piece of carpeting on his arm, for which he asked forty purses. The Prince told him that he could not understand how so small a piece of carpeting could be set at so high a price, unless it had something very extraordinary about it which failed to show in its appearance. "You have guessed right, sir," replied the crier; "whoever sits on this piece of carpeting may be carried in an instant wherever he desires." "If that is so," said the Prince, "I shall not think forty purses too much." "Sir," replied the crier, "I have told you the truth. Let us go into the back warehouse, where I will spread the carpet. When we have both sat down, form the wish to be transported into your apartment at the khan, and if we are not conveyed there at once, it shall be no bargain."

On the Prince agreeing to this, they went into the merchant's back shop, where they both sat down on the carpet; and as soon as the Prince had expressed his wish to be carried to his apartment at the khan, he in an instant found himself and the crier there. After this convincing proof of the virtue of the carpet, he paid over to the crier forty purses of gold, together with an extra purse for himself.

Prince Houssain was overjoyed at his good fortune, never doubting that this rare carpet would gain him the possession of the beautiful Nouronnihar.

After seeing all the wonders of Bisnagar, Prince Houssain wished to be nearer his dear Princess, so he took and spread the carpet, and with the officer whom he had brought with him, commanded the carpet to transport them to the caravansery at which he and his brothers were to meet, where he passed for a merchant till their arrival.

Prince Ali, the second brother, designed to travel into Persia, so, after parting with his brothers, joined a caravan, and soon arrived at Shiraz, the capital of that empire.

Walking through the quarters of the jewelers, he was not a little surprised to see one who held in his hand an ivory tube, about a foot in length, and about an inch thick, which he priced at fifty purses. At first he thought the man mad, and asked him what he meant by asking fifty purses for a tube which seemed scarcely worth one. The jeweler replied, "Sir, you shall judge yourself whether I am mad or not, when I have told you the property of this tube. By looking through it, you can see whatever object you wish to behold."

The jeweler presented the tube to the Prince, and he looked through it, wishing at the same time to see the Sultan his father. Immediately he saw before him the image of his father, sitting on his throne, in the midst of his council. Next, he wished to see the Princess Nouronnihar; and instantly beheld her laughing and talking with the women about her.

Prince Ali needed no other proof to persuade him that this tube was the most valuable of gifts in all the world, and taking the crier to the khan where he lodged, paid him his fifty purses and received the tube.

Prince Ali was overjoyed at his purchase, for he felt fully assured that his brothers would not be able to meet with anything so rare and admirable, and the Princess Nouronnihar would be his. His only thought now was to get back to the rendezvous as speedily as might be, so without waiting to visit any of the wonders of Shiraz, he joined a party of merchants and arrived without accident at the place appointed, where he found Prince Houssain, and both waited for Prince Ahmed.

Prince Ahmed had taken the road to Samarcand, and the day after his arrival went, as his brothers had done, into the merchants quarters, where he had not walked long before he heard a crier, with an artificial apple in his hand, offer it at five-and-forty purses. "Let me see your apple," he said to the man, "and tell me what extraordinary property it possesses, to be valued at so high a rate." "Sir," replied the crier, giving the apple into his hand, "if you look at the mere outside of this apple it is not very remarkable; but if you consider its miraculous properties, you will say it is invaluable. It cures sick people of every manner of disease. Even if a person is dying, it will cure him instantly, and this merely by his smelling of the apple."

"If that be true," replied Prince Ahmed, "this apple is indeed invaluable; but how am I to know that it is true?" "Sir," replied the crier, "the truth is attested by the whole city of Samarcand; ask any of these merchants here. Several of them will tell you they had not been alive today had it not been for this excellent remedy."

Many people had gathered round while they talked, and now confirmed what the crier had declared. One among them said he had a friend dangerously ill, whose life was despaired of; so they could now see for themselves the truth of all that was said. Upon this Prince Ahmed told the crier he would give him forty-five purses for the apple if it cured the sick person by smelling it.

"Come, sir," said the crier to Prince Ahmed, "let us go and do it, and the apple shall be yours."

The sick man smelled of the apple, and was cured; and the prince, after he had paid the forty-five purses, received the apple. He then joined himself to the first caravan that set out for the Indies, and arrived in perfect health at the caravansery, where the Princes Houssain and Ali waited for him.

The brothers embraced with tenderness, and felicitated each other on their safe journeys.

They then fell to comparing gifts. Houssain showed the carpet and told how it had brought him thither. Ali brought out the ivory tube, and nothing would do but they must at once look through it at their beloved. But—alas and alack! for the sight that met their eyes. The Princess Nouronnihar lay stretched on her bed, seemingly at the point of death.

When Prince Ahmed had seen this, he turned to his two brothers. "Make haste," he adjured them, "lose no time; we may save her life. This apple which I hold here has this wonderful property—its smell will restore to life a sick person. I have tried it and will show you its wonderful effect on the Princess, if you will but hasten to her."

"If haste be all," answered Houssain, "we cannot do better than transport ourselves instantly into her chamber on my magic carpet. Come, lose no time, sit down, it is large enough to hold us all."

The order was no sooner given than they found themselves carried into the Princess Nouronnihar's chamber.

Prince Ahmed rose off the carpet, and went to her bedside, where he put the apple to her nostrils. Immediately the Princess opened her eyes, expressed her joy at seeing them, and thanked them all for their efforts in her behalf.

While she was dressing, the Princes went to present themselves to the Sultan, their father. The Sultan received them with joy. The Princes presented each the rarity which he had brought, and begged of him to pronounce their fate.

The Sultan of the Indies considered what answer he should make. At last he said, "I would that I could declare for one of you, my sons, but I cannot do it with justice. It is true, Ahmed, that the Princess owes her cure to your artificial apple; but let me ask you, could you have cured her if you had not known of the danger she was in through Ali's tube, and if Houssain's carpet had not brought you to her so quickly? Your tube, Ali, discovered to you and your brothers the illness of your cousin; but the knowledge of her illness would have been of no service without the artificial apple and the carpet. And as for you, Houssain, your carpet was an essential instrument in effecting her cure. But it would have been of little use, if you had not known of her illness through Ali's tube, or if Ahmed had not been there with his artificial apple. Therefore, as I see it, the carpet, the ivory tube, and the artificial apple have no preference over each other, on the contrary, each had an equal share in her cure."

The story goes on to tell how the Sultan, after repeated trials, finally did choose a husband for the Princess. How Prince Ali wed her. How Prince Ahmed wandered away, disconsolate. How he met the Fairy Princess Banou. And how through her he finally won the greatest prize of all—contact with the Spirit within that knows all, sees all and can do all things.

In *The Secret of the Ages*, I endeavored to show how your subconscious mind can be made to serve as the Ivory Tube, giving you the answer to any problem you may put up to it in the right way.

In later volumes of this set, I shall try to prove to you how the Spirit within can and gladly *will* serve you better than Magic Carpet or Curative Apple. Length of days is in His right hand, freedom from fear, protection from harm, health, happiness and prosperity.

Do I promise too much? Just listen:

"But be ye glad and rejoice for ever in that which I create: for, behold, I create Jerusalem a rejoicing, and her people a joy.

"And I will rejoice in Jerusalem, and joy in my people: and the voice of weeping shall be no more heard in her, nor the voice of crying.

"There shall be no more thence an infant of days, nor an old man that hath not filled his days:

"And they shall build houses, and inhabit them; and they shall plant vineyards, and eat the fruit of them.

"They shall not build, and another inhabit; they shall not plant, and another eat: for as the days of a tree are the days of my people, and mine elect shall long enjoy the work of their hands.

"They shall not labour in vain, nor bring forth for trouble; for they are the seed of the blessed of the Lord, and their offspring with them.

"And it shall come to pass, that before they call, I will answer; and while they are yet speaking, I will hear."—Isaiah 65:18–24

But how to find this Kingdom? Let us see what Jesus says—"Except a man be born again, he shall in no wise enter into the kingdom."

How shall man be born again? "Master," asked His disciples, "do you mean that a person must go back into his mother's body, must have a birth again on this earth, before he can enter into the kingdom of which you tell us?"

"Ye must be born again of water and of the Spirit," Jesus told them.

"Of water and of the Spirit." Let us see how this Spirit came to Jesus Himself.

"Now when all the people were baptized, it came to pass, that Jesus also being baptized, and praying, the heaven was opened.

"And the Holy Ghost descended in a bodily shape like a dove upon him, and a voice came from heaven, which said, Thou art my beloved Son; in thee I am well pleased."—LUKE 3:21–22

"IT IS THE SPIRIT THAT QUICKENETH"

"And Jesus being full of the Holy Ghost returned from Jordan, and was led by the Spirit into the wilderness.

"And Jesus returned in the power of the Spirit into Galilee: and there went out a fame of him through all the region round about."—Luke 4:1, 14

Then Jesus went up into the Temple to preach. "And there was delivered unto him the book of the prophet Esaias. And when he had opened the book, he found the place where it was written."

"The Spirit of the Lord is upon me, because he hath anointed me to preach the gospel to the poor; he hath sent me to heal the broken-hearted, to preach deliverance to the captives, and recovering of sight to the blind, to set at liberty them that are bruised.

"To proclaim the acceptable year of the Lord."—Matthew 61

What, then, shall we do to be saved? How shall we bring the Holy Spirit into our lives? How find the Kingdom here on earth?

Step by step, Jesus showed us the way. He "was led by the Spirit into the wilderness"—into rest, into quiet, into thought. He retired to where he could be alone for a while, where he could concentrate his thoughts without outside distractions, where he could commune with the Father.

"Praying, the heaven was opened, and the Holy Ghost descended upon Him." And if we will pray rightly, the heaven will open to us and the Holy Ghost will come upon us.

But He will never do it for the mere repetition of lip prayers that we have learned by rote.

THE SOUL'S SINCERE DESIRE

[14]Do you know what prayer is? Just an earnest desire that we take to God—to Universal Mind—for fulfillment. As Montgomery puts it—"Prayer is the soul's sincere desire, uttered or unexpressed." It is our Heart's Desire. At least, the only prayer that is worth anything is the prayer that asks for our real desires. That kind of prayer is heard. That kind of prayer is answered.

Mere lip prayers get you nowhere. It doesn't matter what your lips may say. The thing that counts is what your heart desires, what your mind images on your subconscious thought, and through it on Divine Mind.

"And when thou prayest, be not as the hypocrites are; for they love to pray standing in the synagogue and at the corners of the streets, that they may be seen of men. Verily I say unto you, they have their reward."—Matthew 6:5

What was it these hypocrites that Jesus speaks of really wanted? "To be seen of men." And their prayers were answered. Their sincere desire was granted. They were seen of men. "They have their reward." But as for what their lips were saying, neither God nor they paid any attention to it.

"But thou, when thou prayest, enter into thy closet, and when thou hast shut the door, pray to thy Father which is in secret, and thy Father which seeth in secret, shall reward thee openly. But when ye pray, use not vain repetitions, as the heathen do. For they think that they shall be heard for their much speaking. Be not ye therefore like unto them.

---

14. From *The Secret of the Ages*.

For your Father knoweth what things ye have need of, before ye ask Him."—Matthew 6:6–8

Go where you can be alone, where you can concentrate your thoughts on your one innermost sincere desire, where you can impress that desire upon the Spirit within, and so reach the Father.

But even sincere desire is not enough by itself. There must be BELIEF, too. "What things soever ye desire, when ye pray, believe that ye *receive* them and ye shall *have* them." You must realize God's ability to give you every good thing. You must believe in his readiness to do it. Model your thoughts after the Psalmists of old. They first asked for that which they wanted, then killed all doubts and fears by affirming God's power and His willingness to grant their prayers.

What is it you want most right now? Ask yourself frankly—Is it good that I should receive this? Is it right? Will it work no injustice to anyone else? Then have no hesitancy in asking it of the Father—secure in the knowledge that anything of good He will gladly give to you. Here is His promise. Read it, and see if you can still doubt:

"I will say of the Lord, He is my refuge and my fortress: my God; in Him will I trust.

"Surely He shall deliver thee from the snare of the fowler, and from the noisome pestilence.

"He shall cover thee with His feathers, and under His wings shalt thou trust: His truth shall be thy shield and buckler.

"Thou shalt not be afraid for the terror by night; nor for the arrow that flieth by day.

"Nor for the pestilence that walketh in darkness; nor for the destruction that wasteth at noonday.

"A thousand shall fall at thy side, and ten thousand at thy right hand; but it shall not come nigh thee.

"Because thou hast made the Lord, which is my refuge, even the most High, thy habitation.

"There shall no evil befall thee, neither shall any plague come nigh thy dwelling.

"For He shall give His angels charge over thee, to keep thee in all thy ways.

"They shall bear thee up in their hands, lest thou dash thy foot against a stone.

"Thou shalt tread upon the lion and adder: the young lion and the dragon shalt thou trample under foot.

"Because he hath set his love upon me, therefore will I deliver him: I will set him on high, beceause he hath known my name.

"He shall call upon me, and I will answer him: I will be with him in trouble; I will deliver him, and honour him.

"With long life will I satisfy him, and shew him my salvation." —PSALMS 91:6

"Surely goodness and mercy shall follow me all the days of my life. And I will dwell in the house of the Lord forever."—PSALMS 23:6

So far we can follow in the footsteps of Jesus. So far we can contact with the Holy Spirit. But how about His miracles? How about His miraculous cures of the sick, the lame, the halt and the blind? Can we follow Him there, too?

Let us see what He says. "The works that I do shall ye do also, and greater works than these shall ye do."

That was a promise. A promise that was made—not merely to His immediate followers—but to ALL who believed! And that promise held good throughout the first three centuries of the Christian era, while it remained fresh in men's minds. It was only when Christianity became the State religion, and Constantine broidered it with too many forms, that the healing power was forgotten and lost.

Again, when Jesus sent His disciples forth, He told them to—"Go, preach, saying, The kingdom of heaven is at hand. Heal the sick, cleanse the lepers, raise the dead, cast out devils; freely ye have received, freely give."

Nothing indirect or obscure about that, is there? The command to preach the Gospel is no more positive than the command to heal the sick. If one was to be kept up by succeeding generations, surely the other was, too.

And in the way Jesus prepared His disciples for their work, in the directions He gave to them, and in the detailed accounts they have left for us of how Jesus performed his miraculous cures and of how the power came to the Apostles we find, step by step, methods that we too can use.

They were simple folk—these Apostles—unlearned, inexperienced, and until the coming of the Holy Spirit, most amazing timid. Jesus' instructions had need to be plain to be grasped by their unpracticed minds.

Don't you suppose that you, with all the advantages of a modern education, can follow them quite as easily, can practice them just as successfully?

Let's try! In the volumes to come, I am going to do my humble best to show the way.

"All Scripture is given by inspiration of God, and is profitable for doctrine, for reproof, for correction, for instruction in righteousness.

"That the man of God may be perfect, thoroughly furnished unto all good works."—II TIMOTHY 3:16–17

THE PROMISE

"The promise is that we may do all things through the mind that was in Christ Jesus."

Riches Within Your Reach

ROBERT COLLIER

"Would you know Life abundant,
Love doubled for all you give?
There is a means no surer
Than helping someone to live."
(The above verse by Ellen H. Jones expresses so well the whole
purpose of this book, that we gladly subscribe our name to it here.)

Contents

THE SECRET OF POWER

THE LAW OF THE HIGHER POTENTIAL

Prologue

Why is it that most of the great men of the world, most of the unusually successful men, started life under a handicap?

Demosthenes, the greatest orator the ancient world produced, stuttered! The first time he tried to make a public speech, he was laughed off the rostrum. Julius Caesar was an epilectic. Napoleon was of humble parentage, and so poor that it was with the greatest difficulty that he got his appointment to the Military Academy. Far from being a born genius, he stood forty-sixth in his class at the Military Academy. And there were only sixty-five in the class. His shortness of stature and extreme poverty discouraged him to such an extent that in his early letters to friends, he frequently referred to thoughts of suicide.

Benjamin Franklin, Abraham Lincoln, Andrew Jackson and a number of our Presidents started life in the poorest and humblest of homes, with little education and no advantages. Stewart, who started what is now the John Wanamaker Store, came to New York with $1.50 in his pocket, and no place where he could hope to get more until he himself earned it. Thomas Edison was a newsboy on trains. Andrew Carnegie started work at $4 a month. John D. Rockefeller at about $6 a week.

Reza Khan, who became Shah of Persia, started as an ordinary trooper in the Persian army. Mustapha Kemal, Ruler of Turkey, was an unknown officer in the Turkish army. Ebert, first President of Germany after World War I, was a saddle maker. A number of our own Presidents were born in log cabins, without money, without education.

Sandow, the strongest man of his time, started life as a weakling. Annette Kellerman was lame and sickly, yet she became diving champion and one of the world's most perfectly formed women. George Jowett was lame and a weakling until he was eleven years old. An older boy bullied him and beat him until he aroused such a feeling of resentment in young Jowett that he determined to work and exercise until he could pay back that bully in kind. In two years, he was able to beat the bully. In ten years, he was the world's strongest man!

Why is it that men with such handicaps can outstrip all of those naturally favored by Nature? Why is it that the well-educated, well-trained men, with wealthy and influential friends to help them, are so often pushed aside, to make way for some "nobody" whose family no one ever heard of, but whose sheer ability and force make him a power to be reckoned with?

Why? Because men with early advantages are taught *to look to material things for success* . . . to riches or friends or influence or their own training or abilities. And when these fail them, they are at a loss where to turn next.

But when a man has no special skill or ability or riches or influence, he has to look to something outside these for success, something beyond material means. So he turns to the God in him, to his cell of the God-Mind, and of that cell he demands that it bring him fame or fortune or power or position. What is more, if he continues to demand it with persistent faith, HE GETS IT!

You see, in every adversity there lies the seed of an equivalent advantage. In every defeat there is a lesson showing you how to win the victory next time. The turning point in the lives of most successful men has come at some moment of crisis, when everything looked dark, when there seemed no way out. That was when they turned to their inner selves, when they gave up hope in material means and looked to the God in them for help. That was when they were able to turn each stumbling block into a stepping-stone to success.

> 'Isn't it strange that princes and kings,
> And clowns that caper in sawdust rings,
> And common folks like you and me,
> Are builders for eternity?
>
> Each is given a bag of tools,
> A shapeless mass, a book of rules;
> And each must make, ere life is flown,
> A stumbling block or a stepping stone.

You are one with the great "I AM" of the universe. You are part of God. Until you realize that—and the power it gives you—you will never know God. "We are parts of one stupendous whole, whose body Nature is, and God the soul."

God has incarnated Himself in man. He seeks expression. Give Him work to do through you, give Him a chance to express Himself in some useful way, and there is nothing beyond your powers to do or to attain.

It matters not what your age, what your present circumstances or position. If you will seek your help outside your merely physical self, if you will put the God in you into some worthwhile endeavor, and then BELIEVE in Him, you can overcome any poverty, any handicap, any untoward circumstance. Relying upon your personal abilities or riches or friends is being like the heathen of old, whom the Prophet of the Lord taunted. "You have a God whom you must carry," he derided them. "We have a God *who carries us!*"

The God of personal ability or material riches or friends is one that you must continually carry. Drop him, and immediately you lose everything. But there is a God in you who will carry you—and in the doing of it, provide you with every good thing this world can supply. The purpose of this book is to acquaint you with this God *in you, The God That Only The Fortunate Few Know.*

As the poet so well expressed it—

In your own self lies Destiny, Let this
Vast truth cast out all fear, and prejudice,
All hesitation. Know that you are great,
Great with Divinity. So dominate
Environment and enter into bliss.
Love largely and hate nothing. Hold no aim
That does not chord with Universal Good.
Hear what the voices of the Silence say—
All joys are yours if you put forth your claim.
Once let the spiritual laws be understood,
Material things must answer and obey.

Some might think that merely a poet's dream, but along comes Dr. J. B. Rhine of Duke University to prove it scientific fact as well.

In his new book "The Reach of the Mind," Dr. Rhine points out that in the past, Science seemed to feel that man was entirely material. It had discovered how glands regulate personality through their chemical secretions; it had shown that the child mind matures only as the brain develops; that certain mental functions are linked with specific areas of the brain, and that if one of these is injured, the corresponding mental function is lost.

So Science believed that it had accounted for all the processes of thought and action, that it could show a material basis for each.

But now Dr. Rhine and other experimenters have proved that knowledge can be acquired *without the use of the senses!*

Not only that, but they have also proved that the powers of the mind are not bound by space or limited by time! Perhaps their greatest discovery is that the mind can influence matter *without physical means.*

This has been done through prayer, of course, since time began, but such results have always been looked upon as supernatural. Dr. Rhine and other experimenters show that any normal person has the power to influence objects and events.

To quote "The Reach of the Mind"—"As a result of thousands of experimental trials, we found it to be a fact that the mind has a force that can act on matter. . . . There must, therefore, be an energy convertible to physical action, *a mental energy.*"

The one great essential to the successful use of this mental energy seems to be intense interest or desire. The more keyed up a person is, the more eager for results, the more he can influence those results.

Dr. Rhine showed through many experiments that when the subject's interest is distracted, when he lacks ability to concentrate his attention, his mental energy has little or no power over outside objects. It is only as he gives his entire attention to the object in mind, as he concentrates his every energy upon it, that he gets successful results.

Dr. Rhine's experiments prove scientifically what we have always believed—that there is a Power over and above the merely physical power of the mind or body, that through intense concentration or desire we can link up with that Power, and that once we do, nothing is impossible to us.

It means, in short, that man is not at the mercy of blind chance or Fate, that he can control his own destiny. Science is at last proving what Religion has taught from the beginning—that God gave man *dominion* and that he has only to understand and use this dominion to become the Master of his Fate, the Captain of his Soul.

Body and mind and Spirit, all combine
To make the creature, human and Divine.
Of this great Trinity, no part deny.
Affirm, affirm, the great eternal I.

Affirm the body, beautiful and whole,
The earth-expression of immortal soul.
Affirm the mind, the messenger of the hour,
To speed between thee and the Source of Power.
Affirm the Spirit, the eternal I—
Of this great Trinity, no part deny.

—ELLA WHEELER WILCOX

The God *in* You

The God in You

1

The God in You

The Declaration of Independence starts with the preamble that all men are born free and equal. But how many believe that? When one child is born in a Park Avenue home, with doctors and nurses and servants to attend to his slightest want, with tutors and colleges to educate him, with riches and influence to start him in his career, how can he be said to be born equal to the child of the Ghetto, who has difficulty getting enough air to breathe, to say nothing of food to eat, and whose waking hours are so taken up with the struggle for existence that he has no time to acquire much in the way of education!

Yet in that which counts most, these two are born equal, for they have equal access to the God in themselves, equal chance to give Him means of expression. More than that, the God in one is just as powerful as the God in the other, for both are part of that all-powerful God of the Universe who rules the world.

In effect, we are each of us individual cells in the great Mind of the universe— the God Mind. We can draw upon the Mind of the Universe in exactly the same way that any cell in our own body draws upon our brain for whatever it needs outside its immediate surroundings.

All men are born free and equal, just as all the cells in your body are equal. Some of these cells may seem to be more fortunately situated than others, being placed in fatty portions of the body where they are so surrounded with nourishment that they seem assured of everything they can need for their natural lives.

Others may be in hard-worked parts where they are continually having to draw upon the lymph around them, and through it upon the blood stream and the heart, and where it seems as though they cannot be sure of sustenance from one day to the next. Still others may be in little-used and apparently forgotten parts where they seem to have been left to dry up and starve, as in the scalp of the head when the hair falls out and the fatty tissue of the scalp dries, leaving the cells there to shrivel and die.

Yet despite their apparent differences in surroundings and opportunity, all these cells are equal, all can draw upon every element in the body for sustenance at need.

To see how it is done, let us take a single nerve cell in our own brain, and see how it works.

Look up the diagram of a typical nerve cell in any medical work, and what do you find? From one side of the cell, a long fibre extends which makes connection with some part of the skin, or some group of cells such as a muscle. This fibre is part of the nerve cell. It is the telephone line, carrying orders or stimuli from the cell to the muscle it controls, or from the sensory nerve in the skin to the cell in the brain. Thoughts, emotions, desires, all send impulses to the nerves controlling the muscles concerned, and provide the stimuli which set these muscles in action, thus transforming nervous energy into muscular energy.

So if you have a desire which requires the action of only a single muscle, what happens? Your desire takes the form of an impulse to the nerve cell controlling that muscle, the order travels along the cell-fibre to the muscle, which promptly acts in accord with the stimulus given it. And your desire is satisfied.

But suppose your desire requires the action of more than one muscle? Suppose it needs the united power of every muscle in the body? So far we have used only the long nerve fibre or telephone line connecting the nerve cell with the muscle it controls. But on the other side of each nerve cell are short fibres, apparently ending in space. And as long as the nerves are at rest, these fibres do lie in space.

But when you stir up the nerve cells, when you give them a job that is greater than the muscles at their command can manage, then these short fibres go into action. Then they bestir themselves to some purpose. They dig into the nerve cells near them. They wake these and stimulate them in turn to stir up those on the other sides of them until, if necessary, every cell in the brain is twitching, and every muscle in the body working to accomplish the job you command.

That is what happens in *your* body if even a single cell in your brain desires something strongly enough, persistently enough, to hold to its purpose until it gets what it wants. And that is what happens in the God-body when you put the same persistence into your desires.

You see, you are a cell in the God-body of the Universe, just as every cell in you is a part of your body. When you work with your hands, your feet, your muscles, you are using only the muscles immediately connected with your brain cells. When you work with the money you have, the riches or friends or influence you control, you are using only the means immediately connected to your brain cell in the mind of God. And that is so infinitesimally small a part of the means and resources at the command of that Great God-mind.

It is just as though you tried to do all the work required of your body today by using only the tiniest muscle in your little finger, when by stirring up the surrounding nerve cells, you could just as well draw upon the power of the whole mind, or of the entire body if that were needed. It is as though one of your nerve cells undertook to do the work of the whole body, and tried, with the single muscle at its command, to do it!

You'd think that foolish, if one tiny nerve cell out of the billions in your brain, undertook any such gigantic job. You'd know it was hopeless . . . that no one cell, and no one muscle, could ever accomplish all that work. Yet you, as a single cell in the God-mind, have often attempted just as impossible jobs. When all you had to do to accomplish everything you desired was to stir into action the cells around you!

How can you do this? In the same way that any cell in your own brain does it. *Pray!* In other words, get an urgent, insistent desire. The first principle of success is DESIRE—knowing what you want. Desire is the planting of your seed. It needs cultivation, of course, but the first important step is the PLANTING. Desire stirs the nerve cells in your brain to use the muscles under their control to do the work required of them. Desire will set your nerve cell in the God-mind vibrating, using the muscle under its command and stirring into action all the nerve cells around it until they, too, are working with you to bring about the thing you wish.

That is the reason it was said in the Vedas thousands of years ago that if any two people would unite their psychic forces, they could conquer the world! That is the reason Jesus told us—"If two of you shall agree as touching anything they shall ask, it shall be done unto them. For when two or three are gathered together in My name, there am I in the midst of them, and I shall grant their request."

When two or more nerve cells unite for a certain action, they get that action, even if to bring it about they have to draw upon every cell in the whole body for help!

This does not mean that anything is impossible to a single cell or a single person—merely that when two or more are united for a common purpose, the results are easier. But there is no good thing any man can ask, believing, that he cannot get.

In the first chapter of Genesis, it is written that God gave man dominion over the earth. And it is true. It is just as true as that any nerve cell in your whole body has dominion over your body. If you doubt it, let one nerve be sufficiently irritated, and see how quickly it puts every nerve in your body to work to remove that irritation.

One nerve cell in your body, with a strongly held purpose, can bring into action every cell in your body to accomplish that purpose. One nerve cell in the God-body (in other words, one man or woman) with a strongly held purpose, can bring into action every cell in the Universe, if these be necessary to the accomplishment of that purpose!

Does that mean anything to you? Does it mean anything to know that the words of prophets and seers are true, that the promises of the Scriptures can be depended upon, that there really is a Power in the Universe that responds to the urge of the lowliest man or woman just as readily as to the command of the highest?

The world is yours! It matters not whether you be prince or pauper, blue-blooded or red, white-skinned, black, yellow or brown. The God-body of the Universe makes no more distinction between cells than do you in responding to the impulses of the nerve cells in your own body.

Rich or poor—it's all one to you. Highly placed or low—one can cause you as much trouble, or give you as great satisfaction, as another. And the same is true of the God-body of the Universe. All men are created free and equal. All remain free and equal nerve cells in the God-mind of the Universe.

The only difference lies in our understanding of the power that is ours. How much understanding have you? And what are you doing to increase it? "Seek first understanding, and all things else shall be added unto you." Easier to believe that now, isn't it? With the right understanding, you could run the world. Can you think of anything more important than acquiring understanding?

What turned the complaining, discouraged, poverty-stricken and quite ordinary young Bonaparte into the greatest military genius of his age, "Man of Destiny" and master of most of Europe?

The Talisman of Napoleon, the Talisman of every great and successful man, the only Talisman that will stir the whole body of the Universe into action, is the same Talisman as that needed to put the entire physical body at the service of any one nerve cell—*a purpose so strongly held that life or death or anything else seems of small consequence beside it!* A purpose—and the persistent determination to hold to it until it is accomplished.

Love sometimes makes such a Talisman—the love that goes out to dare all and do all for the loved one. Greed oftentimes brings it into being—hence many of the great fortunes of today. The lust for power is a potent Talisman, that has animated men since time began. Greater still is the zeal of one who would convert the world. That Talisman has carried men through fire and flood, into every danger and over every obstacle. Look how Mohammed, a lowly camel driver, became the ruler of and prophet to millions.

Faith in charms, belief in luck, utter confidence in another's leadership, all are Talismans of greater or lesser power.

But the greatest of all is belief in the God inside YOU! Belief in its power to draw to itself every element it needs for expression. Belief in a definite PURPOSE it came here to fulfill, and which can be fulfilled only through YOU!

Have you such a faith? If not, get it! For without such a faith, life is purposeless, meaningless. What is more, until you lay hold of that Talisman, life will never bring anything worth while to you!

What was it won for Grant over his more brilliant opponents? The grim, dogged, persistent purpose to fight it out along those lines if it took all summer! What is it that has made England victor in so many of her wars, in spite of inept leadership and costly blunders? That same bull-dog determination, which holds on in spite of all reverses and discouragements, until its fight is won. What was it that wore out the unjust judge, in the parable that Jesus told?

And he spake a parable unto them to this end, that man ought always to pray, and not to faint; saying, "There was in a city a judge, which feared not God, neither regarded man;

"And there was a widow in that city; and she came unto him, saying, 'Avenge me on mine adversary.'

"And he would not for a while; but afterward he said within himself, 'Though I fear not God, nor regard man; yet because this widow troubleth me, I will avenge her, lest by her continual coming she weary me.'"

And the Lord said, "Hear what the unjust judge saith. And shall not God avenge his own elect, which cry day and night unto him, though he bear long with them?"

If the nerve in a tooth keeps crying out that a cavity in that tooth needs attention, won't you finally drop everything and seek out a dentist who can satisfy that nerve's needs? And if any other nerve prays continuously for attention, won't you do likewise with it?

Well, you are a nerve in the God-body. If you have an urgent need, and keep praying and insisting and demanding the remedy, don't you suppose you will get it just as surely?

A definite purpose, held to in the face of every discouragement and failure, in spite of all obstacles and opposition, will win no matter what the odds. It is the one nerve cell working against the indifference, the inertia or even the active opposition of the entire group. If the cell is easily discouraged, it will fail. If it is willing to wait indefinitely, it will have to wait. But if it keeps stirring up the cells next to it, and stimulating them to stir those beyond, eventually the entire nerve system will go into action and bring about the result that single cell desires—even if it be only to rid itself of the constant irritation.[15]

You have seen young fellows determined to go to college. You have thought them foolish, in the face of the obstacles facing them. Yet when they persisted, you know how often those obstacles have one by one magically disappeared, until presently they found themselves with the fruition of their desires. A strongly held purpose, persisted in, believed in, is as sure to win in the end as the morrow's sun is to rise. And earnest prayer is to the God-body what a throbbing nerve is to yours. Hold to it, insist upon it, and it is just as sure of a hearing. But remember:

He that wavereth is like the wave of the sea, driven by the wind and tossed; yet not that man think that he shall receive anything of the Lord.

All are born free and equal. All may not start with the same amount of wealth or opportunity immediately available to them, but all can go to the Source of these and get just as much of them as is necessary to satisfy their desires.

We are surrounded by riches. We have available unlimited wealth. But we have to learn how to draw it to us.

Years ago, at Kimberley in South Africa, a poor Boer farmer tried to glean

---

15. See parable of the importunate friend, page 492.

a living out of the rocky soil. His boys oftentimes picked up pieces of dirty-looking crystal and used them as pebbles to throw at some wandering sheep. After years of fruitless effort, the farmer abandoned his attempts to make a living out of this rocky soil, and moved to a more fertile spot. Today, the farm he tried so hard to cultivate is the site of the Kimberley Diamond Mines, one of the richest spots on the face of the globe. And the bits of dirty crystal that his boys threw at the sheep turned out to be diamonds in the rough!

Most of us are like that poor Boer farmer. We strive and struggle, and frequently give up, because of ignorance of our powers, ignorance of the good things around us. We remain in poverty until along comes someone and shows that we were standing on a diamond mine all the time.

Russell Conwell tells the story of a Pennsylvania farmer whose brother went to Canada and became an oil driller. Fired with the brother's tales of sudden wealth, the farmer sold his land and went to Canada to make his fortune. The new owner, in looking over the farm, found that where the cattle came to drink from a little creek, a board had been put across the water to hold back a heavy scum which was washed down by the rains from the ground above.

He examined this scum, and thought it smelled like oil. So he had some experts come out and look the ground over. It proved to be one of the richest oil fields in the state of Pennsylvania.

What riches are you overlooking? What opportunities? "Opportunity," says a famous writer, "is like oxygen. It is so plentiful that we fairly breathe it." All that is necessary is a receptive mind, a willingness to try, and the persistence to see things through.

There is some one thing that YOU can do better than anyone else. There is some line of work in which you can excel—if you will just find that one thing and spend all your time and effort in learning to do it supremely well.

Don't worry if it seems to be some humble thing that anyone ought to be able to do. In a magazine some time ago, there was the story of a Polish immigrant who could speak scarcely a word of English, who had no trade or training and had to take any sort of job that offered. He happened to get one in a nursery, digging up dirt for the flowers. He dug so well that soon he was attending to the planting of many of the commoner varieties of flowers.

Among these were the peonies. He loved those big peonies, gave them such careful attention that they thrived and grew more beautiful than ever. Soon his peonies began to attract attention, the demand for them grew, until he had to double and then quadruple the space devoted to them. Today he is half owner of that nursery.

Two artists opened an office together, doing any kind of work they could get. One noticed that wherever he happened to do cartoons for people, the results were so effective that they came back for more. So he made an especial study of cartoon drawing. Today his earnings are in the $25,000 class, while his fellow artist is still barely making ends meet as a jack of all trades.

A retail clerk found that she had a special gift for satisfying complaining customers. She liked to straighten out the snarls that others had caused, and she did it so well that she soon attracted the attention of her employers. Today she is head of the complaint department.

There is the switchboard operator with the pleasing voice, the reception clerk with the cheery smile, the salesman with the convincing manner, the secretary with the knack of saving the boss' time, the drummer with the jolly manner. Every one of us has something. Find out what one thing you can do best, cultivate it and you can be the biggest man in that line in the world.

Success is where you are and within yourself. Don't try to imitate what someone else is doing. Develop what YOU have. There is something in you that will enable you to reach the top in some one line. Put the spot light on your own characteristics, your own abilities. Find what you can do best, what people like you best for. Then cultivate that.

When the great Comstock Lode was first discovered, a fortune was taken out of it. Then the ore petered out. The owners presently gave up and sold out to a new group. These men spent several hundred thousand dollars in a fruitless attempt to locate the rich lode, and they too were ready to give up. But someone thought to try a bore hole to the side of one of the entries, and struck an almost solid mass of ore so rich that nearly $300,000,000 was taken from it.

In the early days of the prairie farms, newcomers were frequently able to buy for a song the homesteads of the original settlers, because the latter had been able to find no water. They had dug wells, but had been unable to reach the streams beneath. Oftentimes, however, by digging only a few feet further, the newcomers found water in abundance. The first settlers had quit when success was almost within their grasp. The greatest success usually comes from one step beyond the point where defeat overtook you. "He who loses wealth, loses much," says an old proverb. "He who loses a friend, loses more. But he who loses his courage, loses everything."

Three things educators try to instil into children:

1st—Knowledge
2nd—Judgment
3rd—Persistence

And the greatest of these is Persistence. Many a man has succeeded without education. Many even without good judgment. But none has ever got anywhere worth while without persistence. Without a strong desire, without that inner urge which pushes him on, over obstacles, through discouragements, to the goal of his heart's desire.

"Nothing in the world can take the place of persistence," said Calvin Coolidge. "Talent will not. Nothing is more common than unsuccessful men with talent. Genius will not; unrewarded genius is almost a proverb. Education will not; the world is full of educated derelicts. Persistence and determination alone are omnipotent. The slogan 'Press on' has solved and always will solve the problems of the human race."

Russell Conwell, the famous educator and lecturer who founded Temple University, gathered statistics some years ago on those who succeed, and his figures showed that of 4043 multimillionaires in this country at that time, only 69 had even a High School education. They lacked money, they lacked training, but they had the URGE to get somewhere, the *persistence* to keep trying . . . and they succeeded!

Compare that with the figures Conwell gathered on the sons of rich men. Only one in seventeen died wealthy! Lacking incentive, having no urge within them to get ahead, they not only failed to make their mark, but they lost what they had.

The first essential of success is a feeling of lack, a need, a *desire* for something you have not got. It is the powerlessness of the cripple or invalid that makes him long for strength, gives him the necessary persistence to work for it until he gets it. It is the poverty and misery of their existence that makes the children of the Ghetto long for wealth, and gives them the persistence and determination to work at anything until they get it.

You need that same urgent desire, that same determination and persistence if you are to get what you want from life. You need to realize that whatever it is you want of life, it is there for the taking. You need to know that you are a cell in the God-mind, and that through this God-mind you can put the whole Universe to work, if necessary, to bring about the accomplishment of your desire.

But don't waste that vast power on trifles. Don't be like the fable of the woodsman who, having worked long and hard for the wishing Fairy and accomplished the task she set him, was told that he might have in reward any three things he asked for. Being very hungry, he promptly asked for a good meal. That eaten, he noticed that the wind was blowing up cold, so he asked for a warm cloak. With his stomach full and a warm cloak about him, he felt sleepy, so he asked for a comfortable bed to lie upon.

And so, with every good thing of the world his for the asking, the next day found him with only a warm cloak to show for his labors. Most of us are like that. We put the mountain in labor, just to bring forth a mouse. We strive and strain, and draw upon all the powers that have been given us, to accomplish some trifling thing that leaves us just where we were before.

Demand much! Set a worthwhile goal. Remember the old poem by Jessie B. Rittenhouse from "The Door of Dreams" published by Houghton Mifflin Co., Boston.

> *I bargained with Life for a penny*
> *And Life would pay no more,*
> *However I begged at evening*
> *When I counted my scanty store.*
>
> *For Life is a just employer;*
> *He gives you what you ask,*
> *But once you have set the wages,*
> *Why, you must bear the task.*
>
> *I worked for a menial's hire,*
> *Only to learn, dismayed,*
> *That any wage I had asked of Life,*
> *Life would have paid.*

Don't you be foolish like that. Don't bargain with Life for a penny. Ask for something worth putting the Universe to work for. Ask for it, demand it—then stick to that demand with persistence and determination until the whole God-mind HAS to bestir itself to give you what you want.

The purpose of Life from the very beginning has been dominion—dominion over every adverse circumstance. And through his part of dominion, his nerve cell in the Mind of God and his ability through it to get whatever action he may persistently demand—man HAS dominion over everything.

There is a Spark of Divinity in YOU. What are you doing to fan it into flame? Are you giving it a chance to grow, to express itself, to become an all-consuming fire? Are you giving it work to do? Are you making it seek out ever greater worlds to conquer? Or are you letting it slumber neglected, or perhaps even smothering it with doubt and fear?

And God said, Let us make man in our image, after our likeness; and let him have DOMINION over the fish of the sea, and over the fowl of the air, and over the cattle, and over all the earth, and over every creeping thing that creepeth upon the earth.

Do you know what is the Unpardonable Sin in all of Nature? Read the following chapters, and you will see!
Affirmation:

And every morning I will say, There's something happy on the way. And God sends love to me. God is the light of my life, the Source of my knowledge and inspiration. God in the midst of me knows. He provides me with food for my thoughts, ideas for excellent service, clear perception, Divine intelligence.

The Goal of Life

Mind is the Master-power that moulds and makes,
And Man is Mind, and evermore he takes
The tool of Thought, and, shaping what he wills,
Brings forth a thousand joys, a thousand ills:—
He thinks in secret, and it comes to pass:
Environment is but his looking glass.

—JAMES ALLEN

"In the beginning God created the heaven and earth. And the earth was without form and void; and darkness was upon the face of the deep. And the Spirit of God moved upon the face of the waters. And God said . . ."

In the beginning was Mind, Energy, without form, without direction . . . like so much static electricity. Then came the Word, the mental image, to make all that power dynamic, to give it form and direction. What matters it the form it took first, so long as it had definite direction? It required an Intelligence to give it shape. That is the first great fact of the Scriptures. NOT that the heavens and earth were created, or light brought forth, but that *any form pre-supposes a Directing Intelligence!*

You cannot have dynamic electricity without a generator—an intelligence to conceive and direct it. No more can you have an earth or a flower, without an Intelligence to give them form from the static energy all about.

In the beginning, not merely was the earth without form and void, but the whole universe was the same way. Just as the interspaces of the universe are to-day. Everything was static—energy in flux. But "the Spirit of God moved upon the face of the waters. And God said, "Let there be light."

St. John puts it—"In the beginning was the Word. And the Word was with God. And the Word was God." And what is the "Word"? As often mentioned before, a word is not a mere sound issuing from the lips, or so many letters written by hand. A word is a mental concept, an idea, an image.

In the beginning was the mental image! Read over that first chapter of Genesis, and you will see that in everything God created, the "Word" came first—then the material form. The "Word" had to come first—you cannot build a house without first having a clear image of the house you are going to build. You cannot make anything, without first conceiving a mental image of the thing to be created. Not even God could do that!

So when God said—"Let the earth bring forth grass," He had in mind a clear mental picture of what grass was like. As the Scriptures put it—"The Lord God made the earth and the heavens, and every plant of the field *before it was in the earth,* and every herd of the field *before it grew.*" First the "Word," the mental image—then the creation.

It requires intelligence to form a mental concept. The animals cannot do it. They can recall images of things they have seen. They cannot conceive concepts from pure ideas. So, as stated above, creation pre-supposes a mental image, and a mental image means a directing Intelligence behind it.

That is the first conclusion that a reading of the Scriptures forces upon us. And the second is that like reproduces like.

Go over that first chapter again, and you will find that no less than six different times is the assertion repeated that "everything reproduces after its kind . . ." "Let the earth bring forth grass, the herb yielding seed, and the fruit tree yielding fruit *after his kind,* whose seed is in itself. . . . Let the earth bring forth the living creature after his kind, cattle, and creeping thing, and beast of the earth after his kind."

Then God made man in His own image, after His likeness. Notice that! After telling us repeatedly that everything reproduced after its own kind, the Scriptures go on to say that God made man *in His own image.* That can mean only one thing—that man, too, is a God! For throughout all nature, hybrids are sterile. Nothing can breed out of its own kind. Different races, different strains of the same species, can interbreed, but all must be of the same kind.

So when God made man in His own image, and bade him be fruitful and multiply, He thereby showed that man was no hybrid, but of the true breed of God. And to prove it, he gave man dominion over the "fish of the sea, and over the fowl of the air, and over every living thing that moveth upon the earth." And He bade man replenish the earth, *and subdue it,* and have dominion.

Simple instructions, and easily carried out—in part—but as for subduing the earth, and having dominion over it, mankind is still in the primer class. Yet if man is a God—*and he is*—then he *can* do it. And anything so worthwhile as that is worth all our effort to learn how to do.

For if we are gods and true sons of God—as the Scriptures frequently assure us—then we must possess all the properties of God. We must be creators. Then why don't we create happier conditions? Why don't we do away with poverty and disease and all unhappiness?

Why? Because it takes understanding and faith to use our powers, and so few have the patience to work for them. Men will study for years to become doctors, or lawyers, or engineers. And they will start the practice of their professions in fear and trembling, realizing that it will be years before they will have gained enough practical knowledge from experience to be really competent in their work.

Yet they will read a book or two on psychology or some of the mental sciences, and if they cannot put the principles into practice next day, they give up in disgust and condemn the principles as tommyrot!

Of all fields of study, none offers such possibilities as the study of the inner powers of man. None offers such sure rewards to the persevering, sincere student. Yet there is no field so neglected by the average man. Nine men out of ten—yes, ninety-nine out of a hundred—merely drift through life. With generators inside them capable of producing power enough to accomplish any purpose, they get nowhere.

They use their generators, of course, but to what purpose? To sigh over some movie idol—or thrill over the exploits of some notorious racketeer—or wax indignant at the thieving of a fat city grafter. Vicarious emotions, all of them—yet because it is so much easier to enjoy one's thrills vicariously, most people go through life experiencing few others.

They speed up their generators, but with no resultant good to themselves. Their experiences are all dream pictures. When they leave the movies, or put

THE GOAL OF LIFE

down their paper or book, they wake up! They never make the effort necessary to bring those thrills into their own lives.

Suppose the envelope of air that surrounds the globe were a great storage battery of electrical energy. Every thought, every fervent desire, every emotion, adds to the energy there. Every time you run your generator—with feelings of love or hate or fear or envy or hope or faith—you put additional energy into that storage battery.

But to draw energy out of this storage battery, you must have good conductors, good wires, the wires of a definite purpose, strongly held. And to keep the energy from dissipating requires the insulation of faith.

You cannot get much current from a storage battery by merely touching your wires to its posts, letting them slip on and off continuously. You have to twist them securely around the posts, fasten them there firmly with the screw cap, to get a constant current.

And you cannot use plain wires, or the current will run off into the first conductor that comes in contact with it. Your wires must be insulated, so the current will go directly from the battery to the appliance you wish it to run.

It is the same with the storage battery of power all around you. You can draw upon it at will, you can get flashes of power from it at the touch of fervent prayer or under the stress of any other high emotion, but if you want a continuous flow of power, you must have first a firmly held purpose, then the insulation of serene faith. Given these, there is no limit to the power you can draw, or the purposes to which it can be put.

Now how would this help if you were out of a job, had a wife and children waiting for something to eat, a home that was about to be taken away from you—and you had been praying and trying in every way you knew to raise the necessary money? How could you use the idea? What would you need to do?

Remember, in the Bible, how it is told that the apostles labored all night long, and caught nothing, yet when Jesus bade them cast their nets on the right side, and they did so, their nets were filled to overflowing?

You have been praying and trying, and you have caught nothing. Now it is your turn to cast your nets on the right side. And casting them there means to disregard the material world around you for a moment, and do your fishing in the world of energy!

All around you is energy—unappropriated energy that you can turn into any form you wish. The same flux out of which God created the world! And you are a god, a creator, a true son of the Father. You have the same power to make of your world what you like that He has. It requires only the same method He used.

First, the "Word," the mental image. What is it you want? Position, power, love, riches, success? Make your mold. The best flux in the world will not make a usable shape unless you have a mold to pour it in. So make your mold, your mental image. See it clearly in your mind's eye. Don't make it the home or position or riches that belong to someone else. Use them as a model, if you like, but make your own out of virgin material.

Second, the flux. "The Spirit of God moved on the face of the waters." Throw your net, your spirit, around as much of the unappropriated energy about as you need to fill your mold. Then hold to it with the dogged grip of the bulldog. It is yours. You have filed your claim upon it, and no one can take it away from you unless you weaken and let go. Hold to that knowledge with grim, unshakable purpose, and there is nothing you cannot get.

"Whatsoever you ask for when you pray, believe that you receive it, and you shall have it." Whatever you want, make your mental hold, then throw your net around the flux necessary to fill it, and hold on to it until that flux has hardened. It is yours. You HAVE it. You have only to believe, to *know that you have it,* in order to give that flux time to harden so that all can see it.

But to lose faith is to pull away the mold while your flux is still liquid. It will run like quicksilver in all directions, and you have to start all over again, making a new mold, casting your net around new energy, starting again to give it time to harden and become manifest.

In every man there is a Seed of Life, with infinite power to draw to itself whatever it conceives to be necessary to its expression. It doesn't matter who you are, what your environment or education or advantages, the Seed of Life in you has the same power for good.

What is it makes a poor immigrant-boy like Edward Bok, overcome every handicap of language and education, to become one of the greatest editors the country has known?

What is it accounts for the fact that, as before-mentioned, of 4043 multi-millionaires in this country a few years before the first World War, all but 69 started so poor that they had not even a high school education?

Isn't it that the more circumstances conspire to repress it, the stronger becomes the urge of the Life in you for expression? The more it lacks channels through which to expand, the more inclined it is to burst its shell and flow forth in all directions?

It is the old case of the river that is dammed, generating the most power. Most of us are so placed that some opportunity for expression is made easy for us. And that little opportunity serves like a safety valve to a boiler—it leaves us steam enough to do something worth while, yet keeps us from getting up enough power to burst the shell about us, and sweep away every barrier that holds us down.

Yet it is only such an irresistible head of steam as that which makes great successes. That is why the blow which knocks all the props from under us is often the turning point in our whole career. Take the case of a man I know who, five years after losing his job, reached his goal as head of a rival company and the greatest authority on his product in the country. Do you suppose he would ever have won these rewards had he continued as salesman for his original company?

No, indeed! He was getting along too well. He had a comfortable home, a fine family, a good income and congenial working conditions. Why should he disturb them? The old fable of the dog with the bone looking at his reflection in the water, keeps many a man from taking a chance at a better opportunity when he has a reasonably good one within his grasp. He's afraid he may be giving up the real for the chimera.

Yet playing safe is probably the most unsafe thing in the world. You cannot stand still. You must go forward—or see the world slide past you. This was well illustrated by figures worked out by one of the big Economic Services. Of all those who have money at 35, 87% lose it by the time they are 60.

Why?—Because the fortunes they have take away the need for initiative on their part. Their money gives to them easy means of expressing the urge in them, without effort on their part. It gives them dozens of safety valves, through which their steam continually escapes.

The result is that they not only accomplish nothing worth while, but they soon dissipate the fortunes that were left them. They are like kettles, the urge of life keeping the water at boiling point, but the open spout of ease letting the steam escape as fast as it forms, until presently there is not even any water left.

Why do the sons of rich men so seldom accomplish anything worth while? Because they don't have to. Every opportunity is given them to express the urge in them through pleasant channels, and they dissipate through these the energies that might carry them to any height. The result? They never have a strong enough "head of steam" left to carry through any real job.

With us ordinary mortals, however, sooner or later comes a crisis in our affairs, and how we meet it determines our future happiness and success. Since the beginning of time, every form of life has been called upon to meet such crises. So the goal of life has always been DOMINION—a means of overcoming all obstacles, of winning dominion over circumstances.

In "Weekly Unity" Magazine, some years ago, there was the story of a couple who wanted to dispose of their house and move to another town. But the so-called "Depression" was on at that time, and houses were a drug on the market. Real Estate Agents held out no hope, so "Why not try prayer?"—a friend asked. "What can we lose?" they asked each other. So they sat down together and tried to realize—

1. That there is only one Mind, that they were parts of that Mind, and that those to whom they must sell were also parts of it.
2. That this God-Mind is working for the good of all—for their good and for that of those who were seeking just such a home as theirs.
3. That this God-Mind was glad to help them, glad to help those seeking such a home, so all they had to do was to put their home in His hands, and leave the working out of the problem confidently and serenely to Him.

Within a short time, they sold the house for a good price for CASH. In another issue, "Unity" told about a dealer who had bought a number of pianos on credit, and borrowed some of the money from the bank to pay for them. The pinch came, and the bank notified him that his note must be paid by a certain date. He went home worried and miserable. With the help of his wife, however, he was able to throw off the worry and put it up to the God Inside Him to find the necessary funds.

That afternoon, one of the clerks came to him and said there was a man cursing and swearing about something he had bought from him the day before. He went over to the man and found him ranting and raging about an inexpensive article he had purchased for his son, on which some of the strings had broken. The shopkeeper promptly gave him a better article to replace it. That took all the wind out of the complaining customer's sails, and he became so apologetic that he felt he had to buy something else to make up for his boorish behavior. It developed that he was planning to get a fine piano for his daughter's birthday, and the money he promptly paid for this proved to be more than enough to take care of the dealer's note at the bank.

The goal of life since the beginning of time has been DOMINION over just such circumstances as these, and only through the God in you can you win it. "My soul, wait thou only upon God," bade the prophet of old, "for my expectation is from Him."

But don't limit the channels through which His help can come to you. Don't insist that it should be through a legacy from some rich uncle, or a raise in your pay or the winning of some prize or order. Develop any channel that looks promising, but leave ALL the channels open. And then act as though *you already possessed the thing you want.*

Don't say—"When this bill is paid—or this crisis past—I shall feel so relieved." Instead, say—"I AM relieved, I feel so content and peaceful now that this load is off my shoulders."

How will you act when you get the thing you want? Well, act that way now, think that way—and before you know it, you will BE that way. Remember the lines by Ella Wheeler Wilcox—

Thought is a magnet; and the longed-for pleasure
Or boon or aim or object is the steel;
And its attainment hangs but on the measure
Of what thy soul can feel.

How would you conduct yourself if you full realized your one-ness with God, if you could truly believe that He is constantly offering you life, love and every good thing your heart can desire? Well, that is exactly what He is doing!

So act as if you already had the thing you want. Visualize it as yours. See the picture clearly in every detail in your mind's eye. Then LET GOD make it manifest. Do what you can, of course, with what you have, where you are, but put your dependence upon God, and LET His good gifts come to you.

Look at the first chapter of the Scriptures. When God wanted light, did He strive and struggle, trying to make light? No, He said—"*Let* there be light."

When you want something very much, instead of trying to MAKE it come your way, suppose you try asking for it and then LETTING it come. Suppose you just relax, and *let* God work through you instead of trying to *make* Him do something for you. Suppose you say to yourself—"I will do whatever is given me to do. I will follow every lead to the best of my ability, but for the rest, it is all up to the God in me. God in me knows what my right work is, where it is, and just what I should do to get it. I put myself and my affairs lovingly in His hands, secure that whatever is for my highest good, He will bring to me."

Emerson used to say that when we discern Truth, we do nothing of ourselves but allow a passage for its beams. They express the same thought in electricity through the equation—$C = E \div R$: The current delivered at any given point is equal to the voltage divided by the resistance. With too much resistance, no current is delivered, no matter how much may be available.

When we worry and are tense and fearful, we set up so great resistance that God finds it difficult to get through to us. We have to LET GO before we can become good conductors. Like John Burroughs, we must be able to say— "Serene I fold my hands and wait, nor care for wind or tide or sea. No more I strive against time or fate, for lo! Mine own shall come to me."

Unity has a favorite Prayer of Faith, written by Hannah More Kohaus, which all of us might well use when we are worried or sick or in need. If you will relax and repeat it slowly aloud, it is calculated to help you in any crisis:

God IS MY help in every need;
God does my every hunger feed;
God walks beside me, guides my way
Through every moment of the day.

I now am wise, I now am true,
Patient, kind, and loving, too.
All things I am, can do, and be,
Through Christ the Truth that is in me.

God is my health, I can't be sick;
God is my strength, unfailing, quick;
God is my all; I know no fear,
Since God and love and Truth are here.

A GOLDEN RULE MOTTO

I shall pass through this world but once.
Any good, therefore, that I can do

Or any kindness that I can show
To any human being
Let me do it now. Let me
Not defer it or neglect it for
I shall not pass this way again.

—ANONYMOUS

ONLY A COG IN A WHEEL

A man there was of unusual gifts
Bearing an honored name,
Life came to him with outstretched hands
Proffering wealth and fame;
But he carelessly turned his head away,
The prize made little appeal,
Contenting himself with a minor part,
He was only a cog in a wheel.

When opportunity knocked at his door,
It found him asleep and deaf;
Long and patiently it waited there,
But he did not come to himself.
His golden chances were wasted like chaff,
He took no account of the real;
Each day a monotonous grind to him,
He was only a cog in a wheel.

In the image of God this man was made,
With power to do and to serve;
Strong of mind and body was he,
But he lacked essential nerve.
So he drifted along from day to day,
Without ambition or zeal,
Playing a dull and nondescript part,
He was only a cog in a wheel.

What place do you fill in life's great machine—
Are you using your gifts aright?
Today have you wrought some truly fine thing—
Can you claim to have fought a good fight?
Will it surely be said that you "played the game"—
That your life was productive and real?
Or will the world say, as it goes on its way,
He was only a cog in a wheel?

—ANONYMOUS

Many versions as to the true description of Christ have been given to the world. Among the most authentic is this one, written by Publius Lentulus, President of Judea, to Tiberius Caesar, and first appeared in the writings of Saint Anselm of Canterbury in the Eleventh Century.

"There lived at this time in Judea a man of singular virtue—whose name is Jesus Christ whom the barbarians esteem as a prophet, but his followers love and adore him as the offspring of the immortal God. He calls back the dead from the graves and heals all sorts of diseases with a word or touch. He is a tall man, well shaped, and of an amiable and reverend aspect—his hair of a color that can hardly be matched, falling into graceful curls, waving about and very agreeably couched about his shoulders, parted on the crown of his head, running as a stream to the front after the fashion of the Nazarites; his forehead high, large and imposing; his cheeks without spot or wrinkle, beautiful with a lovely red; his nose and mouth formed with exquisite symmetry; his beard of a color suitable to his hair, reaching below his chin and parted in the middle like a fork; his eyes bright and blue, clear and serene, look innocent, dignified, manly and mature. Often times however, just before he reveals his divine powers, his eyelids are gently closed in reverential silence. In proportion of body most perfect and captivating; his arms and hands are delectable to behold. He rebukes with majesty, counsels with mildness, his whole address, whether in word or deed, being eloquent and grave. No man has seen him laugh, yet his manners are exceedingly pleasant, but he has wept frequently in the presence of men. He is temperate, modest and wise. A man for his extraordinary beauty and divine perfection, surpassing the children of men in every sense."

3

Your Mental Brownies

Mankind, like Ancient Gaul, can be divided into three parts.

1st—Those who are still in a state of simple consciousness, living, acting and thinking as the animals do. Men and women in this class can be said to exist—nothing more.

2nd—Those in a state of self-consciousness. This comprises the great bulk of the higher races of mankind. They reason, they study, they work, they sorrow and enjoy. But they are forced to depend for all good things upon their own efforts and they are subject to all manner of circumstances and conditions beyond their control. Theirs is a state of struggle.

3rd—Those entering into or who have reached the intuitional or higher consciousness, that state which Jesus termed the Kingdom of Heaven within us.

Just as, in the childhood of the race, there was brought forth an Adam and Eve with such advanced receptual intellects that they presently developed conceptual ideas (i.e. named impressions and the ability to classify them, compare them and draw conclusions from them), so today are to be found here and there the advance guard of the Mental Age—men and women as far ahead of the ordinary conceptual intellect of their fellows as this is in advance of the simple consciousness of the animal.

You see, the animal recognizes only images. Each house is to him a new house, with its own associations of food or famine, of kindness or blows. He never generalizes, or draws conclusions by comparing one house with another. His is the simple or receptual consciousness.

Man, on the other hand, takes his recept or image of a house and tabs it. He names it a house and then classifies it according to its kind. In that way, he turns it from a mere image into an idea or concept. It is as though he were traveling on a railroad train and keeping a tally of every house he passed. To the animal, it would mean filling his mind with the pictures of a hundred or more houses. To a man, it would be merely a matter of jotting down in the tablets of his memory—"100 houses, 25 of the Colonial type, 15 Tudor style, etc."

If his mind were too full of images, there would be no room in it to work out conclusions from those images, so man classifies those images into concepts or ideas, and thus increases his mental capacity a millionfold.

But now the time has come in his mental development when his mind is so full of concepts that a new short cut must be found. Here and there a few have already found this short cut and penetrated to the highest plane of consciousness—the intuitional or "Heaven" consciousness.

What is this higher consciousness? Bucke calls it the Cosmic Consciousness, and defines it as a consciousness of the world about us, a consciousness that does not have to stop and add concept to concept like a column of figures, but which can work out the answer immediately, intuitively, as a "lightning calculator" can work out a problem in mathematics, apparently without going through any of the intermediate stages of addition and subtraction, of labored reasoning from premise to conclusion.

You see, the conscious you is merely that aggregation of images and sensations and concepts known as the brain. But beyond and above this reasoning mind is your intuitive mind—the Soul of you—which is one cell in the great Oversoul of the Universe, God. It is the connecting link between God and you. It is part of Him. It shares in all His attributes, all His power and wisdom and riches. And at need it can draw upon the whole of these. How? In the same way that any cell of your body can draw upon the vitality of the whole body—by creating the need, *by using what it has.*

There is nothing mysterious about the way life works. It is all a logical growth. In the intellect, the young child first registers impressions, then it recognizes and tabs them, finally classifying them and using them as the basis for reasoning out ideas. By the use of impressions and images, the child can know the world it sees and feels. By concepts, it can construct in imagination the world it has not seen. Is this all? Is it the end?

"No!" answers Bucke in "Cosmic Consciousness." "As life arose in a world without life; as simple consciousness came into existence where before was mere vitality without perception; as self-consciousness soared forth over land and sea; so shall the race of man which has been thus established make other steps and attain to a yet higher life than any heretofore experienced or even conceived.

And let it be clearly understood that the new step is not merely an expansion of self-consciousness, but as distinct from it as that it's from simple consciousness, or as is this last from mere vitality without any consciousness at all.

But how shall we know this new sense? How recognize its coming? The signs are evident in every man and woman of high mentality. You have seen accountants who could write down a column of figures and give you the total without consciously adding one to another. You can recall instances when you have anticipated word for word what someone was about to say to you, when you have answered the telephone and known before he spoke who was at the other end of the wire, when you have met a stranger and formed a "snap judgment" of him which afterwards turned out to be marvelously correct. We call this intuition. It is the first stage of the Cosmic Consciousness. It is a perfectly logical step in the growth of the intellect.

In the jump from Simple Consciousness to Self-Consciousness, man combined groups of recepts or images into one concept or idea, just as we combine the three Roman numerals III into the one symbol 3. No longer did he have to hold in his mind each individual tree in a forest. He grouped them all together under one heading of trees, and called the group a forest.

Now he is advancing a step farther. Instead of having to first study each tree individually to learn the properties of that forest, he is getting that knowledge from the soul within him, which is part of the great Oversoul of the forest and of the Universe, and therefore knows all things. In other words, he is getting it intuitively.

That is the first step in reaching the Heaven consciousness—to cultivate your intuitions, to encourage them in every possible way. Your soul is a cell in the great God-body just as every cell in your body is part of you. And as part of the Oversoul of the Universe, it has access to all the knowledge of the Universe. But it needs exercise, it requires development.

When you want to develop any cell or set of cells in your body, what do you do? You exercise them, do you not? You use them to the limit of their abilities. Then what happens? They feel weak, exhausted. They become thin and emaciated. Why? Because you have broken up those cells, used the energy in them, and they have not yet had time to draw upon the blood stream for more. For the first few days or weeks that you continue that hard usage, they remain weak and nerveless. Again why? Because the amount of energy your "governor" is accustomed to apportioning those cells is not sufficient for such heavy work. But keep persevering, and what happens? Those cells not only harden until they are equal to any call you can make upon them, but they grow in size and power. They have put in a permanent order upon the "governor" for more life-giving energy, and as long as they can find use for it, that energy will keep coming to them.

That is the first thing you must do to grow in intuitive consciousness—cultivate what you have, use it on every possible occasion even though you seem to strain it beyond its powers at first. Listen for that still, small voice. And listen *to* it. "And thine ears shall hear a word behind thee," promised the Prophet of old, "saying—This is the way, walk ye in it, when ye turn to the right hand, and when ye turn to the left."

What is the vision of the artist, the inspiration of the writer, the discovery of the chemist or inventor, but his intuitive consciousness at work? Ask almost any great author, and he will tell you that he does not work out his plots. They "come to him"—that's all. "The key to successful methods," says Thomas A. Edison, "comes right out of the air. A real new thing like a general idea, a beautiful melody, is pulled out of space—a fact which is inexplicable."

Inexplicable—yes, from the viewpoint of the conceptual intellect—but quite understandable from the intuitive point of view.

So much for the first step. It is one possible to any man or woman of high intellect. When it involves a problem or a work of art or a story or a new discovery, it requires only filling the mind with all available concepts related to the desired result, then putting it up to the God in you to work out the answer.

The second step is the earnest desire for a higher consciousness. That sounds simple enough. Everybody would like to be able to learn without going through all the labor of adding percept to recept, making concepts of these and then figuring out the answers. So if the earnest desire is all that is needed, it ought to be easy.

Yet it is not. It is the hardest step of all. Why? Because the desire must be your *dominant* desire. It must not be merely a means to the end of obtaining riches or winning to high position.

All agree on this: This Heaven consciousness comes only as the result of a tremendous desire for spiritual truth, and a hunger and thirst after things of the spirit.

Perhaps that can be better understood when you remember how many ordinary people have had partial glimpses of it when almost at the point of death, or when coming out from under the influence of anaesthetics.

What, then, are the necessary conditions?

First, an understanding of the power latent in you, an understanding that, regardless of how much or how little education you have received, there is in you a power (call it the subconscious, or your soul, or your good genii or what you will) capable of contacting the Intelligence which directs and animates all of the universe.

Second, the earnest desire for spiritual growth. To possess this, a man need not be an ascetic, or give up his family or his business. In fact, he should be the better husband and father and business man for it. For the man of business today is no longer engaged in cheating his neighbor before the neighbor can cheat him. He is trying to *serve,* and to the extent that he succeeds in giving more and better service than others, he succeeds. Can you conceive of any finer preparation for the Heaven consciousness?

Third, the ability to thoroughly relax. As Boehme put it—"To cease from all thinking and willing and imaging. Your own 'self-conscious' hearing and willing and seeing hinder you from seeing and hearing God."

"When a new faculty appears in a race," says Bucke, "it will be found in the very beginning in one individual of that race; later it will be found in a few individuals; after a further time, in a larger percentage of the members of the race; still later, in half the members; and so on until, after thousands of generations, an individual who misses having the faculty is regarded as a monstrosity."

The Heaven consciousness, or Cosmic Consciousness as Bucke calls it, has reached the point of being found in many individuals. When a faculty reaches that point, it is susceptible of being acquired by all of the higher type of members of that race *who have reached full maturity.*

And it is never too late to develop this Intuitive Consciousness, for your mind never grows old. In his book, "The Age of Mental Virility," Dr. Dorland points out that more than half of mankind's greatest achievements were accomplished by men over 50 years old, and that more of these were done by men over 70 than by those under 30.

In tests made by Dr. Irving Lorge of Teachers College, Columbia University, it was found that while SPEED of learning might decline with years, the mental powers do not decline. When the speed penalty was eliminated, people of 50 and 60 made higher scores than those around 25. Dr. Lorge sums up his tests in these words:

> As far as mental ability is concerned, there need be no "retiring age." The probabilities are that the older a person becomes, the more valuable he becomes. He possesses the same mental power he had in his young manhood, plus his wealth of experience and knowledge of his particular job. These are things that no youngster, however brilliant, can pick up.

You have an Intuitive Consciousness, which has evidenced itself many a time in "Hunches," and the like. Remains, then, only to develop it. Robert Louis Stevenson pointed the way when he told how he worked out the plot for Dr. Jekyll and Mr. Hyde.

"My Brownies! God bless them!" said Stevenson, "Who do one-half of my work for me when I am fast asleep, and in all human likelihood do the rest for me as well when I am wide awake and foolishly suppose that I do it myself. I had long been wanting to write a book on man's double being. For two days I went about racking my brains for a plot of any sort, and on the second night I dreamt the scene in 'Dr. Jekyll and Mr. Hyde' at the window; and a scene, afterward split in two, in which Hyde, pursued, took the powder and underwent the change in the presence of his pursuer."

You have had similar experiences. You know how, after you have studied a problem from all angles, it sometimes seems worse jumbled than when you started on it. Leave it then for a while—forget it—and when you go back to it, you find your thoughts clarified, the line of reasoning worked out, your problem solved for you. It is your little "Mental Brownies" who have done the work for you!

The flash of genius does not originate in your own brain. Through intense concentration you have established a circuit through your subconscious mind with the Universal, and it is from IT that the inspiration comes. All genius, all progress, is from the same source. It lies with you merely to learn how to establish this circuit at will so that you can call upon IT at need. It can be done.

"There are many ways of setting the Brownies to work," says Dumont in "The Master Mind." "Nearly everyone has had some experience, more or less, in the matter, although often it is produced almost unconsciously, and without purpose and intent. Perhaps the best way for the average person—or rather the majority of persons—to get the desired results is for one to get as clear an idea of what one really wants to know—as clear an idea or mental image of the question you wish answered. Then after rolling it around in your mind—mentally chewing it, as it were—giving it a high degree of voluntary attention, you can pass it on to your Subconscious Mentality with the mental command: '*Attend to this for me—work out the answer!*' or some similar order. This command may be given silently, or else spoken aloud—either will do. Speak to the Subconscious Mentality—or its little workers—just as you would speak to persons in your employ, kindly but firmly. Talk to the little workers, and firmly command them to do your work. And then forget all about the matter—throw it off your conscious mind, and attend to your other tasks. Then in due time will come your answer—flashed into your consciousness—perhaps not until the very minute that you must decide upon the matter, or need the information. You may give your Brownies orders to report at such and such a time—just as you do when you tell them to awaken you at a certain time in the morning so as to catch the early train, or just as they remind you of the hour of your appointment, if you have them all well trained."

Have you ever read the story by Richard Harding Davis of "The Man Who Could Not Lose?" In it the hero is intensely interested in racing. He has studied records and "dope" sheets until he knows the history of every horse backward and forward.

The day before the big race he is reclining in an easy chair, thinking of the morrow's race, and he drops off to sleep with that thought on his mind. Naturally, his subconscious mind takes it up, with the result that he dreams the exact outcome of the race.

That was mere fiction, of course, but if races were run solely on the speed and stamina of the horses, it would be entirely possible to work out the results in just that way. Unfortunately, other factors frequently enter into every betting game.

But the idea behind Davis' story is entirely right. The way to contact your subconscious mind, the way to get the help of the "Man Inside You" in working out any problem is:

First, fill your mind with every bit of information regarding that problem that you can lay your hands on.

Second, pick out a chair or lounge or bed where you can recline in perfect comfort, where you can forget your body entirely.

Third, let your mind dwell upon the problem for a moment, not worrying, not fretting, but placidly, and then turn it over to the "Man Inside You." Say to him—"This is your problem. You Can do anything. You know the answer to everything. Work this out for me!" And utterly relax. Drop off to sleep, if you can. At least, drop into one of those half-sleepy, half-wakeful reveries that keep other thoughts from obtruding upon your consciousness. Do as Aladdin did— summon your Genie, give him your orders, then forget the matter, secure in the knowledge that he will attend to it for you. When you waken, *you will have the answer!*

"The smartest man in the world is the Man Inside," said Dr. Frank Crane. "By the Man Inside I mean that Other Man within each one of us that does most of the things we give ourselves credit for doing.

"I say he is the smartest man in the world. I know he is infinitely more clever and resourceful than I am or than any other man is that I ever heard of. When I cut my finger it is he that calls up the little phagocytes to come and kill the septic germs that might get into the wound and cause blood poisoning. It is he that coagulates the blood, stops the gash, and weaves the new skin.

"I could not do that. I do not even know how he does it. He even does it for babies that know nothing at all; in fact, does it better for them than for me.

"When I practice on the piano I am simply getting the business of piano playing over from my conscious mind to my subconscious mind: in other words, I am handing the business over to the Man Inside.

"Most of our happiness, as well as our struggles and misery, comes from this Man Inside. If we train him in ways of contentment, adjustment and decision, he will go ahead of us like a well-trained servant and do for us easily most of the difficult tasks we have to perform."

Read that last paragraph again. "Most of our happiness, *as well as our struggles and misery,* comes from this Man Inside."

How, then, can we use him to bring us only the good things of life?

By BLESSING instead of ranting and cursing, by TRUSTING instead of fearing. Every man is what he is because of the dominating thoughts that he permits to occupy his mind and thus suggests to the Man Inside.

Those thoughts that are mixed with some feeling of emotion, such as anger or fear or worry or love, magnetize that Man Inside and tend to drive him to such action as will attract to you similar or related thoughts and their logical reactions. All impulses of thought have a tendency to bring about their physical equivalent, simply because they set the Man Inside You to work trying to bring about the physical manifestations of your thought images. Jesus understood this when He said—"By their fruits shall ye know them."

What, then is the answer?

1. Realize that your thoughts are the molds in which the Man Inside You forms your circumstances, that "As a man think-eth, so is he."
2. Remember that there is nothing in all of God's Universe which you need to fear. For God is Love, and you are one with God. So make friends with your problems. Don't try to run away from them. Walk up to them, bring them into the open, and you will find that they are not obstacles, but stepping-stones to something better.
3. If you are worrying or fearful, stop it. Put your affairs into the hands of the God in You—and forget them! Remember that all things are possible with God, and all things are possible with you when you realize that you are one with Him. So look to God instead of to your difficulties. Look to the things you WANT—not to those you fear.
4. Forget the past. Remember—"Now is the accepted time. Now is the day of salvation." Look ahead to the great things that are before you— not backward at the regrets of the past. Look to what you want to see manifested. Think of each day as in itself a life, and say each morning—"I wake to do the work of a man."
5. Bless all things, for under even the most unprepossessing exterior lies a kernel of good. Remember that "When Fortune means to man most good, she looks upon him with a threatening eye."

In "Unity Weekly," the story is told of a farmer who, when he plows a field, blesses every seed he puts into it, and visualizes the abundant harvest it will bring. His neighbors marvel at the size of his crops.

In another issue, they tell of a guest in a western hotel who was impressed by the atmosphere of joy and peace in the room she occupied. Living in it seemed to be an inspiration. She was so filled with the presence of good in it that she asked the maid who had occupied it before, to give it such a restful atmosphere. The maid told her it was not the occupant, but herself; that whenever she worked in a room she blessed it, and as she left it, she stood in the door for a moment affirming peace and restfulness for it and blessing for the one who would occupy it.

Arthur Guiterman has written a blessing for every home that each of us might well use:

Bless the four corners of this house,
And be the Lintel blest;
And bless the hearth, and bless the board,
And bless each place of rest;
And bless the door that opens wide
To stranger, as to kin;
And bless each crystal windowpane
That lets the starlight in;
And bless the rooftree overhead,
And every sturdy wall;
The peace of God, the peace of man,
The peace of love, on all.

CONSECRATION

Laid on Thy altar, my Lord divine
Accept my gift this day for Jesus' sake;
I have no jewels to adorn Thy shrine,
Nor any world-famed sacrifice to make.
But here I bring within my trembling hands
This will of mine—a thing that seemeth small
And only Thou, dear Lord, canst understand
How, when I yield Thee this, I yield mine all.
Hidden therein Thy searching eyes can see
Struggles of passion, visions of delight,
All that I love or am, or fain would be—
Deep loves, fond hope, and longing infinite.
It hath been wet with tears and dimmed with sighs:
Clinched in my grasp till beauty it hath none.
Now, from Thy footstool, where it vanquished lies,
The prayer ascendeth, O, may Thy will be done.
Take it, Oh, Father, ere my courage fail:
And merge it so in Thine own will that e'en

If in some desperate hour my cries prevail
And thou give back my gift, it may have been
So changed, so purified, so fair have grown,
So one with Thee, so filled with peace divine,
I may not know, or feel it as my own,
But gaining back my will, may find it Thine.

—AUTHOR UNKNOWN

4

The Seed of Life

The fundamental law of the Universe is that every form of life holds *within itself* vitality enough to draw to it every element it needs for growth and fruition. But it is only as it casts off all outside support, and puts its dependence solely upon the life force that created it and left its spark within it, that it is able to draw to itself the elements it needs for complete growth and fruition.

Take the giant redwoods of California. By no law known to man can they draw water to their foliage hundreds of feet in the air! Yet they do draw it— hundreds of gallons every day.

It is not done through pressure from below—from the roots. It is done by pull from above! In other words, the need is first established, then the need itself provides the means or the "pull" to draw to it the elements it must have for expression!

All through Nature, you will find that same law. First the need, then the means. Use what you have to provide the vacuum, then draw upon the necessary elements to fill it. Reach up with your stalk, spread out your branches, provide the "pull" and you can leave to your roots the search for the necessary nourishment. If you have reached high enough, if you have made your magnet strong enough, you can draw to yourself whatever elements you need, no matter if they be at the ends of the earth!

God formed a Seed of Himself in you. He gave it power to attract to itself everything it needs for its growth, just as He did with the seed of the tree. He gave it power to draw to itself everything it needs for fruition, just as He did with the tree. But He did even more for you. He gave your Seed of Life power to attract to itself everything it needs for its *infinite expression!*

You see, Life is intelligent. Life is all-powerful. And Life is always and everywhere seeking expression. What is more, it is never satisfied. It is constantly seeking greater and fuller expression. The moment a tree stops growing, that moment the life in it starts seeking elsewhere for means to better express itself. The moment you stop expressing more and more of Life, that moment Life starts looking around for other and better outlets.

The only thing that can restrict Life is the channel through which it works. The only limitation upon it is the limitation you put upon it.

The secret of success lies in this: There is inside you a Seed of God capable of drawing to you any element you need, to bring to fruition whatever of good you desire. But like all other seeds, its shell must be broken before the kernel inside can use its attractive power. And that shell is thicker, harder, than the shell of any seed on earth. Only one thing will break it—*heat from within*—a desire so strong, a determination so intense, that you cheerfully throw everything you have into the scale to win what you want. Not merely your work and your money and your thought but the willingness to stand or fall by the result—to do or to die. Like the Master when He cursed the fig tree for its barrenness, you are willing to demand of the Seed of Life in you that it *bear fruit or perish*.

That is the secret of every great success. That is the means by which all of life, from the beginning of time, has won what it needed.

What was it gave to certain animals protective shells, to others great speed, to still others a sting, to those who needed them claws or horns? What gave to the bold and strong the means to destroy, to the weak and cowardly facilities for hiding or escape? What but the Seed of Life in each, giving to every form of life the means that form craved to preserve its skin.

Since the very creation of the earth, Life has been threatened by every kind of danger. Had it not been stronger than any other power in the Universe—were it not indeed a part of God Himself—it would have perished ages ago. But God who gave it to us endowed it with unlimited resource, unlimited energy. No other force can defeat it. No obstacle can hold it back.

What is it that saves men in dire extremity, who have exhausted every human resource and finally turned to God in their need? What but the unquenchable flame of God in them—the Seed of Life He has given to each of us—with power to draw to us whatever element we feel that we need to save us from extinction.

The story is told of a little girl four years old, who had been taught to believe in a protecting Deity. She got lost one day, and was gone for hours. Her mother was on the verge of desperation when at last she saw her child coming home.

She was all alone, yet seemed to be holding somebody's hand and her lips were moving as if she were carrying on a sprightly conversation. Her mother opened the front door just in time to see her drop the invisible hand and to hear her say:

"You may go now, God. This is where I live. And thank you very much!"

It was all quite simple as she explained it to her mother. She had wandered about until she got tired and hungry. Then she realized that she didn't know the way home.

"I knew I was losted, Mother," she said, "so I asked God to take me home. I knew that He knew the way. Then I started for home and God showed me where to go. And here I am."

"Why, then," some will ask, "does not the God in you exert itself to bring you food when you are hungry, drink when you are thirsty, clothing when you are cold, money when you are in debt?" Why? Because you don't put your dependence upon it for these. You look for these things to your hands or your friends or some means within the power of those around you. It is only when you despair of all ordinary means, it is only *when you convince it* that it must help you or you perish, that the Seed of Life in you bestirs itself to provide a new resource.

That is why psychological or metaphysical means so seldom cure a patient who continues to put some of his dependence upon drugs or treatments. It is not that the spirit in you is a "jealous God." It is that it takes a real need to stir Him into action. As long as you show that you feel there is a chance of your being saved through some other means, the Seed of Life in you is not going to bestir itself to help you. And as long as it sees that you are depending upon your friends or the stock market or some other method to supply your urgent need of money, it is not going to worry itself about it.

"Unity Weekly" tells of a woman alone in a big city, jobless, anxious and discouraged, and worried about her husband who was seeking work in another town.

Because there was no one else to whom she could look for help, she prayed until she was able to put utter faith in God, to believe that He would look after her and to put all her dependence upon Him. Then she was able to go out into the street with springy step, with a heart full of confidence and a face that radiated belief in herself and in her ability to do things. She threw away her sheet of Want Ads, and on impulse, turned into a cheerful looking building and found a desirable job! Within a day or two after, an unexpected check came to her in the mail, and a letter of good news from her husband.

Another case was that of a subnormal boy, about to be rejected by a school. His mother had taught him to believe in God, so he kept repeating to himself—"God will tell me what to do." God did—to such good purpose that a few years later he graduated at the head of his class!

Then there was a woman who was expected to die from a seemingly incurable and painful disease. She asked that her bed be moved to a window, and as she looked out at the starry spaces in the long hours of the night, she thought of God—of His power, of His goodness, of His love for every creature, of Jesus saying that not even a sparrow fell without His marking it. And as she pondered all this, belief in His ability and His willingness to cure her came to her, until presently there began to flow into her consciousness the belief that she WAS cured, and she amazed her attendants by sitting up and asking for something to eat. Today she is alive and well.

How can YOU stir the boundless force of the God in you into action? How can YOU draw upon its infinite resource for your urgent needs?

Utter faith, utter dependence—that is the only answer. No half-way measures will do. If you want help and have exhausted all the methods that physicians and surgeons and practitioners can offer you, and want now to go direct to the Source for new Life, new health and strength, you cannot keep on dabbling with drugs and treatments and hope to stir the Seed of Life in you into action. You must drop everything else. You must put your whole dependence upon the infinite power of that Seed of God in you. You must get the attitude of our revolutionary patriots—"Sink or swim, live or die, survive or perish, I give my hand and my heart to this cause. Either I live by it or I die with it!"

Get that attitude of mind, and the stirring of your Seed of Life into action is simple.

Say to yourself—"I am one with the Life Force that runs the Universe, the great I AM of which Jesus said—'Before Abraham, was I AM.' I AM energy. I AM power. I AM filled with omnipotent life. The vitality of God permeates every fiber of my being. I AM well and whole in every part of my body. I AM made up of billions of cells of Intelligent Life, and that Intelligence is guiding me to Health and Happiness and Prosperity."

E. Stanley Jones, author of "Christ of the Indian Road", tells how he broke down completely with nervous exhaustion and brain fatigue at the end of eight years of missionary work in India, just when he had learned the ways of the people, and conditions seemed ripe for him to do the most good.

He was terribly depressed and disappointed, until one night in the midst of his prayers, he seemed to hear a voice saying—"Are you yourself ready for this work to which I have called you?" "No, Lord," he answered, "I am done for. I have reached the end of my resources." "If you will turn that over to me," the voice told him, "*and not worry about it,* I will take care of it." "Lord," he responded gladly, "I close the bargain right here!"

That was many years ago. The Doctors had just told him he would have to leave India and go back home for a couple of years to rest. Instead, he threw himself with renewed energy into his work, and he never before knew such health as he has had since. He seems to have tapped a new source of life for body, mind and spirit. *Yet all he had to do was to take it!*

Does this mean that you are to make no effort to help yourself? By no means! This was never meant for a lazy man's world. The whole purpose of existence is growth, and all nature is continually growing. Whenever anything stops growing, it starts to die.

We were given hands to work with, brains to think with. We were expected to use these.

For while it is not the roots that send the moisture to the tops of the tall trees, it is the roots that dig down to the moisture and nutriment to start it flowing. It requires an urgent need to draw to you resources beyond the power of your hands, just as it requires the evaporation of the moisture in the leaves to pull the water to the tops of the tallest trees, but unless the hands or the roots do their part first, that need will never be satisfied. The trouble with most people is that they go as far as their hands or their immediate abilities will take them, and stop there. It is as though a tree sent up its stem only as high as the root pressure carried the water from the earth. That would give us a forest of stunted trees, just as dependence upon their hands gives us the masses who live in poverty and misery.

It is only when you multiply your hands by thousands, it is only when you conceive and start great projects impossible of attainment by you alone, that you call forth the power of the Seed of Life in you, to draw to you every element you need for complete growth and fruition.

When George Mueller of England started his first orphanage, he had no money, no backers, no material resources to depend upon. He saw the need, that is all, so he went as far as he could in supplying that need. And each time, when he had reached the end of his resources, yet kept confidently trying, the need was met! In fifteen years, he built five orphanages and spent more than $5,000,000—all without a single visible means of support!

THE SEED OF LIFE

When St. Theresa proposed to build an orphanage, she was asked how much she had on which to start. When it developed that her total wealth was only three ducats, her superiors laughed at the idea. "It is true," she answered them, "that with only three ducats I can do nothing, but with God and three ducats I can do anything!" And she proceeded to prove it by building the orphanage whose good work made her famous.

In the fields of philanthropy and religion, you can find hundreds of similar stories. And in the fields of business, you find many thousands more. How many times have you read of some great institution that was founded on nothing but hard work and the faith of its founder. Henry Ford began on little else. Stewart started what is now the John Wanamaker store with a total cash capital of $1.50.

Sometimes, in fact, it seems to be an advantage not to have enough money when you start a new project. Then you don't put your faith in the money—you put it in IDEAS. In other words, you look to MIND to supply the means.

Someone expressed it well when he said we must work as if everything depended upon us, and at the same time, pray as if everything depended upon God.

What does an oculist do when you go to him for glasses? Fit your eyes with glasses that take away ALL the strain and enable you to see perfectly? No, indeed! The best oculists give you glasses a little short of the strength necessary to take all the strain off your eyes. They relieve you of the heavy burden, but they leave your sight just enough short of perfection to keep your eyes working towards that end.

The result? When you go back six months or a year later, your eyes are stronger—you can take glasses which do less of your work—until in time you do without them altogether.

What do business leaders advise young people today? Live within your income? No, indeed! *Go into debt!* Reach out! Spread yourself! Then dig the harder to catch up!

You are entitled to just as much of the good things of life as Ford or Rockefeller or Morgan, or any of the rich men around you. But it is not THEY who owe it to you. And it is not the world that owes you a living. The world and they owe you nothing but honest pay for the exact service you render them.

The one who owes you everything of good—riches and honor and happiness—is the God inside you. Go to him! Stir him up! Don't rail against the world. You get from it what you put into it—nothing more. Wake up the God inside you! Demand of him that he bring you the elements you need for riches or success. Demand—and make your need seem as urgent as must have been the need of the crustacean to develop a shell, of the bird to grow wings, of the bear to get fur.

Demand—and KNOW THAT YOU RECEIVE! The God in you is just as strong as ever He was in those primitive animals in pre-historic days. If He could draw from the elements whatever was necessary to give the elephant its trunk, the camel its hump, the bird its wings, and to each creature the means it required to enable it to survive, don't you suppose He can do the same today to provide YOU with the factors you consider essential to your well-being?

The answer is that you have already brought into being your "hump" or your "trunk" or whatever it was that you felt you must have. You are, in short, what your thoughts and fears and beliefs have made you. *Your present condition reflects the successful result of your past thought!*

Astonishing as it may sound to many people, you are now living in a world of your own making. But you don't have to keep on living there if you don't like it. You can build a new world in exactly the same way you built that one—only it would be well to build it on a different model.

It is the Einstein doctrine of the extended line, which must return to its source. An evil thought or act goes out upon its course, but the Eternal Law-maker has decreed that it must return to its creator. A good act or thought is governed in the same way. "By their fruits, ye shall know them."

So don't complain of your lot. Don't rail at the difficulties and obstacles that confront you. Smile on them! Treat them as friends. *Bless them*—for they can be made to bless you!

You see, they have not been sent from Heaven to punish you. You asked for them yourself. They are of your own making, and they are your friends, because they call forcibly to your attention some wrong method you have been using. All you have to do is to change your methods, and the results will automatically change with them. It is just as though you were doing some problem in multi-plication, and you kept saying—"One times one is two." That would throw your whole result out of balance, and it would stay out until you learned your mistake and made one times one equal one.

You are not higher than your lowest thought,
Or lower than the peak of your desire.
And all existence has no wonder wrought

To which ambition may not yet aspire.
O Man! There is no planet, sun or star
Could hold you, if you but knew what you are.

What, then, is the method to be used to get what you want from life?

1st—DESIRE. Decide what it is you want. Make it something so worth-while that all other things will seem small and unimportant beside it, something so urgent that you can say to the God Inside You—*"Give me this or I perish!"*

2nd—See *yourself having it.* Visualize the thing you want. See yourself with it. Try to get the FEEL of having it, the joy and thankfulness you would get out of it. In Burton Rascoe's Memoirs, he tells how he worked out his life on a predetermined schedule, in which everything came true because he thought it, he desired it and he BELIEVED it. Here are a few typical lines from it:

> When I was fifteen years old, I wanted to live in Chicago some time and I *knew* I would; the university I wished to go to was the University of Chicago and I *knew* I would; there was only one newspaper in the world I ardently wished to work on—the "Chicago Tribune"—and I *knew* five years in advance that I would some day work there; when I was a reporter I *knew* I would be some day literary editor.
>
> When I was literary editor of the "Chicago Tribune" I *knew* I would some day live in New York and be literary editor of the "New York Tribune."
>
> In 1927 I wanted $50,000 and *knew* I would get it; within less than a year I had over $100,000, almost without any effort on my part.

3rd—*Be thankful for having received it.* Remember the admonition of the Master—"Whatsoever things ye ask for when ye pray, believe that ye RE-CEIVE them, and ye shall have them." You cannot believe that you actually receive the things you ask for without being thankful for them. So give thanks, sincere thanks, for having received the things you prayed for, and try to FEEL grateful. Remember to SMILE! Repeat aloud daily Adelaide Proctor's poem—

My God, I thank Thee, who has made the earth so bright;
So full of splendor and of joy, beauty and light;
So many glorious things are here, noble and right.

I thank Thee too that Thou hast made joy to abound;
So many gentle thoughts and deeds circling us round,
That in the darkest spot of earth Thy love is found.

4th—*Act as though you HAD already received* the thing you asked for. Faith without works is dead. Do some physical thing each day such as you would do if you had the object you prayed for. If you are asking for money, for instance, GIVE a little, even though it be only a dime, just to show the freedom from money worry that is now yours. If you are asking for love, say a kindly word to each of those with whom you come in contact. If you are asking for health, dance about your room, sing, laugh, do some of those things you will do when you have fully manifested the good health you crave.

5th—*Show your affection* for the thing you asked for. Give your love to it, pour it out just as you would if you had the object in your hands. Only by making it REAL to you in your thoughts can you materialize it in your life.

We go, you know, in the direction of our thoughts. What we long for—*and expect*—that we are headed towards. So look for the kind of things you want to see. Look for them in your own life—and in the lives of those around you. Look for them—AND BEGIN DOING THEM! Remember those lines of Goethe's:

Are you in earnest? Seize this very minute;
What you can do, or dream you can, begin it;
Boldness has genius, power, and magic in it.
Only engage, and then the mind grows heated;
Begin, and then the work will be completed.

5

After Its Kind

Do you know what is the most important lesson in the whole Bible? Do you know what principle was considered so vital that God is said to have used it on three of the six days of creation, and it is repeated no less than six times in the first chapter of Genesis alone? Just this:

"Everything Reproduces After Its Kind!"

Go back over the miracles of increase in the Bible. What do you find? When the widow of Zarephath gave Elijah her oil and meal, what did she get? MORE OIL AND MEAL, did she not? Not gold, or riches, but INCREASE AFTER ITS KIND.

When another widow begged Elisha to save her sons from bondage, he asked—"What hast thou in the house?" And when told—"Naught save a pot of oil," it was the *oil* he increased, was it not?

When the multitude lacked for bread and the Apostles asked Jesus what they should do, He did not turn the stones into bread, or bring forth gold with which to buy. No, He asked—"How many loaves have you?" And when told five, and two fishes, He based His increase upon *them*.

You see, it all comes back to terms of electrical energy, for what is energy but power, and what are personality, skill, ability, riches, but different forms of power? If you want to increase your stock of these, what must you do? Put them to work, must you not? Put them out at interest, as in the parable of the talents. No energy ever expanded until it was released. No seed ever multiplied until it was sown. No talent ever increased until it was used.

You want more power, more riches, greater ability, a wider field of usefulness. How are you going to get them? *Only by putting out at interest that which you have!*

And the way to do this lies—NOT in working for riches as such—BUT FOR INCREASE IN THE FORM OF ENERGY YOU HAVE!

Now, what have YOU in the house? What seed can you plant, what service can you give?

In "Weekly Unity" some years ago, there was the story of a mother who had been well-to-do, but had lost everything and was now hard put to it to provide food and clothing for her small boys. It was near Christmas, and she was be-wailing to a friend the fact that she could buy no gifts for her children, much less remember old friends and relatives.

The friend smiled. "Money is not what you need," she told her. "Can money buy the gifts that live in your heart? If I were in your place, I should stop repin-ing and, instead, seek the guidance of your Inner Self."

The mother took the advice, and one night, as she dropped off to sleep after having prayed for guidance, she saw a beautiful tree, lighted with tapers, and beneath each light hung a small envelope. As she looked more closely, she saw that the names written on the envelopes were those of friends and relatives to whom she longed to give.

Opening one of the envelopes, she found a piece of blank paper and she seemed to hear a voice saying: "Write, and let that which you write bear witness of Me. As you write, give from your heart the treasures that are stored there in My name. I will fulfill every blessing according to your word."

The mother woke, and going immediately to her desk, began to write her blessings. She wrote words of life and wholeness for an aunt who had been bound with rheumatism for months; words of courage for an uncle who was having a difficult time with his farm; words of guidance for a young cousin who had seemed to lose her way a bit. Inspired by that Inner Self, she wrote ten blessings that night.

She had never thought that she could write, but her own heart thrilled at the beauty of the words that came to her, and she was lifted up by their power and simplicity. "Don't ever again say you have nothing to give," one of her friends told her later. "I never received so richly in all my life." And throughout the years, the blessings that this mother gave out have continued to bear fruit.

"Give me gold," prayed Levesco, "that I may be helpful, not helpless. Give me gold that I may taste the pure joy of making others happy. Give me gold that I may see the beauties of this world in moments of leisure. Give me gold that I and mine may be secure in our declining years."

A worthy prayer, indeed. But prayer alone is not enough. You must plant the seed before you can hope to reap the harvest. You must give before you can get.

"DO THE THING," said Emerson, "and you shall have the power. But they who do *not* the thing, have not the power. Everything has its price, and if the price is not paid—not that thing but something else is obtained. And it is impossible to get anything without its price.

"For any benefit received a tax is levied. In nature nothing can be given— all things are sold.

"Power to him who power exerts."

Russell Conwell, the famous lecturer, who built the Baptist Temple in Philadelphia and founded Temple University, was in the beginning merely the pastor of a very poor flock. His congregation consisted of working people, and many of them were in need. So he was continually offering prayers for money.

One Sunday, it occurred to him that the old Jewish custom had been to make a gift or offering first, and then pray for what you wanted. So he announced that the following Sunday, he would reverse his usual method of procedure. Instead of offering his prayer first, he would first take up the collection, and he wanted all who had special favors to ask of God to give freely as an "Offering." We quote the result from "Effective Prayer":

> The question was asked afterward if anyone who made a special offering on that particular day had not been answered, and there was no exception in the mass of testimony to the efficiency of each prayer that day. The recitals of the marvels which followed that prayerful offering were too startling for general belief. The people had complied with the conditions, and God had answered clearly according to His promise. They had brought the tithes into the storehouse, and the Lord had poured out the blessings as an infallible result.
>
> Cases of sudden and instantaneous recovery of the sick were related by hundreds. One poor man whose child was insane prayed for her recovery. That afternoon when he went to the sanitarium, she met him in her right mind.
>
> A lady sold her jewelry and brought the proceeds as an offering as she prayed for healing from sciatic rheumatism. She fell going from the Church, and arose to find the rheumatism gone.

One old gentleman involved in a ruinous lawsuit brought all the profits of the previous week and deposited them as he prayed for a just outcome. Within the week, the suit was withdrawn.

A woman with an overdue mortgage on her home determined to risk all on one prayer, and gave all she had as she prayed. When plumbers came to repair a leak the following week, they discovered a loose board in the floor under which her father had hidden all his money. The sum was more than enough to pay off the mortgage in its entirety.

There were probably fifty such cases.

You have to sow before you can reap. You have to give before you can get. And when you sow, when you give, you must give freely with no strings to it. As Jesus put it—"Except a kernel of wheat fall into the ground and die, it abideth alone. But if it die, it beareth much fruit."

You remember the old-fashioned hand-pumps that are still to be found on many farms. To start them, you had to pour in a bucket of water, in order to create a vacuum and thus be able to draw water from the well. The same principle applies in using a siphon. You pour in water to drive out the air and create a vacuum. Once the vacuum is formed, your water flows, and you can get unlimited quantities of it without having to give more. But you get none from pump or siphon until you first give some.

You must give to get. You must sow the seed you have before you can reap the harvest. You cannot merely lend it. You must GIVE it, freely and fully. "Except a kernel of wheat fall into the ground and DIE," said the Master. Except your seed of riches be given freely and fully, you get nothing from it. "But if it die, it beareth much fruit." If it be dead to you—if it is gone beyond hope of return, then you can look for a harvest.

"He that findeth his life shall lose it," said the Master on another occasion, "but he that loseth his life for My sake shall find it." He that gives all he has in the service of his fellows shall find that in so doing, he has planted seeds which will bring him a harvest of happiness and plenty.

You have probably read the story of Charles Page, as given in the "American Magazine" a few years ago. Page was then a millionaire oil operator in Oklahoma, but a few years before he had little or nothing, and his wife was so sick he feared he was going to lose her as well. The surgeons at the hospital had given up hope for her, so as all other avenues seemed closed, Page turned to God.

"Oh, Lord," he prayed, "don't take her away from me. I just couldn't bear it."

The words rang in his ears—and they had an empty ring. As a prayer, it seemed to fall flat. Why should the Lord interfere for him, if the only reason he could offer was that he couldn't bear it? Plenty of husbands just as devoted as he had lost their wives. Why should the Lord specially favor him?

The thought came home to him with the power of a blow. What had he ever done that the Lord should go out of His way to help him? What reason had he to look for special consideration from above? None! He'd been a decent enough citizen, but no more so than the average, and kneeling there he couldn't recall a single thing he had done which would entitle him to ask favors from the Lord.

The thought appalled him. What chance had he? Must he then lose the one dearest to him in all the world, just because he had never done enough to be worthy of keeping her? No! No! That was unthinkable. It wasn't too late. He would start that very minute. What was it the Master had said? "Whatsoever ye do unto the least of these My brethren, ye do it unto Me."

The next morning a poor widow was in transports of joy to find under her doorsill money enough to carry her safely through the winter.

But that evening inquiry at the hospital elicited the information that Page's wife was no better. For a little his faith faltered. Then, as he thought back over the reason for his act, it flamed up anew. Why had he helped the widow? Not because he was interested in her welfare, not even because it was the right thing to do, but because he was trying to buy off the Lord. Thinking of it in that light, it sounded ridiculous. He got down on his knees again.

"I ain't makin' a bargain with You, God," he promised. "I'm doin' this because it's the *right thing* for me to do."

This time it seemed to him his message carried. He felt strangely cheered and relieved. His prayer had gone through.

Now comes the remarkable part of this incident. His wife, much to the astonishment of the surgeons, took a turn for the better, and within a comparatively short time was well!

From that day to this Charles Page has never failed in his Covenant with God. Times there were when everything looked black. Times when it meant a real struggle to find the Lord's share. But his faith never faltered. He knew if he did his part, he could depend upon God for His.

For a long time, he gave a tenth of all his earnings. Then he increased it to a fourth. Later to a half, and finally to all except what he needed for personal and family expenses. He has given away literally millions.

"But don't get the idea," he warns, "that I'm telling you how to get rich. It's the *giving*, not the *getting*, that is important. Personally, I believe that it's only playing fair to tithe, or give a part of your income to God. But it must be a gift, not an investment. Do you get the difference? If you tithe in the right spirit, you will get your reward just as sure as a gun's iron; but the reward may not come in the form of money. Often it's something far better than money . . ."

"What you keep to yourself you lose," wrote Munthe. "What you give away, you keep forever." And Irene Stanley expressed much the same thought in her little poem—

> *You have to let go of the rung below*
> *When you reach for the round above.*
> *There is no other way to climb, you know,*
> *You have to let go of the rung below.*
> *Each upward step brings more of the glow*
> *And warmth of the Sun of Love,*
> *You have to let go of the rung below,*
> *When you reach for the round above.*

You see, God incarnates Himself through you. But He cannot be shut up. He must be given out, expressed. You put Him into everything you do, whether towards failure or success. You are inseparable from the creative force. You are part of the fountain head of supply.

What then must you do to win riches and success? GIVE! Give freely of what you have.

Give, and it shall be given unto you; good measure, pressed down, and shaken together, and running over, shall men give unto your bosom. For with the same measure that ye mete withal it shall be measured to you again.—LUKE 6:38

Does that require too great faith? You do not marvel at the farmer who freely throws all his seed into the ground, knowing he will never see it again, but must depend upon its fruit for his increase. He shows perfect faith. Should you show less?

Remember the first Law of Life, the law that was considered so important that it was repeated six times in the first Chapter of Genesis:

"Everything increases after its kind."

Do you expect that law to be changed for you? Do you expect to reap without sowing? "There is that scattereth and increaseth yet more," said that wisest of ancient sages, King Solomon. "And there is that withholdeth more than is meet, *but it tendeth to poverty.*

"The liberal soul shall be made fat, and he that watereth, shall be watered himself."

You see, Life is logical. Life follows definite, fundamental laws. One of these laws is that you reap as you sow, that "He that hath a bountiful eye shall be blessed."

For all motion is cyclic. It circulates to the limit of its possibilities and then returns to its starting point. Thus any unselfish expenditure of energy returns to you laden with gifts. Any unselfish act done for another's benefit is giving part of yourself. It is an outward flow of power that completes its cycle and returns laden with energy.

Everything we get, we pay for—good or bad. Personal gain comes through impersonal service. Personal loss comes through selfishness.

As Emerson puts it—"A perfect equity adjusts its balance in all parts of life. *Every act rewards itself.*" Any act of ours that injures another, separates us from God. Any act of ours that helps others, brings us closer to God and Good. One may think that his cheating of another is a secret between them, but by his cheating, he has shaken the trust of another in human brotherhood and damaged his idealism. Isn't that a definite affront that is going to stand between him and God when the one who cheated tries to enlist God's help in enlarging the activities of his own life?

Wouldn't it have been better to say to himself: "God gives me all my money. Surely He has given me enough for all the needs of my business, or if He hasn't already given it, it is on the way. If I need more, He will give me more. So I am not even going to think about trying to make 'easy money' by taking advantage of others. God provides me with plenty, and I am going to run this business as if He were always here beside me."

One on God's side is a majority. You are always together with God. So make Him an active partner in your business. Look to Him for its needs, give the same loving service you feel that He would give. Then cast off all worries fears, and *put your business lovingly in His hands.* When the future looks dark, when problems confront you, just say to yourself:

God lights the way; no more I grope,
Nor stumble on in troubled hope.
I sow no seeds of care and strife;
But those of love, and joy, and life.
No more I strive to plan my lot;
The Father fills my cup unsought.

What is the Unpardonable Sin? What but damming the sources of God's supply. What but trying to shut up the God in you, trying to keep Him from expressing Himself.

When the giant monsters of antiquity ceased developing, and depended upon their size and strength and fierceness, they perished. When the vast Empires of China and Greece and Persia and Rome stopped reaching out and tried merely to hold what they had, they died. When the rich man or big business of today stops giving service and merely hangs on to his fortune, he loses it.

You cannot stand still. You must go forward—or die.

There is a God in you seeking expression. You cannot keep Him shut up. You must give Him channels through which to express Himself, or He will rend you and come out of you.

What would you think of a man who spent years in developing great muscles, then tried to keep them great by not using them, by not wearing them out? You'd call him a fool, wouldn't you, because everyone knows that the only way to develop muscles is to use them, the only way to keep them strong is to continually exercise them.

What everyone does not seem to know is that all of life works in the same way. You cannot hold on to anything good. You must be continually giving—and getting. You cannot hold on to your seed. You must sow it—and reap anew. You cannot hold on to riches. You must use them and get other riches in return.

The Unpardonable Sin is to stand in the way of progress, try to stop the cycle of life.

You must give to get. You must sow to reap. The unprofitable servant in Jesus' parable was not the first or the only one to be cast into outer darkness where is weeping and gnashing of teeth, from burying his talent. The ones who became rulers over many things were those who freely used what they had—who started riches *flowing!*

So when a "talent" is given you, don't try to hide it away or bury it. Don't dam up the channels of supply with the few dollars you have, and thus prevent the unlimited riches of God from flowing to you.

Set up your generator, which is the service you have to offer your fellowman. Turn on the steam by giving to it all the power, all the skill, all the intelligence you have. Then start the flow of riches with your faith by cheerfully pouring into the channel of service all that you have. That means buy the things that are necessary to your development and that of your family. Pay your just debts, though it leaves you without a cent in your purse. Put your dependence—NOT on the few dollars you have in hand, but on the great ocean of supply above and about you. Use the few dollars you have to create the vacuum which shall poke a hole in the bottom of that ocean, and start the unending flow of riches pouring into you.

You remember that Jesus once likened the power of God to the leaven in bread. You put a tiny yeast cake into a great pan of dough and it affects the whole mixture. It makes it GROW. Apparently it INCREASES the quantity of flour, milk, eggs and other ingredients—certainly it makes them bulk to several times their original size.

That yeast is the "God in you" that you put into your circumstances, your affairs. Put it into fears and worries, and it will increase them until they can hardly be borne. Put it into your expenses, and it will make them ever greater. Put it into love and life and good work, and it will bring these back to you increased a hundredfold.

"Let's have a league of optimists," writes Elizabeth Swaller in LET'S HAVE IT,

To boost the world along.
We are so weary of the thought
That everything is wrong!

We're surfeited with talk of lack,
Depression, gloom and fear.
If we but think of brighter things,
Good times will soon be here.

'Tis time to turn and face about
And court conditions fine.
By boosting, I shall prosper yours,
And you will prosper mine.

Put your yeast into optimistic thoughts, into kindly words, into loving acts of service. Remember, the hardest part of anything is the start. If you want something, pray for it—*then START* doing, being, giving—whatever is needful to set the yeast acting. *You* don't have to make the dough expand when you put the yeast into it. The yeast attends to that. All you have to do is to give the yeast a chance to get in its work!

So if you want to receive something of good, show your faith by GIVING of what you have. Put a little yeast into your affairs. It doesn't matter how poor you are, how much in debt, how weak or sickly. You can always give something. But remember that everything increases after its kind, so give of what you want to receive. Sow the seeds of the harvest you want to reap, whether it be love, energy, service or money.

And PRAY! Nearly 2,000 years before Christ, it was said in the Vedas that if two people would unite their psychic forces, they could conquer the world. Then came Jesus, to put it even more definitely: "Again I say unto you, that if two of you shall agree on earth as touching anything that they shall ask, it shall be done for them of my Father which is in Heaven. For when two or three are gathered together in my name, there am I in the midst of them."

In one of his books, Russell Conwell tells of a little group in his church who were in such straitened circumstances that they decided to get together and see if, by uniting their prayers, they could not improve their finances.

So they met at the house of one of their number who happened to be a bookbinder by trade, and decided that each week the whole group would unite their prayers to solve the difficulties of some one member.

The bookbinder was the first one chosen. He owed a great deal of money, and had no means of paying his debts. So that evening, the group prayed that he might receive help in meeting his obligations. It was then agreed that at noontime every day until the next meeting, each member would stop whatever he was doing, and spend a minute or two in silent prayer that the bookbinder's needs might be met.

The meeting was on Tuesday evening. The next day after lunch, as was his custom, the bookbinder dropped into a publishing house nearby for a chat with some friends. He met there a man from Washington who told him that "for the first time in his life, he had forgotten his train," and must now get back home on some urgent business, without placing a contract which he had intended to give to a New York bookbinder.

The bookbinder suggested that he also was in that business, and possibly could help him, but the other objected that the particular class of work he wanted could be done only in New York. Upon the binder persisting, however, he explained his needs, and being convinced that they could be filled right there in as satisfactory a way and on more reasonable terms than in New York, he not only gave the binder the contract, *but advanced enough money to more than take care of his difficulties!*

The binder hurried to the other members of his group and told them of his good fortune. His problem was so completely solved that he felt they ought to start work at once for some other member, because all were so badly in need. All felt so elated over their success in helping the binder solve his problem, that they chose the most difficult case of all as the next.

This was a jeweler who had grown so old and forgetful that his business was in a deplorable condition. Bankruptcy seemed so sure that his son had moved out of town to avoid sharing the disgrace.

Two or three days after the group started working on the jeweler's problem, the son came to town for a day to attend a funeral. On the return trip from the cemetery, he fell into conversation with one of the other mourners, in the course of which the latter mentioned that he was looking for an expert in clock-making to superintend a new factory he was erecting in another city.

The son told him his father was a master of that art, but no good at managing finances. The upshot of it was that the jeweler applied for the position, at the same time explaining his present financial difficulties. The manufacturer liked his letter, went over the whole situation with him, and ended by taking over the store as a retail outlet, paying off the old debts, and forming a business connection with the jeweler which prospered both amazingly.

An old lady who owned a small notion store was next. Soon after the group united in prayer for her, a fire destroyed the store next door to her. The owner decided to build bigger than before, and offered her not only an attractive price for her store, but an interest in his business, which paid her enough to live in comfort the rest of her days.

Every member of that group became prosperous!

Do you, too, want something very much? Then give—*and pray!* Get yourself a small toy bank—a paper one will do. Each day put something into it, even though it be only a penny. Give that money to God. Give it to Him at the time you put it into the bank, but leave it there until it amounts to a dollar or more. Then use it for any good charitable purpose that presents itself.

Don't give it to some panhandler. Try to use it where it will do the recipient some good. Use it to help him to help himself, as in buying some book for him that will show him the way out of his difficulties.

And as you give, *pray!* Pray not only for yourself, but for others.

Every morning at seven, we shall pray for protection for our own family, and for all students of this Course who will join with us in "uniting their psychic forces" by "agreeing as to the thing they should ask." For this prayer, you cannot do better than repeat the ninety-first Psalm.

Every day at noon, we shall pray for abundant supply for all of those among our readers who will join with us in praying for the whole group. For this prayer, hold in your hand any money you intend to give that day for any good purpose, and any checks or money you intend to use to pay bills, and say with us:

I bless you . . . and be thou a blessing. May you enrich all who touch you. I thank God for you, but even more I thank Him that there are billions like you where you came from. I bless that Infinite Supply. I thank God for it and I expand my consciousness to take it in. (Here try to see in your mind's eye a Niagara of money flowing to you and to all who are praying with you. See yourself and all of us bringing in a great net full of money like the nets the Apostles pulled in bursting with fish.) I release that Infinite Supply through all my channels and the channels of all the students of this Course just as I freely release the money I hold in my hand, giving it where it will do the most good. The Spirit that multiplied the loaves and fishes for Jesus enters into this money, making it grow and increase and bring forth fruit a hundredfold. All of God's channels are now open and flowing for us. The best in ourselves for the world—the best in the world for us.

Then PREPARE for prosperity. When the Israelites of old were suffering from drought, and begged the Prophet Elisha to help them, what was the first thing he told them to do? Fill the valley with ditches—prepare to RECEIVE the water that they asked for!

You see prayers and affirmations are not for the purpose of influencing God. He has already done His part. All of good is always available to each of us. Our prayers and affirmations are for the purpose of bringing our own minds to the point where we can ACCEPT God's gifts! We don't need to work on conditions—we need only to work on ourselves. The only place we can cure our lacks and our troubles *is in our own minds!* When we have done it there, we shall find that they are cured everywhere.

"Whatsoever things ye ask for when ye pray," the Master assured us, "believe that ye HAVE RECEIVED them, and ye shall HAVE them."

That is the basis of all successful prayer, whether for the healing of our bodies, or for material benefits. Once you convince your Higher Self, which is the God in you, that you HAVE the thing you want, *it will proceed immediately to bring it into being!*

But how, you may ask, can I convince my Higher Self that I have riches or any other good thing, when my common sense tells me that I am in debt up to my ears and creditors are hounding me day and night?

You can't—if you keep thinking and acting DEBTS. But here is a psychological fact: The Higher Self accepts as fact anything that is repeated to it in convincing tones often enough. And once it has accepted any statement as fact, it proceeds to do everything possible to MAKE IT TRUE!

That is the whole purpose of affirmations—to bring the God in You to accept as true the conditions that you desire, to the end that He will then proceed to bring them into being. It is a sort of auto-suggestion. You keep saying to yourself that you ARE rich, that you HAVE the things you desire, until the constant repetition is accepted by the Higher Self and translated into its physical equivalent.

Debts? Don't worry about them. Remember that the shadow of growing grain kills the weeds. Keep your mind on the good you want and it will kill off the evil you fear, just as the turning on of light dispels darkness. A farmer does not have to hoe the weeds out of growing wheat, any more than you have to sweep the darkness out of a room. Neither do you have to worry about debts or lack. Put all your thoughts and all your faith in the riches you are praying for, and let them dispel the debts.

But don't worry if you can't summon such faith right out of the blue. Most of us have to lead up to it gradually. Start with Coue's well-known affirmation— "Every day in every way we are getting richer and richer." Use that to prepare your Higher Self for the stronger affirmations. Then, when your faith has grown stronger, *claim the thing you want!* Affirm that you HAVE it—and insofar as possible, ACT AS THOUGH YOU HAD IT!

Write it in your heart that each day is the best day of the year, that NOW is the accepted time, NOW is the day of salvation. Then thank God for the good you have been praying for, believe that you HAVE received and give thanks.

Remember this: God's will always works when you offer no resistance to it. So pray—and then LET His good come to you. Don't fight the conditions about you. Don't try to overcome the obstacles in your path. BLESS them— know that God is in them—that if you will LET them, they will work WITH you for good. Have faith not only in God, but in people and things. Don't look for a miracle to happen. Don't expect an angel from Heaven to come and open the way. Know that God works through ordinary people and things, and it is through them that your good will come.

So bless THEM. Serve them as you would the Lord, doing each thing that is given you to do as though you were the greatest genius. And all day long, as the thought occurs to you, keep repeating to yourself—"Every day in every way I am getting richer and richer," or whatever it is that you desire.

There is something about praying for *others* that oftentimes does one more good than praying for oneself. You see, you cannot give anything to others without first possessing it yourself. When you wish another evil, you draw that evil to yourself first and you usually get a part of it. When you bring good to another, you bring it through yourself, and you share in it.

Remember the experience of Job in the olden days. Despite his lamentations and prayers, he lost all his riches, and his afflictions remained with him. But then misfortune fell upon his friends as well, and in his sympathy for them, Job forgot his own ailments and prayed for his friends. And it is written that—"The Lord turned the captivity of Job, *when he prayed for his friends*. And the Lord gave him twice as much as he had before."

> *For who upon the hearth can start a fire,*
> *And never warm the stone?*
> *Or who can cheer another's heart,*
> *And not his own?*
> *I stilled a hungry infant's cry,*
> *With kindness filled a stranger's cup,*
> *And lifting others,*
> *Found that I was lifted up!*

6

How to Develop Faith Power for Successful Living

To you, faith has doubtless been a term properly applied in sermons and theological books, but which has but little or no practical place or meaning in the world of action and deeds—in the world in which most of us live most of our time, and perform most of our actions.

We assure you that Faith Power is something having a most intimate and important relation to Personal Power along practical lines, and is something which, in the current phrase, "you need in your business."

Mr. Leon Jolson, president of the huge Necchi Sewing Machine Company, is today worth many millions of dollars. A few years ago he was a poor Polish immigrant who couldn't even speak English. The newspaper account of his spectacular rise to success quoted him as saying, "I had unfaltering faith. I prayed for guidance every step of the way. I used head and foot work."

The general conception of Faith—the idea of Faith held by most persons—is that it is an emotional state independent of, if not indeed actually contrary to Reason. However, we believe that the most important reasoning of practical everyday life is based on Faith. We do not know positively that the sun will rise tomorrow morning—all that we know is that in the history of the race the sun always has risen in the morning, and we "believe" that it will continue the practice on the morrow; but we do not "know" absolutely that such will be the case, we cannot prove it absolutely by argument—even by mathematics—unless we admit the existence of Universal Law, or the law of Causation, whereby "the same causes, under the same conditions will produce the same effects."

You may object to all this as silly—but, instead, it is the strictest application of the rules and laws of practical thought. Of course, you say that we "know" that the sun will rise tomorrow morning, and may even tell to a second the time of its rising. Certainly we "know" this—but we know it only by an act of Faith. That Faith, moreover, is the belief that there exists Universal Law—that "natural things act and move under Law"—that "the same causes, under the same conditions, produce the same results."

In the ordinary affairs of life and action you act according to Faith. You do this so naturally and instinctively, so constantly and habitually, that you are not aware of it. You start on an airline flight. You buy your ticket, having faith that the plane will start from the airport named on the ticket, and approximately on the time noted in it. You have faith that it will proceed to the destination promised. You do not "know" these things from actual experience—for you cannot so know what lies in the future: you take them for granted, you assume them to be true, you act upon Faith.

You take your seat. You do not know the pilot or the co-pilot—you have never seen them, nor do you even know their names. You do not know whether or not they are competent, reliable, or experienced. All that you know is that it is reasonable to suppose that the plane company will select the right kind of men for the task—you act upon Faith, upon Faith rationally interpreted. You have Faith in the company, in the management, in the system of flights, in the equipment, etc. and you stake your life and wholeness of body upon that Faith. You may say that you only "take a chance" in the matter; but, even so, you manifest Faith in that "chance," or else you wouldn't take it. You wouldn't "take a chance" of standing in the path of a rushing express train, or of leaping from the Empire State Building, would you? You manifest Faith in something—even if that something be no more than the Law of Averages.

You place your money in a bank; here again you manifest Faith—Faith rationally interpreted. You sell goods on credit to your customers—Faith again. You have Faith in your grocer, your butcher, your lawyer, your physician, your clerks, your insurance company. That is to say Faith of some kind, or of some degree—else you would not trust anything whatsoever to them. If you "believe" that a man is dishonest, incompetent, or insane, you do not place confidence in him, nor trust your affairs or interests to him; your Faith is in his "wrongness," and not in his "rightness"—but it is Faith, nevertheless. Every "belief" short of actual, positive knowledge, is a form or phase of Faith.

You have the Faith that if you step off a high building into space, you will fall and be injured, perhaps killed: this is your Faith in the Law of Gravitation. You have a similar Faith in certain other physical laws—you have the Confident Expectation that evil results to you will follow certain courses of action concerning these physical laws. You have Faith that poisons will injure or destroy your physical body, and you avoid such. You may object that you "know" these things, not merely "believe" them; but you don't "know" anything directly and immediately until you experience it—and you cannot experience it—and you cannot experience a future happening before its time. All that you can do concerning each and every future experience is to "believe" certain things concerning it—and that "belief" is nothing else but Faith, interpreted more or less rationally and correctly.

You do not "know" certainly and positively, by direct experience, or by pure reason, a single thing about the happenings of tomorrow, or of some day next week, or of the corresponding day of next year. Yet you act as if you did possess such knowledge—but why? Simply because of your Faith in the Law and Order of the Universe; of the operation of the Law of Causation; whereby effects follow causes; of the Law of Probabilities, or of the Law of Averages; or of some other Natural Law. But your knowledge of and belief in such Laws are but forms of your Faith, i.e., Confident Expectation that "things will work out according to the rule observed in past actions." You cannot get away from Faith in your thoughts and beliefs concerning the present and the future, any more than you can run away from your shadow in the bright daylight.

From the foregoing, and the reflections aroused in your mind by the consideration of it, you will perceive that Faith has as true and as sound position and place in the psychology of the human being as have Reason and Intellect.

Without the Confident Expectation of Faith, there will be no kindling of the flame of Insistent Desire—no application of the steel of Persistent Determination. Unless Faith expresses itself in the Confident Expectation of the obtaining or attainment of the thing desired and willed, then will Desire find it difficult to "want it hard enough," and Will will find it impossible to "persistently determine to obtain it." Desire and Will depend upon Faith for their Inspirational Forces—by means of the latter, the Energizing Forces of Desire and the Dynamic Forces of Will are inspired and vitalized, and have the Breath of Life breathed into them.

HOW SICKNESS IS CURED BY FAITH

Among the many phases and forms of the application and manifestation of the mental principle of Faith Power is that important phase or form known generally as "Faith-Cure."

Faith-Cure is a term applied to the practice of curing disease by an appeal to the hope, belief, or expectation of the patient, and without the use of drugs or other material means. Formerly, Faith-Cure was confined to methods requiring the exercise of religious faith, such as the "prayer cure" and "divine healing," but has now come to be used in the broader sense, and includes the cures of Mental Science.

It is now generally agreed that the cures made by the various practitioners of the numerous schools and forms of Faith-Cure have as their underlying effective principle the mental condition or state of Faith; this principle operating so as to call forth the innate power of the mental-physical organism to resist and to overcome the abnormal conditions which manifest as disease. Thus, all cures wrought by the mental forces of the individual, under whatever name or method, are, at the last, Faith-Cures.

This innate power of the organism so lodged in the subconscious mentality, is found to respond readily to the ideas accepted as true by the individual—to his "beliefs," in short. These beliefs are forms of Faith, at the last.

From the psychological point of view, all these different kinds of faith-healing, as indeed all kinds of faith-healing, as indeed all kinds of mind-cure, depend upon suggestion. In faith-healing proper not only are powerful direct suggestions used, but the religious atmosphere and the autosuggestions of the patient co-operate, especially when the cures take place during a period of religious revival or at other times when large assemblies and strong emotions are found. The suggestibility of large crowds is markedly greater than that of individuals, and to this greater faith must be attributed the greater success of the fashionable places of pilgrimage.

Analyzing the phenomena attributed to Suggestion, and reducing the idea of Suggestion to its essential elements, we find that Suggestions consists of: (1) placing a strong idea in the mind—grafting it on the mind, as it were; (2) arousing the Expectant Attention of the results implied or indicated in the suggested idea; and (3) setting into operation the activities of the subconscious mentality in the direction of bringing about the result pictured by the Expectant Attention, which in turn has been aroused by the suggested idea. There you have the whole idea of Suggestion in a nutshell!

Now then, all phenomena of Faith-Cure, and of Suggestion as well, are seen to depend upon the presence and action of the element or principle of Faith Power in the mentality of the individual.

By an application of the first of the above stated elements of this greater principle of your being, and of Nature as a whole, you may keep yourself in health, strength and general desirable physical well-being; or you may bring about by it a gradual return to health and physical well-being if you have lost these; again, if you allow this principle to be directed wrongly and abnormally, you may lose your physical well-being and health, and may start on the downward path of disease, the end of which is an untimely death. Your physical condition is very largely dependent upon the character and kind of the Ideas and Ideals which you permit to be planted in your mind and by the degree of Expectant Attention, or Faith, which you permit to vitalize these Ideas and Ideals.

Briefly stated, the course to be followed by you in this matter is as follows: (1) Encourage Ideas and Ideals of Health, Strength, and Vitality—the ideas of Physical Well-Being—to take lodgment in your mind, there to send forth their roots sprouts, blossoms and fruit; cultivate these Ideas and Ideals and vitalize them with a goodly amount of Expectant Attention, Confident Expectation and Faith along the lines of these conditions which you desire to be present in yourself; see yourself "in your mind's eye" as you wish to be, and "confidently expect" to have these conditions manifested in you by your subconscious mentality; (2) never allow yourself to hold the ideas of diseased abnormal conditions, and, above all, never allow yourself to cultivate the mental habit of "expecting" such conditions to manifest in your body—cultivate the attitude of Faith and Hope, and discard that of Fear; (3) if your mind has been filled with these negative, harmful and destructive mental Ideas and Expectancy, and if your body has manifested Disease in response to them, you should proceed to "kill out" these noxious mental weeds by a deliberate, determined and confident cultivation of the right kind of Ideas and Ideals and states of "Expectancy"; it is an axiom of advanced psychology that "the positives tend to inhibit and to destroy the negatives"—the weeds in the mental garden may be "killed out" by the careful and determined cultivation of the positive plants of Hope, Faith and Confident Expectation of the Good and Desirable.

Faith Power is present and active—it is potent and powerful—and it is friendly to you if you recognize and realize its existence; it is ready to serve you, and to serve you well, provided that you call upon it properly and furnish it with the proper channels through which to flow in its efforts to manifest itself. This is the great truth back of the special lesson of Faith-Cure!

THE MIGHTY SUBCONSCIOUS MIND

The Subconscious—that great field or plane of mental activity—is the seat of far greater power, and the source of far deeper and broader streams of mental force, than the average person even begins to realize. In that field, or on that plane, are performed over seventy-five percent of man's mental activities.

Our mental world is far more extensive than we usually conceive it to be; it has great comparatively unsounded depths, and equally grand comparatively unscaled heights. The explored and charted areas of our conscious mentality are incidental and subordinate to those broad areas of which even the brightest minds of our race have merely explored the borderland; the expanded uncharted interior of the strange country still awaiting the exploring expeditions of the future. Our position in relation to this great *Terra Incognita* of the mind is similar to that of the ancient civilized world toward the earth as a whole; we are as yet awaiting the Columbus who will explore the Western Continent of the mind, and the Livingstones and Stanleys who will furnish us with maps of the mental Darkest Africa.

Yet, even the comparatively small explored areas of the Subconscious have revealed to us a wonderful land—a land filled with the richest raw materials, precious metals, wonderful species of animal and plant life. And our daring investigators have discovered means of applying and using some of the wonderful things which have been discovered in even that borderland of the new mental world.

The Subconscious entertains deep-rooted convictions and beliefs concerning the general success or non-success of the individual. The person who has constantly impressed upon his subconscious mentality that he is "unlucky" and that "Fate is against me," has created a tremendous power within himself which acts as a brake or obstacle to his successful achievement. He has created an enemy within himself which serves to hold him back, and which fights against every inner effort in the direction of success. This hidden enemy hampers his full efforts and cripples his activities.

On the contrary, the person who believes that "luck is running my way," and that "things are working in my favor," not only releases all of his latent energies but also actually stimulates his full powers—along subconscious lines as well as conscious.

Many men have become so convinced of their propitious Destiny that they have overcome obstacles which would have blocked the progress of one holding the opposite conviction. In fact, most of the men who have used their failures as stepping-stones to subsequent success have felt within themselves the conviction that they would triumph in the end, and that the disappointments and temporary failures were but incidents of the game.

Men have believed in their "stars" or in the presence and power of something outside of themselves which was operating in the direction of their ultimate triumph. This has given to them an indomitable will and an unconquerable spirit. Had these same men allowed the conviction of the operation of adverse and antagonistic influences to take possession of their souls, they would have gone down in the struggle—and would have stayed down. In either case, however, the real "something" which they have believed to be an outside thing or entity, has been nothing more nor less than the influence and power of their own Subconscious—in one case pulling with them, and in the other pulling against them.

The man with his Subconscious filled with belief and Faith in his non-success, and in the inevitable failure of his efforts—the man whose Confident Expectation is that of non-success, failure and inability, and whose Expectant Attention is directed toward such an outcome and the incidents and circumstances leading up to it—is like a man in the water who is swimming against the stream. He is opposing the strong current, and his every effort is counteracted and overcome by the adverse forces of the stream. Likewise, the man whose Subconscious is saturated with the conviction of ultimate victory and final success—whose Confident Expectation is directed toward that end, and whose Expectant Attention is ever on the look-out for things tending to realize his inner beliefs—is like the swimmer who is moving in the direction of the current. Such a man not only is not really opposed by the forces of the stream, but, instead, has these forces at work aiding him.

The importance of having the Faith, Confident Expectation and Expectant Attention of the Subconscious directed toward your success, achievement and successful ultimate accomplishment—and the importance of not having these mighty forces operate against yourself—may be realized when you stop to consider that in the one case you have three-quarters of your mental equipment and power operating in your favor, and in the other case you have that three-quarters operating against you. And that three-quarters, in either case, not only is working actively during your waking hours, but also "works while you sleep." To lose the assistance of that three-quarters would be a serious matter would it not? But far more serious is it to have that three-quarters actually working against you—having it on the side of the enemy! This is just what happens when the Subconscious gets into action under the influence of wrongly directed Faith, Expectant Attention and Confident Expectation.

Get busy with your Subconscious. Train it, educate it, reeducate it, direct it, incline it, teach it, suggest to it, along the lines of the Faith in Success and Power and not those of the Faith in failure and weakness. Set it to work swimming with that current. The Subconscious is much given to Faith—it lives on Faith, it acts upon Faith. Then see that you supply it with the right kind of Faith, and avoid as a pestilence that Faith which is based on fear and is grounded in failure and despair. Think carefully—and act!

HOW TO DEVELOP ENTHUSIASM FOR YOUR WORK

Faith is the underlying principle of that remarkable quality of the human mind which is known as Enthusiasm. It is its essence, it is its substance, it is its actuating principle. Without Faith there can be no manifestation of Enthusiasm. Without Faith there can be no expression of the activities of Enthusiasm. Without Faith there can be no exhibition of the energies of Enthusiasm. Without Faith the quality of Enthusiasm remains dormant, latent and static—Faith is needed to arouse it, to render it active, to cause it to become dynamic.

Moreover, the Faith required for the manifestation and expression of Enthusiasm must be positive Faith—Faith in the successful outcome of the undertaking—Faith exhibiting its positive phases—Faith in the attainment of that which is desirable and which is regarded as good. You can never manifest Enthusiasm toward that which you confidently expect to be a failure, nor toward that which you feel will bring undesirable results and effects. Negative Faith has no power to arouse Enthusiasm; the presence of Positive Faith is necessary to awaken this wonderful latent mental or spiritual force.

Enthusiasm is a mental or spiritual force which has always been regarded by mankind with respect—often with a respect mingled with awe. To the ancients it seemed to be a special gift of the gods, and by them it was regarded as animating the individual with almost divine attributes of power, and as causing him to absorb a portion of the essence of the divine nature. Recognizing the fact that men under the influence of Enthusiasm often accomplish almost superhuman tasks, the ancients came to believe that this added power and capacity arose from the superimposition of power from planes of being above that of humanity. Hence, they employed terms to define it which clearly indicated their belief in its transcendent nature.

The term "Enthusiasm," is directly derived from the ancient Greek term meaning, "to be inspired by the gods." The two compositive elements of the original term are, respectively, a term denoting "inspiration," and one denoting "the gods" or "divinity," the two terms in combination meaning literally "inspired by the gods."

You have found that when you become quite intensely interested in a subject, object, study, pursuit or cause, so that your Enthusiasm is thoroughly aroused then there comes to you a highly increased and greatly intensified degree and amount of mental energy and power. At such times your mind seems to work with lightning-like rapidity, and with a wonderful sense of ease and efficiency. Your mental powers seem to be quadrupled—your mental machinery seems to have some miraculous oil poured into the proper place, thus removing all friction and allowing every part of the mechanism to move smoothly and easily and with wonderful speed. At such times you feel, indeed, actually "inspired." You feel that a new world of attainment would be opened to you if you could make this mental condition a permanent one.

Looking around you in your world of practical everyday work and effort, you will see why business men and other men of affairs regard as an important factor of successful work that mental quality known as "enthusiastic interest" on the part of the persons performing that work. This "enthusiastic interest" in the work or task is found to call forth all the mental and physical powers of the worker. He not only puts into his task every ounce of his ordinary capacity, but he also draws upon that hidden reserve force of his Subconscious mentality and adds that to his ordinary full energy. When he approaches the fatigue limit his "enthusiastic interest" carries him on, and before long he has "caught his second wind" and obtained his fresh start.

Ask any successful sales-manager for a list of the essential characteristics of the successful salesman, and on that list you will find this capacity for or habit of "enthusiastic interest" occupying a prominent place. This, not only because of its highly important effect upon the work of the salesman himself, but also because "Enthusiasm is contagious," and the lively, quickened interest of the salesman tends to communicate itself to the subconscious mentality of his customer.

In the same way the Enthusiasm of the public speaker, orator, advocate or statesman energizes and quickens his entire intellectual and emotional nature, thus causing him to do his best, likewise communicating itself to his audience by means of "mental contagion." The man with "his soul afire" tends to fire the souls and hearts of those around him. The spirit of the enthusiastic leader, foreman, or "boss" is "caught" by those under him.

Enthusiasm is clearly a manifestation of the emotional phase of man's mentality, and it appeals directly and immediately to the emotional nature of others. Likewise, it is clearly a product of the subconscious mentality, and accordingly it appeals directly and immediately to the subconscious mentality of others. Its effect is characteristicly animating, energizing, inspiring, "quickening." It not only stirs the feelings and sets fire to the spiritual nature but it also stimulates and vivifies the intellectual faculties. The "live wires" in the world of men are those individuals who possess the quality of "enthusiastic interest" highly developed and habitually manifested when the occasion calls for it. Overdone, it defeats its object—the Golden Mean must be observed; but lacking it the man is what is known in the idiom of practical men as a "dead one."

The man of true Enthusiasm is characterized by his abiding Faith in his proposition or subject; by his lively interest in it; by his earnestness in presenting it and working toward its accomplishment; by his untiring, indefatigable efforts on its behalf. Faith, however, is the foundation upon which all the rest is built; lacking Faith, the structure of Enthusiasm falls like a house of cards.

The more Faith a man has in that which he is doing, toward which he is working, or that which he is presenting to others, the greater will be the manifestation of his own powers and capacity, the more efficient will be his performance of the work, and the greater will be his ability to influence others and to cause them to see things in the light of his own belief and interest. Faith arouses and sustains Enthusiasm; lack of Faith deadens and inhibits it; Unfaith and positive disbelief kill it. It is clear that the first step toward the cultivation and development of Enthusiasm is that of the creation of Faith in the subject or object toward which you wish to manifest and express Enthusiasm.

If you have no Faith in the subject or object of your activities, then you will never be able to manifest Enthusiasm concerning that subject or object.

Life without Faith and Enthusiasm is a living death—persons living that life are mere walking corpses. If you would be a "live wire" instead of a "dead one," you must begin to arouse and develop Enthusiasm in your heart and soul. You must cultivate that keen and quickened Interest, and that lively and earnest Faith in what you are doing, and in the things to which you are giving your time and work. You must mentally "breathe in," and inspire that Spirit of Life which men for many centuries have called "Enthusiasm," and which is the twin-sister of Inspiration. Then will you know the exhilaration of that "enkindled and kindling fervor of soul"—that "ardent and lively zeal"—the mark of true Enthusiasm.

THE FLAME OF DESIRE ESSENTIAL TO FAITH

Desire is the second factor of Mental Power. You must not only "know definitely exactly what you want," and manifest it by means of Idealization; you must also "want it hard enough," and manifest it in Insistent Desire. Desire is the flame and fire which create the steam of Will. The Will never goes out into effective action except when drawn forth by active and sufficiently strong Desire. Desire furnishes the "motive" for Will; Will never becomes active in absence of a "motive." When we speak of a man having a "strong will," we often mean really that he has strong desire—Desire strong enough to cause him to exert every ounce of power and energy in him toward the attainment or accomplishment of the object of Desire.

Desire exerts a tremendous influence upon all of the mental faculties, causing them to put forth their full energies and powers and to perform their work efficiently. It stimulates the intellect, inspires the emotions and quickens the imagination. Without the urge of Desire there would be but little mental work performed. The keynote of Desire is "I Want"; and to gratify and satisfy that "want" the mind puts forth its best energies. Without Desire you would do but little thinking, for there would be no motive for such. Without Desire you would perform no actions, for there would be no moving-reason for such. Desire is ever the "mover to action"—to action mental as well as physical.

Moreover, the degree and the intensity of your work, mental or physical, is determined by the degree of Desire manifested in you concerning the object or end of such work. The more you want a thing, the harder will you work for it, and the easier will such work seem to you to be. The task performed under the influence and incentive of strong Desire will seem much easier than would be the same task performed without such influence and incentive—and infinitely easier than would the same task appear if its end and object were contrary to your Desire. No argument is needed to establish these facts—they are matters of common knowledge and are proved by the experience of everyday life.

The degree of force, energy, will, determination, persistence and continuous application manifested by an individual in his aspirations, ambitions, aims, performances, actions and work, is determined primarily by the degree of his Desire for the attainment of these objects—his degree of "want" and "want to" concerning that object. So true is this principle that some who have studied its effects have announced the aphorism: "You can have or be anything you want—if you only want it hard enough."

Without Faith it is practically impossible for you to manifest strong, ardent, insistent Desire. If you are filled with doubt, distrust, unfaith or disbelief in a thing, or concerning the successful accomplishment or attainment of anything, you will not be able to arouse the proper degree of desire for that thing or for its accomplishment and attainment. Lack of Faith, or, still more, positive disbelief, tends to paralyze the Desire Power; it acts as a brake or as a damper upon its power. Faith, on the contrary, frees the brakes of Desire, or turns on the full draft of its fire.

Here is the principle in concise form: Faith encourages and sustains, promotes and maintains Desire in its highest degree of efficiency; doubt, disbelief, distrust, and unfaith retard and restrict, inhibit and paralyze this efficient manifestation of Desire.

THE MIGHTY POWER OF A STRONG WILL

Will-Action is the third factor of Mental Power. You must not only "know clearly just what you want," and see it in your "mind's eye" in ideal form—you must not only "want it hard enough," and arouse its power to a degree of insistence and demand which will not brook denial or defeat—you must also call into service the persistent, determined, indomitable application of the Will, which will hold your energies and powers steadfastly and relentlessly to the task of accomplishment and attainment. You must "will to will" and must make your Will will itself in the act of Willing.

Will is perhaps the most mysterious of all of the mental powers. It seems to dwell on a mental plane alone by itself. It lies nearer and closer to the "I AM I" or Ego, than does any other phase of mentality. It is the principal instrument of the

"I AM I"—the instrument which the latter employs directly and immediately. Its spirit is Persistent Determination—its essence is Action. Whenever you act, then do you employ your Will. Will Power is the dynamic phase or aspect of Mental Power. All other mental force is more or less static—it is only when the Will becomes involved in the process that Mental Power manifests its dynamic phase or aspect. Wise men have held that "All Power is Will Power at the last"; and that, "All activities are forms or phases of Will-Action, at the last." In the Cosmos, as well as in the individual, Will Power is the essential and basic phase of Power.

HOW TO ATTRACT THE PERSON YOU WANT

The Law of Mental Attraction, or Mental Gravitation, acts along lines very similar to those of the action of physical Gravitation. There is present and active the mutual and reciprocal "pull" between Thoughts and Things, and between Thoughts and Thoughts—Thoughts, however, are Things at the last analysis. This principle extends even to so-called inanimate objects: this mystery is explainable under the now well-established law that there is Mind in everything, even in the apparently inanimate objects of the universe, even in the atoms and particles of which material substances are composed.

Not only do you attract thought-vibrations, thought-waves, thought-currents, thought-atmospheres, etc. of a harmonious character, and to which your thoughts have a natural affinity; you also attract to yourselves (by the power of thought attraction) other persons whose thoughts have an affinity and harmony with your own. In the same way you attract to yourself (and are attracted toward) other persons whose interests run along the same general lines as your own.

You draw to yourself the persons who may be necessary for the successful carrying out of the plans and purposes, the desires and ambitions, which fill your thoughts most of the time; and, in the same way, you are drawn toward those into whose plans and purposes you are fitted to play an important part. In short, each person tends to attract toward himself those other persons whom he needs in order to materialize his ideals and to express his desires—providing that he "wants hard enough" and providing that the other persons are in harmonious affinity with his plans and purposes.

Persons who have had their attention directed toward the operations of the Law of Mental Attraction, and who have learned to apply the principles of its manifestation in their own affairs in life, observe many wonderful instances of its power in the happenings of their everyday life. Books, newspaper items, magazine articles bearing on some subject which is prominent in their thoughts, all these come to hand in an almost uncanny way. Persons who fit into the general scheme of the thought-plan come into one's life. Peculiar "happenings" come to pass in the same way. Things arise which "fit in" with the general idea. Unexpected circumstances arise which, although often at first sight seemingly obstructive and undesirable, in the end are found to dovetail perfectly into the whole scheme of things. No wonder that many persons having these experiences are at first inclined to attribute them to supernatural or superhuman influence—but they are in full accordance with Natural Law, and are a part of the powers of man, when rightly understood.

Your conditions and environment, the circumstances and happenings which come to you, are very largely the result of the operation of the Law of Mental Attraction—and they are accordingly, to a great extent, manifestations in objective, material form of your mental ideas, ideals and pictures, the force and nature of such manifestation depending largely upon the degree of Faith and Confident Expectation possessed and expressed by you in your thoughts upon these subjects and events—or upon the degree of doubt, disbelief, distrust and unfaith, those negative phases of Faith which serve to slow down the action of Faith Power or perhaps even to reverse its machinery.

You create environment, conditions, circumstances, events, assistance, means to ends, by Mental Power operating along the lines of the Law of Mental Attraction. Mental Attraction, like all forms or phases of Mental Power, is the transformation of the subjective Ideal into objective Reality—the thought tends to take form in action, the mental form tends to take on objective materiality and substance. The ideal is represented by the clear, strong, definite, mental picture or ideal form manifested in Idealization. Desire furnishes the flame and heat which generate the steam of Will needed in the creative process; but the Idealization is impaired and weakened, the Desire dies away, the Will loses its determination, unless Faith be there to create the Confident Expectation. The less the Faith and Confident Expectation, or the greater the doubt, disbelief, distrust, unfaith and lack of confidence, the weaker is the Idealization, the weaker the Desire, and the weaker the Will Power manifested.

Without Faith there can be no Confident Expectation; without Faith, the Fires of Desire die away; without Faith, the Steam of Will ceases to be generated; and thus Attainment becomes impossible. Whenever you think of the Law of Mental Attraction, think of Faith—for Faith is its very soul—its inspiration.

BELIEVE IN YOURSELF

Among the many characteristics and qualities which make for success of the individual there is none more fundamental, essential and basic than that of Self Confidence and Self Reliance—both of these terms being but expressions of the idea of Faith in Oneself. The man who has Faith in himself not only brings under his control and direction those wonderful powers of his subconscious mentality, and the full power of his conscious mental faculties and instruments, but also tends to inspire a similar feeling in the minds and hearts of those other individuals with whom he comes in contact in the course of his pursuit of the objects of his endeavors. An intuitive perception and realization of one's own powers and energies, capacity, and efficiency, possibilities and capabilities, is an essential attribute of the individual who is destined to success.

A study of the world of men will disclose the fact that those men who eventually succeed, who "arrive" ultimately, who "do things," are marked by this deep intuitive Faith in themselves, and by their Confident Expectation of Ultimate success. These men rise superior to the incidents of temporary defeat; they use these failures as stepping-stones to ultimate victory. They are living expressions of Henley's *Invictus*—they, indeed, are the Masters of their Fate, the Captains of their Souls! Such men are never really defeated; like rubber balls, they have that "bounce" which causes them to rise Triumphantly after each fall—the harder they are "thrown down," the higher do they rise on the rebound. Such men are always possible—nay, probable and certain—victors, so long as they maintain this intuitive Faith in Self, of Self Confidence; it is only when this is lost that they are really defeated or destroyed.

The failures in life are discovered usually to be either (1) those who have never manifested this Faith in Self, or Self Confidence; or else (2) those who have permitted themselves to lose the same under the "Bludgeonings of Chance."

Those who have never felt the thrill of Faith in Self, or of Self Confidence, are soon labeled by their fellows as lacking the elements of successful achievement—the world soon "gets their number" and places them where they belong. Their lack of Self Faith and Self Confidence is felt by those with whom they come in contact; the world lacks Faith in them and has no Confident Expectation of their success.

The study of the life-story of the successful men in all walks of life will illustrate this principle to you so forcibly that, having perceived it, you will never again doubt its absolute truth. In practically every case you will find that these successful men have been knocked down, and bowled out, many times in the early days of their careers—often even later on in life. But the knock-out, though perhaps dazing them for a short time, never robbed them of their gameness, their will-to-succeed. They always arose to their feet before they were counted out; and they always firmly, but resolutely, faced Fate. Though their "heads were bloody, they were unbowed," as Henley triumphantly chants. Fate cannot defeat such a spirit; in time, Destiny recognizes the fact that "here is a man"—and being feminine, she falls in love with him and bestows her favors upon him.

When you have found your Real Self—"That Something Within"—this "I AM I"—then have you found that Inner and Real Self which has constituted the subject and object of that Faith and Confident Expectation which have inspired, animated, enthused and sustained the thousands of men who have reached the Heights of Attainment by the Path of Definite Ideals, Insistent Desire, Confident Expectation, Persistent Determination, and Balanced Compensation. It is this Intuitive perception and consciousness of the Real Self which has caused men to live out the ideal of *Invictus* in the spirit of that glorious poem of Henley. Nothing but this inner realization would have been sufficient to fill the soul of man with this indomitable spirit and unconquerable will.

INVICTUS
by W. E. Henley

Out of the night that covers me,
Black as the pit from pole to pole,
I thank whatever gods there be
For my unconquerable soul.

In the fell clutch of circumstance
I have not winced or cried aloud;
Under the bludgeonings of chance
My head is bloody but unbowed.

Beyond this vale of doubt and fear
Looms but the terror of the Shade
And, yet, the passing of the years
Finds, and shall find me, unafraid.

It matters not how straight the gate,
How charged with punishments the scroll
I am the Master of my Fate,
I am the Captain of my Soul.

The wise teachers of the race have for centuries taught that this Faith in the Real Self, in the "I AM I," will enable the individual to convert into the instruments of his success even those circumstances which apparently are destined to defeat his purposes; and to transmute into beneficent agencies even those inimical forces which beset him on all sides. They have discovered, and passed on to their followers, the knowledge, that such a Faith is a spiritual Power, a living force, which when trusted and rightly employed will annihilate the opposition of outward circumstances, or else convert them into workers for good.

Your Real Self is a ray from the great Sun of Spirit—a spark from the great Flame of Spirit—a focal point of expression of that infinite SELF OF SPIRIT.

The earnest Faith in your Real Self, and your Confident Expectation concerning its manifestation and expression in your work, your endeavors, your plans, your purposes, serve to bring into action your full mental and spiritual power, energy, and force. It quickens your intellectual powers; it employs your emotional powers efficiently and under full control; it sets into effective action your creative imagination; it places the powers of your will under your mastery and direction. It draws upon your subconscious faculties for inspiration and for intuitive reports; it opens up your mind to the inflow of the illumination of your superconscious spiritual faculties and powers. It sets into operation the Law of Mental Attraction under your direct control and direction, whereby you attract to yourself, or you to them, the circumstances, events, conditions, things and persons needed for the manifestation of your ideals in objective reality. More than this, it brushes away the obstacles which have clogged the channels of your contact with and communication with SPIRIT itself—that great source of Infinite Power which in this instruction is called POWER.

Discover your Real Self, your "I AM I"—then manifest your full Faith in and toward it; and cultivate your full Confident Expectation concerning the beneficent results of that Faith.

7

The Infinite Loves You

BECOME AN INVINCIBLE SOUL

The Message of Truth: You, yourself, in your essential and real being, nature, and entity, are Spirit, and naught but Spirit—in and of SPIRIT; spiritual and not material. Materiality is your instrument of expression, the stuff created for your use and service in your expression of Life, Consciousness and Will: it is your servant, not your master; you condition, limit and form it, not it you, when you recognize and realize your real nature, and awaken to a perception of its real relation to you and you to it. The report of SPIRIT received by its accredited individual centers of expression, and by them transmitted to you is this:

In the degree that you perceive, recognize, and realize your essential identity with ME, the Supreme Presence-Power, the Ultimate Reality, in that degree will you be able to manifest My Spiritual Power. I AM over and above you, under and beneath you, I surround you on all sides. I AM also within you, and you are in ME; from Me you proceed and in Me you live and move and have your being. Seek Me by looking within your own being, and likewise by looking for Me in Infinity, for I abide both within and without your being. If, and when, you will adopt and live according to this Truth, then will you be able to manifest that Truth—in and by it alone are Freedom and Invincibility, and true and real Presence and Power, to be found, perceived, realized and manifested.

Francis Thompson, in his mystic poem entitled *The Hound of Heaven* describes with a tremendous power, and often with an almost terrible intensity, the hunt of Reality for the unwilling individual Self. He pictures Divinity as engaged in a remorseless, tireless quest—a seeking, following, tracking-down of the unwilling individual soul. He pictures the separated spirit as a "strange, piteous, futile thing" that flees from the pursuing Divinity "down the nights and down the days." The individual spirit, not knowing its relation to and identity with the pursuing Absolute, rushes in a panic of terror away from its own good. But, as Emerson says, "You cannot escape your own Good"; and, so the fleeing soul is captured at last. By Faith in the Infinite, however, the individual soul overcomes its terror of the Infinite and, recognizing it as its Supreme Good, it turns and moves toward it. Such is the mystic conception of the effect and action of Faith in the Infinite.

The complete poem, *The Hound of Heaven,* covers five pages; but we here present a condensed version of these beautiful and gripping lines by Francis Thompson. If you are not reciprocating the Great Love of God, you may have a feeling of remorse and resolve to do better. If this feeling does not come to you; you must have a heart of stone.

THE HOUND OF HEAVEN
by Francis Thompson

I fled Him, down the nights and down the days;
I fled Him, down the arches of the years;
I fled Him, down the labyrinthine ways
Of my own mind; and in the mist of tears
I hid from Him, and under running laughter.
Up vistaed hopes I sped;
And shot, precipitated,
Adown Titanic glooms of chasmed fears,
From those strong Feet that followed, followed after.
  But with unhurrying chase,
  And unperturbed pace,
Deliberate speed, majestic instancy,
  They beat—and a Voice beat
  More instant that the Feet—
"All things betray thee, who betrayest Me."

I said to Dawn: Be sudden—to Eve: Be soon;
With thy young skiey blossoms heap me over
  From this tremendous Lover—

  Still with unhurrying chase,
  And unperturbed pace,
Deliberate speed, majestic instancy,
  Came on the following Feet,
  And a voice above their beat—
"Naught shelters thee, who wilt not shelter Me."

In the rash lustihead of my young powers,
I shook the pillaring hours
And pulled my life upon me; grimed with smears,
I stand amid the dust of the mounded years—
My mangled youth lies dead beneath the heap.
My days have crackled and gone up in smoke.
Designer Infinite!—
Ah! must Thou char the wood ere Thou canst limn with it?
My freshness spent its wavering shower in the dust;
And now my heart is as a broken fount.

  Now of that long pursuit
  Comes on at hand the bruit;
That Voice is round me like a bursting sea:
"How little worthy of any love thou art!
Whom wilt thou find to love ignoble thee
  Save Me, save only Me?
All which I took from thee I did but take,
  Not for thy harms,
But just that thou mightest seek it in My arms.
  All which thy child's mistake
Fancies as lost, I have stored for thee at home:
  Rise, clasp My hand, and come!"

  Halts by me that footfall:
  Is my gloom, after all,

Shade of His hand, outstretched caressingly?
"Ah, fondest, blindest, weakest,
I am He Whom thou seekest!
Thou dravest love from thee, who dravest Me."

Prentice Mulford said: "A Supreme Power and Wisdom governs the Universe. The Supreme Mind is measureless and pervades all space. The Supreme Wisdom, Power, and Intelligence are in everything that exists, from the atom to the planet. The Supreme Power has us in its charge, as it has the suns and endless system of worlds in space. As we grow more to recognize this sublime and exhaustless Wisdom, we shall learn more and more to demand that Wisdom, draw it to ourselves, and thereby be ever making ourselves newer and newer. This means ever perfecting health, greater power to enjoy all that exists, gradual transition into a higher state of being, and the development of powers which we do not now realize as belonging to us. Let us then daily demand Faith, for Faith is power to believe and power to see that all things are parts of the Infinite Spirit of God, that all things have Good or God in them, and that all things, when recognized by us as parts of God, must work for our good."

To sum up:

1. There exists a greater underlying Something that is beneficent and well-disposed toward you, and which tries to help, aid and assist you whenever and wherever It can do so.
2. Faith and Confident Expectation regarding the beneficent power of that Something tends to open the channels of Its influence in your life; while doubt, unbelief, distrust, and fear, tend to dam up the channel of its influence in your life, and to rob it of the power to help you.
3. To a great extent, at least, you determine your own life by the character of your thought; by the nature and character of your thoughts you furnish the pattern or mold which determines or modifies the efforts of the Something to aid you, either in the direction of producing desirable results or else in bringing about undesirable results by reason of your damming up the sources of your Good.

In the *Book of Psalms* in our own Scriptures, are to be found several of the great masterpieces of the esoteric teachings concerning Faith Power—in them is given the essence of the Secret Doctrine concerning Faith in the Infinite.

Chief among these are the Twenty-Third Psalm, and the Ninety-first Psalm, respectively. So important are these two great esoteric poems—so filled with practical helpful information are they—that we deem it advisable to reproduce them here that you may avail yourself of their virtue and power at this particular stage of this instruction. Accordingly, they are given on these pages.

THE PSALM OF FAITH

Psalm 23

The Lord is my shepherd; I shall not want. He maketh me to lie down in the green pastures; he leadeth me beside the still waters. He restoreth my soul; he leadeth me in the paths of righteousnes for His name's sake. Yea, though I walk through the valley of the shadow of death, I will fear no evil; for thou art with me; Thy rod and Thy staff they comfort me. Thou preparest a table before me in the presence of mine enemies; Thou anointest my head with oil; my cup runneth over. Surely goodness and mercy will follow me all the days of my life, and I will dwell in the house of the Lord forever.

THE PSALM OF SECURITY

Psalm 91

He that dwelleth in the secret place of the most High shall abide under the shadow of the Almighty. I will say of the Lord, He is my refuge and my fortress: my God in Him will I trust. Surely He shall deliver thee from the snare of the fowler, and from the noisome pestilence. He shall cover thee with His feathers, and under His wings shalt thou trust: His truth shall be thy shield and buckler. Thou shalt not be afraid for the terror by night; nor for the arrow that flieth by day; nor for the pestilence that walketh in darkness; nor for the destruction that wasteth at noonday. A thousand shall fall at thy side, and ten thousand at thy right hand; but it shall not come nigh thee. Only with thine eyes shalt thou behold and see the reward of the wicked. Because thou hast made the Lord, which is my refuge, even the most high, thy habitation. There shall no evil befall thee, neither shall any plague come nigh thy dwelling. For

He shall give His angels charge over thee, to keep thee in all thy ways. They shall bear thee up in their hands, lest thou dash thy foot against a stone. Thou shalt tread upon the lion and the adder: the young lion and the dragon shalt thou trample under feet. Because he hath set his love upon Me, and therefore will I deliver him; I will set him on high, because he hath known My name. He shall call upon Me, and I will answer him and honor him. With long life will I satisfy him, and show him my salvation.

LEAD KINDLY LIGHT

The teachers and students of the Inner teachings, the Ancient Wisdom, the Secret Doctrine, are also aware of the esoteric spiritual significance of the lines of the well-known hymn "Lead Kindly Light," written by Newman in a period of spiritual stress. Few who read or sing this hymn realize its esoteric spirit and meaning—none but "those who know" perceive and recognize that which dwells under the surface of those wonderful words and lines.

THE CHANT OF FAITH POWER

(Lead Kindly Light)
Lead kindly Light, amid the encircling gloom; Lead Thou me on.
The night is dark, and I am far from home; Lead Thou me on.
Keep Thou my feet; I do not ask to see the distant scene; one step enough for me,
Lead Thou me on.

Carry with you ever the spirit of the ancient aphorism of the wise sage, which is; "Faith is the White Magic of Power."

The Magic Word

8

The Law of Increase

I am Success, though hungry, cold, ill-clad,
I wander for a while, I smile and say,
"It is but a time, I shall be glad
Tomorrow, for good fortune comes my way.
God is my Father, He has wealth untold,
His wealth is mine—health, happiness and gold."

—ELLA WHEELER WILCOX

In a pamphlet written by Don Blanding, he tells of a time during the trying years of the Great Depression, when he found himself financially, mentally and physically "broke." He was suffering from insomnia and from a physical lethargy amounting almost to paralysis. Worst of all, he had a bad case of "self-pity," and he felt that the self-pity was fully justified.

He was staying at a small Art Colony (on credit), trying to rebuild his wrecked life and wretched body. Among those at the Colony was Mike, an Hawaiian boy. Mike seemed to be always cheerful. Mike seemed to be always prosperous. And, naturally, Blanding wondered why. For Mike, when he had known him before, had been blessed with few of this world's goods.

So one day he asked Mike what good fairy had waved her wand over him and turned all that he touched into gold.

For answer, Mike pointed to a string of letters he had pasted over his bed—
"L-I-D-G-T-T-F-T-A-T-I-M."

Blanding read them, but could make no sense out of them. "What are they,
the 'Open, Sesame' to the Treasure Cave?"

"They have been the 'Open, Sesame' for me," Mike told him, and went on to
explain how they had helped him. It seems that Mike, too, had experienced his
ups and downs, but in the course of one of his "downs," he had happened upon
a teacher who showed him the power of PRAISE and THANKFULNESS.

"There is an inherent law of mind," says Charles Fillmore, "that we IN-
CREASE whatever we PRAISE. The whole of creation responds to praise, and
is glad. Animal trainers pet and reward their charges with delicacies for acts of
obedience; children glow with joy and gladness when they are praised. Even
vegetation grows better for those who love it. We can praise our own ability,
and the very brain cells will expand and increase in capacity and intelligence,
when we speak words of encouragement and appreciation to them."

God gave you dominion over the earth. Everything is your servant, but
remember it is said in the Scriptures that God brought every beast and fowl to
Adam, *to see what he would call them.* You are like Adam in this, that you can
give to everything and everybody with whom you come in contact the name
you like. You can call them good or bad. And whatever you call them, that is
what they will be—good servants or evil. You can praise or curse them, and as
you do, so will they be to you.

There is one unfailing Law of Increase—"*Whatever is praised and blessed,
MULTIPLIES!*" Count your blessings and they increase. If you are in need of
supply, start in now to praise every small piece of money that comes to you,
blessing it as a symbol of God's abundance and love. Salute the Divinity represented by it. Bless Him and name Him Infinite and Abundant Supply. You will
be surprised how soon that small piece of money will increase to many pieces.
Take God into your business. Bless your store, bless every one that works for
you, each customer that comes in. Know that they represent the Divinity called
Abundance, so bless them as such.

If you are working for someone else and want a better job or more pay, start
by BLESSING and being THANKFUL *for what you have.* Bless the work you
are doing, be thankful for every opportunity it gives you to acquire greater skill
or ability or to serve others. Bless the money you earn, no matter how little it
may be. Be so thankful to God for it that you can give a small "Thank Offering" from it to someone in greater need than yourself.

Suppose the Boss does seem unappreciative and hard. Bless him just the same. Be thankful for the opportunity to SERVE faithfully, no matter how small the immediate reward may seem to be. Give your best, give it cheerfully, gladly, thankfully, and you will be amazed how quickly the INCREASE will come to you—not necessarily from your immediate boss, but from the Big Boss over all.

I remember reading a letter from a woman in the drought belt in which she said that they, unlike most of their neighbors, had an abundant supply of water, and excellent crops. "When my husband plows a field," she writes, "I ask God to bless each furrow. Each seed that goes into the seeder is blessed, and the realization held that it will produce abundantly according to His righteous law. Our neighbors marveled at the abundance of hay that we cut this year. The hay was sold before the third cutting was put up.

"Each day, in the silence, I put the ranch 'Lovingly in the hands of the Father.' I ask God to bless everybody that comes in contact with the ranch."

Few realize the power of praise and blessing. Praise may be called the great liberator. You remember the story of Paul and Silas. They lay in jail bound with chains, but they did not despair. They rejoiced and sang hymns of praise, and lo, the very walls were shaken down and they were set free.

Praise always magnifies. When we praise God and then look about us and praise His invisible presence in all that we see, we find that the good is so magnified that much becomes evident that we ordinarily fail to see. Running through all of Jesus Christ's acts as well as His teachings we find the glowing element of praise. When He looked at five loaves and two small fishes and realized that He had a multitude to feed, His first thought was a thought of praise. "And looking up to heaven, he blessed."

Go back over the Old Testament and see how often you are adjured to "Praise the Lord and be thankful, that THEN shall the earth yield her increase." Probably no life chronicled in the Scriptures was more beset with trials and dangers than that of King David. And what was his remedy? What brought him through all tribulations to power and riches? Just read the Psalms of David and you will see.

> *Jehovah reigneth; let the earth rejoice;*
> *Let the multitude of isles be glad.*
> *Bless Jehovah, O my soul;*
> *And all that is within me, bless his holy name . . .*

Who forgiveth all thine iniquities;
Who healeth all they diseases.

"If anyone could tell you the shortest, surest way to all happiness and all perfection," wrote William Law, "he must tell you to make it a rule to yourself to thank and praise God for everything that happens to you. For it is certain that whatever seeming calamity happens to you, if you thank and praise God for it, you turn it into a blessing. Could you therefore work miracles, you could not do more for yourself than by this thankful spirit; for it turns all that it touches into happiness."

How then can YOU increase your supply? How can you get more of riches and happiness and every good thing of life? In the same way as the Wise Men and the Prophets of old. In the same way that Jesus twice fed the multitudes. In the same way that He filled the disciples' nets to overflowing with fish, after they had labored all night and caught nothing.

By EXPANDING what you have! And the way to expand is through love, through praise and thanksgiving—through saluting the Divinity in it, and naming it Infinite and Abundant Supply.

Throughout the Bible we are told—"In everything by prayer and supplication WITH THANKSGIVING let your requests be made unto God." Again and again the root of inspiration and attainment is stressed. *Rejoice, be glad, praise, give thanks!*

And that was what our Hawaiian boy had done. That was the secret of his prosperity and success. The Talisman he had pasted over his bed meant— "Lord, I do give Thee thanks for the abundance that is mine." Every time he looked upon it, he repeated those words of thankfulness. The happy ending lies in the fact that these words of praise and thanksgiving proved to be as potent a talisman for Don Blanding as they had for Mike, the Hawaiian.

"Whose offereth praise, glorifieth Me," sang the Psalmist of old. And it is as true today as it was thousands of years ago. Praise, thankfulness, understanding— these three supply the golden key to anything of good you may desire of life.

In "Think What You Want" magazine, some time ago, H. W. Alexander told how praise helps. "Sincere praise is money in your pocket," he said.

It is a spiritual and moral uplift. It is a tonic to the giver and the receiver. It rebounds to both a thousand times. I know a company whose sales during the depression went from $2,600,000 a year to $8,000,000. Praise was the inspiration.

In a divorce court not so long ago was recorded the story of a man who from a laborer's job climbed to the Presidency of his business. A friend asked him why he quit his almost lifetime companion, though she was well provided for. Said he, "Well my wife of today appreciates my ability, tells me right along, whereas my childhood sweetheart knows my weaknesses and tells me about them. I like appreciation." His income tax is on a $100,000 salary.

Little things count. Your secretary has a new dress, a new hat, a fashionably fluffy ruffle—tell her so. The file clerk finds your letters quickly—tell her so. The cop on the beat is sure to see the school boys are safely over with a wave of his hand. Tell him he is tops.

One of the finest persons who worked for me was an elderly servant woman. She had a tough time in life, poorly educated, used split infinitives, came early in the morning to clean the house. She often said to me as I left in the morning, "Sure, you look good today. You've got a big job, you work hard, you'll win." She *thought* I was good, and when I went out I *was* good. Top executives who read this know very well the truth of what the chauffeur, maid, gardener—who gives them a cheery word of praise, means to them at market time, conference time, or directors' time—it rings in their mind—oh, yes, they remember. You can't fly too high.

And the mother who *thinks* her boy or girl is about right, aids them on as no one else can.

I have this belief—that big or little, praise does win friends, wins respect for yourself, wins you a monetary return, and it helps a Pullman porter, a housewife, an industrialist to bigger, better things. It costs you nothing but a smile—but do be sincere.

To the wives who may read this: You know your man. He can't fool you. But be just as honest as you can, praise him, send him out to work with a smile, with praise, and you'll wear sables—try it.

Like attracts like. Praise and appreciation bring back greater praise and appreciation to you. If you want health, happiness, in your life, if you are seeking riches and success, attune your thoughts to these. BLESS the circumstances that surround you. Bless and praise those who come in contact with you. Bless even the difficulties you meet, for by blessing them, you can change them from discordant conditions to favorable ones, you can speed up their rate of activity to where they will bring you good, instead of evil. It is only lack of RESPONSIVE-NESS to good that produces the lacks in your life. Good works on the plane of EXPANSION. Good revolves at a high rate of activity. You can key your activity to that same rate by an expectant, confident state of mind. You can bring all your surroundings and circumstances up to that same level by BLESSING them, PRAISING the good in them, saluting the DIVINITY in them.

In the pages that follow, we shall show you how the practice of blessing and praising all things has brought good to all who have tried it, how you can use these same methods to attract every good thing *you* may desire.

Into whatsoever house ye enter, first say—"Peace be to this house!"

9

In the Beginning

For life is the mirror of king and slave,
'Tis just what we are and do;
Then give to the world the best you have,
And the best will come back to you.

We often speak of psychology and metaphysics as new sciences, and think that the study of these began within the last half-century. Yet if you refer to the very first book of the Bible, you find more profound examples of applied psychology than in any textbook of today.

Take the story of Jacob as an instance. You remember how Jacob agreed to serve Laban seven years for the hand of Rachel in marriage. And how, through the guile of his father-in-law, Jacob had to serve a second seven years. Even then, when he would have gone back to his own country, Laban begged him to tarry yet a while longer, and agreed to pay Jacob as wages "all the speckled and spotted cattle and all the brown cattle among the sheep, and the speckled and spotted among the goats."

Since Laban first removed from the herds all cattle of this kind, the chances of Jacob's getting rich on the speckled offspring of solid-colored cattle seemed poor indeed.

But Jacob evidently knew his Scriptures, and the idea we think so new, that first comes the "word" (or mental image), then the physical manifestation, was in his mind even when he made the bargain.

For what did he do?

And Jacob took him rods of green poplar, and of the hazel and chestnut tree; and pilled white strakes in them, and made the white appear which was in the rods.

And he set the rods which he had pilled before the flocks in the gutters in the watering troughs when the flocks came to drink, that they should conceive when they came to drink.

And the flocks conceived before the rods, and brought forth cattle ringstraked, speckled, and spotted.

And Jacob did separate the lambs, and set the faces of the flocks toward the ringstraked, and all the brown in the flock of Laban; and he put his own flocks by themselves, and put them unto Laban's cattle.

As it came to pass, whensoever the stronger cattle did conceive, that Jacob laid the rods before the eyes of the cattle in the gutters that they might conceive among the rods.

But when the cattle were feeble, he put them not in; so the feebler were Laban's, and the stronger Jacob's.

And the man increased exceedingly, and had much cattle, and maidservants, and menservants, and camels, and asses.

You have heard of the English cuckoo. Too lazy to rear and care for its own young, it goes to the nests of other birds when they are off seeking food, notes the markings on their eggs, then comes back later *and lays in their nest eggs of those same exact markings!*

Various saints of the middle ages are said to have had markings on their hands, feet and sides similar to those on the crucified Saviour, acquired from constant contemplation of His image. And only recently I read of an adopted child, which was reported to have developed markings similar in all respects to those of the real son of its foster-parents, although the son had died some months before the adopted child was born. The parents were satisfied it was a case of reincarnation, but it seemed to me merely a materialization in the foster-child of the images in the mother's mind. She had grieved inexpressibly over her loss. She had adopted the waif to try to fill the void left by her own little boy. And striving to see in his every action some reminder of her lost one, those images so strongly held in her mind actually expressed themselves in the body of her foster-child.

It all comes back to that first line of the first chapter of the Gospel of St.

John—"In the beginning was the Word." For what is a "Word"? A mental image, is it not? Before an architect can build a house, he must have a mental image of what he is to build. Before you can accomplish anything, you must have a clear mental image of what it is you want to do.

Turn to the Scriptural account of the creation of the world. What is the outstanding fact you find there?

IN EVERY THING GOD CREATED, THE "WORD" CAME FIRST—THEN THE MATERIAL FORM!

Just listen: "And God said, Let there be light . . . And God said, Let there be a firmament . . . And God said, Let us make man . . ."

First the "word," then the material form. Scientists tell us that words denote ideas, mental concepts—that you can always judge how far a race has advanced in the mental scale by the number of words it uses. Its vocabulary is the measure of its ideas. Few words—few ideas, few mental images.

Therefore, when God said—"Let the earth bring forth grass," He had in mind a clear mental image of what grass was like. In other words, He had already formed the mold. As the Scriptures put it—"The Lord God made the earth and the heavens, and every plant of the field *before it was in the earth,* and every herb of the field *before it* grew." He made the mental image, the mold. It needed then only to draw upon the energy about Him to fill that mold and give it material form.

And that is all you, too, need to do to give your word of power material form—first make the mental image, the mold, then pour into it the elements necessary to make that image manifest for all to see.

What do you want first?—Health—Happiness? Riches?

For perfect health, begin by taking the life out of every distorted image of sickness or imperfection. Charge those nerve centers of yours to withdraw their supporting hands, and let your image of disease collapse like the pricked bubble it is.

THEN IMAGE THE PERFECT MOLD OF WHATEVER ORGAN HAS BEEN DISEASED.

Image the perfect mold of it so vividly that you can clearly see it in your mind's eye, then charge The God in You to reach out with its millions of hands for all the elements it needs to make that perfect image manifest.

First the word (the mental image), then the creation. But the creation will never become manifest without faith. So when you have made your image, when you have set The God in You to work pouring into it the elements it needs for life, *"believe that you receive!"* See with the eyes of your mind that perfect organ functioning as it was meant to, *and thank God for it!*

For riches, the same principle holds true. Take your life out of every image of debt, of lack, of unfulfilled obligation. The God in you is a God of plenty. He cannot owe money. He cannot be limited. There are no circumstances powerful enough to force Him to live in poverty or want.

Yet He, remember, is devoted entirely to your advancement. So how can you be tied down by debt or limitation of any kind?

How? Because YOU have insisted upon it. Instead of a God of plenty, you have worshipped one of want. Instead of reaching out for what you needed, you have tied the hands of The God in You and tried to do their work with the paltry powers of your material hands.

Unloose The God in You! Give Him a job and set Him to work. Make your mental image of the great business or other service you long for, then set The God in You to work bringing to you every element you need to make that image real. And don't wait until you receive the whole of it, but as fast as any element becomes manifest, USE it!

If you have only 10¢, USE it to start your great idea. If you have only the idea, START it, even though you can take only the first step. First the word, remember, then the creation. And there can be no creation without faith.

Show your faith by using each element as fast as it makes itself manifest, even though there be no sign that any other element is following, and before you know it, your whole structure will be complete.

Have you ever read Genevieve Behrend's account of how she got $20,000, when, from all material points of view, her chances of ever seeing that amount of money were just about nil?

"Every night before going to sleep," she writes, in YOUR INVISIBLE POWER:

I made a mental picture of the desired $20,000 which seemed necessary to go and study with Troward. Twenty imaginary $1,000 bills were counted over each night in my bedroom, and then, with the idea of more emphatically impressing my mind with the fact that this twenty thousand dollars was for the purpose of going to England, and studying with Troward, I wrote out my picture, saw myself buying my steamer ticket, walking up and down the ship's deck from New York to London, and finally saw myself accepted as Troward's pupil. This process was repeated every morning and every evening, always impressing more and more fully upon my mind Troward's memorized statement: "My mind is a center of Divine operations." I endeavored to keep this statement in the back part of my consciousness all the time, with no thought in mind of how the money might be obtained. Probably the reason why there was no thought of the avenues through which the money might reach me was because I could not possibly imagine where the $20,000 would come from. So I simply held my thought steady and let the power of attraction find its own way and means.

One day while walking on the street, taking deep breathing exercises, the thought came: "My mind is surely a center of Divine operation. If God fills all space, then God must be in my mind also; if I want this money to study with Troward that I may know the truth of Life, then both the money and the truth must be mine, though I am unable to feel or see the physical manifestations of either. Still," I declared, "it must be mine."

While these reflections were going on in my mind, there seemed to come up from within me the thought: "I AM all the substance there is." Then, from another channel in my brain the answer seemed to come, "Of course, that's it; everything must have its beginning in mind. The Idea must contain within itself the only one and primary substance there is, and this means money as well as everything else." My mind accepted this idea, and immediately all the tension of mind and body was relaxed. There was a feeling of absolute certainty of being in touch with all the power Life has to give. All thought of money, teacher, or even my own personality, vanished in the great wave of joy which swept over my entire being. I walked on and on, with this feeling of joy steadily increasing and expanding until everything about me seemed aglow with resplendent light. Every person I passed appeared illuminated as I was. All consciousness of personality had disappeared, and in its place there came that great and almost overwhelming sense of joy and contentment.

That night when I made my picture of the twenty thousand dollars it was with an entirely changed aspect. On previous occasions, when making my mental picture, I had felt that I was waking up something within myself. This time there was no sensation of effort. I simply counted over the twenty thousand dollars. Then, in a most unexpected manner, from a source of which I had no consciousness at the time, there seemed to open a possible avenue through which the money might reach me.

Just as soon as there appeared a circumstance which indicated the direction through which the twenty thousand dollars might come, I not only made a supreme effort to regard the indicated direction calmly as the first sprout of the seed I had sown in the absolute, but left no stone unturned to follow up that direction, thereby fulfilling my part. By so doing, one circumstance seemed naturally to lead to another, until, step by step, my desired twenty thousand dollars was secured.

For happiness, the method is no different. Your God is a God of love, and real love can know no unhappiness, for love gets its happiness from giving.

There are laws to interfere with almost every other activity of humanity, but none to keep you from giving as much as you like. An unselfish giving results in getting, just as surely as planting results in harvesting. Give with no thought of reward but the good of the one you are helping, and good is bound to flow back to you.

Love begets love, you know, so take your life out of every thought of enmity, of repining, of unhappiness. In place of these, see yourself in your mind's eye giving every manner of happiness to all whom you would have love you. Image that in your mind's eye, then set The God in You to work bringing you opportunities to make all these loved ones happier. And as fast as each opportunity presents itself, USE it! No matter how tiny an opportunity it may be, *use it!* No matter if it be merely the chance to say a pleasant word, to give a kindly smile, to bring a happy thought, *use it!*

And in the using, you will find that doubly great happiness has come to you.

Each of us is a miniature sun, his circumstances and surroundings his solar system. If debts and disease and troubles form part of your system, what is the remedy? *Let go of them, of course!* If you want new planets of riches and youth and happiness, how can you get them? In the same way the sun does, and only in that way—by throwing off from yourself.

Remember this: Nothing can come into your solar system except from you or through you. If it comes from outside, it is not yours and has no power over you until you take hold of it mentally and accept it as yours. If you don't want it, you can refuse to accept it, refuse to take hold of it, refuse to believe in its reality—then put in the place it seems to occupy, the perfect condition of your own imaging.

If there is something lacking in your solar system, you have only to "speak the word"—create the mental image, then hold to that image in serene faith until The God in You has filled it with those elements that make it visible to all.

It is your own fault when you allow yourself to become the victim of personal impotence or of undesirable external situations. As Emerson put it— "Nothing external to you has any power over you." You fear these negative seemings simply because you BELIEVE in them, when all the time it is only that BELIEF that gives them power and authority.

Remember, YOU are the central sun of your own solar system. YOU have dominion over everything within that system. YOU can say what shall enter, what shall stay there. And you have infinite attractive power to draw to you anything of good you may desire. Nothing stands between you and your fondest desires but lack of understanding of or faith in this power of attraction.

But once you send out the desire, you must have perfect faith in the result. You cannot accomplish anything by expressing a desire and then spending your time fearing and worrying lest you will not find the work you seek, or not have the money in time to pay your bills, or that some other evil thing will happen to prevent good from coming to you. The Law of Attraction cannot bring both good and evil at the same time. It must be one or the other. And it is up to YOU to decide which it shall be.

"After any object or purpose is clearly held in thought," says Lilian Whiting, "its precipitation in tangible and visible form is merely a question of time. Columbus saw in vision a path through trackless waters around the world. The vision always precedes and itself determines the realization."

Dare you to say—"Every day in every way I am getting richer and richer"? If you dare—and will follow up the word with the mental image of yourself HAVING all the riches you desire—Spirit substance will make your word manifest and show you the way to riches.

You were designed by the Father to be master of your fate and captain of your soul. If you are not exercising that mastery, it is because you are lying down on the job. Instead of mastering your thoughts and mental images, you are letting them bow down before mere things.

No thing can make you unhappy if you will exercise your divine power of love and blessings towards it. Everything is good in its essence, and that good essence will respond to your call of blessing, and its good will come forth to meet you.

> *The world stands out on either side*
> *No wider than the heart is wide;*
> *Above the world is stretched the sky—*
> *No higher than the soul is high;*
> *The heart can push the sea and land*
> *Farther away on either hand;*
> *The soul can split the sky in two,*
> *And let the Face of God shine through.*

10

Treasure Mapping for Supply

So many people have won to success and happiness by making "Treasure Maps" to more easily visualize the things they wanted, that "Nautilus" magazine recently ran a prize competition for the best article showing how a "Treasure Map" had helped to bring about one's heart's desire. Caroline J. Drake won the contest.

"I had been bookkeeper," she wrote, "in a large department store for seven years when the manager's niece, whose husband had just died, was put in my place.

I felt stunned. My husband had died ten years previously, leaving a little home and some insurance. But sickness and hospital bills had long since taken both home and money. I had supported the family for eight years and kept the three children in school, but had not been able to save any money. The eldest child, a boy, had just finished high school but as yet had found nothing to do to help along.

Day after day I looked for work of any kind to do which might pay rent and give us a living. I was thirty-five years old, strong, capable and willing; but there was absolutely no place for me. For the first time in my life I was afraid of the future. The thought that we might have to go on relief appalled me.

Thus three months passed. I was behind two months with the rent when the landlord told me I would have to move. I asked him to give me a few days longer in which to try and find work. This he agreed to do.

The next morning I started out again on my rounds. In passing a magazine stand I stopped and glanced over the papers and magazines.

It must have been the answer to my many prayers that led me to pick up the copy of a magazine which stared me in the face. Idly I opened it and glanced at the table of contents. My mind was in such a turmoil that I was barely conscious of the words which my eyes saw.

Suddenly my eye was caught by a title about "treasure-mapping" for success and supply. Something impelled me to buy a copy of the magazine, which proved to be the turning point in our lives.

Instead of looking for work, I went home. Still under the influence of that "Something" (which I did not then understand) I began to read the magazine. Strange and unreal as it then seemed, still I did not doubt. I read each article eagerly and in its order. When I came to the article about treasure-mapping to bring success and supply, something about the idea seemed to hold me in its grip. As a child I had always loved games, and this idea of making a treasure-map reawakened that old desire.

I read the article several times. Then, with a bunch of papers which I hunted up, I set to work to make my treasure-map of success and supply. So many things came into my mind to put on that treasure-map! First, there was the little cottage at the edge of town. Then there was a little dress and millinery shop which I had always longed for. Then, of course, a car. And in that cottage would be a piano for the girls; a yard in the back where we could work among the flowers of an evening or a morning. My enthusiasm grew by leaps and bounds. From magazines and papers I cut pictures and words and sentences—all connected with the idea of success and abundance.

HOW I MADE THE "TREASURE-MAP"

Next I found a large sheet of heavy white paper and began building that map. In the center I pasted a picture of a lovely little cottage with wide porches and trees and shrubbery around it. In one corner of the map I put a picture of a little storeroom and underneath I pasted the words, "Betty's Style Shop." Close to this I pasted pictures of a few very stylish dresses and hats.

At different places on the map I placed sentiments and mottoes—all carrying out the idea of success, abundance, happiness and harmony.

I do not know how long I worked on that treasure-map which was to be the means of attracting into our lives the things which we had need of and desired. I could already feel myself living in that cottage and working in the little dress shop. Never had I felt so completely fascinated and thrilled with an idea as with that treasure-map and what I was sure it would bring us. I tacked the map on the wall of my bedroom, right in front of my bed, so that the first thing I saw in the morning and the last thing at night would be that treasure-map of my desires.

Every night and morning I would go over every detail of that map until it fairly seemed to become a part of my very being. It became so clear that I could call it instantly to mind at any moment in the day. Then in my Silence period I would see myself and the children going through the rooms of the cottage, laughing and talking, arranging the furniture and curtains. I would picture my daughters at the piano singing and playing; I would see my son sitting in the library with books and papers all around him. Then I would picture myself walking about my shop, proud and happy; people coming in and going out. I would see them buying the lovely hats and dresses, paying me for them and going out smiling.

During all this time, I was learning more and more of the power of the mind to draw to us the things and conditions like unto our thoughts. I understood that this treasure-map was but the means of impressing upon my subconscious mind the pattern from which to build the conditions of success and harmony into our lives. Always, after each of my Silence periods, I would lovingly thank God that the abundance and harmony and love were already ours. I believed that I *had* received; for mentally living in the cottage and working in the shop was to me the certain fact that I would take possession of them in the material world just as in the mental.

When the children found out what I was doing, they entered heartily into the spirit of the game and each of them soon had a treasure-map of his own.

It was not many weeks before things began to happen. One day I met an old friend of my husband's and he told me that he and his wife were going west for several months and asked if we would come out and take care of their house for the rent. A week later we were settled in that cottage, which was almost the very picture of the one I had on my treasure-map. A little later my son was offered work evenings and

Saturdays in an engineering office, which proved the means of his entering college that fall.

We had been in the cottage nearly two months when I saw an advertisement in the local paper for a woman to take charge of a lady's dress shop. I answered the ad and found that the owner was having to give up the shop for several months, perhaps permanently, on account of her health. Arrangements were quickly made so that I was to run the business and share half the expenses and the profits.

Within six months after we started treasure-mapping for supply, we had accomplished practically everything that map called for. When the owner of the cottage came back several months later, he made it possible for us to buy the place and we are still here.

The business, too, is mine now. The lady decided not to come back, so I bought the business, paying her so much a month. It is a much larger and more thriving business now—thanks to the understanding of the power of thought which I gained through my study and practice.

In another article in "Nautilus," Helen M. Kitchel told how she used a "Treasure Map" to sell her property. She pasted an attractive picture of her house on a large sheet of paper, put a description of it underneath and then surrounded picture and description with such mottoes as—"Love, the Divine Magnet, attracts all that is good"—and others of a similar nature. She hung her map where she could see and study it several times a day, and repeated some of the affirmations or mottoes whenever the thought of making a sale occurred to her.

She also started a little private letter box which she called "God's Box" and in it, whenever the thought occurred to her, she placed a letter written to God telling of her needs and desires. Then each month she went over the letters, taking out and giving thanks for those that had been answered.

Within a year her house was sold, on the very plan she herself had outlined in one of her "Letters to God," on the exact basis and for the exact price she had asked in that letter.

Another method is to "Talk with God." Go somewhere where you can be alone and undisturbed for a little while, and talk aloud to God exactly as you would to a loving and understanding Father. Tell Him your needs. Tell Him your ambitions and desires. Describe in detail just what you want. Then thank Him just as you would an earthly father with whom you had had a similar talk and who had promised you the things you asked for. You will be amazed at the result of such sincere talks.

"My word shall not come back to me void, but shall accomplish that whereunto it was sent." Whatever you can visualize—and BELIEVE in—you can accomplish. Whatever you can see as yours in your mind's eye, you can get. "In the beginning was the Word." In the beginning is the mental image.

Corinne Updegraff Wells had an article in her little magazine "Through Rose Colored Glasses" that illustrates the power of visualizing your ambitions and desires. "Many years ago," she says, "a young girl who lived in a New York tenement was employed by a fashionable Fifth Avenue modiste to run errands, match samples and pull basting threads.

Annie loved her job. From an environment of poverty she had become suddenly and miraculously an inhabitant of an amazing new world of beauty, wealth and fashion. It was thrilling to see lovely ladies arrive in fine carriages, to watch the social elite preen before Madam's big gold framed mirrors.

The little errand girl, in her starched gingham, soon became filled with desire and fired with ambition. She began imagining herself as head of the establishment instead of its most lowly employee. Whenever she passed before mirrors she smiled at a secret reflection she saw of herself, older and more beautiful, a person of charm and importance.

Of course, nobody even suspected the secret existence of this make-believe person. Hugging her precious secret, Annie smiled confidently at that dazzling reflection in the mirror and began playing an exciting game, "I'll pretend I'm already Madam. I'll be polite and look my best and have grand manners and learn something new each day. I'll work as hard and take as much interest as though the shop were really and truly mine."

Soon fashionable ladies began whispering to Madam: "Annie's the smartest girl you've ever had!" Madam herself began to smile and say: "Annie, you may fold Mrs. Vandergilt's gown if you'll be very careful," or, "I'm going to let you deliver this wedding dress," or, "My dear, you're developing a real gift for color and line," and, finally, "I'm promoting you to the work-room."

The years passed quickly. Each day Annie came more and more to resemble the image she alone had seen of herself. Gradually the little errand girl became Annette, an individual; then Annette, stylist; and finally, Madam Annette, renowned costume designer for a rich and famous clientele.

The images we hold steadfastly in our minds over the years are not illusions; they are the patterns by which we are able to mould our own destinies.

You never can tell when you do an act
Just what the result will be,
But with every deed you are sowing a seed,
Though the harvest you may not see.
Each kindly act is an acorn dropped
In God's productive soil;
You may not know, but the tree shall grow
With shelter for those who toil.

You never can tell what your thought will do
In bringing you hate or love,
For thoughts are things and their airy wings
Are swifter than carrier doves.
They follow the law of the universe—
Each thing must create its kind,
And they speed o'er the track to bring you back
Whatever went out from your mind.

—ELLA WHEELER WILCOX

11

"Wanted: Rain!"

From one to two inches, and free from hail if possible. Is badly needed to save remaining crops and fill the reservoirs. Must be delivered soon to do any good. Will pay highest market price.

Can be delivered any place; prefer general rain. Showers gratefully accepted, but prefer real, honest-to-goodness downpour.

This offer made by the following firms for the general good of the community, and in the general belief that anything worth having, is worth asking for.

BELLE FOURCHE, South Dakota needed one thing—RAIN—to save remaining crops and fill the reservoirs. Why not advertise for it, thought L. A. Gleyre, publisher of "The Northwest Post." A novel idea—advertising to the Lord—never been tried in just that way before, but at least there was no harm in trying. The prayerful advertisement reprinted above was the result.

"We proposed to each merchant in town," says Mr. Gleyre, "that he pay $2.50 for his name at the bottom of the page ad, with the provision that if no material rain fell between the date of the advertisement and the following Tuesday midnight, the ad was entirely at our expense."

The idea took immediately . . . we could probably have filled a double truck. While the week was rolling by, our people had a new one to think about—their minds were actually taken off the scarcity of rain and made to function along the line of whether "The Northwest Post" was going to make good with their ad. The majority of our merchants were pleased with the idea. Some actually believed we had some inside information from the weather bureau which prompted our offer. A few, including one or two preachers, while not saying so to us, took occasion to say it was sacrilegious, etc.

During the specified week, light rains fell in some parts of our territory. Belle Fourche had three very light sprinkles—not enough to count, for we agreed that the rain should be a downpour. Toward the end of the week excitement ran rife and interest continued to grow. Some of our warm friends made bets we would win. Others openly hoped we would, while everyone agreed that it would be tremendously helpful if we did win.

We won—but lost. Just six hours after midnight, Wednesday morning, it rained pitch-forks-and-saw-logs-for-handles. It was exactly what we advertised for—a swash-buckling, rip-snortin' downpour of rain. It measured from one-half to two inches, and one remote point reported seven inches of rainfall!

But we didn't charge any merchant a cent. We lost by six hours.

I think it attracted more attention than anything we have done in years. To this day we are asked to advertise for something needed.

Where did that rain come from? Did the advertisement bring it? Does the Rain Dance of the Hopi Indians bring it? Did the prayer of Elijah bring it, as told in the Bible?

Yes! At least, so we believe, and we think we can show you good reason for that belief. Not only that, but we believe that back of these answers to prayer is the fundamental law of life and supply!

For of all the promises of Jesus, there is but one that promises us WHATEVER WE ASK shall be done for us! That one positive assurance is *based on this condition*—"If two of you agree on earth as touching anything they shall ask, it shall be done for them of my Father which is in Heaven."

And again He said—"Where two or three are gathered together in My name, there am I in the midst of them." Why is this? Why the necessity for several to unite in asking for a thing in order to be sure of getting it?

A good many years ago, Professor Henry of Princeton made an experiment with a charged magnet. First he took an ordinary magnet of large size, suspended it from a rafter and with it lifted a few pounds of iron.

Then he wrapped the magnet with wire and charged it with the current from a small battery. Instead of only a few pounds, the now highly charged magnet lifted 3,000 pounds!

That is what happens when one person prays, believing, and another adds his prayers and his faith. In effect, the second person is charging the magnet of the first one with his current, MULTIPLYING the power of the other's prayer a dozen times over.

In "Nautilus" magazine some months ago, Elizabeth Gregg told how five people prayed—agreeing—and the most pressing personal problem of each was soon solved. It seems that the husband of a Mrs. A. had been sick with ulcerated stomach for months. She had prayed repeatedly, without result, so one day she picked four of her friends whom she knew to be badly in need of help in different ways, and got them to agree to meet together on a certain day each week and see if, by uniting their prayers in perfect agreement, they might not improve their condition.

At the first meeting, it was decided to pray for the recovery of Mrs. A.'s husband, so these five women, sitting in silence, mentally pictured the husband strong and well, going about his work in a happy way. Then they gave thanks that their prayer had been answered.

"It was agreed," the article goes on to say, "that promptly at twelve o'clock noon each day until the next meeting, each of the five women would stop whatever she was doing and spend five minutes in silent prayer, agreeing with each other, that the husband be freed from sickness."

Three days after that first meeting, the husband was entirely free from pain. By the end of the week, he was on his way to complete recovery.

Next came the problem of Mrs. B., a widow whose home was to be sold in six weeks for failure to meet her payments. With earnestness and faith the women concentrated at the stated time each day upon the desire that the way would open for her supply. And true to the law, the way did open. Just a day before the week was up a well-to-do lady in the town called and asked Mrs. B. if she would take care of her children, eight and ten, for a few weeks while she, the mother, was away. The sum she offered would take care of the back payments on the home and provide living expenses. Shortly after the lady returned she made arrangements for Mrs. B. to take care of an invalid aunt, which gave the widow a steady and lucrative income.

Next was the problem of Mrs. C., whose husband had been out of work for several months. A few days after the week of agreement was up the husband received a letter from a cousin living at a short distance offering him work in his lumber mill. So, again the law was fulfilled.

Then the case of little Miss D., who for years had been estranged from her family, came under the law for solution. But in this case it was several weeks before any outward sign of fulfillment appeared. However, love had entered the heart of Miss D. during this time and for the first time since the estrangement she gave way to her new feeling and wrote to each of the family asking forgiveness for what she now acknowledged had been intolerance on her part. By return mail came letters from her family, letters also filled with the spirit of love. Thus, for the fourth time in the work of these women did the law work unfailingly.

The last problem was that of Mrs. E., who owned a little dress shop but whose business had been almost ruined since the larger and newer shop just across the street had opened. Envy and hate had filled the heart of Mrs. E. so that she resisted all overtures at friendship which the owner of the new shop had made. Then, from her study of Truth she learned that no one need compete with anyone; that there is full abundance for all when we learn how to claim it. So, instead of envying, she now joined with the others in sending out love and good will to her competitor, as she had called her.

A few weeks later the owner of the new store called and asked if Mrs. E. would take over the management of her store for six months while she was in the East on business. She explained that when she returned it might be advantageous to both of them to form a partnership. This was later done and today Mrs. E. is half owner of a thriving dress and millinery shop and there is perfect harmony between her and the woman she once hated.

Russell Conwell, author of "Acres of Diamonds," tells of dozens of such cases. He tells of a kidnapped child returned unharmed through the power of united prayer; of a lost child found in the same way; of men and women cured of apparently incurable diseases; of businesses saved, of positions won, of love renewed and families reunited. There is no good thing you can ask, believing, that shall not be given you.

"What will you have?" quoth God. "Pay for it and take it." And the paying consists of complying with the law of agreement, by praying—if you pray alone—that the good you are asking for yourself shall be given to all others as well, by "agreeing as to what ye shall ask" if you are praying in a group.

Did you ever read the diary of George Mueller covering the early days of his great work? George Mueller, you know, was the man who started an orphanage with no money in hand, no rich patrons, no prospects—just absolute trust in God. Read the following extracts from his diary and see how that trust was justified:

Nov. 18, 1830. Our money was reduced to about eight shillings. When I was praying with my wife in the morning, the Lord brought to my mind the state of our purse, and I was led to ask Him for some money. About four hours after, a sister said to me, "Do you want any money?" "I told the brethren," said I, "dear sister, when I gave up my salary, that I would for the future tell the Lord only about my wants." She replied, "But He has told me to give you some money." My heart rejoiced, seeing the Lord's faithfulness, but I thought it better not to tell her about our circumstances, lest she should be influenced to give accordingly; and I also was assured that, if it were of the Lord, she could not but give, I therefore turned the conversation to other subjects, but when I left she gave me two guineas.

On March 7. I was again tempted to disbelieve the faithfulness of the Lord, and though I was not miserable, still, I was not so fully resting upon the Lord that I could triumph with joy. It was but one hour after, when the Lord gave me another proof of His faithful love. A Christian lady brought five sovereigns for us.

April 16. This morning I found that our money was reduced to three shillings; and I said to myself, I must now go and ask the Lord earnestly for fresh supplies. But before I had prayed, there was sent from Exeter two pounds, as a proof that the Lord hears before we call.

October 2. Tuesday evening. The Lord's holy name be praised! He hath dealt most bountifully with us during the last three days! The day before yesterday five pounds came in for the orphans. O how kind is the Lord! Always before there has been actual want he has sent help. Yesterday came in one pound ten shillings more. Thus the expenses of yesterday for housekeeping were defrayed. The Lord helped me also to pay yesterday the nineteen pounds ten shillings for the rent.

I saw more clearly than ever that the first great and primary business to which I ought to attend every day was to have my soul happy in the Lord. The first thing to be concerned about was not how much I might serve the Lord, how I might glorify the Lord; but how I might get my soul into a happy state, and how my inner man might be nourished.

REVIEW OF THE YEAR 1838

As to my temporal supplies. The Lord has been pleased to give me during the past year 350 pounds, 4 shillings, 8 pence. During no period of my life has the Lord so richly supplied me. Truly, it must be manifest that, even for this life, it is by far the best thing to seek to act according to the mind of the Lord as to temporal things. We have to make known our need to God in prayer, ask His help, and then we have to believe He will give us what we need. Prayer alone is not enough. We may pray never so much, yet, if we do not believe that God will give us what we need, we have no reason to expect that we shall receive what we have asked for.

"In the heart of man a cry, in the heart of God supply." But as Mueller said, prayer alone is not enough. If we do not BELIEVE that God will give us what we ask for, we have no reason to expect that we shall receive it.

How can we cultivate such belief? Jesus gave us the cue. "Unless ye be converted (turned about) and become as a little child, ye shall in no wise enter the Kingdom of Heaven." And again—"Unless a man be born again, he shall not enter the Kingdom."

How can we become as a little child? How can we be born again? The first essential would seem to be to determine what there is about a child that we must imitate. What one thing is universal with all little children? DEPENDENCE, is it not? Utter dependence upon those around them, utter faith in them to provide their needs. And the greater the Dependence, the better those needs seem to be supplied.

Take the embryonic child in its mother's womb, for instance. At inception, it measures only .004 centimeters. In nine months, it multiplies in size a billion times. That is what happens to it during its state of most utter dependence. In the next eighteen to twenty-one years, when it comes to depend more and more upon itself, it increases only sixteen times.

Does that mean we should make no effort ourselves? By no means! The admonition given us was—"Work and pray!" And the "work" is emphasized first. But it does mean that when we have done all that is in our power, we can confidently and serenely leave to the Lord whatever else is necessary to the accomplishment of our desire.

Three thousand years ago, there was a poor woman whose husband had just died and left her with two small sons and a heavy burden of debt.

The amount was not much, as debts go today, but when you have not a cent, even a small debt looks big as a mountain. And the widow had nothing at all.

So in the fashion of those days, her creditor purposed to sell her sons into bondage. For even in those semi-barbaric times, property was more valuable than life. The right of human beings to life, liberty and the pursuit of happiness had never even been heard of. So she, having nowhere else to turn, went to the Prophet Elisha, and begged him to help her in her need.

And what do you suppose Elisha did? Took up a collection? Or appealed to the fund for widows and orphans? Not he! "What have you in the house?" he asked.

He believed in using the means at hand, believing that God always provides unlimited supply if we but have the courage and faith to use what we have.

So he merely asked what the widow had to start with, and when told— "Naught save a pot of oil," he bade her borrow vessels from the neighbors *and pour out into them the oil that she had.* In other words, she was to *start the flow.* And it is written that so long as she had vessels to receive it, *the oil kept flowing.*

When the vessels were all filled, Elisha bade her sell the oil and pay her debt, and then start afresh with her sons beside her.

What have YOU *in your house?* When troubles assail you, do you sit back and bemoan your fate, waiting for some friend to help, or do you take stock of what you have, and set to work using it?

You remember the story of the man who came from the hospital after an accident, completely paralyzed. Of all his body, he could move only one finger. In those circumstances, wouldn't you have given up? But he didn't. "If I can move but one finger," he decided, "I'll use it to do more than one finger ever accomplished before!" He did—and lo and behold! In a little while, the fingers next that one began to show life, too. Before many months had passed, he was using every muscle in his body.

I know of a man who lost everything he had in the clothing business. From an expensive apartment, he had to move his family into the poorest rooms in town, where they and their neighbors did not know from one day to another, where the next meal was coming from. They were downcast—yes. But discouraged? No!

He went around to some of his old creditors—got them to trust him for a few knit neckties that they could not sell anywhere else—found a printer who would give him credit for a few hundred envelopes, letterheads and postage—and sent those ties to lists of men culled from the occupational directory of the telephone book. As fast as the money for them came back, he bought more ties and mailed them out, he and his family doing the work of enclosing, addressing and stamping in their cramped little apartment. Before that type of selling became passé, *he had made two hundred thousand dollars out of it.* Yet most men in the same circumstances give up and quit. Life's biggest mistakes, according to Harrington Emerson, is to under-estimate your power to develop and to accomplish. Ella Wheeler Wilcox says:

Ships sail east, and ships sail west,
By the very same breezes that blow;
It's the set of the sails, and not the gales,
That determine where they go.

Success is not a thing—not a guerdon that awaits you at some far-off shrine. Success lies in doing well whatever thing you are doing *now.* It is more a matter of mental attitude than of mental or physical capacity. You have all the fundamentals of it right now. But it is only the USE of them that can make you successful.

"All very well," perhaps you say, "but look at the handicaps I am under. There is Jim Jones, whose father left him a million—and all mine left was some debts to add to my own."

Have you ever read Emerson's comparison of Alaska and Switzerland? Alaska, according to him, is in six respects much better off than Switzerland. It has tremendous resources of virgin forests; Switzerland has practically none. It has great stores of gold and silver and copper and lead and tin and coal; Switzerland has practically none. It has fisheries—the greatest in the world; Switzerland has none.

It has in proportion to its area, greater agricultural possibilities than Switzerland—over a hundred thousand square miles suitable for agriculture. It has a tremendous seacoast; Switzerland none. And yet if Alaska were supporting the same number of people to the square mile as Switzerland, it would have 120,000,000 inhabitants.

Now the Swiss have marketed what? Natural resources? No! The Swiss are a people who take a block of wood that was worth ten cents and convert it into a carving worth a hundred dollars.

They will take a ton of metal, steel, brass and so on, and put it together in such form as to make it worth several million dollars.

They take cotton thread that they buy from this country at twenty cents a pound, and they convert it into lace worth a couple of thousand dollars a pound.

And because as a nation they have learned the art of utilizing their latent capacities, they have prospered abundantly.

What is the moral? Simply this: It is not money that counts. It is not natural resources. It is the way *you use what you have!* You can succeed with what you have at this moment, if only you learn to use it rightly.

"Ask not for some power that has been denied you. Ask what ability you have which can be made to develop into something worth while. *What is in your hand?*"

"We are too apt to think," says Bruce Barton, "that if we had some other man's equipment or opportunity, we could do great things. Most successful men have not achieved their distinction by having some new talent or opportunity presented to them. They have developed the opportunity that was at hand."

Great successes are simply a group of little successes built one upon another, in much the same way that John MacDonald's first great subway was merely a long line of little cellars—*strung together!* As Professor James put it—

> As we become permanent drunkards by so many separate drinks, so we
> become saints in the moral, and authorities and experts in the practical
> and scientific spheres, by so many separate acts and hours of working.
> Let no one have any anxiety about the upshot of his work or education,
> whatever the line of it may be. If he keeps faithfully busy each hour of the
> working day, he may safely leave the final result to itself. He can with
> perfect certainty count on waking some fine morning, to find himself one
> of the competent ones of his generation, in whatever pursuit he may have
> singled out.

What makes a great musician? Practice—keeping everlastingly at it until playing becomes second nature. What makes a great artist, a great lawyer, a great engineer, a great mechanic or carpenter? Persevering study and practice. You may have a natural liking for a subject, so the study of it is easier to you than to others, but the big successes in life have seldom been the brilliant men, the natural wonders, the "born orators" or the talented artists. The great successes have been the "grinds."

"A few years ago," said Dr. John M. Thomas, president of Rutgers University, "Rutgers had a student called a 'greasy grind' by some of his classmates. This was S. Parker Gilbert, Agent-General for Reparations under the Dawes plan. He may have been a 'greasy grind,' but at thirty-two he was earning $45,000 a year. And, according to Owen D. Young, Chairman of the Board of Directors of the General Electric Company, Gilbert held for several years the most important political position in the world."

A good many men in and out of college have an idea that to study is foolish. "No one ever gets anywhere from studying," they say. S. Parker Gilbert is only one of thousands of cases that prove to the contrary.

The most important job in the world for you is the one above yours. And the way to get it is to study—to "grind"—until you can put more of knowledge, more of skill, more of initiative into it than any man around you. Only thus can you win success.

Why do so many fail? Because they do not try hard enough, work persistently enough. The doors of opportunity are always closed. They have been since the world began. History tells us of no time when you could walk down a street and find any doors of opportunity standing open and inviting you to come in. Doors that are worth entering are usually closed, but the resolute and courageous knock at those doors, and keep knocking persistently until they are opened.

You remember the parable of the importunate friend:

And He said unto them, Which of you shall have a friend, and shall go unto him at midnight and say unto him, Friend, lend me three loaves; for a friend of mine in his journey is come to me, and I have nothing to set before him?

And he from within shall answer and say, Trouble me not; the door is now shut, and my children are with me in bed; I cannot rise and give thee.

I say unto you, though he will not rise and give him because he is his friend, yet because of his importunity he will rise and give him as many as he needeth. And I say unto you, Ask, and it shall be given you; seek, and ye shall find; knock and it shall be opened to you.

Why do so many fail to receive that for which they ask? Because they are not importunate enough. They do not convince the God in them that their prayer is something they MUST have. They ask and knock once or twice, and because the door is not immediately opened, they give up in despair. Remember—"He that wavereth is like a wave of the sea, driven with the wind and tossed. Let not that man think that he shall receive anything of the Lord."

If you have faith in God or man or self,
Say so; if not, push back upon the shelf
Of silence all your thoughts till faith shall come.
No one will grieve because your lips are dumb.

—ELLA WHEELER WILCOX

12

Catalysts of Power

Doubt not, fear not, work on, and wait;
As sure as dawn shall conquer dark,
So love will triumph over hate,
And Spring will bring again the lark.

—DOUGLAS MALLOCH

Nearly two thousand years before Christ, it was said in the Vedas (the sacred Hindu writings) that if any two people would unite their psychic forces, they could conquer the world, even though singly they could do nothing.

Then came Jesus to tell us even more positively that if two of us agree as touching anything we may ask, it shall be done for us.

Jesus never made any such positive promise of certain results when we pray alone. Why should it be necessary for two to unite their desires or prayers in order to be sure of results? If you add 2 to 2, you get only 4. If you add your muscular power to mine, you can lift only twice as much as either of us could lift alone. Yet if you add your prayers to mine, you get—not merely twice the power, but a hundred or a thousand times as much.

Why should this be? We have the word of many great psychologists that it is so. Judge Troward of England, who was to the British Empire what Professor Wm. James was to America, is authority for the statement, as is Brown Landone and a score of psychologists of lesser note. What is the reason?

Perhaps the answer lies in what the chemists call CATALYSTS. In chemistry there are certain substances which, when added to others, release many thousands of times as much power as they themselves contain. These catalysts, without losing any of their own energy, multiply the energy in other substances by thousands and sometimes even by millions! Perhaps that is what happens when two or more unite as touching the thing they shall pray for. Perhaps one is a CATALYST, multiplying the power of the other by thousands upon thousands of times. Certain it is that even Jesus, when those about Him were not in sympathy with Him and did not believe in Him, as on the occasion of His visit to Nazareth, worked no mighty works. Perhaps that is why, when He sent out His disciples to heal the sick, He sent them out "two by two."

Be that as it may, one thing is sure: If two or more of you will get together for a minute or two each day, and really agree as touching the thing you shall ask and the way you shall ask for it, you will get amazing results. Mind you, it is not enough to merely pray together for the same thing. You must unite your thought. You may ask me to pray with you that you may be healed of an ulcerated stomach, and when we pray, you may be picturing those sores and thinking of the pain and trouble they have been causing, while I am picturing the perfect organ that God gave you. That is not uniting our forces. That is setting them in opposition. We must both think health. We must both see in our mind's eye the thing we WANT—not the one we fear or wish to be rid of.

The same is true of debts. You may be thinking of all the money you owe, of the mortgage that is falling due, of the cut in pay you had to take, while I am trying to help you by thinking of the Infinite Supply that God is sending you. We'll never accomplish much that way. We've BOTH got to think of and visualize RICHES—not debts or lack. We've got to remember that the debts or other wrong conditions are merely the LACK of riches or health or other good thing, and that when we provide the good, the evil disappears as naturally as darkness disappears when you turn on the light. So what we must think of and see in our mind's eye is the light—i.e. the riches or the perfect health or the love or other good thing we desire.

If two can unite in doing that, there is no good thing they can ask, believing, that they cannot get. In the preceding chapter, we quoted the article by Elizabeth Gregg in "Nautilus," telling how five women prayed together, and every prayer was answered. And in Chapter Five, we told of a similar group in Russell Conwell's church who accomplished even more marvelous results through united prayer.

You have problems too great to be solved by you alone. And you have friends with problems that they are unable to handle. Why not get together and unite your forces? Why not meet for fifteen minutes once a week, talk over your difficulties, decide upon the case that seems most pressing, and then at a certain time each day, all of you drop whatever you are doing and give a minute or two to uniting your thought and your prayers? You CAN do it, and you will be amazed at the power of your united prayers. There is nothing of good you can ask, believing, that cannot and will not be done for you.

No star is ever lost we once have seen.
We always may be what we might have been.

13

The First Commandment

If with pleasure you are viewing
Anything a man is doing,
If you prize him, if you love him,
Tell him now.
Don't withhold your approbation
Until the Parson makes oration
And he lies with many lilies on his brow.

For no matter how you shout it
He won't really know about it,
He won't count the many teardrops
That you shed.
If you think some praise is due him,
Now's the time to pass it to him.
For he cannot read his tombstone when he's dead.

"What shall I do to be saved?" asked the rich young man of Jesus 1900 years ago. And today most of us are asking essentially the same question—"What shall I do to be saved from poverty and sickness and unhappiness, here and now as well as in the hereafter?"

"Keep the commandments!" was the Master's answer to the rich man. And later, when asked—"What is the greatest commandment," He told His hearers: "Thou shalt love the Lord thy God with all thy heart, and with all they soul, and with all thy mind: *This is the first and great commandment.* And the second is like unto it. Thou shalt love thy neighbor as thyself. On these two command-ments hang all the Law and the Prophets."

Sounds simple enough, but just what is "loving God"? Is it going to Church and being a professed Christian? Or is it simply BEING THANKFUL AND HAPPY!

Going to Church and being an example to your neighbors is excellent, but is there any way in which you can show your love for God better than by being happy? Happiness implies praise, satisfaction with what God has done, thank-fulness for His good gifts. Happiness means that you are enjoying life, appreci-ating it to the full, radiating joy to all about.

And loving your neighbor is just making him happy, too—praising him and blessing him and doing what you can to help him.

Can you think of any commandment, any law, that would do as much to-wards universal peace, towards settling the strife between labor and capital, towards bringing the millennium, as these two?

1. Be thankful and happy yourself.
2. Try to make your neighbor happy.

"On these two commandments hang all the Law and the Prophets."

Someone has wisely said that the first step towards universal peace is to have peace in our own hearts—to wish our neighbors well, to bless and praise even those who have used us despitefully. Evelyn Gage Browne expressed the thought when she wrote—

This old world needs the tender touch,
The kindly word, the lifting hand,
The love that blesses us so much,
And friendly hearts that understand.

It is said that a woman once went to Krishna and asked him how to find the love of God. "Who do you love most?" he inquired. "My brother's child," she answered. "Go back and love him more," advised Krishna. She did so, and lo! Behind the boy, she saw the form of the Christ child.

The same thought is expressed in the old legend of the group that went out to find the Christ child. There were knights and great ladies and monks and clergymen and all manner of people, and among the latter was a kindly old shoemaker. Everyone laughed at the idea of his going out when so many of the great ones of the earth were ahead of him. But after they had all come back disappointed, the bent little shoemaker walked joyfully in, accompanied by the Christ child himself.

"Where did you find Him?" they asked. And the Christ Child answered for him—"I hid myself in common things. You failed to find me because you did not look with the eyes of love."

Millions of books have been written about love, but most of them know not even the meaning of the word. To them, love is passion, self-gratification. Real love is not that. Real love is GIVING. It seeks only the good of the loved one. Yet in giving love freely, you get it, for it is like energy in that it expands only as it is released. It is like a seed in that it multiplies only when you sow it. As Ella Wheeler Wilcox put it—

Give love, and love to your heart will flow,
A strength in your utmost need;
Have faith and a score of hearts will show
Their faith in your word and deed.

Carlyle defined wealth as the number of things a man loves and blesses, *which he is loved and blessed by.*

Who are the unhappiest creatures on earth? Not the poor or the sick—but those who keep all their love for themselves. They may be worth millions, they may have dozens of servants to attend to their every want, but they are bored to extinction. They are miserable. Why? Because they have stopped giving, and as the words of a beautiful hymn express it—

For we must share, if we would keep
That blessing from above.
Ceasing to give, we cease to have—
Such is the Law of Love.

Life is expansion, mentally and physically. When you stop growing, you die. That is literally true in the case of your body cells, and figuratively true mentally, for when you cease to progress mentally, you are as good as dead. The undertaker may not call for a year or two, but so far as useful purposes are concerned, you might as well be buried.

And just as life is action, so is happiness service. For in helping and praising others and making them happy, you win happiness for yourself. Charles
Kingsley once said that we knew our relations to God only through our relations with each other. No man can love God while he hates his neighbor. No
man can love God while he is himself unhappy or deliberately makes another
unhappy.

To be unhappy implies a criticism of God. An unhappy man cannot be
grateful, he cannot be trustful, he cannot be at peace—and without these, how
can he love God?

Yet if he lives only for himself, he is bound to be unhappy. "For whosoever
shall save his life shall lose it," said the Master. "But whosoever shall lose his
life for My sake, the same shall save it." He who loses himself in the service of
others shall find therein life and love and happiness.

Longfellow tells of sending first an arrow into the air, and then a song, and
seeming to lose them. But presently he found the arrow in an oak tree, and the
song, from beginning to end, he found in the heart of a friend.

"He prayeth well," wrote Coleridge, "who loveth well both man and bird
and beast.

> *He prayeth best, who loveth best*
> *All things both great and small;*
> *For the dear God who loveth us,*
> *He made and loveth all.*

When Jane Addams graduated from college, the doctors told her she had
only six months to live. If a doctor told you that, what would you do? Most of
us would simply sit down and die, and feel very sorry for ourselves in the doing
of it.

Not so Jane Addams. "If I have only six months to live," she said, "I'll use
those six months to do just as much as I can of the things I want most to do
for humanity."

And she so lost herself in the work that she forgot to die. Eight years after
the time predicted for her demise, she started Hull House, the Chicago settlement that is known the world over. Not only that, but her health was as good
or better than that of the doctors who had prophesied her end.

Everyone has heard of Luther Burbank and of the marvelous success he had in growing things. He could take even a prickly cactus plant and from its shoots grow a plant without thorns or prickers, from which cattle could get sustenance on even the dryest soil.

How did he work such wonders with all manner of growing things? Through the magic of love! He blessed each little plant, he praised and nursed and loved it. And the life in it responded by giving him such results as no man before him had ever dreamed of. Here is the message that Luther Burbank sent to his friends on his last birthday:

As you hold loving thoughts toward every person and animal and even toward plants, stars, oceans, rivers and hills, and as you are helpful and of service to the world, so you will find yourself growing more happy each day, and with the happiness comes health and everything you want.

"Love and you shall be loved," said Emerson. "All love is mathematically just, as much as the two sides of an algebraic equation." The old philosopher who said—"Take out of life anything you want, *and pay for it*," stated an eternal truth. You get as you give. It is well to remind one's self of this frequently by repeating now and then, when inclined to be disturbed by seeming difficulties—"I so love that I see all good and give all good, *and all good comes back to me.*"

The most universal desire in all the world is man's natural desire for happiness. It is the purpose of existence. It is God's plan—to make man WIN happiness through struggle and service, through adding to the happiness of others.

Why is it that a moving-picture actor makes a thousand times as much as a teacher, or as an average business man or even a clergyman? Because he makes many thousand times as many people happy. He enables them to forget their troubles, to live their ideals, their dreams, through his picturing of them. When the rest of us find some way to make as many people happy, we shall share in like rewards.

A long time ago, Emerson wrote—"He who addresses himself to modes and wants that can be dispensed with, builds his house off the road. But he who addresses himself to problems every man must come to solve, builds his house on the road, and every man must come to it."

Just ask yourself—What have I to GIVE that will add to the happiness of those around me? You will be surprised how many simple little ways of brightening the lives of others will present themselves, and how great the reward these ways can bring, when multiplied by hundreds or thousands.

A man down in Washington was too poor to buy his child toys, yet he wanted above everything to make that child happy. So with his pocket-knife, he carved out of discarded pieces of lumber a rough sort of Kiddie-car. It made such a hit, not only with his own youngster but with every child around, that he took it to a manufacturer and made a fortune out of it.

Years ago, a young veterinary over in England had a mother who was confined to a wheel chair. To soften the jolts for her, he fastened a strip of rubber around the iron tires. Those strips of rubber, through constant improvement, developed into the famous Dunlop tire, which have sold by the million.

There are similar stories to be found by the hundred. The only limit to your opportunities is the limit of human happiness. And that has not yet been reached.

"My husband died a short time ago," writes a poor, harassed widow, "leaving his estate so involved that it looks as though we shall lose everything. What can I do? I have two young children to clothe and feed and educate, and I've never made a penny in my life. Tell me, is it wrong to pray for death, for I don't know what else we can do?"

Is it wrong to pray for death? What do *you* think? Is praying for death showing love for God, confidence in Him? What did the Prophet of old, in similar case? "My husband is dead," wailed the widow to Elisha, "and the creditor is come to take unto him my two sons to be bondmen." Did Elisha demand that God rain down gold upon her? On the contrary—he asked what she had in the house, and with it he helped her to win her own salvation.

Read the story of Mary Elizabeth, and you will find an almost exact parallel. A widow with three children, no money, and the creditor "Poverty" demanding those children for bondservants. But the oldest of them asked herself—"What have we in the house?"—and found an ability to make others happy through delicious candy. Today the whole family is independently wealthy.

> *You have no talent? Say not so.*
> *A weaker brother you can lift*
> *And by your strength help him to go*
> *Renewed and blessed—this is your gift.*

No talent? Some one needs a word
Of courage, kindness, love, and cheer—
Which only you can speak—to gird
His spirit against grief and fear.

Yours is a special gift that none
But you can use. Oh, lift your heart!
So much of good will be undone
Unless you do your own great part.

You are God's helper day by day;
He comforts, guides, and speaks through you;
He needs just you in this blest way.
No talent? Oh, that is not true!

—EVELYN GAGE BROWNE

The ancient Greeks had a legend that all things were created by love. Everyone was happy, because love was everywhere, and each vied with the other to make those around him happy.

Then one night while love slept, fear crept in, and with it came disease and lack and all unhappiness. For where love attracts, fear repels. Where love gives freely, fear is afraid there will not be enough for all, so holds on to everything it has.

What was the knowledge of good and evil against which God warned Adam in the Garden? Wasn't it a knowledge of things to *fear?*

In the second chapter of Genesis, we are told that Adam and Eve were naked and were not ashamed. Why? Because they knew no evil—therefore they feared no evil.

But they ate of the Tree of Knowledge of good and evil. They learned about evil. They hid themselves in the Garden in fear of evil. And immediately evil things began to happen to them, and have continued happening to their descendants ever since.

In the Garden of Eden, everything was abundance. The earth gave of its fruit bountifully. Then man learned fear. And having been given dominion over the earth, his fear reacted upon it. He feared it would hold back its fruits.

He feared there would not be enough for all. He feared the snake and the wild animal, which before had been docile to his love.

What was the result? Instead of giving of its abundance gladly, he had to wrest its fruits from the earth. Instead of the luscious fruits and herbs of the Garden, the earth gave him the product of his fears—thorns and thistles. Instead of friendship between him and the beasts of the forest, there was the natural fruit of fear—suspicion and enmity.

From the time he ate of the Tree of Knowledge of Good and Evil, man has reaped the fruits of fear. And as long as his belief in evil holds, he will continue to reap the fruits of fear.

God is love. And what is the first characteristic of love? *To give.* God is constantly giving to us *all that we will accept.*

But that is, alas, woefully little. For the first characteristic of fear is to shut up every opening, whether of income or outgo. Fear repels. Fear holds on to what it has, lest it should be unable to get more. Fear takes only what it can grab. It will not open its doors and let good come in. It is too much afraid of evil.

The result is that good comes to us through fear only after great struggle and suffering, even though the good be all the time trying to manifest itself. It is like a fortress built upon the highest peak of a great mountain. It is so fearful of evil coming to it that it has put itself as far as possible away from good as well.

Love opens the petals of the flowers and the leaves of all growing things to the sun, giving freely of its fragrance, and thereby draws to itself every element it needs for growth and fruition.

Love asks—What have we in the house that will make others happy?—and thereby attracts to itself everything necessary for its own happiness.

What is the first and greatest commandment? To give out love, to make the world a happier place than you found it. Do that, and you cannot keep happiness from coming to you, too.

"I often wonder," says Andrew Chapman, "why people do not make more of the marvelous power there is in Kindness. It is the greatest lever to move the hearts of men that the world has ever known—greater by far than anything that mere ingenuity can devise, or subtlety suggest. Kindness is the kingpin of Success in life; it is the prime factor in overcoming friction and making the human machinery run smoothly. If a man is your enemy, you can not disarm him in any other way so surely as by doing him a kind act."

THE LADY OR THE TIGER

In ancient times, it is said that there lived a king whose methods of administering justice were original in the extreme.

He built a huge arena to seat himself and all his people. Under it, he put two doors. When a culprit was brought before him, accused of any crime, the king gave him his choice of which door he would open. If the accused man chose the right door, there came forth from it a beautiful lady, who was forthwith wed to him. But if he chose the wrong door, there came out of it a fierce and hungry tiger, which immediately tore him to pieces.

The king had a beautiful daughter, and upon a time it came to pass that a handsome young courtier fell in love with her and she with him. That was a grievous crime, for it did not at all suit the king's plans that his daughter should marry a commoner, no matter how well favored he might be. So the poor suitor was promptly clapped into a cell, and informed that on the morrow he must stand trial in the arena like any common culprit.

The princess was heartbroken. She tried prayers, she tried tears, but her father was adamant. Any common man who dared lift his eyes to her deserved death, and death he should have—death, or marriage to someone in his own station.

Failing to move her father, the princess tried the guards. But no amount of gold would persuade them to free her lover. This much she did accomplish, though—she learned from which door the tiger would come, from which the lady. More, she learned who the lady was, and horror of horrors, it was one she had seen more than once casting amorous glances at her lover!

The morning found her torn between love and jealousy. She could not see her lover killed before her eyes—and yet, would it not be better to suffer that moment of agony, and be able to remember him as loving only her, than to see him day after day in the arms of another, see the triumph in that other's eyes, see his own eyes turn away from her to the beauty in his arms?

As in a dream, she took her place on the dais at her father's right hand. As in a dream, she saw her lover step forth, saw him look to her for a sign, saw herself signal to him to choose the right hand door—then hid her face that she might see no more.

Which had she chosen—the Lady or the Tiger? Which would you choose in like circumstances? Judging from the newspapers of the day, all too many, even in our so-called civilization, would choose the tiger. Why? Because they would rather see their lover dead than in the arms of another. Their idea of love is passion, self-gratification, and if they can't have their loved one for themselves, they don't want anyone else to have him, regardless of how he or the other may suffer.

At some time and in one modified form or another, that choice of the Lady or the Tiger comes to most people, and your answer depends solely upon what kind of love yours is. If it is real love, you will not hesitate for a moment, for real love is selfless and free from all fear. (And that is all jealousy is—*fear!*) Real love gets its happiness from giving. It lavishes itself upon the object of its affections without thought of return. And by its very prodigality, it brings back real love to itself.

For love is a magnet. Like the magnet of iron which gives off electricity, by its very giving it draws to itself its own. And again like the iron magnet, when its strength is done, when all power has gone out of it, it has only to rub against a stronger magnet to be renewed!

What is it that makes men and women fall in love? Not beauty; that attracts attention. But love requires more than beauty. Love requires personality, *charm*, MAGNETISM!

And what is magnetism? What but the power you GIVE OUT! It is vitality, it is abounding interest in people and things, it is LOVE!

You cannot be self-centered and still give out magnetism. You cannot think only of the gratification of your own desires and still expect to win or hold another's love.

Love gives out a current of love, and all who come within its aura are attracted to it. Selfishness, jealousy, hate, are like layers of insulation around a magnet. They not only shut off all love from going out, but they keep any from getting in. A selfish man, a jealous man, an angry man, has no magnetism. He repels everyone he comes in contact with. He has shut off his own current, and insulated himself against any from the outside.

I remember reading a story of a man who had become involved in a serious law-suit. He was bitter and resentful, for he felt that his opponents had been most unfair and unjust. But the suit was apparently going against him.

He went to a teacher of the mental sciences and laid his case before him. The teacher told him he would never get anywhere with his case until he rid himself of his resentment and hatred. "Bless your opponents," he advised. "Know that in some way not yet apparent they are doing you a favor. Say to yourself, whenever thoughts of resentment creep in—'I live by the law of love.' And then try to do just that."

The man tried it, and found that he could not keep saying and using this affirmation without its affecting everything he did. There came a most unexpected opportunity to do a great favor for his opponents. Reluctantly he did it, and lo and behold, it opened the way to a fair settlement of the whole case—a settlement that proved eventually far more profitable to him than winning the case would have done.

"Doubt not, fear not, work on and wait; as sure as dawn shall conquer dark, so love will triumph over hate." So writes Douglas Malloch, and in a recent issue of "Nautilus" magazine, Sonia Shand tells of a "Love Game" which bears out the same idea.

It is based, she says, on Shakespeare's "Taming of the Shrew." You remember, in the play, no matter what Katharine said or did, Petruchio acted as though she were falling in with his wishes, and the more contrary she became, the more he would praise her for her sweet submission to his every wish. Well, this game is as simple as that. No matter what happens during the time you are playing your game of Love, you smile and say it is good and wonderful.

Whether a feared bill collector comes blustering to your door, or the neighbors' children pull up your favorite flowers, or any one of the hundred annoying things that are part of your daily existence happen, just smile and give thanks for them as though they were great blessings instead of annoying trials.

Release the feeling of love toward each and every annoying thing as though it were the best that ever happened to you. You will be amazed at the results that come from this little game, because in love, no matter how tiny the grain of it, there is unlimited power for good, and it is never wasted.

You have heard the old adage that a soft answer turneth away wrath. This game has the same principle incorporated in it, with a lot more added to it. Nonresistance is one thing, but by itself it is negative. Add your praise and blessings to it, and you turn it into a positive force for good.

To love all things is our natural heritage. It was what made Adam and Eve so happy in the Garden of Eden. The snake of Fear crept into their hearts and turned them out of Eden, but we can each of us get back in if we will use the game of Love.

Try it. And while you are playing it, be sure to glorify *yourself*. See yourself as the perfect individual you always had hoped some day to become. Be the charming, gracious, noble self, who is raised by the powers of Love to a level above all sordid, petty, annoying and ugly things of life. Be that for one hour each day, and you will be amazed how quickly you will be that all the day.

You can use this Love Game in the home, in business, in whatever you are doing and wherever you are working.

If you are a business man, perhaps worried by a heavy load of debts and obligations, bless your creditors with the thought of abundance as you begin to accumulate the wherewithal to pay off your obligations. Keep the faith they had in you by including them in your prayer for increase. Begin to free yourself at once by doing all that is possible with the means you have, and as you proceed in this spirit the way will open for you to do more. For through the avenues of Spirit, more means will come to you and every obligation will be met.

If you are a creditor, be careful of the kind of thoughts you hold over your debtor. Avoid the thought that he is unwilling to pay you or that he is unable to pay you. One thought holds him to be dishonest and the other holds him to be subject to lack, and either of them tends to close the door to the possibility of his paying you soon.

Declare abundant supply for both creditors and debtors, and thus help them to prosper. Pray and work for their good as well as for your own, for yours is inseparable from theirs. You owe your debtor quite as much as he owes you and yours is a debt of love. Pay your debt to him and he will pay his to you.

Take anything in your life that seems not to be going well, and give a few minutes each day to "treating" it. Remind yourself first that harmony and true success are the Divine purpose of your life, that there are no exceptions to this law, therefore this particular difficulty must come under it. That being so, this thing that troubles you cannot be inharmonious or negative, once you know the truth about it. Know, therefore, the truth must be that in some way this difficulty is working out for your good, that beneath its hard and ugly outer shell, there is a kernel of perfect good for you. So bless the good within.

How does the kernel of the black walnut break its tough shell and send up a green shoot that presently grows into a great tree? By heating within! And that is the way you have to break the shell of every difficulty and trial that confronts you—by BLESSING the kernel of good you know to be within it, by praising and loving it until it expands and bursts its shell and springs forth as the fragrant plant of good for you.

Praise, blessing, thanksgiving, LOVE—these will solve any difficulty, tame any shrew of sickness or trouble. Start each day by saying—"This is the day which Jehovah hath made; I will rejoice and be glad in it. I thank God for abundant life, I thank God for enduring love. I thank God for joy, I thank God for glorious health, I thank God for infinite supply. I have awakened to a new day. I join the birds and all created things in glorious praise and thanksgiving. Lord, I do give Thee thanks for the abundance that is mine."

> If I have faltered more or less
> In my great task of happiness;
> If I have moved among my race
> And shown no glorious morning face;
> If beams from happy human eyes
> Have moved me not; if morning skies,
> Books and my food, and summer rain
> Knocked on my sullen heart in vain;
> Lord, Thy most pointed pleasure take
> And stab my spirit broad awake.

—ROBERT LOUIS STEVENSON

EXERCISE FOR CHAPTER THIRTEEN

Remember, in "Vanity Fair," the owner of a fine estate who always carried acorns in his pocket, and when strolling about his grounds, if he came to a vacant spot, he would dig a little hole with his foot and drop an acorn into it. "An acorn costs nothing," he was fond of saying, "but it may spread into a prodigious bit of timber."

The same is true of words of praise, of blessing. They cost nothing, but when planted in the waste places of human consciousness, they become tremendously productive of happiness. As Willa Hoey expressed it—

> It's the little things we do and say
> That mean so much as we go our way.
> A kindly deed can lift a load
> From weary shoulders on the road,
> Or a gentle word, like summer rain,

May soothe some heart and banish pain.
What joy or sadness often springs
From just the simple, little things!

Write it on your heart that each day is the best day of the year. There is no tomorrow, you know; there is no yesterday. There is only the eternal NOW. So make the most of your happiness *now,* while you can.

You create your own environment, so only YOU are to blame if some existing situation seems unhappy. That being so, only YOU can rectify it. You must cure it in your own thought before it can be remedied anywhere else. "Nothing is evil, but thinking makes it so."

Instead of thinking unhappy thoughts, sickly thoughts, thoughts of poverty and lack, talk to the God in You about the good things you want. Start with what you have, and suggest to him each day that you are getting stronger, healthier, richer, happier. Talk to Him as to a rich and loving Father, describing the improvements you see in your affairs, the finer body you have in your mind's eye, the more important work you should be doing, the lovelier home, the richer rewards. Talk them over for ten minutes each day when you are alone with Him. You will be amazed at how readily He will help you to carry out your suggestions.

Don't worry about how He is to bring about the conditions you desire. Just talk to Him confidently, serenely, happily—and then leave the rest to Him. And for your prayers, here is an affirmation used by Unity which has been found unusually effective:

"My Father-God, I place all my dependence in Thee, Thou giver of every good and perfect gift. Thou who art the source of my being art also the source of my supply. All that I shall ever need is in Thy mind for me, prepared for me from the beginning. Omnipresent substance, the garment with which Thou clothest Thy universe, with which Thou nourishest all Thy creation, is also mine to have and to use for my every desire and for the blessing of others of Thy children. I open myself fully through my faith in Thee, through my vision of Thy abundance, through my expectancy of its manifestation for me. I open my hands, my pocketbook, my wardrobe, my business, my bank account, and from Thy rich storehouse Thou dost fill every vessel that I hold out to Thee full to overflowing with Thine own omnipresent good and in Thine own good measure, pressed down, shaken together, running over. I thank Thee, my Father-God, that through the Christ in me I can touch Thine omnipresent substance and all my world be clothed with Thy opulence. I praise and give thanks that now and throughout eternity I am one with Thee and that in this union all Thine is mine and mine is Thine forever and ever."

Throughout this book, we shall give you numbers of affirmations to use for different conditions. Don't try to use them all at once. Use one until it becomes so familiar that you find yourself repeating it too parrotlike. Then change to another. All are helpful. The mere statement—"I am good," "I am strong," "I am capable," is an upbuilding affirmation that tends to start your subconscious trying to bring about that condition in you, just as negative statements such as "I am poor or sick" tend to make those conditions true. So try to remember always to PRAISE God in every thing and every condition that confronts you. Praise Him and look for the Divinity in each.

Praise God that Good is everywhere;
Praise to the Love we all may share—
The Life that thrills in you and me;
Praise to the Truth that sets us free.

14

The Three Laws of Life

For thousands of years, philosophers have wrangled over the problem of why men without scruple or conscience should so often succeed, while good men of equal ability fail. Some tell us it is because the wicked have their innings in this world and will suffer for it through eternity, while we shall have our turn at happiness and plenty then. That is a bit unsatisfying, especially when those near and dear to us are suffering for lack of things we should be able to give them. But for many, it has to suffice.

But not for all! A few have learned that there are definite laws governing success—just as definite and just as certain of results as the laws of Physics.

These basic laws govern everything you do. They rule all of mankind, whether mankind likes it or not. They are unlike man-made laws in that they govern high and low alike. They defer neither to rich nor to poor, to weak nor to powerful—only to those with an understanding heart. It was with them in mind that the wisest of ancient kings bade us seek first understanding, and all things else would be added to us. Summed up, those laws are:

1. *The Law of Averages,* under which man in the mass is no better off than the animals, his chances of happiness and success in life but little better than one in a hundred.
2. *The Law of Tendency,* which is towards Life-GIVING. To the extent that a man allies himself with this great fundamental force of nature, to that extent he improves his chances for success.
3. *The Law of Capillary Attraction,* which gives to every nucleus the power to draw to itself those things necessary for its growth and fulfillment. It is through this third law that man is able to rise above the Law of

Averages. It is by using it with the Law of Tendency that he is able to reach any height, attain any goal.

Under the Law of Averages, man in the mass is subject to alternate feast or famine, happiness or misery—just as the animals are. Nature seems carelessly profligate. She brings forth enough fish to choke the sea—then lets the many die that the few may live. She gives life with a prodigal hand—then seems entirely careless of it, letting the mass suffer or perish so long as the few survive.

To man she has given inexhaustible riches—but the few have most of it while the many toil to serve them.

That is Nature's Law of Averages in the animal kingdom. That is Nature's Law of Averages for man in the mass. But for man the individual she reserves a different fate.

As long as he chooses to be governed by the Law of Averages, man must be content with his one chance in a hundred of prosperity and happiness. But let him separate himself from the mass, and he can choose his own fate.

And the way to separate himself from the mass is—not to journey to some desert or forgotten isle, not to mew himself up in a solitary cell—but to hitch his wagon to the star of some strong purpose, and thereby pull himself out of the mass of self-centered, self-seeking, merely animal humanity, and ally himself with the great fundamental Law of the Universe, which carries all mankind upon its crest.

The word "Man," you know, means steward or distributor. The purpose of man here on earth is to utilize and distribute God's good gifts. To the extent that he cooperates in this purpose, he is allying himself with the forces behind all of nature. To the extent that he looks out only for his own selfish ends, he is opposing it. "I came," said Jesus, "that they might have life, and have it more abundantly." And He demonstrated His mission by giving more of life to all who sought it.

And what is "Life"? Life is energy. Life is power. Life is supply. Life is the creative force out of which the world and everything in it was made in the beginning, and is made now.

As I see Him, God is the Life-Principle which permeates and directs the universe. His "sons" are the individual subconscious minds or Spiritual Selves back of each of us, pouring Life into us, guiding and governing (to the extent we permit them) all the complicated functions of our bodies, all our outward circumstances and conditions.

These "sons" are like vast Genii, possessing all riches, all happiness, all wisdom on their own plane, but forced to reflect those God-like gifts upon the material plane only as we (their mirrors) can understand and express them.

They pour their Life-Energy through us in a continuous stream, like the strips of steel that are fed into stamping machines in a steel mill. Going in, it is potential life, potential power, potential riches. But like the strips of steel, coming out it is only what we have expressed through it—what our stamping machine (our innermost beliefs) has impressed upon it.

Whatever we truly believe, whatever we love and bless and hold constantly in thought as our own, it brings into being in our lives, in our bodies, in our circumstances. Like light shining through a prism it is broken up into its component colors in passing through our conscious minds. But like the prism, our minds can be darkened by fear and worry to shut off all the happier colors. It is a perfect stream of Life-Energy that starts through us, but just as a poorly made die in a stamping machine can cut crude and ugly patterns on the best of steel, just as a faulty prism can turn beams of sunshine into shadows, so can your beliefs turn perfect Life-Energy into manifestations of sickness and poverty and misery. God does not inflict them upon you—you do.

The first essential, then, is to change the pattern—to watch your beliefs as the Director of the U. S. Mint watches the molds which cast the coins he turns out. Instead of picturing the things you FEAR, and thus stamping their mold upon the Life-Energy passing through you, picture the conditions you WANT. "What things soever ye ask for when ye pray," said Jesus, "believe that ye RE-CEIVE them, and ye shall HAVE them!"

What do YOU want? Know that your spiritual self HAS it. Like the perfect flower in the tiny unopened bud, it is all there, needing only the sunshine of your faith to bring it forth.

You have seen trees in the winter, all the twigs bare, with no sign of the brilliant foliage soon to spring from them. Yet the leaves are already there, perfectly formed, waiting only for the warm sunshine to bring them out. In the same way, the things YOU want are already around you, no matter how bare everything may look. They need only the sunshine of your faith to bring them forth.

That is the first step, *to have faith!* That is the pattern which molds all your circumstances—*your beliefs.* Get that pattern right. It is there that unscrupulous men get ahead of their less understanding brethren. Knowingly or unknowingly, they have hit upon the fact that the first essential of material success is to believe in themselves, believe that the world belongs to them, believe that it *owes* them a living. They may not knowingly BLESS the things they want, but they LOVE them, long for them, put them above everything else in life, and since God is love, it sometimes seems that we have only to love a thing greatly to get it.

To that extent, they are right. Their trouble is that they do not bother to look around for right sources from which to draw their supply. They take whatever is not nailed down, and sooner or later they run afoul of the Law of Tendency and end in ruin.

This Law of Tendency is our next step, for it *requires co-operation* with the Life-Giving forces of the universe—*swimming with the tide.*

The Law of Tendency is based upon the fact that the whole purpose of Life is growth. The forces of nature are Life-GIVING forces. Its fundamental trends are towards the advancement of life, the good of the world. Those businesses and those individuals whose work is in line with that tendency are swept forward by the great tide of good. Those whose work tends to hinder the forward movement of life are sooner or later brushed aside and cast upon the rocks.

Ella Wheeler Wilcox expressed the thought beautifully when she wrote—

The world has a thousand creeds, and never a one have I, Nor church of my own, though a million spires are pointing the way on high.

But I float on the bosom of faith, that bears me along like a river:

And the lamp of my soul is alight with love, for life, and the world and the Giver.

"But," I can hear you say, "I know many worthy men whose efforts were always for good, yet who are hopeless failures." True—but so do I know many swimmers who cannot keep afloat a hundred yards, even with the strongest tide behind them. The tide is the second step. The first step is to get your pattern right—in other words, learn how to swim. And having the tide with you makes that first step none the less necessary.

Believe in yourself. Look upon yourself as one of the Lords of the Universe. Know that it belongs to you. BELIEVE THAT YOU *HAVE* the things you want. Love them. Bless them. Thank God for them, even before they seem to manifest. "Lord, I do give Thee thanks for the abundance that is mine."

That is the first essential. The second is to USE your powers for good—*get on the side of the Life-GIVING forces.*

"Sounds well," perhaps you will say, "but I'd like you to tell me how I am going to use riches for good, when my principal reason for taking this course is to learn how to GET riches to keep the wolf from my own door!"

The first essential in the creation of anything—be it a house or an automobile or a fortune—is the mental picture or image. Before God made man, He "imaged" him—He formed a mental picture of him. Then He poured His Life-Energy into that image, and it became man. Before an architect builds a house, he draws a mental picture of it, he "images" it upon paper. Then he pours materials and energy into that image and it becomes a house. Before you can build a fortune, you must form it in your mind's eye. You must "image" it on the mental plane, and in that mental image you must think of it as already yours. In other words, "believe that you HAVE it!" An easy way to do this is the "Treasure Mapping" outlined in Chapter 10.

One of the startling facts of modern science is that this universe is not a finished product. Creation is going on all around us—new worlds being formed, cosmic energy taking shape in a million different molds.

But a far more startling fact to most of us is that WE ARE CREATORS, and that we can form today the world we personally shall be living in tomorrow.

People blame their environment, their education, their opportunities, their luck, for their condition. They are wrong. There is one person to blame—and only one—THEMSELVES. They are today the result of their thoughts of yesterday and the many yesterdays that preceded it. They are forming today the mold for what they will be in the years to come.

For there is no such thing as failure. Whether you are poor and sickly, or rich and strong, you have succeeded in one thing. You have compressed the cosmic energy about you into the mold that you held before the mind's eye of your inner self. You have named the forces that worked with you "good" or "bad," and as you named them, so have they been to you as servants—Good, or Evil.

But there is a happy ending. You don't need to leave things as they are. If you don't like the present results you can rename those servants. You can bless and praise the good, no matter how tiny it may seem, and by your praise and blessing, you can expand it a thousand-fold.

Which brings us to the third step—"The Law of Capillary Attraction."

Plant a seed of corn in the ground, and it will attract to itself from the earth and the water and the air everything it needs for its growth. Plant the seed of a desire in your mind and it forms a nucleus with power to attract to itself everything needed for its fulfillment. But just as the seed of corn needs sunshine and air and water from which to draw the energies necessary to bring forth the perfect ear, so does your seed of desire need the sunshine of a perfect faith, the fruitful soil of a will-power held steadfast to the one purpose.

This is the Alpha and Omega of all accomplishment—that every seed has in it the perfect plant, that every right desire has in it the perfect fulfillment, for Desire is God's opportunity knocking at your door. The seed must be planted, it must have nourishment and sunshine. The desire must be definitely planted by the work of starting the initial step in its accomplishment, it must be nourished by a will-power which holds it to its purpose, and it must have the warm sunshine of perfect faith. Given these, it will attract to itself whatever else is necessary to its fulfillment.

You see, the Law of Capillary Attraction is based upon the principle of growth from the vitality inherent in the seed or idea itself. It is like a snowball which starts with only a handful of snow, yet by gathering to itself all it comes in contact with, ends as an avalanche!

First the seed, the desire. Next, the planting—the initial step necessary to start its accomplishment. Third, the cultivation—the continual working towards the one end. You can't just WILL a thing into existence, you know. But you can use the will as the machinist uses a vise—to hold the tool of your purpose until it accomplishes its end. Fourth, the sunshine—FAITH—without which all the others are as nothing. Without sunshine, the seed will rot in the ground, the plant will wither on the stalk. Without faith, your desire will die still-born. Believe that you RECEIVE. See the perfect plant in the seed. See the perfect accomplishment in the desire.

Prof. Wm. James of Harvard, the greatest psychologist this country has known, wrote—"If you only care enough for a result, you will almost certainly attain it. If you wish to be rich, you will be rich; if you wish to be learned, you will be learned; if you wish to be good, you will be good. Only you must, then, really wish these things, and wish them exclusively, and not wish at the same time a hundred other incompatible things just as strongly."

But be careful that your desire tends towards Life-GIVING, towards the furtherance of Good. You can't make much of a snowball pushing up hill. If you do, it will presently grow bigger than you, get beyond your control, and engulf you in the resultant catastrophe. The fruit you bring forth is going to partake of the same nature as the seed you plant. If there is no kindliness in the seed, no love of your fellow-man, nothing but self-gratification, the fruit of your tree will be the same kind. It will be bitter to others—it will turn bitter in your own mouth.

Now how does this apply to you? There are certain things you want from life—Success, Riches, Fame, Honor, Love, Happiness, Health, Strength. All of these are worthy desires. All of them are entirely possible of fulfillment for you. How are you to go about getting them?

Your job here on earth is to distribute certain God-given gifts—certain goods, certain services, certain abilities—to the end that the world may be more livable for your having been in it.

In ancient Egypt, it was believed that each person was given at birth a "Ka" or "Double," which was his REAL SELF. It had infinite power for good. The body was merely its reflection, seen through the glass of the conscious mind.

So it is with you. Your REAL Self is God's image of you—the God in You. He gave it dominion over all the earth. Can you imagine it, then, as powerless under any circumstances, as poverty-stricken, as in doubt where its supply is coming from?

If you believe in God at all, you must believe in His intelligence. And if He is intelligent, He made nothing without a purpose. Everything fits into His plan. YOU, for instance—He created you for the purpose of performing certain work. That being so, it would seem pretty certain that He gave you every ability, every means necessary for the perfect performance of that work, would it not?

But how are you to know what that work is? Easily enough, if you stop to analyze your ambitions and desires. They are your subconscious promptings. Not, of course, the merely selfish desires for the gratification of some personal vanity or passion. But the big, deep down ambitions that come to you in exalted moments. They are the promptings of The God in You, urging you to EXPRESS on the material plane the work he is already doing in the mental realm.

You have an idea, let us say, which will short-cut the work of the world, make life easier and happier for any number of its inhabitants. You take whatever steps seem good to you to accomplish that idea. But you presently reach a point where lack of money or lack of knowledge or other circumstances leave you high and dry—seemingly at your rope's end. What are you to do then?

PRAY! And how are you to pray? Jesus gave us the formula—"Whatsoever things ye ask for when ye pray, believe that ye RECEIVE them, and ye shall HAVE them."

But how can you believe that you HAVE when you are at the end of your resources and there is no possible way out in sight? How? By knowing that The God in You, your REAL SELF, already HAS the answer in the realm of the REAL. By seeing the finished result there, imaging it in your mind's eye, and then putting it up to that God in You to show you the next step necessary to reflect that result on the material plane, in the serene confidence that, since he has worked out the answer, the EXPRESSION of it step by step through you is simple.

Tell yourself—and KNOW—you ARE rich, you ARE successful, you ARE well and happy and possessed of every good thing you desire. Use your "Treasure Map" to picture these things—then believe that you HAVE them.

No matter how limited your education, no matter how straitened your circumstances, the God in You HAS the knowledge and the means and the power to accomplish any right thing you may desire. Give him a job—and it is DONE! You HAVE it! And you have only to see that finished result in your mind's eye—"BELIEVE THAT YOU RECEIVE"—in order to begin to reflect it on the material plane.

Therein lies the nucleus of every success—the nucleus which has such life that it draws to itself everything it needs for its full expression—*the belief that you HAVE*. It is the secret of power, the Talisman of Napoleon. To acquire it takes just three things.

1. Know that this is a world of Intelligence. Nothing merely happens. You were put here for a purpose, and you were given every qualification and every means necessary to the accomplishment of that purpose. So you need never fear whether you are big enough, or smart enough, or rich enough to do the things required of you. "The Father knoweth that ye have need of these things," so do the things that are given you to do in the serene knowledge that your needs will be met.

2. Know that The God in You which is your REAL Self is already DOING this work you were given to do, so all that is required of you is to SEE that accomplished result, and REFLECT it step by step on the material plane, as the way is opened to you. "And thine ears shall hear a word behind thee, saying—This is the way. Walk ye in it."

3. Have serene faith in your God's ability to express the finished results through you. When you can SEE that result in your mind's eye as already accomplished, you will realize that you don't need to fear or worry or rush in and do things foolishly. You can go serenely ahead and do the

things that are indicated for you to do. When you seem to reach a cul-de-sac, you can wait patiently, leaving the problem to The God in You in the confident knowledge that at the right time and in the right way He will give you a "lead" showing what you are to do.

The fundamental Law of the Universe, you remember, is the Law of Attraction. You attract to you whatever you truly love and bless and believe is YOURS.

Knowing that The God in You has the fruition of your desire—knowing that the perfect leaf is in the bare twig of your present circumstances—it is easy to pour such life, love and blessings into that leaf that it bursts its bonds and blossoms forth for all to see.

So, like the Egyptians of old, let us commune with The God in Us night and morn, much as our reflection in the mirror might commune with us:

Reality of me, I greet you and salute you the perfect "me" God created. You have a perfect body, made in the image and likeness of God. Make that perfect body manifest in me. You have infinite riches—dominion over all things. Use that dominion, I pray you, to uncover and bring out in my life, my work and my surroundings the perfect reflection of (whatever your particular desire may be).

Then SEE, in your mind's eye, The God in You doing those things you wish to do, emphasizing the traits you wish to cultivate, displaying the riches or possessions you want. Know that he HAS these. And that as soon as you can SEE them through the prism of your conscious mind, as fast as you can *realize* their possession, *you, too, will reflect them for all the world to see!*

OUR PRAYERS ARE ANSWERED
by Bonnie Day

Our prayers are answered: each unspoken thought
And each desire implanted in the mind
Bears its own harvest, after its own kind;
Who dreams of beauty has already caught
The flash of angel wings. Who seeks to find
True wisdom shall assuredly be taught.
But thorns of fate have thorny thoughts behind;

For out of our own hearts our lives are wrought.
Be on thy guard, my soul, lest wind-blown seed
Into the fertile soil of thought should fall
And lodging place within the garden wall
Be given to bitter rue or noxious weed.
Unspoken prayers bear fruitage. Love thoughts call
Forth into being every loving deed.
Idle or earnest, still our prayers are all
Answered according to our inward creed.

15

A Prayer for Work

Lord give me work. All work is Thine.
Help me to make Thy business mine.
Give me my part, and let me share
Thy joy in making life more fair;
My part, and with the part the will
To make my life Thy plan fulfill.
Thus every day, Lord, help me see
My simplest task as done for Thee.

—ESTHER ANN CLARK

All day long and every day, the God in You keeps repeating—"I AM." But He lets YOU end the sentence. You can add "poor" or "rich," "sad" or "happy," "sick" or "well," as YOU choose. God can do for you only what you ALLOW Him to do THROUGH you. You praise and bless Him, only when you see the good and true and beautiful. You dishonor Him when you call yourself weak or sick or poor.

So claim the good! Praise God for it, thank Him and bless Him for all His good gifts.

If you are out of work at the moment, know that the Spirit of the Lord is upon you, directing you to your right work. The Spirit of God goes before you to make plain your way. It works through you to make you efficient, successful, prosperous and of real worth to your employer and associates.

Know this—and then open your channels! Give of what you have of service to others. Start where you are. Distant fields always look greener, but opportunity lies right where you are. Take advantage of every opportunity of service, even if it be only to wash dishes or do chores around your own home. Show God that you are a channel for good NOW. The more you can prove that, the greater will be your opportunities, and soon those opportunities will take the form of just the right job for you.

Each night and morning, and whenever the need for a job occurs to you, repeat this affirmation:

"God in me knows what my right work is, where it is and what I ought to do to be actually engaged in it. Let this knowledge be quickened in me as a revelation to my conscious mind so I shall know what is my right work, where it is and what there is for me to do to be established in it."

Remember it is from within, and not from without, that you get in touch with all of Good. Every ill, every lack, every discordant condition, must be cured in your own thought first. It is like a radio. The programs of all the world are in the air about you, but you have to tune in on the one you want. When you turn on the radio, the program that comes to you may be some sordid tale of crime or unhappiness, or it may be merely static noises. If so, that is all you will get—until you turn the dial. But you CAN get the program you want, if you keep turning away from the others and persistently try until you find the one you want.

But you must both affirm and ACT the part. To affirm prosperity and then act like a pauper with what substance you have is to show that you do not believe your own affirmation and do not expect anything from it. It doesn't matter if you have to force yourself to take some appropriate action. Take it—and thereby increase your faith.

Every affirmation should be matched by some action expressing the faith that you HAVE received or ARE receiving, action of the sort you would engage in if the affirmed good were visibly and tangibly present.

That doesn't mean you must spend a lot of money recklessly, buy a lot of things such as you will when you have the riches you crave. It does mean you must take the mental attitude of BEING rich, HAVING the right sort of job, sprucing up, being confident and serene and unworried.

You can help others get the sort of place they want in the same way you can yourself. Here is an affirmation to use for others:

Infinite Spirit, open the way for So-and-so's right position (or home or abundance or what-not), the position he is best fitted to fill, the position that needs him and which no one else can fill so well as he. Let him be led to the right people, the right place where he can give good service for good pay. Lead him to make the right contacts. I leave it with you, and I know all is well.

In a recent issue of "Nautilus" magazine, Dortch Campbell tells how he prayed for a home—and found the one he had always dreamed of.

"The whole secret," he says, "lies in that beautiful thing called love. I prayed for a home. Every element in the answer that came was in accord with justice. The quality of love was not strained.

A house that you can call your own home is not so easy to obtain these days. For me it was most difficult. Conditions have been serious in the Mississippi Valley for nearly a decade; the cotton problem has become acute. But the house where I had lived for a long time was taken away from me. I was homeless; there was no other available, for people have not been building houses in my country.

I had to build my own home to find a roof for myself and my loved ones. But there was no mortal way to build that home. I had not sufficient money to buy even a lot. Yet the home of my own became a reality in answer to my prayers as simply and as unostentatiously as a rose unfolds.

I felt that we are far too selfish in our prayers, so I prayed for others when I prayed for myself. I asked that the contractor who should build my home should be blessed through me. I prayed for the owner of the land. I prayed for a harmonious association with the contractor. I asked that there be love and friendship between us and between all who might be associated in the undertaking. I prayed that he might find a way to finance my home and that I in turn should help him to succeed. I prayed for others as earnestly as I prayed for myself. I prayed for the landowners that they, through me, might sell other lots.

I prayed in this fashion, loving them that they in turn might love me. Deep within me, I desired that all of us might equally profit in the building of my home. This was all. There was no domination on my part, no attempt to influence or control them, no direct thought to them.

Step by step, that home came about. I obtained the lot for a very small outlay—a lot worth three times what I paid. The contractor himself actually gave me the money I required. The home became mine in such a gentle fashion that I, accustomed to prayer, stand amazed. Things—for example—like a driveway, were contributed free.

But it was not only I who was helped, and this to me is the most beautiful part of the answer to that prayer. It has been my privilege since the house was constructed to help those who helped me in getting my home. More lots have been sold, more will be sold. The contractor has closed several contracts as a result of building my home.

What we need is to be not only hearers but DO-ERS of the Word. We find Truth by trying to live it. Since God is love, it may be that we have only to love a thing greatly to get it. Can it be that the long-lost key to attainment through prayer is in feeling the loving power of God within to give us that which the heart desires?

If I can do some good today,
If I can serve along life's way,
If I can something helpful say,
Lord, show me how.

If I can right a human wrong,
If I can help to make one strong,
If I can cheer with smile or song,
Lord, show me how.

If I can make a burden less,
If I can aid one in distress,
If I can spread more happiness,
Lord, show me how.

If I can do a kindly deed,
If I can sow a fruitful seed,
If I can help someone in need,
Lord, show me how.

If I can feed a hungry heart,
If I can give a better start,
If I can fill a nobler part,
Lord, show me how.

—GRENVILLE KLEISER

16

First Causes

How can I tell if I am working a-right?"—many students ask us.

And "How can I be sure I am following correct lines?"—is the question in the mind of many a man and woman when confronted by some unusual problem.

In his Edinburgh Lectures, Judge Troward gave so clear an answer to this question that I quote it here:

If we regard the fulfillment of our purpose as contingent upon any circumstances, *past, present, or future, we are not making use of First Cause. We have descended to the level of* Secondary Causation, *which is the region of doubts, fears and limitations.*

What is First Cause? Judge Troward defined it, too.

If a lighted candle is brought into a room, the room becomes illuminated; if the candle is taken away, it becomes dark again. Now the illumination and the darkness are both conditions, the one positive resulting from the presence of the light, the other negative resulting from its absence. From this simple example we therefore see that every positive condition has an exactly opposite negative condition corresponding to it, and that this correspondence results from their being related to the same cause, the one positively and the other negatively; and hence we may lay down the rule that all positive conditions result from the active presence of a certain cause, and all negative conditions from the absence of such a cause. A condition, whether positive or negative, is never primary cause, and the primary cause

*of any series can never be negative, for negation is the condition which
arises from the absence of active causation.*

How can you be sure that you are working a-right? By asking yourself one
question: "On what am I putting my dependence for the riches, or the health,
or the success I am seeking?" If the answer is—"Upon my ability, or my doctor, or his drugs, or the help of my friends," then you can rate your chances of
success as not more than one in ten, for you are working with secondary causes,
and secondary causes are always undependable.

But if your answer is—"I am throwing everything I have into my work, but
I am putting my dependence for success—NOT on these *means*—but on the
unquenchable, irresistible power of the Seed of Life working through me," why
then you can count your chances of success as nine out of ten.

You see, it all comes back to the Fundamental Law of the Universe—that
each nucleus, each seed, contains within itself vitality enough to draw to it
every element it needs for its complete growth and fruition.

But the seed must germinate, the nucleus must start whirling, before either
has the slightest attractive power. Until they do that, they are so much congealed life, with no more "pull" to them than any other bit of inanimate matter
around them.

Suppose you want something badly—more than anything else life can offer
you at the moment. The desire for that something forms a nucleus, a seed, and
like every other seed, it has latent in it the power to draw to itself the elements
necessary for its complete growth and fruition. But until you *do* something
about it, it is an inanimate nucleus, a seed that has not been planted, a nucleus
with no power of attraction because no one has taken the trouble to start it
whirling.

How can you put it to work? By PLANTING your seed—in other words,
by making your start. What is the first thing you would do if you KNEW you
would get your desire? What is the first step you would take in its accomplishment? TAKE IT! Do something to start, no matter on how small a scale. To
begin, you know, is to be half done. Make the accomplishment of that desire
the *sine qua non* of your existence, give to it all the thought and energy and
riches you have to bring it into being, leave all other considerations in second
place until you have won what you want.

That is the way great fortunes are made. That is the way miracles are performed. That is the only way you can put life into the nucleus of your desires

and start them whirling and drawing to you whatever things you need for their manifestation.

Conditions, obstacles—they don't matter. Disclaim them, disregard them, and lay claim to the thing you want regardless of conditions. Like the seed in rocky soil, they may force your nucleus to work harder, to whirl faster, but give it vitality enough, and it will draw what it needs from the ends of the earth!

So don't work on poverty. Don't work on debts. That will merely bring more of these undesirables to you. Work on your idea, work on your nucleus—*believe that you receive*—and you will speedily draw to you all the riches you need to fill out the vacuums now caused by poverty and debts.

You have seen shoots of trees spring up on rocky ledges where there was scarcely enough nourishment to keep a bit of moss alive. And you have known such shoots to grow into mighty trees. How do they do it?

The seed of a tree is a nucleus. Plant it, and the first thing it does after it heats and germinates is to burst its shell and send forth a shoot—*upward*—using for that purpose the energy latent in the seed itself. In other words, it reaches out first to express life. It uses all the power it has to bring forth fruit. When it finds it has not enough energy in itself to accomplish this, it puts forth roots to draw the necessary elements from the soil about.

But if it happens to have fallen on a rocky ledge, it soon finds there is not enough soil to give it moisture or nourishment. Does it then despair? Not a bit of it! It sends its roots into every tiny crevice until they reach moisture and nourishment. It actually splits giant rocks asunder in its search for nutriment. It burrows through or around any obstacle until it exhausts the last flicker of life in itself or gets what it wants. Wherever they are, whatsoever may stand between, the shoot of the tree sends its roots seeking every element it needs for its growth and fruition.

First the stalk—then the roots. First the need—then the means to satisfy that need. First the nucleus—then the elements needed for its growth. The seed is a primary cause. The need, the nucleus, both are primary causes. Conditions—they are secondary. Given enough life in the nucleus, it will draw to itself the necessary means for growth regardless of conditions. The life in the seed is what counts—not the place where it falls.

All through Nature, you will find that same law. First the need, then the means. Use what you have to provide the vacuum, then draw upon the necessary elements to fill it. Reach up with your stalk, spread out your branches, provide the "pull" and you can leave to your roots the search for the necessary nourishment. If you have reached high enough, if you have made your magnet strong enough, you can draw to yourself whatever elements you need, no matter if they be at the ends of the earth!

God formed a Seed of Life which is you. He gave it power to attract to itself everything it needs for its growth, just as He did with the seed of the tree. He gave it power to draw to itself everything it needs for the fruition of its DESIRES, just as He did with the tree. But He did even more for you. He gave your Seed of Life power to attract to itself everything it needs for its *infinite expression!* He asks of you only that you make your desires strong enough, your faith in their drawing power great enough, to attract to you anything necessary to their fruition.

You see, Life is intelligent. Life is all-powerful. And Life is always and everywhere seeking expression. What is more, it is never satisfied. It is constantly seeking greater and fuller expression. The moment a tree stops growing, that moment the life in it starts seeking elsewhere for means to better express itself. The moment you stop expressing more and more of Life, that moment Life starts looking around for other and better outlets.

The only thing that can restrict Life is the channel through which it works. The only limitation upon it is the limitation you put upon it.

Over in Japan, they have taken the shoots of oak trees, and by binding a wire tightly around the main root at the point where the trunk begins, they have stunted the growth to such an extent that instead of great oaks eighty or a hundred feet high, these shoots reproduce all their qualities in dwarfed trees twelve or fourteen inches in height! These stunted trees live as long as regular trees, but they express only the millionth part of the life an oak should manifest.

We look upon that as abnormal, and so it is, yet it is being done all around us every day. Men bind their subconscious minds with wires of fear and worry. They put clamps of limitation upon their channels of supply. Then they wonder why they don't express more life in their bodies, why more of happiness and comfort is not evidenced in their surroundings.

God put a seed of Himself into you. That seed He called DESIRE. He gave it infinite power to draw to itself whatever it needs for expression. But He gave you free will—in other words, He left it with you to direct that expression—to draw upon it to the full or to put clamps upon it, as you like.

There lies in you the aegis of a Napoleon, a Lincoln, an Edison—anything you wish. All that is necessary is to stir up the Seed of God in you, and give it channels for expression. You can be what you want to be, if you want it strongly enough, if you believe in it firmly enough to make it your dominant desire.

How did Annette Kellerman, from a hopelessly crippled child, become one of the world's most perfectly formed women? By stirring up the Seed of Life in her limbs, through her earnest DESIRE for strength and beauty, by giving them work to do, ways in which to express life! How did George Jowett, from a cripple at eleven, become the world's strong man at twenty-one? By stirring up the Seed of Life in him through his overmastering DESIRE to be strong—by giving his muscles first a little, then more and more of work to do.

How did Reza Khan, from an ordinary trooper in the Persian army, rise to the rulership of Persia? How did a water boy win the throne of Afghanistan?

One and all, they stirred up the Seed of Life in them through DESIRE and Faith. One and all, they reached up and out, using freely all the power they had in the serene confidence that there was plenty more behind. Obstacles? They knew that obstacles were merely negative conditions that would disappear as darkness disappears when you turn on the light. It was the *prize* they kept their eyes upon. And it was the *prize* that they reached out for and plucked!

A few years ago, if anyone had told the neighbors of these men that today they would be rulers, he would have been laughed at as crazy. "Why, just look at their position," he would have been told. "Look at their circumstances, their surroundings. Look at the condition of the country. Consider their lack of training, of experience."

Conditions—all of them. Secondary causes. And these men had the vision to see beyond them—to go back to the *primary cause*—the Seed of God in themselves. They opened new channels for it to express itself. They reached up their stalks and spread out their branches and the Seed of Life in them drew to itself every element needed to bring forth their fruit.

At the heart of you is a seed—the Seed of God, the Seed of Life. In it is a perfect body, just as in every acorn there is a perfect oak. Not only that, but there is the power in it to draw to you every element you need to manifest a perfect body.

What do you care if circumstances have conspired to make you sick, or crippled or weak or infirm or ugly or old? If you are, it is because you or those around you have put the clamps of your fears or wrong beliefs upon the Seed of Life in you, and certain of your organs are stunted or dying.

The remedy? It is simple. Remove the clamps! Disregard your infirmity? It is only a condition—a LACK of Life. Then stir up the Seed of Life in you. Stir it up and charge it to draw to itself every element necessary to fill out the perfect image of your body that is in the seed.

Impossible? Have you ever heard of anything that is impossible to God? It is a Seed of God that is in you, and there is NOTHING of good it cannot draw to you!

The Law is—Use what you have, and more will be given you.

> *Let me not ask how difficult may be*
> *The work assigned to me.*
> *This only do I ask:*
> *Is this my task?*
>
> *Let me not ask if I be strong enough,*
> *Or if the road be rough.*
> *I only ask today,*
> *Is this the way?*

—CLAUDE WEIMER

"Every good tree bringeth forth good fruit," said Jesus. "But a corrupt tree bringeth forth evil fruit. Every tree that bringeth not forth good fruit is hewn down and cast into the fire. Wherefore by their fruits ye shall know them."

What did Jesus mean by "Bearing fruit"? Didn't He have in mind methods of expressing the Seed of Life in you, making opportunities for it to expand and reach out to all those you come in contact with, doing something that makes this world a better place to live in?

And how does a tree go about the bearing of fruit? It brings forth a fragrant blossom first, does it not? When the blossom goes, it leaves the pistil, which gradually ripens into the luscious fruit.

The blossom is any idea of service, any means for making life more comfortable or enjoyable for those you live or deal with. The pistil is the action of turning that blossom into the beginning of the fruit by taking the first step to start the service, no matter how small that step may be. The luscious fruit is the finished service.

"That's fine!" I can hear many say, "I have the blossom—oh, a most fragrant blossom—but no means for turning it into the pistil or the fruit."

What does the branch have with which to start fruit? Enough nourishment for a start, but nothing over. Do you see the branch worrying on that account? Not a bit of it! It uses cheerfully everything it has, serene in the knowledge that providing more is the vine's problem. The branch has only to supply the *need*. The more it finds use for, the more it gets. Another branch may be just as big, but if the first one bears twice as much fruit, it will get twice as much nourishment, for the vine apportions its life-giving forces—not by size, but by needs. Wasn't it Jesus who said—"I am the vine, ye are the branches." Can you draw on Him for more than He can provide?

"Straight from a mighty bow this truth is driven: They fail, and they alone, who have not striven." They have a proverb in the East that a road of a thousand miles begins with a single step. Goethe expressed the thought when he wrote—

Are you in earnest? Seize this very minute;
What you can do, or dream you can, BEGIN it!
Boldness has genius, power and magic in it.
Only engage, and then the mind grows heated;
BEGIN, and then the work will be completed.

"If ye abide in me," promised the Master, "and my words abide in you, ye shall *ask what ye will*, and it shall be done unto you. For herein is my Father glorified, that ye bear much fruit."

If you stir up the Seed of Life in you by strong DESIRES, if you provide it channels through which to express itself by taking the first step towards the accomplishment of those desires, you can ask for any element you need, and it will be given you.

But if you lose this day loitering, it will be the same story tomorrow and the day after. That which you are today is the fulfillment of yesterday's aspirations; that which you are tomorrow will be the achievement of today's vision. You can't stand still. You must go forward—or backward. Eternal progress is the Law of Being. If you meet its call, you will never fail to go on and on to greater and greater heights. As Florence Taylor so aptly put it—

Success is the sum of small efforts,
Repeated day in and day out,
With never a thought of frustration,
With never a moment of doubt.
Whatever your cherished ambition,

Begin now to make it come true,
Through efforts, repeated, untiring,
Plus faith in the thing that you do.

Health, riches, love—they are all *means* to an end, they are all conditions. The Seed of Life in you is the only thing that counts—that, and the channels you give it for expression. There is your PRIMARY CAUSE—all else is secondary. So disregard all else, and keep going back to it.

Do you want love? The mere desire is a proof of the availability of the love you want, for someone has rightly defined desire as God tapping at your door with His infinite supply. So plant the seeds of love by giving it to all you come in contact with. Plant the seeds freely, serenely, believingly, and the harvest is as sure as when you plant seeds of wheat in fertile ground.

Make it a practice to appreciate things and people. Use it all through the day whenever anything occurs that pleases you. Say silently, if you cannot do so audibly, "I appreciate you." And never miss an opportunity to say a kindly word of praise or thanks to those around you. As Amy Bower puts it—

We never know
How far kind words may go.
There is no way to measure
Friendly smiles. They carry treasures
Of courage, faith and love of man.
And we may watch them grow
Until their warmth
Infolds a multitude; returns to bless
The giver too with bread of happiness.

A good affirmation to use is—"I so love that I see all good and give all good, and all good comes back to me."

Do you want riches? Wealth is largely a matter of consciousness. Many persons who want money, and who are striving for money, actually tend toward driving it away from them by reason of their tenseness of thought and their failure to realize the "money consciousness." In order to handle millions, one must learn to think in the terms and ideas of millions. Harriman once expressed this pregnant truth when he said: "It is just as easy to think and to talk in millions as in single dollars." This wizard of finance, whose feats were regarded by the public as closely approaching those of legerdemain, made this adage one of his cardinal principles of thought and action. He "thought and talked in millions," and his thought took form in action—his mental states took on material form—his ideals became realities.

There are many men in this country—in every city in this country—who have within them the germ-powers which, if allowed to develop and grow, would cause these men to become second Harrimans, or second Morgans, or even second Rockefellers. But practically none of these persons ever will really develop into this stage; in fact, the probability is that they will evolve merely into successful small shopkeepers, small news-stand keepers, or even small peanut-stand men—successful, in each case, but always on a small scale. They are content to think in single dollars—even in dimes—instead of thinking in millions. They manifest realities in the direct ratio of their ideals. Their thought takes form in actions of like calibre. Their mental states are reproduced in material form, but they are the same size in both subjective pattern and objective form.

Just where thou art, shine forth and glow;
Just where thou art, 'tis better so;
Serve thou the Lord with perfect heart,
Not somewhere else, but where thou art.

Emerson had a saying that you could travel the world over in search of beauty, but unless you had it within yourself, you would never find it, and the same is true of every good thing of life. The first step to success lies right where you are and in what you are doing. Until you have learned the lesson your present work holds for you, until you have learned to do it joyfully, lovingly, as to the Lord, you have not taken that first step towards the goal of your ambitions. You have not really begun.

Supply is an active force. It goes only to those who are alive, who are providing so many and such powerful magnets for it that they can "pull" it to themselves regardless of what obstacles may come between.

But suppose it is health you want? Suppose you are crippled or blind or bedridden. What then?

Why, then your remedy lies in breaking up the congealed life in your afflicted organ, and pouring it anew into the perfect mold.

And the way to break it up is by giving all you have of life to that one desire, by working up so intense a FEELING that it shall presently burst its shell and draw to it every element it needs for its perfect expression.

You can't do that by dabbling in mental work, while you are depending partly upon drugs, partly upon other means. You must FEEL so strongly that your salvation lies in the Seed of God within you, you must BELIEVE so utterly in its power, that you are willing to sink or swim by it alone. Like Grant, you must have the grim determination to "fight it out along those lines, if it takes all summer!"

But it will not take "all summer." Once you get the spirit of it, you will find it by far the speediest and surest method there is. Often your relief will be immediate.

A writer in "Unity" tells of a friend who was suffering from a physical inharmony that threatened to become malignant, when all at once the thought came to her—"If God can't heal me, what can *this* do?" "This" referred to the drugs she was taking. Immediately she applied a cleansing substance to the troublous part, threw away the drugs and from that day had no further trouble.

In THE FORUM, recently, Winifred Rhoades told of an amusing happening in India. It seems that a pack animal slipped at a ferry in India some years ago, and a case of medicines was spilled. The colored pills were picked up and returned to their appropriate bottles, but with the white pills it was impossible to tell one kind from another. However, a young native gathered them up, and in spite of the missionary doctor's warning of the danger of using them ignorantly, he promptly made them the foundation of a widespread reputation.

When the missionary next appeared in that region, the young native greeted him with joy. "I owe all my prosperity to you!" he exclaimed. It seems that the bottle containing the assorted white pills he had picked up was the favorite in his shop. Patients came from far and near to get them. And in answer to the horrified doctor's question as to how he could administer them if he didn't know what they were meant for, he announced that he gave them to patients only when he didn't know what was the matter with them.

Dr. Richard C. Cabot of Harvard told a gathering of his fellow-medicos— "The body has a super wisdom and force which are biased in favor of life rather than death. What is this force? It is God, the healing power which supplies 90 percent of recovery." And on another occasion, he said—"If nature, assisted by the proper mental and emotional moods, is capable of curing an ulcer in three or four weeks, why isn't it possible for the same force to heal the same ulcer in three or four minutes, when the curative processes have been speeded up abnormally by the subject's passing through an intense religious *(emotional)* experience?" In "Man, the Unknown," Dr. Alexis Carrel told of having actually seen a cancerous growth on a man's hand cured in a few minutes.

You see, underneath all its seeming hardness, life is really a kindly force. Life is love. It is supply. It is health. It has in it every element we need to satisfy any right desire. So there is no need to look to this man, or that drug, or some outside agency, for the things you need. Go to the Primary Cause. Go to Life. Go to God!

"There is a time in every man's education," said Emerson, "when he arrives at the conviction that he must take *himself* for better or for worse *as his portion; that* though the wide universe is full of good, no kernel of nourishing corn can come to him but through his toil on that plot of ground given to him to till.

"The power which resides in him is new in nature, and none but he knows what he can do. *Nor does he know until he has tried."*

"You are sick," they said, "But that isn't the truth"—
And the woman shook her head.
"The Bible declares, he that dwelleth in God
Shall not say, I am sick," she said.
And she held to the truth through a starless night,
Till morning proved that her words were right.

"You are tired," they said. But she smiled at that.
"How can I be tired," said she,
"When the only work is work for God,
And He is my life, you see?"
And she quietly went her busy way,
With a happy song in her heart all day.

"You are poor," they said. But she only thought,
"How little they know! God speed
The day when the world awakes to find
That love is its only need."
And she still maintained, as her fortune grew,
Not money but love—if they only knew!

For the world knows not of the peace that comes
To a soul at one with God.
It is only those who are toiling on
In the path the Master trod
Who can feel, through the dark, that loving hand,
And holding it fast, can understand.

What was it that made Napoleon Master of most of Europe? Not native genius. Not brilliant intellect. In his class at the Military Academy, he stood forty-sixth—and there were only sixty-five in the class!

The genius that made Napoleon was first his intense DESIRE for power, and then *his colossal belief in his own destiny!* He had no fear in battle, because he believed the bullet was not made that could kill him. He had no hesitation in attempting the seemingly impossible, because he believed the very stars in their courses would stoop to sweep the obstacles from his path.

You see, the secret of success lies in this: There is inside you a Seed of Life capable of drawing to you any element you need, to bring to fruition whatever of good you desire. But like all other seeds, its shell must be broken before the kernel inside can use its attractive power. And that shell is thicker, harder, than the shell of any seed on earth. Only one thing will break it—heat from WITHIN—a *desire* so strong, a determination so intense, that you cheerfully throw everything you have into the scale to win what you want. Not merely your work and your money and your thought, but the willingness to stand or fall by the result—to do or to die. Like the Master when He cursed the fig tree for its barrenness, you are willing to demand of the Seed of Life in you that it *bear fruit or perish.*

That is the secret of every great success. That is the means by which all of life, from the beginning of time, has won what it needed.

What was it gave to certain animals protective shells, to others speed, to still others a sting, to those who needed them claws or horns? What gave to the bold and strong the means to destroy, to the weak and cowardly facilities for hiding or escape? What but the Seed of Life in each, giving to every form of life the means that form craved to preserve its skin.

Always the seed in each form of life responded to the call of that life—*"Give me so-and-so or I perish."*

Since the very creation of the earth, Life has been threatened by every kind of danger. Had it not been stronger than any other power in the Universe—

were it not indeed a part of God Himself—it would have perished ages ago. But God who gave it to us endowed it with unlimited resource, unlimited energy. No other force can defeat it. No obstacle can hold it back.

What is it that saves men in dire extremity, who have exhausted every human resource and finally turned to God in their need? What but the unquenchable flame of God in them—the Seed of Life He has given to each of us—with power to draw to us whatever element we feel that we need to save us from extinction.

What do business leaders advise young people today? Live within your income? No, indeed! *Go into debt!* Reach out! Spread yourself! Then dig the harder to catch up!

You are entitled to just as much of the good things of life as Ford or Rockefeller or Morgan, or any of the rich men around you. But it is not THEY who owe it to you. And it is not the world that owes you a living. The world and they owe you nothing but honest pay for the exact service you render them.

The one who owes you everything of good—riches and honor and happiness—is the Seed of Life inside you. Go to it! Stir it up! Don't rail against the world. You get from it what you put into it—nothing more. Wake up the Seed of God inside you! Demand of it that it bring you the elements you need for riches or success. Demand—and make your need seem as urgent as must have been the need of the crustacean to develop a shell, of the bird to grow wings, of the bear to give it fur.

Demand—and KNOW THAT YOU RECEIVE! The Seed of Life in you is just as strong as ever it was in those primitive animals of pre-historic days. If it could draw from the elements whatever means it required to enable them to survive, don't you suppose it can do the same today to provide you with the factors you consider essential to your well-being?

True, these factors are different from those called for in primitive times, but do you suppose that matters to the Seed of Life? Everything in this world is made up of energy. Don't you suppose it is as easy to pour that energy into one mold as into another?

Many seem to think that riches and success are a matter of luck. They are not luck. They are a matter of DEMANDING MUCH from the Seed of God inside you, and then insisting upon those demands being met.

The trouble with most people is that they are looking to some force outside themselves to bring them riches or happiness. The superstitious carry a rabbit's foot or an amulet, believing it will bring them luck. The religious carry medals or images or the relic of some Saint. It never occurs to them that they have the means of going direct to God. God seems too impalpable, too shadowy and far away. His apparent isolation, His seeming detachment from their work-a-day world, makes Him appear too unsubstantial to depend upon in real need. They want something they can see and feel and talk to. Something with a substance like their own. Hence the demand for statues and pictures and shrines and relics. Hence, too, the need for Saints and Priests—intercessors, nearer to the Great One than ordinary mortals can hope to reach.

But direct contact is always better than even the most potent intermediary. And you HAVE the direct contact, any time you want to use it.

You are a Tree of Life. The seed of you is a Seed of God—part of Him as much as the acorn is part of the oak. And that Seed has all the properties of God, just as the acorn has all the potential properties of the oak. It can draw to you every element you need to make yours the most perfect tree in the garden, the most fruitful.

So, instead of depending upon the stars, or a rabbit's foot, or an amulet, or even the Saints, put your faith in the Seed of God, which is the animating part of you. No matter what your circumstances may be, no matter what obstacles may conspire to hold you down, look—NOT merely to the means at hand, NOT to circumstances or conditions—but to that never-failing power of the Seed inside you to draw to you any element you believe you MUST have to survive.

That is the way to make your "Star," your "Destiny," work for you. Only the "Star," the "Destiny," is right inside YOU. It is the Seed of God, the Seed of Life in YOU which your desire, your faith and your need have started into action. It is stronger than any circumstances. It can overcome any condition. So bless it and baptize it, *and stir it up!*

Bless it morning and evening, but when the urgent need arises—DEMAND! Demand that it bestir itself. Demand that it draw to you whatever elements you need. Demand—and *give all* as you demand all—make it a matter of life or death, survive or perish.

There is a point in the tree, you know, below which the "pull" of the leaves has little power. That is the point to which the roots must deliver the water, or the tree will never flower or bear fruit.

There is a point in your circumstances or your business at which the pull of your Seed of Life does not make itself felt. That is the point to which your efforts must deliver the fruit of your work, or your desire will die still-born.

So when you demand, first GIVE—throw every bit of effort you have into reaching the point at which the Seed of Life will take over the work. Give all that you can to the work in hand, and don't forget to give to the Lord as well.

It is this which makes so successful the prayers of those who, demanding riches, throw all their scanty store into the plate, and depend solely upon that Seed of God in them to supply their needs. When you can do this, believing, the world is yours.

> When things go wrong, as they sometimes will,
> When the road you're trudging seems all up hill,
> When the funds are low and the debts are high,
> And you want to smile, but you have to sigh,
> When care is pressing you down a bit,
> REST—if you must—but don't you quit.
>
> Success is failure turned inside out—
> The silver tint of the cloud of doubt,
> And you never can tell how close you are,
> It may be near when it seems afar.
> So stick to the fight when you're hardest hit—
> It's when things seem worse that you mustn't quit.

EXERCISE FOR CHAPTER SIXTEEN

All things therefore whatsoever ye would that men should do unto you, even so do ye also unto them; for this is the law and the prophets.

Someone in Omaha studied that Golden Rule, and out of it found the solution to much of Nebraska's jobless problem in the last big depression. He brought together a number of jobless men and women, and started them doing things to help others!

Forgetting their own troubles, they looked about them for ways to help others more unhappy and unfortunate than themselves and organized the All Omaha Self Help Society. They do farming, craft work and canning. They build houses, repair them, tend yards, do housework, care for children, and perform any service that offers which is of value to the community. Where money is available, they accept pay for their services and turn it into wheat and flour and fuel and shelter. They have improved their condition and that of all around them, without waiting for business to pick up or for some government agency to give them a lift. And in scores of parts of the country, similar groups have done the same.

In times of quandary, when you seem at the end of your rope, if you will only stop and think awhile, you will nearly always find that you have the BEGIN-NINGS of the solution of your problem in your mind, or somewhere ready to your hand. Use that beginning to start—no matter on how small a scale.

Alice Foote MacDougall built a business that, before the depression of the '30's, was worth $5,000,000. Yet she started with a little booth in Grand Central Station where she sold coffee. One blustery winter's day, everyone that came in seemed so cold and hungry that she sent home for her waffle iron and the necessary ingredients, and served waffles free to all who came for coffee. Those free waffles made her famous. They were the start that built for her a string of restaurants and a good-sized fortune.

The stories of that kind we might tell are legion. There was the poor farmer's wife who gave some of the strawberry preserves she was making to a youngster from High School who had stopped by for a drink. He thought them so good that he asked if he couldn't sell some of them to neighbors. From that start she built a profitable business.

The famous Jones Farm Sausage got its start from the talk of neighbors and friends who had tasted this delicious sausage at the Jones' table. And many another successful business has started on as small a scale.

The great thing is the start—to see an opportunity for service, and to start doing it, even though in the beginning you serve but a single customer—and him for nothing.

> *In life's small things be resolute and great*
> *To keep thy muscles trained.*
> *Knowst thou when Fate thy measure takes?*
> *Or when she'll say to thee*
> *"I find thee worthy, do this thing for me!"*

17

Strong Desire Essential
to Success

Desire Power is one of the many phases of Personal Power—of that Personal Power which flows into and through the individual from that great source of the All-Power of All-Things which in this instruction is known as POWER.

You do not create your own Personal Power of any kind, though you may modify it, adapt it, develop it, and direct it. POWER, the source of All-Power, has always existed and will always exist. You generate Personal Power by drawing upon the great Source and Fount of All-Power; by opening your natural channels to its inflow; and by supplying it with the proper physical and mental mechanism by means of which it is enabled to express and manifest itself efficiently.

An old writer once said: "Few speakers succeed who attempt merely to make people think—they want to be made to feel. People will pay liberally to be made to feel or to laugh, while they will begrudge a sixpence for instruction or talk that will make them think. The reasons are palpable and plain: it is heart against head; soul against logic; and soul is bound to win every time." Cardinal Newman once said: "The heart is commonly reached, not through reason, but through the imagination, by means of direct impressions, by descriptions. Persons influence us, voices melt us, deeds inflame us."

One has but to recall instances of the great influence exerted over the public mind by the emotional appeals to affection or dislike, to prejudices for or against, to desires, ambitions, aspirations, cravings, longings and things eagerly "wanted," made by orators, politicians, statesmen, actors and preachers, in order to realize the potent effect of Emotion, Affection and Desire upon men's thoughts, opinions, beliefs and convictions.

A modern writer says: "A large part of the business of life consists in moving the emotions and desires of men so as to get them to act." Another says: "The successful man is he who is able to persuade the crowd that he has something that they want, or that they want something that he has." The successful salesman, advertising man or any other man who has things to sell other men, all bring into play the force of Desire in those whom they are seeking to interest in their projects. They appeal to the "want" or "want to" side of the mind of men. They play upon men's sympathies, their prejudices, their hopes, their fears, their desires, their aversions.

Men "do things" and "act" because of the motive power of their emotional nature, particularly in the form of Affection and Desire. This is the only reason impelling or influencing men to "do things." Were this motive power absent, there would be no action or doing of things; there would be no reason or cause for such action or doing, in that event. We act and do solely because we "like" and "want." Were the emotional element absent, there would be no element of volition. Without Desire we would make no choices, would exercise no decision, would perform no actions. Without the "want" and "want to," there would be no "will to do," and no "doing." Desire is the motive power of Action; take away the motive power and there cannot be and will not be any movement, activity or volition. Without the motive power of Desire, the machinery of voluntary action ceases to operate, and comes to a complete standstill.

An old writer, whose words have been preserved for us though his name is unknown to the present writers, enunciates a profound truth in the following rather startling statement:

"Every deed that we do, good or bad, is prompted by Desire. We are charitable because we wish to relieve our inner distress at the sight of suffering; or from the urge of sympathy, with its desire to express its nature; or from the desire to be respected in this world, or to secure a comfortable place in the next one. One man is kind because he desires to be kind—because it gives him satisfaction and content to be kind. Another man is unkind because he desires to be so—because it gives him satisfaction and content to be so. One man does his duty because he desires to do it—he obtains a higher emotional satisfaction and content from duty well done than he would from neglecting it in accordance with some opposing desires. Another man yields to the desire to shirk his duty—he obtains greater satisfaction and content from refraining from performing his duty, in favor of doing other and contrary things which possess a greater emotional value to himself.

> *The religious man is religious in his actions, because his religious desires are stronger than are his irreligious ones—he finds a greater satisfaction and content in religious actions than in the pursuits of the worldly-minded. The moral man is moral because his moral desires are stronger than his immoral ones—he obtains a greater degree of emotional satisfaction and content in being moral than in being immoral. Everything we do is prompted by Desire in some shape or form, high or low. Man cannot be Desireless, and still act in one way or another—or in any way whatsoever. Desire is the motive-power behind all action—it is a natural law of Life. Everything from the atom to the monad; from the monad to the insect; from the insect to man; from Man to Nature; and possibly from Nature to God; everything from lowest to highest and from highest to lowest—everything that is—is found to act and to do things, to manifest action and to perform work, by reason of the power and force of Desire. Desire is the animating power, the energizing force, and the motive-power in, under, and behind all natural processes, activities and events.*

There is a general rule concerning Desire which it is important that you should note and remember. The rule is as follows: *"The degree of force, energy, will, determination, persistence and continuous application manifested by an individual in his aspirations, ambitions, aims, performances, actions and work is determined primarily by the degree of 'want' and 'want to' concerning that object."*

So true is this principle that some who have studied its effects have announced the aphorism: *"You can have or be anything that you want—if you only want it hard enough."* To "want a thing hard enough" is equivalent to "paying the price" for it—the price of the sacrifice of lesser desires and "wants"; the casting off of the non-essentials, and the concentration of Desire upon the one essential idea or thing, and the application of the will to its attainment or accomplishment.

Much that we have been in the habit of ascribing to the possession and the manifestation of a "strong will" has really been due to the element of Will which is called Conation, i.e., Desire tending toward expression in Will-action. The man filled with an ardent, fierce, burning, craving and urge for and toward a certain object, will call to his aid the latent powers of his Will, and of his Intellect—these under the motive power and stimulus of Desire will manifest

RICHES WITHIN YOUR REACH

unusual activity and energy toward the accomplishment of the desired end. Desire has well been called the Flame which produces the heat which generates the Steam of Will.

Very few persons, comparatively, know how to Desire with sufficient intensity and insistence. They content themselves with mere "wishing" and mild "wanting." They fail to experience that Insistent Desire, which is one of the important elements of the Master Formula of Attainment. They do not know what it is to feel and manifest that intense, eager, longing, craving, insistent demanding, ravenous Desire which is akin to the persistent, insistent, ardent, overwhelming desire of the drowning man for a breath of air; of the shipwrecked or desert-lost man for a drink of water; of the famished man for bread and meat; of the fierce, wild creature for its mate; of the mother for the welfare of her children. Yet, if the truth were known, the desire for success of the men who have accomplished great things has often been as great as these.

We are not necessarily slaves to our Desires; we may master the lower or disadvantageous desires by Will, under the Power of the "I AM I," or Master Self. We may transmute lower desires into higher, negatives into positives, hurtful into helpful, in this way. We may become Masters of Desire, instead of being mastered by it. But before we may do so, we must first desire to do so, to accomplish and to attain this end. We may even rise to the heights of Will—the place where the "I AM I" may say, truthfully, "I Will to Will" and "I Will to Desire"; but even there we must first desire to so "Will to Will" and "Will to Desire."

Even at these sublime heights of Egohood, we find Desire to be the fundamental and elemental Motive Power: this because it abides at the very heart of things—the heart of ourself—the Heart of Life. Even there, we essay and accomplish the highest deeds and acts of Will solely and simply because they serve to "content our spirit," to give us the highest degree of "self satisfaction"—to gratify, satisfy and give expression and manifestation to our greatest, most insistent, most persistent and strongest "want" and "want to."

18

Magnetic Power of Desire

The strongest and most persistent desires of the individual tend to attract to him (or him to) that which is closely related to or correlated with those desires." That is to say: the strong insistent desires of a person tend to attract to him those things which are closely related to such desires; and, at the same time, tend to attract him toward those related things. The Attractive Desire of Desire operates in two general ways, viz., (1) to attract to the individual the things closely related to his desires; and (2) to attract the individual to such related things.

In your own experience, in all probability, you have experienced many cases of the operation of this subtle law of Nature. You have become intensely interested in some particular subject, and your desire for further progress and attainment along the lines of that subject has been actively aroused. Then you have noticed the strange and peculiar way in which persons and things related to that subject have come under your observation and attention—sometimes even being apparently forced upon you apart from any act on your part. In the same way, you have found yourself attracted in certain directions in which, unknown to you, were to be found persons or things related to the subject of your desire, information concerning that subject, conditions in which the subject was involved or being manifested. In short, you have found that things happened "as if" you were either attracting persons, things and circumstances to you, or else that you were being attracted, drawn or "led" to such persons, things or circumstances.

Under such conditions, you will find arising on all sides certain events connected with and related to the subject of your desire; books containing information concerning it; persons having some connection with it; conditions in which that subject plays an important part. You will find, on the one hand, that you seem to have become a center of attraction for things, persons and circumstances related to that subject; or, on the other hand, that you are being attracted to certain centers of attraction related to that subject. In short, you will discover that you have set into operation certain subtle forces and principles which have "correlated" you with all related to that subject.

More than this, you will find that if you will maintain for a considerable time a continuous and persistent interest and desire in that particular subject, you will have established a vortex-center of attraction for that which is related to the subject. You will have set into operation a mental whirlpool, steadily spreading its circumference of influence, which draws into itself and to your central point the related and correlated things, persons and circumstances. This is one of the reasons why after you "get things going" in any particular line of interest and desire, things tend to "come easier" to and for you as time passes. In such cases, that which required enormous effort in the earlier stages seems to move almost automatically in the later ones. These are matters of common and almost universal experience with those who have been actively engaged in any particular line of work in which strong interest and insistent desire have been aroused and maintained.

So, you see, Desire Power tends not only to develop and evolve within you the qualities and powers necessary to enable you to manifest and express yourself along the lines of the desires persistently held by you; it also tends to attract to you, and you to them, the things, persons, circumstances and conditions related to or correlated with the subject of such desires. In other words, Desire Power employs every means at its disposal in order to express and manifest itself more fully, and (through you) to attain its object and end—its greatest possible degree of satisfaction and realization. When you have thoroughly aroused Desire Power within you, and have created for it a strong, positive focal center of influence, you have set into operation powerful forces of Nature, operating along subconscious and invisible lines of activity. In this connection, remember the adage: *"You may have anything you want—if you only want it hard enough."*

The attractive force of Desire Power operates in many different ways. In addition to the "drawing power" operating along the lines of "something like telepathy" of which we have spoken, it also operates in other ways on the subconscious planes of the mind in order to influence, guide and direct the person to the other persons, things, conditions and circumstances related or correlated to or with the particular desire which is being persistently and insistently held by that person. Under its influence, the subconscious mentality raises to the levels of consciousness new ideas, thoughts, plans, which if applied will tend to "lead" the person in the direction of the things which will serve to aid him in the realization of those desires which he is insistently harboring.

In this way, the person is led to the related things, just as in the other ways the things are led to him. Desire Power pushes, as truly as it pulls—it urges you forward as truly as it attracts things to you. In some cases the process is entirely subconscious, and the person is amazed when he finds "by chance" (!) that he has "stumbled upon" helpful things in places in which he had least expected to find them, and in places to which he had apparently been led by Chance. But there is no Chance about it; persons are undoubtedly "led to" helpful things and conditions, but by Desire Power operating along the lines of the subconscious mentality, and not by Chance.

Many successful men could tell how often in their respective careers, at critical times, the most peculiar happenings have been experienced by them, seemingly "by chance" or "by accident," which served as the means of transforming defeat into victory. In this way they acquired "by chance" some important bit of information serving to supply the missing link in their mental chain, or else giving them a clue to that which had previously escaped their thought. Or, perhaps, they unexpectedly "ran into" the person who afterward turned out to be the one particular person who alone could have helped them in certain ways. Or, again, they have picked up at random the particular newspaper, magazine or book which either gave them the required information, or else mentioned some other book or thing which filled the need.

These things happen so often, and in such a striking way, that many men of active experience have learned to expect them, to rely upon them, and to act upon them. Not knowing the true underlying causes of the happenings, they usually refrain from mentioning their experiences to their friends for fear of being regarded as superstitious or credulous; but if the subject happens to be introduced in confidential conversation between men of this kind, it will be found that the instances cited are numerous, and are so strikingly similar in general nature that the careful thinker is forced to the conclusion that there is some fundamental principle involved in the events, and that there is a logical sequence of cause and effect indicated.

Not knowing the true cause of these happenings, men are prone to ascribe them to "luck," fate, destiny, chance or else to think of them simply as "one of those things beyond explanation." Some men who have become familiar with them have learned to recognize them readily when they experience them, by reason of a "feeling" that "here is another of those things." They learn to distinguish between a mere general and vague notion, and a "sure enough hunch." Sometimes, men think that these things are the result of the aid of a kindly Providence operating in their behalf; others feel that they have helpers "on the other side"; still others feel that there is "something almost uncanny" about the whole thing; but so long as it is perceived to operate in their behalf all are willing to take advantage of the aid of the Unknown Power.

Of course, the subconscious mentality of the individual is the "helper," or "directing genius" in such cases, and the happenings are merely phases of the general phenomena of the Subconscious. But, nevertheless, Desire Power is the animating principle involved. The subconscious mentality, like the conscious mentality, is energized and aroused into activity by the urge of Desire Power. Desire Power employs every possible form of energy, activity and motive-power at its command; and also presses into service all kinds of machinery and instruments, mental and physical. The Fire of Desire kindles every faculty of the mind, on conscious and subconscious planes, and sets them all into active work on its behalf. Without Desire Power in some form or phase, none of these faculties would manifest activity; where activity is manifested by them, there is always implied the presence and urge of Desire Power.

Sometimes Desire Power will operate in strangely indirect ways in order to accomplish its results. By means of the "under the surface" perception of the subconscious faculties, Desire Power seemingly perceives that "the longest way 'round is the quickest way home," and it proceeds to cause the individual to pursue that "longest way 'round" in order to attain his desire in the shortest possible time. In such cases it often acts so as to upset and overturn the plans which one has carefully mapped out; the result makes it seem to one that failure and defeat, instead of victory and success, have come to him. It will sometimes tear the person away from his present comparatively satisfactory environment and conditions, and then lead him over rock roads and hard trails; and finally, when he has almost despaired of attaining success, he finds it literally thrust upon him.

Such instances are not invariable, of course, but they occur sufficiently often and with such characteristically marked features that they must be recognized. It often happens that, as one who has experienced it has said, "It seems as if one were grabbed by the back of his neck, lifted out of his set environment and occupation, dragged roughly over a painful road, and then thrust forcibly but kindly upon the throne of success or at least into the throneroom with the throne in plain sight before him."

But, at the last, those who have experienced these strenuous activities of Desire Power operating through the subconscious nature and in many other ways are found to agree universally in the statement, "The end justified the means; the thing is worth the price paid for it." It requires philosophy and faith to sustain one when he is undergoing experiences of this kind, but the knowledge of the law and principle in operation will of course greatly aid him. The right spirit to maintain in such cases is that expressed in the phrase, "It's a great life, if you don't weaken."

Desire Power employs freely the subconscious faculties in its work of Realization through Attraction. It employs these in man just as it employs them in the case of the homing pigeon, the migrating birds, the bee far from its hive—it supplies the "homing instinct" to the man seeking success, as well as to the animal seeking refuge. It is said that animals separated from their mates, seemingly are attracted to them over long distances. Lost animals find their way home, though many miles over strange country have to be traveled. Let a person establish a "refuge" for birds, and the birds will soon begin to travel toward it—even strange species from long distances putting in an appearance. Water fowls travel unerringly toward water; the roots of trees manifest the same sense of direction toward water and rich soil.

In high and low, the Law of Desire Attraction manifests its power. Man is under the law, and may even cause the law to work for him when he understands its nature. Man may harness Desire Power just as he has harnessed other great forces of Nature—may harness it and set it to work for him. Once set to work for him, this power will work "without haste, and without rest" toward the end impressed upon it—it will work for him while he is awake and working otherwise, and when he is asleep and resting from his conscious work. Desire is the "force of forces," because it is the inmost kernel of all the other forms of natural force, physical or mental. All force depends upon inner Attraction or Repulsion—and these are but the manifestation of Desire Power, positive or negative.

19

The Master Formula for Getting What You Want

The Master Formula of Attainment, stated in popular form, is as follows:

"You may have anything you want, provided that you (1) know exactly what you want, (2) want it hard enough, (3) confidently expect to attain it, (4) persistently determine to obtain it, and (5) are willing to pay the price of its attainment."

We shall now ask you to consider three of the above five elements of the Master Formula of Attainment, viz., the element of Definite Ideals, or "knowing exactly what you want"; the element of Insistent Desire, or "wanting it hard enough"; the element of Balanced Compensation, or "being willing to pay the price of its attainment." Each of these three elements is highly important, and should be carefully examined and considered. Let us begin with the first requisite, i.e. "Knowing exactly what you want."

When you consider the question, "Exactly what do I want?" you will be apt to regard it as one quite easy to answer. But after you begin to consider the question in detail, and in real earnest, you will discover two very troublesome obstacles in your way on the road to the correct answer. The two obstacles are as follows: (1) the difficulty in ascertaining a clear and full idea of your desires, aspirations, ambitions, and hopes; and (2) the difficulty in ascertaining which ones of a number of conflicting desires, aspirations, ambitions, and hopes you "want" more than you do those opposing them.

You will find yourself with "the divine discontent" of a general dissatisfaction with your present condition, circumstances, possessions and limitations. You will feel, perhaps strongly, the "raw desire" of the elemental Desire Power within you, but you will not have clearly outlined in your mind the particular directions in which you wish that elemental force to proceed into manifestation and expression.

You will often feel that you wish that you were somewhere other than where you now are; that you were doing something different from what you are now doing; that you possessed things other and better than you now possess; or that your present limitations were removed, thus giving you a wider and fuller expression and manifestation of the power which you feel to be within you: all these general feelings will be experienced by you, but you will not be able to picture clearly to yourself just what "other things" you really want to take the place of those which are now your own.

Then, when you attempt to form the clear picture, and definite idea, of what you want, you will find you want *many* things, some of them opposing each other, each offering attractive features, each bidding actively for your favor and acceptance—thus rendering a choice and definite decision very difficult. You find yourself suffering from an embarrassment of riches. Like the perplexed lover in the song, you say, "How happy would I be with either, were t'other fair charmer away." Or, like the psychological donkey who was placed at an equidistant point between two equally tempting haystacks, and who died of hunger because he couldn't make up his mind which one he wanted most, you may remain inactive because of strong conflicting desire-motives.

It is because of one or both of the above-mentioned conditions that the great masses of persons do not avail themselves of the great elemental urge of Desire Power. It is there, ready to exert its power, but they lack definite direction and power of decision, and so remain, like the vegetables or the lower animals, content to allow Nature to work along the instinctive lines of self-protection, propagation, etc., without employing initiative or self-direction.

The few of the race who break these barriers, and who strike out for themselves, are found to have known very clearly "just what they wanted," and to have "wanted it hard," and to have been willing to pay the price of attainment. In order to set to work the forces of Desire Power in a special direction, the individual must make clear an ideal path over which they may travel, as well as to arouse the forces so as to cause them to travel over that path.

Self-Analysis. You will find that a scientific application of the principle of Self-Analysis, or mental stock-taking, will aid you materially in overcoming the two great obstacles in the Path of Attainment, which we have just mentioned.

Self-Analysis in this case consists of a careful analysis of your elements of Desire, to the end that you may discover which of these elements are the strongest, and that you may clearly understand just what these strongest elements are really like in character. You are advised to "think with pencil and paper" in this work of self-analysis—it will greatly aid you in crystallizing your thought and, besides, will give a definite and logical form to the results of your work. The following suggestions and advice will aid you materially in this task.

Begin by asking yourself the question: *"What are my strongest desires? What do I 'want' and 'want to' over and above anything and everything else? What are my highest Desire-Values?"* Then proceed to "think with pencil and paper," and thus to answer your important question above stated.

Take your pencil and begin to write down your strongest desires—your leading "wants" and "want tos"—as they come into your consciousness in response to your inquiry. Write down carefully the things and objects, the aims and ideals, the aspirations and ambitions, the hopes and confident expectations, which present themselves for notation in the course of your mental stock-taking. Note all of them, without regard to the question of whether or not you ever expect to be able to secure or attain them.

Put them all down on the list, no matter how ridiculous and unattainable they may seem to you at the time. Do not allow yourself to be overcome by the magnificent aims and ideals, aspirations and ambitions, which thus present themselves. Their very existence in your Desire-nature is, in a measure, the prophecy of their own fulfillment. As Napoleon once said: "Nothing is too magnificent for a soldier of France!" You are that soldier of France! Do not impose limitations on your Desire-nature in this way. If a magnificent desire is within you, it should be respected—so put it down on the list.

By this process of Self-Analysis you bring to the surface of your consciousness all the various feelings, desires, longings and cravings which have been dwelling in your subconscious mind. Many of these deep desires are like sleeping giants—your exploration of your subconscious mental regions will arouse these—will cause them "to sit up and take notice," as it were. Do not be frightened by these awakening sleepers. Nothing that you find there is alien to you. Even though you may find it necessary to transmute them, or to inhibit them in favor of more advantageous desires, at a later stage of your work, do not now deny them a place on your list—put them down on paper. The list must be an honest one, therefore be honest with yourself in the analysis.

At first, you will find that your list is a more or less higgledy-piggledy con-
glomeration of "wants" and "want tos," apparently having but little or no logical
order or systematic relation. Do not let this disturb you, however—all this will
be taken care of as you proceed; order and arrangement will establish themselves almost automatically when the proper time arrives. The main thing at
this stage is to get all of your stronger desires into the list. Be sure to exhaust
your subconscious mind of strong desires—dig out of that mine anything and
everything that has strength in it.

The next step is that of the cold-blooded, ruthless, elimination of the weakest desires, with the idea and purpose that in the end there will be a "survival of
the fittest" on your list. Begin by running over your list, striking off the weaker
and less insistent—the mere temporary and passing—desires, and those which
you clearly recognize as likely to bring you but little if any permanent satisfaction, continued happiness and lasting content.

In this way you will create a new list of the stronger desires, and those having a greater permanent and satisfying value. Then, examining this list, you
will find that some of the items will still stand out from the others by reason
of their greater comparative strength and greater degree of permanent value.
Make a new list of these successful candidates, including only those possessing
the greatest strength and value to you, and dropping the others from the list.
Then continue this process of elimination of the weakest and the least satisfying until you reach that point where you feel that any further elimination
would result in cutting away live wood.

By this time you will have become aware of a most significant and important fact, namely, that as your list has grown smaller, the strength and value of
the surviving desires have grown greater. As the old gold-miners expressed it,
you are now "getting down to pay dirt"—getting down to the region in which
the nuggets and rich ore abide. When you have reached this stage, you will do
well to stop work for the time being; this will give you a needed mental rest,
and will also furnish your subconscious mentality with the opportunity to do
some work for you along its own particular lines.

When you again take up your list for consideration, you will find a new
general order and arrangement of its items pictured in your mind. You will
find that these remaining desires have grouped themselves into several general
classes. Your subconscious mental faculties will have performed an important
task for you. Then you will be ready to compare these general classes, one with

the other, until you are able to select certain classes, which seem stronger than the others. Then you will be ready to proceed to the task of eliminating the weaker general classes, making a new list of the stronger ones.

After working along these general lines for a time, with intervals of rest and recuperation, and for subconscious digestion and elimination, you will find that you have before you a list composed of but a comparatively few general classes of "wants" and "want tos"—each of which possesses a far greater degree of strength and value than you had previously suspected. Your subconscious mind has been working its power upon these classes of desires, and they have evolved to a higher stage of strength, definiteness, clearness and power. You are beginning at last to find out "just what you want," and are also well started on your way to "wanting it hard enough."

General Rules of Selection. In your task of selection, elimination, "boiling down" and chopping away the dead wood, etc., you will do well to observe the three following general Rules of Selection:

I. *The Imperative Requisite.* In selecting your strongest desires for your list, you are not required to pay attention to any fears lurking in your mind that any of the particular desires are apparently unattainable—that they are beyond your power of achievement, and are rendered impossible by apparently unsurmountable obstacles. You are not concerned with such questions at this time and place—ignore them for the present. You are here concerned merely with the question of whether or not your "want" or "want to" concerning a certain thing is felt "hard enough" for you to sacrifice other desirable things—whether you feel that the particular desire is of sufficient value for you to "pay the price" of its attainment, even though that price be very high. Remember the old adage: "Said the gods to man, 'Take what thou wilt—but pay for it!'" If you are not willing to "pay the price," and to pay it in full, then you do not "want it hard enough" to render it one of your Prime Desires.

II. *The Test of Full Desire.* We have told you that, *"Desire has for its object something that will bring pleasure or get rid of pain, immediately or remote, for the individual or for some one in whom he is interested."* Therefore, in passing upon the comparative strength and value of your respective desires, or general classes of desires, you must take into consideration all of the elements of Desire noted in the above definite statement—the indirect as well as the direct elements of personal satisfaction and content.

You must weigh and decide the value of any particular desire, or class of desires, not only in the light of your own *immediate* satisfaction and content, but also in the light of your own *future* satisfaction and content; not only in the light of your own *direct* satisfaction and content, but also in the light of your *indirect* satisfaction and content derived from the satisfaction and content of others in whom you are interested. Your future satisfaction and content often depend upon the sacrifice of your present desire in favor of one bearing fruit in the future. You may be so interested in other persons that their satisfaction and content has a greater emotional value to you than the gratification of some desire concerned only with your own direct satisfaction and content. These Desires-values must be carefully weighed by you. If you leave out any of these elements of Desire, you run the risk of attaching a false value to certain sets of desires. You must weigh and measure the value of your desires by the use of the standard of the full content of Desire.

III. *Seek Depth of Desire.* You will find it advisable to omit from your list all purely superficial and transient feelings, emotions and desires. They have but a slight value in the case. Instead, plunge into the deep places of your mental being or soul; there you will find abiding certain deep, essential, basic, permanent feelings, emotions and desires. In those regions dwell the "wants" and the "want tos" which when aroused are as insistent and as imperative as are the want of the suffocating man for air; the want of the famished man for food; the want of the thirsting man for water; the want of the wild creature for its mate; the want of the mother for the welfare of her child.

These deep desires are your real emotional elements—the ones most firmly and permanently imbedded in the soil of your emotional being. These are the desires which will abide when the transient, ephemeral ones have passed and are forgotten. These are the desires for which you will be willing to "pay the price," be that price ever so high in the form of the sacrifice and relinquishment of every other desire, feeling or emotion. Measure your desires by their essential depth, as well as by their temporary weight. Select those which are embedded so deeply in the soil of your emotional being that they cannot be uprooted by the passing storms of conditions and circumstances.

The Struggle for Existence. You are now approaching the final stages of your discovery of "just what you want." You now have a list of Insistent Desires— the survivors in the Struggle for Existence on the part of your many desires and classes of desires. If you have proceeded earnestly and honestly in your work of Self-Analysis and Selection, you will have a group of sturdy Desire-giants before you for final judgment. By a strange psychological law these surviving candidates have taken on much of the strength and energy of those which they have defeated in the struggle; the victors will have absorbed the vitality of those whom they have defeated, just as the savage hopes to draw to himself the strength of the enemies killed by him in battle. Your Desire Power has now been concentrated upon a comparatively small group of desires, with a consequent focusing of power.

You will now find that your "wants" and "want tos" have arranged themselves into two great classes, viz., (1) the great class of those desires which while *different* from other desires, or classes of desires, are not necessarily *contradictory* to them nor *directly opposed* to them; and (2) the great class of those desires which are not only *different,* but are also actually *contradictory* and *opposed* to other desires or classes of desires.

The merely *"different"* classes may abide in mutual harmonious existence and relation with or to each other, just as do light and heat, or the color and odor of a flower. But two *contradictory* and *opposing* classes of desires cannot co-exist and coordinate their energies in the same individual; both remaining in the fore, there will be friction, inharmony, strife, and mutual interference.

One might as well try to ride two horses moving in different directions, as to try to maintain in equal force two opposing or contradictory sets of desires. The two sets, each one pulling in an opposite direction and with equal strength, will bring the Will to a standstill. The individual, in such a case, will either oscillate between the two attracting poles, or else he will come to a "dead center" between them. Something must be done when you find an opposing set of desires of this kind well to the fore in your category of strong desires. You must set in operation a process of competition, from which one set must emerge a victor and the other set be defeated.

In this process of competition, you will need to employ your best and keenest powers of analysis and judgment. In some cases the matter may be settled quickly, and the decision easily arrived at, because when your full attention is turned upon the two competitors, one will be seen to stand out so much more clearly than the other that the latter will be almost automatically retired. The full power of Reason and Feeling focused in such a case will usually result in a quick and sure decision.

But there are instances in which both of the opposing sets of desires seem to possess an equal power and value in your emotional and intellectual scale. Here you are apparently in the condition of the poor donkey, previously mentioned, who starved to death because he was unable to decide which of the two haystacks was to be eaten. The matter must be decided by the introduction of an additional element which will add weight to one set or the other, and thus bring down the balance on that particular side. This added element is usually found in one or the other of the following two classes of mental processes, viz., (1) Imagination, and (2) Association. Let us consider each of these.

The Element of Imagination. The imagination, employed in the case of the desire-conflict now before us, usually is very effective in bringing about a decision. In employing it, you have but to imagine yourself, first, in the actual possession of the object of the one set of desires; and then, instead, in possession of the object of the second set. In this process you draw upon your own recollections and experiences, and upon your recollection of the experiences of others. You imagine "how it would feel" to have attained the object of, first, *this* "want" or "want to," and then *that* one. You place yourself in imagination in the position that you would occupy in case you should attain the object of *this* desire, or of *that* one. Then you pass judgment as to which seems to be the better, i.e., to afford the greater degree of satisfaction and content, present and future, direct and indirect.

This process has the advantage of overcoming the handicap placed upon a future satisfaction in favor of a present one. The future experience is brought into the field of the present, and thus may be compared with a present experience relieved of the handicap of time. This is a matter of great importance, for ordinarily the present-time value of an emotional feeling or desire is far greater than that of a past-time or future-time value of a similar experience. The test of imagination usually results in (1) strengthening the present value of a really advantageous emotional feeling and desire, and (2) in weakening the present value of an apparently advantageous, but really disadvantageous, one. The use of the memory and the imagination is to be highly recommended in the task of deciding the real and actual value of an emotional state or desire.

The Element of Association. The element of association introduced into a desire-conflict will often result speedily in a determination and decision in favor of one side as against the other. Association will add strength to one set of desires, and will weaken the opposing set, in most cases. The Association of Ideas is that psychological law which binds one set of ideas, or mental states, to others; so that by bringing one set into consciousness we tend to bring there also the associated sets. In the present case we bring into consciousness the associated consequences of each set of desires.

You may proceed to apply the test of Association as follows: Seek to uncover and discover as many as possible of the associated results of the attainment of the set of desires in question—strive to think of "what else will happen" in case you attain that set of desires. This is something like inquiring into the family and social connections of two rival suitors or sweethearts—weighing their respective relations and associations and the probable future consequences of marriage with either of them.

It is always well, in cases of doubt concerning the comparative value of conflicting sets of desires, to consider carefully just what other things are associated with each of the two respective sets of desires—just what other results are likely to accompany the attainment of the object or end of each set of desires under consideration. In other words, you should ascertain the kind of relations and friends possessed by each of the rival suitors or sweethearts. In this way you will often find that one of the two apparently equal sets of desires has some very agreeable and advantageous relations and associates, while the other has some very disagreeable and disadvantageous ones.

You thus discover, figuratively speaking "just what kind of family you are marrying into"; and you thus take stock of the respective associated and related "in laws," friends, associates and entanglements of each of the suitors. This is of great value, since in spite of the oft asserted statement that "I am not marrying the whole family," one usually really does do just that very thing.

The idea of the application of the test of Association in such cases may be expressed in a few words, as follows: The real test of any particular desire depends not alone upon the immediate results likely to accompany its attainment, but also upon the associated and related results which follow in its train of association and correlation—the results which necessarily "go with it," and which are so closely bound up with it that they cannot easily be detached from it. In some cases, the test of Association will reveal the fact that the price of the attainment of a certain set of desires is excessive—often actually prohibitive. In other cases, on the contrary, you will find by this test that you are getting a great bargain by reason of the "extras" which go with the thing itself. The objects of some desires are thus found to be "damaged goods"; while those of others are found to have an associative value not apparent to the casual observer.

An Appeal to the Touchstone. In cases in which careful analysis, deliberation, the tests of imagination and association, and all other means of weighing and measuring, trying and testing, fail to reveal the advantage of one set of desires over the opposing set, resort must be had to the Touchstone of Positivity so often referred to in this instruction. The Touchstone by which the Positivity of any mental state, thought, feeling, desire or action is determined is as follows:

"Will this tend to make me stronger, better and more efficient?" In the degree that any mental state meets the requirements of this test, so is its degree of Positivity and consequent desirability.

In testing two sets of conflicting desires in this way, you ask yourself: *"Which of these two desires, if attained, will tend to make me stronger, better and more efficient?"* This is the Test Question. The answer should represent your final decision in the matter. The Touchstone is your Court of Last Resort, to be appealed to when all other tests have failed. Its report represents the best, highest and most valuable elements, mental, moral and spiritual, within your nature; all that is worst in you is absent therefrom. It represents your Summum Bonum—your Chief Good.

The Survival of the Fittest. By this time, your list of desires has resolved itself into a schedule or inventory of a few strong, dominant, prime desires, and of a larger number of lesser ones. The strongest desires should be finally tested in order to discover whether they are merely "different" from each other, or whether they are essentially mutually antagonistic and contradictory.

If they come under the latter category, then they must be pitted against each other until one of the pair wins the victory, and one goes down in defeat; for two sets of this kind must not be permitted to dwell permanently in your region of Desire: "a house divided against itself shall not stand." There must be fought a fight to the finish. One of the opposing sets must be rolled in the dust, while the other stands proudly erect as the victor. The defeated one, thereafter, must be compelled to say, "After you, monsieur," as our French cousins politely express it.

If two sets of desires are merely "different,"' and are not essentially and necessarily conflicting and antagonistic, then they may be permitted to remain dwelling in mutual peace and harmony, at least for the time being. This permission, however, is conditioned by the fact that there must not be too many of such sets occupying the front seats of Desire at the same time. The tendency should always be in the direction of concentration and focused energy; you should beware of scattered power and energy arising from a great diversity of desires and aims.

If you discover that there are too many strong "different" desires left after you have reached this stage of selection and elimination, you should carefully weigh each remaining set, subjecting it to the tests of memory, imagination, association and rational judgment, discarding all that are not found profitable and sufficiently advantageous. If you find that any of your desires cost you more than you get out of them; get rid of all those which do not pay for their keep.

Continue until you have left only a comparatively few sets of desires, all of proved value and superlative emotional strength and depth. These should be recognized as well worth the price which you are prepared to pay for their maintenance and support. Treat in the same way any new desires which arise within you. Test them just as you have tested their predecessors, and insist that they prove that they are "worth while" before you decide to keep them. If they cost you more than you get out of them, discard them. Insist that they shall "pay their keep" and yield you some emotional profit beside. Run your emotional and desire establishment on business principles.

You have now finally reached the stage in which you have on your list nothing but your Dominant Desires—the survivors in the Struggle for Existence—the Survival of the Fittest. These Dominant Desires must thereafter rule your emotional realm. Any new comer must prove its worth by a test of strength with these Dominant Desires—if it shows its strength, and is able to hold its place, very well; it may be added to the list. Those going down in defeat must be eliminated. This will require strength and determination on your part—but you are a strong and determined individual, or at least are becoming one.

The process of Self-Analysis and Selection which you just considered will furnish you with two classes of reports, viz., (1) it will demonstrate to you your strongest classes of desires—your Dominant Desires; and (2) it will cause you clearly and definitely to picture and form a strong idea of each of such Dominant Desires. In both reports it will cause you to "know exactly what you want," which is the first requisite of the Master Formula of Attainment.

20

Putting Power into Your Desire

According to the Master Formula you must not only "know exactly what you want," but must also "want it hard enough," and be "willing to pay the price of its attainment." Having considered the first of the above stated three requisites for obtaining that which you want, we ask you now to consider the second requisite, i.e., that of "wanting it hard enough."

You may think that you "want it hard enough" when you have a rather keen desire or longing for anything, but when you compare your feeling with that of persons manifesting really strong, insistent desire, you will find that you are but merely manifesting a "wish" for that for which you have an inclination or an attachment. Compared to the insistent "want" or "want to" of thoroughly aroused Desire, your "wish" is but as a shadow. The chances are that you have been a mere amateur—a dilettante—in the art and science of "wanting" and "wanting to." Very few persons really know how to "want" or "want to" in such manner as to arouse fully the elemental forces of Desire Power.

An old fable illustrates the nature of Desire aroused to its fullest extent. The fable relates that a teacher took his pupil out on a deep lake, in a boat, and then suddenly pushed him overboard. The youth sank beneath the surface of the water, but rose in a few seconds, gasping for breath. Without giving him time to fill his lungs with air, the teacher forcibly pushed him under once more. The youth rose to the surface the second time, and was again pushed under. He rose for the third time, almost entirely exhausted; this time the teacher pulled him up over the side of the boat, and employed the usual methods to restore him to normal breathing.

When the youth had fully recovered from his severe ordeal, the teacher said to him: "Tell me what was the one thing that you desired above all other things before I pulled you in—the one desire to which all other desires seem like tiny candles compared with the sun?" The youth replied, "Oh, sir; above all else I desired air to breathe—for me at that time there existed no other desires!" Then said the teacher, "Let this, then, be the measure of your desire for those things to the attainment of which your life is devoted!"

You will not fully realize the measure of Desire pointed out in this fable, unless you employ your imagination in the direction of feeling yourself in the drowning condition of the youth—until you do this, the fable is a mere matter of words. When you can realize in feeling, as well as recognize in thought, the strength of the desire for air present in that youth, then, and then only, will you be able to manifest in expression a similar degree of Desire for the objects of your prime "wants" and "want tos." Do not rest satisfied with the intellectual recognition of the condition—induce the corresponding emotional feeling in yourself to as great a degree as possible.

Varying the illustration, you will do well to induce in yourself (in imagination) the realization of the insistent, paramount desire for food experienced by the starving man lost in the dense forest in mid-winter. The chances are that you never have been actually "hungry" in the true sense of the term; all that you have mistaken for hunger is merely the call of appetite or taste—the result of habit. When you are so hungry that an old, stale, dry crust of bread will be delicious to your taste, then you are beginning to know what real hunger is. Those men who, lost in the forest or shipwrecked, have tried to satisfy intense hunger by gnawing the bark of trees, or chewing bits of leather cut from their boots—these men could give you some interesting information concerning hunger. If you can imagine the feelings of men in this condition, then you may begin to understand what "insistent desire" really means.

Again, the shipwrecked sailors adrift at sea with their supply of water exhausted; or the desert-lost man wandering over the hot sands with a thirst almost inconceivable to the ordinary person; those men know what "insistent desire" means. Man can live many days without food; but only a few days without water; and only a few minutes without air. When these fundamental essentials of life are withdrawn temporarily, the living creature finds his strongest and most elemental feelings and desires aroused—they become transmuted into passions insistently demanding satisfaction and content. When these elemental emotions and desires are thoroughly aroused, all the derivative emotional states are forgotten. Imagine the emotional state of the starving man in sight of food, or the thirst-cursed man within reach of water, if some other person or thing intervenes and attempts to frustrate the suffering man's attainment of that which he wants above all else at that time.

Other examples of insistent desire may be found in the cases of wild animals in the mating season, in which they will risk life and defy their powerful rivals in order to secure the chosen mate. If you ever have come across a bull-moose in the mating season, you will have a vivid picture and idea of this phase of elemental desire raised to the point of "insistent demand."

Again, consider the intense emotional feeling, and the accompanying desires experienced by the mother creature in connection with the welfare and protection of her young when danger threatens them—this will show you the nature and character of elemental desire aroused to its fullest extent. Even tiny birds will fight against overwhelming odds in resisting the animal or man seeking to rob their nests. It is a poor spirited mother-animal which will not risk her life, and actually court death, in defense of her young. The female wild creature becomes doubly formidable when accompanied by her young. "The female of the species" is far "more deadly than the male" when the welfare of its young is involved. There is a well-known proverb: "It is a very brave, or a very foolish, man who will try to steal a young tiger-cub while its mother is alive and free in the vicinity."

We have called your attention to the above several examples and illustrations of the force of strongly aroused elemental emotions and desires, not alone to point out to you how powerful such desires and feelings become under the appropriate circumstances and conditions, but also to bring you to a realization of the existence within all living things of a latent emotional strength and power which is capable of being aroused into a strenuous activity under the proper stimulus, and of being directed toward certain definite ends and purposes indicated by the stimulus. That this strength and power is aroused by, and flows out toward, the particular forms of stimulus above indicated is a matter of common knowledge. But that it may be aroused to equal strength, power, and intensity by other forms of stimulus (such stimulus having been deliberately placed before it by the individual) is not known to the many; only the few have learned this secret.

We ask you to use your imagination here, once more, for a moment. Imagine an individual who has "his mind set upon" the attainment of a certain end or purpose to such a degree that he has aroused the latent Desire Power within him to that extent where he "wants" or "wants to" that end or purpose in the degree of strength, power, insistency and fierceness, manifested by the drowning man who "wants" air; by the desert lost man who "wants" water; by the starving man who wants food; by the wild creature who "wants" its mate; by the mother animal who "wants" the welfare of its young. This is the individual in whom the elemental Desire Power has been aroused to such an extent, and directed toward the attainment or achievement of his Dominant Desire. How would you like to compete with such a man for the attainment of that object of his Desire Power? How would you like to be the opposing obstacle standing directly in his path of progress and attainment? How would you like to play with him the part analogous to that of one who would try to snatch away the bone from a starving wolf, or pull the tiger cub from the paws of its savage mother?

This is an extreme case or illustration, of course. Very few individuals actually reach the stage indicated—though it is not impossible by any means; but many travel a long way along that road. The strong, successful men who have "made good," who have "arrived," who have "done things," in any line of human endeavor, will be found to have travelled quite a distance in that direction, on the road of Desire. They have aroused within themselves the strong, elemental Desire Power which abides in latency in the depths of the mental and emotional being—the "soul," if you will—of every human creature; and have caused that elemental force to pour through the channels of the particular Dominant Desires which they have brought to the surface of their nature from the depths of the subconscious self.

Look in any direction you may, and you will find that the strong, masterful, dominant, successful men are those in whom Desire Power has been aroused and directed in this way. These men "know what they want"—just as the drowning man, the starving man, the thirst-cursed man, the wild mating creature, the mother creature, each knows what he or she wants—they have no doubts concerning their Dominant Desires. And these men also "want hard enough" that which represents their Dominant Desires—just as did the drowning man, the starving man, and the rest of our illustrative examples. And, like those examples, these men were also "willing to pay the price."

Run over the list of the successful men and women with whose careers you are acquainted. Place on that list the great discoverers, inventors, explorers, military men, business men, artists, literary men and women, all those who have "done things" successfully. Then check off name after name, as you discover the biographical report of the Desire Power manifested by these individuals. You will find that in each and every case there were present the "Definite Ideals, Insistent Desire, Confident Expectation, Persistent Determination, and Balanced Compensation," which constitute the Master Formula of Attainment of our instruction. And this second requisite—the "Insistent Desire"—is found to be this elemental Desire Power directed into the appropriate channels of manifestation and expression. These individuals "knew just what they wanted"; they "wanted it hard enough"; and they were "willing to pay the price."

It is this spirit of "wanting it hard enough" that distinguishes the men and women of strong purpose and determination from the common herd of persons who merely "wish for" things in a gentle, faint, conventional way—that distinguishes the true "wanters" from the dilettante "wishers." It was the recognition of this spirit in men that caused Disraeli to say that long meditation had brought him to the conviction that a human being with a settled purpose, and with a will which would stake even existence itself upon its fulfillment, must certainly accomplish that purpose.

"But," you may say, "admitting the truth of your premise, how am I to proceed in order to arouse the dormant latent Desire Power within me, and to cause it to flow forth in the direction of the attainment of my Dominant Desires?" Answering the question, we would say, "Begin at the very beginning, and proceed to arouse and draw forth the latent Desire Power, by presenting to it the stimulus of suggestive and inciting ideas and pictures." For, from beginning to end, there prevails the principle expressed in that axiom of psychology which says: *"Desire is aroused and flows forth toward things represented by ideas and mental pictures; the stronger and clearer the idea or mental picture, the stronger and more insistent is the aroused desire, all else being equal."*

You should proceed to apply this principle from the very beginning even at the stage of semi-awakened Desire Power. There abides within you a great store of latent, dormant Desire Power—a great reservoir of Desire Power which is almost dormant, but which contains within itself the latent and nascent powers of wonderfully diversified manifestation and expression. You will do well to begin by "stirring up" this great reservoir of Desire Power—arousing it into activity in a general way, to the end that you may afterward direct its power and cause it to flow forth into and along the channels of expression and manifestation which you have provided for it.

In the great crater of a mighty volcano of Hawaii, in plain sight of the daring visitor to the rim of the abyss, there abides a large lake of molten lava, seething and bubbling, boiling and effervescing in a state of hissing ebullience—a lake of liquid fire, as it were. This great fiery lake is comparatively calm on its surface, however, the ebullition proceeding from its depths. The whole body of fiery liquid manifests a rhythmic tide-like rise and fall, and a swaying from side to side of the crater. The observer is impressed with the recognition of a latent and nascent power of almost immeasurable possibilities of manifestation and expression. He feels borne upon him the conviction that this seething, rising and falling, swaying, tremendous body of liquid fire, if once fully aroused into activity, would boil and seethe up to the edge of the crater, and overflowing, would pour down into the valleys beneath carrying before it and destroying every obstacle in its path.

This great lake of molten lava—this great body of liquid fire—is a symbol of the great body of latent and nascent Desire Power abiding within every individual—within YOU. It rests there, comparatively inactive on the surface, but ever manifesting a peculiar churning ebullition proceeding from its great depths. It seethes and boils, effervesces and bubbles, rises and falls in tide-like rhythm, sways in rhythmic sequence from side to side. It seems ever to say to you, "I am here, restless and disturbed, ever longing, craving, hankering for, hungering and thirsting for, desiring for expression and manifestation in definite form and direction. Stir me up; arouse my inner force; set me into action; and I will rise and assert my power, and accomplish for you that which you direct!"

Of course, we realize that this stirring up or agitation of your latent Desire Power is apt to—in fact, certainly will—create additional Discontent on your part; but what of it? Some philosophers praise the Spirit of Contentment, and say that Happiness is to be found only therein. Be that as it may, it may be as positively asserted that all Progress proceeds from Discontent.

While admitting the value of Content, at the same time we believe in preaching the "Gospel of Discontent" to a sane degree and extent. We believe that Discontent is the first step on the Path of Attainment. We believe that it is just this very Divine Discontent that causes men and women to undertake the Divine Adventure of Life, and which is back of and under all human progress. Content may be carried quite too far. Absolute Content results in Apathy and Lethargy—it stops the wheels of Progress. Nature evidently is not Content, else it would cease to manifest the process of Evolution. Nature has evidently been ever filled with the Spirit of Discontent, judging from her invariable manifestation of the Law of Change. Without Discontent and the Desire to Change, there would be no Change in Nature. The Law of Change shows plainly Nature's opinion on the subject, and her prevailing feelings and desires in the matter.

You will do well to begin by "treating" your great body of elemental Desire Power for increased activity, and for the transmutation of its static power into dynamic power—bringing it from its state of semi-rest into the state of increased restlessness and tendency to flow forth into action. You may do this in the same way that you will later employ in the case of specific, particular and definite desires, i.e., *by presenting to it suggestive and inciting ideas and mental pictures!*

Begin by presenting to your elemental Desire Power the suggestive idea and mental picture of itself as akin to the great lake of molten lava, or liquid fire, filled with latent and nascent energy, power and force; filled with the elemental urge toward expression and manifestation in outward form and action; able and willing to accomplish anything it desires to do with sufficient strength, providing a definite channel is provided for its flow of power. Show it the picture of itself as ready and willing to transmute its static energy into dynamic force, and to pour forth along the channels which you will provide for it—and above all else, quite *able* to do this if it will but arouse itself into dynamic action. In short, present to its gaze your idealistic and ideative mental equipment in the form of the surface of a great mirror, reflecting the picture of the elemental Desire Power as it presents itself to that mirror—let Desire Power see itself as it is. Supply Desire with its complementary Idea.

You will do well to accompany this mental picture with a verbal statement or affirmation of the details of that picture. Treat your elemental Desire Power as if it were an entity—there is a valid psychological reason for this, by the way—and tell it in exact words just what it is, what are its powers, and what is its essential nature displaying the disposition to express and manifest itself in outward form and activity. Pound these suggestive statements into it, as firmly, earnestly and persistently as you can. Supply the Desire Power with the element of Idea and Mental Pictures. Give it the picture of what it is, and the pattern or diagram of what it can do if it will.

The result of this course of "treatment" applied to your elemental Desire Power will soon show itself in an increased feeling of more vigorous rhythmic tidal-movement and side-to-side movement, as previously described; and in an increased rate and vigor of its seething, boiling, effervescing ebullition. From its depths will arise mighty impulses and urges, upheavals and uprisings. The great molten-lake of Desire Power will begin to boil with increased vigor, and will show an inclination to produce the Steam of Will. You will experience new and strange evidences of the urge of Desire Power within you, seeking expression and manifestation along the channels which you have provided for it.

But before reaching this stage, you must have created the channels through and in which you wish the overflowing Desire Power to flow when it reaches the "boiling over" stage. These channels must be built along the lines of those desires which you have proved to be your Dominant Desires. Build these channels, deep, wide and strong. From them you can afterward build minor channels for your secondary and derivative desires arising from your Dominant Desires. At present, however, your main concern is with your main channels. Let each channel represent the clear, deep, strong idea and mental picture of "just what you want" as you clearly see and know it. You have found out exactly what you want, when you want it, and how you want it; let your channels represent as closely as may be just these ideas. Build the banks high, so as to obviate any waste; build the walls strong, so as to stand the strain; build the channel deep and wide, so as to carry the full force and quantity of the current.

By "creating the channels" of your Dominant Desires, we mean establishing the paths to be traversed by the overflowing current of Desire Power which you have aroused from its latent and nascent condition. These channels or paths are created mentally by the employment of Creative Imagination and Ideation. These mental forces proceed to manifest in the direction of creating and presenting to your consciousness the ideas and mental pictures of your Dominant Desires which you have discovered in your process of Self-Analysis. The work of creating these channels is really but a continuation of the mental work performed by you in the discovery of your Dominant Desires.

In creating these channels you should observe three general rules, as follows:

(1) *Make the Channels Clear and Clean* by creating and maintaining a clear, clean, distinct, and definite idea of each of your Dominant Desires, in which idea the entire thought concerning the Dominant Desire is condensed, and in which there is no foreign or non-essential material.

(2) *Make the Channels Deep and Wide* by forming mental pictures or suggestive ideas appealing to the emotional feelings associated with the Dominant Desires, and thus tempting the appetites of those desires by the representation of the objects of their longing, and by the presentation of imaginative pictures of the joys which will attend their final achievement and attainment.

(3) *Make the Banks Strong* by means of the employment of the Persistent Determination of the Will, so that the powerful swift current may be confined

within the limits of the Dominant Desire and not be permitted to escape and waste itself by scattering its energy and force over the surrounding land.

When your current is flowing freely, you will find it necessary to build minor channels serving to bring about the attainment of objects and ends helpful to the accomplishment of the objects and ends of the major channels. In building these minor channels, follow the same general rules and principles which we have given you. From the great main channels down to the tiniest canal the same principle is involved. *Always build clear and clean, by means of definite ideas and aims; always build deep and wide, by means of suggestive ideas and mental pictures; always build strong banks, by means of the determined will.*

In concluding this consideration of the second requisite, i.e., the element of "wanting it hard enough," we wish to impress upon your mind the tremendous vitalizing and inciting power exerted by Suggestive Ideas and Mental Pictures upon Desire Power. Suggestive Ideas and Mental Pictures act upon Desire Power with a tremendous degree of effect in the direction of inciting, arousing, stirring, stimulating, exciting, spurring, goading, provoking, moving, encouraging, animating and urging to expression and manifestation. There are no other incentives equal to these. All strong desires are aroused by such incentives, consciously or unconsciously applied.

For instance, you may have no desire to visit California. Then your interest in that part of the country is aroused by what you read or hear concerning it, and a vague desire to visit it is aroused in you. Later, information in the direction of giving you additional material for suggestive ideas and mental pictures serves to arouse your desire to "go to California." You begin to search eagerly for further ideas and pictures, and the more you obtain the stronger grows the flame of your desire. At last, you "want to hard enough," and brushing aside all obstacles you "pay the price" and take the trip across the plains. Had you not been furnished with the additional suggestive ideas and mental pictures, your original desire would soon have died out. You know by experience the truth of this principle; you also know how you would use it if you wished to induce a friend to visit California, do you not? Then start to work using it on your Desire Power when you wish to incite it into "wanting hard enough" something that you know to be advantageous to you!

It is customary to illustrate this principle by the figure of pouring the oil of Idea upon the flame of Desire, thereby keeping alive and strengthening the power of the latter. The figure of speech is a good one—the illustration serves well its purpose. But your memory and imagination, representing your experience, will furnish you with one a little nearer home. All that you need do is to imagine the effect which would be produced upon you if you were hungry and were able to form the mental picture or create the suggestive idea of a particularly appetizing meal. Even as it is, though you are not really hungry, the thought of such a meal will make your mouth water.

Again, you may readily imagine the effect produced upon you, when you are parched and intensely thirsty on a long ride, by the vivid mental picture or strong suggestive idea of a clear, cold spring of mountain water. Or, again, when in a stuffy, ill-ventilated office you think of the fresh air of the mountain-camp where you went fishing last Summer,—when you picture plainly the joys of the experience—can you deny that your Desire Power is intensely aroused and excited, and that you feel like dropping everything and "taking to the woods" at once.

Raising the principle to its extreme form of manifestation, try to imagine the effect upon the famishing man of a dream of plentiful food; the dream of the thirst-cursed man in which is pictured flowing fountains of water. Try to imagine the effect upon the mate-seeking wild bull-moose of the far-off bellow of the sought-for mate—would you like to impede his path on such an occasion. Finally, picture the emotional excitement and frenzy of desire on the part of the tigress when she comes in sight of food for her half-starved cubs; or her force of desire when she hears afar-off the cry of distress of her young ones.

In order to "want" and "want to" as hard as do these human beings and wild things which we have employed as illustrations, you must feed your Desire Power with suggestive ideas and mental pictures similar in exciting power to those which rouse into action their dominant and paramount "want" and "want to." Of course, these are extreme cases—but they serve to illustrate the principle involved.

In short, in order to "want it hard enough," you must create a gnawing hunger and a parching thirst for the objects of your Dominant Desires; this you must intensify and render continuous by repeatedly presenting with suggestive ideas and mental pictures of the Feast of Good Things, and the Flowing Fountain, which awaits the successful achievement or attainment of the desires.

Or, you must be like the half-drowned youth wanting "a breath of air" above all else—wanting it with all the fierce energy of his soul and being; and you must ever keep before you the suggestive idea and mental picture of "all the air there is" which is to be found just above the surface of the water of Need in which you are now immersed. When you can create these mental and emotional conditions within yourself, then, and then only, will you really know just what it is to "want hard enough."

Think well over this idea, until you grasp its full meaning!

HOW TO OVERCOME TEMPTATIONS THAT SIDETRACK YOUR AMBITIONS

According to the Master Formula, "In order to get what you want you must not only know exactly what you want," not only "want it hard enough," but also "be willing to pay the price of its attainment." We have considered the first and second of these elements of successful attainment; let us now consider the third one, and learn what it means to "be willing to pay the price of attainment."

This final element of successful attainment—this last hurdle in the race—often is the point at which many persons fail; riding gallantly over the first several hurdles, they stumble and fall when they attempt to surmount this final one. This, not so much because of the real difficulty in passing over this obstacle, but rather because they are apt to underestimate the task and, accordingly, to relax their energies. Thinking that the race is practically over, they fail to observe care and caution and thus meet failure. With the prize almost in hand, they relax their efforts and lose it.

The Law of Compensation is found in full operation in the realm of Desire, as well as in every other field and region of life and action. There is always present that insistence upon Balance which Nature invariably demands from those who seek her prizes. There is always something to be given up, in order that something else may be gained. One cannot have his pie and his dime at the same time—he must spend the dime if he would buy the pie. Neither can one keep his dime and yet spend it. Nature boldly and plainly displays her sign, "Pay the Price!" Once more let us quote the old adage: "Said the gods to man, 'Take what thou wilt; but pay the price.'"

When in actual experience you perform the process of selection of the Dominant Desires, with its attendant Struggle for Existence and Survival of the Fittest among the competing desires, even then you are beginning to "pay the price" of the attainment of your Dominant Desires; this because you are setting aside and relinquishing one or more sets of desires in favor of a preferred set. Every set of desires has its opposing set, and also other sets which would to some extent interfere with its full manifestation; you must "pay the price" of attainment of the one set of desires by relinquishing the other sets.

In order to attain the object of your desire for wealth, you must "pay the price" of relinquishing desires for certain things which would prevent you from accumulating money. In order to attain the object of your desire for all possible knowledge in some particular field of study and research, you must "pay the price" of relinquishing your desires for a similar degree of knowledge in some other field of thought and study. In order to attain the object of your desire for business success, you must "pay the price" of hard work and the passing by of the objects of your desires for play, amusement, and enjoyment which would necessitate the neglect of your business. And so on; to attain the object of any one set of desires, you must always "pay the price" of the relinquishing of the objects of other sets of desires.

In some cases, this process of the inhibition of opposing desires is akin to that of weeding your garden, or of pruning your trees—getting rid of the useless and harmful growths which interfere with the growth and development of the useful and advantageous thing. In other cases, however, the desires which you must inhibit and put away from you are not in themselves harmful or useless. On the contrary, they may be very advantageous and useful in themselves, and may be actually worthy of being adopted as Dominant Desires by others; but, at the same time, they are of such a nature as to prove an obstacle to your progress along the line of your own chosen Dominant Desires.

Things may oppose and antagonize each other without either of them being harmful or "bad" in themselves. You cannot travel at the same time both forks of the road; nor can you travel north and south on any road at the same time; though either of these courses of travel may be good in itself. You cannot very well be a successful clergyman and a successful lawyer at the same time; if you have strong desires for both of these careers, you must choose the one you desire more and set aside the other. The girl with the two attractive suitors—the man with the two delightful sweethearts—the child with the dime, gazing longingly at the two different tarts—each must choose one and pass by the other, and thus "pay the price."

Not only in the preliminary process of discovering and identifying your Dominant Desires are you called upon to "pay the price," but you are equally called upon to do so at almost every subsequent step and stage of your progress in actual experience. There is always something presenting itself to tempt you into "sidetracking" your Desire Power; some alluring desires which beckon you from the straight Path of Attainment. Here you will find that it is hard to "pay the price"; and often you will gravely question yourself, asking if the things represented by the Dominant Desires are, after all, worth the price you are being called on to pay for them. These temptations and struggles come to all—they constitute one of the tests whereby it is determined whether you are strong or whether you are weak in regard to your Desire Power. Here is the real test of whether or not you "want it hard enough" to make you willing to "pay the price."

Particularly difficult to overcome and conquer are those temptations which induce you to relinquish your desire for future attainment in favor of the gratification of present desires; or which tempt you to forego the attainment of permanent future benefits in favor of temporary, ephemeral benefits. The tempter whispers in your ear that you are foolish to content yourself with the skim-milk of the present in the hope of obtaining the full cream of tomorrow. The ever-present suggestion to "Eat, drink, and be merry, for tomorrow we die" must be boldly confronted and conquered if you wish to attain the object of that which your reason and judgment, as well as your self-analysis, has shown that you really want above everything else. The habit of saying: "Get thee behind me Satan!" must be cultivated; and when you have got him behind you, look out lest he give you a push from behind!

Here you determine whether or not you really "want it hard enough." The drowning man is in no doubt concerning the value of the breath of air. He is willing to "pay the price of it," no matter how high that price may be. The famishing man knows the value of food—the parched man knows the value of water: they are willing to "pay the price," and are not liable to be sidetracked from their Dominant Desire. The bull-moose seeking his mate is willing to "pay the price" of danger and possible death lying in his path—but you cannot sidetrack him. The mother tiger cannot be sidetracked from the pursuit of food for her hungry cubs—she is willing to "pay the price" of risk of life without hesitation. When you begin to "want it hard enough" along the same lines, and reaching toward the same degree of intensity and insistence manifested by these creatures, then you will not hesitate to "pay the price"—to pay it in full, and without hesitation; when you reach this stage the tempter will whisper into ears deaf to his voice.

In order to hold the current of Desire Power within the bounds of your channels of Dominant Desire, the banks must be erected and kept in a state of strength by Will Power. The "Will to Will" must be called into manifestation.

While Desire is one of the fundamental elements of Will, it is not all of Will. Will is a subtle combination of Conative Desire and of Purposeful Determination. It springs from Desire, but it evolves into something which is capable of mastering Desire by its power of "Willing to Will."

Here follow three general rules which you should note very carefully in connection with the subject of inhibiting and setting-aside the temptations of conflicting desires—of those desires which are constantly springing up and tempting you to forego "paying the price," or to become "sidetracked" from the Path of Attainment of your Dominant Desires. Two of these rules are along the lines of which we have spoken in connection with the influence of Representative Ideas upon Desire Power.

1. *Under temptation by sidetracking desires, use every effort to feed the Flame of Desire of your Dominant Desires, by an increased supply of suggestive ideas and mental pictures tending to stimulate its heat and incite its energy.*

2. *At the same time, strenuously avoid feeding the flame of the tempting desires by suggestive ideas and mental pictures likely to arouse or incite them. On the contrary, carefully and positively refuse to admit such ideas and pictures to your mind so far as is possible; seek to starve the fires of such desires by withholding from them the fuel necessary for their continuance and support.*

The third rule involves another psychological principle, and is as follows:

3. *So far as is possible, transmute the sidetracking desires into forms more in accordance with general trend of the Dominant Desires, thereby converting them into helpful rather than harmful emotional energy.*

In the case of the first rule above stated, you tend to inhibit the energy of the sidetracking desires by imparting additional energy to the Dominant Desires. When the attention is strongly attracted or held by the suggestive ideas and mental pictures of a strong set of desires, it is not easily diverted by those of a weaker set. The strong light of the former tend to cast the latter into a comparative shadow. The attention firmly concentrated and held upon one particular set of ideas and mental pictures refuses to accept the demand of another set. Keep the attention busy with the advantageous set, and it "will have no time" for the consideration of the opposing set. With these opposing suggestive ideas and mental pictures kept out of the field of conscious attention, the desires associated with them tend to die down and finally to disappear.

In the case of the second rule above stated you deliberately and determinedly refuse to feed the flame of the sidetracking desires with the fuel of suggestive ideas and mental pictures. Instead, you proceed deliberately and determinedly to starve that flame. No flame of desire can long continue to burn vigorously if its supply of suggestive fuel be cut off from it. Cut off the fuel supply of any desire, and it will begin to decrease in vigor and force. Refuse to allow your mind to dwell upon the ideas or mental pictures tending to suggest the sidetracking desires. When such ideas and pictures intrude themselves and seek to attract the attention, you must deliberately turn your attention to something else—preferably to the suggestive ideas and pictures of your Dominant Desires.

The Roman Catholic Church evidently recognizes the value of this rule, for its teachers instruct their pupils to form the habit of turning their attention to prayers and certain forms of devotional exercises when temptations assail them. The attention being directed to and held firmly upon the devotional exercise or ceremony, it is withheld from the suggestive ideas and mental pictures of the tempting desire; and, accordingly, the latter loses strength and in time dies away. Without detracting from the value of the religious element involved, we may say that it is certain that the purely psychological effect of such course is highly advantageous. You would do well to apply the principle in your own case.

In the case of the third rule above stated, you transmute the energy of the sidetracking desire into that of desires more in accordance with the general trend of your Dominant Desires. In this way you not only obviate the danger of the interference and distraction of the sidetracking desires, but also actually employ the basic energy of Desire Power to feed the flame of the advantageous desires. Here, the principle involved is not so well known as are those involved in the other rules; but that principle is sound, nevertheless, and is capable of being employed with remarkable results by the individual possessing sufficient will power and determination to apply it.

As an example of this principle of the transmutation of the form of Desire Force, let us point you to a fact well known to scientific observers, viz., that the energy of the sexual passions may be transmuted into the energy of any kind of mental or physical creative work. This fact is also known to priests and others who are called on for advice from those wishing to control passions of this kind. The explanation probably lies in the fact that sexual desire is essentially *creative* in its fundamental nature, and therefore is capable of being diverted to other forms of creative activity. But whatever may be the true explanation, it is a fact that the person experiencing strong intruding sexual desires may proceed to master and control them by means of engaging in some form of creative work in which the elemental creative energy is transmuted into other forms of creative force.

For instance, one may *create* by writing, musical composition, artistic work, or making and constructing things with the hands—in fact, by any kind of work in which things are made, put together, constructed or created in any way. In all of such work, provided that sufficient interest is thrown into the task, it will be found that the strong impulse of the intruding sexual passions will gradually lose its force, and that the person will then experience a sense of new energy in the creative work which he has undertaken in order to transmute the previous form of Desire Power.

The experienced physician knows that the best possible prescription for certain classes of cases of this kind coming to him for treatment and advice is that of "interesting work" for head or hands or both. There is much truth in the old saying that "An idle brain is the devil's workshop," and the similar one that "The devil finds plenty of work for idle hands to do." This principle may be set to work against "the devil," by simply reversing its action by giving head and hands plenty to do.

Another illustration of this principle is found in the case of the beneficial effect of certain games—in fact, of nearly all games played in moderation. Here the sidetracking and distracting desires which seek to take one away from his appointed tasks, and from the manifestation of his Dominant Desires, are transmuted into the interest, feeling, and desires of Play. Play is a safety-valve of emotional feeling. It serves to transmute many a distracting desire into the conative energy expressing itself in an interesting game. This is true of games involving purely mental skill, as well as those in which physical skill is also involved. Baseball has been a wonderful benefit to the American people in this way. Golf is playing an important part in the direction of affording a "transmutation channel" of energy for busy men who tire under the somewhat monotonous strain of the strenuous pursuit of the object of their Dominant Desires. In cases of this kind, not only are the distracting desires transmuted in this way, but the games themselves give recreation, exercise and a restful change of occupation to the individual.

"Paying the price" of your Dominant Desires does not necessarily imply

that you must give up everything in life not actually concerned in further-
ing the interests of those particular desires—in such case, indeed, you would
probably actually injure your own interests by too closely restricting your circle
of interest and attention. The real meaning of the injunction is that you must
"pay the price" of *giving up, inhibiting, or at least transmuting any and all desires
which directly and certainly oppose and seriously interfere with the attainment of
the objects of your Dominant Desires.* That price, indeed, you must be prepared
to pay. In many cases, such desires may be transmuted into forms which will in
a sense "run along with" the pursuit of the objects of your Dominant Desires,
and thus be rendered helpful rather than harmful. Many emotional elements
may be turned to account in this way by the process of transmutation. You
should give some thought to this matter of transmutation when you are threatened by distracting and sidetracking desires.

Another form of "paying the price" is that of the labor and work to be performed by the individual in his task of attainment of the object of his Dominant
Desires. This work and labor, however, is not alone performed by the exercise of
the Persistent Determination of the Will, though this is the active element involved; there is needed also the inhibition and starving out of the conflicting or
sidetracking desires which strive to draw the individual away from his appointed
tasks and toward the actions requiring less work, and which for the time being
seem to be richer in promise of pleasure and satisfaction.

The price paid by the men and women who have achieved marked success
almost always is found to include self-denial, and sometimes even actual priva-
tion during the earlier days of the undertaking; work far in excess of that rightfully demanded of the wage earner, both in amount and in time is demanded
of them; application and unwearied perseverance are required of them; indomitable resolution and persistent determination must be "paid" by them. There is
here the constant giving up of the present pleasure in favor of that hoped for in
the future. There is here the constant performance of tasks which might easily
be avoided, and which are really avoided by the average person, but which are
required to be performed by the individual who is inspired by the Dominant
Desire and who is working for the accomplishment of "the one big thing."

Napoleon "paid the price" in his earlier days when he refused to indulge in
the frivolous pursuits of his fellow-students at Brienne, and instead, deliberately devoted his spare time to the mastery of the elements of military science
and history. Abraham Lincoln "paid the price" when he studied the few books
he could find by the light of the fireplace, instead of indulging in the pleasures

and dissipations of the other young men of his neighborhood. Read the history of any successful man and you will find this invariable "paying the price" of study, application, work, self-denial, economy, thrift, industry and the rest of the needful things.

Never delude yourself with the thought that you can escape "paying the price" of the attainment of the objects of your strong desires. The price must always be paid—the greater the object of attainment the greater is the price demanded. But you will find that if you have learned how to "want it hard enough" then the price will be comparatively easy to pay—the thing will be deemed well worth it.

If you feel that the price that you are being called upon to pay for the object of your Dominant Desires is more than the thing is worth, then there is something wrong about the whole matter. In such case, you should carefully "take stock" of your feelings, weighing and comparing them carefully as we have suggested in our consideration of Self-Analysis, and selection of Dominant Desires. You may find that what you had supposed to be a Dominant Desire is not really such at all. Or you may find that you have failed to include some necessary element or phase of the Dominant Desire. Or, that you have failed to make some possible transmutation of distracting desires; or have failed to inhibit or starve out sidetracking desires. Or, possibly, that you have failed to feed the flame of your Dominant Desire properly. At any rate, there is something wrong in such a case, and you should seek the remedy.

While the Law of Nature provides that you must "pay the price" of any and all desires, it also provides that the attainment must always be worth the price. If you find that the present and probable future value of any object of your desire is not worth the price you must be called upon to pay for it, then you should carefully consider the whole matter most critically, viewing it from all angles, and in the light of all possible relations and associations, with full deliberation concerning the probable consequences of an opposite course, and with thoughtful judgment concerning all alternative courses. The dissatisfaction may be merely temporary and passing, or on the other hand, it may be growing in strength and promise of permanency.

Any desire which upon careful consideration, deliberation, and judgment may seem not to "pay for its keep"—to be not worth its storage charges or floor space in your emotional nature—is a fit object for a final retrial upon its merits, a re-valuation of its points, in order to decide whether it shall be retained and treated for additional strength, energy and emotional value, or else discarded and rejected. The test should always be: *"Is this really worth while—worth the price I am called on to pay for it; would its rejection cost me more than its retention?"* The Touchstone of Merit should be: *"Does this render me stronger, better and more efficient—and, therefore, more truly and permanently happier?"*

SUMMARY

You have seen that Desire is that emotional state which is represented by the phrase, *"I want!"* You have seen that *"Desire has for its object something which will bring pleasure or get rid of pain, immediate or remote, for the individual or for some one in whom he is interested."* You have seen that *"You always act according to your greatest 'like' or 'dislike' of which you are cognizant at the time."* You have seen that *"The degree of force, energy, will, determination, persistence, and continuous application manifested by an individual in his aspirations, ambitions, aims, performances, actions and work is determined primarily by the degree of his desire for the attainment of the objects thereof—his degree of 'want' and 'want to' concerning that object."* You have seen that *"Desire is the Flame that produces the Steam of Will,"* and that, therefore, Desire is the source from which all human action springs.

You have seen that not only does Desire Power directly or indirectly cause all human action, but that it also sets into operation the Life Forces which develop the mental and physical faculties and powers of the individual along lines designed to further and more efficiently manifest and express the dominant desires of the individual. You have seen how Desire Power presses into service the powers of the subconscious mentality in the work of manifesting and expressing the strong desires. You have seen how the subconscious powers act so as to attract to the individual the things, person, conditions and circumstances serving to enable him to better manifest and express his sovereign desires; and how, in the same way, they tend to attract the individual to those things, persons, conditions and circumstances. You have seen how Desire Attraction works silently, even when one is asleep, toward the end impressed upon it by the character of the strong desires.

You have discovered the importance of "knowing exactly what you want," and have learned how to gain such important knowledge by Self-Analysis and Selection. You have discovered the importance of "wanting it hard enough," and have learned how to feed the Flame of Desire so as to cause it to burn fiercely. You have learned how to set into motion and activity the great body of Elemental Desire, and how to cause it to flow forth through the channels of manifestation and expression which you have carefully built for its flood. You have discovered the necessity of "paying the price of attainment" of the objects of your desire, and have learned the general rules concerning such payment.

You have been informed concerning the tremendous power of the Desire Power within your being, and have become acquainted with the laws governing its manifestation and expression, and the rules regulating its control and direction. If you have entered into the spirit of this instruction, and have allowed its influence to descend into the subconscious depths of your mentality, you have already become aware of the aroused energy of the Desire Power in those depths. You will have found yourself filled with a new and unfolding consciousness of Personal Power within you. You will have experienced that intuitive feeling that there have been set into operation in you certain subtle but dynamic forces which will tend to make you "stronger, better and more efficient."

As you proceed to arouse into further activity these great forces of your nature, and to direct their channel of manifestation and expression, you will from time to time receive actual evidence and proof that you are travelling along the right road, and are employing the proper methods. You will be astonished to receive proofs and actual results in the most unexpected manner, and from sources and directions never dreamt of before. You will realize more and more, as you proceed, that you have set into operation one of Nature's most potent forces, in fact, "the force of forces." Finally, you will begin to realize that the very actual presence within you of a Dominant Desire which has won its place in the "struggle for existence," and which has stood all the tests, is practically "the prophecy of its own fulfillment."

You have been asked to consider the facts which have been discovered concerning the nature, character and modes of activity of Desire Power, that great elemental psychic energy which is seen to pervade all existence and to be present universally. Analyze the actions of any or every living thing, and you will find Desire Power inspiring and motivating it. Nay, examine the motions of the so-called inanimate objects of Nature, and you will find even there the energizing forces of "something like Desire Power."

If Nature be regarded as a magnificent Cosmic Machine—then Desire Power is the motive-power that runs that universal machinery. If Nature be regarded as a Living Macrocosm—then Desire Power is the living motive-power inspiring and causing its activities. From whatever angle Nature may be viewed, under whatever hypothesis or theory it may be regarded, Desire Power is perceived to be the Something or Somewhat directly responsible for making "the wheels go 'round." The old Hermetic axiom, "As above, so below; as within, so without; as in great, so in small," is seen to apply here: the individual and the Cosmos both are seen to have as their essential motive-power that original, aboriginal, elemental, fundamental Something which we know as Desire Power.

In view of this fact, you scarcely need to be urged to study the methods of operation of this mighty force, so that you may harness it to your machinery of life and action. Like Gravitation or Electricity, its power is available to all who have the courage, intelligence and perseverance to master it and to press it into service. It is as free as the air or the sunshine; it costs nothing to run your living machinery with it—nothing but persistence and determination. You do not have to supply it with power, or to add energy to it: it has within itself far more power, energy or force than you will ever have occasion to make use of. All that you need do is to tap on to its free energy, and to set it to work for you in the direction of running the mental and physical machinery with which you have provided it.

Let us ask you to consider the following remarkable statement of Wr. Wilfrid Lay. Speaking of the Desire Power of the Subconscious, Dr. Lay says:

> I call your attention to the enormous power of the Subconscious. It is the accumulated desire in each one of us, of aeons of evolution, the present form, in each individual, of that vital force which has kept itself immortal through thousands of generations of men behind us, and millions of generations of animals behind them. It need not be anything but a source of power to us, power that we can draw upon, if we rightly understand it, just as we can turn on power from a steam pipe or an electric wire. It need not be destructive, indeed it is not destructive, except in the most distracted souls, but on the contrary ought in each one of us, when we have learned to manage it rightly, to be as much and as completely at our command as is the power in the automobile. As in the automobile, there are a few simple things that we have to learn and the rest is furnished by the maker of the car, and we do ill to tamper with it. The experience of having a two-hundred-horsepower car placed at one's command (if it is to be driven by oneself) is a situation into which there are many persons,

*both men and women, who are very loath to enter. And similarly there
are many persons who for various causes would not be willing to have
developed the two-hundred-thousand-generation-power which resides in
them. To all intents and purposes, and as far as human flesh is able to
bear the strain, this power which is largely in the hands of the Subconscious in most men and women is illimitable.*

Desire Power is a Cosmic Force designed for the controlled and directed
use of the strong. It is at the disposal of all—but only few are courageous
and determined enough to avail themselves of its services. The masses of
men merely dally with it, play with it, handle it gingerly: the Masters of Men
boldly grasp its controlling levers, and turn its power into their mental and
physical machinery. It is a Master Force fitted only for the service of Masters.
It is the rightful servant only of those whose slogan is: "I Can, I Will; I Dare,
I Do!"

You can be a Master of Desire Power, and thus a Master of Men, a Master
of Circumstances, a Master of Life, if you but will to be so. You are the Master of your Fate—the Captain of your Soul—if you will but recognize, realize
and manifest the Power of the "I AM I" which is your Real Self, and of which
Desire Power is the willing servant.

YOUR SILENT PARTNER WITHIN

While the mental planes lying outside of and beyond the field of ordinary consciousness have been until recent years comparatively unexplored by psychologists, and in fact have been almost entirely ignored by western psychology until
modern times, the best thought of the present time is in practical agreement
upon the fact that on those hidden planes of mentality are performed the major
portion of our mental work, and that in their field are in operation some of the
most important of our mental processes.

The exploration of these obscure regions of the mind has been one of the
most fascinating tasks of modern psychology; and the mines have yielded rich
material in abundance. Many mental phenomena formerly either denied as impossible by the orthodox psychologists, or else regarded by the average person
as evidence of supernatural agencies and forces, are now seen to fit perfectly
into the natural order of things, and to operate according to natural law and

order. Not only have such investigations resulted in a greater increase of the scientific knowledge concerning the inner workings of the mind, but they have also served to place in the hands of the more advanced psychologists the material which they have turned to practical and efficient use by means of scientific methods of application.

The effect of these discoveries has been the presentation of an important truth to the thinking individual—the truth that his mental realm is a far greater and grander land that he has heretofore considered it to be. No longer is the Self held to be limited in its mental activities to the narrow field of ordinary consciousness. Your mental kingdom has suddenly expanded until it now constitutes a great empire, with borders flung wide and far beyond the boundaries of the little kingdom which you have been considering as the entire area of the field of the forces, powers and activities of the Self.

The Self has often been likened to the king of a great mental kingdom; but, in view of the discovery of the new facts concerning the wonderful field of the unconscious, subconscious and superconscious mental activities, the Self is now more properly to be represented as a mighty emperor of a vast empire of which only a comparatively small portion has as yet been explored. You are being called upon to appreciate more fully the ancient aphorism: "You are greater than you know." Your Self is like a new Columbus, gazing at the great new world which it has discovered around itself, and of which it is the owner and the ruler.

Employing the term, "The Subconscious," to indicate the entire field of activities of the mind which are performed below, above or in anyway "outside of" the field or plane of the ordinary consciousness of the individual, we soon discover that the activities of the Subconscious extend over a very wide range of manifestation, and embrace a great variety of forms of expression.

In the first place, the Subconscious presides over the activities of your physical organism; it is the animating spirit of your physical processes. It performs the manifold tasks of digestion, assimilation, nutrition, elimination, secretion, circulation, reproduction—in short, all of your vital processes. Your conscious mentality is thus relieved of these great tasks.

Again, the Subconscious supervises the performance of your instinctive actions. Every action that you perform automatically, instinctively, "by habit," "by heart" and without conscious employment of thought and will, is really performed by your subconscious mentality. Your conscious mentality, thus relieved of this work, is able to concentrate upon those other tasks which it alone can perform. When you learn to perform an action "by heart," or "by habit," the conscious mentality has turned over this particular work to your Subconscious.

Again, the Subconscious is largely concerned with the activities of your emotional nature. Your emotions which rise to the plane or level of consciousness are but the surface manifestations of the more elemental activities performed in the depths of the ocean of the Subconscious. Your elemental and instinctive emotions have their source and home in the Subconscious; they have accumulated there by reason of habit, heredity or racial memory. Practically all the material of your emotional activities is stored on the planes and levels of the Subconscious.

Again, the Subconscious presides over the processes of Memory. The subconscious planes or levels of the mind constitute the great storehouse of the recorded impressions of memory. Moreover, on those planes or levels is performed the work of indexing and cross-indexing the memory-records, by means of which subsequent recollection, recognition and remembrance are rendered possible. These regions of your subconscious mentality contain not only the recorded impressions of your own personal experience, but also those racial memories or inherited memories which manifest in you as "instinct," and which play a very important part in your life.

Again, the Subconscious is able to, and frequently does, perform for you important work along the lines of actual "thinking." By means of "mental rumination" it digests and assimilates the materials furnished by your conscious mentality, and then proceeds to classify these, to compare them, and to proceed to form judgments and decisions upon them and from them—all below the levels of your ordinary consciousness. Careful psychologists have decided that by far the greater part of our reasoning processes are really performed on mental levels and planes outside of the field of the ordinary consciousness. Much of your creative mental work, particularly that of the constructive imagination, is performed in this way, the result afterward being raised to the levels of conscious thought.

Finally, there are levels and planes "above" those of the ordinary consciousness, just as there are those "below" the latter. Just as the lower levels are largely concerned with working over the stored-up materials of the past, so these higher levels are concerned with reporting that which may be considered to represent the future conscious activities of the human race. These higher regions of the Subconscious may be said to contain the seed or embryo of the higher faculties and powers which will unfold fully in the future stages of the mental evolution of the race; many of these higher faculties and powers are even now beginning to manifest in occasional flashes in the minds of certain individuals, and, as a consequence, such individuals are frequently regarded as "inspired" or as possessing that indefinable quality or power known as "genius."

On these higher planes of the Subconscious abide certain marvelous powers of the Self, which powers manifest and express themselves in that which we call genius, inspiration, illumination—the exceptional mental achievements of certain intellects which stamp them as above the average. On these high planes abide and are manifested those wonderful mental activities which we attempt to explain under the term "Intuition." These activities, however, are not contrary to reason, though they may seem to transcend it at times; it is better to consider them as the manifestation of a Higher Reason. The investigation and exploration of these higher realms of the Subconscious form one of the most interesting and fascinating tasks of modern psychology. Even now, the reports of the investigators and explorers are of surpassing interest; those which confidently may be looked for in the future bid fair to constitute a marvelous contribution to the pages of the history of modern scientific research.

We shall ask you to accompany us in an exploration of the various regions of the Subconscious—those wonderful realms of your mind—from the highest to the lowest. In this new land there are valuable deposits of material useful to you and to all mankind. It is our purpose to point out these to you, and to instruct you in the most approved methods of mining and converting them to practical uses. You are interested in the matter of being led directly to the mines containing these rich deposits, and in being told just how to conduct the mining operations and the converting processes. In this spirit, then, our journey of exploration shall be conducted.

The Secret Forces of the Great Subconscious, like all other great natural forces, may be harnessed and pressed into service by you. Like electricity, they may be so managed and directed into the proper channels that they may be set to work by and for you. You have been employing these forces, to a greater or less extent, in very many of your mental activities; but, in all probability, you have been employing them instinctively and without a full knowledge of the laws and principles involved in them. When you understand just what these forces are, how they work, and the methods best calculated to produce efficient results and effects, then you may proceed to employ them intelligently, deliberately and with conscious purpose and intent, end and aim.

The average man employs but about 25 per cent of the Subconscious Power.

The man who understands the principles and methods to which we have just referred will be able to employ 100 per cent of his available Subconscious Power. This means that he will be able to increase fourfold his Subconscious mental work and activity, with correspondingly increased results and effects. Inasmuch as at least 75 per cent of man's mental processes are performed on the plane or level of the Subconscious, it will be seen that the benefits arising from quadrupling his Subconscious mental activities and available power are almost beyond the power of adequate calculation. This increased power and efficiency, moreover, are not obtained at the cost of increased effort and mental wear and tear: on the contrary, the man effectively employing his Subconscious relieves himself of a great portion of the mental strain incident to the employment of the conscious mentality.

In addition to the offices and powers of the Superconscious which we have mentioned, there is another and a most important function of that phase of the mentality which may be called "the protective power." Many persons, most persons in fact, have at times experienced this beneficent power. They have felt strongly that they were in close contact with a force, power or entity of some kind which was in some way higher than themselves, but which was concerned with their welfare. This beneficent presence has been interpreted in various ways in accordance with the trend of thought of those experiencing it. Some of the ancients called it "the kindly genius"; others termed it "the guardian angel"; still others have thought of it as "my spirit friend"; while many others, though quite vividly conscious of its presence and power, have failed to give it a special name.

But by whatever name it may have been thought of, or even when no name at all has been applied to it, the mysterious something has been recognized as a beneficent presence-power—a hovering and brooding Something or Somewhat animated by a warm, kindly interest in the individual, and seemingly devoted to his interests and disposed to render to him useful services.

This beneficent presence-power has often acted as a warning guardian in the lives of many persons. In other cases it has been felt to have acted subtly to bring about advantageous results and conditions for the persons whom it protected. It has led some into circumstances and conditions calculated to be of advantage to them; it has drawn others away from conditions and circumstances calculated to bring harm to them. In short, it has played the part of "the kindly genius" or "the guardian angel" to many an individual.

The touch of this Unseen Hand has been felt by countless individuals—very likely by you who are now reading these lines. It has cheered men when the tide of circumstances seemed to be running against them; it has animated them with a new lively spirit, has encouraged them to renewed endeavor, has filled them with new courage when they needed it most. It has seemingly led persons into the presence of other persons and things, into conditions and environments, which have proved advantageous to them. Men in all ages—some of the most practical and "hard headed" men of affairs, among others—have felt the touch of this Unseen Hand, and have gratefully acknowledged its help in times of need, even though they have been perplexed concerning its real character.

To many careful thinkers who have earnestly investigated this phenomenon, it has seemed that this beneficent presence-power—this Unseen Hand that has reached out in times of need—is not an external power, nor an entity outside of themselves, but is rather a manifestation of that part of man's mental nature which we have here considered under the term "The Superconscious." Instead of being an entity outside of us, it is believed to be a part of ourselves—a phase, part or aspect of our Self that manifests above the levels or planes of the ordinary consciousness. In short, this "kindly genius" or "guardian angel" is your own Superconscious Self, manifesting on some of its higher levels or planes of activity and power.

In this Higher Self you have a friend far truer, more constant and more loyal than can be any other friend—for it is Yourself, in its essence and substance. Your interests are its interests, for you are one with it in essential being and power. It will manifest a fidelity to you, and a watchfulness over your real interests which is amazing in its devotion and constancy. It will manifest toward you, in turns, the protecting care of a father; the brooding watchful, loving care of a mother; and the helpful, fraternal care of a brother. It will be all of these things to you—and more—if you will but give it the chance to unfold its presence and to manifest its power in your life.

This Higher Self—this phase of your Superconscious—needs but the encouragement of your recognition and realization in order to manifest its power in your behalf. It is seemingly discouraged, disheartened and abashed by your indifference, unbelief and the failure to recognize its presence and to realize its power. It does not need "training" or "developing"—all that it asks is to be recognized and realized by you, and to have from you a kindly, sympathetic reception. It has done much for you in the past—it will do more for you in the future, if you will but meet it half way.

This higher part of your Self is full of discernment, and of cold, keen-edged wisdom. It can see far ahead, and is able to discern and select the right road for you to travel, and then to lead you into that road and to keep your feet on its solid substance, in spite of your efforts to take a side path or to wander into the ditches which lie on either side of the road. You will do well to "get off by yourself" once in a while, then and there to commune with your Higher Self—to have a little "heart-to-heart" visit with it. You will find this Higher Self to be a wonderful companion—one closer to you than can be any human being—for it is Yourself, and nothing but Yourself, manifesting on the higher planes and levels of your being. You will emerge from these periods of self-communion with renewed strength and vigor, filled with new hope and faith, animated by new ambitions and purposive determination.

We have presented to you a view of your New Mental Empire—a view of its lowest and its highest planes and levels, of its highlands and its lowlands. It is your own empire—YOURS! Yours it is to rule and to govern, to explore and to cultivate. You are at home in it. The many wonderful phenomena manifested in its immense region are your phenomena—yours to control, direct, develop, cultivate; yours to restrict, restrain, inhibit; at your will, as you will, by your will.

Do not allow yourself to be tempted by the wonderful powers manifested by some of your subordinate mental machinery or instruments; do not allow yourself to fall under the spell of any of the phenomenal manifestations in your mental wonderland. View all; respect all; use all; demand and secure aid and work from all; but never lose sight of the fact that YOU, your Real Self—the "I am I"—is the Master of this land, the ruler of this Empire, and that you rightfully have power and dominion over it, all its inhabitants and all contained in its realm.

Your "I am I," your Real Self—YOU—are a centre of consciousness and will, of Personal Power, in that Infinite and Eternal Power, that Ultimate POWER from which all things proceed, and in which we live, and move, and have our being. Your physical body and your physical energies; your mental mechanism and its energies, manifesting on any or all the planes or levels of consciousness, subconsciousness or superconsciousness; all these are but instruments or channels of expression of your Real Self, the "I AM I," of YOU.

YOU, the "I AM I" are the centre of your personal world of experience and manifestation. Keep ever your rightful place at the center of that world; observe all the rest whirling and revolving around that center, as the planets revolve, whirling, around the sun. YOU are the Sun! Do not lose your balance, nor be induced to move away from your central position to accommodate any of your subordinate planets—not even the greatest of them.

Hail! Mighty Emperor! Enter into and possess, rule and govern, your New Mental Empire! It is YOURS!

Let us remind you of the truth of the ancient aphorism: "You are greater than you know!"

The Secret *of* Power

Introduction

What is the strongest political trend in the world today?

After the last war, it was towards democracy. But somehow democracy failed the average man. When the depression came and he found himself unable to provide food and shelter for his loved ones, he demanded something more than equality of opportunity. He demanded SECURITY from want.

To answer that demand came "Strong Men," so-called, Mussolinis and Hitlers and Antonescus and Francos and the like, and Fascism was born. Men achieved security, of a kind, but they bartered their freedom for it. And soon they learned that power feeds on power, and the only end of dictatorship is war, which destroys all.

And the reason? The same reason that has impelled man since time began—the longing for security, security for the home, security against want, security for old age.

Since time began, the search for security has been one of the strongest urges in all of nature. You see it in the animal in the way it conceals its nest and tries to make it safe from predatory creatures—man or animal. You see it in the records of early man in the caves he dug into the sides of the mountains, in the tree huts, in the cliff dwellings. You follow it down through the ages to the walled cities, the turreted castles, the inaccessible mountains in which men made their homes.

Throughout history, you see this search for security as one of the dominant characteristics of all human kind. And now that the common man has realized his power, you find him all over the world banding together to take over all property, to the end that he and his may find that security from want that he has so long worked for.

What he does not seem to realize is that the mere redistribution of property never has and never will solve his problem. It will provide him with temporary supply, yes—but supply is a continuing problem, and when his small share of the general distribution is gone, he will be worse off than he was before, because production will have either ceased or been greatly curtailed.

Redistribution is not the answer. It has been tried repeatedly, and always failed. You must go farther back than that. You must start with the source of things. And that is what we shall try to do in the following pages.

Know this, ye restless denizens of earth,
Know this, ye seekers after joy and mirth,
Three things there are, eternal in their worth—
LOVE, that outreaches to the humblest things:
WORK, that is glad in what it does and brings;
And FAITH, that soars upon unwearied wings.
Divine the powers that on this trio wait,
Supreme their conquest, over time and fate.
LOVE, WORK and FAITH, these three alone are great.

21

The Creative Force

The Spirit of the Lord is upon me,
Because he anointed me to preach good tidings to the poor:
He has sent me to proclaim release to the captives,
And recovering of sight to the blind,
To set at liberty them that are bruised,
To proclaim the acceptable year of the Lord.
In the beginning was the Word. And the Word was with God.
And the Word was God.

—ST. JOHN

What is a word? A mental concept or image, is it not? In originating language, words were coined to represent certain images or objects. The word horse, for instance, calls to mind the image left upon the retina and the brain by what one has seen of that quadruped.

But what if there were no horses? What if one were called upon to create a horse, with no previous knowledge of such an animal? You'd have to build up a clear mental image of him first, would you not? You'd have to work out a mental picture of every part of his anatomy, every physical outline. You'd need a perfect mental concept of everything that is comprised in the word horse.

And that was what happened when God created the world. In the beginning was the "Word," the mental concept, the image in God's mind of what He planned. "And the Word was made flesh." It took on shape and substance. It grew into an habitable world. It developed creatures like the fish in the sea, the birds in the air, the beasts of the field. And finally man.

Life then, as now, was a continually developing process. Those early forms of life were threatened by every kind of danger—from floods, from earthquakes, from droughts, from desert heat, from glacial cold, from volcanic eruptions—but each new danger was merely an incentive to finding some new resource, to putting forth their Creative Force in some new shape.

To meet one set of needs, the Creative Force formed the Dinosaur; to meet another, the Butterfly. Long before it worked up to man, we see its unlimited resourcefulness in a thousand ways. To escape danger in the water, some forms of Life sought land. Pursued on land, they took to the air. To breathe in the sea, the Creative Force developed gills. Stranded on land, it perfected lungs. To meet one kind of danger, it grew a shell. For another, it developed fleetness of foot, or wings that carried it into the air. To protect itself from glacial cold, it grew fur. In temperate climes, hair. Subject to alternate heat and cold, it produced feathers. But ever, from the beginning, it showed its power to meet every changing condition, *to answer every creature need*.

Had it been possible to stamp out this Creative Force, or halt its constant upward development, it would have perished ages ago, when fire and flood, drought and famine followed each other in quick succession. But obstacles, misfortunes, cataclysms, were to it merely new opportunities to assert its power. In fact, it required difficulties or obstacles to stir it up, to make it show its energy and resourcefulness.

The great reptiles, the monster beasts of antiquity, passed on as the conditions changed that had made them possible, but the Creative Force stayed, changing as each age changed, always developing, always improving.

When God put this Creative Force into His creatures, He gave to it unlimited energy, unlimited resource. No other power can equal it. No force can defeat it. No obstacle can hold it back. All through the history of life and mankind, you can see its directing intelligence rising to meet every need of life.

No one can follow it down through the ages without realizing that the purpose of existence is GROWTH, DEVELOPMENT. Life is dynamic, not static. It is ever moving forward—not standing still. The one unpardonable sin in all of nature is to stand still, to stagnate. The Gigantosaurus, that was over a hundred feet long and as big as a house; the Tyrannosaurus, that had the strength of a locomotive and was the last word in frightfulness; the Pterodactyl or Flying Dragon—all the giant monsters of pre-historic ages—are gone. They ceased to serve a useful purpose. They stood still while the life around them passed them by.

Egypt and Persia, Greece and Rome, all the great empires of antiquity, perished when they ceased to grow. China built a wall around herself and stood still for a thousand years. In all of Nature, to cease to grow is to perish.

It is for men and women who are not ready to stand still, who refuse to cease to grow, that this book is written. Its purpose is to give you a clearer understanding of your own potentialities, to show you how to work with and take advantage of the infinite energy and power of the Creative Force working through you.

The terror of the man at the crossways, not knowing which way to turn, should be no terror for you, for your future is of your own making. The only law of infinite energy is the law of supply. The Creative Principle is your principle. To survive, to win through, to triumphantly surmount all obstacles has been its everyday practice since the beginning of time. It is no less resourceful now than it ever was. You have but to supply the urge, to work in harmony with it, to get from it anything you need. For if this Creative Force is so strong in the lowest forms of animal life that it can develop a shell or a poison to meet a need; if it can teach the bird to circle and dart, to balance and fly, if it can grow a new limb on a spider or crab to replace a lost one; how much more can it do for YOU—a reasoning, rational being, with a mind able to work with this Creative Force, with energy and purpose and initiative to urge it on!

The evidence of this is all about you. Take up some violent form of exercise, and in the beginning your muscles are weak, easily tired. But keep on a few days, and what happens? The Creative Force in you promptly strengthens them, toughens them, to meet their need.

All through your daily life, you find this Force steadily at work. Embrace it, work with it, take it to your heart, and there is nothing you cannot do. The mere fact that you have obstacles to overcome is in your favor, for when there is nothing to be done, when things run along too smoothly, the Creative Force seems to sleep. It is when you need it, when you call upon it urgently, that it is most on the job.

It differs from Luck in this, that fortune is a fickle jade who smiles most on those who need her least. Stake your last penny on the turn of a card—have nothing between you and ruin but the spin of a wheel or the speed of a horse—and the chances are a hundred to one that luck will desert you.

It is just the opposite with the Creative Force in you. As long as things run smoothly, as long as life flows along like a song, this Creative Force seems to slumber, secure in the knowledge that your affairs can take care of themselves. But let things start going wrong, let ruin or death stare you in the face—then is the time this Creative Force will assert itself if you but give it the chance.

There is a Napoleonic feeling of power that insures success in the knowledge that this invincible Creative Force is behind your every act. Knowing that you have with you a force which never yet has failed in anything it has undertaken, you can go ahead in the confident knowledge that it will not fail in your case. The ingenuity which overcame every obstacle in making you what you are, is not likely to fall short when you have immediate need for it. It is the reserve strength of the athlete, the second wind of the runner, the power that, in moments of great stress or excitement, you unconsciously call upon to do the deeds which you ever after look upon as superhuman.

But they are in no wise superhuman. They are merely beyond the capacity of your conscious self. Ally your conscious self with that sleeping giant within you, rouse him daily to the task and those superhuman deeds will become your ordinary, everyday accomplishments.

It matters not whether you are banker or lawyer, business man or clerk, whether you are the custodian of millions or have to struggle for your daily bread. The Creative Force makes no distinction between high and low, rich and poor. The greater your need, the more readily will it respond to your call. Wherever there is an unusual task, wherever there is poverty or hardship or sickness or despair, there this Servant of your mind waits, ready and willing to help, asking only that you call upon him. And not only is it ready and willing, but it is always ABLE to help. Its ingenuity and resource are without limit. It is mind. It is thought. It is the telepathy that carries messages without the spoken or written word. It is the sixth sense that warns you of unseen dangers. No matter how stupendous and complicated, or how simple your problem may be, the solution of it is somewhere in mind, in thought. And since the solution does exist, this mental giant can find it for you. It can know, and it can do, every right thing. Whatever it is necessary for you to know, whatever it is necessary for you to do, you can know and you can do if you will but seek the help of this Genie-of-your-mind and work with it in the right way.

To every living creature, God gave enough of this Creative Force to enable it to develop whatever it felt that it needed for survival. Behind and working through every living thing was this Creative Force, and to each was given the power to draw upon it at need. With the lower forms of life, that call had to be restricted to themselves, to their own bodies. They could not change their environment.

They could develop a house of shell in which to live, like the crustaceans or the snail or the turtle. They could use the Creative Force to develop strength or fleetness or teeth and claws—anything within or pertaining to themselves. But aside from building nests or caves or other more or less secure homes, they could not alter conditions around them. To man alone was given the power to make his own environment. To him alone was given dominion over things and conditions.

That he exercises this power, even today, only to a limited extent, does not alter the fact that he has it. Man was given dominion. "And God said—Let us make man in our image, after our likeness, and let them have dominion over the fish of the sea, and over the fowl of the air, and over the cattle, and over all the earth, and over every creeping thing that creepeth upon the earth."

Of course, few believe in that dominion. Fewer still exercise it for their own good or the good of all. But everyone uses the Creative Force in him to an extent. Everyone builds his own environment.

"Don't tell me," some will say indignantly, "that I built these slums around me, that I am responsible for the wretched conditions under which I work, that I had anything to do with the squalor and poverty in which my family have to live." Yet that is exactly what we do tell you. If you were born in poverty and misery, it was because your parents imaged these as something forced upon them, something they could not help, a condition that was necessary and to be expected. Thinking so, they used the Creative Force working through them to fasten those conditions upon themselves as something they were meant to suffer and could do nothing about.

Then you in your turn accepted those conditions as what you were born to, and fastened them upon yourself by your supine acceptance of them, by failing to claim better ones, by making no great or sustained efforts to get out of them.

All history shows that the determined soul who refuses to accept poverty or lack can change these to riches and power if he has the determination and the perseverance. The great men of the world have almost all come up from poverty and obscurity. The rich men of the world have mostly started with nothing.

"Always the real leaders of men, the real kings, have come up from the common people," wrote Dr. Frank Crane. "The finest flowers in the human flora grow in the woods pasture and not in the hothouse; no privileged class, no royal house, no carefully selected stock produced a Leonardo or a Michelangelo in art, a Shakespeare or Burns in letters, a Galli Curci or Paderewski in music, a Socrates or Kant in philosophy, an Edison or Pasteur in science, a Wesley or a Knox in religion."

It is the NEED that calls forth such geniuses, the urgent need for development or expression, and it is because these men drew powerfully upon the Creative Force within them that they became great. As the poet put it:

There is Power within me which is Life itself;
I can turn to it and rest on it;
As I turn to it and rest on it,
It helps me and heals me all the time.

There is Wisdom itself within me which is Life itself;
I can turn to it and rest on it;
As I turn to it and rest on it,
It helps me and heals me all the time.

There is Love itself within me which is Life itself;
It can turn to it and rest on it;
As I turn to it and rest on it,
It helps me and heals me all the time.

"Look within," said Marcus Aurelius. "Within is the fountain of all good. Such a fountain, where springing waters can never fail, do thou dig still deeper and deeper."

God gave to man, and to man alone, the power to make his own environment. He can determine for himself what he needs for survival, and if he holds to that thought with determination, he can draw whatever is necessary from the Creative Force working through him to make it manifest. First the Word, the mental image, then the creation or manifestation.

Professor Michael Pupin says—"Science finds that everything is a continually developing process." In other words, creation is still going on, all around you. Use your Creative Force to create the conditions you desire rather than those you fear. The life about you is constantly in a state of flux. All you have to do is create the mental mold in which you want the Creative Force to take form, and then hold to that mold with persistence and determination until the Creative Force in it becomes manifest.

Dr. Titus Bull, the famous neurologist, says—"Matter is spirit at a lower rate of vibration. When a patient is cured, it is spirit in the cell doing the healing according to its own inherent pattern. No doctor ever cured a patient. All he can do is to make it possible for the patient to heal himself."

And if that is true of the body, it is just as true of conditions around you. Matter—physical materials—is spirit or Creative Force at a lower rate of vibration. The spirit or Creative Force is all around you. You are constantly forming it into mental molds, but more often than not these are dictated by your fears rather than your desires. Why not determinedly form only good molds? Why not insist upon the things you want? It is just as easy, and it works just as surely.

"There is no great and no small," writes Emerson,

> To the soul that maketh all;
> And where it cometh, all things are;
> And it cometh everywhere.
> I am the owner of the sphere,
> Of the seven stars and the solar year,
> Of Caesar's hand, and Plato's brain,
> Of Lord Christ's heart, and Shakespeare's strain.

"Give me a base of support," said Archimedes, "and with a lever I will move the world."

And the base of support is that all started with *mind*. In the beginning was nothing—a fire mist. Before anything could come of it there had to be an idea, a mental model on which to build. *The God Mind* supplied that idea, that model. Therefore the primal cause is mind. Everything must start with an idea. Every event, every condition, every thing is first an idea in the mind of someone.

Before you start to build a house, you draw up a plan of it. You make an exact blue-print of that plan, and your house takes shape in accordance with your blue-print. Every material object takes form in the same way. Mind draws the plan. Thought forms the blue-print, well drawn or badly done as your thoughts are clear or vague. It all goes back to the one cause. The creative principle of the universe is mind, and thought forms the molds in which its eternal energy takes shape.

But just as the effect you get from electricity depends upon the mechanism to which the power is attached, so the effects you get from mind depend upon the way you use it. We are all of us dynamos. The power is there—unlimited power. But we've got to connect it with something—set it some task—give it work to do—else are we no better off than the animals.

The "Seven Wonders of the World" were built by men with few of the opportunities or facilities that are available to you. They conceived these gigantic projects first in their own minds, pictured them so vividly that the Creative Force working through them came to their aid and helped them to overcome obstacles that most of us would regard as insurmountable. Imagine building the Pyramid of Gizeh, enormous stone upon enormous stone, with nothing but bare hands. Imagine the labor, the sweat, the heartbreaking toil of erecting the Colossus of Rhodes, between whose legs a ship could pass! Yet men built these wonders, in a day when tools were of the crudest and machinery was undreamed of, by using the unlimited power of the Creative Force.

That Creative Force is in you, working through you, but it must have a model on which to work. It must have thoughts to supply the molds.

There are in Universal Mind ideas for millions of wonders greater far than the "Seven Wonders of the World." And those ideas are just as available to you as they were to the artisans of old, as they were to Michelangelo when he built St. Peter's in Rome, as they were to the architect who conceived the Empire State Building, or the engineer who planned the Hell Gate Bridge.

Every condition, every experience of life is the result of our mental attitude. We can *do* only what we think we can do. We can *be* only what we think we can be. We can *have* only what we think we can have. What we do, what we are, what we have, all depend upon what we think. There is only one limit upon the Creative Force, and that is the limit we impose upon it.

We can never express anything that we do not first believe in. The secret of all power, all success, all riches, is in first thinking powerful thoughts, successful thoughts, thoughts of wealth, of supply. We must build them in our own mind first. As Edgar A. Guest so well expressed it,

You can do as much as you think you can,
But you'll never accomplish more;
If you're afraid of yourself, young man,
There's little for you in store.
For failure comes from the inside first,
It's there if we only knew it,
And you can win, though you face the worst,
If you feel that you're going to do it.

William James, the famous psychologist, said that the greatest discovery in a hundred years was the discovery of the power of the subconscious mind. It is the greatest discovery of all time. It is the discovery that man has within himself the power to control his surroundings, that he is not at the mercy of chance or luck, that he is the arbiter of his own fortunes, that he can carve out his own destiny. He is the master of the Creative Force working through him. As James Allen puts it:

Dream lofty dreams, and as you dream, so shall you become. Your vision is the promise of what you shall one day be; your Ideal is the prophecy of what you shall at last unveil.

For matter is in the ultimate but a product of thought, the result of the mold into which you have put the Creative Force working through you. Even the most material scientists admit that matter is not what it appears to be. According to physics, matter (be it the human body or a log of wood—it makes no difference which) is made up of an aggregation of distinct minute particles called atoms. Considered individually, these atoms are so small that they can be seen only with the aid of a powerful microscope, if at all.

Until comparatively recent years, these atoms were supposed to be the ultimate theory regarding matter. We ourselves—and all the material world around us—were supposed to consist of these infinitesimal particles of matter, so small that they could not be seen or weighed or smelled or touched individually—but still particles of matter *and indestructible.*

Now, however, these atoms have been further analyzed, and physicists tell us that they are not indestructible at all—that they are mere positive and negative buttons of force or energy called protons and electrons, without hardness, without density, without solidity, without even positive actuality. In short, they are vortices in the ether—whirling bits of energy—dynamic, never static, pulsating with life, but the life is *spiritual!* As one eminent British scientist put it—"Science now explains matter by *explaining it away!*"

And that, mind you, is what the solid table in front of you is made of, is what your house, your body, the whole world is made of—*whirling bits of energy!*

To quote the "New York Herald-Tribune":

We used to believe that the universe was composed of an unknown number of different kinds of matter, one kind for each chemical element. The discovery of a new element had all the interest of the unexpected. It might turn out to be anything, to have any imaginable set of properties.

That romantic prospect no longer exists. We know now that instead of many ultimate kinds of matter there are only two kinds. Both of these are really kinds of electricity. One is negative electricity, being, in fact, the tiny particle called the electron, familiar to radio fans as one of the particles vast swarms of which operate radio vacuum tubes. The other kind of electricity is positive electricity. Its ultimate particles are called protons. From these protons and electrons all of the chemical elements are built up. Iron and lead and oxygen and gold and all the others differ from one another merely in the number and arrangement of the electrons and protons which they contain. That is the modern idea of the nature of matter. *Matter is really nothing but electricity.*

Can you wonder then that scientists believe the time will come when mankind *through mind* can control all this energy, can be absolute master of the winds and the waves, can literally follow the Master's precept—"If ye have faith as a grain of mustard seed, ye shall say unto this mountain, Remove hence to yonder place; and it shall remove; and nothing shall be impossible unto you."

For Modern Science is coming more and more to the belief that what we call *matter is a force subject wholly to the control of mind.*

So it would seem that, to a great degree at least, and perhaps altogether, this world round about us is one of our mind's own creating. And we can put into it, and get from it, pretty much what we wish. "Nothing is," said Shakespeare, "but thinking makes it so." And the psychologist of today says the same in a different way when he tells us that only those things are real to each individual that he takes into his consciousness. To one with no sense of smell, for instance, there is no such thing as fragrance. To one without a radio, there is no music on the air waves.

To quote from "Applied Psychology," by Warren Hilton:

The same stimulus acting on different organs of sense will produce different sensations. A blow upon the eye will cause you to "see stars"; a similar blow upon the ear will cause you to hear an explosive sound. In other words, the vibratory effect of a touch on eye or ear is the same as that of light or sound vibrations.

The notion you may form of any object in the outer world depends solely upon what part of your brain happens to be connected with that particular nerve-end that received an impression from the object.

You see the sun without being able to hear it because the only nerve-ends tuned to vibrate in harmony with the ether-waves set in action by the sun are nerve-ends that are connected with the brain center devoted to sight. "If," says Professor James, "we could splice the outer extremities of our optic nerves to our ears, and those of our auditory nerves to our eyes, we should hear the lightning and see the thunder, see the symphony and hear the conductor's movements."

In other words, the kind of impressions we receive from the world about us, the sort of mental pictures we form concerning it—in fact, the character of the outer world, the nature of the environment in which our lives are cast—all these things depend for each one of us simply upon how he happens to be put together, upon his individual mental make-up.

In short, it all comes back to the old fable of the three blind men and the elephant. To the one who caught hold of his leg, the elephant was like a tree. To the one who felt of his side, the elephant was like a wall. To the one who seized his tail, the elephant was like a rope. The world is to each one of us the world of *his individual perceptions*.

You are like a radio receiving station. Every moment thousands of impressions are reaching you. You can tune in on whatever ones you like—on joy or sorrow, on success or failure, on optimism or fear. You can select the particular impressions that will best serve you, you can hear only what you want to hear, you can shut out all disagreeable thoughts and sounds and experiences, or you can tune in on discouragement and failure and despair if these are what you want.

Yours is the choice. You have within you a force against which the whole world is powerless. By using it, you can make what you will of life and of your surroundings.

"But," you will say, "objects themselves do not change. It is merely the difference in the way you look at them." Perhaps. But to a great extent, at least, we find what we look for, just as, when we turn the dial on the radio, we tune in on whatever kind of entertainment or instruction we may wish to hear. Who can say that it is not our thoughts that put it there? And why shouldn't it be? All will agree that evil is merely the lack of good, just as darkness is the lack of light. There is infinite good all about us. There is fluid cosmic energy from which to form infinitely more. Why should we not use our thoughts to find the good, or to mold it from the Creative Force all about us? Many scientists believe that we can, and that in proportion as we try to put into our surroundings the good things we desire, rather than the evil ones we fear, *we will find those good things.* Certain it is that we can do this with our own bodies. Just as certain that many people are doing it with the good things of life. They have risen above the conception of life in which matter is the master.

Just as the most powerful forces in nature are the invisible ones—heat, light, air, electricity—so the most powerful forces of man are his invisible forces, his thought forces. And just as electricity can fuse stone and iron, so can your thought forces control your body, so can they win you honor and fortune, so can they make or mar your destiny.

From childhood on we are assured on every hand—by scientists, by philosophers, by our religious teachers, that "ours is the earth and the fulness thereof." Beginning with the first chapter of Genesis, we are told that "God said, Let us make man in Our image, after Our likeness; and let them have dominion over the fish of the sea, and over the fowl of the air, and over the cattle, and over all the earth—and over every living thing that moveth upon the earth." All through the Old and the New Testament, we are repeatedly adjured to use these God-given powers. "He that believeth on Me," said Jesus, "the works that I do shall he do also; and greater works than these shall he do." "If ye abide in Me, and My words abide in you, ye shall ask what ye will, and it shall be done unto you." "For verily I say unto you, that whosoever shall say unto this mountain, Be thou removed, and be thou cast into the sea; and shall not doubt in his heart, but shall believe that those things which he saith shall come to pass; he shall have whatsoever he saith." "The kingdom of God is within you."

We hear all this, perhaps we even think we believe, but always, when the time comes to use these God-given talents, there is the "doubt in our heart."

Baudouin expressed it clearly:

To be ambitious for wealth and yet always expecting to be poor; to be always doubting your ability to get what you long for, is like trying to reach east by travelling west. There is no philosophy which will help a man to succeed when he is always doubting his ability to do so, and thus attracting failure.

You will go in the direction in which you face. . . .

There is a saying that every time the sheep bleats, it loses a mouthful of hay. Every time you allow yourself to complain of your lot, to say, "I am poor; I can never do what others do; I shall never be rich; I have not the ability that others have; I am a failure; luck is against me"; you are laying up so much trouble for yourself.

No matter how hard you may work for success, if your thought is saturated with the fear of failure, it will kill your efforts, neutralize your endeavors and make success impossible.

What was it made Napoleon the greatest conqueror of his day? Primarily his magnificent faith in Napoleon. He had a sublime belief in his destiny an absolute confidence that the obstacle was not made which Napoleon could not find a way through, or over, or around. It was only when he lost that confidence, when he hesitated and vacillated for weeks between retreat and advance, that winter caught him in Moscow and ended his dreams of world empire. Fate gave him every chance first. The winter snows were a full month late in coming. But Napoleon hesitated—and was lost. It was not the snows that defeated him. It was not the Russians. It was his loss of faith in himself.

THE KINGDOM OF HEAVEN

"The Kingdom of Heaven is within you." Heaven is not some faraway state— the reward of years of tribulation here. Heaven is right here—here and now! In the original Greek text, the word used for "Heaven" is "Ouranos." Translated literally, Ouranos means EXPANSION, in other words, a state of being where you can expand, grow, multiply and increase. This interpretation is strengthened by Jesus' own description of what the Kingdom of Heaven is like. "The Kingdom of Heaven is like to a grain of mustard seed, which a man took, and sowed in his field; which indeed is the least of all seeds, but when it is grown, it is the greatest among herbs, and becometh a tree so that the birds of the air come and lodge in the branches thereof." "The Kingdom of Heaven is like unto leaven, which a woman took and hid in three measures of meal, until the whole was leavened."

What is the property of a mustard seed? *It spreads*—a single seed will grow into a tree, a single tree will produce enough seeds to plant a great field. And what is the property of leaven or yeast? *It expands*—in a single night it can expand a hundred times in size. So when Christ said that Heaven was within us,

He meant just what He said—the power to multiply our happiness, to increase our good, to expand everything we need in life, is within each one of us.

That most of us fail to realize this Heaven—that many are sickly and suffering, that more are ground down by poverty and worry—is no fault of His. He gave us the power to overcome these evils; the Kingdom of Expansion is within us, the power to increase anything we have. If we fail to find the way to use it, the fault is ours. If we expand the evil instead of the good, that is our misfortune. To enjoy the Heaven that is within us, to begin here and now to live the life eternal, takes only the right understanding and use of the Creative Force working through us.

Even now with the limited knowledge at our command, many people control circumstances to the point of making the world without an expression of their own world within where the real thoughts, the real power, resides. Through this world within, they find the solution of every problem, the cause for every effect. Discover it—and all power, all possession is within your control.

For the world without is but a reflection of that world within. Your thought *creates* the condition your mind images. Keep before your mind's eye the image of all you want to be and you will see it reflected in the world without. Think abundance, feel abundance, BELIEVE abundance, and you will find that as you think and feel and believe, abundance will manifest itself in your daily life. But let fear and worry be your mental companions, thoughts of poverty and limitation dwell in your mind, and worry and fear, limitation and poverty will be your constant companions day and night.

Your mental concept is all that matters. Its relation to matter is that of idea and form. There has got to be an idea before it can take form.

The Creative Force working through you supplies you with limitless energy which will take whatever form your mind demands. Your thoughts are the mold which crystallizes this energy into good or ill according to the form you impress upon it. You are free to choose which. But whichever you choose, the result is sure. Thoughts of wealth, of power, of success, can bring only results commensurate with your idea of them. Thoughts of poverty and lack can bring only limitation and trouble.

"A radical doctrine," you'll say, and think me wildly optimistic. Because the world has been taught for so long to think that some must be rich and some poor, that trials and tribulations are our lot. That this is at best a vale of tears.

The history of the race shows that what is considered to be the learning of one age is ignorance to the next age.

Dr. Edwin E. Slosson, Editor of SCIENCE SERVICE, speaking of the popular tendency to fight against new ideas merely because they are *new,* said: "All through the history of science, we find that new ideas have to force their way into the common mind in disguise, as though they were burglars instead of benefactors of the race."

And Emerson wrote: "The virtue in most request is conformity. Self-reliance is its aversion. It loves not realities and creators, but names and customs."

In the ages to come, man will look back upon the poverty and wretchedness of so many millions today, and think how foolish we were not to take advantage of the abundant Creative Force all about us. Look at Nature; how profuse she is in everything. Do you suppose the Mind that imaged that profuseness ever intended you to be limited, to have to scrimp and save in order to eke out a bare existence?

There are hundreds of millions of stars in the heavens. Do you suppose the Creative Force which could bring into being worlds without number in such prodigality intended to stint you of the few things necessary to your happiness or well-being?

Nature is prodigal in all that she does. Many insects increase at such a marvelous rate that if it were not for their almost equal death rate, the world would be unable to support them. Rabbits increase so rapidly that a single pair could have 13,000,000 descendants in three years! Fish lay millions of eggs each year. Throughout Nature, everything is lavish. Why should the Creative Force working through you be less generous when it comes to your own supply?

Take as an example the science of numbers. Suppose all numbers were of metal—that it was against the law to write figures for ourselves. Every time you wanted to do a sum in arithmetic you'd have to provide yourself with a supply of numbers, arrange them in their proper order, work out your problems with them. If your problems were too abstruse you might run out of numbers, have to borrow some from your neighbor or from the bank.

"How ridiculous," you say. "Figures are not things; they are mere ideas, and we can add them or divide them or multiply them as often as we like. Anybody can have all the figures he wants."

To be sure he can. And when you learn to use the Creative Force, you will find that you can multiply your material ideas in the same way. You will EXPAND the good things in your life even as Jesus did the loaves and fishes.

Thought externalizes itself, through the Creative Force working through us. What we are depends entirely upon the images we hold before our mind's eye. Every time we think, we start a chain of causes which will create conditions similar to the thoughts which originated it. Every thought we hold in our consciousness for any length of time becomes impressed upon our subconscious mind and creates a pattern which the Creative Force weaves into our life or environment.

All power is from within and is therefore under our own control. When you can direct your thought processes, you can consciously apply them to any condition, for all that comes to us in the world without is what we've already imaged in the world within.

The source of all good, of everything you wish for, is Mind, and you can reach it best through your subconscious.

Mind will be to you whatever you believe it to be—the kind and loving Father whom Jesus pictured, always looking out for the well-being of his children—or the dread Judge that so many dogmatists would have us think.

When a man realizes that his mind is part of the God Mind, when he knows that he has only to take any right aspiration to this Universal Mind to see it realized, he loses all sense of worry and fear. He learns to dominate instead of to cringe. He rises to meet every situation, secure in the knowledge that everything necessary to the solution of any problem is in Mind, and that he has but to take his problem to Universal Mind to have it correctly answered.

For if you take a drop of water from the ocean, you know that it has the same properties as all the rest of the water in the ocean, the same percentage of sodium chloride. The only difference between it and the ocean is in volume. If you take a spark of electricity, you know that it has the same properties as the thunderbolt, the same power that moves trains or runs giant machines in factories. Again the only difference is in volume. It is the same with your mind and the God Mind. The only difference between them is in volume. Your mind has the same properties as the God Mind, the same creative genius, the same power over all the earth, the same access to all knowledge. Know this, believe it, use it, and "yours is the earth and the fulness thereof." In the exact proportion that you believe yourself to be part of the God Mind, sharing in Its all-power, in that proportion can you demonstrate the mastery over your own body and over the world about you.

All growth, all supply is from the Creative Force working through you. If you would have power, if you would have wealth, you must first form the mold in this world within, in your subconscious mind, through belief and understanding.

If you would remove discord, you must remove the wrong images—images of ill health, of worry and trouble from within. The trouble with most of us is that we live entirely in the world without. We have no knowledge of that inner world which is responsible for all the conditions we meet and all the experiences we have. We have no conception of "the Father that is within us."

The inner world promises us life and health, prosperity and happiness—dominion over all the earth. It promises peace and perfection for all its offspring. It gives you the right way and the adequate way to accomplish any normal purpose. Business, labor, professions, exist primarily in thought. And the outcome of your labors in them is regulated by thought. Consider the difference, then, in this outcome if you have at your command only the limited capacity of your conscious mind, compared with the boundless energy of the subconscious and of the Creative Force working through it. "Thought, not money, is the real business capital," says Harvey S. Firestone, "and if you know absolutely that what you are doing is right, then you are bound to accomplish it in due season."

Thought is a dynamic energy with the power to bring its object out from the Creative Force all about us. Matter is unintelligent. Thought can shape and control. Every form in which matter is today is but the expression of some thought, some desire, some idea.

You have a mind. You can originate thought. And thoughts are creative. Therefore you can create for yourself that which you desire. Once you realize this, you are taking a long step toward success in whatever undertaking you have in mind. You are the potter. You are continually forming images—good or bad. Why not consciously form only good images?

More than half the prophecies in the scriptures refer to the time when man shall possess the earth, when tears and sorrow shall be unknown, and peace and plenty shall be everywhere. That time will come. It is nearer than most people think possible. You are helping it along. Every man who is honestly trying to use the power of mind in the right way is doing his part in the great cause. For it is only through Mind that peace and plenty can be gained. The earth is laden with treasures as yet undiscovered. But they are every one of them known to the God Mind, for it was this Mind that first imaged them there. And as part of Universal Mind, they can be known to you.

"TO THE MANNER BORN"

Few of us have any idea of our mental powers. The old idea was that man must take this world as he found it. He'd been born into a certain position in life, and to try to rise above his fellows was not only the height of bad taste, but sacrilegious as well. An All-wise Providence had decreed by birth the position a child should occupy in the web of organized society. For him to be discontented with his lot, for him to attempt to raise himself to a higher level, was tantamount to tempting Providence. The gates of Hell yawned wide for such scatterbrains, who were lucky if in this life they incurred nothing worse than the ribald scorn of their associates.

That is the system that produced aristocracy and feudalism. That is the system that feudalism and aristocracy strove to perpetuate.

What was it that Jesus taught which aroused the wrath of the Priests and the Rulers? What was it that made them demand His blood? NOT the doctrine of the One God. NOT the teachings of love instead of hate. But the fact that He went up and down the length and breadth of the land teaching that all men were equally the Sons of God. That would never do. That would ruin their system, spread discontent, cause uprisings against their authority. It must be stopped at any cost.

Yet Jesus' teaching has lived to become the basis of all democracies—that man is not bound by any system, that he need not accept the world as he finds it. He can remake the world to his own ideas. It is merely the raw material. He can make what he will of it.

It is this idea that is responsible for all our inventions, all our progress. Man is satisfied with nothing. He is constantly remaking his world. And now more than ever will this be true, for psychology teaches us that each one has within himself the power to use the Creative Force to become what he wills.

LEARN TO CONTROL YOUR THOUGHT. Learn to image upon your mind only the things you want to see reflected there.

You will never improve yourself by dwelling upon the drawbacks of your neighbors. You will never attain perfect health and strength by thinking of weakness or disease. No man ever made a perfect score by watching his rival's target. You have to think strength, think health, think riches. To paraphrase Pascal—"Our achievements today are but the sum of our thoughts of yesterday."

For yesterday is the mold in which the Creative Force flowing through us took shape. And cosmic energy concentrated for any definite purpose becomes power. To those who perceive the nature and transcendency of this Force, all physical power sinks into insignificance.

What is imagination but a form of thought? Yet it is the instrument by which all the inventors and discoverers have opened the way to new worlds. Those who grasp this force, be their state ever so humble, their natural gifts ever so insignificant, become our leading men. They are our governors and supreme law-givers, the guides of the drifting host that follows them as by an irrevocable decree. To quote Glenn Clark in the ATLANTIC MONTHLY,

> *Whatever we have of civilization is their work, theirs alone. If progress was made, they made it. If spiritual facts were discerned, they discerned them. If justice and order were put in place of insolence and chaos, they wrought the change. Never is progress achieved by the masses. Creation ever remains the task of the individual.*

Our railroads, our telephones, our automobiles, our libraries, our newspapers, our thousands of other conveniences, comforts and necessities are due to the creative genius of but two per cent of our population.

And the same two per cent own a great percentage of the wealth of the country.

The question arises, Who are they. What are they? The sons of the rich? College men? No—few of them had any early advantages. Many of them have never seen the inside of a college. It was grim necessity that drove them, and somehow, some way, they found a method of drawing upon their Creative Force, and through that Force they reached success.

You don't need to stumble and grope. You can call upon the Creative Force at will. There are three steps necessary:

First, to realize that you have the power.

Second, to know what you want.

Third, to center your thought upon it with singleness of purpose.

To accomplish these steps takes only a fuller understanding of the Power-that-is-within-you.

So let us make use of this dynamo, which is *you*. What is going to start it working? Your *Faith*, the faith that is begotten of understanding. Faith is the impulsion of this power within. Faith is the confidence, the assurance, the enforcing truth, the knowing that the right idea of life will bring you into the reality of existence and the manifestation of the All power.

All cause is in Mind—and Mind is everywhere. All the knowledge there is, all the power there is, is all about you—no matter where you may be. Your Mind is part of it. You have access to it. If you fail to avail yourself of it, you have no one to blame but yourself. For as the drop of water in the ocean shares in all the properties of the rest of the ocean water, so you share in that all-power, all-wisdom of Mind. If you have been sick and ailing, if poverty and hardship have been your lot, don't blame it on "fate." Blame yourself. "Yours is the earth and everything that's in it." But you've got to *take* it. The Creative Force is there—but *you* must *use* it. It is round about you like the air you breathe. You don't expect others to do your breathing for you. Neither can you expect them to use the Creative Force for you. Universal Intelligence is not only the mind of the Creator of the universe, but it is also the mind of MAN, *Your* intelligence, *your* mind. "Let this mind be in you, which was also in Christ Jesus."

> *I am success, though hungry, cold, ill-clad,*
> *I wander for awhile, I smile and say,*
> *"It is but a time, I shall be glad*
> *Tomorrow, for good fortune comes my way.*
> *God is my Father, He has wealth untold,*
> *His wealth is mine, health, happiness and gold."*

—ELLA WHEELER WILCOX

So start today by *knowing* that you can do anything you wish to do, have anything you wish to have, be anything you wish to be. The rest will follow.
"Ye shall ask what ye will and it shall be done unto you."

A FUNNY WORLD

> *There is a world, a funny world, that's not a world at all;*
> *A world that has no shape nor size, that's neither sphere nor ball;*
> *You think at first that it exists; you think it very true;*
> *Then, finally, you see the point: that it's just fooling you.*
> *Perhaps, you once lived in this world with all its hates and fears;*
> *You were a glum and saddened soul, believed in pains and tears;*
> *You thought you had to be diseased and thought there was a hell;*
> *When, all at once, you learned the truth. This world just went pell-mell.*

And, then, this world, this shadow world, just disappeared from sight;
And in its place a world of joy, of health, of love and light
Came into view right where you were; you came to understand
That you abide in Heaven now and God is right at hand.

—FRANK BLENLARRY WHITNEY

THE GOAL

If you think success—success has begun;
If you think you can win, your battle is won!
Whatever you need you can have, you'll find:
It's all in the way you set your mind.

If you feel that your part in the world is small,
You may never achieve your work at all;
But feel that your life, of God's life is a part—
Then you'll work in the way you have set your heart.
If you know you are great, you will do great things;
Your thoughts will soar on eagle's wings;
Your life will reach its destined goal,
If you know the way to set your soul.

—KATHERINE WILDER RUGGLES

22

The Urge

What is the strongest force in life? What is the power that carries those who heed it from the bottom-most pits of poverty to the top of the world—from the slums and ghettos to governorships and presidencies and the rulership of kingdoms?

The URGE for SECURITY—for ASSURED SUBSISTENCE AND SAFETY!

When the first primitive water plants appeared, living in the saturated soil along the shores of the waters, you might think the Creative Force would have rested content for a while. It had created something that lived and grew and reproduced itself. It was the first form of life upon this earth—the thallophytes.

As with the water plants, there came next the multiple-celled creature, each dependent for life upon drawing its own nourishment from the waters about. Then a central system corresponding with the stem and roots of the fern, finally evolving into distinct organs to take care of each function of life. And so was laid the foundation for all forms of animal life that have developed from this simple beginning. The principle had been perfected—it remained now only to develop every possible ramification of it, until the highest form should be reached.

When means of protection were found necessary for survival, the Creative Force developed these too. For those subject to the abrasive effects of sand and rocks, it developed shells. To the weak, it gave means of escape. To the strong, teeth and claws with which to fight. It fitted each form to meet the conditions it had to cope with. When size was the paramount consideration, it made the Gigantosaurus, over a hundred feet long and as big as a house and all the other giant monsters of antiquity. When smallness was the objective, it developed the tiny insects and water creatures, so that it takes a powerful microscope to see them, yet so perfectly made as to form organisms as exact and well-regulated as the greatest.

Size, strength, fierceness, speed—all these it developed to the last degree. It tried every form of life, but each had its weaknesses, each was vulnerable in some way. The Creative Force might develop forms that would grow, but nothing physical could be made that would be invulnerable, that would ever attain SECURITY.

To man has been given the job of emulating his Maker—of becoming a creator, finding new and broader and better ways through which to express the Creative Force in him. His is the work of creating beauty, or bringing more of comfort, of joy and happiness into the world.

To every living thing on earth is given a measure of Creative Power. Of the lower forms of life all that is required is that they bring forth fruit according to their kind—"some thirty, some sixty, some an hundred fold."

Of you, however, much more is expected. To bring forth fruit according to your physical kind is good—but that is no more than the animals do. More is required of you. You must bring forth fruit, according to your *mental* kind as well! You are a son of God, a creator. Therefore creation is expected of you. You are to spread seeds not merely of human kind, but of the intellect as well. You are to leave the world a better place than you found it, with more of joy in it, more of beauty, of comfort, of understanding, of light.

The real purpose of Life is expression, the constant urge onward and upward. Even in the smallest child, you see evidence of this. It plays with blocks. Why? To express the urge in him to build something. The growing boy makes toys, builds a hut. The girl sews dresses, cares for dolls, cooks, plays house. Why? To give vent to the inner urge in each, struggling for expression.

They reach the period of adolescence. They dance, they motor, they seek all manner of thrill. Why? Again to satisfy that constant craving of the Creative Force in them for *expression!*

True—at the moment, it is mostly a physical urge. But in some way, that urge must be translated into a mental one—*and satisfied!* It must be given an outlet for expression. It must be brought into the light of day, given useful, uplifting work to do, and it will then bring forth abundant fruit of happiness and accomplishment. Because no matter how it is repressed, no matter how deep it is buried in dark cellars, the Creative Force will still bring forth fruit—only then it may be fungus growths of sin and misery.

Through every man there flows this Creative Force, with infinite power to

draw to itself whatever is necessary to its expression. It doesn't matter who you
are, what your environment or education or advantages, the Creative Force in
you has the same power for good or evil. Mind you, that Force never brings
forth evil. Its life is good. But just as you can graft onto the trunk of the finest
fruit tree a branch of the upas tree, and thereupon bring forth deadly fruit, so
can you engraft upon the pure energy of your Creative Force any manner of
fruit you desire. But if the fruit be bad, it is *you* who are to blame, not the perfect Force that flows through you.

> To every man there openeth
> A high way and a low,
> And every man decideth
> The way his soul shall go.

What is it makes a poor immigrant boy like Edward Bok overcome every
handicap of language and education, to become one of the greatest editors the
country has ever known?

Isn't it that the more circumstances conspire to repress it, the stronger becomes the urge of the Creative Force in you for expression? The more it lacks
channels through which to expand, the more inclined it is to burst its shell and
flow forth in all directions.

It is the old case of the river that is dammed generating the most power. Most
of us are so placed that some opportunity for expression is made easy for us. And
that little opportunity serves like a safety valve to a boiler—it leaves us steam
enough to do something worth while, yet keeps us from getting up enough power
to burst the shell about us, and sweep away every barrier that holds us down.

Yet it is only such an irresistible head of steam as that which makes great
successes. That is why the blow which knocks all the props from under us is
often the turning point in our whole career.

As Walt Whitman put it—

> Oh, while I live, to be the ruler of life, Not a slave.
> To meet life as a powerful conqueror . . .
> And nothing exterior shall ever take command of me.

You cannot stand still. You must go forward—or see the world slide past
you. This was well illustrated by figures worked out by Russell Conwell years

ago. Of all the thousands who are left fortunes through the deaths of relatives, *only one in seventeen dies wealthy!*

Why?—Because the fortunes left them take away the need for initiative on their part. Their money gives to them easy means of expressing the urge in them, without effort on their part. It gives them dozens of safety valves, through which their steam continually escapes.

The result is that they not only accomplish nothing worth while, but they soon dissipate the fortunes that were left them. They are like kettles, the urge of life keeping the water at boiling point, but the open spout of ease letting the steam escape as fast as it forms, until presently there is not even any water left.

Why do the sons of rich men so seldom accomplish anything worth while? Because they don't have to. Every opportunity is given them to turn the Creative Force in them through pleasant channels, and they dissipate through these the energies that might carry them to any height. The result? They never have a strong enough "head of steam" left to carry through any real job.

"What shall I do to be saved?" begged the rich young man of Jesus. "Sell all that thou hast, give it to the poor and follow Me," the Master told him. Churches have used that to prove that poverty is necessary to salvation. But is that the lesson the Biblical writer meant to convey? If so, why is there no record of Jesus having ever given similar advice to Nicodemus, or Joseph of Arimathea, or any others of the rich who sought counsel of Him and at whose houses He frequently stopped?

Isn't the difference that these latter had made their mark in the world—expressed the Creative Force in them to some worth-while purpose—and in the expressing of it, the Creative Force had increased and multiplied and brought back to them goodly harvests of riches?

The young man, on the other hand, had done nothing to earn all the good things that were his. His life had been cast in pleasant places. The Spirit in him urged its need of expression, but Jesus saw that only by getting away from his life of ease was any worth-while expression possible. And the young man had not courage enough for that. Truly it is harder for a camel to go through the eye of the needle than for such a rich man to enter into the Kingdom of Heaven—the Land of Accomplishment.

You will be what you will to be;
Let failure find its false content

In that poor word 'environment,'
But Spirit scorns it, and is free.

It masters time, it conquers space,
It cows that boastful trickster Chance,
And bids the tyrant Circumstance
Uncrown and fill a servant's place.

Be not impatient in delay,
But wait as one who understands;
When Spirit rises and commands
The gods are ready to obey.

—ELLA WHEELER WILCOX

You are a channel for power. There is no limit to the amount of Creative Force that will flow through you. The only limit to what you *get,* is the amount that you *use.* Like the widow's cruse, no matter how much you pour out, there is just as much still available, but unlike the cruse of oil, your channel and your power grow with use!

What are *you* doing to satisfy the urge in you? What are you doing to give expression—*and increase*—to the Creative Force working through you?

Many a man and woman has the urge to write—or paint—or sing—or do some other worth-while thing. But does he? No, indeed. He is not well enough known, or has not the right training, or lacks education or opportunity or influence. Or else he has tried once or twice and failed.

What does that matter? It is not your responsibility if others fail in their appreciation. Your job is to express the Creative Force surging through you, to give it the best you have. Each time you do that, *you* are the better for it, whether others care for it or not. And each time you will give more perfect, more understanding expression to the Creative Force working through you, until sooner or later ALL appreciate it.

You don't suppose the great writers, the successful artists, were born with the ability to write or paint, do you? You don't suppose they had all the latest books or finest courses on the art of expression? On the contrary, all that many of them had was the URGE! The rest they had to acquire just as you do.

The Creative Force flowing through you is as perfect as the rose in the bud.

But just as the life in the rose bush evolved through millions of less beautiful forms before it perfected the rose, so must you be satisfied to model but crudely at first, in the sure knowledge that if you keep giving of your best, eventually the product of your hands or your brain will be as perfect as the rose.

Every desire, every urge of your being, is Creative Force straining at the bonds of repression you have put upon it, straining for expression. You can't stand still. You can't stop and smugly say—"Look what I did yesterday, or last week, or last year!" It is what you are doing *now* that counts.

The Creative Force is dynamic. It is ever seeking expression—and when you fail to provide new and greater outlets for it, it slips away to work through some more ambitious soul who will. Genius is nothing but the irresistible urge for one particular channel of expression—an urge so strong that it is like a mountain torrent in flood, sweeping trees and bridges and dams and everything else before it.

So don't worry about whether those around you recognize your talents. Don't mind if the world seems indifferent to them. The world is too busy with its own little ways of expressing life to pay much attention to yours. To get under its skin, you must do something to appeal to its emotions.

You see, the world in the mass is like a child. Prod it, and you make it angry. Preach to it, or try to teach or uplift it, and you lose its attention. You bore it. But appeal to its emotions—make it laugh or weep—and it will love you! Love you and lavish upon you all the gifts in its power to give. That is why it pays a Crosby millions, and a great educator only hundreds. Yet the name of the educator may live for ages, while the entertainer will be remembered only until a better one displaces him.

So forget the immediate rewards the world has to offer, and give your energies to finding ways of better expressing the Creative Force in you. You are expressing it every day and hour. Try to express it better, to find ever greater channels through which to work. If your urge is to write a story, put into it the best you have, no matter if you know you could get by with a third of the effort. Work always for perfection, knowing that thus only can you be sure of the greatest help of the Creative Force working through you. "I can do all things through Christ which strengtheneth me," said Paul. And you can do all things through the Creative Force working through you.

That Creative Force is striving for a perfect body, perfect surroundings, perfect work. It is not its fault when you manifest less than these. Depend upon it, it is not satisfied with anything less. So don't *you* be! If you have the courage to refuse anything short of your ideal, if you have the dogged perseverence to keep trying, there's no power in the heavens or the earth that can keep you from success!

It's the way every great success has been won. Do you suppose if Michelangelo or Da Vinci had an off day and painted some imperfect figures into a painting, he left them there? Do you think he explained to his friends that he was under the weather that day, and so, while he was sorry it spoiled the picture, he could not be held accountable for it?

Just imagine one of these great painters letting something less than his best go over his name! Why, he would cheerfully destroy a year's work rather than have that happen. The moment he noticed it, he would hasten to scratch out the offensive figure, lest others might see it and judge his work by it. Or even if no one was ever to see it, he would do it because it failed to express the genius that was his!

That is how you must feel about your work before ever it can attain greatness. The Creative Force working through you is perfect, all-powerful, without limit. So don't ever be satisfied with less than its best! Follow its urge. Use every atom of strength and skill and riches you have to express it, serene in the knowledge that, like Paul, you can do anything through the Christ working in you.

Andrew Carnegie said:

> *Here is the prime condition of success, the great secret: Concentrate your energy, thought, and capital exclusively upon the business in which you are engaged. Having begun on one line, resolve to fight it out on that line, to lead in it, adopt every improvement, have the best machinery, and know the most about it. Finally, do not be impatient, for, as Emerson says, "No one can cheat you out of ultimate success but yourself."*

Have you ever climbed a high mountain? Did you notice, as you kept getting higher and higher, how your horizon rose with you? It is the same with life. The more you use the Creative Force, the more you have to use. Your skill and power and resources grow with your use of them.

From earliest infancy, the Creative Force is trying to express something through you. First it is purely physical—a perfect body, and through it the generation of other perfect bodies. But gradually it rises above the physical plane, and strives to express itself in some way that will leave the world a better place for your having been in it—a memory of noble thoughts, of splendid deeds, of obstacles conquered and ideals won.

Do your part by never falling short of your best, no matter in how small a thing you may express it. Perfection, you remember, is made up of trifles, but perfection is no trifle.

It doesn't matter how small or seemingly unimportant your job may be. You have the same chance to attain perfection in it as the greatest artist has in his work. It doesn't matter how little others may believe that any good or great thing can come from you. It was said in the Scriptures of a far greater than you—"Can there any good thing come out of Nazareth?"

Who knows what good things may come from you?

There's nothing to fear—you're as good as the best,
As strong as the mightiest, too.
You can win in every battle or test;
For there's no one just like you.
There's only one you in the world today;
So nobody else, you see,
Can do your work in as fine a way;
You're the only you there'll be!
So face the world, and all life is yours
To conquer and love and live;
And you'll find the happiness that endures
In just the measure you give:
There's nothing too good for you to possess,
Nor heights where you cannot go;
Your power is more than belief or guess—
It's something you have to know.
There's nothing to fear—you can and you will,
For you're the invincible you.
So set your foot on the highest hill—
There's nothing you cannot do.

—ANONYMOUS

23

The Mental Equivalent

All the world's a stage,
And all the men and women merely players.

What part are you acting in the theater of life? What place have you assigned to yourself on that stage? Are you one of the stars? Do you bear one of the important parts? Or are you merely one of the "mob" scene, just background for the action, or one of the "props" for moving the scenery around?

Whatever part is yours, it is you who have given it to you, for as Emerson says, and the whole Bible teaches from one end to the other, "Man surrounds himself with the true image of himself."

"Every spirit builds itself a house," writes Emerson, "and beyond its house a world, and beyond its world a heaven. Know then that the world exists for you. For you is the phenomenon perfect. What we are, that only can we see. All that Adam had, all that Caesar could, you have and can do. Adam called his house, heaven and earth. Caesar called his house, Rome; you perhaps call yours a cobbler's trade; a hundred acres of plowed land; or a scholar's garret. Yet line for line and point for point, your dominion is as great as theirs, though without fine names. Build therefore your own world. As fast as you conform your life to the pure idea in your mind, that will unfold its great proportions."

All men are created free and equal, in that all are given the only tool with which you can really build your life. That tool is your thought. All have the same material with which to build. That material is the Creative Force working through you. As your interior thought is, so will your exterior life be. The Creative Force takes shape in the mold your thoughts give it. "We think in secret and it comes to pass; environment is but our looking glass."

"In all my lectures," declared Emerson, "I have taught one doctrine—the infinitude of the private man, the ever-availability to every man of the divine presence within his own mind, from which presence he draws, at his need, inexhaustible power."

Think big, and your deeds will grow;
Think small, and you'll fall behind;
Think that you can, and you will—
It's all in the state of mind.

"What sort of mental image do you hold of yourself?" Emmett Fox asks in one of his helpful books.

Whatever your real conviction of yourself is, that is what you will demonstrate.

Whatever enters into your life is but the material expression of some belief of your own mind. The kind of body you have, the kind of home you have, the kind of job you have, the kind of people you meet with, are all conditioned by and correspond to the mental concept you are holding. The Bible teaches that from beginning to end.

About twenty years ago, I coined the phrase "mental equivalent." And I am going to say that anything that you want in your life, anything that you would like to have in your life—a healthy body, a satisfactory vocation, friends, opportunities, above all the understanding of God—if you want these things to come into your life, you must furnish a mental equivalent for them. Supply yourself with a mental equivalent and the thing must come to you. Without a mental equivalent, it cannot come to you.

And what is this "Mental Equivalent"? What but your mental image of what you hope to be, plan to be. "Think and forms spring into shape, will and worlds disintegrate."

God hid the whole world in your heart, as one great writer tells us, so when any object or purpose is clearly held in thought, its manifestation in tangible and visible form is merely a question of time. Cause and effect are as absolute and undeviating in the hidden realm of thought as in the world of visible and material things. Mind is the master weaver, both of the interior garment of character and the outer garment of circumstance. Thinking for a purpose brings that purpose into being just as surely as a hen's "setting" on an egg matures and brings the chicken into being.

"Amid all the mysteries by which we are surrounded," wrote Herbert Spencer, "nothing is more certain than that we are ever in the presence of an infinite and eternal energy from which all things proceed."

That infinite and eternal energy or Creative Force is molded by our thought. For thousands of years, men of wisdom have realized this and have molded their own lives accordingly. The Prophets of old did their best to impress this fact upon their people. "My word (my thought or mental image) shall not come back to me void, but shall accomplish that whereunto it was sent," says one. And in a hundred places, you will find the same thought expressed. You are molding your tomorrows, whether you realize it or not. Make them the good you desire—not the evil you fear.

Clarence Edwin Flynn expresses something of the power of thought in his little poem:

Whenever you cultivate a thought
Remember it will trace
With certain touch, its pictured form
A story on your face.

Whenever you dwell upon a thought,
Remember it will roll
Into your being and become
A fiber of your soul.

Whenever you send out a thought,
Remember it will be
A force throughout the universe,
For all eternity.

Remember that this holds good in all of your affairs. In your own thoughts, you are continually dramatizing yourself, your environment, your circumstances. If you see yourself as prosperous, you will be. If you see yourself as continually hard up, that is exactly what you will be. If you are constantly looking for slights, if you seek trouble in your thoughts, you will not be long in finding them in your daily life. Whatever part you give yourself in the drama of life in your own thought, that part you will eventually act out on the stage of life.

So give yourself a good part. Make yourself the hero of the piece, rather than the downtrodden member of the mob or the overworked servant. Set your lines in pleasant places. It is just as easy as laying them in the slums. As long as you are bound to dramatize yourself and your surroundings and circumstances anyway, try this:

1. Dramatize yourself, in your mind's eye, with the people and surroundings and things you want most, doing the things you would like most to do, holding the sort of position you long for, doing the work you feel yourself best fitted to do. Some may call it day-dreaming, but make it day-dreaming with a purpose. Make the picture as clear in your mind's eye as though you saw it on the screen of a motion picture theater. And get all the enjoyment out of it that you can. Believe in it. Be thankful for it.

2. Prove your faith in your dream by making every logical preparation for the material manifestation of your desires. Just as the kings of old did when they prayed for water, dig your ditches to receive it.

3. Alter minor details of your drama as you like, but stick to the main goal. Make it your objective, and like Grant in his successful campaign, resolve to stick to it "though it takes all summer."

4. Be a finisher as well as a beginner. Remember that one job finished is worth a dozen half finished. The three-quarter horses never win a prize. It is only at the finish that the purse awaits you. So complete your drama mentally before you begin to act it out, and then stick to it actually until you've made it manifest for all to see.

5. Keep that mental drama to yourself. Don't tell it to others. Remember Samson. He could do anything as long as he kept his mouth shut. Most people's minds are like boilers with the safety valve wide open. They never get up enough of a head of steam to run their engines. Keep your plans to yourself. That way they'll generate such power that you won't need to *tell* others about them—they'll see the result for themselves.

"The imagination," says Glenn Clark in "The Soul's Sincere Desire," "is of all qualities in man the most God-like—that which associates him most closely with God. The first mention we read of man in the Bible is where he is spoken of as an "image." "Let us make man in our image, after our likeness." The only place where an image can be conceived is in the imagination. Thus man, the highest creation of God, was a creation of God's imagination.

The source and center of all man's creative power—the power that above all others lifts him above the level of brute creation, and that gives him dominion, is his power of making images, or the power of the imagination. There are some who have always thought that the imagination was something which makes-believe that which is not. This is fancy—not imagination. Fancy would convert that which is real into pretense and sham; imagination enables one to see through the appearance of a thing to what it really *is*.

There is a very real law of cause and effect which makes the dream of the dreamer come true. It is the law of visualization—the law that calls into being in this outer material world everything that is real in the inner world by directing your Creative Force into it. Imagination pictures the thing you desire. VISION idealizes it. It reaches beyond the thing that is, into the conception of what can be. Imagination gives you the picture. Vision gives you the impulse to make the picture your own by directing your Creative Force into it.

Make your mental image clear enough, picture it vividly in every detail, then do everything you can to bring that image into being, and the Creative Force working through you will speedily provide whatever is necessary to make it an everyday reality.

The law holds true of everything in life. There is nothing you can rightfully desire that cannot be brought into being through visualization and faith.

The keynote of successful visualization is this: See things as you would have them be instead of as they are. Close your eyes and make clear mental pictures. Make them look and act just as they would in real life. In short, day-dream—but day-dream purposefully. Concentrate on the one idea to the exclusion of all others, and continue to concentrate on that one idea until it has been accomplished.

Do you want an automobile? A home? A factory? They can all be won in the same way. They are in their essence all of them ideas of mind, and if you will but build them up in your own mind first, complete in every detail, you will find that the Creative Force working through you can build them up similarly in the material world.

"The building of a trans-continental railroad from a mental picture," says C. W. Chamberlain in "The Uncommon Sense of Applied Psychology,"

gives the average individual an idea that it is a big job. The fact of the matter is, the achievement, as well as the perfect mental picture, is made up of millions of little jobs, each fitting in its proper place and helping to make up the whole.

A skyscraper is built from individual bricks, the laying of each brick being a single job which must be completed before the next brick can be laid.

It is the same with any work, any study. To quote Professor James:

As we become permanent drunkards by so many separate drinks, so we become saints in the moral, and authorities and experts in the practical and scientific spheres, by so many separate acts and hours of working. Let no youth have any anxiety about the upshot of his education whatever the line of it may be. If he keep faithfully busy each hour of the working day he may safely leave the final result to itself. He can with perfect certainty count on waking some fine morning, to find himself one of the competent ones of his generation, in whatever pursuit he may have singled out. . . . Young people should know this truth in advance. The ignorance of it has probably engendered more discouragement and faintheartedness in youths embarking on arduous careers than all other causes taken together.

Remember that the only limit to your capabilities is the one you place upon them. There is no law of limitation. The only law is of supply. Through mind you can draw upon the Creative Force for anything you wish. Use it! There are no limitations upon it. Don't put any on yourself.

Aim high! If you miss the moon, you may hit a star. Everyone admits that this world and all the vast firmament must have been thought into shape from the formless void by some God-Mind. That same God-Mind rules today, and it has given to each form of life power to attract to itself as much of the Creative Force as it needs for its perfect growth. The tree, the plant, the animal—each one finds supply to meet its need.

You are an intelligent, reasoning creature. Your mind is part of the great God-Mind. And you have the power to *say* what you require for perfect growth.

Don't be miserly with yourself. Don't sell yourself for a penny. Whatever price you set upon yourself, life will give. So aim high. Demand much! Make a clear, distinct mental image of what it is you want. Hold it *in your thoughts.* Visualize it, see it, *believe it!* The ways and means of satisfying that desire will follow. For supply always comes on the heels of demand.

It is by doing this that you take your fate out of the hands of chance. It is in this way that you control the experiences you are to have in life. But be sure to visualize *only what you want.* The law works both ways. If you visualize your worries and your fears, you will make them real. Control your thought and you control circumstances. Conditions will be what you make them.

To paraphrase Thackeray—

"The world is a looking glass, and gives back to every man the reflection of his own thought."

Philip of Macedon, Alexander's father, perfected the "phalanx"—a triangular formation which enabled him to center the whole weight of his attack on one point in the opposing line. It drove through everything opposed to it. In that day and age it was invincible. And the idea is just as invincible today.

Keep the one thought in mind, SEE it being carried out step by step, and you can knit any group of workers into one homogeneous whole, all centered on the one idea. You can accomplish any one thing. You can put across any definite idea. Keep that mental picture ever in mind and you will make it as invincible as was Alexander's phalanx of old.

> *It is not the guns or armament*
> *Or the money they can pay,*
> *It's the close cooperation*
> *That makes them win the day.*
> *It is not the individual*
> *Or the army as a whole*
> *But the everlasting team work of every bloomin' soul.*

—J. MASON KNOX

The error of the ages is the tendency mankind has always shown to limit the power of Mind, or its willingness to help in time of need.

"Know ye not," said Paul, "That ye are the temples of the Living God?"

No—most of us do not know it. Or at least, if we do, we are like the Indian family out on the Cherokee reservation. Oil had been found on their land and money poured in upon them. More money than they had ever known was in the world. Someone persuaded them to build a great house, to have it beautifully furnished, richly decorated. But the Indians, while very proud of their showy house, continued to *live in their old sod shack!*

So it is with many of us. We may know that we are "temples of the Living God." We may even be proud of that fact. But we never take advantage of it to dwell in that temple, to proclaim dominion over things and conditions. We never avail ourselves of the power that is ours.

The great prophets of old had the forward look. Theirs was the era of hope and expectation. They looked for the time when the revelation should come that was to make men "sons of God." "They shall obtain joy and gladness, and sorrow and sighing shall flee away."

Jesus came to fulfill that revelation. "Ask and ye shall receive, that your joy may be full."

The world has turned in vain to materialistic philosophy for deliverance from its woes. In the future the only march of actual progress will be in the mental realm, and this progress will not be in the way of human speculation and theorizing, but in the *actual demonstration* of the power of Mind to mold the Creative Force into anything of good.

The world stands today within the vestibule of the vast realm of divine intelligence, wherein is found the transcendent, practical power of Mind over all things.

What eye never saw, nor ear ever heard,
What never entered the mind of man—
Even all that God has prepared for those who love him.

24

I Am

Years ago, Emile Coué electrified the world with his cures of all manner of disease—solely through the power of SUGGESTION!

"Nobody ought to be sick!" he proclaimed, and proceeded to prove it by curing hundreds who came to him after doctors had failed to relieve them. Not only that, but he showed that the same methods could be used to cure one's affairs—to bring riches instead of debts, success instead of drudgery.

Originally, Coué was a hypnotist. In his little drug store, he found occasional patients whom he could hypnotize. He hypnotized them—put their conscious minds to sleep—and addressed himself directly to their subconscious.

To the subconscious, he declared that there was nothing wrong with whatever organ the patient had thought diseased, and the subconscious accepted the statement and molded the Creative Force within accordingly. When the patient came out from under the hypnotic influence, he was well! It remained then only to convince his conscious mind of this, so he would not send through new suggestions of disease to his subconscious, and the patient was cured!

How account for that? By the fact that the disease or imperfection is not so much in your body as in your mind. It is in your rate of motion, and this is entirely mind-controlled. Change the subconscious belief, and the physical manifestations change with it. You speed up your rate of motion, and in that way throw off the discordant elements of disease. Doctors recognize this when they give their patients harmless sugar pills, knowing that these will dispel fear, and that when the images conjured up by fear are gone, the supposed trouble will go with them.

But Coué found many patients whom he could not hypnotize. How treat them? By inducing a sort of self-hypnosis in themselves. It is a well-known fact that constant repetition carries conviction—especially to the subconscious mind. So Coué had his patients continually repeat to themselves the affirmation that their trouble was passing, that they were getting better and better. "Every day in every way I am getting better and better." And this unreasoning affirmation cured thousands of ills that had been troubling them for years.

What is back of that success? A law as old as the hills, a law that has been known to psychologists for years—the law that the subconscious mind accepts as true anything that is repeated to it *convincingly* and *often*. And once it has accepted such a statement as true, it proceeds to mold the Creative Force working through it in such wise as to MAKE IT TRUE!

You see, where the conscious mind reasons inductively, the subconscious uses only deductive reasoning. Where the reasoning mind weighs each fact that is presented to it, questions the truth or falsity of each and then forms its conclusions accordingly, the subconscious acts quite differently. IT ACCEPTS AS FACT ANY STATEMENT THAT IS PRESENTED TO IT CONVINCINGLY. Then, having accepted this as the basis of its actions, it proceeds logically to do all in its power to bring it into being.

That is why the two most important words in the English language are the words—"I AM." That is why the Ancients regarded these two words as the secret name of God.

You ask a friend how he is, and he replies carelessly—"I am sick, I am poor, I am unlucky, I am subject to this, that or the other thing,"—never stopping to think that by those very words he is fastening misfortune upon himself, declaring to the subconscious mind within him that he IS sick or poor or weak or the servant of some desire.

"Let the weak say—'I am strong!'" the Prophet Joel exhorted his people thousands of years ago. And the advice is as good today as it was then.

You have seen men, under hypnotic suggestion, perform prodigies of strength. You have seen them with their bodies stretched between two chairs, their heads on one, their feet on another, supporting the weight of several people standing on them, when they could not ordinarily hold up even their own bodies in that position. How can they do it? Because the hypnotist has assured their subconscious that they CAN do it, that they have the strength and power necessary.

"Therefore I say unto you, what things soever ye desire when ye pray, BELIEVE THAT YE RECEIVE THEM, and ye shall HAVE them." That was the assurance given us by the Master Psychologist of all time, the Great Healer, the Worker of Miracles. Again and again He told those He healed that it was their FAITH that made them whole. And where such faith was lacking, as when He went back to Nazareth, the home of his childhood, it is written that "There He did no mighty works."

How can you work up the necessary faith to accomplish the things you desire? By taking the advice of the wise men of old, of the Prophet Joel, of Jesus—by *claiming* it as yours, and setting your subconscious mind to work making those claims come true.

It is a sort of self-hypnosis, but so is all of prayer. Away back in 1915, the head of the Warsaw Psychological Institute conducted a series of experiments from which he concluded that the energy manifested by anyone during life is in direct ratio with his power for plunging himself into a condition of autohypnosis. In simple language, that means convincing yourself of the possibility of doing the things you want to do.

The subconscious in each of us HAS the knowledge, HAS the power to do any right thing we may require of it. The only need is to implant in it the confidence—the "BELIEVE THAT YOU RECEIVE" which Jesus taught.

In a case cited by Baudouin, the famous psychologist, a woman after using autosuggestion as a means of helping herself, declared: "I can do twice as much work as before. During vacation, I have been able to go through two extensive tasks, such as a year ago I should never have attempted. This year I systematized my work and said, 'I can do it all; what I am undertaking is materially possible, and therefore must be morally possible; consequently I ought not to experience, and shall not experience, discouragement, hesitancy, annoyance, or slackness.'" As a result of these affirmations, the way to her inner powers was opened and she was able to say truly, "Nothing could stop me, nothing could prevent my doing what I had planned to do; you might almost have said that things were done by themselves, without the slightest effort on my part." Not only did she find herself working with a high degree of success heretofore unknown, but with a certainty and calmness of mind beyond her previous attainment.

Emerson, with his genius for condensing great truths into a few words, wrote—"Do the thing and you shall have the power."

The wise men of old learned thousands of years ago that life is like an echo. It always returns the call sent out. Like the echo, the response is always the same as the call, and the louder the call, the greater the response.

You say—"I am sick, I am poor," and your words are forerunners of your circumstance. "Every idle word that men shall speak, they shall give account of in the day of judgment." And that day of judgment comes sooner than most people think.

Be careful to speak only those words which you are willing to see take form in your life, for remember the words of wise old Job: "Thou shalt also decree a thing, and it shall be established unto thee." Never speak the word of lack or limitation, for—"By thy words shalt thou be justified, and by thy words shalt thou be condemned."

Affirm constantly—"I have faith in the power of my word. I speak only that which I desire to see made manifest." Remember, "Behind you is Infinite Power, before you is endless possibility, around you is endless opportunity. Why should you fear?"

C. G. Tanner expresses the idea beautifully—

If you have faith in what you want to do,
If you behold yourself a king's own son,
Then you have asked God's power to work through you,
And pledged yourself to see that it is done.
'With faith I place it in God's hands,' you say?
God's hands are yours! Your good must come through you!
God has no other hands with which He may
Give unto you your sonship's rightful due.

Faith and persistence travel hand in hand,
The one without the other incomplete.
If you would reach success, then take the stand,
'This I will try once more,' and no defeat
Can cloud that beacon gleaming bright and clear,
Or conjure up dread failure's haunting wraith!
You rest secure with God. No thought of fear
Can dim the shining armor of your faith.

Most people seem to think that we work to live, but there is a deeper purpose in life than that. What we really work for is to call forth the talents that are within our own soul, to give expression to the Creative Force working through us. That is the one big purpose for which we were born—to express the Creative Force in us, to give God the chance to express Himself through us. And we CAN do it. As the famous English poet Shelley put it—"The Almighty has given men arms long enough to reach the stars, if they would but put them forth."

And the first step lies in using what you have. The key to power lies in using, not hoarding. Use releases still more power for ever greater works. Hoarding builds a hard shell around the thing hoarded and prevents more from coming in. You may have what you want, if you are willing to use what you have now. You can do what you want to do if you are willing to do what there is to do right now. "The one condition coupled with the gift of truth," says Emerson, "*is its use.*"

Professor William Bateson of the British Society for Scientific Research said: "We are finding now beyond doubt that the gifts and geniuses of mankind are due not so much to something added to the ordinary person, but instead are due to factors which in the normal person INHIBIT the development of these gifts. They are now without doubt to be looked upon as RELEASES of powers normally suppressed."

And why are they suppressed? Because of doubt, of fear of failure, of procrastination, of putting things off till the morrow. "Straight from a mighty bow this truth is driven: They fail, and they alone, who have not striven."

> *Tomorrow you will live, you always cry;*
> *In what far country does this morrow lie,*
> *That 'tis so mighty long ere it arrive?*
> *Beyond the Indies does this morrow live?*
> *'Tis so farfetched, this morrow, that I fear*
> *'Twill be both very old and very dear.*
> *Tomorrow I will live, the fool does say;*
> *Today itself's too late; the wise lived yesterday.*

—ABRAHAM COWLEY

"To begin," said Ausonius, "is to be half done." "Greatly begin!" wrote another sage. "Though thou have time for but a line, be that sublime." And the Easterners have a proverb that the road of a thousand miles begins with one step.

So make your start, and don't allow any thought of failure to stop you. Have faith—if not in yourself—then in the Creative Force working through you. Many a splendid work has been lost to mankind because the faith of its originator was not strong enough to release the Creative Force that would have enabled him to make his dream come true.

Remember that you cannot talk failure, or think failure, and reap success. You'll never reach the top of the ladder if doubt and fear and procrastination make you hesitate to put your foot on the first rung.

There is a Power working through you that can accomplish any aim you may aspire to. But to energize that power, you must harness it up with Faith. You must have the will to believe, the courage to aspire, and the profound conviction that success is possible to anyone who works for it persistently and believingly.

Three hundred and forty years ago, there sailed from Spain the mightiest fleet the world had ever known, Spanish galleasses, Portuguese caracks, Florentine caravels, huge hulks from other countries—floating fortresses, mounting tier upon tier of mighty cannon—140 great ships in all, manned to the full with sailors and soldiers and gentlemen adventurers.

The treasure of the Incas, the Plunder of the Aztec, had gone into the building and outfitting of this vast Armada. No wonder Spain looked upon it as invincible. No wonder England feared it. For this was the Armada that was to invade England and carry fire and sword through town and countryside. This was the Armada that was to punish these impudent Britons for the "piratical" raids of Sir Francis Drake, Morgan and all those hardy seamen who had dared death and slavery to pull down treasure ships on the Spanish Main.

The iron hand of Philip II of Spain rested heavily upon the Netherlands. It dominated all of Europe. Now he confidently looked forward to the time when England, too, would groan beneath its weight.

But he reckoned without one thing—faith! He put in charge of this invincible Armada, the Duke of Medina Sidonia, a man who had no faith in himself, no faith in his ability, no faith in his men. And when he did that, he blunted the point of every pike; he dulled the cutting edge of every sword; he took the mightiest naval weapon ever forged, and deliberately drew its sting.

Is that putting it too strongly? Just listen. Here is the letter the Duke wrote to the King, upon being notified of his appointment to the command:

My health is bad and from my small experience of the water I know that I
am always seasick. . . . The expedition is on such a scale and the object is of
such high importance that the person at the head of it ought to understand
navigation and sea fighting, and I know nothing of either. . . . The Ad-
elantado of Castile would do better than I. The Lord would help him, he
is a good Christian and has fought in naval battles. If you send me, depend
upon it, I shall have a bad account to render of my trust.

He had everything to succeed with—everything but faith in himself. He
expected failure—and disastrous failure met him at every turn.

One hundred and forty mighty ships—the greatest ever built. And England, to meet that splendid Armada, had only 30 small ships of war and a few
merchantmen outfitted and manned by private gentlemen. Yet England, while
alarmed, was yet courageous and hopeful. For had not England Sir Francis
Drake? And Lord Charles Howard? And a dozen other mighty fighters who
had met and bested the Spaniards a score of times on the Spanish Main? And
could they not do the same again?

So said England, believing in her leaders. And her leaders echoed that sen-
timent. Are not English sailors the hardiest seamen and finest fighters afloat,
they asked. And believed in their men.

The English had 30 or 40 little ships against the Spaniards' 140 mighty
men-of-war. The English had scarce two days' powder aboard—so penurious
was their Queen—while the Spanish were outfitted with everything a ship-of-
war could ask.

But Howard and Drake were not depending upon any Queen to fight their
battles. They were not worrying about the size of the enemy. They were thinking—
"There are the Spaniards. Here are we. We have fought them and whipped them
a dozen times before. We can do it now. So let's get at them!"

They went out expecting victory. And victory met them at every turn.

From the Lizard in Cornwall to Portland, where Don Pedro de Valdes and
his mighty ship were left; from Portland to Calais, where Spain lost Hugo de
Moncado with the galleys which he captured; from Calais, out of sight of England, around Scotland and Ireland, beaten and shuffled together, that mighty
Armada was chased, until finally the broken remnants drifted back to Spain.

With all their vast squadron, they had not taken one ship or bark or pinnace
of England. With all those thousands of soldiers, they had not landed one man
but those killed or taken prisoner.

Three-fourths of their number lost or captured, their mighty fleet destroyed. And why? Because one man lacked faith. Spanish soldiers were proving on a dozen fields that no braver fighters lived anywhere. The "Spanish Square" had withstood infantry, cavalry, artillery—then carried all before it. Yet these same soldiers, afloat in their huge fortresses, were utterly defeated by less than a fourth their number.

And the reason? Because they were a spear without a head—an army without a leader—riches and power without faith. Was ever a better example of the power of belief?

Men go all through life like the Duke of Medina Sidonia—looking ever for the dark side of things, expecting trouble at every turn—and usually finding it. It is really lack of courage—courage to try for great things, courage to dare disappointment and ridicule to accomplish a worthy end. Have you ever sat in a train and watched another train passing you? You can look right on through its windows to the green fields and pleasant vistas beyond. Or you can gaze at the partitions between the windows and see nothing but their dingy drabness. So it is with everything in life. You can look for the good, the joyful and happy—and not merely see only these but manifest them in your daily life. Or you can look for trouble, for sickness and sorrow—and find them awaiting you around every corner.

Pessimists call this the "Pollyanna Age" and ridicule such ideas as this. But ridicule or not, it works—in one's personal life as well as in business—and thousands can testify to its efficacy.

Perhaps one of the best examples of the difference that outlook makes is in the lives of Emerson and Thoreau. Emerson's philosophy of living can best be expressed in his own words—"Nerve us with incessant affirmatives. Don't bark against the bad, but chant the beauties of the good." And his tranquil and serene life reflected that attitude throughout.

Thoreau, on the other hand, was constantly searching out and denouncing evil. With motives every whit as high as Emerson's, he believed in attacking the problem from the opposite angle, with the result that he was constantly in hot water, yet accomplished not a tenth of the good that Emerson did. Like the man in d'Annunzio's play, LA CITTA MORTA—"Fascinated by the tombs, he forgot the beauty of the sky."

It is necessary at times to clean up evil conditions in order to start afresh. It is necessary to hunt out the source of pollution in order to purify a stream. But it should be merely a means to an end. And the end should always be—

not negative like the mere destruction of evil, but the positive replacing of evil with good.

If you have ever walked across a high trestle, you know that it doesn't pay to look down. That way dizziness and destruction lie. You have to look forward, picking out the ties you are going to step on ten or twenty feet ahead, if you are to progress.

Life is just such a trestle. And looking downward too much is likely to make one lose his balance, stumble and fall. You must gaze ever forward if you are to keep your perspective.

There's a little poem by Edgar Guest[16] that exemplifies the idea:

Somebody said that it couldn't be done,
But he with a chuckle replied
That 'maybe it couldn't,' but he would be one
Who wouldn't say so till he'd tried.
So he buckled right in with the trace of a grin
On his face. If he worried he hid it.
He started to sing as he tackled the thing
That couldn't be done, AND HE DID IT.

Most of the world's progress has been made by just such men as that. Men like Watt, who didn't know that steam could not be made to accomplish any useful purpose, and so invented the steam engine. Men like Fulton, who didn't know that it was foolish to try to propel a boat with wheels—and so invented the steamboat.

Men like Bell, Edison, Wright, who didn't know how foolish it was to attempt the impossible—and so went ahead and did it.

"For God's sake, give me the young man who has brains enough to make a fool of himself!" cried Stevenson. And when they succeed, the whole world echoes that cry.

There is no limit upon you—except the limit you put upon yourself. You are like the birds—your thoughts can fly across all barriers, unless you tie them down or cage them or clip their wings by the limitations you put upon them.

There is nothing that can defeat you—except yourself. You are one with

---

16. From "The Path to Home." The Reilly & Lee Co.

the Father. And the Father knows everything you will ever need to know on any subject.

Why then, try to repress any right desire, any high ambition? Why not put behind it every ounce of energy, every bit of enthusiasm, of which you are capable?

Mahomet established a larger empire than that of Rome on nothing but enthusiasm. And Mahomet was but a poor camel-driver. What then can *you* not do?

Men repress their power for good, their capacity for success, by accepting suggestions of inferiority; by their timidity or self-consciousness; by fear; by conservatism.

Never mind what others think of you. It is what *you* think that counts. Never let another's poor opinion of you influence your decisions. Rather, resolve to show him how unfounded is his opinion.

People thought so poorly of Oliver Cromwell that he could not win permission to emigrate to the Colonies. When he raised his regiment of cavalry, that later won the name of "Ironsides" because of its practical invincibility, the old soldiers and the dandies of the day laughed at it. Seldom had a lot of more awkward-looking countrymen been gathered together.

Any soldier might have trained them. But the thing that made them invincible, the thing that enabled them to ride over and through all the legions of King Charles, was not their training, but their fervent belief in the justice of their cause, in their leader and in their God.

"Hymn-singing hypocrites," their enemies called them. But here were no hypocrites. Here were men who were animated by a common faith that God was with them as with the Israelites of old—and that with God on their side, nothing could withstand them.

That was the faith of Cromwell. And he instilled that faith into every man in his regiment.

And while Cromwell lived to keep that faith alive, nothing *did* withstand them. They made the man who was not good enough to emigrate to America, Ruler of England!

Nothing worth while ever has been accomplished without faith. Nothing worth while ever will.

Why do so many great organizations go to pieces after their founder's death? Why do they fail to outlive him by more than a few years?

Because the ones who take up his work lack the forward look, the faith, to carry on. His idea was one of service—theirs is to continue paying dividends. His thought was to build ever greater and greater—theirs to hold what he won.

"The best defensive is a strong offensive." You can't just hold your own. You can't stand still. You've got to go forward—or backward!

Which is it with you? If forward, then avoid the pessimist as you would the plague. Enthusiasm, optimism, may make mistakes—but it will learn from them and progress. Pessimism, conservatism, caution, will die of dry rot, if it is not sooner lost in the forward march of things.

So be an optimist. Cultivate the forward look.

> *The Optimist and Pessimist,*
> *The difference is droll,*
> *The Optimist sees the doughnut,*
> *The Pessimist—the hole!*

The good is always there—if you look for it hard enough. But you must look for *it*. You can't be content to take merely what happens to come into your line of vision. You have got to refuse to accept anything short of good. Disclaim it! Say it is not yours. Say it—*and believe it*. Then keep a-seeking—and the first thing you know, the good you have been seeking will be found to have been right under your nose all the time.

What is the backbone of all business? Credit. And what is credit but faith—faith in your fellow-man—faith in his integrity—faith in his willingness and his ability to give you a square deal?

What do you base credit-faith upon? Upon hearsay—upon what your prospective customer has done for others, his promptness in paying them, his willingness to cooperate with them. In many cases you have never seen him—you can't be certain of your own personal knowledge that such a person exists—but you believe in him, you have FAITH. And having faith, your business grows and prospers.

If you can have such faith in a man you have never seen, as to trust large portions of your earthly goods in his hands, can you not put a little trust in the Father, too?

True, you have not seen Him—but you have far greater proof of His being than of that of your customer thousands of miles away. You have far greater proof of His reliability, of His regard for you, of His ability and His willingness at all times to come to your assistance in any right way you may ask. You don't need money with Him. You don't need high standing in your community. You don't need credit.

What is it makes a successful salesman? Faith in his house. Faith in the goods he is selling. Faith in the service they will render his customers. Faith in himself. Have you faith in your "house"—in your Father—in the manifold gifts He offers you so freely?

Men can sell for a little while solely on faith in their own ability, they can palm off anything that will show a profit to themselves. But they never make successful salesmen. The inevitable reaction comes. They grow cynical, lose all faith in others—and eventually lose faith in themselves as well. The successful salesman must have a fourfold faith—faith in his house, faith in his product, faith in the good it will do his customer, faith in himself. Given such a faith, he can sell anything. Given such a faith in the Father, *you* can do anything.

It wasn't superior courage or superior fighting ability that enabled Washington's half-trained army to beat the British. English soldiers were showing all over the world that they were second to none in fighting qualities. And the American soldiers were, for the most part, from the same sturdy stock. It was their faith in a greater Power outside themselves.

What is it differentiates the banker from the pawnbroker? Both make loans. Both require security. But where the pawnbroker must have tangible, material property that he can resell before he will lend a cent, the really great banker bases his loans on something bigger than any security that may be offered him—his faith in the borrower.

America was built on faith. Those great railroad builders who spanned the continent knew when they did it that there was not enough business immediately available to make their investment profitable for a long time to come. But they had faith—a faith that was the making of our country.

That same faith is evident on every hand today. Men erect vast factories—in the faith that the public will find need for and buy their products. They build offices, apartments, homes—in the faith that their cities will grow up to the need of them. They put up public utilities capable of serving twice the number of people in their territories—in the faith that the demand will not only grow with the population, but the availability of the supply will help to create new demands.

Faith builds cities and businesses and men. In fact, everything of good, everything constructive in this old world of ours is based on faith. So if you have it not, *grow it*—as the most important thing you can do. And if you have it, *tend it,* water it, cultivate it—for it is the most important thing in life.

When nothing seems to help, I go and look at a stonecutter hammering away at his rock, perhaps a hundred times without as much as a crack showing in it. Yet at the hundred and first blow, it will split in two, and I know it was not that blow that did it, but all that had gone before.

—J. A. RIIS.

25

Talisman

What is the eternal question which stands up and looks you and every sincere man squarely in the eye every morning?

"How can I better my condition?" That is the real life question which confronts you, and will haunt you every day until you solve it.

The answer to that question lies first in remembering that the great business of life is thinking. Control your thoughts and you mold circumstance.

Just as the first law of gain is desire, so the first essential to success is FAITH. Believe that you *have*—see the thing you want as an existent fact—and anything you can rightly wish for is yours. Belief is "the substance of things hoped for, the evidence of things not seen."

You have seen men, inwardly no more capable than yourself, accomplish the seemingly impossible. You have seen others, after years of hopeless struggle, suddenly win their most cherished dreams. And you've often wondered, "What is the power that gives new life to their dying ambitions, that supplies new impetus to their jaded desires, that gives them a new start on the road to success?"

That power is belief—*faith*. Someone, something, gave them a new belief in themselves and a new faith in their power to win—and they leaped ahead and wrested success from seemingly certain defeat.

Do you remember the picture Harold Lloyd was in some years ago, showing a country boy who was afraid of his shadow? Every boy in the countryside bedeviled him. Until one day his grandmother gave him a talisman that she assured him his grandfather had carried through the Civil War and which, so she said, had the property of making its owner invincible. Nothing could hurt him, she told him, while he wore this talisman. Nothing could stand up against him. He believed her. And the next time the bully of the town started to cuff him around, he wiped up the earth with him. And that was only the start. Before the year was out he had made a reputation as the most daring soul in the community.

Then, when his grandmother felt that he was thoroughly cured, she told him the truth—that the "talisman" was merely a piece of old junk she'd picked up by the roadside—that she knew all he needed was *faith in himself,* belief that he could do these things.

Stories like that are common. It is such a well-established truth that you can do only what you think you can, that the theme is a favorite one with authors. I remember reading a story years ago of an artist—a mediocre sort of artist—who was visiting the field of Waterloo and happened upon a curious lump of metal half buried in the dirt, which so attracted him that he picked it up and put it in his pocket. Soon thereafter he noticed a sudden increase in confidence, an absolute faith in himself, not only as to his own chosen line of work, but in his ability to handle any situation that might present itself. He painted a great picture—just to show that he *could* do it. Not content with that, he visioned an empire with Mexico as its basis, actually led a revolt that carried all before it—until one day he lost his talisman. Then the bubble burst.

It is your own belief in yourself that counts. It is the consciousness of dominant power within you that makes all things attainable. *You can do anything you think you can.* This knowledge is literally the gift of the gods, for through it you can solve every human problem. It should make of you an incurable optimist. It is the open door to welfare. *Keep it open*—by expecting to gain everything that is right.

You are entitled to every good thing. Therefore expect nothing but good. Defeat does not *need* to follow victory. You don't have to "knock wood" every time you congratulate yourself that things have been going well with you. Victory should follow victory.

Don't limit your channels of supply. Don't think that riches or success must come through some particular job or some rich uncle. It is not for you to dictate to the Creative Force the means through which it shall send Its gifts to you. There are millions of channels through which It can reach you. Your part is to impress upon Mind your need, your earnest desire, your boundless belief in the resources and the willingness of the Creative Force to help you. Plant the seed of desire. Nourish it with a clear visualization of the ripened fruit. Water it with sincere faith. But leave the means to the Creative Force.

Open up your mind. Clear out the channels of thought. Keep yourself in a state of receptivity. Gain a mental attitude in which you are constantly *expecting good*. You have the fundamental right to all good, you know. "According to your faith, be it unto you."

The trouble with most of us is that we are mentally lazy. It is so much easier to go along with the crowd than to break trail for ourselves. But the great discoverers, the great inventors, the great geniuses in all lines have been men who dared to break with tradition, who defied precedent, who believed that there is no limit to what Mind can do—and who stuck to that belief until their goal was won, in spite of all the sneers and ridicule of the wiseacres and the "It-can't-be-doners."

Not only that, but they were never satisfied with achieving just one success. They knew that the first success is like the first olive out of the bottle. All the others come out the more easily for it. They realized that they were a part of the Creative Force and Intelligence of the Universe, and that the part shares all the properties of the whole. And that realization gave them the faith to strive for any right thing, the knowledge that the only limit upon their capabilities was the limit of their desires. Knowing that, they couldn't be satisfied with any ordinary success. They had to keep on and on and on.

Edison didn't sit down and fold his hands when he gave us the talking machine. Or the electric light. These great achievements merely opened the way to new fields of accomplishment.

Open up the channels between your mind and the Creative Force, and there is no limit to the riches that will come pouring in. Concentrate your thoughts on the particular thing you are most interested in, and ideas in abundance will come flooding down, opening up a dozen ways of winning the goal you are striving for.

But don't let one success—no matter how great—satisfy you. The Law of Life, you know, is the Law of Growth. You can't stand still. You must go forward—or be passed by. Complacency—self-satisfaction—is the greatest enemy of achievement. You must keep looking forward. Like Alexander, you must be constantly seeking new worlds to conquer. Depend upon it, the power will come to meet the need. There is no such thing as failing powers, if we look to the Creative Force for our source of supply. The only failure of mind comes from worry and fear—and disuse.

William James, the famous psychologist, taught that—"The more mind does, the more it can do." For ideas release energy. You can *do* more and better work than you have ever done. You can *know* more than you know now. You know from your own experience that under proper mental conditions of joy or enthusiasm, you can do three or four times the work without fatigue that you can ordinarily. Tiredness is more boredom than actual physical fatigue. You can work almost indefinitely when the work is a pleasure.

You've seen sickly persons, frail persons, who couldn't do an hour's light work without exhaustion, suddenly buckle down when heavy responsibilities were thrown upon them, and grow strong and rugged under the load. Crises not only draw upon the reserve power you have but they help to create new power.

IT COULDN'T BE DONE

It may be that you have been deluded by the thought of incompetence. It may be that you have been told so often that you cannot do certain things that you've come to believe you can't. Remember that success or failure is merely a state of mind. Believe you cannot do a thing—and you can't. Know that you *can* do it—and you *will*. You must *see yourself doing it.*

> *If you think you are beaten, you are;*
> *If you think you dare not, you don't;*
> *If you'd like to win, but you think you can't,*
> *It's almost a cinch you won't;*
> *If you think you'll lose, you've lost,*
> *For out in the world you'll find*
> *Success begins with a fellow's will—*
> *It's all in the state of mind.*

Full many a race is lost,
Ere even a race is run,
And many a coward fails
Ere even his work's begun.
Think big, and your deeds will grow,
Think small and you fall behind,
Think that you can, and you will;
It's all in the state of mind.

If you think you are outclassed, you are;
You've got to think high to rise;
You've got to be sure of yourself before
You can ever win a prize.
Life's battle doesn't always go
To the stronger or faster man;
But sooner or later, the man who wins
Is the fellow who thinks he can.

There's a vast difference between a proper understanding of one's own ability and a determination to make the best of it—and offensive egotism. It is absolutely necessary for every man to believe in himself, before he can make the most of himself. All of us have something to sell. It may be our goods, it may be our abilities, it may be our services. You've got to believe in yourself to make your buyer take stock in you at par and accrued interest. You've got to feel the same personal solicitude over a customer lost, as a revivalist over a backslider, and hold special services to bring him over into the fold. You've got to get up every morning with determination, if you're going to go to bed that night with satisfaction.

There's mighty sound sense in the saying that all the world loves a booster. The one and only thing you have to win success with is MIND. For your mind to function at its highest capacity, you've got to be charged with good cheer and optimism. No one ever did a good piece of work while in a negative frame of mind. Your best work is always done when you are feeling happy and optimistic.

And a happy disposition is the *result*—not the *cause*—of happy, cheery thinking. Health and prosperity are the *results* primarily of optimistic thoughts. *You* make the pattern. If the impress you have left on the world about you seems faint and weak, don't blame fate—blame your pattern! You will never cultivate a brave, courageous demeanor by thinking cowardly thoughts. You cannot gather figs from thistles. You will never make your dreams come true by choking them with doubts and fears. You've got to put foundations under your air castles, foundations of UNDERSTANDING AND BELIEF. Your chances of success in any undertaking can always be measured by your BELIEF in yourself.

Are your surroundings discouraging? Do you feel that if you were in another's place success would be easier? Just bear in mind that your real environment is within you. All the factors of success or failure are in your inner world. *You* make that inner world—and through it your outer world. You can choose the material from which to build it. If you've not chosen wisely in the past, you can choose again now the material you want to rebuild it. The richness of life is within you. No one has failed so long as he can begin again.

> *For yesterday is but a dream,*
> *And tomorrow is only a vision.*
> *And today well-lived makes*
> *Every yesterday a dream of happiness,*
> *And every tomorrow a vision of hope.*

Start right in and *do* all the things you feel you have it in you to do. Ask permission of no man. Concentrating your thought upon any proper undertaking will make its achievement possible. Your belief that you *can* do the thing gives your thought forces their power. Fortune waits upon you. Seize her boldly, hold her—and she is yours. She belongs rightfully to you. But if you cringe to her, if you go up to her doubtfully, timidly, she will pass you by in scorn. For she is a fickle jade who must be mastered, who loves boldness, who admires confidence. Remember, you can have what you want if you will use what you have now. You can do what you want if you will do what there is to do right now. Take the first step, and your mind will mobilize all its forces to your aid. But the first essential is that you *begin*. Once the battle is started, all that is within and without you will come to your assistance, if you attack in earnest and meet each obstacle with resolution. But *you* have to start things. As the poet so well expresses it:

> *Then take this honey from the bitterest cup,*
> *There is no failure save in giving up—*
> *No real fall so long as one still tries—*

For seeming set-backs make the strong man wise.
There's no defeat, in truth, save from within:
Unless you're beaten there, you're sure to win.

The men who have made their mark in this world all had one trait in common—*they believed in themselves!* "But," you may say, "how can I believe in myself when I have never yet done anything worth while, when everything I put my hand to seems to fail?" You can't, of course. That is, you couldn't if you had to depend upon your conscious mind alone. But just remember what One far greater than you said—"I can of mine own self do nothing. The Father that is within me—He doeth the works."

That same "FATHER" is within you, and back of Him and of you is all the Creative Force in the universe. It is by knowing that He is in you, and that through Him you can do anything that is right, that you can acquire the belief in yourself which is so necessary. Certainly the Mind that imaged the heavens and the earth and all that they contain has all wisdom, all power, all abundance. With this Mind to call upon, you know there is no problem too difficult to undertake. The *knowing* of this is the first step. *Faith.* But St. James tells us—"Faith without works is dead." And Emerson expressed it in the modern manner when he said: "He who learns and learns, and yet does not what he knows, is like the man who plows and plows, yet never sows." So go on to the next step. Decide on the one thing you want most from life, no matter what it may be. There is no limit, you know, to Mind. Visualize this thing that you want. See it, feel it, BELIEVE in it. Make your mental blue-print, and *begin to build!* And not merely a mental blue-print, but make an actual picture of it, if you can. Cut out pictures from magazines that symbolize what you want. Paste them on a large sheet of paper and pin them up where you can see them often. You'll be surprised how such pictures help you to form the mental mold, and how quickly the Creative Force will take shape in that mold.

Suppose some people DO laugh at your idea. Suppose Reason does say—"It can't be done!" People laughed at Galileo. They laughed at Henry Ford. Reason contended for countless ages that the earth was flat. Reason said—or so numerous automotive engineers argued—that the Ford motor wouldn't run. But the earth *is* round—and some millions of Fords did run—and are running.

Let us start right now putting into practice some of these truths that you have learned. What do you want most of life right now? Take that one desire, concentrate on it, impress it upon your subconscious mind in every way you can, particularly with pictures. Visualizing what you want is essential, and pictures make this visualizing easier.

Psychologists have discovered that the best time to make suggestions to your subconscious mind is just before going to sleep, when the senses are quiet and the attention is lax. So let us take your desire and suggest it to your subconscious mind tonight. The two prerequisites are the earnest DESIRE, and an intelligent, understanding, BELIEF. Someone has said, you know, that education is three-fourths encouragement, and the encouragement is the suggestion that the thing can be done.

You know that you can have what you want, if you want it badly enough and can believe in it earnestly enough. So tonight, just before you drop off to sleep, concentrate your thought on this thing that you most desire from life. BELIEVE that you have it. SEE it in your mind's eye, and see YOURSELF possessing it. FEEL yourself using it.

Do that every night until you ACTUALLY DO BELIEVE that you have the thing you want. When you reach that point, YOU WILL HAVE IT!

> *"Do you accept the Power within,*
> *Or do you say—'Tomorrow,*
> *Or after that, I will begin,'*
> *And try from time to time to borrow*
> *Sweet, precious moments, quickly sped,*
> *On futile paths by error led?*
>
> *"Our God has willed a legacy*
> *To all of those believing.*
> *So why not change your 'it might be'*
> *To just 'I am receiving*
> *A guiding hand in every task,*
> *And full returns for all I ask.'*
>
> *"Do you desire success to win?*
> *Humbly accept the Power within."*

—JOHN GRAHAM

26

The Perfect Pattern

In Chapter 4, we quoted Baudouin to show how a person can hypnotize himself into health, happiness, success.

This is not as foolish as it sounds, for self-hypnosis is nothing more nor less than deep concentration, and it is a well-known fact that we go in the direction of our thoughts. What we long for, or dread or fear—that we are headed towards.

You see, man is inseparable from the Creative Force. God has incarnated Himself in man, and God is dynamic—not static. He cannot be shut up. He must be expressed in one way or another. We put His power into all that we do—whether towards failure or success.

How then can we use this Creative Power for good? How can we put it into our efforts toward success?

First, by convincing ourselves that we ARE successful, that we are on the road to riches or health or power. We must "believe that we receive." And the quickest, easiest, surest way to do this is through repetition. It is now generally known and accepted that one comes to believe whatever one repeats to oneself sufficiently often, whether the statement be true or false. It comes to be the dominating thought in one's mind.

Such thoughts, when mixed with a strong feeling of desire or emotion, become a magnet which attracts from all about similar or related thoughts. They attract a host of their relatives, which they add to their own magnetic power until they become the dominating, motivating master of the individual.

Then the second law begins to work. All impulses of thought have a tendency to clothe themselves in their physical equivalent. In other words, if the dominating thought in your mind is riches, that thought will tend to draw to you opportunities for riches that you never dreamed of. Just as the magnet attracts iron, so will you attract money and ways of making more money. Or if health be your dominating thought, ways and means of winning new health and strength will come to you. The same is true of love, of happiness, of anything you may greatly desire of life.

On the other hand, if you fill your mind with fear, doubt and unbelief in your ability to use the forces of Infinite Intelligence, these in turn will become your dominating thought and form the pattern for your life.

You will be lifted up, or pulled down, according to the pattern of your thought. There are no limitations upon the Creative Force working through you. The limitations are all in you, and they are all self-imposed. Riches and poverty are equally the offspring of your thought.

So if you desire anything of good, the first and most important thing you must do is to develop your faith that *you can have that good*. Faith, like any other state of mind, can be induced by suggestion, by repetition. Tell yourself often enough that you HAVE faith, and you will have it, for any thought that is passed on to the subconscious often enough and convincingly enough is finally accepted, and then translated into its physical equivalent by the most practical method available.

You remember the story of the king who felt that his child, if brought up in the court, would be spoiled by overmuch attention. So he put him in the family of an honest peasant, and had him raised as the peasant's own child. The boy had all the power, all the riches of the kingdom at his disposal—yet he knew it not. He was a great prince, yet because he knew nothing of it, he worked and lived as a lowly peasant.

Most of us are like that young prince, in that we are ignorant of our Divine parentage. We know nothing of the power that is ours, so we get no good from it. God is working through us, and there is nothing He cannot do, yet because we know nothing of Him, we are powerless.

There is no such thing as a human nobody. All have the Divine spark in them, all can kindle it into a glowing flame through faith. People let themselves be hypnotized by fear and anxiety, fear of poverty, of failure, of disease. They continually visualize these, and thus make them their dominant thought, using it as a magnet to draw these things to them.

Whatever form your thoughts and beliefs take, the Creative Force working through you uses as a mold in which to form your life and your surroundings. If you want to be strong, think of yourself as perfect. If you want to be prosperous, think not of debts and lacks, but of riches and opportunity. We go in the direction of our dominating thought. It strikes the keynote of our life song.

"The chief characteristic of the religion of the future," wrote Dr. Eliot, "will be man's inseparableness from the great Creative Force." We are in partnership with the Fountain Head of all good.

Emerson said that Christ alone estimated the greatness and the divinity of man. Christ constantly emphasized man's unlimited possibilities. He saw that God incarnated Himself in man.

Emerson goes on to say that man is weak when he looks for help outside himself. It is only as he throws himself unhesitatingly upon the Creative Force within himself that he finds the springs of success, the power that can accomplish all things. It is only when he realizes that all outside help amounts to nothing compared with the tremendous forces working through him that he stands erect and begins to work miracles.

Nearly every man has a habit of looking back and saying—"If I had that period of my life to live over again, if I could go back and take advantage of the chance at fortune I had then, I'd be rich and successful today."

Yet a year from now, or five or ten years from now, most of you who read this will be saying the same thing of today.

Why? Because your future depends upon the foundations you are digging NOW. Yesterday is gone. There is no recalling it. And tomorrow has not come. The only time you have to work with is right now, and whether you will go up or down tomorrow, whether you will be rich or a failure, depends upon your thoughts today.

It took mankind thousands of years to learn how to control matter, how to provide comfort and safety and some degree of financial security. It has taken less than a generation to learn how to control one's own future. The knowledge is so new that most people are not yet aware of it. As David Seabury put it in his book—"They know that science and mechanics have made over the face of the earth. They do not know that psychology and its kindred sciences are making a like change in man's handling of his own nature."

Do you know why so few people succeed in life? Because it is so EASY that most people cannot believe in the methods that really make men successful. They prefer to look upon success as something arduous, something practically impossible for them to attain—and by looking upon it that way, make it so for themselves.

YOU CAN HAVE WHAT YOU WANT—if you know how to plant the

seeds of it in your thought. To know that is the most important thing that anyone can learn. It is not fate that bars your path. It is not lack of money or opportunity. It is yourself—your attitude towards life. Change it—and you change all.

Ask yourself this important question: Are you a victim of self-pity? Are you
embittered at life and at those more successful than yourself? Do you think
fortune has played you a scurvy trick? Or are you cheerfully, steadfastly, confidently working out ways of meeting and bettering the situations that life presents to you?

Most people will dodge that question. They are more concerned in defend-
ing their ego and putting the blame for their failures on something outside
themselves than they are in getting ahead. Failure comes from the inside first.
It cannot be forced upon a resolute, dauntless soul.

How about YOU? Will you give yourself an honest answer to this important question—"Are you a victim of self-pity?"

Think of the times when you have yearned for a future—when you have
grown impatient with the barriers that seemed to hold you down—when
you have heard of the success of some acquaintance whom you knew to be
inwardly no more capable than yourself. Are you willing to keep on *wishing*
and *envying* and looking to the future for your success? Or will you start that
success in the only time that will ever be yours to work with—the everlasting
NOW?

Remember what Emerson told us: "There is one Mind common to all
individual men. Every man is an inlet to the same and to ALL of the same.
He that is once admitted to the right of reason is a freeman of the whole
estate. What Plato has thought, he may think; what a Saint has felt, he may
feel; what has at any time befallen any man, he can understand. Who hath
access to this Universal Mind is a party to all that is or can be done; for this
is the only and sovereign agent—of this Universal Mind each individual is
one more incarnation."

The Creative Force of the Universe is working through you. You can be as
great an outlet for IT as anyone who has ever lived. You have only to provide
the mold in which it is to take shape, and that mold is formed by your thoughts.
What is your dominant desire? What do you want most? *Believe in it*—and you
can have it. Make it your dominating thought, magnetize your mind with it,
and you will draw to you everything you need for its accomplishment.

"There is not a dream that may not come true," wrote Arthur Symons, "if we have the energy which makes or chooses our own fate. We can always in this world get what we want, if we *will* it intensely and persistently enough. So few people succeed because so few can conceive a great end and work towards it without deviating and without tiring. But we all know that the man who works for money day and night gets rich; and the man who works day and night for no matter what kind of material power, gets the power. It is only the dreams of those light sleepers who dream faintly that do not come true."

Knowing these things, can you ever again limit yourself, when you have such unlimited possibilities? Sure, there are times when you feel inferior. Everyone does. Just remember that, and realize that *you* are superior, one of the efficient few who take advantage of the Infinite Power inside them to carry you on to the heights of success.

Plato held, you remember, that in the Divine Mind are pure forms or Archetypes according to which all visible beings are made. And most of the great Mystery Schools of the older world held similar opinions. They taught growth by intent rather than by accident, a development from birth all through life towards the perfect image or Archetype of each of us that is held in Divine Mind. They visioned each of us growing into a destiny that had been imaged for him long before he was born.

Progress was movement in the direction of the perfect Archetype. Man became nobler as the interval between him and his perfect pattern grew less. To the Greeks, happiness meant peace between a man and his pattern, whereas if you lived in a manner inconsistent with your Archetype, you suffered from inharmonies of various kinds. They believed that it was not so much what you do that causes you to suffer, as it is the inharmony between what you do and what you SHOULD DO to match your perfect pattern.

There is a perfect pattern for YOU in the Divine Mind, a perfect Archetype that you CAN match. It has perfect form, perfect intelligence, all power necessary to make your surroundings perfect. Why not make yourself like it?

You CAN! Just let your Archetype be your model. Fill your mind with thoughts of its perfection, make it your dominant thought, and you can draw to yourself whatever elements you need to manifest that perfect image. And not merely the perfect image of yourself, but all that goes to make your surroundings and circumstances just as perfect. Remember, the only limit upon the Power working through you is the limit you impose.

Bear these facts in mind:

1. Your subconscious mind is constantly amenable to control by the power of suggestion.
2. Its power to reason deductively from given premises to correct conclusions is practically perfect.
3. It is endowed with a perfect memory.
4. It is the seat of your emotions.
5. It has the power to communicate and receive intelligence through other than the recognized channels of the senses.

"Man contains all that is needful within himself," wrote Emerson. "He is made a law unto himself. All real good or evil that can befall him must be from himself. The purpose of life seems to be to acquaint a man with himself. The highest revelation is that God is in every man."

27

To Him That Hath

Jesus gave us the Fundamental Law of Increase when He told us that—"Unto everyone that hath shall be given, and he shall have abundance, but from him that hath not shall be taken away even that which he hath."

Sounds simple, doesn't it, yet it is the basic law of all success, all riches, all power. It is the way the whole universe is run. You live by it, whether you like it or not, or you die by it.

To many, this law seems unfair, but in this, as in all things, Nature is logical, and when you understand exactly how the law works, you will agree that it is eminently just and right.

You see, everything consists primarily of electricity—of tiny protons and electrons revolving about each other. It is of these that your body is made, it is of these that all plant life is made, it is of these that all so-called inanimate life is made. Wherein, then, is the difference between all these forms of life? Largly in their RATE OF MOTION!

Remember this: Starting with the individual cell in your mother's womb, you attract to yourself only those elements that are identical in quality and character with yourself, and that are revolving at the same rate of speed. Your selective ability is such that you are able to pick such material as will preserve your quality and identity.

This is true of your body, of your circumstances, of your environment. Like attracts like. If you are not satisfied with yourself as you are, if you want a healthier body, more attractive friends, greater riches and success, you must start at the core—within YOURSELF!

And the first essential to putting yourself in harmony with the Infinite Good all about you is to relax, to take off the brakes. For what is worry or fear or discouragement but a brake on your thinking and on the proper functioning of your organs, a slowing down of your entire rate of activity.

"Get rid of your tensions!" says the modern psychologist. By which he means—think more about the agreeable things and less about the disagreeable ones. You know how martial music stirs your pulses, wakes even the tiredest man into action. Why? Because it tends to increase the rate of motion in every cell in your body. You know how good news has often cured sick people, how sudden excitement has enabled paralyzed people to leap from their beds. Why? Because good news makes you happy, speeds up your rate of motion, even as sudden excitement stirs up the whole organism. You know how fear, hatred and discouragement slow you down. Why? Because those feelings put a definite clamp upon your rate of motion.

Remember this: Hatred, anger, fear, worry, discouragement—all the negative emotions—not only slow down your rate of motion, and thus bring on sickness and make you old before your time, but they definitely keep the good from you. Like attracts like, and the good things you desire have a different rate of motion from these negative ones.

Love, on the other hand, attracts and binds to you the things you love. As Drummond tells us—"To love abundantly is to live abundantly, and to love forever is to live forever." And Emerson expresses the same idea—"Love and you shall be loved. All love is mathematically just, as much as the two sides of an algebraic equation."

> Whate'er thou lovest, man,
> That, too, become thou must;
> God, if thou lovest God,
> Dust, if thou lovest dust.

And that, again, is strictly logical, strictly in accord with Nature's law that like attracts like. Whatever your rate of motion, the elements of like quality with that rate of emotion will be attracted to you.

Which brings us back to the law enunciated by Jesus—"Unto everyone that hath shall be given, and he shall have abundance, but from him that hath not shall be taken away that which he hath."

Read the parable of the Talents, which brought forth this pronouncement of Jesus, and you will see that it is not mere money or possessions that attracts more money—it is the USE to which these are put. You can't bury your talent and expect increase. You must put it to good use. It is the rate of motion that attracts increase, what the modern merchant would call the "turn-over." The oftener he turns over his stock of goods, the more money he makes on his invested capital. But if he fails to turn it over, if his goods lie dormant on his shelves, they will gather dust or mold and presently be worthless.

The servant in the parable who had five talents put them to work and attracted five more; the servant with two talents did likewise and increased his by two more. But the servant with only one talent buried his in a field and let it lie idle. He got nothing, and the talent he had was taken away from him.

We see the same thing happening every day. Statistics show that of all those who inherit money, only one in seventeen dies with money; of all those possessed of fortunes at the age of 35, only 17 per cent have them when they reach 65.

The old adage used to be—"Three generations from shirtsleeves to shirtsleeves," but the modern tempo has speeded this up until now most fortunes hardly last out a single generation. Why is this? Because of the old law of the Rate of Motion, The man who makes the money has set in motion some idea of service that has attracted riches to him. More often than not, it is the idea or the service that is important in his mind. The money is incidental, and is attracted to him with other things of good because he has set in motion an idea that is bringing good to others.

But when he dies, what happens? Too often the business is carried on solely with the thought of how much money can be made out of it. Or the business is sold, and the money put out at interest, with the sole idea of hanging on to the money in hand. Naturally its rate of movement slows down. Naturally it begins to disintegrate and its parts are gradually drawn away by the stronger forces around it, until of that fortune there is nothing left.

You see exactly the same thing in Nature. Take any seed of plant life; take an acorn, for instance. You put it in the ground—plant it. What happens? It first gives of all the elements it has within itself to put forth a shoot, which in turn shall draw from the sun and the air the elements that they have to give; and at the same time, it puts out roots to draw from the earth the moisture and other elements it needs for growth. Its top reaches upward to the sun and air, its roots burrow deeply into the ground for moisture and nourishment. Always it is reaching out. Always it is creating a vacuum, using up all the materials it has on hand, drawing to itself from all about every element it needs for growth.

Time passes. The oaktree stops growing. What happens? In that moment, its attractive power ceases. Can it then live on the elements it has drawn to itself and made a part of itself through all those years? No, indeed! The moment growth stops, disintegration starts. Its component elements begin to feel the pull of the growing plants around them. First the moisture drains out of the tree. Then the leaves fall, the bark peels off—finally the great trunk crashes down, to decay and form soil to nourish the growing plants around. Soon of that noble oak, nothing is left but the enriched soil and the well-nourished plants that have sprung from it.

The Fundamental Law of the Universe is that you must integrate or disintegrate. You must grow—or feed others who are growing. There is no standing still. You are either attracting to yourself all the unused forces about you, or you are giving your own to help build some other man's success.

"To him that hath, shall be given." To him that is using his attractive powers, shall be given everything he needs for growth and fruition. "From him that hath not, shall be taken away even that which he hath." The penalty for not using your attractive powers is the loss of them. You are demagnetized. And like a dead magnet surrounded by live ones, you must be content to see everything you have drawn to yourself taken by them, until eventually even you are absorbed by their resistless force.

That is the first and fundamental Law of the Universe. But how are you to become an Attracter? How are you to make your start? In the same way that it has been done from the beginning of time.

Go back to the first law of life. Go back to the beginning of things. You will find Nature logical in all that she does. If you want to understand how she works, study her in her simplest, most elementary forms. The principles established there hold good throughout the universe. The methods there used are used by all created things, from the simplest to the most complicated.

How, for instance, did the earliest forms of cell life, either plant or animal, get their food? By absorbing it from the waters around them. How does every cell in your body, every cell in plant or tree or animal, get its food today? In exactly the same way—by absorbing it from the lymph or water surrounding it! Nature's methods do not change. She is logical in everything. She may build more complicated organisms, she may go in for immense size or strange combinations, but she uses the same principles throughout all of life.

Now, what is Nature's principle of Increase? From the beginning of Time, it has been—

DIVIDE—AND GROW!

That principle, like every other fundamental Law of Nature, is the same in all of life. It has remained unchanged since the first single-celled organism floated on the surface of the primordial sea. It is the fundamental Law of Increase.

Take the lowest form of cell life. How does it grow? It DIVIDES—each part grows back to its original size—then they in turn divide and grow again.

Take the highest form of cell life—MAN. The same principle works in him in exactly the same way—in fact, it is the only principle of growth that Nature knows!

How does this apply to your circumstances, to the acquisition of riches, to the winning of success?

Look up any miracle of increase in the Bible, and what do you find? First division—then increase.

When Russell Conwell was building the famous Baptist Temple in Philadelphia, his congregation was poor and greatly in need of money. Through prayer and every other means known to him, Conwell was constantly trying to help his flock.

One Sunday it occurred to him that the old Jewish custom had been, when praying to God, to first make an offering of the finest lamb of the flock, or of some other much-prized possession. Then, after freely giving to God, prayer was made for His good gifts.

So instead of first praying, and then taking up the collection, as was the custom, Conwell suggested that the collection be taken first and that all who had special favors to ask of the Creator should give freely as a "Thank Offering."

A few weeks afterwards, Conwell asked that those who had made offerings on this occasion should tell their experiences. The results sounded unbelievable. One woman who had an overdue mortgage on her home found it necessary to call in a plumber the following week to repair a leak. In tearing up the boards, he uncovered a hiding place where her late father had hidden all his money—enough to pay off the mortgage and leave plenty over!

One man got a much-needed job. A servant some dresses she badly needed. A student the chance to study for his chosen vocation. While literally dozens had their financial needs met.

They had complied with the law. They had sown their seed—freely—and they reaped the harvest.

"Except a kernel of wheat fall into the ground and die," said the Master, "it abideth alone. But if it die, it beareth much fruit." You can't put strings on your seeds. You can't sow them and say—"I'll give you a chance to sprout and bring forth increase, but if you fail, I'll take you back and use you to make bread." You must give that seed freely, fully. It must be dead to you, before you can hope to get back from it a harvest of increase.

Many people will tell you—"I don't see why God does not send me riches, I have prayed for them, and promised that if I get them, I will use them to do good." God enters into no bargains with man. He gives you certain gifts to start, and upon the way you use these depends whether you get more. You've got to start with what you have.

And the place to start is pointed out in a little poem by Nina Stiles:

The land of opportunity
Is anywhere we chance to be,
Just any place where people live
And need the help that we can give.

The basis of all work, all business, all manufacturing, is SERVICE. Every idea of success must start with that. Every nucleus that is to gather to itself elements of good must have as its basis service to your fellow man. Carlyle defined wealth clearly when he said that "the wealth of a man is the number of things he loves and blesses, which he is loved and blessed by."

And that is the only kind of wealth that endures. Love and blessings speed up your rate of motion, keep your nucleus active, keep it drawing to you every element of good that you need for its complete and perfect expression. They are, in effect, a constant prayer—the kind of prayer Coleridge had in mind when he wrote—

He prayeth well who loveth well
Both man and bird and beast.
He prayeth best who loveth best
All things both great and small;
For the dear God who loveth us,
He made and loveth all.

Remember that the only word often used in the Old Testament to signify "prayer" means, when literally translated—"To sing a song of joy and praise."

In other words, to speed up your rate of motion with joy and thanksgiving. And you have only to read the Old Testament to know how often the great characters of the Bible had recourse to this method.

What do *you* want from life? Speed up your rate of motion and overtake it. Is it health you want? Then start by relaxing, by letting go of all your fears and worries. In a recent article, I read: "Dr. Loring Swaim, director of a famous clinic in Massachusetts, has under observation 270 cases of arthritis which were cured when they became free from worry, fear, and resentment. He has come to the conclusion after some years that no less than 60 per cent of his cases are caused by moral conflict."

In the Reader's Digest some months ago, it was stated that "Personal worry is one of the principal causes of physical ailments which send people to hospitals. It is literally possible to worry yourself sick; in fact, the chances are better than even that if you are ill, worry is causing the symptoms."

That is not a modern discovery, by any means. In Proverbs, you will find the statement—"A merry heart causeth good healing, but a broken spirit drieth up the bones." And Plato observed 19 centuries ago—"If the head and the body are to be well, you must begin by curing the soul."

So the first essential in curing yourself of any ailment would seem to be to let go of your resentments, your worries and fears. Make peace within yourself, within your thoughts. Laugh a little, sing a little. Dance a little, if you can. Exercise speeds up your rate of motion, but it should be joyous exercise. Do something you enjoy, something that speeds up your mind as well as your muscles. Dance, if you like dancing. Swim, ride horseback, play tennis—do something exhilarating to the spirit as well as the body. Mere routine exercises that soon become a chore do little good and often are harmful. Unless you can get mental as well as physical exhilaration out of your exercise, don't bother with it at all.

Do you want money, riches? Then use what you have, no matter how little it may be. Speed up your rate of turnover, as the merchant speeds the turnover of his stocks. Money is now your stock. Use it! Pay it out joyfully for any good purpose, and as you pay it, BLESS IT! Bless it in some such wise as this:

I bless you . . . and be thou a blessing; May you enrich all who touch you. I thank God for you, but I thank Him even more that there is unlimited supply where you came from. I bless that Infinite Supply. I thank God for it, and I expand my consciousness to take in as much of it as I can use . . . As I release this money in my hand, I know that I am opening the gates of

Infinite Supply to flow through my channels and through all that are open
to receive it. The Spirit that multiplied the loaves and fishes for Jesus is
making this money attract to itself everything it needs for growth and
increase. All of God's channels are open and flowing freely for me. The best
in myself for the world—the best in the world for me.

There is no quicker way of speeding up your rate of motion than by *giv-*
ing. Give of your time, of your money, of your services—whatever you have
to give. Give of that you want to see increased, for your gift is your seed, and
"everything increaseth AFTER ITS KIND!"

Solomon was the richest man of his day, and he gave us the key to his riches
and success when he wrote:

There is that scattereth, and increaseth yet more. And there is that withol-
deth more than is meet. The liberal soul shall be made fat, and he that
watereth, shall be watered himself.

And one even wiser than Solomon told us: "Give, and it shall be given unto
you, good measure, pressed down and shaken together and running over, shall
men give into your bosom. For with the same measure that ye mete withal, it
shall be measured to you again."

Do you want power, ability, greater skill in what you are doing? Then use
what you have, use it to the greatest extent of which you are capable. The Sunshine Bulletin had an excellent little piece along these lines:

There is a task for today which can be done now better than at any other
time. It is today's duty. And we are writing now a judgment upon our
lives by our faithfulness or unfaithfulness at the present moment.

This moment has its own priceless value, and if wasted, it can no
more be recovered than jewels that are cast into the depths of the ocean.

Each day has its share in the making of our tomorrow; and the
future will be nobler or meaner by reason of what we now do or leave
undone.

What is ambition but the inner urge that speeds up your rate of motion and
makes you work harder and longer and more purposefully to the end that you
may accomplish something worth while? What is perseverance but the will to

carry on in spite of all difficulties and discouragements? Given that ambition and that perseverence, there is nothing you cannot accomplish, nothing with a rate of motion so high that you cannot overtake it.

It is in loving, not in being loved,
The heart is blessed.
It is in giving, not in seeking gifts,
We find our quest.

If thou art hungry, lacking heavenly bread,
Give hope and cheer.
If thou art sad and wouldst be comforted,
Stay sorrow's tear.

Whatever be thy longing or thy need,
That do thou give.
So shall thy soul be fed, and thou indeed
Shalt truly live.

—M. ELLA RUSSELL

28

Everything Has Its Price

Dear God, help me be wise enough to see
That as I give so it is meted out to me!
Help me to know that with my every thought
The good or ill that's mine myself I've wrought!
Help me to place all blame of lack on me,
Not on my fellow man, nor yet on Thee.
Give me the courage, God, truly to know
That as I'd reap in life thus must I sow!

—VERA M. CRIDER

In his essay on Compensation, Emerson says:

"What will you have?" quoth God
"Pay for it, and take it!"

How can we buy the things we want at the counter of God? What pay can we offer?

Perhaps the answer lies in the ancient Law of Karma. Karma is Sanskrit, you know, and means "Comeback." It is one of the oldest laws known to man. It is the law of the boomerang. Jesus quoted it when He said—"Whatsoever a man soweth, that shall he also reap."

In the parlance of today, it is—"Chickens come home to roost." Even in science we find it, as Newton's Third Law of Motion—"Action and reaction are equal to each other." Ella Wheeler Wilcox expressed the Law beautifully when she wrote—

There are loyal hearts, there are spirits brave,
There are souls that are pure and true;
Then give to the world the best you have,
And the best will come back to you.

Give love, and love to your heart will flow,
A strength in your utmost need;
Have faith, and a score of hearts will show
Their faith in your word and deed.

For life is the mirror of king and slave,
'Tis just what you are and do,
Then give to the world the best you have
And the best will come back to you.

One of the best illustrations of the working of the Law lies in the two seas of Palestine, the Sea of Galilee and the Dead Sea. The Sea of Galilee contains fresh water and is alive with fish. Green trees adorn its banks and farms and vineyards spread all around it. The River Jordan flows into it, and all the little rivulets from the hills around feed its sparkling waters.

The Dead Sea, on the other hand, knows no splash of fish, has no vegetation around it, no homes, no farms or vineyards. Travelers give it a wide berth, unless forced by urgent business to use its shores. The air hangs heavy, and neither man nor beast will drink of the waters.

What makes the difference? The River Jordan empties the same good waters into both seas. So it is not the river. And it is not the soil or the country round about.

The difference lies in the fact that the Sea of Galilee gives as it receives; for every drop of water that flows into it, another flows out. Whereas the Dead Sea holds on to all it receives. Water leaves it only through evaporation and seepage. It hoards all it gets, and the result is that the water stagnates, turns salt and is good for naught.

"Unless a kernel of wheat fall into the ground and die," Jesus told us, "it abideth alone. But if it die, it beareth much fruit." In other words, if you put your kernel of wheat safely away to keep, you will never have anything but a kernel of wheat, and in time it will mould and rot away, but if you sow it freely (let it die to you), it will bear much fruit. It is another way of saying—"Cast thy bread upon the waters and it will return to you after many days increased an hundredfold."

In all of Nature, the only known law of increase is that you must give to get. If you want to reap a harvest, you must first plant your seed. If you want to increase your strength, you must first break up the muscle cells, and stimulate them to divide and grow.

Division and growth is the way that all of life increases. Watch a single cell at work in your body, in a plant, or in any form of life. What happens? It first divides, then each half grows until it reaches its normal size, when it divides and starts growing again. Without division, there is no growth—only atrophy and decay. You must divide to grow, you must give to get.

John Bunyan knew nothing of the law of cell growth, but he expressed it just as well when he wrote—

A man there was and they called him mad;
The more he gave, the more he had.

And Moffatt had the same thought in his couplet:

One gives away, and still he grows the richer;
Another keeps what he should give, and is the poorer.

Even the thoughts we send forth return to us laden with a harvest of their kind. That which we put into our thought comes back into our own lives, because for every thought there is a response, a return of the pendulum we have started swinging. It is the Einstein doctrine of the extended line, which must return to its source.

There is no use saying you have not enough money or abilities to be worth starting with. Just remember the parable of the talents. The servant who was given five talents put them out at interest and made more, as did the one who was given two talents. But the servant who received only one talent felt that it was too little to do much with, so he buried it. And you know what happened to him when the Master came back.

Start with what you have and plant your seed, no matter how small and unimportant it may seem. You remember Jesus told us that the Kingdom of Heaven (or Expansion) is like a mustard seed—"Which indeed is the least of all seeds, but when it is grown, it is the greatest among herbs, and becometh a tree, so that the birds of the air come to lodge in the branches thereof."

What you have to start with can hardly be smaller than the tiny mustard seed. If it can grow into a tree, think what your seed may grow into.

"*Do the thing* and you shall have the power," says Emerson. "But they that do not the thing have not the power. Everything has its price, and if the price is not paid—not that thing but something else is obtained. And it is impossible to get anything without its price. For any benefit received, a tax is levied. In nature, nothing can be given—all things are sold. Power to him who power exerts."

> *You are not higher than your lowest thought,*
> *Or lower than the peak of your desire.*
> *And all existence has no wonder wrought*
> *To which ambition may not yet aspire.*
> *Oh man! There is no planet, sun or star*
> *Could hold you, if you but knew what you are.*

The key to power lies in using what you have, for use releases more power, just as using your muscles builds them into greater muscles, and failing to use them makes them weak and useless. "The one condition coupled with the gift of truth," Emerson tells us, "is its USE! That man shall be learned who reduces his learning to practice."

And Goethe expressed it even more strongly when he wrote—

> *Lose this day loitering, it will be the same story*
> *Tomorrow, and the rest more dilatory;*
> *Thus indecision brings its own delays*
> *And days are lost tormenting over other days.*
> *Are you in earnest? Seize this very minute;*
> *What you can do, or dream you can, begin it;*
> *Boldness has genius, power, and magic in it;*
> *Only engage and then the mind grows heated;*
> *Begin, and then the work will be completed.*

29

Yesterday Ended Last Night

*I said to the man who stood at the gate of the year: "Give me a light that
I may tread safely into the unknown." And he replied: "Go out into the
darkness and put your hand into the hand of God. That shall be to you
better than a light and safer than a known way."*

What do you want from life? Whatever it is, you can have it—and you have the
word of no less an authority than Jesus for that.

"Seek ye first the Kingdom of God and His Righteousness," He told us,
"and all these things (all the riches and power and other material things you
have wanted) shall be added unto you."

Does that mean that you must become saintly in order to amass material
possessions? Experience would seem to indicate that it seldom works out that
way. The saintly are not often burdened with worldly goods. No, saintliness is
not the answer. Then what is?

Let us examine the meaning of "righteousness" and see if the answer does
not lie in it. The word used for "righteousness" in the ancient Greek text of the
original Gospels is "dikaiosune," which, literally translated, means the absolute
dictatorship of the spirit within you.

Translated thus the passage reads—"Seek ye first the Kingdom of God and
His absolute dictatorship of the spirit within you, and all these things shall be
added unto you." In other words, put the problem up to God in You, the part
of Divinity that is the Creative Force in you, and leave it to Him to work out
while you rest in serene faith that it IS done.

How would this work out in practice? There was an article in UNITY recently that exemplified the idea so well that I quote it here:

Let us say we are planning a business venture, or a social event, or a religious meeting, or the recovery of the sick. We are ready to pray over the situation. Now instead of futurizing our prayers and asking for something to take place tomorrow, let us imagine (imagination is an aid to the release of faith power) that everything has turned out just as we desired it. Let us write it all down as if it were all past history. Many of the Bible predictions are written in the past tense. Let us try listing our desires as if they had already been given us.

Of course we shall want to write down a note of thanksgiving to God for all that He has given us. He has had it for us all the time or else we should not have received it. More than this, God has it for us or we could not even desire it now or picture it in our imagination.

What happens? After we have written down our desires in the past tense, read them over carefully, praised God for them, let us then put away our paper and go on about our business. It will not be long before we actually see the desired events taking place in ways so natural that we may even forget that God is answering our prayers.

Imagination helps us to have faith, for it pictures the thing desired and helps make it real. After we have tried this experiment a few times we shall find that our imagination has increased our faith, and faith has turned to praise, and praise has opened our eyes to see what God has for us.

The habit of thanking God ahead of time for benefits about to be received has its firm basis in past experience. We can safely look upon it as a sure formula for successful prayer because Christ used it. David always praised and thanked God when he was in trouble. Daniel was saved from the lions through the praise of God. Paul sang songs of praise and liberated himself from prison. And don't you, and everyone else, find satisfaction in being praised for a task well done?

Wrote William Law:

If anyone could tell you the shortest, surest way to all happiness and all perfection, he must tell you to make it a rule yourself to thank and praise God for everything that happens to you. For it is certain that whatever seeming calamity happens to you, if you thank and praise God for it, you turn it into a blessing. Could you therefore work miracles, you could not do more for yourself than by this thankful spirit; for it . . . turns all that it touches into happiness.

And Charles Fillmore adds:

Praise is closely related to prayer; it is one of the avenues through which spirituality expresses itself. Through an inherent law of mind, we increase whatever we praise. The whole creation responds to praise, and is glad. Animal trainers pet and reward their charges with delicacies for acts of obedience; children glow with joy and gladness when they are praised. Even vegetation grows better for those who love it. We can praise our own ability, and the very brain cells will expand and increase in capacity and intelligence, when we speak words of encouragement and appreciation to them.

So don't let anything that has happened in your life discourage you. Don't let poverty or lack of education or past failures hold you back. There is only one power—the I AM in you—and it can do anything. If in the past you have not used that power, that is too bad as far as the past is concerned, but it is not too late. You can start NOW. "Be still, and know that I AM God." What more are you waiting for? God can do for you only what you allow Him to do through you, but if you will do your part, He can use you as a channel for unlimited power and good.

The difference between failure and success is measured only by your patience and faith—sometimes by inches, sometimes by minutes, sometimes by the merest flash of time.

Take Lincoln. He went into the Black Hawk War a Captain—and came out a private. His store failed—and his surveyor's instruments, on which he depended to eke out a livelihood, were sold for part of the debts. He was defeated in his first try for the Legislature. Defeated in his first attempt for Congress. Defeated in his application for Commissioner of the General Land Office. Defeated for the Senate. Defeated for the nomination for the Vice Presidency in 1856. But did he let that long succession of defeats discourage him? Not he. He held the faith—and made perhaps the greatest President we have ever had.

Then there was Grant: He failed of advancement in the army. Failed as a farmer. Failed as a business man. At 39, he was chopping and delivering cordwood to keep body and soul together. Nine years later he was President of the United States and had won a martial renown second in this country only to Washington's.

Search the pages of history. You will find them dotted with the names of men whom the world had given up as failures, but who held on to their faith, who kept themselves prepared—and when their chance came they were ready and seized it with both hands.

Napoleon, Cromwell, Patrick Henry, Paul Jones—these are only a few out of thousands.

When Caesar was sent to conquer Gaul, his friends found him one day in a fit of utter despondency. Asked what the matter was, he told them he had just been comparing his accomplishments with Alexander's. At his age, Alexander had conquered the entire known world—and what had Caesar done to compare with that? But he presently roused himself from his discouragement by resolving to make up as quickly as might be for his lost time. The result? He became the head of the Roman Empire.

The records of business are crowded with the names of middle-aged nobodies who lived to build great fortunes, vast institutions. No man has failed as long as he has faith in the Father, faith in the great scheme of things, faith in himself.

YESTERDAY ENDED LAST NIGHT

When Robert Bruce faced the English at the battle of Bannockburn, he had behind him years of failure, years of fruitless efforts to drive the English out of Scotland, years of heart-breaking toil in trying to unite the warring elements among the Scotch themselves. True, at the moment a large part of Scotland was in his hands, but so had it been several times before, only to be wrested from him as soon as the English brought together a large enough army.

And now in front of him stood the greatest army England had ever gathered to her banners—hardy veterans from the French provinces, all the great English nobles with their armored followers, wild Irish, Welsh bowmen—troops from all the dominions of Edward II, over 100,000 men.

To conquer whom Bruce had been able to muster but 30,000 men, brave and hardy, it is true, but lacking the training and discipline of the English.

Was Bruce discouraged? Not he. What though the English had the better archers. What though they were better armed, better trained, better disciplined. He was fighting for freedom—and he *believed* in himself, he believed in his men, he believed in the God of battles.

And, as always, weight, numbers, armament, proved of no avail when confronted with determination and faith. The vast English host was completely defeated and dispersed. Bruce was firmly seated upon the throne of Scotland, and never more did an invading English army cross its borders.

It matters not how many defeats you have suffered in the past, how great the odds may be against you. Bulow put it well when he said—"It's not the size of the dog in the fight that counts, so much as the size of the fight in the dog." And the size of fight in you depends upon your faith—your faith in yourself, in the Creative Force working through you and in your cause. Just remember that yesterday ended last night, and yesterday's defeats with it.

Time after time throughout the Bible we are told that the battle is not ours—but the Lord's. But like all children, we know better than our Father how our affairs should be handled, so we insist upon running them ourselves.

Is it any wonder they get so tangled as to leave us in the depths of discouragement?

When the Black Prince with his little army was penned in by Philip of France, most men would have felt discouraged. For the hosts of France seemed as numerous as the leaves on the trees. While the English were few, and mostly archers. And archers, in that day, were believed to stand no chance against such armored knights as rode behind the banners of Philip.

The French came forward in a great mass, thinking to ride right over that little band of English. But did the Black Prince give way? Not he. He showed the world that a new force had come into warfare, a force that would soon make the armored knight as extinct as the dodo. That force was the common soldier—the archer.

Just as the Scotch spearmen overthrew the chivalry of England on the field of Bannockburn, just as infantry have overthrown both cavalry and artillery in many a later battle, so did the "common men" of England—the archers—decide the fate of the French at Crecy. From being despised and looked down upon by every young upstart with armor upon his back, the "common men"—the spearmen and archers—became the backbone of every successful army.

And from what looked like certain annihilation, the Black Prince by his faith in himself and his men became one of the greatest conquerors of his day.

Troubles flocked to him, but he didn't recognize them as troubles—he thought them opportunities. And used them to raise himself and his soldiers to the pinnacle of success.

There are just as many prizes in business as in war—just as many opportunities to turn seeming troubles into blessings. But those prizes go to men like the Black Prince who don't know a trouble when they meet it—who welcome it, take it to their bosoms, and get from it their greatest blessings.

What is the use of holding on to life—unless at the same time you hold on to your faith? What is the use of going through the daily grind, the wearisome drudgery—if you have given up hoping for the rewards, and unseeing, let them pass you by?

Suppose business and industry did that? How far would they get? It is simply by holding on hopefully, believingly, watchfully—as Kipling put it: "Forcing heart and nerve and sinew to serve your turn long after they are gone, and so hold on when there is nothing in you except the will which says to them: 'Hold on'!"—that many a business man has worked out his salvation.

It is not enough to work. The horse and the ox do that. And when we work without thought, without hope, we are no better than they. It is not enough to merely hold on. The poorest creatures often do that mechanically, for lack of the courage to let go.

If you are to gain the reward of your labors, if you are to find relief from your drudgery, you must hold on hopefully, believingly, confidently—knowing that the answer is in the great heart of God, knowing that the Creative Force working through you will give it to you, the moment you have prepared yourself to receive it.

It is never the gifts that are lacking. It is never the Creative Force that is backward in fulfilling our desires. It is we who are unable to see, who fail to recognize the good, because our thoughts are of discouragement and lack.

So never let yesterday's failure discourage you. As T. C. Howard wrote in "Forbes" magazine:

Yesterday's gone—it was only a dream;
Of the past there is naught but remembrance.
Tomorrow's a vision thrown on Hope's screen,
A will-o'-the-wisp, a mere semblance.

Why mourn and grieve over yesterdays ills
And paint memory's pictures with sorrow?
Why worry and fret—for worrying kills—
Over things that won't happen tomorrow?

Yesterday's gone—it has never returned—
Peace to its ashes, and calm;
Tomorrow no human has ever discerned,
Still hope, trust, and faith are its balm.

This moment is all that I have as my own,
To use well, or waste, as I may;
But I know that my future depends alone
On the way that I live today.

This moment my past and my future I form;
I may make them whatever I choose
By the deeds and the acts that I now perform,
By the words and thoughts that I use.

So I fear not the future nor mourn o'er the past
For I do all I'm able today,
Living each present moment as though 'twere my last;
Perhaps it is! Who knows! Who shall say?

"Duty and today are ours," a great man once wrote. "Results and the future belong to God." And wise old Emerson echoed the same thought. "All that I have seen," he said, "teaches me to trust the Creator for all I have not seen." In short, a good daily prayer might be one I read in a magazine recently—"Lord, I will keep on rowing. YOU steer the boat!"

Easy enough to say, perhaps you are thinking, but you never knew such disaster as has befallen me. I am broken down with sickness, or crippled by accident, or ruined financially, or something else equally tragic. Shakespeare wrote the answer to your case when he told us—"When Fortune means to man most good, she looks upon him with a threatening eye."

In the town of Enterprise, Ala., there is a monument erected by its citizens for services done them. And you could never guess to whom it is dedicated. To the Boll Weevil!

In olden days, the planters living thereabouts raised only cotton. When cotton boomed, business boomed. When the cotton market was off—or the crop proved poor—business suffered correspondingly.

Then came the Boll Weevil. And instead of merely a poor crop, left no crop at all. The Boll Weevil ruined everything. Debt and discouragement were all it left in its wake.

But the men of that town must have been lineal descendants of those hardy fighters who stuck to the bitter end in that long-drawn-out struggle between North and South. They got together and decided that what their town and their section needed was to stop putting all their eggs into one basket.

Instead of standing or falling by the cotton crop, diversify their products! Plant a dozen different kinds of crops. Even though one did fail, even though the market for two or three products happened to be off, the average would always be good.

Correct in theory, certainly. But, as one of their number pointed out, how were the planters to start? They were over their heads in debt already. It would take money for seeds and equipment, to say nothing of the fact that they had to live until the new crops came in.

So the townsfolk raised the money—at the Lord only knows what personal sacrifices—and financed the planters.

The result? Such increased prosperity that they erected a monument to the Boll Weevil, and on it they put this inscription:

In profound appreciation of the Boll Weevil, this monument is erected by the citizens of Enterprise, Coffee Co., Ala.

Many a man can look back and see where some Boll Weevil—some catastrophe that seemed tragic at the time—was the basis of his whole success in life. Certainly that has been the case with one man I know.

When he was a tot of five, he fell into a fountain and all but drowned. A passing workman pulled him out as he was going down for the last time. The water in his lungs brought on asthma, which, as the years went on, kept growing worse and worse, until the doctors announced that death was only a matter of months. Meantime, he couldn't run, he couldn't play like other children, he couldn't even climb the stairs!

A sufficiently tragic outlook, one would say. Yet out of it came the key to fortune and success.

Since he could not play with the other children, he early developed a taste for reading. And as it seemed so certain that he could never do anything worth while for himself, what more natural than that he should long to read the deeds of men who had done great things. Starting with the usual boy heroes, he came to have a particular fondness for true stories of such men as Lincoln, Edison, Carnegie, Hill and Ford—men who started out as poor boys, without any special qualifications or advantages, and built up great names solely by their own energy and grit and determination.

Eventually he cured himself completely of his asthma—but that is another story. The part that is pertinent to this tale is that from the time he could first read until he was seventeen, he was dependent for amusement almost entirely upon books. And from his reading of the stories of men who had made successes, he acquired not only the ambition to make a like success of himself, but the basic principles on which to build it.

Today, as a monument to his Boll Weevil, there stands a constantly growing, successful business, worth millions, with a vast list of customers that swear by—not at—its founder.

And he is still a comparatively young man, healthy, active, putting in eight or ten hours at work every day, an enthusiastic horseman, a lover of all sports.

"There is no handicap, either hereditary or environmental, which cannot be compensated, if you are not afraid to try." Thus wrote one of New York's greatest psychiatrists. "No situation in our heredity or in our environment can compel us to remain unhappy. No situation need discourage one or hold him back from finding a degree of happiness and success."

Age, poverty, ill-health—none of these things can hold back the really determined soul. To him they are merely stepping-stones to success—spurs that urge him on to greater things. There is no limit upon you—except the one you put upon yourself.

> Ships sail east, and ships sail west,
> By the very same breezes that blow;
> It's the set of the sails,

And not the gales,
That determine where they go.

Men thought they had silenced John Bunyan when they threw him into prison. But he produced "Pilgrim's Progress" on twisted paper used as a cork for the milk jug.

Men thought that blind Milton was done. But he dictated "Paradise Lost."

Like the revolutionist of whom Tolstoy wrote—"You can imprison my body, but you cannot so much as approach my ideas."

You cannot build walls around a thought. You cannot imprison an idea. You cannot cage the energy, the enthusiasm, the enterprise of an ambitious spirit.

This it is that distinguishes us from the animals. This it is that makes us in very truth Sons of God.

Waste no tears
Upon the blotted record of lost years,
But turn the leaf
And smile, oh, smile to see
The fair, white pages that remain for thee.

—ELLA WHEELER WILCOX

30

The Undying Fire

I want to do one kindly deed each day
To help someone to find a better way.
I want to lend a hand to one in need
Or find some lonely stray that I may feed.
I want to sing for someone a loved song
To give them courage when the road is long.
If just one smile of mine can lighten pain
Then I shall feel I have not lived in vain.

—LENA STEARNS BOLTON

In an old newspaper clipping, I read of a fire on the hearth of a farmhouse in Missouri, that has not been out for a hundred years.

When the builder of that old homestead left Kentucky with his young bride a hundred years ago, he took with him some live coals from the home fireplace, swinging in an iron pot slung from the rear axle of his prairie schooner.

Matches were unknown in those days, and the making of fire from flint and steel was too uncertain. So all through the long trek from Kentucky to Missouri, he kept that little fire alive, finally transferring it to his new log cabin home.

There his children grew and prospered. There he lived and there he died—by the light and warmth of that living fire. And so it must be with love—an undying fire.

The ancient Greeks had a legend that all things were created by love. In the beginning, all were happy. Love reigned supreme, and life was everywhere. Then one night while Love slept, Hate came—and everything became discordant, unhappy, dying.

Thereafter, when the sun of Love rose, life was renewed, happiness abounded. But when the night of Hate came, then came discord also, and sorrow and ashes. And truly without love, life would be dead . . . a thing of wormwood and death.

I have seen tenderness and pity trace
A line of beauty on a homely face,
And dull and somewhat ordinary eyes
Made brilliant by a flash of glad surprise,
And lips relax and soften happily
At unexpected generosity.
But, oh, what strange, delightful mystery
Is there in love's breath-taking alchemy,
With power to take a drab, gray chrysalis
And form such radiant loveliness as this!

—OPAL WINSTEAD

The most fascinating women in history—Cleopatra, Helen of Troy, Catherine the Great, Queen Elizabeth, the Pompadour—none of them had beautiful features. Cleopatra's nose was much too big—but that didn't keep her from holding the ruler of the then-known world under her thumb for ten long years, and after his death, subjugating Anthony in his turn.

Of course, she had something else—as did all these famous women of history—something stronger, more subtle, more fascinating than beauty. She had charm—that enticing, bewildering thing called feminine charm. The same charm that is born in every daughter of Eve who has the brains to use it.

What is charm? Charm is something in the glance of the eyes, the turn of the head, the touch of the hand, that sends an electric thrill through every fiber of the one at whom it is directed, that speeds up his rate of motion. Charm is taking the gifts that God has given you and keeping them supernally young and fresh and alive. Charm is being so exquisitely buoyant and full of life, *keeping the magnet within you so surcharged with the joy of life,* that even poor features are lost sight of in the bewitching attraction of the whole.

Charm is keeping your loveliness all through life. It is holding on to your ability to stir the pulses and speed up the rate of motion of the one you love.

> *For those we love, we venture many things,*
> *The thought of them gives spirit flaming wings,*
> *For those we love, we labor hard and long,*
> *To dream of them stirs in the heart a song.*
> *For those we love, no task can be too great,*
> *We forge ahead, defying adverse fate.*
> *For those we love, we seek Life's highest goal,*
> *And find contentment deep within the soul.*

"Though we travel the world over to find the beautiful," wrote Emerson, "we must carry it with us or we find it not." Charm is not to be bought in jars or bottles. Nor is beauty. Both must come from within. Both spring from that magnet of life which is the Creative Force within us.

There are women who seem to have been born tired—never exactly sick, never entirely well. They don't go out because they don't get any fun out of play. They are sallow, listless, having neither charm nor personality, because they have allowed the magnet of life within them to run down. To them I would say—renew your health first, renew your energy and vigor, renew your interest in those around you, speed up your own rate of motion—*then* begin to look for love. "For love," says Browning, "is energy of life."

> *For life, with all it yields of joy or woe*
> *And hope and fear,*
> *Is just our chance of the prize of learning love—*
> *How love might be, hath been indeed, and is.*

How to inspire love in another? By first cultivating it in yourself. Love begets love, you know. Charge your mental magnet with thoughts of unselfish love and devotion, give to the loved one in your thoughts the admiration, the appreciation, the idealized service you would like to give in reality—and as you give, love will come back to you.

Love is giving. It cannot be jealous, for it seeks only the good of the one loved.

"Blessed is he that truly loves and seeketh not love in return," said St. Francis of Assisi. "Blessed is he that serves and desires not to be served. Blessed is he that doeth good unto others and seeketh not that others do good unto him."

Love such as that is never lost or wasted. It comes back as surely as the morrow's sun—oftentimes not from the one to whom you sent it, but it comes back, nevertheless, blessed and amplified. As Barrie says—"Those who bring happiness into the lives of others, cannot keep it from themselves."

And Ella Wheeler Wilcox wrote—

Who giveth love to all
Pays kindness for unkindness, smiles for frowns
And lends new courage to each fainting heart,
And strengthens hope and scatters joy abroad.
He, too, is a Redeemer, Son of God.

A woman once went to Krishna and asked him how to find the love of God. He inquired of her—"Whom do you love most?" "My brother's child," she answered. "Then go," he told her, "and love the child still more!" She did so, and behind the figure of the child, she presently saw the form of the Christ child.

True happiness doth lie in store
For those who love their neighbor more;
'Tis blessed more to give than get.
Come, do your part, our cause abet.

'Tis blessed more—and it does more to speed up your rate of motion. Though that statement would seem to be belied, at times, by young mothers who work so hard over their families.

Why is it that many married women grow old quickly, lose their youthful lines and rounded cheeks, get sallow and wan while their husbands are still in their prime?

Bearing children? There are thousands of women with three and four and five children who still look as youthful as when they married.

Work? A reasonable amount of work is good for every woman.

Then what is the reason?

STRAIN—unending, unceasing strain. There is not a servant in this country that you could hire to work every day and all day, without any period of freedom, any day of rest. Yet many men think nothing of making their wives do it.

When Taylor, the great efficiency engineer, was called in to re-organize the work of a certain foundry, he found a number of men with wheel-barrows engaged in carting pig iron from the pile in the yard to the cupola. They worked continuously, without rest except for lunch, and careful checking showed that each man carted from twelve to fifteen tons of pig iron a day. At the end of the day they were worn out.

Taylor took one of the men (an entirely average man), stood over him with a watch and had him work exactly in accordance with his directions. He would have him load his barrow with pig iron, wheel it over to the cupola, dump it— then sit down and rest, utterly relaxing for a minute or more. When the minute was up, he would go through the same performance—and again rest.

It took two or three days to figure out the best periods of rest, but at the end of the week, Taylor's man was carting forty-five tons of pig iron every day, where before he had carted twelve to fifteen! And at the end of the day he was still fresh, where before he had been worn out.

If you have ever seen an army on the march, you know that no matter how great the hurry, the men are allowed to fall out for five minutes in every hour, and completely relax. Why? Because it has been found that this relaxation and rest enables them to march farther and faster.

There is not an organ in the body that does not require and take its period of rest, from the heart and lungs to the stomach and digestive tracts. Yet many a wife and mother goes all day and every day with never a moment of relaxation, never a minute when her nerves are not taut with strain. Is it any wonder they grow old years before their time? Is it any wonder they are nervous and irritable, unhappy themselves and making those around them depressed and unhappy?

To every such mother, I would say, first—relax! Sit down, lie down, every chance you get—*and just let go!* Don't listen for the baby—don't worry about dinner. Just blissfully relax—even if only for a minute or two at a time. If you can multiply those minutes by a dozen times a day, you will be surprised how much better you feel when night comes.

Give your inner magnet a chance to renew itself. Remember, the first essential toward speeding up your rate of motion is to relax, to get rid of your tensions, to LET the Creative Force work through you. Only then can you draw to you kindred elements of good.

I pray the prayer the Easterns do,
May the peace of Allah abide with you.
Wherever you stop—wherever you go—
May the beautiful palms of Allah grow;
Thru days of love and nights of rest
May the love of sweet Allah make you blest.
I touch my heart as the Easterns do
May the love of Allah abide with you.

31

Prayer

But the stars throng out in their glory,
And they sing of the God in man;
They sing of the mighty Master,
Of the loom His fingers span,
Where a star or a soul is part of the whole,
And weft in the wondrous plan.

—ROBERT SERVICE

If you would know the surest way of speeding up your rate of motion, and overtaking the things you desire, try PRAYER!

But when I say "prayer," I don't mean the begging kind. I don't mean a lot of vain repetitions, that seldom have the attention even of the one repeating them, much less of the Lord. Go to the Bible, and you will learn how to pray.

Out of 600,000 words in the Old Testament, only six, when literally translated, mean to "ask for" things in prayer, and each of these six is used but once.

Against that, the word "palal" is used hundreds of times to signify "to pray." And "palal" means—"To judge yourself to be a marvel of creation; to recognize amazing wonders deep within your soul."

Wouldn't that seem to indicate that prayer was meant to be a realization of the powers deep within you? Wouldn't you judge that all you need to do is to expand your consciousness to take in whatever it is that you desire?

"What things soever you ask for when you pray, believe that ye receive them, and ye shall have them." You are not to think of your lacks and needs. You are to visualize the things you want! You are not to worry about this debt or that note, but mentally see the Infinite Supply all about you. "All that you need is near ye, God is complete supply. Trust, have faith, then hear ye, dare to assert the 'I.'"

Remember this: If you pray to God, but keep your attention on your problem, you will still have your problem. You'll run into it and continue to run into it as long as you keep your attention focussed upon it. What you must do is fix your attention upon God—upon His goodness, His love, His power to remedy any ill or adjust any untoward condition. Focus your attention upon these, and these are the conditions you will run into.

Prayer is expansion, and expansion of yourself into the Godself all around you. As Kahlil Gibran describes it in his great book "The Prophet"—

For what is prayer but the expansion of yourself into the living ether.
When you pray, you rise to meet in the air those who are praying at that
very hour, and whom save in prayer you may not meet. Therefore let your
visit to the temple invisible be for naught save ecstasy and sweet commu-
nion. I cannot teach you to pray in words. God listens not to your words
save when He Himself utters them through your lips.

Prayer is a realization of your Oneness with God, and of the infinite power this gives you. It is an acceptance of the fact that there is nothing on earth you cannot have—once you have mentally accepted the fact that you CAN have it. Nothing you cannot do—once your mind has grasped the fact that you CAN do it.

Prayer, in short, is thanksgiving for the infinite good God *has* given you. The word most often used for "prayer" in the Old Testament means—"To sing a song of joy and praise."

And how often you see that method used by every great character of the Bible. Running through all of Jesus Christ's acts, as well as His teachings, you find the glowing element of praise and thanksgiving. When He looked at five loaves and two small fishes and realized that He had a multitude to feed, His first thought was a thought of praise. "And looking up to Heaven, He blessed." When He raised Lazarus from the dead, He first praised and thanked God.

When Paul and Silas lay in jail, bound with chains, did they repine? Did they get down on their knees and beg for help? On the contrary, they sang hymns of praise, and the very walls were shaken down and they were set free. "The righteous doth sing and rejoice." "The sons of God shouted for joy."

Go back over the Old Testament and see how often you are adjured to "Praise the Lord and be thankful, that THEN shall the earth yield her increase." Probably no life chronicled in the Scriptures was more beset with trials and dangers than that of King David. And what was his remedy? What brought him through all tribulations to power and riches? Just read the Psalms of David and you will see.

> *Jehovah reigneth; let the earth rejoice;*
> *Let the multitude of isles be glad.*
> *Bless Jehovah, O my soul;*
> *And all that is within me,* bless *His holy name . . .*
> *Who forgiveth all thine iniquities;*
> *Who healeth all thy diseases.*

Throughout the Bible we are told—"In everything by prayer and supplication WITH THANKSGIVING let your requests be made known unto God." Again and again the root of inspiration and attainment is stressed: *Rejoice, be glad, praise, give thanks!* "Prove me now herewith, saith the Lord of Hosts, if I will not open you the window of Heaven and pour you out a blessing, that there shall not be room enough to receive it."

The most complete interpretation of prayer I have heard came from the man who wrote—"Once I used to say 'Please.' Now I say, 'Thank you.'" "Enter into His gates with thanksgiving," the Psalmist bade us, "and into His courts with praise. Be thankful unto Him and bless His name." And Christ's apostles tell us the same thing—"Let us offer up a sacrifice of praise to God continually. In everything by prayer and supplication *with thanksgiving* let your requests be made known unto God."

Someone has said that prayer is the spirit of God pronouncing His works good. "This is the day Jehovah hath made. We will rejoice and be glad in it." It is sound psychology as well, as Prof. Wm. James of Harvard testified. "If you miss the joy," he wrote, "you miss all."

Complete, wholehearted reliance upon God—that is the prayer of faith. Not an imploring of God for some specific thing, but a clear, unquestioning recognition that the power to be and do and have the things you want is inherent in you, that you have only to recognize this power and put your trust in it to get anything of good you wish.

But perhaps you have prayed long and fervently for some particular thing, and it has not come? What then? Has it ever occurred to you that the answer was there, but you didn't receive it because you were not ready or willing to accept it?

God always answers prayer. Over and over He tells us this. The answer to your prayer is as sure as tomorrow's sunrise. YOU are the one who is not sure. You are not sure, and so you do not accept the answer.

If you accepted it, you would act on it, wouldn't you? Did you ever act upon the answer to those long and fervent prayers of yours? Yet that is the way it must be, if you are to pray for an answer—and GET it. If you pray for health, you must accept health. You must act as though you already had it. If you pray for other things, you must accept them at once and start doing—even on the smallest scale—the things you would do when the answer to your prayer became evident.

Dr. Alexis Carrel, the brilliant scientist who for many years headed the Rockefeller Institute, stated that "prayer is the most powerful form of energy one can generate."

"The influence of prayer on the human mind and body," Dr. Carrel went on to say,

> is as demonstrable as that of secreting glands. Its results can be measured in terms of increased physical buoyancy, greater intellectual vigor, moral stamina, and a deeper understanding of the realities underlying human relationships. . . . Prayer is as real as terrestrial gravity. As a physician, I have seen men, after all other therapy had failed, lifted out of disease and melancholy by the serene effort of prayer. It is the only power in the world that seems to overcome the so-called "laws of nature," the occasions on which prayer has dramatically done this have been termed "miracles." But a constant, quieter miracle takes place hourly in the hearts of men and women who have discovered that prayer supplies them with a steady flow of sustaining power in their daily lives.

An old peasant was kneeling alone in a village church, long after the services had ended. "What are you waiting for?" the priest asked him. "I am looking at Him," the peasant replied, "and He is looking at me." That is prayer, of the kind that Emerson said—"No man ever prayed without learning something."

I never try to do my work by my own power alone.
When I begin I make my prayer before God's holy throne.
I ask that His Almighty power may work its will through me
And so each task is done with ease; I'm charged with power, you see.

—HANNAH ORTH

In the eighteenth chapter of St. Matthew, Jesus gives us a method of praying that He assures us will bring us anything we ask for: "Again I say unto you, that if two of you shall agree on earth as touching anything they shall ask, it shall be done for them of My Father which is in Heaven. For where two or three are gathered together in My name, there am I in the midst of them."

That would seem simple enough, for two or three to gather together and agree upon some one thing that all should ask for. It is simple, too, and when properly done, it works wonders. In "The Magic Word," we give a number of true experiences in which little groups of people got together and prayed for the particular needs of some one of their number, with seemingly miraculous results.

It is the most effective method of prayer known, and the only reason it is not used oftener is that people so seldom agree upon what they shall ask for. They will get together and agree to pray for the health of some of their number, but where one may be thinking of health and strength, another will be dwelling upon his suffering, or the hardships it has brought upon his family or any one of a dozen other negative images. To get results, all must think of the health and strength they are praying for—not the sickness. They must dwell upon the power of God to heal the sick one, not upon the misery his sickness has caused.

Two thousand years before Christ, it was said in the Vedas that if two people would unite their forces, they could conquer the world, though singly they might be powerless. And psychologists and metaphysicians everywhere agree that the power of two minds united in a single cause is not merely their individual powers added together, but multiplied manifold.

Perhaps this can best be explained in terms of electrical power. Take an ordinary magnet capable of lifting, let us say, ten pounds of iron. Wrap this magnet with wire and charge it with the current from a small battery, it will lift—not merely ten pounds, but a hundred pounds or more!

That is what happens when one person prays and believes, and another adds his prayer and his faith. Why did Jesus send out his disciples, two and two? Why was it that on the one occasion He went alone among a crowd of scoffers, He was able to do no mighty works—on the occasion of His visit to His home town of Nazareth? You find the answer written in the Bible—"Because of their unbelief!"

Before a miracle could be wrought, there had to be faith—not only on Jesus' part, but on the part of someone around Him. Read how often He told those He cured—"Thy faith hath made thee whole."

If you were stuck in a muddy road with a heavily loaded two-horse wagon, and I were stuck with another right behind you, what would be the quickest way out? To unhitch my horses, would it not, couple them on to your wagon tongue and let the two teams pull you out. They could then take my wagon in its turn and pull it onto solid ground. What neither team could accomplish alone, the two pulling together could easily do.

Have you ever noticed a locomotive pulling a long train of cars? To START such a train takes 90 per cent of the locomotive's power. To keep it running on a smooth stretch takes less than 1 per cent. So a freight locomotive must have nearly a hundred times as much power as it needs for ordinary smooth running.

You are like a locomotive in that. To start you on the road to success requires every bit of energy you can muster. To keep you there, once you have reached the top, needs only a fraction of your abilities. The locomotive must carry its extra 99 per cent of power as a reserve, to start it again when it stops for orders or water or to pick up or unload freight, or to carry it over a heavy grade. It can do nothing with all that extra energy at other times, except blow off steam.

But what about you? You need your full 100 per cent to get started. Probably there are many times when you draw upon all of it to carry you through some grave difficulty, to push aside some obstacle that bars your way. But for the most part, you just carry that extra energy as reserve. What can you do with it? Find outlets for it!

All around you are men and women—earnest, hardworking men and women—who have put their hearts into their work, but lack some of the 100 per cent energy that would start them on the road to success. They are like freight locomotives that are perfect engines, but not quite up to the task of starting as heavy a train as has been given them. Give them a push, help them to get started or over the hump of some obstacle or difficulty, and they will go far. But getting started is too much for them alone.

Why should you do this? Because only thus can you profit from that excess energy you have to carry for emergencies, but which you so seldom use. How do you profit? Through the additional reserve power it brings you. A stalled train is a useless thing. Worse than that, it is an encumbrance, in the way of everything else that uses the line. It may be generating all but 10 per cent of the power required to move it, but without that 10 per cent, the 90 per cent is useless. So the 10 per cent you furnish to get it started is of as much value to it as the 90 per cent it furnishes, and is entitled to as great reward. When you help another in that way, you have in effect grub-staked him, and you share in the spiritual power that his success brings him. As Edwin Markham put it in his little poem—

There is a destiny that makes us brothers;
No man goes his way alone;
All that we send into the lives of others
Comes back into our own.

So whenever you have some earnest purpose, or want to help a friend or loved one to accomplish some greatly-cherished ambition, follow the advice Jesus gives us and unite in prayer for a few minutes each day until you have brought about the answer to that desire.

And when praying alone, remember:

First, center your thoughts on *the thing that you want*—not on your need.

Second, read the 91st and the 23rd Psalms, just as a reminder of God's power and His readiness to help you in all your needs.

Third, *be thankful,* not merely for past favors, *but for granting of this favor you are now asking.* To be able to thank God for it sincerely, in advance of its actual material manifestation, is the finest evidence of belief.

Fourth, BELIEVE! Picture the thing that you want so clearly, see it in your imagination so vividly, that you can actually BELIEVE THAT YOU HAVE IT!

It is this sincere conviction, registered upon your subconscious mind, that brings the answer to your prayers. Once convince your subconscious mind that you HAVE the thing that you want, and you can forget it and go on to your next problem. Mind will attend to the rest. So "sing and rejoice" that you HAVE the answer to your prayer. Literally shout for joy, as did the Sons of God in days of old.

Fifth, remember Emerson's advice—"Do the thing and you shall have the power." Start doing—even on a small scale—whatever it is that you will do when the answer to your prayer is materially evident. In other words, ACCEPT the thing you have asked for! Accept it—and start using it.

If you have faith in God, or man, or self,
Say so; if not, push back upon the shelf
Of silence all your thoughts till faith shall come.
No one will grieve because your lips are dumb.

—ELLA WHEELER WILCOX

The Law *of the* Higher Potential

32

P-R-A-I-S-E

Did you ever notice that if you leave off the "P" from the word Praise, what you have left is *"Raise"*?

That is no mere accident, for wise men have realized for thousands of years that to praise is to raise the spirits and increase the power of the one praised. In the same way, praise of God and thankfulness for His gifts raises the spirits of the one who sings those praises to the heights of rare accomplishment.

Just as praise and thanksgiving freed Paul and Silas from the chains of the dungeon, so can they free you from worry and fear and the dungeons of dark despair. "I will sing unto Jehovah," sang the Psalmist of old, "because He hath dealt bountifully with me." And if we would have Him deal bountifully with us, it behooves us to praise and be thankful for the good we now have, no matter how small that good may seem to be.

"The righteous doth sing and rejoice," we are told in the Scriptures. And the Hebrew word used for "sing" means "to sing out loud, even to shout for joy." To sing with joy is one of the long-neglected truths of POWER. "The Sons of God shouted for joy."

The Kingdom of Heaven is the Kingdom of Expansion, and the way to expand what we have is through praise and joy and thanksgiving. Seldom indeed in the Bible do you find that God provides supply out of thin air. Almost always He requires the recipients of His bounty to start with what they have. The widow with the oil and meal, that other widow with a little oil, the feeding of the multitudes with the loaves and fishes, and scores of other cases, all started with the supply in hand. God expanded what they had. And God will expand what you have, if you rightly use the power of praise and thanksgiving.

But mere expansion is not enough. You might expand all the water in the world into steam, and get no good from it—if you had no engine in which to use the steam. You must have a purpose in mind if you are to get the utmost of good from your expansion. You must set a goal. You must plan the *form* in which that expanded energy is to make itself manifest. It can be in your body, in your circumstances, in your surroundings—in anything of good you may desire.

Some years ago the "Journal of Education" had a story that expressed this idea clearly. "There was once a prince," it read,

> who had a crooked back. He could never stand straight up like even the lowest of his subjects. Because he was a very proud prince, his crooked back caused him a great deal of mental suffering.
>
> One day he called before him the most skilful sculptor in his kingdom and said to him: "Make me a noble statue of myself, true to my likeness in every detail, with this exception—make this statue with a straight back. I wish to see myself as I might have been."
>
> For long months the sculptor worked, hewing the marble carefully into the likeness of the prince, and at last the work was done, and the sculptor went before the prince and said: "The statue is finished; where shall I set it up?" One of the courtiers called out: "Set it before the castle gate where all can see it," but the prince smiled sadly and shook his head. "Rather," said he, "place it in a secret nook in the palace garden where only I shall see it."
>
> The statue was placed as the prince ordered, and promptly forgotten by the world, but every morning and every noon and every evening, the prince stole quietly away to where it stood and looked long upon it, noting the straight back and the uplifted head and the noble brow. And each time he gazed, something seemed to go out of the statue and into him, tingling in his blood and throbbing in his heart.
>
> The days passed into months and the months into years; then strange rumors began to spread throughout the land. Said one: "The prince's back is no longer crooked or my eyes deceive me." Said another: "Our prince has the high look of a mighty man." And these rumors came to the prince, and he listened with a queer smile.
>
> Then went he out into the garden to where the statue stood and behold, it was just as the people said, his back had become straight as the

statue's, his head had the same noble bearing; he was, in fact, the noble man his statue proclaimed him to be.

2500 years ago, in the Golden Age of Athens, when its culture led the world, Grecian mothers surrounded themselves with beautiful statues that they might bring forth perfect children and that the children in turn might develop into perfect men and women.

Eleven months from now, YOU will have an entirely new body, inside and out. Not a single cell, not a single bit of tissue that is now in you will be there then. What changes do you want made in that new body? What improvements?

Then start right now getting that new model clearly in mind. Buy yourself a scrap book. Cut from the magazines a picture of the finest figure of a man or woman that you can find, and paste it on page one. Cut out other pictures, that show clearly different parts of your body that need developing or perfecting, and paste them on other pages. Then cut pictures of people doing the sort of things you would love to do—dancing, swimming, riding horseback, rowing, fishing, playing golf or tennis, anything you like—and paste them on different pages of your scrap book.

At the top and bottom of each page, or alongside the pictures, put such reminders and affirmations as these:

Father God, I thank Thee for my glorious strength, my abiding health, my tireless energy.

Vitalize Thy perfect image in me in perfect form.

I am strong in the Lord and the power of His might.

God made me in His own image. He is my strength and power. He maketh my way perfect. The joy of the Lord is my strength.

Know ye not that ye are the temple of God and that the Spirit of God dwelleth in you?

Divine Love protects and sustains me. I am the open channel through which the healing currents of life are now flowing. God is my life. God is my health. In God is my trust.

Under a picture showing someone with a splendid chest, taking breathing exercises, put—

The Spirit of the Lord hath made me, and the breath of the almighty giveth me life.

Under one bathing—

Wash me and I shall be whiter than snow.

Under a picture of the eyes—

Open thou mine eyes, that in Thy light I may see the light.

Or, if your eyes are weak or troublesome, put—

Jehovah openeth the eyes of the blind. Blessed are the pure in heart, for they shall see God. I see God in my eyes, in their perfect life and strength and wholeness. If thou can'st believe, all things are possible to him that believeth. According to thy faith be it done unto you.

Under picture at a well-filled table—

Thou shalt eat thy bread with joy.

Under sleep—

They that rest in the Lord shall renew their strength like the eagle. They shall walk and not faint, they shall run and not be weary. Thy Spirit strengthens both my soul and my body, and I rest in peace of wholeness and health.

Under vigorous, happy, healthy older people—

As my days, so shall my strength be. Behold, all things are becoming new. Thou shalt make me full of joy in Thy presence. Passing years have no effect upon my spiritual body. I am alive in Jesus Christ forever. I am a tower of strength and stability in the realization that God is my health. God's life is constant, unbroken, eternal. I am quickened in His consciousness of life. His constant power and strength sustain me and I am healed. I AM a perfect idea of God and all of life is with me now and always.

A long time ago, Epictetus said: "God has delivered YOU to YOUR care, and this is what He says to you—'I have no fitter to trust than YOU. Preserve this body for me just as it is by nature; modest, beautiful, faithful, noble, tranquil.'"

You will find many affirmations to paste in your scrap book. Use any and all that seem helpful. But that saying of Epictetus is a good one to paste on the last page—a good one to bear always in mind. "God has delivered you to your care." And God gave you dominion. So think of yourself as well and strong. Think of your body as spiritual substance that is not subject to the ills of the flesh. Think of it as constantly changing, continually GROWING into the perfect image that you are holding before it.

The Kingdom of Heaven is the Kingdom of Expansion. If you have but a single perfect cell in your whole body, you can expand that cell into a perfect body, provided only that you hold before it the image of health and strength—not of sickness; provided only that you BELIEVE! "God made man but little lower than the Angels."

"Give Us This Day Our Daily Bread"

For your Prosperity and Abundant Supply Scrap Book, you cannot do better than start with that line from the Lord's Prayer—"Give us this day our daily bread."

Get a picture of a horn of plenty—a cornucopia—with all manner of good things pouring out of it, and paste it on the first page of your Scrap Book. Line the page with pictures of sparrows and lilies of the field, to remind you of Jesus' promise, and then put at the bottom of the page something like this:

O God, beginning now I shall forever LET Thy Spirit Infinite become the sole dictator of my soul; and I shall never more take anxious thought of anything, but grow as the lilies grow, in peace and power, so that I shall have all I need, forever more.

The next page, I'd head with the line—"I can have what I want—*if I plant it.*" Under it, paste pictures of farmers or gardeners planting seed, only take a pen or pencil and change those seeds into $$$. Under these pictures, put— "The riches of the Spirit now fill my mind and affairs. I think prosperity, I talk prosperity and I know that prosperity and success are mine."

On other pages, show pictures of growing grain or other plants, with $$$ at the top instead of the usual grain or fruit. Use such affirmations as—"God is my inexhaustible and omnipotent source of abundant supply." "I accept the will of God, which is abundant prosperity for me." "If I continue to desire you, I shall have you, because I trust in God for all things I desire."

Then on succeeding pages, show pictures of great piles of money—bags of money, piles of paper money and currency all around the pages, and pictures of yourself pasted in the center, surrounded by riches. If you can find pictures of men digging up treasure hoards, put them in. Put in all kinds of pictures that imply riches and prosperity. Put in pictures of the sort of surroundings you will have, when you have manifested the riches you desire. Get pictures of a beautiful home—the home of your dreams. Show if possible, each room as you would have it furnished. Show the outside, with a wide driveway, bordered by a beautiful lawn, shrubbery around the house, trees in the background, the kind of car you would like to own drawn up before the house. Show even the wardrobes of fine clothes you would have, show horses or bicycles or whatnot for the children, show the flowers in your garden.

"When I got the Lessons of THE GOD IN YOU," wrote Mrs. Caroline Kroll of Indianapolis, in December, 1939, "I had only $12.00 a month. Now I have a nice home and everything is paid for. I am so happy." Mrs. Kroll had written us in the fall of '37 expressing her great desire for a home, and we suggested to her this Treasure Mapping method. She says in her last letter—"I never faltered in my home making, and tonight I am sitting in a good home of my own and never was any happier in my youth."

Remember, the first step in supplying a need is to know that it IS already supplied in the Mind of God. God has already given you all of good. It is yours for the taking, and the most perfect prayer is the deep realization that your need is already supplied. You don't have to waste energy wondering about the supply. All you have to do is to focus your energy upon *being* one with it.

Your desires are like acorns—visions of the mighty oaks they can grow to be. What you desire is and always has been yours. What man can conceive, man can achieve. It is the eye that makes the horizon. No man ever bettered his position by limiting himself in his own mind to the one he had. No man ever made a success of his business by thinking failure. Every success is achieved first in your own thoughts. You must work first on yourself, because all trouble, limitation and the like are states of consciousness. Change your thought and you change all. You get the conditions that belong to your consciousness. As Emerson put it—"No man was ever ridden down or talked down by anything but himself."

Look within yourself for the source of all power. I AM the great power of God expressing as ME. I AM the great abundance for all my needs and a surplus to spare. That to which I give my attention reveals itself. So give your attention to the things you want! Fill your Scrap Book with pictures of them. Put over and under and around them such affimations as these:

God is able to do exceeding abundantly above all that we ask or think, according to the Power that worketh in us. I rejoice in the bounty of God, constantly manifesting to meet my every need.

If ye abide in Me and my words abide in you, ye shall ask what ye will and it shall be done unto you. For herein is the Father glorified, that ye bear much fruit. Your Father knoweth what things ye have need of before you ask Him. Fear not, for it is the Father's good pleasure to give you the Kingdom. All that the Father hath is yours, and you are in all ways prospered.

I will give thee hidden riches of secret places, that thou mayest know that I am the God of Israel. If thou return to the Almighty, then shalt thou lay up gold as dust, and the gold of Ophir as the stones of the brooks. I will sing unto Jehovah, because He hath dealt bountifully with me.

Remember that—"According to thy faith be it done unto you." So believe that you RECEIVE! If your beliefs are all for the future, you will get them in the distant future but never NOW You will never quite catch up with them. "Now is the accepted time. Now is the day of salvation." Realize that all these good things are NOW coming into manifestation in your life. Bless and thank God for them NOW.

Instead of pleading, "God bless me,"
And making such a weary fuss,
How much better off we'd be
If we would smile awhile and say,
"I thank you, God, for blessing us today."

Instead of begging, "God, give me
And mine the things which our hearts crave,"
How much happier we'd be

If we would laugh with life, and say,
"We thank you, God, for what we have today."

—MARION B. SHOEN

"But what shall we do about pressing debts?" many will ask. First, make a list of all of them. Then, thank God for having sent such trustful people to your aid, thank Him for the confidence they have shown in you. Next, see yourself in your mind's eye going the rounds of all your creditors, paying them in full. See their thankful, smiling faces. Hear yourself expressing to them your appreciation of their courtesy and forbearance, hear them telling you that they were glad to be of help, will be glad to extend the same credit to you in the future. Get pictures of people paying money over to merchants, paste in your own features over those of the debtors, and under them put such affimations as these:

Divine Love prospers all of us together NOW. God is our supply, through each of us to all, and through all of us to each. I speak for all of us the word that multiplies money to all of us. And my word accomplishes that whereunto I send it. In God is my trust.

When I worry, I am not trusting God. When I trust God, I have nothing to worry about.

I put the payment of these debts lovingly in the hands of the Father with a child-like trust. That which is for my highest good will come to me.

Then do your part by using some of whatever money you receive to pay these just debts, and as you pay out the money, bless it in some such wise as this: "I bless thee . . . and be thou a blessing! As I pay out this money, I bless it. May it enrich everyone who touches it. The value of this substance I hold in my hand is this day magnified, for I perceive that it is truly a symbol of my heavenly Father's inexhaustible riches. Go forth, increase, multiply and bring forth fruit and hundredfold!"

Here is a prayer suggested by R. A. D., in a recent issue of NAUTILUS, to be used in connection with your list of debts:

Father, I thank Thee that thou hast opened the way for me to pay every bill on this list, sending the money for each one before it is due. I place this expense sheet absolutely and unconditionally in Thy hands, and from the depths of a rich consciousness, I thank and praise Thee that the money for each separate item already is provided, awaiting only my claim to bring it into evidence. The glory of Thy radiance shining before me, Infinite Father, has opened the way for my unfailing prosperity and for a success greater than I ever before have experienced. I put from me every thought of limitations or lack and go free to have an abundance of all good.

The right job is the most pressing problem for many people. And you can help yourself or others to that right work through "Treasure Mapping" in the same way that you can bring riches or health or any other good thing.

The first essential, of course, is to know what you want. What kind of work would you most like to do? What are you best fitted for? What is your ultimate ambition? Get a Scrap Book and paste in it first a picture of yourself. After deciding on the line of work you want to devote yourself to, take inventory of yourself and think in what position you are now fitted to start. Then get a picture from the magazines of someone working in that position, paste it in your Scrap Book, and if you have a snap-shot of yourself that you can substitute for the face in the picture, do so.

Decide then what is the next position you will be fitted for in the line of work you have adopted, and paste a picture of someone in that position on the next page of your Scrap Book. Fill succeeding pages with logical steps in your progress, right on up to the very top. When you feel that your work will entitle you to a private office, paste in a picture of someone representing yourself seated at a desk in a sumptuously furnished office, with his title lettered on the door or on the side of the desk, and then letter in your name over the title.

And remember, no one ever got a good job by limiting himself mentally to a poor one. Admit to yourself that you are good. Then let others find it out by the service you give. That is the key to any door you wish to unlock. Yourself PLUS is your fortune. Your affairs PLUS is success.

Paste over and under and around your pictures such affirmations as these: "God is with me in all that I do." "If God be for you, who can be against you?" "Know ye not that ye are Gods, sons of the Most High?" What should your situation be like? What is it like in the Divine Mind, in the Eternal Plan? "Your Father knoweth what things ye have need of before you ask Him. Fear not, for it is the Father's good pleasure to give you the Kingdom. All that the Father has is yours, and you are in all ways prospered." "If ye abide in Me and My words abide unto you, ye shall ask what ye will and it shall be done unto you. For herein is the Father glorified, that ye bear much fruit." "With good will, doing service as to the Lord and not to man." "Whether therefore ye eat or drink, or whatever ye do, do all to the glory of God."

The same principles that help you to a better position will help you to make your business grow and prosper, when you have a business of your own. Many a man has started with practically nothing, and built a fortune, simply by taking God into partnership with him.

Start your Scrap Book with a picture of yourself and of your business as it is now. Then on each succeeding page, show it growing bigger and better. Picture the service you want to give your customers. Picture thousands of them taking advantage of that service. Picture yourself and your helpers serving ever greater numbers, picture your product in the hands of more and more users, picture its manufacture in great volume, its shipping, its sale, everything you can connected with it. And let every picture show progress, growth, *expansion*. See yourself serving the world.

Under those pictures, put inspiring affirmations. "I am a partner and co-worker with God." It is the purpose of Universal Mind to see men prosper, that they may express more of life, love, happiness and understanding, thus reflecting more of God. Our product is the connecting link between this demand and God's supply. The need is expanding continually and we have the will and the intelligence to see and meet it. Therefore, there is a continually growing demand for our product, that increases as I realize the spiritual significance of my work and make better products for my customers. It is in my power to make my customers better qualified, through the equipment that I provide, for prosperity and success. I delight in that power. I increase that power by using it for the honor, glory and pleasure of my customers and myself.

"Father, this business has to be good, so You handle it for me. I put it and all my affairs lovingly in Your hands, with a child-like faith. That which is for my highest good will come to me. One on God's side is a majority, and I am together with You, so all things are working together for my good and I am working with them in the wisdom and the power of the Spirit."

"God is in control. God is Spirit, good omnipotent. Apart from Him, there is no overcoming power. God is life, love and peace. God's will now fulfilled in me is abundant work for our business."

"The Spirit that multiplied the loaves and fishes for Jesus increases my sub-stance, and I manifest prosperity."

But remember to give "good measure" to all, customers and co-workers alike, for "All who joy would win must share it—*Happiness was born a twin*."

Many who have no business to worry about have homes or pieces of prop-erty or whatnot that they wish to sell, and at times this is a problem. Yet it is a problem that lends itself to the same methods outlined above, as you can judge from the following letter dated May 15th, 1940, from one of the subscribers to THE GOD IN YOU:

> When I received Robert Collier's Course THE GOD IN YOU, we were in debt and sometimes wondered what the next meal was to be, even though we owned our cottage and three lots. It seemed we couldn't get a buyer, nor could we even borrow on the property, even though it was clear, as it was in a run-down neighborhood.
>
> Since reading the Course, we have sold all St. Louis County prop-erty and purchased this 96-acre farm at Belle, paying cash for it and clearing ourselves of debt, as we sold most of the property for cash, a thing we could not have done without the help of THE GOD IN YOU. I believe we are about to see another manifestation of God's goodness as we have deposits under our ground which may indeed show God's goodness through riches to us.

The first essential is to BLESS the property you wish to sell. Know that it is a perfect image in the Divine Mind, made for the express purpose of man-ifesting good to someone, and declare that it is now sold to the right party at the right price.

Paste a picture of it in your Scrap Book. Think of every possibility for its development, and paste such pictures in your book, too. Show pictures of people looking at similar properties, of a sale being made, of the developments that will take place on it.

L. C. B. told in a recent issue of UNITY how she put her house "lovingly in the hands of the Father," then used this affirmation: "You, Christ, will find for us the perfect purchasers, who will love our home as we have loved it and rec-ognize it for theirs and have sufficient cash to pay for it and have it NOW. Only through You are we fully aware of our omnipresent good." Within a short time, the article states, the house was sold for cash, and at their own price!

In "Nautilus" sometime ago, there was a similar story, the affirmation used in that case being the following:

> God's loving Presence in all of us brings the right buyer NOW, who will pay the right price for the property and who will make money on the deal, while at the same time I will make money, God's money, in the selling. Divine Love now multiplies God's money and His Good to both buyer and seller, so that all shall be satisfied. All things now work together for good to me and to the new buyer of this property. We are the open channels through which Divine Love is now flowing to this property and through it to all the world. All the barriers are now dissolved by Divine Love and my customer comes quickly and gloriously. God is our prosperity here and now. In God I trust and I know that all things work together to manifest the good we desire.

Whatever your problem, whatever your difficulty, you can get guidance if you will seek it. Give the facts to the God in You, ask Him for the solution, then leave the problem with Him and FORGET it in the serene confidence that He can and will find the answer. Never force the issue. Have faith in that God in You, and wait for a leading. "And thine ear shall hear a voice behind thee saying, this is the path; walk ye in it."

Our physical senses are able to discern only such objects as are on the same or a lower material plane than ourselves. Our ears, for instance, are attuned to but a few octaves of sound. Those of higher or lower wave lengths are inaudible to us. Yet the radio has taught us that all about us are sounds of music, of laughter, of drama and instruction.

The same is true with our eyes. We see only those things that are on the median light waves. The air may be full of television pictures, yet with our unaided eyes, we get none of them. Is it therefore so hard to believe that when the servant of the Prophet Elisha was fearful, because of the enemies all around, Elisha prayed and said—"Lord, I pray thee, open his eyes, that he may see. And the Lord opened the eyes of the young man; and he saw; And behold, the mountain was full of horses and chariots of fire round about Elisha."

May not the air around you be just as full of God's angels? May not Elisha's advice be just as good today—"Fear not, for they that be with us are more than they that be with them."

The Psalmist of old testified, you remember—"I have been young, and now am old, yet have I not seen the righteous forsaken, nor his seed begging bread."

Paste in your Scrap Book some of those old Biblical pictures of Angels guiding the children of God, of Guardian Angels, and over and under them put such affirmations as these: "God goes before me and opens the way." "Infinite Wisdom tells me just what to do." "I thank you, God, that you are here with us, and no matter what happens, we are all right." "Thou shalt not be afraid for the terror by night, nor for the arrow that flieth by day. He will cover thee with his pinions, and under his wings shalt thou take refuge."

Grace Crowell had a beautiful little poem along these lines in Unity Weekly:

So often through God's Holy Book there shines
Some clear-cut word, some strong and simple phrase
That gleams like diamonds gathered from deep mines,
Set polished there to light our earthly days;
"And God was with the lad." The words, how brief,
And yet what vital meaning in their sound,
As spoken of that ancient child of grief
Once left to die upon the hot, parched ground.

"And God was with the lad," One need not look
For further information; all is told.
No gifted hand on earth could pen a book
Of strange biography that would unfold
With clearer words, nor could it tell as well
The God-companioned life of Ishmael.

Such affirmations cannot help but bring you peace and serenity. In "Esquire" magazine some time ago there was an article telling about the fear-scent the body gives off, which is exceedingly irritating to any animal that senses it. "It is this fear-scent," said the article, "which causes dogs to attack people who have not molested them. A dog will respond quickly both in friendship and in training when he is approached without fear, but no one can fool him for a minute with a fearless exterior concealing a quaking heart, for the fear-scent is there.

It is usually the fear that a canoe will tip over that causes the occupant to move suddenly in the wrong direction and thereby upset it. The fear of drowning, when suddenly thrown into the water, causes one to struggle frantically, and incidentally force himself under. It is an interesting scientific fact that a baby, until 24 hours old, can swim. Beyond that, it starts to realize fear and will sink. Fear is really the mental hazard of crossing your bridges before you come to them.

Is it not likely that the strong odor of our "fear-scent" registers on all we come in contact with, even though it be but subconsciously with human beings? Certain it is that when we approach people fearfully, we seem to repel them, for we seldom make a favorable impression, seldom get from them what we want.

The remedy? To BLESS the Divinity in all we come in contact with. You remember how often Jesus used the greeting—"Peace!" "Peace I leave with you; my peace I give unto you." And to the wind and waves, He bade—"Peace! Be still." And immediately the storm abated. "Acquaint now thyself with God and be at peace."

When trouble threatens in your home or your business, bless all concerned and mentally affirm—"Peace! The love of God is at work here. All of my forces are peaceful and harmonious. There is no resistance in me against the Spirit of God's peaceful life. Every anxious thought is stilled. Thy mighty confidence and Thy peace enfold me. The Spirit of God fills my mind, and abundance is everywhere manifest." Then go up to the thing you fear, confidently, serenely. Or if it is something you must do, do it! Once you have lost the fear of it, you will find it easy.

Evil? There is really no such thing. It is merely the lack of Good. Summon the Good and the evil vanishes. The same is true of enemies. Summon love for them, salute the Divinity in them and bless them, and you will find hate turned to love. Say mentally to the Divinity in those who appear to be your enemies—"I recognize you. You can't disguise yourself. You are a radiant child of God. God's creations are all excellent. I bless you in the name of Jesus Christ. Because you are a child of God, you speak the truth and you are ever honest, just and harmonious. My world is filled with splendid people, and I love them all."

Be noble, and the nobleness that lies in other men, sleeping but never dead, will rise in majesty to meet thine own. Trust men, and they will be true to you. Treat them greatly, and they will show themselves great.

Love overcometh, for all motion is cyclic. It circulates to the limits of its possibilities and then returns to its starting point. Thus any unselfish expenditure of energy returns to you laden with gifts. Any unselfish act done for another's benefit is giving part of yourself. It is an outward flow of power that completes its cycle and returns laden with energy.

The thoughts that we send forth always return with a harvest of their kind. That which we put into the thought comes back into our life. For our every thought there is a response, a return of the pendulum that we have started swinging. It is Emerson's Law of Compensation.

So you can see the wisdom in the dictum—"Into whatsoever house ye enter, first say—'Peace be to this house!'"

But do more than bless those you come in contact with. *Act* the part. Think kindly of them as well.

> *Believe not each accusing tongue,*
> *As most weak people do;*
> *But still believe that story wrong*
> *Which ought not to be true.*

It is as easy to add, you know, as it is to subtract. Love adds. Fear and hatred subtract. You can reinforce your efforts with all the universe through love, as easily as you can separate yourself from everyone through hatred and fear.

Remember, evil is usually in the eye of the beholder. There is an old poem that depicts this graphically:

> *Mistress Polly Wittenhouse*
> *Lived on Whetstone Alley,*
> *And she was like an angel*
> *To little orphan Sally,*
> *And she was like a harlot*
> *To the lass across the way,*
> *A "good 'un" to the slavey*
> *Who made her bed each day.*
> *And she was like a siren*
> *With the devil in her eye*
> *To any roving sailor man*
> *As he was passing by.*

So Mistress Polly Wittenhouse
Was either good or bad,
According to the need or greed
Each of her judges had,
According as her living
Threw a shadow on their own.
The sailors flung her kisses
And the lass she cast a stone.
And Sally and the slavey
They prayed for her each night,
And all of them that judged her
Knew that they judged her right.

A Scrap Book on Love is probably the most valuable one you can make. Put in it pictures of all your friends, all those you would have for friends. Paste in it pictures of the home of your dreams, of each separate room in it, of the furnishings, of everything about it.

Put in it every motto of peace and love and happiness you can find. Put in it pictures of children and toys and fireside scenes, dinners and parties and all the intimate happy things you can think of. Love that house and everything about it. Live in it mentally. Believe in it, and before long you will find that you ARE in it in actuality.

God lights the way, no more we grope
Nor stumble on in troubled hope.
We sow no seeds of care or strife,
But those of love and joy and life.
No more we strive to plan our lot,
The Father fills our cup unsought.

Sow the seeds in your Scrap Book and in your life of love and joy and happiness, then leave it to the Father to provide the means of making these seeds grow and bear fruit. "I have planted, Apollos watered, but God gaveth the increase."

Remember, the I AM in you is your part of Divinity. Some sage put it—"Whatever the Creator is, I AM." How often have you said—"I AM poor, I AM sick, I AM ignorant, I AM weak"—and thus fastened these evils upon yourself?

You acknowledged a lack of something. What can you build with minus quantities? Only emptiness, void.

Reverse all that. Whenever you say "I AM," whenever you thus call upon the God in You, make it something you WANT. "I AM rich. I AM powerful. I AM well and whole and strong. I AM happy. I AM perfect in every way."

Make an I AM Scrap Book, with your picture on the first page, then pictures of supermen or genii or whatever your idea of power may be scattered throughout the pages of the book. Put in it pictures of all the things you would like to be and do. And fill it with such affirmations as these:

The Spirit of Prosperity fills my mind and overflows into my affairs. God is my perfect will; through me it is done. There is only one Presence and one Power in my life—God, the Good Omnipotent. God is my inexhaustible source of abundant supply. The riches of the Spirit now fill my mind and affairs. I think prosperity. I talk prosperity, and I know that prosperity and success are mine.

If we but touch the garment's hem,
Comes power surging through.
Try—play the part—stretch out your hand,
Then quiet—wait what comes to you.

God gave man power and dominion over all that is below him. "I said—Ye are Gods, and all of you Sons of the Most High." "As many as received Him, to them gave He power to become the Sons of God, even to them that believe on His name."

Will YOU receive Him? Will you believe in and accept the power He offers you? "God is able to do abundantly above all that we ask or think, according to the Power that worketh in us." Will you accept His Divine Sonship? Will you BE the God-man you were intended to be? Then cast off all fear of debt and lack and sickness and evil. Live in the world of love and plenty that was intended for you. Use the God-given power that is yours to first visualize the things you want—"In the beginning was the Word," the mental image, you remember—and then bring those mental images into actuality through your faith and your work.

Treasure Maps help to re-educate your mind, help you to visualize and hold in thought the images you wish to create. But visualizing and asking God's guidance is only half the battle. The other half is to make your start, to dig in and DO the first thing necessary towards bringing your desires into actuality.

The Kingdom of Heaven is the Kingdom of Expansion, but there must be something to expand. You can start a house with a single brick. You can start a fortune with a single dollar. But there must be that brick or that dollar or that first step to put your leaven into before you can make it expand and grow into the perfect structure of your dreams.

So do the thing, whatever it may be, that is necessary to your start. Make your picture, draw your Treasure Map, then take the first step that may be necessary towards bringing it into actuality. To begin is to be half done. You will be amazed how quickly you will reach your goal.

> To every man God gives a gift tonight;
> To king and peasant and to you and me:
> A shining year, clean, white, as crystal clear
> As tropic pools or stars above the sea.
>
> Oh, let us promise all the coming days
> To keep them pure, to keep them ever white!
> As, heaven born, one comes to us each morn,
> God, help us use it wisely in Thy sight.
>
> Whatever task, whatever joy be ours
> Throughout the year that now has scarce begun,
> Let us steadfastly claim in His own name
> The promised presence of the Holy One.

—BERTHA M. RUSSELL

33

The Kingdom of Expansion

Here is a secret of riches and success that has been buried 1,990 years deep.

Since time began, mankind has been searching for this secret. It has been found—and lost again—a score of times. The Ancients of all races have had some inkling of it, as is proven by the folktales and legends that have come down to us, like the story of Aladdin and his wonderful lamp, or Ali Baba and his "Open Sesame" to the treasure trove.

Every nation has such legends. Every nation has had its Wise Men, its men of genius and vision who glimpsed the truth that is buried in these old folktales and who understood at least something of how it works.

But it remained for Jesus to re-discover this secret in its entirety and then to show us clearly, step by step, how we might use it to bring us anything of good we might desire.

Make no mistake about this: The miracles of Jesus were not something super-natural that could be performed only by Him, else how could He have picked seventy disciples—ordinary men, uneducated, untaught, fishermen, farmers, tax-gatherers and the like—and sent them out two by two to perform miracles and wonders second only to His own so that they returned to Him with joy, saying, "Lord, even the devils are subject to us through Thy name." How could He have assured us—"The things that I do shall ye do also, and greater things than these shall ye do." The miracles of Jesus were divinely NAT-URAL. Instead of being departures from natural law, they were demonstrations of what the law will do for you—if you understand how to use it!

God does not deal in exceptions. Every force in Nature works along definite, logical lines, in accord with certain principles. These forces will work for any-one who possesses the key to their use, just as Aladdin's fabled Genie would

respond to the call of anyone who rubbed the magic lamp. They can be neglected and allowed to lie idle, they can be used for good or evil, but the laws
themselves do not change. It is merely the methods of using them that change.

An airplane or an automobile would have seemed as great a miracle to the
people of Jesus' day as the curing of a leper. Sending sound waves through
the ether, to be picked up by a little box called a radio, would have been as
wonderful to our fathers as is the sending of our voice over a beam of light to
us today. Yet there is nothing super-natural about either of these. The forces of
Nature have always been there, ready for our use. It is our understanding of
them that has changed, our knowledge of how to USE them.

Man in ancient times looked upon the lightning as the wrath of God, just
as many deeply religious people look upon poverty and sickness and calamities
today in the same way, as visitations of God. Yet man has learned to harness the
lightning and make it serve him.

The laws governing electricity were there all the time, waiting only for the
understanding of someone wise enough to show us how to put them to good
use. Just so the power to BE and HAVE what you want is right here, needing
only for you to learn how it works.

Nineteen hundred years ago, there came to this earth a Son of Man who
proclaimed that His mission was—"That ye might have LIFE, and have it more
ABUNDANTLY."

NOT, mind you, that you might learn how to die, and thus reach Heaven
and a life of comfort, but that you might have LIFE—here and now. Over and
over again He told us—"What things soever ye desire . . . ye shall have them,"
and lest you might think that this referred to some future state, He assured
us—"If two of you shall agree ON EARTH as touching anything they shall
ask, it shall be done for them."

Furthermore, He gave exact instructions as to how to go about getting the
things you desire. When you want more of the good things of life, when happiness or success or riches seem to elude you, there is a definite formula for you
to use. "Seek ye first the Kingdom of Heaven," Jesus directed, "and all these
things shall be added unto you."

"Ah ha!" you say. "There it is. You do have to die and go to Heaven in order
to get the good you want." But Jesus must have anticipated that you might
think just that, for He pointed out specifically that the Kingdom of Heaven is
not afar off, in the clouds or in the next world. "The Kingdom of Heaven com-

eth not with observation," He said. "Neither shall they say, Lo here, lo there! For behold, the Kingdom of Heaven is within you."

WHAT IS HEAVEN?

That word "Heaven" is perhaps the most misunderstood word in the Bible. In the original Greek text, the word used for "Heaven" is OURANOS, which, translated literally, means EXPANSION. And what is expansion? It is increasing, spreading out, multiplying, is it not? "Seek ye first the Kingdom of EXPANSION, and all these things shall be added unto you." Seek a place or a state of being where you can expand, grow, increase, multiply, bring forth fruit.

But we don't need to seek such a place, for Jesus assured us that the Kingdom of Heaven is already within us. We must therefore look within ourselves for this faculty of expansion.

Now what, within us, has unlimited power to expand? Our muscles are elastic, our lungs and many of our organs can be expanded to an extent, but none of them can expand greatly without harm to itself and to the body.

The only thing in this body of ours that can expand without limit is our MIND, our imaging faculties. So Jesus' advice might be paraphrased—"Seek ye first the Kingdom of Mind, of imagery, and all these things shall be added unto you."

That would seem to fit in with Jesus' own description of what the Kingdom of Heaven is like. "The Kingdom of Heaven is like to a grain of mustard seed, which a man took, and sowed in his field; which indeed is the least of all seeds, but when it is grown, it is the greatest among herbs, and becometh a tree, so that the birds of the air come and lodge in the branches thereof." "The Kingdom of Heaven is like unto leaven, which a woman took and hid in three measures of meal, until the whole was leavened."

What is the property of a mustard seed? *It spreads*—a single seed will grow into a tree, a single tree will produce enough seeds to plant a great field. And what is the property of leaven or yeast? *It expands*—in a single night it can expand a hundred times in size.

Go back over any of the miracles of increase in the Bible and see if they are not all miracles of EXPANSION. How did Elijah make the oil and meal last, so that one measure of oil and a little meal fed him and the widow and her son for an indefinite period? How did Elisha increase the pot of oil for that other widow who came to him to save her sons from bondage, so that she had enough to fill all the vessels she could borrow from her neighbors?

By EXPANDING them, did they not? And that is how you can increase your substance, your happiness, your every good thing.

When the disciples asked Jesus how to pray, what did He teach them? "Our Father which art in Heaven, hallowed be Thy name, Thy Kingdom come, *Thy will be done on earth as it is in Heaven*." In other words, may the good that you have imaged for me in the Heaven of your consciousness be made manifest here on earth.

God is MIND, and He dwells in the Kingdom of Mind or Heaven. There—in the mind and thoughts of God—all is good. He images you as perfect, your surroundings pleasant and comfortable, all your ways cast in pleasant places. He does not think up sickness and troubles for you. He images you as His perfect child, happy and care-free, with everything of good that makes life desirable. He is your Father, and what father, even among us here on earth, would plan anything but good for his children? As Jesus reminded us—"What man is there of you, whom if his son ask bread, will he give him a stone? Or if he ask a fish, will he give him a serpent? If ye then, being evil, know how to give good gifts unto your children, how much more shall your Father which is in heaven give good things to them that ask Him?"

In short, when you pray . . . "Thy will be done . . ." you are asking that everything of good that the Father has imaged for you in His mind should be made manifest for you here on earth. For His will, like that of every father, is that His children should be contented and happy, that they should have everything that is for their good.

How can we help to bring this about? By putting our own lives and especially our thoughts on the plane of the Kingdom of Heaven—in other words, by starting here and now to *live* in that Kingdom of Heaven.

When you meet evil on its own level, you meet it at a disadvantage. You may overcome it, but only after a terrific struggle. The only sure way to overcome evil is to get above it—to use the Law of the Higher Potential not merely to defeat the evil that confronts you, but to replace it with the perfect condition you desire.

That is what Jesus bade us do when He told us to "Seek first the Kingdom of Heaven (of expansion, of mind, of the imaging faculties)."

Seek in your own mind the ideal condition you would have, expand your thoughts to image it in every detail, see it as part of the Kingdom of Heaven, so that you can be thankful for it and praise God for it. See it, believe in it, until you can be happy over it and no longer fearful or worrying about seeming conditions around you.

In the beginning all was void—space—nothingness. How did God construct the planets, the firmaments, the earth and all things on and in it from this formless void? By first making a mental image on which to build.

That is what you, too, must do. You control your destiny, your fortune, your happiness to the exact extent to which you can think them out, VISUALIZE them, SEE them, and allow no vagrant thought of fear or worry to mar their completion and beauty. The quality of your thought is the measure of your power. Clear, forceful thought has the power of attracting to itself everything it may need for the fruition of those thoughts. As W. D. Wattles puts it in his "Science of Getting Rich":

> There is a thinking stuff from which all things are made and which, in its original state, permeates, penetrates, and fills the interspaces of the universe. A thought in this substance produces the thing that is imagined by the thought. Man can form things in his thought, and by impressing his thought upon formless substance, can cause the thing he thinks about to be created.

The connecting link between your conscious mind and the Kingdom of Heaven is thought, and every thought that is in harmony with progress and good, every thought that is freighted with the right idea, can penetrate to the Heaven Mind. And penetrating to it, it comes back with the power of God to accomplish it. You don't need to originate the ways and means. God knows how to bring about any necessary results. There is but one right way to solve any given problem. When your human judgment is unable to decide what that one right way is, turn to the Lord for guidance. You need never fear the outcome, for if you heed His advice you cannot go wrong.

Always remember—your mind is but a conductor—good or poor as you make it—for the power of the Universal Mind or God. And thought is the connecting energy. Use that conductor, and you will improve its conductivity. Demand much, and you will receive the more. The Lord is not stingy in any of His gifts. "Ask and ye shall receive, seek and ye shall find, knock and it shall be opened unto you."

That is the law of life. And the destiny of man lies not in poverty and hardship, but in living up to his high estate in unity with the Heaven Mind, with the Power that governs the universe.

To look upon poverty and sickness as sent by God and therefore inevitable, is the way of the weakling. God never sent us anything but good. What is more, He has never yet failed to give to those who would use them the means to overcome any condition not of His making. Sickness and poverty are not of His making. They are not evidences of virtue, but of weakness. God gave us everything in abundance, and he expects us to manifest that abundance. If you had a son you loved very much, and you surrounded him with good things which he had only to exert himself in order to reach, you wouldn't like it if he showed himself to the world half-starved, ill-kempt and clothed in rags, merely because he was unwilling to exert himself enough to reach for the good things you had provided. No more, in my humble opinion, does God.

Man's principal business in life, as I see it, is to establish a contact with the Heaven Mind. It is to acquire an understanding of this power that is in him. "With all thy getting, get understanding," said Solomon.

Happy is the man that findeth wisdom,
And the man that getteth understanding.
For the gaining of it is better than the gaining of silver.
And the profit thereof than fine gold.
She is more precious than rubies:
And none of the things thou canst desire are to be compared unto her.
Length of days is in her right hand:
In her left hand are riches and honor.
Her ways are ways of pleasantness,
And all her paths are peace.
She is a tree of life to them that lay hold upon her.
And happy is every one that retaineth her.

—PROVERBS

When you become conscious, even to a limited degree, of your one-ness with this God Mind, your ability to call upon It at will for anything you may need, it makes a different man of you. Gone are the fears, gone are the worries. You know that your success, your health, your happiness will be measured only by the degree to which you can impress the fruition of your desires upon mind.

The toil and worry, the wearisome grind and the backbreaking work, will go in the future as in the past to those who will not use their minds. The less they use them, the more they will sweat. And the more they work only from the neck down, the less they will be paid and the more hopeless their lot will become. It is Mind that rules the world.

You see, from an ordinary earthly point of view, any savage or even many animals are to all intents as good as you or I. They are stronger, have greater vitality, live longer comparatively, and some are surer of their sustenance. The only faculty in which we are their superior is our mind.

And the only faculty that can make us superior to those around us, that can keep us from being the sport of circumstance and lift us above all danger of want or sickness, is that same mind.

Why is it that fervent prayer often works what seems to us to be a miracle? Why does Treasure Mapping bring such marvelous results? Because both put us upon the Heaven-plane, the plane where the Father works with us to bring about the object we desire.

When you pray earnestly, you see in your mind's eye the condition or result you desire. When you Treasure Map, you picture on paper the condition you want to see realized. And that is exactly how God worked when He created the world. "In the beginning was the word (the mental image)." In the beginning, He formed a picture in His own mind of what He wanted to create. "And the word (the mental image) was made flesh." It was made manifest, became reality for all to see.

Your word—your mental image—can be made flesh in the same way. All it needs is to get on the same plane that God is on when He creates—the plane of the Kingdom of Heaven—of imagery and faith. Remember the words of the Psalmist—"In Thy Book, all my members were written, *when as yet there was none of them.*" And elsewhere in the Scriptures, you find—"The Lord made the earth and the heavens, and every plant of the field *before it was in the earth*, and every herb of the field *before it grew.*"

That is the way you must create the conditions you desire. Create them in your own mind first.

"The imagination," says Glenn Clark in "The Soul's Sincere Desire," "is of all qualities in man the most Godlike—that which associates him most closely with God. The first mention we read of man in the Bible is where he is spoken of as an 'image.' 'Let us make man in our image, after our likeness.' The only place where an image can be conceived is in the imagination. Thus man, the highest creation of God, was a creation of God's imagination.

> *The source and center of all man's creative power—the power that above all others lifts him above the level of brute creation, and that gives him dominion, is his power of making images, or the power of the imagination. There are some who have always thought that the imagination was something which makes-believe that which is not. This is fancy—not imagination. Fancy would convert that which is real into pretense and sham; imagination enables one to see through the appearance of a thing to what it really is.*

There is a very real law of cause and effect which makes the dream of the dreamer come true. It is the law of visualization—the law that calls into being in this outer material world everything that is real in the inner world. Imagination pictures the thing you desire. VISION idealizes it. It reaches beyond the thing that is, into the conception of what can be. Imagination gives you the picture. Vision gives you the impulse to make the picture your own.

34

As a Man Thinketh

We cannot change the past experience, but we can determine what the new ones shall be like. We can make the coming day just what we want it to be. We can be tomorrow what we think today. For the thoughts are causes and the conditions are the effects.

Thought is the only force. Just as polarity controls the electron, gravitation the planets, tropism the plants and lower animals—just so thought controls the action and the environment of man. And thought is subject wholly to the control of mind. Its direction rests with us.

Walt Whitman had the right of it when he said—"Nothing external to me has any power over me."

Each of us makes his own world—and he makes it through mind.

Thoughts are the causes. Conditions are merely effects. We can mold ourselves and our surroundings by resolutely directing our thoughts towards the goal we have in mind.

Ordinary animal life is very definitely controlled by temperature, by climate, by seasonal conditions. Man alone can adjust himself to any reasonable temperature or condition. Man alone has been able to free himself to a great extent from the control of natural forces through his understanding of the relation of cause and effect. And now man is beginning to get a glimpse of the final freedom that shall be his from all material causes when he shall acquire the complete understanding that mind is the only cause and that effects are what he sees.

"We moderns are unaccustomed," says one talented writer,

to the mastery over our own inner thoughts and feelings. That a man should be a prey to any thought that chances to take possession of his

mind, is commonly among us assumed as unavoidable. It may be a matter of regret that he should be kept awake all night from anxiety as to
the issue of a lawsuit on the morrow, but that he should have the power
of determining whether he be kept awake or not seems an extravagant
demand. The image of an impending calamity is no doubt odious, but
its very odiousness (we say) makes it haunt the mind all the more pertinaciously, and it is useless to expel it. Yet this is an absurd position for
man, the heir of all the ages, to be in: Hag-ridden by the flimsy creatures
of his own brain. If a pebble in our boot torments us, we expel it. We
take off the boot and shake it out. And once the matter is fairly understood, it is just as easy to expel an intruding and obnoxious thought
from the mind. About this there ought to be no mistake, no two opinions. The thing is obvious, clear and unmistakable. It should be as easy
to expel an obnoxious thought from the mind as to shake a stone out of
your shoe; and until a man can do that, it is just nonsense to talk about
his ascendancy over nature, and all the rest of it. He is a mere slave, and
a prey to the bat-winged phantoms that flit through the corridors of his
own brain. Yet the weary and careworn faces that we meet by thousands, even among the affluent classes of civilization, testify only too
clearly how seldom this mastery is obtained. How rare indeed to find a
man! How common rather to discover a creature hounded on by tyrant
thoughts (or cares, or desires), cowering, wincing under the lash.

   It is one of the prominent doctrines of some of the oriental schools
of practical psychology that the power of expelling thoughts, or if need
be, killing them dead on the spot, must be attained. Naturally the art
requires practice, but like other arts, when once acquired there is no
mystery or difficulty about it. It is worth practice. It may be fairly said
that life only begins when this art has been acquired. For obviously
when, instead of being ruled by individual thoughts, the whole flock
of them in their immense multitude and variety and capacity is ours to
direct and despatch and employ where we list, life becomes a thing so
vast and grand, compared to what it was before, that its former condition may well appear almost ante-natal. If you can kill a thought dead,
for the time being, you can do anything else with it that you please.
And therefore it is that this power is so valuable. And it not only frees
a man from mental torment (which is nine-tenths at least of the torment of life), but it gives him a concentrated power of handling mental

work absolutely unknown to him before. The two are co-relative to
each other.

There is no intelligence in matter—whether that matter be electronic energy
made up in the form of stone, or iron, or wood, or flesh. It all consists of Energy,
the universal substance from which Mind forms all material things. Mind is the
only intelligence. It alone is eternal. It alone is supreme in the universe.

When we reach that understanding, we will no longer have cause for fear,
because we will realize that Universal Mind is the Creator of life only; that death
is not an actuality—it is merely the absence of life—and life will be ever-present.
Remember the old fairy story of how the Sun was listening to a lot of earthly
creatures talking of a very dark place they had found? A place of Stygian blackness. Each told how terrifically dark it had seemed. The Sun went and looked for
it. He went to the exact spot they had described. He searched everywhere. But
he could find not even a tiny dark spot. And he came back and told the earth-
creatures he did not believe there was any dark place.

When the sun of understanding shines on all the dark spots in our lives,
we will realize that there is no cause, no creator, no power, except good; evil
is not an entity—it is merely the absence of good. And there can be no ill effects
without an evil cause. Since there is no evil cause, only good can have reality or
power. There is no beginning or end to good. From it there can be nothing but
blessing for the whole race. In it is found no trouble. If God (or Good—the two
are synonymous) is the only cause, then the only effect must be like the cause.
"All things were made by Him; and without Him was not anything made that
was made."

35

The Master of Your Fate

Orison Swett Marden wrote—"A highly magnetized piece of steel will attract and lift a piece of unmagnetized steel ten times its own weight. De-magnetize that same piece of steel and it will be powerless to attract or lift even a feather's weight.

Now, my friends, there is the same difference between the man who is highly magnetized by a sublime faith in himself, and the man who is de-magnetized by his lack of faith, his doubts, his fears, that there is between the magnetized and the de-magnetized pieces of steel. If two men of equal ability, one magnetized by a divine self-confidence, the other de-magnetized by fear and doubt, are given similar tasks, one will succeed and the other will fail. The self-confidence of the one multiplies his powers a hundred-fold; the lack of it subtracts a hundred-fold from the power of the other.

When Frank A. Vanderlip, former President of the National City Bank, was a struggling youngster, he asked a successful friend what one thing he would urge a young man to do who was anxious to make his way in the world. "Look as though you have already succeeded," his friend told him. Shakespeare expresses the same thought in another way—"Assume a virtue if you have it not." Look the part. Dress the part. Act the part. Be successful in your own thought first. It won't be long before you will be successful before the world as well.

David V. Bush, in his book "Applied Psychology and Scientific Living," says: "Man is like the wireless operator. Man is subject to miscellaneous wrong thought currents if his mind is not in tune with the Infinite, or *if he is not keyed up to higher vibrations* than those of negation.

A man who thinks courageous thoughts sends these courageous thought waves through the universal ether until they lodge in the consciousness of someone who is tuned to the same courageous key. Think a strong thought, a courageous thought, a prosperity thought, and these thoughts will be received by someone who is strong, courageous and prosperous.

It is just as easy to think in terms of abundance as to think in terms of poverty. If we think poverty thoughts we become the sending and receiving stations for poverty thoughts. We send out a "poverty" mental wireless and it reaches the consciousness of some poverty-stricken "receiver." We get what we think.

It is just as easy to think in terms of abundance, opulence and prosperity as it is to think in terms of lack, limitation and poverty.

If a man will *raise his rate of vibration* by faith currents or hope currents, these vibrations go through the Universal Mind and lodge in the consciousness of people who are keyed to the same tune. Whatever you think is sometime, somewhere, received by a person who is tuned to your thought key.

If a man is out of work and he thinks thoughts of success, prosperity, harmony, position and growth, just as surely as his thoughts are things—as Shakespeare says—someone will receive his vibrations of success, prosperity, harmony, position and growth.

If we are going to be timid, selfish, penurious and picayunish in our thinking, these thought waves which we have started in the universal ether will go forth until they come to a mental receiving station of the same caliber. "Birds of a feather flock together," and minds of like thinking are attracted one to the other.

If you need money, all you have to do is to send up your vibrations to a strong, courageous receiving station, and someone who can meet your needs will be attracted to you or you to him.

When you learn that you are entitled to win—in any right undertaking in which you may be engaged—you will win. When you learn that you have a right to a legitimate dominion over your own affairs, you will have dominion over them. The promise is that we can do all things through the Mind that was in Christ.

The Heaven Mind plays no favorites. No one human being has any more power than any other. It is simply that few of us *use* the power that is in our hands. The great men of the world are in no wise SUPER Beings. They are ordinary creatures like you and me, who have stumbled upon the way of drawing upon their subconscious mind—and through it upon the God Mind. Speaking of Henry Ford's phenomenal success, his friend Thomas A. Edison said of him—"He draws upon his subconscious mind."

The secret of being what you have it in you to be is simply this: Decide now what it is you want of life, exactly what you wish your future to be. Plan it out in detail. Vision it from start to finish. See yourself as you are now, doing those things you have always wanted to do Make them REAL in your mind's eye—feel them, live them, believe them, especially at the moment of going to sleep, when it is easiest to reach your subconscious mind—and you will soon be seeing them in real life.

It matters not whether you are young or old, rich or poor. The time to begin is NOW. It is never too late. Remember those lines of Appleton's:[17]

> *I knew his face the moment that he passed*
> *Triumphant in the thoughtless, cruel throng—*
> *I gently touched his arm—he smiled at me—*
> *He was the Man that Once I Meant to Be!*
>
> *Where I had failed, he'd won from life, Success;*
> *Where I had stumbled, with sure feet he stood;*
> *Alike—yet unalike—we faced the world,*
> *And through the stress he found that life was good.*
> *And I? The bitter wormwood in the glass,*
> *The shadowed way along which failures pass!*
> *Yet as I saw him thus, joy came to me—*
> *He was the Man that Once I Meant to Be!*
>
> *We did not speak. But in his sapient eyes*
> *I saw the spirit that had urged him on,*

---

17. From "The Quiet Courage." D. Appeleton & Co., New York.

The courage that had held him through the fight
Had once been mine. I thought, "Can it be gone?"
He felt that unmasked question—felt it so
His pale lips formed the one-word answer, "No!"

Too late to win? No! Not too late for me—
He is the Man that Still I Mean to Be!

The secret of power lies in understanding the infinite resources of your own mind. When you begin to realize that the power to do anything, to be anything, to have anything, is within yourself, then and then only will you take your proper place in the world.

As Bruce Barton put it—"Nothing splendid has ever been achieved except by those who dared believe that something inside them was superior to circumstance."

36

The Master Mind

The connecting link between the human and the Divine, between the formed universe and formless energy, lies in your imagining faculty. It is, of all things human, the most God-like. It is our part of Divinity. Through it we share in the creative power of the Heaven Mind. Through it we can turn the most drab existence into a thing of life and beauty. It is the means by which we avail ourselves of all the good which God is constantly offering to us in such profusion. It is the means by which we can reach any goal, win any prize.

Do you want happiness? Do you want success? Do you want position, power, riches? *Image* them! How did God first make man? "In his image created He him." He "imaged" man in His Mind.

And that is the way everything has been made since time began. It was first imaged in Mind. That is the way everything you want must start—with a mental image.

So use your imagination! Picture in it your Heart's Desire. Imagine it—daydream it so vividly, so clearly, that you will actually BELIEVE you HAVE it. In the moment that you carry this conviction to your subconscious mind—in that moment your dream will become a reality. It may be a while before you realize it, but the important part is done. You have created the model. You can safely leave it to your subconscious mind to do the rest.

Every man wants to get out of the rut, to grow, to develop into something better. Here is the open road—open to you whether you have schooling, training, position, wealth or not. Remember this: Your subconscious mind knew more from the time you were a baby than is in all the books in all the colleges and libraries of the world.

So don't let lack of training, lack of education, hold you back. Your mind can meet every need—and will do so if you give it the chance. The Apostles were almost all poor men, uneducated men, yet they did a work that is unequalled in historical annals. Joan of Arc was a poor peasant girl, unable to read or write—yet she saved France! The pages of history are dotted with poor men, uneducated men, who thought great thoughts, who used their imaginations to master circumstances and became rulers of men. Most great dynasties started with some poor, obscure man. Napoleon came of a poor, humble family. He got his appointment to the Military Academy only through very hard work and the pulling of many political strings. Even as a Captain of Artillery he was so poverty-stricken that he was unable to buy his equipment when offered an appointment to India. Business today is full of successful men who have scarcely the rudiments of ordinary education. It was only after he had made his millions that Andrew Carnegie hired a tutor to give him the essentials of an education.

So it isn't training and it isn't education that make you successful. These help, but the thing that really counts is that gift of the Gods—Creative Imagination!

You have that gift. Use it! Make every thought, every fact, that comes into your mind pay you a profit. Make it work and produce for you. Think of things—not as they are but as they MIGHT be. Make them real, live and interesting. Don't merely dream—but CREATE! Then use your imagination to make that CREATION of advantage to mankind—and, incidentally, yourself.

Get *above* your circumstances, your surroundings. Get above your troubles—no matter what they may be. Remember, the Law is that Power flows only from a higher to the lower potential. Use your imaging faculty to put yourself and keep yourself on a higher plane, *above* trouble and adversity. "Circumstances?" exclaimed Napoleon when at the height of his power. "I make circumstances!" And that is what you too must do.

"As the rain cometh down and the snow from heaven, and returneth not thither, but watereth the earth, and maketh it bring forth and bud, and giveth seed to the sower and bread to the eater; so shall my word be that goeth forth out of my mouth: it shall not return unto me void, but it shall accomplish that which I please, and it shall prosper in the thing whereto I sent it."—Isaiah.

DO YOU HAVE MONEY WORRIES?

Say to yourself and believe—"There is no lack in the Kingdom of Heaven." Then make a Treasure Map as suggested in The Magic Word, showing all the riches and supply you may long for. All this must start, you know with an idea, a mental image.

"All that the Father hath is mine," said Jesus. And all that the Father hath is yours, too, for all He has to begin with is IDEAS, *mental images,* and you can create these as easily as He. Make your mental image of the thing you want, picture it on paper in so far as you can to make it more real and vivid to you, then have FAITH!

Faith starts you DOING the things you need to do to bring your ideas into realities. Faith brings to you the opportunities and people and things you need to make your images realities.

All that the Father hath is yours—all the ideas, all the mental images, all the power to make them manifest.

Do you want riches? They are yours for the making. The ancient Alchemists who spent their lives trying to turn base metals into gold were trying and working from the bottom up. Power does not flow that way. You must start ABOVE the thing you want, working from the higher potential to the lower.

Riches, health, happiness, power, all are yours if you work for them in the right way—if you make them yours in Heaven first and then use your faith and your abilities to make them manifest here on earth.

"Thy will be done on earth as it is in Heaven," God's will for you is for riches, for happiness, for health. If you haven't these now, deny the lack. Deny the wrong conditions. Say to yourself—"There is no lack in Heaven. There is no disease there, no weakness, no trouble or conflict, no worries of any kind. There is only love and plenty."

Then take your beliefs out of the images around you, which are merely the result of your previous belief objectified and put all your faith, all your hopes, all your strength and abilities into making your new Heaven images come true.

You CAN do it. But you must believe so firmly that you can actually ACT the part. As the Prophet Noel told us "Let the weak say—I am strong!" And the poor say, I am rich. And the sick say, I am well. And the miserable say, I am happy. Say it, repeat it until you believe it—then *ACT the part!*

In one of Edgar Rice Burroughs' Martian stories, he told of a great walled city that had outlived its usefulness and was now peopled by only a few old men. But every time an invading army appeared before this city, it was driven away by hordes of archers that manned every foot of the walls and even swarmed out through the gates to meet the enemy in the open. When the enemy fled, the archers disappeared!

Where did the archers come from? According to the story, they came entirely from the minds of the old men who still lived in that almost-deserted city. These old men remembered the huge armies that had garrisoned the town in its heyday. They remembered former invasions when their soldiers had repelled every assault and then dashed out through the gates and swept the invaders into the sea. And by gathering together and visualizing those mighty armies of theirs as once more existent, they brought them into being so that their enemies too could see them and be driven into flight by them.

Does that sound far-fetched? Then remember that you have only to go back to the Bible to find a parallel. Just turn to II Kings, Chapter 6, and you will read how the King of Syria sent his horses and chariots and a great host to capture the Prophet Elisha, and how in the night they compassed him around.

And when the servant of the man of God was risen early, and gone forth, behold, an host compassed the city both with horses and chariots. And his servant said unto him, Alas, my master, what shall we do?

And he answered, Fear not! For they that be with us are more than they that be with them.

And Elisha prayed, and said, Lord, I pray thee, open his eyes, that he may see. And the Lord opened the eyes of the young man; and he saw: and behold, the mountain was full of horses and chariots of fire around Elisha.

Again, when the High Priest sent his soldiers to seize Jesus, and Peter struck one of the soldiers with his sword, Jesus rebuked him, saying: "Thinkest thou that I cannot now pray to My Father, and He shall presently give Me more than twelve legions of angels?"

The mountains can be full of chariots of fire for you, too. The Father can send to your help as many legions of angels as you may need. All it requires is the power to visualize what you want, the faith to believe that you receive, the serenity to sit back and LET God work through you.

However meager be my worldly wealth,
Let me give something that shall aid my kind,
A word of courage, or a thought of health,
Dropped as I pass for troubled hearts to find.
Let me tonight look back across the span
'Twixt dawn and dark, and to my conscience say—
Because of some good act to beast or man—
The world is better that I lived today.

—ELLA WHEELER WILCOX

About the Author

Born in St. Louis, Missouri, in 1885, Robert Collier trained to become a priest early in his life, before settling on a career in business, achieving success in the fields of advertising, publishing, and engineering. After recovering from a chronic illness with the help of mental healing, Collier began studying New Thought, metaphysical, and success principles. He distilled these theories into widely popular and influential works that included *The Secret of the Ages* and *Riches Within Your Reach*. Collier died in 1950.